A Genealogy of the Good and Critique of Hubris

A Genealogy of the Good and Critique of Hubris

A History of the Discourse on Social Welfare in the United States

PHILLIP DYBICZ

OXFORD
UNIVERSITY PRESS

OXFORD
UNIVERSITY PRESS

Oxford University Press is a department of the University of Oxford. It furthers
the University's objective of excellence in research, scholarship, and education
by publishing worldwide. Oxford is a registered trade mark of Oxford University
Press in the UK and certain other countries.

Published in the United States of America by Oxford University Press
198 Madison Avenue, New York, NY 10016, United States of America.

© Oxford University Press 2023

Library of Congress Cataloging-in-Publication Data
Names: Dybicz, Phillip, author.
Title: A genealogy of the good and critique of hubris : a history of the discourse
on social welfare in the United States / Phillip Dybicz.
Description: New York, NY : Oxford University Press, [2023] |
Includes bibliographical references and index.
Identifiers: LCCN 2022040658 (print) | LCCN 2022040659 (ebook) |
ISBN 9780197670071 (hardback) | ISBN 9780197670118 (epub) |
ISBN 9780197670132 (online)
Subjects: LCSH: Public welfare—United States—History. |
Social service—United States—History. | United States—Social policy.
Classification: LCC HV91 .D93 2023 (print) | LCC HV91 (ebook) |
DDC 361.973—dc23/eng/20220919
LC record available at https://lccn.loc.gov/2022040658
LC ebook record available at https://lccn.loc.gov/2022040659

DOI: 10.1093/oso/9780197670071.001.0001

1 3 5 7 9 8 6 4 2

Printed by Integrated Books International, United States of America

I'd like to dedicate this book to the social workers and social welfare agents in society: past, present, and future. Their tireless efforts in seeking the good for society too often go unsung.

Contents

Foreword

When I decided to pursue an M.S.W. degree, I had no idea what I was getting myself into. My passion for helping and serving others, particularly those who are oppressed or disadvantaged, led me here; I simply listened to my gut and followed. My undergraduate degree and my background were not in social work, and I knew very little about the field or the profession. But I took a chance. In my first semester at the University of North Alabama, I was given what I'd call the social work crash course—introduced to the National Association of Social Workers' *Code of Ethics* and learned what it means to be a social worker and how to display professionalism in the field. But the burning question in my mind, the one I wanted an answer to the most, was how did this all begin and why? More importantly, where do we go from here?

I eventually found my answer in a course entitled Foundations of Social Work History, Policy, and Philosophy taught by none other than Dr. Dybicz, the author of this book. As the reader, you are about to embark on the same journey that I took, a journey that greatly shaped my view of social work practice. My first piece of advice is to forget everything that you think you know. Start by reading each chapter with an open mind and a willingness to learn from a new perspective. This text may not be what you are used to reading, and it can seem overwhelming and intimidating, even to those of us who are fascinated by history. Unlike a traditional textbook that may focus on teaching specific practice models, techniques, or interventions, this text provides an opportunity for self-reflection and self-discovery. This text challenges us to be aware of our own hubris and to always be on guard for moral blind spots. Rather than focusing solely on sharpening our skills or techniques, we are provided the unique opportunity to gain wisdom that will aid us in avoiding the pitfall of moral blind spots.

With that said, I challenge each of you to immerse yourself in the discourse of every era. The chapters might seem lengthy and time-consuming at first glimpse, but it's due to great care and attention to detail—each era is broken down fully, providing an overview of the economic, political, and social conditions; their needs; and the prominent ideologies of the time. All of these factors intertwine to influence and shape society during that given period, and thus shape social welfare practices. By having such a detailed and nuanced understanding of society during each era, you can truly place yourself in their shoes and see the world as they saw it through their eyes. Fully embrace it. If you can do that, you will be able to better understand each era's practices and why social welfare was carried out in the manner that it was. This will in turn allow you to reflect upon and be critically aware of the "why" social work is carried out presently. This will help you to avoid present moral blind spots—such as inadvertently acting as an agent of social control rather than an agent of change—and to free your mind to consider alternate possibilities.

This journey is what I would consider the "evolution of social work," progressing from the colonial era into our current modern era, then going even further to offer a glimpse at what the future could look like in the postmodern era, placing you on the cutting edge of innovations in practice. Right now, you may be asking yourself what the benefit in learning about the past is; what relevance does any of this have with right now, with today? While I understand your hesitation, I can attest that what you are about to read changed my perspective of social work and what it means to help others completely. As you begin the readings, you will be transported back in time to the colonial era. While this era may seem so distant from our current society, the lessons we can learn through their eyes, from their practice, still hold relevance today, despite the centuries of time separating us. You probably wouldn't expect to learn a lesson on how to be more responsive to LGBTQ+ individuals from social welfare practices in colonial America, but it's there, along with critical lessons on the dangers of hubris: Sometimes as social welfare agents, despite our best intentions, values, and level of expertise, we can still inflict harm upon those we serve. Even today, that danger persists.

As you near the end of this book, you will start to see the way that social work, when practiced unwisely, can lead us into seeking out deficits in our clients and pathologizing them, rather than seeing them as whole and human. This text offers you the chance to gain valuable insight into how to be a better social worker and how to provide more comprehensive, compassionate care and interventions to clients. By choosing this field and this profession, we have assumed responsibility for the grave task of aiding and assisting others without controlling or forcing our own views and beliefs on them. You will come to see that there is a very fine line between providing assistance and service to others and practicing social control. Throughout these readings, you will develop the wisdom to know when you are in danger of crossing this line.

As you begin this journey, I can only hope that each of you takes away as much as I took away from this text. If you are willing to put in the time and effort to engage and understand the discourse of each era, you will be better off for it. It is up to all of us to learn from the history of our past and build a better future. What will the future of social work look like? That's for us to decide and create, and this book gives you the tools that will assist you in this creation.

Bethany Turner

Preface

As a Ph.D. student at the University of Kansas, I fondly recall being exposed to Michel Foucault's *The Order of Things*. I was immediately hooked. I had already developed a passion for history while pursuing my master's degree at the University of Houston, thanks to the influence of Dr. Robert Fisher—one of just a handful of social work historians that remained in academia at the time. My advanced research course was in historical research, and Dr. Fisher was well positioned to teach it, as he had earned his Ph.D. in history and only later was recruited to teach in the Department of Social Work.

I was drawn to the University of Kansas due to the prominent scholars being steeped in postmodernism—a topic that fascinated me—and having applied their insights to create the Strengths Perspective. They are the ones who introduced me to the works of Foucault. Other social work scholars drawn to postmodern thought had already begun offering penetrating applications of Foucault's ideas to social work, most prominently with the recent publication of *Reading Foucault for Social Work*. Yet, I felt that I was uniquely positioned to make an important contribution all my own. You see, the social work scholars writing on Foucault inevitably approached him as a philosopher and sought to apply his various philosophical insights to social work. I, on the other hand, wished to approach him as a historian. His research methodology in the form of conducting a genealogy—a process he created on his own—is what fascinated me. Social work scholars steeped in the historical method were (and still are unfortunately) a rare breed in social work academia. And of these, very few have embraced postmodern forms of historical research.

Fortunately for me, serendipity struck again when I met Dr. Benjamin Sax in the History Department at the University of Kansas. His expertise was in the intellectual history of the social sciences. I had the pleasure of sitting in on many of his seminars, wherein we discussed works such as Aristotle's *Poetics*; St. Thomas Aquinas' *Confessions*; Kant's *Critique of Pure Reason*, *Critique of Practical Reason*, and *Critique of Judgment*; Goethe's *the Sorrows of Young Werther*; Herder's *Philosophical Writings*; Heidegger's *Being and Time*; Gadamer's *Truth and Method*; Foucault's *The Order of Things* and *The Birth of the Clinic*; and Ricœur's *Time and Narrative*. Left to my own devices, I would have been poorly situated to attempt to access the deeper insights from these works on my own. But Dr. Sax's brilliant mind unlocked the many secrets in these works for me and, thus, granted me access to begin applying their deep insights to my concerns of social welfare. While many social work scholars were conducting statistical analyses, I began writing about Socrates (in my early article entitled "An Inquiry into Practice Wisdom"). Hence, one might easily conclude that my preparation as a social work scholar was highly atypical, and perhaps, even unique.

With my dissertation, I now began my own journey of genealogical research in social welfare. It helped lay a sparse but solid foundation for this work. After a decade in the field, I was ready to take up the project once again. Typical of most solid and thorough historical investigations, this entailed a lengthy process. It took five additional years of intensive research and writing to transform my dissertation into the work that stands before you. As you might surmise, this was a labor of love and my gift to the field of social work. My hope is that it is well received.

1
Overview

"Is this intervention effective?" This is a question that social workers have asked themselves since the birth of the profession and which social welfare agents have asked since the birth of our country. In our attempts at advancing the social welfare of the client and society, it is essential that we constantly evaluate the impact of our interventions. Over the years, however, this question has yielded some surprising answers. During the Colonial Era, those individuals suffering from mental illness who demonstrated a proclivity for aberrant and sometimes harmful behaviors were locked away in barns or small rooms.[1] During the late 1800s in New York City, social welfare agents organized the orphan trains, sending poor immigrant children—many of whom were not orphans— out to the more "wholesome" environment of family farms in the Midwest.[2] In the 1950s, social workers placed themselves in the role of social police by conducting midnight "raids" (i.e., unscheduled visits at midnight) at the homes of welfare recipients to ensure that welfare mothers were not benefiting from a man's company in secret and, thus, disqualifying themselves from receiving aid.[3] Looking upon these interventions with our present eyes, from a viewpoint firmly grounded in notions of self-determination and empowerment, our profession can easily see their moral failings. From these examples, as a profession we are able to note that simply applying good intentions—by themselves—is not adequate to ensure effective and worthy interventions. We are also able to note that simply having an outcome measure is not enough to ensure the worthiness of an intervention, as the examples above contained easily measured outcomes.

Upon recognizing these and other past failings, it is deceptively easy to take comfort in the stance that we have moved beyond them as we have progressed as a profession. That even though we still have a lot to do and learn, we can mark how far we have come. Most historical views of our profession take this same approach,[4] that of a Kantian view of historical progress revealed through historicization.[5] This view asserts that as we continually gain experience and knowledge, we increase our expertise. Consequently, our evaluation of effective interventions becomes more refined and better informed: a natural and beneficial result of the steady accumulation of a body of knowledge. So, for example, Walter I. Trattner's *From Poor Law to Welfare State* has been well recognized in our profession as providing a broad yet thorough history of social welfare in America. Beginning with the colonial era and proceeding up until the present day, Trattner sketches

A Genealogy of the Good and Critique of Hubris. Phillip Dybicz, Oxford University Press. © Oxford University Press 2023.
DOI: 10.1093/oso/9780197670071.003.0001

out a winding road of overall progress in our attempts to address the issue of social welfare.[6] In terms of causality, it is an attempt to accurately portray events and enumerate the effects they had on this overall progress. In short, it seeks to explain why things happened as they did. It is hoped that this knowledge will better inform our future attempts in addressing social welfare by enabling us to recognize our successes and to not repeat past mistakes. Continuing in this tradition of the historicization of social welfare, Phillip R. Popple (2018) offers the most recent example with his work *Social Work Practice and Social Welfare Policy in the United States: A History*. In addition, Popple takes the purposeful step of including and emphasizing the voice of the front-line worker as the means to capture a richer fabric to social welfare history.[7]

This present book does not seek to deny the proposition that accumulating a body of knowledge for the profession leads to advancement of theoretical developments and refinement of practice techniques and skills, as well as measures for evaluating them. Yet can it be stated with certainty that accumulating a body of knowledge also naturally contributes to the *moral* progress of the profession? There are some who argue that it has not, that we continue to make various mistakes due to value biases inherent in our culture.[8] What may be required instead is not a research endeavor that seeks to add to the profession's body of knowledge but rather one that seeks to promote moral reflection and insight. This is the task that this book seeks to accomplish. Granted, the National Association of Social Workers provides a code of ethics that is prominently embraced within our profession as a guide to intervening.[9] But is a code of ethics alone all that is needed to keep our profession morally alert? Some of the practices discussed in this book speak to the contrary. And what about seeking to progress morally? How will this occur, unless through focused inquiry and research? Yet, when our profession turns to conducting research, inevitably the task seems to turn to adding to the social work body of technical knowledge, and thus increasing our expertise.

Cultural histories represent a first step toward promoting this moral insight and reflection. These are histories that seek cultural interpretations of historical experiences, in effect allowing the reader to step inside the shoes of a typical person from a historical era and thus see the world through their eyes. These works place less emphasis on explaining causality and instead seek to open up a window to another viewpoint; this is done by describing a particular culture and time period via its relationship to a specific issue. It should be noted that as we consider this different approach to historical inquiry, most cultural histories on social welfare have been written by historians.[10] For example, David Rothman's *The Discovery of the Asylum* offers a rich description of the cultural climate during the Jacksonian era (1820s and 1830s), the time in which prisons and asylums were first established in America. Eschewing one-dimensional explanations—that they emerged from progressive Enlightenment notions or, more negatively, that they were coercive devices aimed at disciplining the labor force in a capitalist society—Rothman offers a deep and rich cultural picture of the time period.[11] From this description, one is better able to understand how individuals from that time period viewed the creation of asylums and prisons. While Rothman and the other trained historians are able to offer much in terms of the rigor brought to bear in these studies, a social worker also possesses current and firsthand experience of the profession. Such firsthand experience in doing social work as well as being well versed in current and past social work literature grants the social work historian intimate knowledge of the vital concerns of our profession regarding values such as respecting diversity and fostering empowerment.

Phillip R. Popple, Leslie Leighninger, and Robert Leighninger's cultural history *Social Work, Social Welfare, and American Society* offers an excellent illustration of this dynamic. As social work historians, they are able to take historical insights and connect them directly to these vital concerns, focusing and targeting moral reflection in a way that is both accessible and relevant to the average social work practitioner.[12] To give such moral reflection prominence, I have dedicated a section to this task under the heading *Reflections* when discussing the social welfare practices for each era (Chapters 3, 5, 7, and 9).

While cultural histories represent a first step toward promoting moral reflection, critical histories take this moral reflection further by not only exploring cultural interpretations of past events but also offering a critique on how these events result from cultural biases and create moral blind spots. In addition to stepping in the shoes of someone from this era, a critical historian brings the viewpoint of someone from outside this era as a means to critique various shortcomings. Three studies representing historical research on social welfare in this vein are as follows. In their work *Regulating the Poor*, Francis F. Piven and Richard Cloward were able to describe historical, structural forces at work in society—below the conscious awareness of social workers employing interventions—that, by circumscribing their actions, could easily make them unwitting agents of social control. By describing forces at work below the conscious awareness of individuals, an analysis such as Piven and Cloward's explores a moral ground that is not captured by the conscious implementation of a code of ethics.[13]

Leslie Margolin's *Under the Cover of Kindness* examines social work practices alongside their aims for "doing good." The critique that he provides is the following: The very quality that enables us to be most effective as a social worker—building rapport and trust with the client—also increases the domination we exert as social control agents. Briefly, his argument contains the following points. The casework method (with the recording that it involves) and the practice of the home visit were adopted in order to respect the uniqueness of individuals and to best address their particular circumstance. Thus, this approach arose from the application of social work values, is based in good intentions, and is a reflection of currently understood best practices. However, it also accomplished the goal of extending political surveillance of oppressed groups (which heretofore was restricted to the public sphere of streets, schools, and businesses) into the private sphere of their homes. The emphasis on respecting the uniqueness of the individual also encourages the individualizing of blame for their circumstances. The very act of building rapport and trust with the client opens up wider this private sphere of the individual and, thus, increases the range of surveillance that social workers inevitably exert. And finally, he states that there exists a level of consistency in this dynamic throughout the various decades in social work.[14] From the friendly visitors of the early 1900s to the focus midcentury on the hard-to-reach client to the emphasis on empowerment in the 1970s and beyond, he argues that the result is the same: "I show that despite superficial shifts in claims and style, the basic practice is the same: people from one social class go into the homes of people belonging to another; they write biographies of these people; they judge what is normal and abnormal; they call it 'doing good.'"[15]

As with most cultural histories on social welfare, neither of these two critical histories were written by someone who identifies themselves as a social worker.[a] The deficiency arising from an outsider's limited and less intimate understanding of social work is particularly apparent in Margolin's work. While he is able to unearth a number of important historical insights, when taking the step of applying a critique in which to promote moral reflection these insights are applied to a caricature of social work, thus diluting their impact and relevance, as attested by the various book reviews by social workers.[16]

The third example of a critical history I wish to share is written by a social worker and serves to fortify the point made earlier as to the importance of the author having an intimate knowledge of social welfare. This is Ken Moffat's *A Poetics of Social Work: Personal Agency and Social Transformation in Canada, 1920–1939*. By focusing upon the activities of four prominent individuals in social work over a two-decade span, Moffat seeks to trace the epistemological influences shaping social work practice in Canada and, by so doing, to lend greater voice to less privileged knowledges in social work.[17] The critical history of social welfare in the United States I am attempting to offer via this book also seeks to trace the epistemological influences shaping social work practice over the years. In so doing, I have drawn heavily upon the genealogical method of

---

[a] Piven and Cloward were sociologists. Margolin did earn an M.S.W. and had limited experience working in psychiatric hospitals as a social worker; however, he earned his Ph.D. in sociology. He does not identify himself as a social worker and thus only has a tenuous connection to the profession.

inquiry developed by Michel Foucault, while seeking additional inspiration from Thomas Kuhn and Fernand Braudel. As such, it is the first such genealogy by a social work historian.

While not addressing social work directly, Foucault has also described historical, structural forces at work—linguistic structures embedded in culture in the form of a dominant Discourse—that serve to circumscribe how we shape our thoughts, order our knowledge, and, consequently, intervene to promote social welfare.[18] As the concept of *discourse* will be central in the historical analyses provided in this investigation, I offer the following provisional definition:

A discourse is an epistemological framework consisting of both linguistic and nonlinguistic (i.e., material) elements that order knowledge in a particular manner, legitimizing some knowledges while subjugating others.

Under this definition, it is important to note that a discourse is not a theoretical or philosophical framework. So, for example, the strengths perspective itself does not represent a discourse. Rather, there is a discourse that supports the strengths perspective and legitimizes its schema for ordering knowledge. A discourse operates as a structure within language itself and, hence, is comprised of elements that are value-laden: The creation of these value schemas is influenced by the unique conditions (both linguistic and material) of one's culture and time period. In addition, as it is structural in nature, the dominant Discourse on social welfare operates below the conscious awareness of those employing the theoretical or philosophical models that it supports: It represents the inherent cultural biases we possess concerning ordering knowledge and, hence, the values we use to determine which types of knowledge are seen as legitimate and which types are not. Critical reflection on the part of the social worker is necessary to unearth and recognize these biases.

The stronger the dominance that a Discourse exerts, the less likely one is to gain awareness of its influence, and thus the less likely one will be to question its basic tenets. This is where the role of the historian comes in. By providing a historical analysis via conducting a genealogy, the historian is able to uncover and thus describe these Discourses at work—raising awareness of these biases. In such analyses as offered by Foucault, moral progress does not naturally flow from advancement of knowledge and experience. Rather, a particular cultural era has prominent value schemas in which certain knowledges as well as certain interpretations of values are pressed to the fore, while others recede to the background.

Foucault's major insight in introducing his genealogical method was his novel conception of power as a force that legitimates these schemas, and thus supports a particular discourse and thrusts it into the role of exerting a dominant status concerning truth claims. This type of power (operating at the epistemological level) does not lie in the hands of an individual or group; rather, it is "a machine in which everyone is caught."[19] This is because power operates below the conscious awareness of individuals and circulates within culture as a whole. Consequently, it is not to be viewed as a tangible force for social cohesion or repression. Neither should this type of power be viewed as a commodity that is possessed by some and lacking in others. Rather, it is viewed as something that circulates within the discourse. Individuals are not objects upon which power acts but rather vehicles for its expression and articulation. This is because power influences how knowledge is ordered (recognizes some while subjugating others), thus facilitating the production of recognized knowledge. This knowledge that is produced serves to further fuel the mechanisms of power. This creates a reciprocal relationship that cannot be untangled: "The exercise of power perpetually creates knowledge and, conversely, knowledge constantly induces effects of power. . . . It is not possible for power to be exercised without knowledge, it is impossible for knowledge not to engender power."[20] In short, power arises out of relationships—in fact, power is these relationships, a self-organizing cluster of relationships of meaning that arise between various value schemas and events that serve to complement and reinforce each other.[21]

As an example, in *Madness and Civilization: A History of Insanity in the Age of Reason* and *The Birth of the Clinic: An Archaeology of Medical Perception* Foucault uncovers the following: Positivism's stress on objective measurement, intersecting with medicine's concern for understanding insanity and disease, resulted in truth claims being based upon the concept of the norm. In *Discipline and Punish: The Birth of the Prison*, Foucault outlines how power works to reinforce this concept of the norm. He describes a carceral network that emerged in modern society, one that supports the claims to truth of normalization via structures and mechanisms of discipline. Mutually reinforcing, this network gained justification from medicine's and psychiatry's view of deviance grounded in science and the judicial view of deviance grounded in law—all the while providing knowledge to further justify these views in return.

The brilliance in Foucault's works is that he is able to demonstrate that these truth claims are not resting upon a universal ground of truth but, rather, are arbitrary in nature. He does this by describing opposing truth claims from a different cultural era and illustrating how they were determined by that particular culture and time period. He then goes on to describe how the truth claims that we currently operate under are being shaped by our current culture and time period. The resulting conclusion is that these current truth claims must be arbitrary in nature as well, thus attacking the hubris that we *know* and, hence, sparking a critical consciousness. This dynamic is what is at the heart of a rhetoric of truth,[22] which I will speak more upon shortly in this chapter. It is important to note that in representing this genealogical approach Foucault is not seeking to offer judgment that one particular discourse for establishing truth is better than another or that a particular discourse in and of itself is undesirable—such evaluations lie outside a genealogical analysis. Rather, he seeks to attack the dominance of a Discourse (and hence hubris) by revealing its arbitrary nature. As Foucault so eloquently states in his preface to *Birth of the Clinic,*

> I should like to make it plain once and for all that this book has not been written in favour of one kind of medicine as against another kind of medicine, or against medicine and in favour of an absence of medicine. It is a structural study that sets out to disentangle the conditions of its history from the density of discourse, as do others of my works.[23]

It is within this spirit of seeking a rhetoric of truth that this investigation is based; it seeks to attack the hubris that *we know* what comprises an effective intervention and what consists of best practices. Applying such an analysis to the examples given earlier yields the following interpretation. The locking away of the mentally ill, the creation of orphan trains, and the practice of midnight raids do not represent naive attempts at intervention during a nascent stage of our development, one in which we are steadily growing wiser in our practice as social workers. Rather, each is viewed as an egregious example of a moral blind spot that existed during that particular era. These moral blind spots arise due to a level of hubris concerning our relationship to knowledge, that is, how we order it and thus what we consider legitimate and true. The blind spots that gave rise to locking away the mentally ill and placing street youth on orphan trains have disappeared as the schemas to which they belonged have since been replaced by our present schemas—which contain blind spots of their own (as evidenced by the former practice of midnight raids). Describing these schemas and corresponding blind spots thus is the task of this book's research endeavor, an endeavor aimed at promoting moral reflection and insight concerning current social work practices.

As mentioned briefly, these cultural biases inherent to a particular dominant Discourse also serve to delegitimize knowledge that is produced by values contrary to these biases; Foucault calls this delegitimized knowledge *subjugated knowledge.*[24] In order to increase one's awareness to present subjugated knowledge, we may also examine from previous eras past interventions not considered morally bereft in our present eyes but which have fallen out of sync with today's notions of effective practice. For example, during the early 1900s at the settlement houses, one of the main requirements for social workers was that they live at the settlement houses, and thus in the neighborhoods of the people they served. In the 1950s, the youth director of the YMCA outreach program in Los Angeles for runaway youth "would bring runaways back to his home, a practice now widely frowned upon by youth-service workers."[25] Looking upon these examples, one is prompted to ask how the value that precipitated these actions—fostering human fellowship on either a community or an individual level—is voiced in the actions of today's social workers. Has the knowledge that this value promotes become delegitimized and thus subjugated?

Starting in the 1990s, drawing upon Foucault for inspiration, a number of scholars in the profession began to examine this notion of subjugated knowledge. Ann Weick explores how the values of social caretaking, shared experiences, and relationship-building—and the knowledge that they promote—are subjugated by a professional Discourse that currently prizes rationality and logic.[26] Dennis Miehls and Ken Moffat, as well as Dennis Saleebey, examine the value of honoring the voice of clients and the local knowledge that they possess.[27] Lastly, an entire book, *Reading Foucault for Social Work*, offer chapters from numerous different authors, all of whom explore this notion of subjugated knowledge.[28] These scholars speak out against a professional Discourse that restricts the personal voice of clients to that of a data source for diagnostic measures and consequently offers no venue for clients to be equal contributors, and thus co-creators, in knowledge generation. And as Thomas Holbrook reveals, even the agency forms that social worker's use reflect this value schema's cultural bias—pointing out that there is no role for a client to be a co-contributor when conducting assessments and creating case records.[29] Building upon the insights offered by the above authors, Bob Peace warns of the dangers of social workers unwittingly disempowering the clients with whom they work by only giving credence to the profession's expert knowledge, and thus delegitimizing the client's role in knowledge generation.[30]

In order to evaluate an intervention as effective and worthy, we as social workers must appeal to knowledge that we have collected. In determining what knowledge is useful and appropriate for making our evaluation and which knowledge is not, certain value standards are embraced. These value standards are a product of our present time period and culture—and the inherent biases that it contains. Heightened awareness of current biases we hold concerning social welfare interventions is stimulated through the examination of past dominant Discourses. These previous eras, much different from our own, offer a unique vantage in which to view and critique the biases operating in the present dominant Discourse within which we are currently enmeshed (in effect, stepping into the shoes of someone from a different era and then turning back to view our present Discourse). Such an analysis attempts to define the boundaries, or "box," we as social workers operate within when conceiving of effective interventions. By increasing our awareness of these biases, we deflate any hubristic notions we may have concerning effective interventions (i.e., that there is no need to look outside this box for answers). Hence, this project seeks to act as a spark toward innovation: By defining the "box" we are currently operating within, it hopes to facilitate one's ability to "think outside the box."

The goals of this research project are the following: (1) to effectively describe the current dominant Discourse on social welfare interventions, and thus the "box" we operate within concerning effective interventions; (2) as a result of this description, to facilitate awareness of the biases we hold concerning social welfare interventions and, consequently, our evaluations of effective interventions and the moral blind spots that may result from them; (3) as a result of this awareness, to deflate any hubristic notions we hold concerning the determination of effective interventions, thus increasing our sensitivity and respect for answers presented to us by clients or circumstances concerning effective interventions which are currently subjugated because they lie outside this "box"; and (4) as a result of this awareness, to spark innovation concerning novel conceptions of best practice.

Seeking a Rhetoric of Truth

The particular philosophical framework that will inform this inquiry is that of poststructuralism, as elaborated within the writings of Foucault.[31] Within this framework, the main concept of import to this investigation is that of epistemological causality. Unlike traditional notions of causality (what I term here as *ontological causality*), inquiry guided by epistemological causality does not seek to add to a body of knowledge as this is typically understood—that is, to increase one's expertise on a topic. Historians pursuing ontological causality—the most common approach to inquiry and likely the most familiar to the reader—examine historical events and seek to trace the forces involved that caused the particular events to arise. By contrast, historians pursuing epistemological causality examine historical events as a means to trace the forces at work shaping and ordering the value judgments being made about the events at the time of their occurrence. Consequently, via seeking epistemological causality, postmodern historians do not seek to contribute to a body of knowledge;[b] instead, their aim is to contribute to a rhetoric. But this is not a rhetoric of persuasion, where one orders knowledge into an argument in order to convince another of one's position. Rather, it is a rhetoric of truth, along the lines of a Socratic inquiry: We seek an aporia with the goal of sharpening our awareness.[32] Michel Foucault expounds upon this concept as it applies to his work:

[b] Doing so would treat knowledge as a product (i.e., being ontological in nature—and so appropriate for an ontologically based causality).

As for what motivated me, it is quite simple; I would hope that in the eyes of some people it might be sufficient in itself. It was curiosity—the only kind of curiosity, in any case, that is worth acting upon with a degree of obstinacy: not the curiosity that seeks to assimilate what it is proper for one to know, but that which enables one to get free of oneself. . . . There are times in life when the question of knowing if one can think differently than one thinks, and perceive differently than one sees, is absolutely necessary if one is to go on looking and reflecting at all.[33]

This endeavor at describing epistemological causality and contributing to a rhetoric of truth is best modeled by the early Socratic dialogues written by Plato. When Socrates approaches Euthyphro in the agora and asks him "What is piety?" Euthyphro believes that he already knows the answer. This is the starting point of the inquiry. At the end of the inquiry, Euthyphro no longer believes that he knows the answer and leaves very confused. Thus, by employing a rhetoric of truth, the purpose of Socrates' inquiry—and mine for this research endeavor—is not to increase one's expertise but rather to increase one's confusion.

But this confusion is of a specific type: that of a philosophical aporia. A philosophic aporia, as promoted by Socrates, arises when a fundamental truth with which one is familiar and comfortable (defined in this book as a cultural bias stemming from a dominant Discourse) suddenly comes under doubt. This state of aporia is a condition that is specifically sought by Socrates. Through the process of dialogue he seeks to offer an elenchus—a statement that one also finds to be fundamentally true yet contradicts the first fundamental truth that one holds. Confusion arises because these contradictory statements both appear to be equally true. In the present book, this contradiction occurs via the historical comparisons of various Discourses, each claiming a privileged position in defining what comprises effective interventions. The confusion that arises, however, serves a positive purpose. It makes one more aware and sensitive to the potential bias one holds, while also spurring one to greater depths of self-reflection in order to resolve the contradiction. In simpler terms, this condition of aporia seeks to attack one's hubris that one *knows*. An important assumption underlying this approach, and postmodern inquiry in general, is that we cannot step out of either culture or language to get an objective view when conducting inquiry. As human beings, we exist in both culture and language—which inevitably give us a biased view of the world. Thus, it is important to seek and actively maintain a condition in which we are sensitive to the biases influencing our actions.

When Euthyphro leaves Socrates, his attitude toward piety has changed. He no longer views piety as something easy to define, and thus merely needing common sense to guide him in his actions. Since he has become aware how his previous

assumptions have the power to easily mislead him, he will extend more careful-
ness, more thought, more awareness, and more heed in his future actions that are
guided by piety. Thus, the purpose of Socrates' inquiry is not to make Euthyphro
and himself greater experts on piety (as is the purpose of an inquiry that seeks to
increase one's technical knowledge). Rather, it is to make themselves both wiser
in their actions guided by piety. This wisdom can be described as the awareness
one is able to maintain of the assumptions (based in culture) under which one
operates,[c] thus allowing one to be more flexible toward other ways of ordering
knowledge. Consequently, the purpose of this book's historical inquiry is not to
make social workers greater experts on social welfare interventions; rather, it is to
promote moral reflection and insight, and thus make social workers wiser when
employing social welfare interventions. This is accomplished through increasing
awareness to the value standards being used to evaluate effective interventions.

Thus, describing a dominant Discourse serves to outline how culture
influences our interpretations of reality. Under the rubric of epistemological causality, knowledge serves as an elenchus (which, as a rhetorical device, makes it
epistemologically based). It causes us to question what we know and serves as
"the bite or sting that wakes us from our complacency, arouses us to excellence,
to learn and discover and inquire."[34] Consequently, the purpose of research in
this paradigm is to attack any hubris we may have concerning our technical
knowledge (via ontological causality), and thus promote a level of wisdom
when looking to act with such incomplete and biased knowledge. Genealogical
research seeks to contribute to maintaining this awareness by constantly
questioning the dominant Discourse influencing our thought.

It is through his unique conception of power and the analysis of its workings
that Foucault is able to build upon the more fundamental dynamic reminiscent
of the Socratic dialogue.[d] By unearthing the various value schemas of a particular era, the historian is able to offer an elenchus to the current Discourse.
Via an analysis of power through a genealogy, the historian is able to offer a
critique of the current Discourse as well. This critique fits within the notion of
a critique as adopted by Immanuel Kant: It is a thorough mapping out of the
boundaries within which the topic of the critique operates—not a critique that
employs evaluative judgment in terms of good/bad or useful/useless.[35] Kant

---

[c] In the early Socratic dialogues themselves, Plato does not specifically address the issue of culture.
The methodological approach pursued in this study builds upon the dynamic of a Socratic elenchus
by adding a postmodern perspective of culture.

[d] Foucault, *Power–Knowledge*, 114–15. It is with his conception and analysis of power that
Foucault marks his break with Plato. In the later Socratic dialogues, Plato turns to semiotics in an
attempt to move beyond the condition of aporia. Foucault embraces this condition of aporia and then
offers a critique of discourse via the analysis of power: "The history which bears and determines us
has the form of a war rather than that of a language: relations of power, not relations of meaning . . .
'semiology' is a way of avoiding its [conflict's] violent, bloody and lethal character by reducing it to
the calm Platonic form of language and dialogue."

concerned himself with a critique of reason; a genealogist is able to offer a critique of a particular Discourse. This critique provides a thorough description of the "box" that the Discourse creates; thus, by the same measure, the critique also helps to spur innovation by allowing one to explore ways of "thinking outside the box."

Cultural Humility

It should be noted that while the history of social welfare in the United States offered in this book covers a broad time span—from colonial America to the present—it is primarily a social history of White persons' attempts at promoting social welfare. This is both a limitation and a strength. The big limitation is the consequent lack of attention to the rich cultural histories offered by historically oppressed groups in American society. While groups such as Native Americans, African Americans, and other minorities may have shared some broad historical, social, political, and economic events in common with White Anglo-Saxon Protestant America, their unique American experiences would have produced quite different discourses on promoting social welfare. Examination of the historical discourses informing these various groups would serve to provide many additional vantage points from which to expose biases operating in the current dominant Discourse circulating in American society as well as spark additionally unique ideas of innovation. As I myself identify as a White, male, heterosexual, I leave such explorations to other authors better positioned to comment upon these matters than I.

The main strength is that by historically targeting the majority group's dominant Discourses on social welfare, the various social work practices arising from these Discourses, whether for good or ill, have had some impact on all groups in American society. Consequently, the need to attack hubris lies greatest among the majority group as the cultural biases inherent to this group have the broadest reach on social welfare overall and less often come under critical scrutiny by the various social and political forces operating in society. Such critical scrutiny helps to promote cultural humility. As reflected in current social work literature, the fostering of cultural humility is the primary means to apply the core social work value of respecting diversity in the clients whom we serve.[36] In the chapters that follow, when applying the concept of cultural humility to the insights offered by the readings, I will be drawing upon the following definition offered by Dorothy E. Stubbe: "Cultural humility involves entering a relationship with another person with the intention of honoring their beliefs, customs, and values. It entails an ongoing process of self-exploration and self-critique combined with a willingness to learn from others."[37]

The 1970s marked a turn in social work consciousness on the importance of attending to culture when seeking to apply normative models to the helping situation. This idea was first captured by the term *cultural awareness*, that is, the idea of maintaining an awareness on how the client's culture may serve to modify certain aspects of the model, and hence one's practice intervention. By the 1990s, this idea was refined and evolved into the term *cultural competence*.[38] Cultural competence took this one step further by stating that the social worker must be more than just aware of the need to modify the normative model; they also must develop the competence to effectively modify it to the client's culture. More recently, this idea has been refined once again and is now captured by the term *cultural humility*.[39] Cultural humility takes the stance that it is a mark of hubris to believe one can achieve true competence in the culture of another in such a manner. Rather than attempting to apply a normative model to the client's situation, the social worker's gaze is turned inward toward developing an awareness of their own cultural biases that are being brought to the helping situation and prompting an examination of how these biases might be interfering with clients' attempts to define their actions in relation to their sense of cultural identity.[40] In short, it is an exercise in attacking the hubris that one *knows*.

The genealogical analysis offered in this book can be viewed as an extended exercise in cultural humility. In the nature of our work today, it is common for a social worker to come across a client exhibiting behaviors that society views as odd or strange. This is typical as our profession's mission as currently defined is to aid clients' adjustment to their environment brought about through some type of conflict—and atypical behaviors on the part of the client are often the source of such conflict. Cultural humility asks that instead of immediately labeling such atypical behaviors as dysfunctional or abnormal, one takes a step back and attempts to view the behavior through the client's cultural lens. Social welfare practices from a hundred years ago and beyond offer such a long historical distance that practices of that time easily appear odd or strange to our present eyes. A genealogical analysis allows the reader to step inside the shoes of a typical person from a historical era and thus see the world through their eyes. Thus, as such, it becomes an exercise in cultural humility.

By way of example, let's take the practice from colonial America of requiring dispossessed individuals seeking relief to wear a red or blue letter "P" on their clothing to indicate that they belonged to this group of the poor. Upon hearing of such a practice, a first reaction by students, and even some historians,[41] is that it was demeaning and unnecessarily stigmatizing. One of our cultural experiences fueling such a view is the practice that occurred in Nazi Germany of requiring those of the Jewish faith to wear a Star of David on their clothing. The inhumane treatment and genocide that followed serve to further stain this practice with a sense of evil. Yet Nazi Germany was not part of colonial America's cultural consciousness. As we will see in Chapter 2, once we as the reader step into the cultural consciousness of colonial America, we are able to see that through the eyes of American colonists this practice was neither cruel, demeaning, nor stigmatizing. Coming around to such a realization, first by questioning the hubris that one *knows* and then exploring the cultural aspects defining these individuals' experiences, is a firm example of an exercise in cultural humility. To help promote such an exercise, at the beginning of each chapter describing the dominant Discourse of that era I will start by describing a few practices from that era, thus giving the reader the opportunity to reflect upon their initial reaction to these practices before taking the step of understanding them through the cultural consciousness of that era.

With the above preface in mind, the following statements comprise the rationale for reaching the aforementioned goals of this research project: (1) Determining effective interventions is an essential element to social work practice—a genealogical study on social welfare interventions will uncover the cultural biases we hold regarding our current notions of effective interventions. (2) Acting hubristically may interfere with effectively meeting the needs of our clients; hence, our professional code of ethics states, "Social workers should understand culture and its function in human behavior and society."[42] A genealogical study seeks to attack our notions of hubris by revealing that our biases arise from a specific historical and cultural context and form as a result of power, thus acting to dispel any notions that they arise out of a universal notion of truth. (3) Innovations concerning effective interventions are important because social workers intervene in a culture and society that is constantly changing—identifying our biases will enable us to use those biases in a productive manner by stimulating us to expand our horizons of thinking about effective interventions.

Describing the Discourse

This book's research endeavor of mapping epistemological causality leading to a dominant Discourse draws upon the following precepts from cultural and critical histories. As a cultural history, this study's design borrows from precepts developed by the *Annales* school of France—a movement of historical method founded in France in the early 1900s.[43] The first precept borrowed is that of the *longue durée*. It speaks to the notion that a long time span must be investigated if one is seeking out the movement of underlying structures—both linguistic and material—within a society. Furthermore, I draw upon the specific approach of the *Annales* historian Fernand Braudel, most notable in his book *The*

Mediterranean, for inspiration in including the geography, economics, politics, and social conditions of an era as important underlying non-discursive material structures comprising a Discourse. The second precept borrowed from *Annales* is that the time period is chosen to fit the problem rather than the other way around. In addition, while not reflective of the *Annales* school, I take inspiration from Thomas Kuhn's *The Structure of Scientific Revolutions* by including the role of prominent intellectual thought and the establishment of a philosophical paradigm as additional elements of a Discourse.

Finally, as this is a critical history that is seeking epistemological causality and the effects of power, its research method has followed that of a genealogical investigation as employed by Michel Foucault, most notably in his works *Discipline and Punish* and *The History of Sexuality*, volume 1. In his genealogical method, Foucault employs the design precepts of the *Annales* school, but he also adds one more: the examination of the underlying linguistic structures of society. This leads to another design precept, that the subject is chosen to fit the problem rather than the other way around. In other words, the parameters for defining the subject itself emerge as part of the investigation. For example, during the course of this investigation the concept of a "world" in which human beings perceive themselves as existing was identified as a key element in the Discourse, and thus became part of the subject under study. Thus, the corpus of source data to be examined at the beginning of an investigation fell within loose parameters and emerged as the investigation proceeded. And it seeks to examine a power–knowledge dynamic as defined by Foucault as the means to describe the epistemological causality at work.

It may be worthwhile to elaborate a bit more on Foucault's concept of a power–knowledge dynamic in order to better illustrate the notion of epistemological causality at work. Foucault's concept of epistemological causality which guides this research inquiry stems from poststructuralist thought that flows from the work of the prominent Swiss linguist Ferdinand de Saussure and the constructivist thought that followed in its wake. Saussure contributes two main principles of thought that are pertinent to this research study. First is that language can be thought of as a system of signs, a system that can be studied as an object of culture (versus merely studying the mechanics and nomenclature of language).[44] Second is "that the meaning which a particular item has depends in some way on its intralinguistic relations to other items in the language";[45] thus, meaning for a sign is influenced by the sign's relationship to other signs: This places emphasis on a spatially oriented causality when seeking epistemological causality rather than that of a time-oriented causality (i.e., event A must precede event B to state that A causes B) that comprises traditional historical endeavors which seek to explain why a historical event happened (i.e., ontological causality).

From these two principles, the following premise is derived: "a linguistic sign is a psychological entity related systematically to other linguistic signs to form a system, and furthermore one whose signifying features depend on the ways in which it is related to those other signs."[46] Saussure employs an excellent metaphor to illustrate this point: that of a chess game.[47] While the ontology of a chess piece never changes (how it is defined, how it moves and captures other pieces), the value or importance of a given piece is determined by its relationship to all the other pieces on the chessboard—with those pieces in the center of the chessboard typically exerting greater power. This metaphor also nicely illustrates the prominence of a spatially oriented causality vis-à-vis a time-oriented causality: The moves that led to the current system (i.e., arrangement of pieces) are irrelevant; value is determined by the current relationship of the pieces only. This conceptual model developed by Saussure plays a prominent role in establishing standards of rigor for a genealogical analysis.

Foucault builds upon concepts of Saussure in a number of crucial ways— moving away from the structuralist stance embodied by Saussure to one that is distinctly poststructuralist. Whereas Saussure applies his principles to abstract concepts in language, Foucault applies them to actual practices engaged in by individuals. By framing these practices within the context of culture and examining the language used to justify them, Foucault is able to describe how culture influences the alignment of linguistic signs within the system: creating not language in the abstract but, rather, a discourse that circumscribes our thought. From the perspective of a historical analysis, this discourse is made up of structures that can be studied—structures that are both discursive (e.g., intellectual thought) and non-discursive (e.g., economic conditions and technological advances) and whose relationship to each other causes empirical knowledge to be ordered in a particular manner. The power arising from these relationships acts to legitimate or delegitimate certain types of knowledge. Legitimated knowledge will then guide actions that will produce similar legitimated forms of knowledge, whereas delegitimated knowledge produces less influence over actions. Thus, an interplay occurs which is sustaining and reinforcing to some structural elements, while debilitating to others. As a result of this interplay, a particular Discourse will arise as dominant for the historical era in question.

The power at work in the epistemological ordering of knowledge via the interplay of various elements of the Discourse is well illustrated when a new dominant Discourse arises replacing the old. Discursive elements prominent within the old Discourse do not fade from human knowledge; rather, they are pushed to an obscure corner of the "chessboard," where their influence on practices becomes greatly diminished. So, for example, in colonial America knowledge promoting belief that one possesses a soul held a prominent position on the "chessboard" of epistemological ordering, and hence played a great role in shaping social welfare practices of that era. Today, knowledge promoting belief that one possesses a soul is still widely held by most Americans;[48] however, in our present era, this knowledge no longer exerts a significant influence on shaping social work practices. The ontology of this "chess piece" has not changed; what has changed is simply its relationship to other pieces on our "chessboard."

The structural elements (or "chess pieces" to continue Saussure's metaphor) that arose as subjects in this study concerning the Discourses on social welfare are the following.

The Geographic, Economic, Political, and Social Conditions of the Historical Era

Quite simply, these represent the state of affairs in each sphere (geographic, economic, political, social) which serve to structure everyday existence. The first of these structural elements—geographic conditions—takes a look at how geography affects communication and interactions between members of society. Social welfare requires a coordinated effort; this coordinated effort relies upon communication and transportation. Thus, technological innovations in transportation and communication are examined regarding their influence on facilitating this interaction and communication. In addition, population demographics are examined. Population density speaks to both needs and logistics of communication and transportation, while population characteristics serve to resonate with and shape the cultural milieu.

The second structural element—economic conditions—speaks specifically to the economic interactions that occur in society. Economic well-being is a central goal of social welfare. The examination of economic conditions takes a look at the philosophy and practices adopted in that era as the means to achieve this goal. How they are impacted by and influence in turn technological innovation, political policies, and social conditions serve to help flesh out the broader description of the Discourse.

The third element—political conditions—speaks to how society organizes itself to promote social welfare. Advancing individual rights that promote one's full participation in society is another central goal of social welfare. The story of the American experience is one of an ongoing experiment with democracy; hence, one facet to be examined is how this democracy unfolds in a particular era to promote this full participation. Additionally, the level and extent of government involvement in promoting this participation are other facets to be examined. As with the economic examination, how political conditions are impacted by and influence in turn the other conditions serve as means to flesh out the description of the Discourse.

The final element—social conditions—speaks to the cultural milieu shaping society's understanding of social welfare. One's sense of community plays a large role in shaping attitudes and practices that serve to promote the welfare of one's fellow citizens who are in need. Media serves as a primary means through which cultural attitudes are dispersed within society and also serves to engender a sense of community; hence, innovations in and growth of media are facets that are examined. Cultural practices that speak to a sense of community represent another facet that is explored. And as in the previous examinations, how social conditions are impacted by and influence in turn the other conditions round out the analysis. The confluence of the geographic, economic, political, and social conditions serves to create what Michel Foucault terms an *urgent need* for that particular era.[49]

Urgent Need

This is a concept borrowed directly from Foucault. The urgent need of an era is society's major preoccupation in very broad terms on the topic of study, the topic of study in this book being social welfare. This urgent need reflects society's viewpoint of what is most important to promote a robust society so that society can stave off existential threats to its survival. In short, social welfare is seen as being advanced by society's attempts to address this urgent need. This urgent need is something broadly understood and accepted by society. Even though it is never explicitly stated as such in writings of that era, everyday practices are organized around attempts to meet this urgent need. The other structural elements (outlined below) that best align with this urgent need coalesce into a Discourse which consequently dominates the ordering of knowledge for that era.

Intellectual Thought

Intellectual thought is something that is seized upon and thrust into prominence by its ability to address the urgent need. Thus, it should be noted that intellectual thought of a particular Discourse is introduced and developed well before its rise to dominance in terms of organizing everyday practices. It takes some time for these ideas to trickle down into the consciousness of broad swaths of society. In addition, prominent changes occurring in society will prompt a new conceptualization of the urgent need to be addressed, and thus a reassessment of what type of intellectual thought best does so.

Defining Cultural Current of the Era

This comes in the form of a major, widely held cultural belief that aligns itself with the urgent need. It can be seen as a defining cultural feature of its time. This will not necessarily be the most important or most prominent cultural feature defining the era overall; rather, it is the one that resonates most strongly with the other elements of the social welfare Discourse.

Paradigm of Understanding

The paradigm of understanding, as defined in this book, consists of fundamental philosophical assertions concerning reality (i.e., ontology), knowledge (i.e., epistemology), and causality. This represents the everyday person's understanding of the world in which they live. Most people from a particular era may not know the names or substantive rationales for each of these fundamental philosophical assertions; however, the basic premises will have been handed down and communicated to them nonetheless as it is impossible to navigate the world in which one lives without holding some basic understanding of it.

Conceptions of the Self

Similar to a paradigm of understanding, one cannot help but have a conception of self in terms of one's existence in the world as this also is essential in navigating everyday experiences. Consequently, these conceptions of self will be articulated at a very fundamental level. Such conceptions of self will resonate with one's understanding of community.

Rules of Right

In addition to producing an urgent need, the confluence of the various structural elements just outlined also serves to produce what Foucault labels as *rules of right*.[50] Rules of right speak to rules concerning which knowledge is privileged over others. They are the value judgments that a culture adopts that serve to sort knowledge along degrees of validity and measures of truth. These value judgments, or rules of formation, begin to operate at the very first step of inquiry—that of problematization: that is, what are valid questions to ask and how they should be phrased. Since these values are readily accepted and embraced, they often operate below the conscious awareness of individuals, lying deeply embedded in their cultural milieu. Seeking epistemological causality then becomes a process of unearthing these rules of right that lie below the conscious surface—remnants of a culture that must be dug up.

Theme of the Discourse

This represents my endeavor at applying narrative theory to Foucault's notion of a Discourse. As is the case with rules of right, the coalescing of discursive and non-discursive elements will give rise to a broad theme for the Discourse. Elaborating a theme is a succinct way in which to describe the main insight being promoted by the Discourse, and thus the understanding being employed in shaping one's actions. Examination of this theme will prove useful when studying the transitional period from when the next dominant Discourse begins to challenge its predecessor.

A Note on Plato

As the aim of this research is to conduct a genealogy of the good—in the form of social welfare—I have decided to layer my analysis by drawing upon the Platonic framework distinguishing knowledge into the categories of knowledge of the True, knowledge of the Good, and knowledge of the Beautiful. To be clear, this Platonic framework is not being offered as a structural element comprising a Discourse, as is the case for the previous descriptions. Rather, it offers a lens through which to elaborate the workings of the Discourse in terms of its knowledge generation.

The Layout of the Book

Both footnotes and endnotes are used liberally throughout this book. Endnotes are used extensively throughout the narrative. Each section contains its own endnotes, which are designated by numbers. The endnotes themselves will typically not elaborate upon the narrative. Rather, I am primarily using endnotes to simply mark a statement as a truth claim—based upon the citation information contained in the endnote. Footnotes are designated by lowercase letters of the alphabet and are found at the bottom of the page on which they appear. I use the footnotes to expand upon the narrative in some manner—yet they are not crucial to either the layout of the data or the flow of the argument.

Also, I adopt the convention used by Foucault in using a capital letter "D" for Discourse as a means to signify that Discourse's position of dominance. It should be noted that the Discourse represents something completely different than a historical era. Thus, for example, when referring to the Modern Discourse I am referring to the apparatus itself (comprised of the eight elements mentioned above) that orders knowledge in a particular pattern. When I refer to the *Modern Era*, I am referring to the time period within which the corresponding Discourse dominates.

Hence, the names of each of the eras under study (Colonial, Premodern, Modern, and Postmodern) derive from my attempts at naming the dominant Discourse, and thus are completely arbitrary in this regard. So, for example, the field of history has never adopted the term *premodern* to designate a particular time period. It is a name that is purely my invention. Additionally, the time period I use to designate the Modern Era (1920–present) does not align with the time period recognized by historians using this same descriptor.

The study contains eight major chapters, with two chapters each devoted to describing a distinct time period of data analysis: the Colonial America Discourse (c. 1620–1819), the Premodern Discourse (c. 1820–1919), the Modern Discourse (c. 1920–present), and the Postmodern discourse (representing a recently emerging discourse that has not yet achieved dominance). The first chapter for each era provides a thorough description of the dominant Discourse using the eight categories of structural elements described above. As this study concerns social welfare interventions, the urgent need to which the Discourse responds is expressed in terms of the survival and stability of the social order existing at the time. Evidence that supports the description of the various structural elements comprising the Discourse is cited using endnotes.

The second chapter for each era begins by outlining the various social welfare practices operating during this historical era, along with offering commentary explaining the practices based upon the previous chapter's description of the Discourse. This endeavor comprises the bulk of the chapter. Following this is a brief description of the time period covering the transition period between dominant Discourses. This is a time in which the current dominant Discourse begins to wane, and a new emerging discourse begins to compete for dominance. The interaction and interplay between these discourses yield important insights as to what occurs during the transition from one dominant Discourse to another— as the reigning Discourse attempts to incorporate various insights arising from the theme of the emerging discourse. This has particular relevance for today in that we exist in a time period in which the Modern Discourse exerts dominance in social welfare but is facing competition from the emerging Postmodern discourse. This then leads into a section examining the strengths and weaknesses of the Discourse in terms of its ability to address previous moral blind spots (i.e., strengths) and the manifestation of new moral blind spots (i.e., weaknesses). Lastly, I offer a few reflections as a social work historian on how insights from the examination of the Discourse can be applied to inform present-day social work practice with clients.

Notes

1. Schneider, *The History of Public Welfare*, 81.
2. Brace, *The Dangerous Classes*, 246–70.
3. Margolin, *Under the Cover*, 92–94.
4. Leiby, *History of Social Welfare*; Leighninger, *Social Work: Search for Identity*; and Trattner, *From Poor Law*. These serve as some examples.
5. Kant, "An Old Question."
6. Trattner, *From Poor Law*.
7. Popple, *Social Work Practice*.
8. Margolin, *Under the Cover*; Wagner, *What's Love Got?*.
9. National Association of Social Workers, *Code of Ethics*.
10. Boyer, *Urban Masses*; Rothman, *Discovery of the Asylum*; Stansell, *City of Women*; Wagner, *What's Love Got?*. All serve as examples of works that fall into this category.
11. Rothman, *Discovery of the Asylum*.
12. Popple, Leighninger, and Leighninger, *Social Work, Social Welfare*.
13. Piven and Cloward, *Regulating the Poor*.
14. Margolin, *Under the Cover*.
15. Margolin, 9.
16. Archenbaum, "Review"; Wakefield, "Foucauldian Fallacies."
17. Moffat, *A Poetics of Social Work*.
18. Foucault, *Discipline and Punish*; Foucault, *The Birth of the Clinic*; Foucault, *The Order of Things*. Each illustrates this.
19. Foucault, *Power–Knowledge*, 156.
20. Foucault, *Discipline and Punish*, 52.
21. Foucault, *Power–Knowledge*, 154–58.
22. Reeve, *Socrates in the Apology*, 18–19.
23. Foucault, *The Birth of the Clinic*, xix.
24. Foucault, *Power–Knowledge*, 81–82.
25. Ruddick, *Young and Homeless*, 137.
26. Weick, "Guilty Knowledge"; Weick, "Hidden Voices."
27. Miehls and Moffat, "Constructing Social Work Identity"; Saleebey, "Culture, Theory, and Narrative."
28. Chambon, Irving, and Epstein, *Reading Foucault for Social Work*.
29. Holbrook, "Finding Knowledge."
30. Pease, "Rethinking Empowerment."
31. Foucault, *Power–Knowledge*; Foucault, *The Order of Things*; Foucault, *Discipline and Punish*. These serve as good examples.

32. Reeve, *Socrates in the Apology*.
33. Foucault, *The Use of Pleasure*, 8.
34. McAvoy, *The Profession of Ignorance*, 19.
35. Kant, *Critique of Pure Reason*.
36. Hook et al., "Cultural Humility"; Ross, "Notes from the Field."
37. Stubbe, "Practicing Cultural Competence," 49.
38. Abrams and Moio, "Critical Race Theory"; Gallegos, Tindall, and Gallegos, "The Need for Advancement." These serve as two examples.
39. Tervalon and Murray-Garcia, "Cultural Humility versus Cultural Competence," 117.
40. Danson, "Cultural Competence and Cultural Humility"; Fisher-Borne, Cain, and Martin, "From Mastery to Accountability"; Ross, "Notes from the Field."
41. Axinn and Levin, *Social Welfare*, 14; Axinn and Stern, *Social Welfare*, 21; Schneider, *The History of Public Welfare*, 64.
42. National Association of Social Workers, *Code of Ethics*, 9.
43. Burke, *The French Historical Revolution*.
44. Saussure, *Course in General Linguistics*.
45. Holdcroft, *Saussure: Signs, System*, 49.
46. Holdcroft, 49.
47. Saussure, *Course in General Linguistics*.
48. Murphy, "Most Americans Believe"; Weldon, "Paradise Polled."
49. Foucault, *The Order of Things*; Foucault, *Discipline and Punish*.
50. Foucault, *The Order of Things*; Foucault, *Discipline and Punish*.

References

Abrams, Laura, and Jenè Moio. "Critical Race Theory and the Cultural Competence Dilemma in Social Work Education." *Journal of Social Work Education* 45 (2009): 245–61.

Archenbaum, Walter. "Review of *Under the Cover of Kindness: The Invention of Social Work*, by Leslie Margolin." *Journal of Social History* 32 (1999): 957–99.

Axinn, June, and Herman Levin. *Social Welfare: A History of the American Response to Need*. New York: Harper & Row, 1975.

Axinn, June, and Mark Stern. *Social Welfare: A History of the American Response to Need*. 5th ed. Needham Heights, MA: Pearson, 2000.

Boyer, Paul. *Urban Masses and Moral Order in America, 1820–1920*. Cambridge, MA: Harvard University Press, 1978.

Brace, Charles Loring. *The Dangerous Classes of New York and Twenty Years' Work among Them*. New York: Wynkoop and Hallenbeck, 1872.

Braudel, Ferdinand. *The Mediterranean and the Mediterranean World in the Age of Philip II*. 2 vols. New York: HarperCollins, 1975–76.

Burke, Peter. *The French Historical Revolution: The Annales School 1929–89*. Stanford, CA: Stanford University Press, 1990.

Chambon, Adrienne, Allan Irving, and Laura Epstein, eds. *Reading Foucault for Social Work*. New York: Columbia University Press, 1999.

Danson, Ransford. "Cultural Competence and Cultural Humility: A Critical Reflection on Key Cultural Diversity Concepts." *Social Work* 18 (2016): 410–30.

Fisher-Borne, Marcie, Jessie M. Cain, and Suzanne L. Martin. "From Mastery to Accountability: Cultural Humility as an Alternative to Cultural Competence." *Social Work Education* 34 (2014): 165–81.

Foucault, Michel. *Power–Knowledge: Selected Interviews & Other Writings 1972–1977.* Edited by Colin Gordon. New York: Pantheon Books, 1981.

Foucault, Michel. *Madness and Civilization: A History of Insanity in the Age of Reason.* New York: Vintage Books, 1988.

Foucault, Michel. *The History of Sexuality.* Vol. 1, *An Introduction.* New York: Vintage Books, 1990.

Foucault, Michel. *The History of Sexuality.* Vol. 2, *The Use of Pleasure.* New York: Vintage Books, 1990.

Foucault, Michel. *Discipline and Punish: The Birth of the Prison.* New York: Vintage Books, 1991.

Foucault, Michel. *The Birth of the Clinic: An Archaeology of Medical Perception.* New York: Vintage Books, 1994.

Foucault, Michel. *The Order of Things: An Archaeology of the Human Sciences.* New York: Vintage Books, 1994.

Gallegos, Joseph, Cherie Tindall, and Shiela A. Gallegos. "The Need for Advancement in the Conceptualization of Cultural Competence." *Advances in Social Work* 9 (2008): 51–62.

Holbrook, Thomas. "Finding Knowledge: Personal Document Research." *Social Work* 40 (1995): 746–51.

Holdcroft, David. *Saussure: Signs, System, and Arbitrariness.* New York: Cambridge University Press, 1991.

Kant, Immanuel. "An Old Question Raised Again: Is the Human Race Constantly Progressing?" In *Kant: On History.* Edited by Lewis Beck. Translated by Robert Anchor. Upper Saddle River, NJ: Prentice Hall, 2001. First published 1798.

Kant, Immanuel. *Critique of Pure Reason.* Translated by Norman Smith. New York: Penguin, 2007. First published 1781.

Kuhn, Thomas. *The Structure of Scientific Revolutions.* Chicago: University of Chicago Press, 1962.

Leiby, James. *A History of Social Welfare and Social Work in the United States.* New York: Columbia University Press, 1978.

Leighninger, Leslie. *Social Work: Search for Identity.* New York: Greenwood Press, 1987.

Lubove, Roy. *The Professional Altruist: The Emergence of Social Work as a Career, 1880–1930.* Cambridge, MA: Harvard University Press, 1965.

Margolin, Leslie. *Under the Cover of Kindness: The Invention of Social Work.* Charlottesville: University Press of Virginia, 1997.

McAvoy, Martin. *The Profession of Ignorance: With Constant Reference to Socrates.* Lanham, MD: University Press of America, 1999.

Miehls, Dennis, and Ken Moffatt. "Constructing Social Work Identity Based on the Reflexive Self." *British Journal of Social Work* 30 (2000): 339–48.

Moffat, Ken. *A Poetics of Social Work: Personal Agency and Social Transformation in Canada, 1920–1939.* Toronto: University of Toronto Press, 2001.

Murphy, Caryle. "Most Americans Believe in Heaven . . . and Hell." Pew Research Center. Last modified November 10, 2015, https://www.pewresearch.org/fact-tank/2015/11/10/most-americans-believe-in-heaven-and-hell/.

National Association of Social Workers. *Code of Ethics of the National Association of Social Workers*. Washington, DC: NASW Press, 1999.

Pease, Bob. "Rethinking Empowerment: A Postmodern Reappraisal for Emancipatory Practice." *British Journal of Social Work* 32 (2002): 135–47.

Piven, Francis F., and Richard Cloward. *Regulating the Poor: The Functions of Public Welfare*. New York: Pantheon Books, 1971.

Popple, Phillip R. *Social Work Practice and Social Welfare Policy in the United States: A History*. New York: Oxford University Press, 2018.

Popple, Phillip R., Leslie Leighninger, and Robert D. Leighninger. *Social Work, Social Welfare, and American Society*. 9th ed. Hoboken: Pearson, 2019.

Reeve, David. *Socrates in the Apology: An Essay on Plato's Apology of Socrates*. Indianapolis: Hackett Publishing Company, 1989.

Ross, Laurie. "Notes from the Field: Learning Cultural Humility Through Critical Incidents and Central Challenges in Community-Based Participatory Research." *Journal of Community Practice* 18 (2010): 315–35.

Rothman, David. *The Discovery of the Asylum: Social Order and Disorder in the New Republic*. 3rd ed. New York: Walter de Gruyter, 1971.

Ruddick, Susan. *Young and Homeless in Hollywood: Mapping Social Identities*. New York: Routledge, 1996.

Saleebey, Dennis. "Culture, Theory, and Narrative: The Intersection of Meanings in Practice." *Social Work* 39 (1994): 351–59.

Saussure, Ferdinand. *Course in General Linguistics*. Translated by Wade Baskin. New York: McGraw-Hill Book Company, 1959. First published 1916.

Schneider, David M. *The History of Public Welfare in New York State 1609–1866*. Chicago: University of Chicago Press, 1938.

Stansell, Christine. *City of Women: Sex and Class in New York, 1789–1860*. New York: Knopf, 1986.

Stubbe, Dorothy E. "Practicing Cultural Competence and Cultural Humility in the Care of Diverse Patients." *Focus: The Journal of Lifelong Learning in Psychiatry* 18 (2020): 49–51.

Tervalon, Melanie, and Jann Murray-Garcia. "Cultural Humility versus Cultural Competence." *Journal of Healthcare for the Poor and Underserved* 9 (1998): 117–25.

Trattner, Walter I. *From Poor Law to Welfare State: A History of Social Welfare in America*. 4th ed. New York: Free Press, 1989.

Wagner, David. *What's Love Got to Do with It? A Critical Look at American Charity*. New York: New Press, 2000.

Wakefield, Jerome C. "Foucauldian Fallacies: An Essay Review of Leslie Margolin's *Under the Cover of Kindness*." *Social Service Review* 72 (1998): 545–87.

Weick, Ann. "Guilty Knowledge." *Families in Society* 80 (1999): 327–32.

Weick, Ann. "Hidden Voices." *Social Work* 45 (2000): 395–402.

Weldon, Kathleen. "Paradise Polled: Americans and the Afterlife." HuffPost. Last modified December 6, 2017. https://www.huffpost.com/entry/paradise-polled-americans_b_7587538.

2

The Colonial American Discourse (c. 1620–1820)

In 1786 in the town of Malden, Massachusetts, Mary Degresha having recently been widowed found herself in a position in which she was unable to support herself. Having no family within the community in whom to seek succor, she appealed to the town selectmen for aid. Their response was to place her up for auction. She went to reside in the household of the winning bidder, wherein she would be expected to perform domestic duties and obey the master of the household.[1] This practice of auctioning off the poor was common throughout the colonies.

The colonists also embraced a criminal justice policy of strict and severe corporal punishment. The following passages, taken from court documents illustrate the workings of criminal justice in the colonies, which heavily relied upon corporal punishment. Alice Thomas found herself convicted of a number of crimes: abetting petty theft by buying stolen goods, promoting carnal wickedness (i.e., sex) by hosting lewd and lascivious persons in her house, selling alcohol without a license, entertaining indentured servants and children without their master's/father's permission, and profanation of the Sabbath by entertaining persons in her home and conducting business on Sundays. Her sentence was as follows:

> Alice Thomas being accused of severall shamefull notorious crimes & high misdemeanors. . . . The Court vpon due consideration of this Verdict Sentenced her to restore to Jon Pinchen Junr forty one pounds fifteen shillings and three pence to Thomas Beard thirteene pounds seaven shillings and eight pence to Capt Jon Hull twelve pounds, all in money being ye proportion of that 3.fold restitution ye Law requireth also to pay fivety pounds fine in money to ye County and fees of Court and prison. Alsoe to bee carried from the prison to ye Gallows, and there stand one hour wth a rope about her necke, one end fastened to ye sd Gallowes, and thence to bee returned to prison. & alsoe to bee carried from the prison to her one house and brought out of the gate or fore-doore strip't to the waste, & there tyed to a Cart's Taile, and soe to be whip't through ye Streete to the prison wth not undr thirty nine Stripes, & there in prison to remaine during the pleasure of this court.[2]

A Genealogy of the Good and Critique of Hubris. Phillip Dybicz, Oxford University Press. © Oxford University Press 2023. DOI: 10.1093/oso/9780197670071.003.0002

John Veering was convicted of being drunk and verbally abusing both his wife and fellow church members with the following result:

John Veering presented for beeing drunck & abuseing his wife in bad language calling her whore & a reproaching mr Allen & Church members in saying mr Allen was a black hypocriticall Rogue, of all which hee was convict in Court. The Court Sentanceth him to bee whip' t with thirty Stripes severely laide on & to stand in the open market place in Boston, exalted upon a Stoole for an houres time on a thursday after Lecture; with a paper fastned to his breast, with this inscription in a Lardge character "A Prophane & Wicked Slandered & Impious Reviler of a minister of the Gosple & Church-members"; & to pay charges of Witnesses & Fees of Court.[3]

Beginning in the 1700s, some cities and counties began erecting alms houses as an alternative means to provide poor relief. Being introduced first in New York in 1707 and subsequently in other cities and counties as the century progressed, there were statutes on the books requiring those seeking poor relief from almshouses to wear a badge of poverty upon their right shoulder. The badge of poverty consisted of a large letter "P" signifying "Pauper" in either red, blue, or green cloth along with the first letter of the person's town of residence.[4] Refusal to wear the badge could result in financial support being withdrawn.[5]

It is not uncommon for those first reading about these three practices— auctioning off a poor person seeking relief from the state, administering corporal punishment in the form of whip lashings to offenders, and requiring the poor to wear a badge of poverty on their shoulder—to come away with an impression that colonial Americans had a pronounced cruel streak when dealing with their fellow citizens in need. One may think that perhaps the harsh conditions under which they lived along with religious zealotry combined to create an environ- ment in which such barbaric acts were deemed necessary. What may surprise the reader is that the colonists themselves did not view these practices as either cruel or barbaric. Quite the contrary, they viewed these practices as quite humane and flowing from a generous heart. To understand how this might be so, one needs to examine the dominant Discourse within which the colonists operated.

To be sure, there was a sprinkling of diversity among immigrants reaching American shores during the Colonial Era.[6] Diverse religious affiliations such as Quakers and Catholics settled among the Protestants. In addition, while most arriving in New England were escaping religious persecution, most settling in the southern colonies were not. The social elites in the southern colonies embraced more the role of cavalier from Renaissance times rather than that of pious Puritan seeking to establish the shining city on a hill.[7] Yet as historian Paul Goodman notes, "Despite religious beliefs and aspirations which distinguished

Puritans from others, most Englishmen shared similar assumptions about the nature and purpose of government and the relationship between the individual and the community."[8] Thus, despite any minor differences, they all shared in a common dominant Discourse in their approach to social welfare.[9] The elements of this Discourse are described in the pages that follow.

Conditions in Colonial America

Geographic Conditions

Historian Robert Weibe uses the metaphor of "island communities" to capture the overall relationship between the various towns and communities established during the Colonial Era.[10] This is a very apt metaphor.

Population Demographics

Even toward the end of the historical era being described here, colonial towns and communities represented small outposts along a frontier, closely knit and small in population.[11] By 1754, Salem was the largest town north of Boston yet only had a population of 3,462, whereas most colonial towns and villages by this time had a population ranging from a few hundred to just over 1,000 people.[12] As most residents lived their entire lives in these communities, it was not difficult for these individuals to learn all of their neighbors' names, personal histories, and particular idiosyncrasies through the various roles and contexts in which they interacted.[13] Throughout the colonies, the church was the central feature to village life. The founding of villages in colonial America—especially those in New England—was undertaken by people who all belonged to a single congregation.[14] Thus, one's identity as a resident of the town had both a social and a spiritual aspect to it. This served to enhance the cohesiveness already brought on by the small size and relative isolation of the community as one's neighbor was also a fellow church member. As new people settled in the village, they would inevitably be accepted into this congregation.[15] Once the population of villages grew beyond a few hundred individuals, a second and then third congregation might be added, yet these additional congregations would be of the same denomination.[16] Only in the towns that grew into cities—such as Boston, New York, and Philadelphia—might you find congregations of different denominations.[17]

Transportation and Communication

Travel between communities was problematic and not undertaken lightly. Being situated on a frontier, early American communities in North America were mainly connected by land via existing Native American footpaths.[18] Traveling by water via boat or canoe offered a bit speedier method, again relying upon routes and portage sites established by Native Americans.[19] Even when rudimentary roads began being built in the 1700s between the established communities on the New England seaboard,[20] only those of middle to upper class could afford a horse for travel; the vast majority of colonists when needing to ply these roads did so by foot.[21] Thus, the next community could be anywhere between a half-day's to a full-day's travel. Even travel within cities was problematic, evidenced by the fact that as late as 1761 in Philadelphia, the largest city at the time with a population of just under 20,000, there were only thirty-eight carriages in the entire city.[22] This geographic isolation experienced between communities, on par with that occurring between a grouping of islands, had a second layer of geographic isolation added on top of this local experience via the American colonies' connection to their mother country of Great Britain and other countries in Europe: The average Atlantic crossing could take between six weeks and six months.[23] Consequently, communication between communities as well as communication between a community and its various seats of government was highly limited.

Nevertheless, trade prospered. Yet, while many a farmer would produce more than was needed to maintain the family and thus would look to barter and trade the surplus,[24] most would not leave their community to do so. The arduous and sometimes dangerous conditions of travel meant that very few people traveled far from their homes and community.[25] Travel on a regular basis between communities was expensive and thus primarily undertaken by merchants conducting business and government officials performing an official duty.[26] Nonetheless, residents of communities would see the occasional traveler of common means. Those seeking residency in a new community—such as newly arrived immigrants, those who finished up their indentured contract and were moving on, and those with little inheritance seeking a better life on the frontier—would make a one-time trip for this purpose and thus pass through many communities before reaching their destination.[27] However, such regularly occurring travel by these more common folk provided cover for the various rogues, vagabonds, and runaway indentured servants who plied the roads as well, seeking to con and deceive the country folk whom they encountered.[28] Thus, while colonists were very liberal with their hospitality toward the common traveler simply passing through,[29] they looked with a more discerning eye at those individuals seeking an extended stay or residency.[30] This insular quality of colonial communities brought on by the geographic isolation of being situated along a frontier wilderness continued throughout this era. It was not until 1740 that settlements in Connecticut filled up the last of its frontier, while the colony of Georgia was first issued its charter in 1732.[31]

Economic Conditions

As was still the case in the Old World whence the colonists came, the main unit of economic production was the family.[32] Being far and wide an agrarian society, in the colonial towns and villages even those practicing a profession, such as a blacksmith, were also farmers. Thus, for all practical purposes, the colonial family was self-sufficient in terms of meeting its fundamental material wants and needs.[33] Besides growing their own food, each family processed a number of dairy items as well as manufactured wool and cloth garments.[34] The family provided the framework within which labor was organized; and everyone in the household— father, mother, children as young as six years, and servants—worked toward the same common purpose of advancing the bounty of the family.[35]

Merchants conducted trade with Great Britain and across the colonies; hence, it was not uncommon for the typical family to trade for needed goods, services, or the occasional luxury item.[36] Circulating money was scarce however; thus, trade within and across communities occurred primarily through barter.[37] Despite these ties by trade to the outside world, colonists understood that their geographic isolation placed their economic survival in a precarious position; the least bit of misfortune could place them in peril. Every colonist could look back upon lean and starving times when their very survival and that of the community was vigorously tested.[38] During these times, outside aid was not readily or speedily available. Consequently, each family strove for self-sufficiency, as did the community as a whole. During personal misfortunes or widespread hard times, community members took care of their own as outside help could not be relied upon.[39]

Political Conditions

The relative geographic isolation of the various communities throughout the American colonies meant that government power devolved greatly to local rule. This political self-sufficiency extended as far as to matters of defense, with each community forming its own militia.[40] For the average colonist, especially when it came to social welfare needs, the town's system of government had a far greater impact on their lives than any colony-wide institutions.[41] In New England, town hall meetings were held regularly wherein freemen were allowed to speak upon matters and vote on policy.[42] The term *freeman* originally was a designation indicating one as a member of a commercial entity, as most colonies were established by corporate charters granted by the king of England.[43] Yet soon thereafter, the term *freeman* came simply to mean a citizen of the state, someone who held the right to vote and to hold office.[44] Freeman status was granted to male heads of households who were members of the town's congregation.[45] Women, servants, and others were given the status of *inhabitant*, which granted the individual such things as protection and equality under the law as well as the right to own property yet offered no voting rights or voice in government.[46] Notwithstanding these limitations on enfranchisement, a greater share of the town's population had a voice in government when compared to communities back in England.[47]

During these town hall meetings, the freemen would elect a number of town selectmen or magistrates.[48] These town selectmen would vote on urgent matters arising between meetings, as well as implement policy by deciding upon matters such as granting residency status or the disbursement of poor relief.[49] When necessary, they would appoint a person to the paid position of overseer of the poor. This overseer would then handle the logistics of delivering the poor relief granted by the town selectmen as well as investigate and communicate new needs that arose—similar to the role that social work case managers play today.[50]

As will be discussed more fully in the upcoming section on the intellectual thought influencing this time period, the town's system of government derived its authority not primarily from political charter but rather as a system ordained by God. While men were given the freedom to decide on the particularities of the system, colonists believed that God ordained all persons to live under the rule of government and to willingly subject themselves to those placed in positions of authority.[51] Government was seen as a necessary check to humans' natural proclivity to fall under the sway of original sin.[52] And while the colonists readily borrowed from English law and common law, it was the bible that served as the main source of inspiration and authority when crafting their rules for society.[53]

Social Conditions

The social cohesiveness of village life fostered strong bonds of interdependence among its members. While each family household strove for economic self-sufficiency, help from neighbors was readily available when needed. Thus, the raising of a barn or other new building would become a community project; neighbors could be called upon to help with harvest for those who, due to misfortune, fell short of the required labor; simple products such as soap and candles were bartered, eliminating the need for family to produce every single product they needed; and when personal tragedies befell a family, such as the death of a spouse or child, neighbors would provide emotional support and succor.[54]

As noted so far, due to the relative isolation of communities and the situation of living on a frontier, members of a community were engaged in a mutual struggle for survival. The success of this struggle rested upon maintaining a strong interdependence on a number of levels: economic interdependence through a barter system for basic goods and services to promote bounty and stave off want, political interdependence through the creation of a militia to combat existential threats and through a welfare system to combat the vicissitudes of fortune, and a spiritual interdependence to keep in God's good graces and avoid provoking His wrath upon the community. The health and vibrancy of this network of interdependency vitally depended upon the maintenance of a strong level of social cohesiveness. And the colonists believed that this strong social cohesiveness was achieved through the maintenance of a clearly established social hierarchy.[55] The reason behind this central importance given to maintaining the social hierarchy was the fact that colonists viewed their community in an organic fashion; the community was not simply made up of a collection of individuals but, rather, functioned like an organism made up of interdependent parts.[56] The ordering of these parts into a hierarchical whole naturally created various levels of social superior/inferior relationships.[57] Each position in the hierarchy contributed toward the health of the whole, and every person in the community had a place and role to fulfill.[58]

It will come as no surprise that this social hierarchy had a heavily patriarchal cast to it.[59] The colonists used their spiritual relationship with God as the model for how to conduct their social relations.[60] Spiritually, they sought to subject themselves to the will of an all-knowing Father. When this concept was translated to the social level, the result was a hierarchical system of social relations in which inferiors were expected to obey the will of superiors.[61] At the family level, this put the father at the head of the household. As still reflected in traditional marriage vows today, the wife was expected to love, honor, and *obey* the husband (similar to the notion as a church member to love, honor, and obey the will of God).[62] However, as mother, she was in a superior position to the children, who in turn were expected to love, honor, and obey her.[63] Additionally, as mistress of the household, servants were expected to honor and obey her (as long as such wishes did not contradict those of the master of the household).[64]

Drawing still upon a medieval heritage, colonists embraced a social stratification at the community level as well, which combined social, economic, and political dimensions into a single unit.[65] Thus, the gradations marking levels of economic power also marked levels of political power and of social standing.[66] Similar to the structure within a family, the community hierarchy comprised relationships between inferiors and superiors.[67] The bottom level of this hierarchy was occupied by servants, children, and the poor (slaves were considered chattel and hence were not part of the social hierarchy); the middle of the hierarchy was comprised of yeoman farmers and artisans; and the upper echelons were occupied by educated elite—landed gentry, ministers, and town selectmen.[68]

One important way in which the American colonists broke away from their medieval heritage was in the fluidity of positions one might obtain in the social hierarchy.[69] Thus, unlike the feudal structure from the Middle Ages wherein if one was born a peasant, one remained a peasant for one's entire life, conditions in colonial America fostered a more fluid movement within the social hierarchy. So, for example, many individuals who came to America's shores did so as an indentured servant.[70] Once their term of service was up, they moved from the status of servant to that of yeoman. If yeomen fell into poverty and sought relief from the community, this could entail them to move back down into the role of servant, as is illustrated by the practice of auctioning off the poor.[71] Also, there was no titled nobility laying claim to the land. Hence, if one prospered economically, a yeoman could enter the upper class, whereas if one experienced economic misfortune, one could fall from the upper class back into the status of a yeoman.[72]

Lastly, within each level of the social hierarchy there were further gradations of inferiority along the lines of gender, ethnicity, religion, and race. As noted above, the status of yeowomen was inferior to that of yeomen inhabiting the same social level as well as being inferior to both the men and women comprising the genteel class. Yet the status of yeowomen was superior to that of those positioned lower in the hierarchy (e.g., children and servants). In addition, the early American colonists were highly ethnocentric and comprised of predominantly White, Anglo-Saxon Protestants (i.e., often referred to as WASPs).[73] The more one deviated from these categories, the lower one sank. Hence, colonists who were White and Protestant yet not Anglo-Saxon—such as the Scots, Welsh, and Germans—occupied a lower rung in the hierarchy level to which they belonged.[74] Those who were White but neither Anglo-Saxon nor Protestant—such as the Irish—occupied a still lower rung. And those who were neither White nor Anglo-Saxon nor Protestant or even Christian—such as Native American Indians and Africans—dropped so low in the hierarchy that they breached the social level below them. So, for example, manumitted slaves gained the status of yeoman; however, they were still viewed as occupying a position of inferiority relative to White servants.[75] Such a view also is what moved those Native Americans and Africans forced into servitude at the lowest level to fall completely off the social hierarchy representing the community "family" and thus no longer occupy a place within it. This moved them from being of the category of "servant" to the category of "slave," and slaves were merely considered chattel of their owners.[76] Native Americans along the frontier were seen as godless pagans whose liberties and rights need not be respected.[77] Also falling off the social hierarchy representing the community "family" were those who led a rootless existence—termed *rogues* and *vagabonds* by the American colonists. They were unwelcome in communities and quickly told to leave.[78]

It must be noted that this relationship between social inferiors and social superiors consisted of *reciprocal* obligations: Each side had both various rights to claim as well as responsibilities to uphold.[79] Reflective of the positions of status themselves, these rights and responsibilities were grounded upon a threefold base: on a social level in the form of cultural custom, on a political level in the form of laws, and on a spiritual level in the form of religious duty.[80] Hence, the duty to honor and obey one's mother and father gained its legitimacy not only from social custom but also as a legal requirement whose maximum criminal penalty was death; and finally, it was also viewed as a religious duty necessary for one's salvation.[81] In addition to applying to children and servants in the household, the prescription to honor and obey one's mother and father was applied metaphorically to the social hierarchy at the community level.[82] Thus, the duty of social inferiors to honor and obey their social superiors carried with it this same threefold force of weight.

The spiritual dimension to this prescription to honor and obey is especially useful in understanding the colonial mindset. Obedience was not simply a recognition of the power inherent in the superior position. Rather, obedience was seen as a form of liberty. When one subjected oneself completely to the will of God, this was viewed as a liberating experience, allowing one the freedom to confidently walk the righteous path. As the following quote attests, this same understanding was applied to social relationships:

> This liberty [civil and federal] is maintained and exercised in a way of subjection to authority; it is of the same kind of liberty wherewith Christ hath made us free. The woman's own choice makes such a man her husband; yet being so chosen, he is her lord, and she is to be subject to him, yet in a way of liberty, not of bondage; and a true wife accounts her subjection her honor and freedom, and would not think her condition safe and free, but in her subjection to her husband's authority.[83]

This right of those in a superior position to the honor and obeisance of those in an inferior position carried with it the reciprocal responsibility to care for the physical, economic, and spiritual well-being of those in the inferior position. So, for example, the master of a household was tasked with providing basic necessities such as food, clothing, and shelter for all those underneath his roof.[84] He was also tasked with adequately preparing his children and servants to enter a livelihood upon leaving the household; in fact, part of the indentured servant contract included the bestowing of a care package upon completion of service that would serve as a starter kit to help the person establish themselves.[85] Lastly, the master of the household was charged with the education of his children (and servants if needed) so that they may read and understand the Bible in order to see for themselves the opportunities for one's salvation as well as what sins God forbade.[86] This responsibility too carried with it the threefold weight of social custom, legal requirement, and religious duty. Thus, it was not unheard of for an indentured servant to file a complaint of mistreatment with the court against his master.[87] At the community level, this translated into the responsibility of social superiors to provide poor relief to those in need.[88] This rule of charity was viewed as a sacred and solemn duty and, as will be fully elaborated later in Chapter 3, resulted in the colonists adopting a very tolerant and amicable attitude toward the poor.[89]

Lastly, the breach of one's responsibility was viewed as a major threat to the social order and was met with severe consequences. Hence, as related above, failure to live up to one's duty to honor and obey one's father and mother was a capital crime. And as related above by the example of an indentured servant filing a complaint with the court, the failure of a social superior to live up to one's duty to promote the welfare of those under his care enabled those in the inferior position to seek redress in the courts and, failing that, to rebel against the authority of the superior and thus make the relationship null and void. This premise of a breach of duty by a social superior is what led our founding fathers toward their decision to break away from rule under King George III of England.[90]

The Urgent Need

As stated in Chapter 1, Foucault's historical approach in mapping the dominant Discourse operating during a particular era proposes that the Discourse achieves dominance due to its ability to most adequately respond to the perceived urgent need of that era.[91] This urgent need reflects society's viewpoint of what is most important to promote a robust society so that society can stave off existential threats to its survival. From the evidence presented thus far concerning the various conditions shaping the colonial experience, the urgent need of this era begins to become apparent. As noted above, life in a colonial community was built upon a network of interdependent relationships. Since American colonists were living within the relative isolation of an "island" community, this interdependence was seen as the main force combatting the various existential threats potentially faced by the community. Thus, economic interdependence served to support members who fell on hard times and to help the community weather lean years of harvest. Political interdependence was necessary to foster order within a community based upon local rule as well as to protect against outside threats via the formation of a militia. And spiritual interdependence was seen as aiding one's salvation by offering a healthy check on one's proclivity to be tempted to sin as well as serving to buffer against the possibility of God visiting wrath upon the community by helping one's neighbors and oneself to stay in God's good graces. It was only through the cooperation of all the individuals in the community that the community would thrive under God's guidance.[92] Thus, maintaining this interdependence was seen as vital to promoting the social welfare and social order of the community.

The social hierarchy, with its division into levels of superiors/inferiors and the establishment of rights and responsibilities for each, was seen as providing the necessary structure for this interdependence to grow and prosper. Thus, the urgent need of this historical era was *the maintenance of the social hierarchy*. As noted earlier, mobility within the hierarchy occurred, so maintenance of the hierarchy meant simply preservation of the hierarchy itself as an organizing feature of society. This position is summed up by historian Paul Goodman as follows: "Yet two basic aspects of seventeenth-century social philosophy which affected everyone must be kept in mind: first, the universal acceptance of the concept of social gradation and a complete belief in its rightness; and second, the belief held simultaneously, that differences in rank, although normally to be observed, were not unalterable."[93] Or as William Hubbard wrote in 1621 in his sermon entitled "The Happiness of a People In the Wisdom of their Rulers DIRECTING And in the Obedience of their Brethren ATTENDING Unto what Israel ought to do," "so that it appears, whoever is for a parity in any Society, will in the issue reduce things into an heap of confusion."[94]

Ideas or efforts that sought to undermine the social hierarchy were viewed as an existential threat. Thus, for example, in the 1730s–1740s the First Great Awakening proposed such parity at the spiritual level by advocating that anyone could speak with God directly and receive guidance from the Holy Spirit concerning their salvation—thus eliminating the need for a pastor to provide this guidance. In addition, anyone who was particularly moved by the Holy Spirit could become a preacher without the need of systematic education (whose access was restricted to the elite) to prepare oneself for this role.[95] This prompted a strong reaction against it by the established clergy and town elites, which resulted in the movement being snuffed out, only to re-emerge at the end of the century as the Second Great Awakening when a new discourse more conducive to this message began to arise and vie for dominance.

At a more micro level, individuals who did not adequately fit into the social hierarchy or who rebelled against it were seen as subversive and viewed as an "other." Thus, those women most likely to be accused of witchcraft were women who challenged their place in the social hierarchy either by refusing to show deference to men occupying positions of authority or by acting contentious and aggressive when asserting their opinions.[96] These "faults" were compounded if the woman had passed menopause and was widowed as she was no longer able to fulfill her role in procreating; also, she lacked a husband to control her susceptibility to the abovementioned base proclivities as well as to provide a respected voice in which to counter any malicious accusations.[97] As historian Richard Godbeer notes, "Colonists associated subversive women with witchcraft because they seemed to re-enact the behavior of Eve and of the Devil, both of whom were real historical figures in the minds of New Englanders."[98] In addition, other social mechanisms were used to put down rebellious women. In 1637, Anne Hutchinson was convicted of heresy and ostracized from Boston for daring to offer her interpretations of scripture.[99] During the 1650s, Elizabeth Hooton responded to a "call" from God to preach; her outspokenness landed her in court on a number of occasions.[100] And twice, first in Boston and later in Cambridge, authorities took her on a two-day walk deep into the forest and then abandoned her, with the Cambridge authorities first whipping her as they passed through three towns on the way to the forest.[101]

Also as stated previously, Africans and Native Americans often fell completely off the social hierarchy, resulting in either their enslavement, forced ouster from lands they once held, or mass annihilation. And lastly, as will be explored more fully in the next chapter, itinerant workers and vagabonds—individuals who did not seek a permanent place in the community's social hierarchy—were unwelcome guests in communities and told to leave in a process known as *warning out*.[102]

Intellectual Thought

While many works of Enlightenment thought were produced in this era, as noted in Chapter 1, it would take many decades for predominant movements of intellectual thought to trickle down to the community level and shape everyday behaviors and practices. Enlightenment thought began to exert an influence toward the end of the eighteenth century (as will be outlined in Chapter 3); however, it would not be until the nineteenth century (Chapter 4) when within a new dominant Discourse it would rise to prominence. Consequently, the intellectual thought that influenced the everyday life of the colonial American community was predominantly religious thought. And though various religious denominations settled in America—such as Puritan, Anglican, Quaker, Presbyterian, Reformed, Lutheran, Catholic, and Pietist—most were Protestant, and they all shared Christian roots.[103] First, it will be useful to examine the broad movement in Christian moral philosophy that shaped the understanding by colonial Americans of what moral actions were needed to achieve the good.

Next, worthy of examination are some common broad intellectual concepts that existed between the various denominations, concepts that were pressed to the foreground within the Colonial Discourse on social welfare: These were concepts of divine order, covenant theology, and original sin.

Moral Philosophy

Moral action by definition is what leads to goodness (i.e., social welfare) in society. It lays out the pathway to guide individual actions on what ought to be done in order to achieve the desired effect of social harmony. The broad movement in moral philosophy that guided the actions of the colonial Americans was grounded in scholastic–Aristotelian philosophy and is known as *natural law theory*. Back in the thirteenth century, St. Thomas Aquinas was the first to locate natural law theory within the Christian tradition.[104] Over the years many others would continually refine this theory of natural law, with the works of Martin Luther and John Calvin in the sixteenth century having the most direct impact on the colonial mindset.

Natural law in this theory is conceived as a set of unchanging moral principles that universally apply to human conduct necessary to achieve good in society. Within the Christian tradition, it was accepted that God was the source of these unchanging moral principles. Natural law theory postulates that moral action arises out of obedience to this natural law. Luther would add an element of voluntarism to this obedience.[105] Starting from the position that God's design for the universe was unknowable by the human mind, Luther concluded that while the use of reason had a role in guiding our actions in secular affairs, we cannot solely employ reason to guide us in spiritual affairs, which included moral action. Luther postulated that love for God, the giving of oneself fully over to God, replaced reason as the means to effect moral action. Hence, through love of God one voluntarily embraced obedience to God's natural law.

In accordance with Luther, Calvin proposed that the elect (those granted divine grace) would obey natural law out of love. Calvin concluded that while we are able to control our passions so that our outward actions are in moral accordance with the law, the attainment of a proper inner state was beyond one's power. For that, we needed God to grant us the gift of divine grace.[106] The effect of this understanding of morality on colonial Americans was that obedience was a moral imperative. This moral imperative of obedience translated directly not only to God's word but also to obedience to one's social superiors as the social hierarchy was a manifestation of God's divine ordering of the universe. Only under the condition of a broken covenant—that is, when the social superior failed to live up to their duty toward the social inferior—could this obedience be questioned. Thus, one displayed love for God by respecting God's ordering of society.

Divine Providence

One of the major concepts influencing society was that God created a divine order to the universe and circumscribed each individual's place in this order.[107] From the Middle Ages, this notion was captured by the concept of the Great Chain of Being. The Great Chain of Being offered an elaborate and detailed hierarchy of all things and beings on earth and between heaven and hell. Consequently, it was concluded that human society should be constructed along serried ranks following this same premise.[108] Respect for the maintenance of the hierarchical order was viewed as a spiritual imperative in one's attempt to follow God's will.[109] Thus, the concept of a divine order to the universe lent credence to the notion that maintaining this social hierarchy was of vital importance and further buttressed the strength of its acceptance arising from the economic, political, and social conditions shaping the colonial experience. The following 1743 quote by the minister Charles Chauncy illustrates the importance placed on maintaining this hierarchy:

> Good order is the Strength and Beauty of the World. The Prosperity of both *Church* and *State* depends very much upon it. And can there be Order, where Men transgress the Limits of their Station, and intermeddle in the Business of others? So far from it, that the only effectual Method, under God . . . is, for *every one* to be faithful, in doing what is *proper* for him in his *own Place*.[110]

The Bible served as an essential tool in helping one to interpret the wishes of God's will as reflected in God's divine plan for the universe and as an aid to understand one's place within it.[111] Hence, the colonists turned to the Bible in their efforts to determine God's will concerning the rights and responsibilities assigned to each social station (e.g., "honor thy mother and father") as well as to determine the penalties that followed for breaching such responsibilities.[112] Lastly, God's divine plan laid out the conditions necessary for one to achieve salvation. Now, while many colonists believed in a Calvinist notion of predestination—that before being born, God had already ordained whether or not your soul would enter heaven—it was believed that God's chosen would reveal themselves through their sincere striving to follow God's will and to battle temptation.[113] Such endeavors prepared one's heart and soul to receive God's grace.[114] Thus, while doing good works and striving to follow God's will would not guarantee one's salvation, those chosen to be saved would only arise from this group. So predestination, rather than being an impediment to one's motivation to do good, actually spurred one to employ a constant vigilance in one's works and deeds.[115]

Covenant Theology

The second major principle supported in this Discourse was the notion of a covenant.[116] A covenant was a solemn agreement between inferiors and superiors which delineated the duties and rights of each position within this divine hierarchy; thus, the salvation that rested upon fulfilling God's plan translated into fulfilling one's duties and responsibilities—one's covenants—accorded to one's position.[117] The ultimate covenant was the one which you as an individual made with God. This covenant of grace called for the complete subjection to God's will and trust in God's wisdom; in return, God would see to one's prosperity and salvation.[118] As was the case with the divine hierarchy, one's covenant with God was seen as the model for directing social relations. Thus, membership in a community was viewed as a social covenant that bound individuals together within a recognized hierarchy.[119] Colonial writings are replete with covenant terminology; they speak of social covenants, church covenants, and national covenants.[120] Fulfilling the responsibilities of each of these covenants was viewed as one's attempt to follow God's will; hence, all covenants had a spiritual component to them which served to make them more than simple legal agreements, and more like sacred vows.

Now what made this subjection of one's will to a social superior palatable in the eyes of the American colonists was the recognition that such covenants were entered into voluntarily.[121] Hence, for example, a man and a woman would freely enter into marriage, upon which point they would assume the duties of husband and wife to each other; the marriage vow itself represented this voluntary acceptance of the covenant (wherein the wife, in the inferior position, promised to honor and obey her husband). Similarly, one's decision to become a member of a church was seen as a voluntary act, as was one's decision to reside in a particular community or to enter a contract as an indentured servant. This premise of voluntarily entering into a covenant also serves to explain how slaves—being forced into servitude and thus not party to a covenant—fell off the social hierarchy and thus were merely considered chattel.

Original Sin

Lastly, the doctrine of original sin was widely recognized.[122] This was viewed as a broken covenant on the part of Adam and Eve.[123] Consequently, every man and woman inherited an innate moral corruption from Adam and Eve, which could only be overcome through the acceptance of God's grace.[124] This doctrine underscored the importance of fulfilling one's covenants in order to achieve salvation. It also had a profound effect upon the colonists' views on crime; that is, it caused them to equate crime with sin.[125] As every individual in the community was tainted with original sin, criminal activity did not mark one as deviant. However, penitence for one's crime was essential.[126] Crime was seen as straying from God's plan—a form of covenant breaking—and thus could bring down God's wrath upon the whole community if proper penance was lacking.[127] Lastly, for the colonials it further supported the already existing notion that women occupied an inferior status to men; hence, the docile obedience of the female sex was mirrored not only in nature but also through the doctrine of original sin as it was seen as a lasting penance for Eve's disobedience in the Garden of Eden.

Defining Cultural Feature: The Family as a Little Commonwealth

The family was held as being the most signature feature of God's plan for creating order in the universe. The colonists' believed that God had appointed humankind to live in societies as a means to provide a check against the inherent stain of original sin and one's proclivity to fall prey to it.[128] The family was regarded as the first and primary form of "society" within which human relations were organized.[129] Beyond interpretations of the Bible in this regard, the colonists found plenty of evidence in God's ordering of nature to support this notion reflected in their everyday experience with various animals.[130] The second type of society God directed humankind to live within was that of the church, with the third being the organization of a commonwealth.[131] Due to its primacy as the "first society," the structure of the family was turned to as the model upon which these other social relations in the community would be organized.[132] Reflecting this notion, the family was typically referred to as "a little commonwealth."[133] Thus, membership within a church was seen as belonging to a church "family," and membership in a commonwealth was seen as belonging to an extended family of sorts.[134]

The main organizational feature of the family—again, readily reflected in nature—was that it was organized along hierarchical lines.[135] Unsurprisingly, this hierarchy was shaped along patriarchal lines.[136] The father served as the head of the household, followed by the mother, with the children occupying the lowest rung.[137] Individuals, such as indentured servants, living within a household who were not biologically related to the father and mother carried the broad designation of "servant" and occupied this third rung along with the children.[138] However, all living in the same household—father, mother, children, and servants—were seen as a member of that family.[139] Lastly, the observation that children grew to adulthood and then became heads of their own household served to reinforce the acceptance of mobility within the hierarchy that characterized the colonial experience.

This hierarchical structure was adopted to organize the church congregation: pastors and church elders filling the role of "father" and thus occupying the top rung, adult members filling the second rung, and once again children occupying the lowest rung.[140] The political organization of the commonwealth was viewed in these terms as well.[141] At a local level, town selectmen, overseers, and town elders occupied the top rung; freemen and freewomen occupied the second rung; and all others occupied the third rung.[142] And at the national level, monarchs were often referred to as the "father" of the country, government officials occupied the second rung, while subjects occupied the third rung.[143] And socially, this organization was reflected in the acceptance of an elite class— from which most political and spiritual leaders arose—who possessed formal education and economic resources placing them above the status of common folk occupying the second rung, with the poor (i.e., those unable to support themselves) occupying the lowest rung.[144]

As was noted above when describing the social conditions of this era, each station in the hierarchy contained certain rights and responsibilities. Reflecting the workings of the family, those of a lower rank were expected to obey the wishes of those of a higher rank. Thus, it is not surprising that upon reading the dictum in the Bible to "honor thy mother and father," the colonists interpreted this to apply to the spiritual, political, and social "families" to which they belonged, with those of a higher rank representing the father.[145] And as we shall see in the next chapter concerning poor relief, those of a higher rank felt the responsibility to care for those in need at the lower rank.

The reverence for the family as representing the locus of social order for the community translated into great suspicion of single adults (e.g., bachelors, spinsters, widows without adult children, etc.) who chose to establish a residence and live alone.[146] In fact, many communities in the New England colonies passed laws forbidding the practice, requiring those of 21 years or older to live within a familial household.[147] In addition, free adults who were judged to be unable to fulfill the responsibilities of their station could be disenfranchised of their freedom and, thus, faced with either having to leave the community or being bound to service within a well-governed family.[148] Furthermore, it was not simply sufficient for individuals to create a new household through marriage; they had to live together in peace and harmony. Thus, the village elders representing the court took it upon themselves to intervene when the peace and harmony of a household began to seriously deteriorate.[149] This reverence for family, and its extension to that of a congregational and community family, also serves to explain how itinerant individuals—whom colonists labeled as rogues and vagabonds—fell outside this family structure and were viewed with utmost suspicion due to the rootless existence their traveling engendered.[150]

Lastly, the importance of the family as a social institution—exhibited not only by household families but also by the congregational family and local commonwealth family—is highlighted by the fact that in this era there was little in the way of hospitals, poor houses, or any other type of specialized social welfare institutions.[151] Consequently, the family structure was seen as the primary means by which to attend to the social welfare of those in need. Thus, for example, the parents of a household were seen as being responsible for the education and vocational training of their children and of any servants.[152] This also begins to shed some light on the case of Mary Degresha (mentioned at the beginning of the chapter) in explaining why it was deemed necessary to place her in the household of another family. Being recently widowed and unable to support herself and having no immediate family in the community offering a household for her to join, elders of her community family—who in their position felt the responsibility to provide for her needs—arranged for her to live in the household of another.

Paradigm of Understanding

For any historical era, those seeking knowledge undergo a quest for certainty. There is the belief that reality can be grasped by the human mind and the underlying truths explored and discovered. Individuals navigate their world and interpret their everyday experiences based upon a shared fundamental paradigm of understanding. Consequently, society as a whole will reflect this shared understanding among individuals; and thus, it will serve and shape the dominant Discourse that arises. My attempt to describe this shared paradigm of understanding includes the elaboration of three fundamental philosophical categories employed when seeking to navigate one's world: the theory of what comprises reality (ontology), the theory of how knowledge is captured by the human mind (epistemology), and the theory of causality used to explain human actions. For the Colonial Discourse, these theories are as follows.

Theory of Ontology: Divine Providence

The colonists' belief in divine providence meant that they conceived of reality as a product of God's will. Thus, all objects in the universe, in addition to being comprised of matter, bore a spiritual essence that served as a marker of God's will. In human beings, this spiritual essence was one's soul, whereas in all other living and inanimate things, this marker served as an extension of God's direct will. Thus, there was no randomness to how reality would unfold or, as Cotton Mather once colorfully put it, "not a sparrow falls to the ground without the will of God directing it."[153] This also serves to explain the colonists' belief in magic, witchcraft, and the existence of spiritual forces acting in the world, as even Satan himself was seen as a tool and unknowing agent in God's plan for the universe.[154] Despite the introduction of Enlightenment thought, divine providence held sway in the American colonies as the defining conceptual understanding of reality throughout the seventeenth and eighteenth centuries. And while doubt in supernatural forces began growing in educated circles, belief in witchcraft and witches would continue throughout this era.[155] In fact, as late as 1787 in Philadelphia, citizens lynched a woman whom they suspected of witchcraft not far from where the Constitutional Convention was being held.[156]

Theory of Epistemology: Hermeneutics

With the understanding of reality as being directed by God's will and each object being imbued with a spiritual essence that served as a marker for God's will, correct understanding of said reality depended upon one's ability to correctly interpret the will of God acting in the universe. As noted above, with such a divine order in place, American colonists did not believe in the randomness of events. Thus, for each object and event that occurred, a spiritual meaning was attached to it. So, for example, when disease or famine ravished a particular community, it was seen as an act of God's wrath.[157] Thus, to correctly understand the reality of one's world, one was tasked with the endeavor to understand God's will. Hermeneutics is the philosophy of how to correctly interpret meaning; thus, it was employed to authenticate knowledge of reality as represented by God's divine order. The Bible, seen as the word of God, was thus turned to as the preeminent source for understanding and validating truth claims. Thus, the Bible served as the inspiration for criminal codes and justice, for organization of society along hierarchical lines and of the various obligations assigned to those in the hierarchy, as well as for the care of one's soul and its salvation.[158] Such an outlook puts great importance on correctly determining the true identity of those running afoul with community norms in terms of this spiritual essence (e.g., incorrigible sinner or truly repentant individual, vagabond or good Christian, etc.) as this correct identification was necessary to advance God's will according to the divine plan.

Theory of Causality: Divine Grace and Free Will

As illustrated by Cotton Mather's colorful phrase that not a sparrow falls to the ground without the will of God directing it, the colonists believed that all actions in the universe were a direct result of God's will. Thus, the answer to any question concerning "Why does this happen?" would always be "because God wills it." This is not surprising considering that during the Colonial Era, the colonists' understanding of their world was dominated by religious thought. Most of the various religious denominations embraced the concept of predestination in one form or another, which meant that at birth it had already been decided by God whether or not one's soul would enter heaven. Yet, for the time that they spent on earth, it was recognized that God had granted human beings free will in determining their actions.

This apparent contradiction between God's will directing all action and the role of free will in determining human actions was resolved via the concept of divine grace. Through the taint of original sin, humans inherited a proclivity to fall into sinful behavior. A modern parallel to such a notion would be the idea of inheriting natural instincts at the biological level. As can be expected, colonists viewed this natural tendency toward sin completely in negative terms—a natural tendency that needed to be overcome. And the way to overcome this natural tendency was through inviting God's grace into one's heart.

Thus, the exercise of free will to which the colonists strived was that of its voluntary subjugation to the will of God. In short, they based their actions upon their understanding of what God expected of them. As noted above in the theory of epistemology for this era, this understanding they sought was derived from correctly divining the signs, or markers, left by God in the natural world and through correctly interpreting the Bible. This dynamic is best illustrated in the Colonial Era by the concept of God speaking to individuals via a calling.

The most common expression of yielding to this calling was the selection of a profession or following one's calling in life. Colonists believed that to appropriately follow God's divine plan, each individual was to serve society and themselves through learning and adopting the productive occupation chosen for them by God.[159] Hence, while the Bible served to provide the directive to choose a profession as the means to find salvation, specific knowledge of God's wishes particular to the individual was a more private matter and resulted from correctly interpreting the signs left for that individual in the world.[160] This notion of a calling extended to actions related to social welfare as well as common everyday actions. If a person felt justified in taking a certain act, it was due to perceiving a call to do it, whereas if a person doubted the appropriateness of taking a certain action, it was ascribed to feeling no call to do it.[161] Thus, as illustrated in a letter from Lucy Downing to Sir Winthrop, she ascribes her son's hesitancy in taking a voyage to the West Indies as stemming from not feeling a call to do it.[162]

Conceptions of the Self

The colonists of this era can be best described as possessing a bifurcated sense of self: one part anchored in a social world, and the other part anchored in a spiritual world.[163] The sense of self anchored in the social world, as is implied by the name, was public in nature. As may be recalled, God's divine plan directed humankind to live in societies—the premier of which being the family, the second being the church congregation, and the third being that of a political commonwealth.[164] Living in these societies was seen as providing a buffer against the influence of the inherited taint of original sin. Colonists consequently derived a sense of identity from the various roles in which they were placed within the social hierarchy.[165] Thus, roles such as magistrate, minister, father, mother, brother, yeoman, servant, etcetera, were the particular modalities in which a person derived one part of identity and how they were primarily viewed by others.

The sense of self anchored in the spiritual world derives from a belief in the soul as an active agent in directing one's actions; this idea is captured by the metaphor commonly held by the colonists of one's body representing a ship, whereas one's soul represented the captain. As a spiritual essence was found in all things, it is not difficult to understand how a person's spiritual essence, in the form of a soul, was a prominent component of the self. The ultimate goal or destination for the soul was salvation and (which despite being a predestined outcome) occurred only to those who successfully entered a covenant of grace with God. Thus, one's sense of identity within the spiritual realm derived from where one believed oneself to fall upon the continuum between incorrigible sinner and saint. Consequently, while the social self had a very public character to it, the spiritual self existed in a very private inner world.[166] This is best reflected by the common practice among colonists of keeping diaries, wherein one reflected upon one's various lapses into immorality and what the proper penance for them should be, as well as one's displays of faith that served as evidence of times when one had successfully invited God into one's heart and soul.[167]

We can further draw upon the notion of a "calling" from God as a useful illustration of how these two parts of the bifurcated self—social and spiritual—worked in tandem. So, for example, choosing a vocation for oneself or one's child involved correctly interpreting the signs left by God in the form of the talent he bestowed upon the individual; thus, finding one's calling in life was a spiritual endeavor.[168] However, at the same time, the vocation needed to be something useful for society and appropriate to one's station in life—thus, it was also a public endeavor at finding one's proper place within the social hierarchy.[169] Of particular interest to note is that, unlike in modern times, the colonists did not have a sense of identity that was prominently anchored in the natural world. So concepts such as nature and nurture did not exist for them; rather, human actions that served to define the individual were solely viewed through a social or spiritual lens.

Rules of Right

In Chapter 1, it was noted that according to Michel Foucault a Discourse forms as a response to the urgent need of an era. And the urgent need in colonial American society was identified as *the maintenance of the social hierarchy*. Furthermore, Foucault then goes on to stipulate that there arise very broad organizing principles directing knowledge formation and understanding toward meeting this urgent need: He labels these organizing principles as *rules of right*. There is sufficient evidence at this point in this analysis to identify the rules of right operating in this era. The two most prominent rules of right operating within the Colonial Discourse were *determining identity* and *determining rights and responsibilities*.

Determining Identity

This rule of right refers not to personal identification such as one's correct name but, rather, to correctly identifying the type of person one was and the qualities one possessed. Determining identity through the examination of characteristics was an important first step in the classification of the individual. This was an important first step toward maintaining the social hierarchy as the correct identification of the individual in these terms ensured their proper placement within the social hierarchy. We shall see shortly, once we get into the extended descriptions of colonial social welfare practices in Chapter 3, how this organizing principle cut across all aspects of social welfare. Thus, when it came to criminal justice, society bent its efforts on determining whether the accused was an incorrigible sinner or a repentant sinner. When it came to poverty relief, as is illustrated by the variations of the English Poor Laws adopted by the various colonies, society spent an inordinate amount of effort outlining the residency requirements to be accepted into the community "family." Acceptance into this social hierarchy carried with it one set of responsibilities concerning poverty relief, whereas another set of responsibilities was applied to nonresidents.

This rule of right also served to mark deviance: Those identified as not having a place in the social hierarchy were seen as existential threats. Thus, one of the greatest threats to the social order was that of the vagabond or rogue. The vagabond did not belong to a congregation, had no community membership, and very often traveled apart from family. Communities had no place for vagabonds within their social order and thus took great measures to exclude them from joining the community. On the transcendental level of existence, the greatest threat was that of the incorrigible sinner. The acts of an incorrigible sinner could bring down the wrath of God on the community. There was no place for this individual within the divine order—at least not on earth: Exclusion from the social hierarchy translated oftentimes into being ostracized from the community or, at the very worst, capital punishment.

Determining Rights and Responsibilities

One's placement within either the social or the divine hierarchy is what determined the rights and responsibilities that one had. Thus, the rules of right operating in an era serve to reinforce each other: Correctly determining an individual's identity is what led to proper placement within the social hierarchy and proper understanding of one's placement in the divine hierarchy. Once an individual was properly placed in the hierarchy, the proper determination of their rights and responsibilities could take place. The rights and responsibilities one maintained served to promote and solidify the interdependence crucial to the survival of the social hierarchy and to maintain respect for the divine hierarchy. Much of the determination of rights and responsibilities was well established and standardized, such as the wife's responsibility to honor and obey her husband and her right for her general welfare to be provided by him.

However, as noted earlier, colonial writings concerning agreements were replete with covenant terminology. The act of entering a covenant was an endeavor at entering an agreement concerning rights and responsibilities. These writing thus were the colonials' attempt to iron out the various rights and responsibilities being accepted by the parties in question for more particular or less standardized arrangements. Thus, when it came to poverty relief, while the responsibility to care for the poor of one's community "family" was a well-established standard, the particular form that this poverty relief took would need to be worked out on a case-by-case basis.

Theme of the Discourse: Salvation

The theme arising from the Colonial Discourse on social welfare is that of salvation. This guiding concept permeated colonial society and strongly influenced the actions of all of its members. The soul was not simply a substance deposited in the body at conception that then waited for death for its release. Rather, the soul was viewed as the primary animating force guiding one's actions: the "captain" in charge of guiding the ship. Thus, advancing social welfare was seen as an endeavor at tending to the soul. A core insight arising from this notion of tending to the soul is that social welfare practices benefited the giver of aid equally to, or even more so than, the receiver of aid. Social welfare agents in their delivery of aid were seen as meeting the responsibilities of their station as divinely ordered by God, and thus tending to their own souls in addition to the souls of recipients. Hence, for example, if God happened to bless one with bounty, one had the responsibility to share that bounty with those who were in need. As an oft-quoted saying from the Bible attests, "For it is easier for a camel to go through the eye of a needle than for a rich man to enter the kingdom of God" (Mathew 19:24). Recipients of aid also had responsibilities in this relationship (e.g., to obey one's social superiors), and it was the meeting of these responsibilities that served to tend to their souls. Thus, a covenant was formed. Material improvements in the recipients' lives were simply the vehicle allowing one the opportunity to tend to one's soul through the honoring of the covenant.

This theme of salvation had profound implications in the shaping of colonial Americans' conception of what comprised knowledge of the Good. As social welfare seeks to promote the good of society and individuals, the theme of salvation served to define this good in religious terms: that of the glorification of God. Thus, religion was turned to when seeking knowledge of the Good in which to promote social welfare. The particular experience of settling in a new land served to provide a tabula rasa in which to create the perfect society according to God's plan: the *shining city on the hill* described in a sermon by John Winthrop[170] and so often quoted by future politicians.

Notes

1. "Town Meeting Auctions," Mass Moments, 2005.
2. Johnson, *Reading the American Past*, 68–69.
3. Johnson, 70.
4. Goodwin, *The Colonial Cavalier*, 245; Pennsylvania Statute (1718) as quoted in Axinn and Levin, *Social Welfare*, 14; New York Common Council (1707) as quoted in Schneider, *History of Public Welfare*, 64.
5. Goodwin, 245; Schneider, 64.
6. Singer, "Scottish-Irish in America," 264; Sweet, *Religion in Colonial America*.
7. Goodwin, *The Colonial Cavalier*, 7–12.
8. Goodman, *Essays in American Colonial*, 137.
9. Goodman, 201.

10. Wiebe, *The Search for Order.*

11. Axinn and Levin, *Social Welfare,* 11; Rothman, *Discovery of the Asylum,* 12.

12. Ulrich, *Good Wives,* 52.

13. Godbeer, *The Salem Witch Hunt,* 14; Ulrich, 52.

14. Demos, *A Little Commonwealth,* 8.

15. Demos, 8.

16. Demos, 8.

17. Bonomi, "Religious Pluralism."

18. Morgan, *The Puritan Family,* 58.

19. "Colonial Travel," Chronicles of America, 7th paragraph.

20. Bridenbaugh, *Early Americans,* 149, 181; Lockridge, *A New England Town,* 80.

21. "Colonial Travel," ConstitutionFacts.com, subheading "Who Could Travel."

22. Channing, *A History,* 529; "Colonial Travel," ConstitutionFacts.com, 1st paragraph.

23. Morgan, *The Puritan Family,* 48; Smith, *The Lower Sort,* 42.

24. Taylor, *Colonial America,* 104; Ulrich, *Good Wives,* 14.

25. "Colonial Travel," ConstitutionFacts.com, 1st paragraph.

26. "Colonial Travel," ConstitutionFacts.com, subheading "Who Could Travel."

27. Lockridge, *A New England Town,* 139–40; Moraley, *The Infortunate,* 73.

28. Bridenbaugh, *Early Americans,* 122, 149, 180; Jernegan, *Laboring and Dependent Classes,* 202.

29. Moraley, *The Infortunate,* 52–53.

30. Abramovitz, *Regulating the Lives,* 79; Jernegan, *Laboring and Dependent Classes,* 192.

31. Goodman, *Essays in American Colonial,* 300, 385; Lockridge, *A New England Town,* 139–40.

32. Abramovitz, *Regulating the Lives,* 51–52; Bremner et al., *Children and Youth,* 103; Demos, *A Little Commonwealth,* 183.

33. Demos, 183.

34. Abramovitz, *Regulating the Lives,* 89; Ulrich, *Good Wives,* 15.

35. Bremner et al., *Children and Youth,* 103; Demos, *A Little Commonwealth,* 183.

36. Taylor, *Colonial America,* 104.

37. Bridenbaugh, *Early Americans,* 73.

38. Goodman, *Essays in American Colonial,* 102.

39. Abramovitz, *Regulating the Lives,* 79, 84; Ulrich, *Good Wives,* 14, 59.

40. Bridenbaugh, *Early Americans,* 178.

41. Demos, *A Little Commonwealth,* 7; Goodman, *Essays in American Colonial,* 100; Kelso, *History of Public Poor,* 35; Ver Steeg, *The Formative Years,* 273; Trattner, *From Poor Law,* 17.

42. Demos, 7.

43. Morgan, *The Puritan Family,* 80.

44. Morgan, 80.

45. Ulrich, *Good Wives,* 81.

46. Miller, "The Puritan State," 51.

47. Morgan, *The Puritan Family,* 81.

48. Demos, *A Little Commonwealth,* 7.

49. Bremner et al., *Children and Youth*, 68; Jernegan, *Laboring and Dependent Classes*, 193, 207; Morgan, *The Puritan Family*, 146.

50. Abramovitz, *Regulating the Lives*, 84; Katz, *In the Shadow*, 14; Trattner, *From Poor Law*, 19.

51. Goodman, *Essays in American Colonial*, 139; Miller, "The Puritan State," 42, 49.

52. Goodman, 139; Miller, 41, 43.

53. Goodman, 144–45; Miller, 47.

54. Godbeer, *The Salem Witch Hunt*, 14.

55. Miller, "The Puritan State," 43; Morgan, *The Puritan Family*, 17; Bouwsma, *Waning of the Renaissance*, 146, 150.

56. Miller, 42.

57. Demos, *A Little Commonwealth*, 100; Miller, 42; Morgan, *The Puritan Family*, 19.

58. Godbeer, *The Overflowing of Friendship*, 149; Miller, 42; Morgan, 18.

59. Abramovitz, *Regulating the Lives*, 52–54; Godbeer, *The Salem Witch Hunt*, 12.

60. Morgan, *The Puritan Family*, 19; Ulrich, *Good Wives*, 6.

61. Goodman, *Essays in American Colonial*, 141; Miller, "The Puritan State," 43; Morgan, *The Puritan Family*, 18.

62. Winthrop, "Authority and Liberty," 39; Ulrich, *Good Wives*, 6.

63. Demos, *A Little Commonwealth*, 100, 104; Morgan, *The Puritan Family*, 19.

64. Abramovitz, *Regulating the Lives*, 53; Bremner et al., *Children and Youth*, 104; Morgan, 117.

65. Goodman, *Essays in American Colonial*, 100, 141, 274; Morgan, 17, 18.

66. Goodman, 274.

67. Goodman, 100; Miller, "The Puritan State," 42; Morgan, *The Puritan Family*, 17–18.

68. Bremner et al., *Children and Youth*, 104; Goodman, 100.

69. Goodman, 100.

70. Demos, *A Little Commonwealth*, 107; Morgan, *The Puritan Family*, 109.

71. Bremner et al., *Children and Youth*, 64; Records of Fitchburg (1812) as quoted in Kelso, *History of Public Poor*, 109; Trattner, *From Poor Law*, 18.

72. Goodman, *Essays in American Colonial*, 524, 525.

73. Goodman, 241.

74. Goodman, 241.

75. Goodman, 227; Smith, *The Lower Sort*, 3.

76. Bremner et al., *Children and Youth*, 104; Goodman, 239.

77. Goodman, 228–29; Morgan, *The Puritan Family*, 14, 34; Taylor, *Colonial America*, 54.

78. Abramovitz, *Regulating the Lives*, 79; Jernegan, *Laboring and Dependent Classes*, 193; Morgan, "The Protestant Ethic," 184.

79. Demos, *A Little Commonwealth*, 100–04; Godbeer, *The Overflowing of Friendship*, 149.

80. Goodman, *Essays in American Colonial*, 274; Ulrich, *Good Wives*, 6.

81. Cotton, *Spiritual Milk*, 4; Demos, *A Little Commonwealth*, 100–04.

82. Cotton, 4; Miller, "The Puritan State," 42; Morgan, *The Puritan Family*, 19.

83. Morgan, 39.

84. Demos, *A Little Commonwealth*, 104; Morgan, 65; 117; Taylor, *Colonial America*, 59.

85. Bremner et al., *Children and Youth*, 105; Demos, *A Little Commonwealth*, 104; Taylor, 59.
86. Bremner et al., 105; Morgan, *The Puritan Family*, 64–65, 88.
87. Moraley, *The Infortunate*, 33; Morgan, 117.
88. Abramovitz, *Regulating the Lives*, 77; Demos, *A Little Commonwealth*, 79; Ulrich, *Good Wives*, 14.
89. Abramovitz, 84; Jernegan, *Laboring and Dependent Classes*, 208; Ulrich, 59.
90. Morgan, "The Protestant Ethic," 196–97.
91. Foucault, *Order of Things*.
92. Winthrop, "Model of Christian Charity," 28; Zuckerman, *Peaceable Kingdoms*, 54.
93. Goodman, *Essays in American Colonial*, 201.
94. Hubbard (1621) as quoted in Morgan, *The Puritan Family*, 18.
95. Kidd, *The Great Awakening*.
96. Godbeer, *The Salem Witch Hunt*, 12.
97. Godbeer, 12.
98. Godbeer, 13.
99. Mays, *Women in Early America*, 188–89.
100. Graves, *Elizabeth Hooton*.
101. Graves.
102. Axinn and Levin, *Social Welfare*, 15; Jernegan, *Laboring and Dependent Classes*, 193; Trattner, *From Poor Law*, 19.
103. Singer, "Scottish-Irish in America," 264; Sweet, *Religion in Colonial America*.
104. Schneewind, *The Invention of Autonomy*, 19–21.
105. Schneewind, 29–31.
106. Schneewind, 34.
107. Bremer, *The Puritan Experiment*, 27; Sweet, *Religion in Colonial America*, 98, 101.
108. Goodman, *Essays in American Colonial*, 141; Miller, "The Puritan State," 42–43; Morgan, *The Puritan Family*, 17, 19.
109. Bremer, *The Puritan Experiment*, 22; Mardsen, "America's 'Christian' Origins," 245, 255; Morgan, 18–19; Rothman, *Discovery of the Asylum*, 10–11.
110. Chauncy (1743) as quoted in Rothman, 10–11.
111. Goodman, *Essays in American Colonial*, 144–5; Miller, "The Puritan State," 47; Morgan, *The Puritan Family*, 71–72.
112. Mardsen, "America's 'Christian' Origins," 244; Morgan, 71–72; Sweet, *Religion in Colonial America*, 98.
113. Godbeer, *The Salem Witch Hunt*, 8; Miller, "The Puritan State," 47.
114. Goodman, *Essays in American Colonial*, 161–63; Bulkeley, "Willing and Voluntary Subjection," 34; Morgan, *The Puritan Family*, 7.
115. Abramovitz, *Regulating the Lives*, 77; Goodman, *Essays in American Colonial*, 161; Miller, "The Puritan State," 49.
116. Miller, 48; Singer, "Scottish-Irish in America," 281; Zuckerman, *Peaceable Kingdoms*, 54–55.
117. Bremer, *The Puritan Experiment*, 81; Miller, "The Puritan State," 48.
118. Kidd, *The Great Awakening*, 4; Bulkeley, "Willing and Voluntary Subjection," 34; Morgan, *The Puritan Family*, 15.

119. Bremer, *The Puritan Experiment*, 89; Miller, "The Puritan State," 48.

120. Bremer, 18; Gildrie, *Salem Massachusetts, 1626-1683*.

121. Goodman, *Essays in American Colonial*, 180–81; Miller, "The Puritan State," 48–50.

122. Miller, 41; Sweet, *Religion in Colonial America*, 99; Zuckerman, *Peaceable Kingdoms*, 61.

123. Bremer, *The Puritan Experiment*, 18.

124. Godbeer, *The Overflowing of Friendship*, 3–4; Godbeer, *The Salem Witch Hunt*, 2; Morgan, *The Puritan Family*, 15.

125. Winthrop (1645) as excerpted in Haskins, *Law and Authority*, 40, see also 52; Rothman, *Discovery of the Asylum*, 15, 51.

126. Oberholzer, *Delinquent Saints*, 38–42; Zuckerman, *Peaceable Kingdoms*, 61–64.

127. Bremer, *The Puritan Experiment*, 91; Morgan, *The Puritan Family*, 64.

128. Bremner et al., *Children and Youth*, 27; Miller, "The Puritan State," 43; Morgan, 18–19, 133.

129. Bremner et al., 27; Morgan, 18–19, 133.

130. Abramovitz, *Regulating the Lives*, 53; Bouwsma, *Waning of the Renaissance*, 148–49.

131. Morgan, *The Puritan Family*, 18–19, 133.

132. Abramovitz, *Regulating the Lives*, 52–53; Godbeer, *The Overflowing of Friendship*, 113; Morgan, 143.

133. Bremner et al., *Children and Youth*, 27; Demos, *A Little Commonwealth*; Taylor, *Colonial America*, 58.

134. Cotton, *Spiritual Milk*, 4; Godbeer, *The Overflowing of Friendship*, 8, 113.

135. Abramovitz, *Regulating the Lives*, 53; Morgan, *The Puritan Family*, 18–19.

136. Abramovitz, 54; Goodman, *Essays in American Colonial*, 531; Bouwsma, *Waning of the Renaissance*, 149.

137. Abramovitz, 53; Bremner et al., *Children and Youth*, 104.

138. Bremner et al., 104; Demos, *A Little Commonwealth*, 65.

139. Bremner et al., 104; Demos, 65; Moraley, *The Infortunate*, 46.

140. Goodman, *Essays in American Colonial*, 274; Morgan, *The Puritan Family*, 19.

141. Axinn and Levin, *Social Welfare*, 22; Rothman, *Discovery of the Asylum*, 13.

142. Miller, "The Puritan State," 42; Morgan, *The Puritan Family*, 18.

143. Godbeer, *The Overflowing of Friendship*, 8; Morgan, 18–19.

144. Godbeer, *The Salem Witch Hunt*, 12; Goodman, *Essays in American Colonial*, 100; Morgan, 18.

145. Cotton, *Spiritual Milk*, 4; Bremner et al., *Children and Youth*, 32.

146. Demos, *A Little Commonwealth*, 67, 78; Morgan, *The Puritan Family*, 64–65.

147. Abramovitz, *Regulating the Lives*, 53; Demos, 78; Morgan, 146; Plymouth Colony Records (1670) as excerpted in Kelso, *History of Public Poor*, 32.

148. Records of Plymouth Colony (1659) as excerpted in Kelso, 32.

149. Demos, *A Little Commonwealth*, 93.

150. Abramovitz, *Regulating the Lives*, 79; Bridenbaugh, *Early Americans*, 87, 122; Morgan, Edmund S. "The Protestant Ethic," 184.

151. Demos, *A Little Commonwealth*, 81; Trattner, *From Poor Law*, 16.

152. Bremner et al., *Children and Youth*, 105; Demos, 183; Morgan, *The Puritan Family*, 88.

153. Godbeer, *The Salem Witch Hunt*, 8, 41.
154. Godbeer, 8.
155. Godbeer, 30.
156. Godbeer, 30.
157. Godbeer, 8.
158. Miller, "The Puritan State," 47; Morgan, *The Puritan Family*, 71.
159. Bremner et al., *Children and Youth*, 109; Mather, "A Christian at His Calling," 122; Morgan, 35.
160. Morgan, 69–70; Sherwood, *Self in Early Modern*, 21–22.
161. Morgan, 69.
162. Morgan, 69.
163. Mather, "A Christian at His Calling," 122; Sherwood, *Self in Early Modern*, 43–44.
164. Morgan, *The Puritan Family*, 18–19.
165. Morgan, 18; Sherwood, *Self in Early Modern*, 21–22.
166. Demos, *A Little Commonwealth*, 8; Sherwood, 43–44.
167. Morgan, *The Puritan Family*, 5.
168. Bremner et al., *Children and Youth*, 109; Bulkeley, "Willing and Voluntary Subjection," 35.
169. Schlatter, "The Puritan Strain," 8; Morgan, *The Puritan Family*, 35.
170. Winthrop, "Model of Christian Charity."

References

Abramovitz, Mimi. *Regulating the Lives of Women: Social Welfare Policy from Colonial Times to the Present*. Brooklyn: South End Press, 1988.

Axinn, June, and Herman Levin. *Social Welfare: A History of the American Response to Need*. New York: Harper & Row, 1975.

Bonomi, P. "Religious Pluralism in the Middle Colonies." Divining America, TeacherServe©: National Humanities Center. Accessed May 22, 2019, http://nationalh umanitiescenter.org/tserve/eighteen/ekeyinfo/elinksmidcol.htm.

Bouwsma, William. *The Waning of the Renaissance, 1550–1640*. New Haven: Yale University Press, 2002.

Bremer, Francis J. *The Puritan Experiment: New England Society from Bradford to Edwards*. Hanover, NH: University Press of New England, 1995.

Bremner, Robert H., John Barnard, Temara K. Hareven, and Robert M. Mennel, eds. *Children and Youth in America*. Vol. 1, *1600–1865*. Cambridge, MA: Harvard University Press, 1970.

Bridenbaugh, Carl. *Early Americans*. New York: Oxford University Press, 1981.

Bulkeley, Peter. "Willing and Voluntary Subjection." In *Puritanism and the American Experience*, edited by Michael McGiffert, 33–37. Reading, MA: Addison-Wesley, 1969.

Channing, Edward. *A History of the United States: The American Revolution, 1761–1789*. Norwood, MA; Norwood Press, 1912.

"Colonial Travel." Chronicles of America. Accessed May 22, 2019, http://www.chronicl esofamerica.com/colonial_folkways/colonial_travel.htm.

"Colonial Travel." ConstitutionFacts.com. Accessed May 22, 2019, https://www.constituti onfacts.com/founders-library/colonial-travel/.

Cotton, Thomas. *Spiritual Milk for Boston Babes*. Cambridge: Samuel Green, 1656. https:// digitalcommons.unl.edu/cgi/viewcontent.cgi?article=1018&context=etas.

Demos, John. *A Little Commonwealth: Family Life in Plymouth Colony*. 2nd ed. New York: Oxford University Press, 1999.

Foucault, Michel. *The Order of Things: An Archaeology of the Human Sciences*. New York: Vintage Books, 1994.

Gildrie, Richard. *Salem Massachusetts, 1626–1683: A Covenant Community*. Charlottesville: University of Virginia Press, 1975.

Godbeer, Richard. *The Overflowing of Friendship: Love Between Men and Women and the Creation of the American Republic*. Baltimore: Johns Hopkins University Press, 2009.

Godbeer, Richard. *The Salem Witch Hunt: A Brief History with Documents*. New York: Bedford/St. Martin's, 2011.

Goodman, Paul. *Essays in American Colonial History*. New York: Holt Rinehart and Winston, 1967.

Goodwin, Maud. *The Colonial Cavalier or Southern Life Before the Revolution*. Kindle ed. Seattle: Amazon Digital Services, 2012. First published 1895.

Graves, Dan. "Elizabeth Hooton, 1st Woman Preacher." Christianity.com, 2007. Accessed May 22, 2019http://www.christianity.com/church/church-history/timeline/1601-1700/elizabeth-hooton-1st-woman-preacher-11630150.html.

Haskins, George. *Law and Authority in Early Massachusetts: A Study in Tradition and Design*. New York: Macmillan Company, 1960.

Jernegan, Marcus. *Laboring and Dependent Classes in Colonial America, 1607–1783: Studies of the Economic, Educational, and Social Significance of Slaves, Servants, Apprentices and Poor Folk*. Chicago: University of Chicago Press, 1931.

Johnson, Michael P. *Reading the American Past: Selected Historical Documents*. Vol. 1, *To 1877*, 5th ed. New York: Bedford/St. Martin's, 2012.

Katz, Michael B. *In the Shadow of the Poorhouse: A Social History of Welfare in America*. 10th anniv. ed. New York: Basic Books, 1996.

Kelso, R. W. *The History of Public Poor Relief in Massachusetts, 1620–1920*. New York: Houghton Mifflin, 1922.

Kidd, Thomas S. *The Great Awakening: A Brief History with Documents*. New York: Bedford/ St. Martin's, 2007.

Lockridge, Kenneth. *A New England Town, the First Hundred Years: Dedham, Massachusetts 1636–1736*. New York: W. W. Norton & Company, 1970.

Mardsen, George. "America's 'Christian' Origins: Puritan New England as a Case Study." In *John Calvin: His Influence in the Western World*, edited by W. Stanford Reid, 241–62. Grand Rapids, MI: Zondervan, 1982.

Mather, Cotton. "A Christian at His Calling." In *Puritanism and the American Experience*, 122–28. Reading, MA: Addison-Wesley, 1969. First published 1701.

Mays, Dorothy. *Women in Early America: Struggle, Survival, and Freedom in a New World*. Santa Barbara: ABC-CLIO, 2004.

Miller, Perry. "The Puritan State and Puritan Society." In *Puritanism and the American Experience*, edited by Michael McGiffert, 41–51. Reading, MA: Addison-Wesley, 1969.

Moraley, William. *The Infortunate: The Voyage and Adventures of William Moraley, an Indentured Servant*. Edited by Susan E. Klepp and Billy Gordon Smith. 2nd ed. University Park: Pennsylvania State University Press, 2005. First published 1743.

Morgan, Edmund S. *The Puritan Family: Essays on Religion and Domestic Relations in Seventeenth-Century New England*. Eastford, CT: Martino Fine Books, 1944.

Morgan, Edmund S. "The Protestant Ethic. The Puritan Ethic and the American Revolution." In *Puritanism and the American Experience*, edited by Michael McGiffert, 182–97. Reading, MA: Addison-Wesley, 1969.

Oberholzer, Emil. *Delinquent Saints: Disciplinary Action in the Early Congregational Churches of Massachusetts*. New York: Columbia University Press, 1956.

Rothman, David J. *The Discovery of the Asylum: Social Order and Disorder in the New Republic*. 3rd ed. New York: Walter de Gruyter, 2002.

Schlatter, Richard. "The Puritan Strain." In *Puritanism and the American Experience*, edited by Michael McGiffert, 3–13. Reading, MA: Addison-Wesley, 1969.

Schneewind, Jerome B. *The Invention of Autonomy: A History of Modern Moral Philosophy*. Cambridge: Cambridge University Press, 1997.

Schneider, David M. *The History of Public Welfare in New York State 1609–1866*. Chicago: University of Chicago Press, 1938.

Sherwood, Terry G. *Self in Early Modern Literature: For the Common Good*. Pittsburgh: Duquesne University Press, 2007.

Singer, Gregg. "The Scottish-Irish in America." In *John Calvin: His influence in the Western World*, edited by W. Stanford Reid, 263–88. Grand Rapids, MI: Zondervan, 1982.

Smith, Billy G. *The Lower Sort: Philadelphia's Laboring People, 1750–1800*. New York: Cornell University Press, 1994.

Sweet, William Warren. *Religion in Colonial America*. New York: Cooper Square, 1965.

Taylor, Alan. *Colonial America: A Very Short Introduction*. New York: Oxford University Press, 2012.

"Town Meeting Auctions Poor Woman to Lowest Bidder." Mass Moments. Accessed May 22, 2019, http://www.massmoments.org/moment.cfm?mid=301.

Trattner, Walter I. *From Poor Law to Welfare State: A History of Social Welfare in America*. 4th ed. New York: Free Press, 1989.

Ulrich, Laurel T. *Good Wives: Image and Reality in the Lives of Women in Northern New England, 1650–1750*. New York: Vintage, 1991.

Ver Steeg, Clarence L. *The Formative Years 1607–1763*. New York: Hill and Wang, 1964.

Wiebe, Robert. *The Search for Order: 1877–1920*. New York: Hill and Wang, 1967.

Winthrop, John. "A Model of Christian Charity." In *Puritanism and the American Experience*, edited by Michael McGiffert, 27–32. Reading, MA: Addison-Wesley, 1969. First published 1630.

Winthrop, John. "Authority and Liberty." In *Puritanism and the American Experience*, edited by Michael McGiffert, 38–40. Reading, MA: Addison-Wesley, 1969. First published 1645.

Zuckerman, Michael. *Peaceable Kingdoms: New England Towns in the Eighteenth Century*. New York: Alfred A. Knopf, 1970.

3

Social Welfare Practices in Colonial America (c. 1620–1820)

With a thorough description of the Colonial Discourse, we are now better prepared to step into the shoes of colonial Americans so as to view these practices from their eyes. The main social problems of concern to colonial Americans were those of poverty and crime. There was no special attention given to mental illness as the concept of mental illness did not exist at this time. Those individuals afflicted with a mental illness who did not exhibit harm to themselves or others were simply classified among the poor and viewed as paupers:[1] persons unable to properly care for themselves. Relief was provided for their care and upkeep, as would be the case for any long-term pauper (e.g., a widow).[2] However, the response toward less compliant mentally ill individuals would be much different: They were caged, placed in locked rooms, barns, or other small dwellings.[3] Such arrangements made their care ripe for neglect.[4] Similarly, as there were no hospitals in these isolated communities, health care was a form of relief: If your family was not able to adequately care for your health care needs, then you would be boarded in another's home at the community's expense, or for more unique needs, money would be given to pay for expenses to visit a doctor in the closest city.[5] Also, there was not yet a concept for child welfare. Dependent children of this era were also simply classified as paupers and were treated similarly to children from poor families.[6] Town magistrates would intervene for severe cases of neglect, and the children would be taken from the parents and placed in a more properly run household—the main goal being the alleviation of their poverty.[7]

The main policies among the various colonies for addressing the issue of poverty were all modeled after the English Poor Laws of the Elizabethan era. The prominence that they played in shaping social welfare practices of that era makes them worthy of a separate examination. A common stance among social work historians has been that the Poor Laws were used to separate the worthy poor from the unworthy poor based upon a moral calculus. As we shall see in Chapter 5, this was certainly the case for the various charity organization societies of the late 1800s. However, I argue here that this viewpoint did not arise until after the age of industrialization and urbanization and that the historical evidence does not support applying this same conclusion to the Colonial Era.

A Genealogy of the Good and Critique of Hubris. Phillip Dybicz, Oxford University Press. © Oxford University Press 2023.
DOI: 10.1093/oso/9780197670071.003.0003

The Settlement Laws (i.e., Colonial Poor Laws)

The laws set forth by colonial governing bodies concerning relief to the poor are sometimes referred to by social welfare historians as the *Poor Laws*.[8] Yet while the titles of these laws speak of poor relief, their main concern was directed toward establishing qualifications for residency or settlement.[9] The act of 1683 in New York is a typical example; entitled, "An Act . . . for maintaining the poore, & preventing vagabonds"[a] the provisions for maintaining the poor are vague, and little space is given to their elaboration. The vast majority of the space in the document was devoted to outlining residency requirements—that is, the criteria that must be met to be considered a resident of the community. The act called for the annual election of commissioners of the poor and a treasurer in each local community; thus, local responsibility for poor relief was firmly stated and established.[10] However, how provisions for the poor were to be accomplished was left open, the act saying no more than "the respective Commissioners . . . shall make provision for the maintenance support of their poor respectively."[11] This stance held sway among all the colonies as they became established.[12] In fact, North Carolina's 1754 law, entitled "An Act for the Restraint of Vagrants, and for making Provision for the Poor," forgot entirely to discuss the poor, concentrating solely upon residency requirements.[13]

Elaborate measures were spelled out in detail concerning either the acceptance or rejection of a stranger into the community.[14] These included the following: posting a monetary security for a period of time, notifying the constable within a certain period of time of one's arrival and then submitting to an examination of one's character and economic standing, purchasing land equal to a particular monetary value, and/or producing a residency certificate documenting one's good standing in one's previous town.[15] These settlement acts would be updated as the years passed—each time this update would consist of further elaborations concerning residency requirements; nothing would be added concerning elaboration of poor relief.[16]

So why do the various colonial Poor Laws spend an inordinate amount of time detailing the various provisions for residency and so little time in detailing the nature of poor relief? An understanding of the dominant Discourse on social welfare operating during this era, as described in Chapter 2, provides some ready answers. First, through their readings of history in the Bible, the colonists came to the understanding that poverty had always been present in human societies. This knowledge combined with their belief in a divine order to the universe led

---

[a] Schneider, *The History of Public Welfare*, p. 35. The full title of this act is as follows "An Act for the Defraying of the publique & necessary Charge of each respective City, towne and County throughout this Province & for maintaining the poore, & preventing vagabonds."

them to conclude that poverty must be part of God's plan. Also part of God's plan was the notion of a social hierarchy being needed to organize society. The very first line of John Winthrop's famous sermon "A Model of Christian Charity" (1630), written aboard the *Arabella* when traveling to the New World, illustrates this acceptance of the poor in one's midst quite clearly: "GOD ALMIGHTY in his most holy and wise providence, hath soe disposed of the condition of' mankind, as in all times some must be rich, some poore, some high and eminent in power and dignitie; others mean and in submission."[17] Thus, within this social hierarchy the poor had a legitimate place.[18] From this, it can be concluded that, while colonial Americans most likely pitied the poor, there was no stigma attached to being a pauper. Colonists did not view these individuals as being mainly or solely responsible for their condition; they did not see poverty as arising from individual moral or other failings. Again, we can turn to Winthrop's famous sermon to illustrate this:

> Thirdly, that every man might have need of others, and from hence they might be all knit more nearly together in the bonds of brotherly affection. From hence it appears plainly that no man is made more honorable than another or more wealthy etc., out of any particular and singular respect to himself, but for the glory of his Creator and the common good of the creature.[19]

So it is clear that the colonists readily accepted the duty to provide relief to the poor and that all members of society were equally honorable; hence, in the minds of the colonists there were no such designations as "worthy" and "unworthy" of poor relief. As historian Marcus Jernegan notes, "Both regions, however, accepted responsibility for the support of their poor and there is little evidence of real suffering for lack of support."[20]

Another consequence arising from their acceptance of poverty in their midst was that there were no lofty goals to eradicate poverty, as it was part of God's plan. This meant that social welfare efforts were mainly geared toward alleviating the suffering caused by poverty, with little in the way of large-scale efforts to prevent it. The theme of salvation running through this Discourse further buttresses these conclusions. The experience of those in poverty was interpreted as God providing instruction regarding care for one's soul and the nature of sacrifice—as the sacrificing of one's will to that of God's was seen as necessary for inviting divine grace to enter one's soul.[21] The story of Job from the Bible serves to illustrate this notion that an individual could be subjected to this instructive suffering without it being due to moral failing.

For the giver of aid, this theme of salvation served also as an opportunity to care for one's soul. The well off viewed the presence of paupers in their midst as God providing them the opportunity to practice beneficence. It was well understood that those who were blessed with God's bounty had a responsibility to share this bounty with those who were less fortunate.[22] The great silence and vagueness on how to address the issue of poverty within the various colonial Poor Laws speaks volumes: This was due to the widely accepted and well understood notion that members of the community had the responsibility to care for its less fortunate members—and that the act of providing relief was seen as benefiting both parties.

And what of the obsession with various residency requirements outlining the process by which a member is accepted into the community? This is where the cultural feature of conceiving the community as an extended family lends insight. Achieving residency meant that one was accepted into this community family. And like one's biological family, once one gained a place within this hierarchy, membership was practically irrevocable. Hence, if you should happen to fall prey to misfortune and enter the ranks of the poor, then you would be able to lay a claim on the well-off members to provide you with relief.[23] However, if one was not a resident and thus not part of this family, the claim for charity would be much weaker and, if granted, very temporary in nature.[24] Therefore colonial Americans paid close attention to who they would or would not let enter their community family[25]—as is reflected in the amount of space in the various Poor Laws dedicated to addressing this concern. We also see in the construction of these Poor Laws the two rules of right from this Discourse actively at work: *determining rights and responsibilities* and *determining identity*. Correctly identifying those worthy of joining one's community family served to attend to the urgent need: *the maintenance of the social hierarchy*. The rights and responsibilities concerning the care for the poor within the social hierarchy were already well established and understood, and thus did not need further elaboration within the Poor Laws. Thus, if one was going to attempt to apply the calculus of worthy and unworthy poor to the Colonial Era, those worthy of relief were those individuals who were part of your community family, and those unworthy of relief were those individuals who were not. However, even this application of this calculus does not fully hold up as colonial Americans were often generous in their provision of aid to those in need but merely traveling through (as we shall see in the following section concerning the story of William Moraley) as well as those in need from neighboring communities when the community as a whole befell misfortune (such as suffering from an attack by indigenous Native Americans).

The longer that a community had been established, the more fixed its social order became; consequently, the ability to fit into that social order became more and more difficult. Thus, newly established communities on the frontier itself usually were open to most anybody willing to settle and contribute to the development of the community.[26] Villages that were only recently established were fairly open to those with a proven craft.[27] Villages that were well settled would require years of residency in good standing before accepting one as an official member of the community.[28] If the individual did not meet the criteria necessary to qualify for residency or a probationary period, they would be told to leave town—a process referred to as *warning out*.[29] As the name implies, those warned out were told to leave the town within a specified number of days.

An individual seeking residency could be from any one of a number of different groups: Some were honest laborers seeking to build a new life; some were recent immigrants; some were simply itinerant workers; yet others were social outcasts or families who met their misfortune and became destitute before finding a place to settle; while still others were runaway slaves or bond servants or petty criminals who had been "warned out" of other settlements.[30] Furthermore, from the early days of colonization, England adopted a practice of sending its vagrants and criminals to be dumped upon America's shores.[31] Consequently, proper classification of every new individual who entered the community— through the ever increasingly detailed settlement laws—was important in *determining their identity* in terms of how and if they might fit into the social order of the community.[32] The language used to denote the greatest threat in this arena facing the community—"vagabonds" and "rogues" (individuals who belong to no social institution)—further illustrates the importance given to hierarchical social institutions as the basis for the welfare of the community.

Poverty Relief

While the American colonists readily embraced their responsibility for caring for their less fortunate neighbors,[33] a calculus was applied to determine the type of aid to be given. However, once again, decisions were not based upon a moral calculus applied to the recipient of aid (i.e., those morally worthy and those unworthy). Rather, the decision on the type of aid was based upon what was the most pragmatic and economical for that particular situation.[34] Thus, the most common form of poverty relief given was that of "outdoor relief": the colonists' term for direct aid.[35] One estimate, applied to the years 1764–1769, calculates that approximately 75% of those seeking aid received this type of relief.[36] This often translated into providing direct relief to families in the form of either goods or money.[37] It also might take the form of an exemption from taxes or public restrictions (e.g., cutting firewood from a restricted area).[38] The pragmatic and economic calculus applied for receiving direct relief applied to situations in which the individual or family was deemed to have met with temporary misfortune. Simply providing the recipient with what was needed in order to make it through this rough patch was the most pragmatic approach to addressing this misfortune.

Women suffering the misfortune of the death of a husband were entitled to receive aid for the rest of their life or until the time they remarried and thus entered a new household.[39] Long-term direct relief was given to widows who were deemed capable of continuing to maintain their home—those who were hale and hearty and who had children to help with the labor required to maintain the household—or to those who were able to join the household of a relative. The economic calculus applied to these situations is that the widow would only receive aid as needed. This aid could take many forms: food, clothing, fuel, other essentials, medical care, and cash payments.[40] Taking a look at the relief roles in Philadelphia from the period 1650–1700, historian Billy Smith notes the case of a woman named Sarah, in which her and her child received aid intermittently over the span of a decade and a half.[41]

Lastly, direct relief was also given in the form of food and lodging to travelers passing through towns. The pragmatic calculus here arose from the fact that the remoteness and relative small size of most villages precluded most from containing an inn within which travelers might board; thus, those travelers needing to stay for a night or two would be boarded in someone's private home. The economic calculus being applied was that this relief was restricted to a few days at most. This generosity exhibited toward travelers is notably captured by the reflections of William Moraley in 1743, who upon terminating his period of indenture sought to travel to the coast in order to book passage on a ship to return to England. Speaking upon the generosity he received, William Moraley noted in his diary, "And the hospitable Inhabitants dispense their Favours to the Traveller, the Poor, and the Needy. . . . In short, it is the best poor Man's Country in the World."[42]

There were, however, situations that would arise wherein providing direct relief was not the most pragmatic solution. Such was the case for Mary Degresha mentioned at the beginning of Chapter 2. After the death of her husband, Mary was the only member of her household as there were no children living with her. Neither her children nor other family members were living in the same community as her; thus, there was no household containing relatives that she might join. The town readily accepted responsibility to provide relief and support for Mary for the rest of her life; however, it was impractical to simply give her direct relief as she was not able to maintain a house and a farm on her own. Thus, the town selectmen set about to find a household which Mary could join.

Similar to foster parents in today's society, the community would pay the head of the household a monthly stipend to accept this non-relative into their home and assume the responsibility as their caregiver.[43] Thus, applying the pragmatic calculus to Mary's relief called for her to be housed in someone else's home. The economic calculus to relief was applied in their method for determining which household Mary would join: The town held an auction wherein families willing to accept the town's charge into their household placed a bid reflecting how much money they would need to receive as a payment for assuming the responsibility of the charge's care.[44]

Thus, Mary Degresha was sent to the household who bid the *lowest*; that is, the household willing to assume the responsibility for her care and asking the least amount of money from the community to do so. In being placed within the social hierarchy of this new household, Mary would adopt the status of *servant* and thus was expected to obey the wishes of the master and mistress of the household. However, it must be noted that the status of *servant* in the Colonial Discourse meant more than just hired help. It was a position within the social hierarchy of a family household, and thus a de facto family member, carrying with it the right to decent treatment and the responsibility to obey one's superiors in the household.[45] This attitude of being considered a de facto family member is also captured by William Moraley in his diary, wherein using the descriptor *our family* to denote all members living in the household, he noted that in addition to the master of the household, "Our Family consisted of a Wife and two Daughters, with a Nephew, a Negro Slave, a bought Servant, and myself, with the aforesaid Gentlewoman."[46]

This vendue system of auctioning off the poor was also the primary means by which to provide care for dependent children. Children who had lost one or both parents or those suffering from neglect would be auctioned off to serve a period of indentured service until reaching adulthood.[47] The colonists took their responsibility seriously of stamping out any instances of neglect of a child's welfare. A typical statute pertaining to this social problem stated that the children would be auctioned off for indenture when parents "are not able to provide Competent and convenient food and raiment for theire Children."[48] Another stated, "Taking into consideration the great neglect of many parents and masters in training up their children in learning, and labor, and other implyments which may be profitable to the common wealth," it was ordered that the selectmen of every town "shall henceforth stand charged with the care of the redresse of this evill."[49]

Oftentimes, parents facing economic hardship would look to indenture out their children themselves, rather than waiting for the town selectmen to step in.[50] In this way, the parents had some say as to which household their child would be sent. In some cases, the youth being indentured would actually represent a valuable contribution to the household in terms of labor. In such instances, when auctioning off such a youth, the bid would be bid down to zero and then bid up—representing sums the household was willing to pay the community for the indentured contract.[51] Reflecting upon the operation of the Colonial Discourse, there were a number of factors that made the auctioning off of these individuals both practical and humane in the eyes of the colonials. As noted earlier, hard currency was scarce. Most economic transactions were handled through a barter system, in which labor served as a commodity to be bartered. Most people traveling to the colonies did so through accepting an indentured period of service—which both paid for their passage over as well as set themselves up with "employment" upon arriving. For those persons born and raised in the colonies, it was not uncommon for parents to indenture out their children upon coming of age in order to learn a trade. Hence, most colonists had at some point in their lives adopted the role of *servant* in the social hierarchy of a household.[52] Consequently, not only was this a well-recognized position in the family social hierarchy but most persons could respect and empathize with the individual serving in such a role.

As described earlier, direct relief in terms of goods was the most popular form of poverty relief in colonial America. The second most used was the placing of a person in another's household under terms of indentured service. The final and least used method to provide poor relief was that of sending the person to an almshouse. First, it should be noted that the almshouses found in colonial America were of much different character than those appearing in the nineteenth century, in which reform and rehabilitation were part of the mission. Colonial Americans accepted poverty in their midst as part of God's divine plan, and thus did not take up the struggle of attempting to reform and rehabilitate the recipient. Rather, there was a pragmatic and economic calculus applied when choosing this method. Thus, in colonial America, the almshouse served as a de facto family household in which to place the recipient.[53] An overseer of the poor (along with any family members comprising their household) was paid to live within the almshouse and assume the position of master of the household in the social hierarchy. There were two circumstances which prompted the creation of almshouses during this period. Both were a pragmatic and economical response to the situation of attempting to provide relief to a large number of recipients at the same time. For towns that grew into cities—such as Boston, New York, and Philadelphia—the number of poor needing to be boarded in another's home also grew. Thus, it became much more pragmatic and economical to simply build a residence to house them all rather than attempting to individually place each of them in a private household.[54] Thus, almshouses became a permanent fixture in the few cities that were established in this era. Smaller towns and villages—where the vast majority of the population lived—adopted this method only when faced with a sudden influx of refugees needing relief (such as when a nearby town or village fell prey to a large attack by Native Americans). But for all practical purposes, the almshouses mimicked the social hierarchy of a family household: the colonials' ideal social institution for maintaining the social order.

Now a particular logistics problem arose concerning employing this method: How was the overseer to distinguish between those persons who applied for and were legitimately granted relief by the community and the various strolling vagabonds and rogues who might seek to take advantage of the community's generosity? This era did not have identification cards or papers to label oneself as a legitimate recipient. Some other manner was necessary to legitimately establish a person's identity as a recipient of aid. The colonists came up with the simple method of providing recipients a cloth letter "P" to stitch upon their clothing along with the initials of their community.[55] Some historians have equated this with a badge of shame forced upon these poor individuals.[56] Fueling this interpretation is the additional evidence that in some instances colonial Americans adopted a similar procedure as a form of penance for certain crimes: such as wearing a cloth "A.D." for adultery,[57] a practice made famous by Hawthorne's tale *The Scarlet Letter.*

But if we look to the Discourse dominating this era, *the determination of identity* was a rule of right: The colonists strived to place individuals in their correct position in the social order. Thus, this rule of right cut across all practices related to social welfare. Yet, as already has been established, poverty was not seen by colonists as arising from personal moral failings (unless one purposefully chose the lifestyle of a rogue or vagabond). The poor had a legitimate place within the social hierarchy. Thus, the practice of wearing a cloth letter "P" was more akin to the clothing identification of a military uniform wherein the single stripe of a private designates that individual's place in the military hierarchy; however, the wearing of this stripe—while required—does not carry with it the stigma of a badge of shame. This is further reflected by the fact that refusal to wear the letter "P" simply resulted in the consequence of not receiving relief, as now one's identity was suspect.[58] As we shall see shortly, true criminal acts received much harsher measures. Also, once the individual had been settled into the almshouse for some time and the overseer began to recognize the individual, it became less important for persons to wear the letter "P" as a means to establish their identity as a legitimate recipient of aid and, thus, the practice was less enforced.

Crime as Sin

Colonial society viewed criminal activity as an act of sin: a moral failure to live up to one's social duties and one's duties before God.[59] In fact, little difference was made between acts that violated religious prohibitions and those that violated civil laws.[60] Since community membership necessarily entailed congregational membership, there was much overlap between these social and divinely ordained duties. So, for example, the biblical prescription to *honor one's mother and father* was also a law.[61] And, as was noted previously, this biblical prescription was extended to include anyone who was one's superior in the social hierarchy.[62] And since this was one of the Ten Commandments, the maximum penalty for this law was death—indicating the level of threat perceived by the colonists that the breaking of this law would have on maintaining the social hierarchy, and thus the social order.

In fact, numerous criminal offenses—over 20% of listed offenses in some areas—carried a maximum penalty of death by hanging.[63] Upon surface examination, this high percentage of capital crimes would make the American colonists appear to be a bloodthirsty lot. However, as we shall see presently with the case of Nicolas Senison, while various laws carried a maximum penalty of death, this maximum penalty was rarely enforced. So, for example, there are no known instances of someone being sentenced to hang during this period for breaking the law by not honoring one's mother, father, or social superior. Rather, assigning a maximum penalty of death was simply a way to communicate the level of importance of the moral imperative embodied in the law. As honoring one's mother and father was one of the Ten Commandments, its moral imperative was naturally granted a high level of importance.

Thus, closer examination reveals that the American colonists actually adopted a reasonably tolerant attitude toward crime. This is because the various religious groups that settled in America all embraced the doctrine of original sin.[64] Since everyone was born with the stain of original sin, its expression by a particular individual did not mark them as a deviant individual belonging to a separate class.[65] Consequently, measures to address criminal behavior were modeled along the lines of doing penance.[66] These measures were determined by the community magistrates and might take the form of any of the following: a harsh admonition by the magistrates, the levying of a fine, or various forms of corporal punishment such as whip lashings or being placed in the stocks.[67] Later generations would look upon the vast array of capital crimes and the colonists' fondness for corporal punishment and deem them barbaric. This may well have been the view of the reader upon reading the cases of Alice Thomas and John Veering at the beginning of Chapter 2. Yet the important distinction to keep in mind was that these physical acts of contrition were seen not primarily as a form of discipline by which to shape wayward behavior but rather as a form of penance to demonstrate one's remorse for having sinned. And due to accepting the doctrine of original sin, it was expected that *everyone* would at some point sin.

Hence, communities, embracing the metaphor of the community as a family, approached criminal punishment as a form of family discipline. Just as no parents carry the expectation that their child will live a perfect childhood and never misbehave, lapses by community members were seen as inevitable (due to original sin). The ways the colonists decided to deal with such lapses show many similarities to those of a family today attempting to address the wayward behavior of their child through the use of corporal punishment. First of these similarities is the use of corporal punishment as a form of discipline.[68] Corporal punishment was the common practice for disciplining children in the family as well as for the wayward member in the community. Hence, jails of this time period were simply holding areas for a suspect until they received their day in court; no one was sentenced to serve time in prison[69]—this would be neither practical nor economical for the community.

Second was the emphasis placed upon having the wayward member confess to the wrongdoing, often publicly, in order to demonstrate that they were truly repentant.[70] Thus, courts in colonial America were not primarily about establishing the guilt of the suspect; the nature of a small town meant that knowledge of the suspect's guilt had usually been established before entering court. Rather, they served as forums for the suspect to genuinely display their remorse—hence the great importance placed upon extracting a confession from the suspect as opposed to simply establishing guilt. Similarly to the situation of disciplining one's child, merely establishing the child's guilt is not the only goal of the parent. Rather, one looks for the child to offer genuine remorse as the means to demonstrate that they have clearly understood the moral transgression arising from their act. Hence, in colonial America the penance/punishment for a crime was treated as a moral educational lesson for the wayward member.[71]

Third, the clergy used the public nature of these punishments as a platform to preach moral lessons for the entire community concerning the folly of sin.[72] Similarly, a child's punishment for misbehavior is used as an example for the other children in the family to learn from as well. Lastly, once the penance/punishment was complete, the offending member was accepted back into the community fold, retaining their previous status in the social hierarchy.[73] Thus, using the comparison once again of disciplining one's child, once remorse has been communicated and the penance served, the child does not return to the family fold as a "lesser" member than before, forever stigmatized for having morally transgressed. Rather, the child is welcomed back into the family and assumes the place they had before.

So, just like what takes place in a family today, conformity to the roles and responsibilities of the existing social order was at all times stressed. Yet, as is sometimes the case with a particularly wayward member of a family, there are some transgressions that cannot be forgiven. While rare, it is not unheard of that parents will take the step of disowning their adult child. Colonial Americans labeled the wayward member who had moved beyond any hope for forgiveness as an incorrigible sinner[74]—a designation that had no place in the existing social and divine order. In such cases there were two possible outcomes. The offending member—after receiving a healthy dose of corporal punishment—would be "warned out" of town, and thus ostracized from the community family. If the crime was particularly heinous and the magistrates felt that they could not inflict such an individual upon another community, the penalty would be death by hanging. This stance sheds some light on why over 20% of criminal acts carried a maximum penalty of death. Some criminal acts, such as murder, were unforgivable sins and thus always carried the maximum penalty of capital punishment.[75] Other criminal acts, such as petty thievery, carried a penalty dependent upon the individual who committed it.

Thus, touching upon the rule of right for this Discourse of *determining identity*, the punishment for a crime was less dependent upon the transgression itself and more dependent upon the identity of the person who committed the act. Hence, if the magistrates judged it as an act from a wayward individual, then petty thievery could carry a punishment as simple as a harsh admonition or a whip lashing.[76] If this was a repeat offense, and thus the offender was deemed particularly in need of moral instruction, they would be indentured for a period of time in a morally upstanding household.[77] Moral instruction would be provided through the discipline process of the family.[78] However, if the magistrates found out that the individual committed many such acts—and thus determined that the most recent violation simply reflected the actions of an incorrigible sinner[79]—the penalty would be either to be warned out of town or a trip to the gallows. As was the case for all criminal punishments, warning out and capital punishment served as a platform to preach upon the folly of sin to the community at large.[80] While being put to death or the ostracism of being warned out of town would not help the offender (who was perceived as beyond help), it could still serve the community by acting as a lesson to others. Thus, even these harsh sentences served the urgent need of the Discourse: maintaining the strength of the social hierarchy through excising the destabilizing individual from it.

The fact that fairly innocuous laws—such as the admonition to honor one's mother and father—carried with them a maximum penalty of death would seem to belie the stance that colonial Americans had a reasonably tolerant attitude toward individuals who committed a crime. Yet, part of the reason for this tolerance was the fact that serious crime was a rarity in these close-knit communities. When in 1771 the case of Bryan Sheenan of the village Marblehead resulted in a conviction in the Essex County courthouse on charges of rape, the press marked him as "the first Person, as far as we can learn, that has been convicted of Felony in this large county, since the memorable year [of witchcraft trials], 1692."[81] This marked a span of eighty years without the occurrence of a felony. Another indication of this tolerance is reflected in their stance toward addressing juvenile delinquency. Those juveniles 16 years of age or under were statutorily exempt from all but the most heinous of crimes.[82] Rather than prosecute juveniles through the court system for their infractions, they were deemed a matter to be taken care of through the discipline of the family.[83]

Finally, we can examine the case of Nicolas Senison as the means to illustrate this tolerance toward crime at work. In 1667, Nicolas Senison was brought to court and found guilty of attempted sodomy.[84] First, his case serves as a good example of the conflation between sin and crime that marked the Colonial Discourse. As will be no surprise to the reader, the conservative religious culture of this time period viewed such types of sexual relations as sin. Yet Senison was notorious in Windsor for his "sodomitical actings," engaging in many such behaviors over a span of decades, for which he was informally admonished by neighbors.[85] The town elders stepped in on two occasions, once in the late 1640s and again in the 1660s, to investigate Senison's activities, which resulted in simply informally reprimanding him for his sin.[86]

It was only when his behavior was deemed socially disruptive—by making untoward advances to Nathaniel Pond, an indentured servant in Senison's household—that he was brought up on charges.[87] Senison's behavior was now viewed by the community as violating the rights and responsibilities inherent in the social hierarchy of the household by violating the duty to protect and care for those family members in an inferior position of the family hierarchy; thus, Senison's act was now viewed as a threat to the social order. Thus, in determining punishment, the community's main concern was focused upon compensating Pond, rather than punishing Senison: They ordered Senison to shorten Pond's term of indenture by one year and to pay him forty shillings as compensation for suffering abuse by the master of the household.[88]

For all of the seventeenth century in the American colonies, there are only two recorded cases of sodomy that resulted in execution: those of William Plaine and John Knight.[89] Both of these individuals were deemed to be incorrigible sinners, and this determination is what brought on the capital punishment as they were seen to be a major threat to the social hierarchy. William Plaine was judged irredeemable due to his influence in corrupting the youth of Guilford by, "masturbations, which he had committed, and provoked others to the like above a hundred times."[90] Thus, the incorrigible aspect of his acts stemmed from the vast number of repeat offenses of masturbation and "corrupting" others to the practice as well. The fact that he was charged with having engaged in sodomy with two persons in England was merely a footnote to this greater threat.[91] John Knight was judged irredeemable due to both being a repeat offender and, more importantly, the fact that he displayed no signs of remorse for having committed this sin.[92]

Strangers or visitors who committed a crime—by not holding the identity of "community member" and thus not being a part of the existing social hierarchy—were simply excised from the community: After receiving their penance, they would be warned out of town.[93] Communal life through a social hierarchy, and the interdependence that it engendered, was so central to colonists' concepts of social order and welfare, as well as of one's salvation, that they could not conceive of any reasons, other than nefarious ones, why anyone would select a more mobile lifestyle. Such individuals were viewed with suspicion and distrust and labeled as either *rogues* (i.e., confidence men practicing some form of deceit), *beggars* (i.e., those in need of relief but not electing to indenture themselves in return), or *vagabonds* (those electing not to join a community family).[94] This resulted in great intolerance for those choosing such a lifestyle, with all being lumped together as petty criminals. It is against these individuals that the settlement laws sought so vigorously to guard against acceptance into the community. Thus, as stated earlier, they were commonly "warned out" of town when their identity was determined to be one of these three types of petty criminals. In some instances, such as Massachusetts in 1699, this intolerance led to the establishment of workhouses, specifically to suppress and punish those deemed as being either a rogue, beggar, or vagabond.[95]

Lastly, a discussion on crime in colonial America would not be complete without including the topic of witchcraft. While the Salem witch trials of 1692 represented a panic, the concern of colonists to root out witches spanned the entire seventeenth and eighteenth centuries.[96] Over sixty witchcraft trials were held in New England in the decades prior to 1692.[97] And these beliefs lasted well into the eighteenth century, with one woman in Philadelphia being lynched for witchcraft as late as 1787.[98] So why did witchcraft gain prominence in the minds of the American colonists, and why did this prominence fade in the minds of Americans beginning in the early nineteenth century? The simple answer is that the Colonial Discourse gave strength and reality to notions of witchcraft, whereas the Premodern Discourse replacing it in the nineteenth century did not.

Examining various elements of the Colonial Discourse provides insight on this matter. First was the understanding that supernatural forces were at work in the world. By adopting divine providence as their philosophical understanding of reality, God's will was actively at work in the world shaping events according to a divine plan of the universe. Thus, the colonists firmly believed that everything happened for a reason, with this reason ultimately being tied to some type of supernatural force at work. As part of the divine plan, God had allowed evil to exist in the world as a means to test the faith of men and women, with the Bible specifically mentioning the existence of witches.[99] Thus, by accepting the proposition that God actively exerted his will in the world, it was a small step to accept that supernatural evil forces—embodied by Satan—were also at work in the world.

By adopting hermeneutics as their philosophical understanding of how truth and the understanding of reality is obtained, the colonists tasked themselves with correctly divining the nature of events by correctly interpreting the supernatural forces at work. Consequently, acts that sought to undermine the social order of the community by questioning the established social hierarchy (which was viewed as the bedrock of this order) were interpreted as being evil forces at work. The unrepentant person committing such subversive acts was thus seen as an agent of Satan. Such an understanding did not bode well for individuals who did not comfortably fit into the existing social hierarchy, most notably women. Those women who most strongly questioned the patriarchal nature of this social hierarchy were prone to being labeled as witches.[100]

c. 1770–1820: A Discourse in Transition

The distinction of classes begins to disappear.
—George Washington to Brissot de Warville, 1788[101]

In the latter part of the eighteenth century and the early part of the nineteenth century, a new discourse began to challenge the existing Colonial Discourse, eventually replacing it and becoming the new dominant Discourse. This period of transition provides an excellent window through which to examine the dynamics at play between two competing discourses during such a transition period. The changing geographic, political, social, and economic landscapes of this time would give birth to a new urgent need, a need most ably met by the emerging discourse. This new, emerging discourse—the topic of the next two chapters—offered a radically different paradigm for understanding the world. This understanding was heavily informed by Enlightenment thought, with prominence given to the role of reason in understanding reality and navigating one's world. The Colonial Discourse would continue to dominate into the early nineteenth century; however, during this period of transition it would be cross-fertilized with insights from the new, emerging discourse.

Reason—An Old Concept in a New Guise

This new prominence given to the role of reason does not mean that under the Colonial Discourse the colonists did not employ reason when understanding their world. So, for example, the colonists prided themselves on the fact that in their town hall meetings any freeman could speak on an issue and, through the use of a reasoned argument, seek to move others to his position.[102] In fact, they believed that this interplay of reasoned argument led to the best decision-making. Thus, the colonists employed and valued the use of reason. In fact, the use of reason is recognized as an inherently human trait and can be traced back to ancient Greece and the earliest civilizations. So this is the first insight to be gleaned: The new knowledge and understanding offered by an emerging discourse arises not from a new human trait or ability that was not used before but rather from a new role being created for that trait. Ferdinand Saussure's metaphor of a chess game is apropos here: A chess piece (in this case, reason) retains its nature in terms of its movement no matter what space on the board it occupies; however, the space it occupies combined with its relationship to the other pieces on the board determines the power and influence exerted by the chess piece and thus its value and role in the game.

The New Role for Reason

In the Colonial Discourse, reason's main role was its employment hermeneutically to decode the will of God. With the embrace of divine providence, the Bible was quite literally viewed as the word of God concerning how the world should be ordered. The faculty of reason was relied upon to correctly interpret the Bible in order to understand this divine order and the role one was to play in it.[103] From the magistrates down to children, the Bible prescribed rights and responsibilities for every position in the social hierarchy; all were bound by its tenets concerning social relations.[104] Thus, reason was the vehicle one used to determine one's identity in the social hierarchy and to understand the rights and responsibilities of that position. The use of reason in interpreting these tenets offered direction concerning codes of punishment, beneficence for those in need, and respect given to superiors to achieve an ordered society.[105]

Within the emerging, competing discourse of this period of transition (which I name the *Premodern Discourse* when describing its dominance in Chapters 4 and 5), rather than being a hermeneutical tool in which to understand the world, reason was employed directly upon nature and society to uncover the secrets of the universe (still believed to be created by God) and to properly navigate one's world. Turning back to the metaphor of a chess game, there are two chess pieces worthy of examining: divine providence and reason. The key element in determining the prominence they achieved in shaping human action and society was the role that each played in determining one's identity.

The notion of divine providence did not die out within the Premodern Discourse; however, it was moved from its central place on the board to an obscure corner. During the Colonial Discourse, divine providence played a central role in shaping human action and society because it determined one's identity by outlining the various rights and responsibilities inherent to one's position. Reason was merely a vehicle through which to arrive at this understanding of one's place in the world. Within the Premodern Discourse, these roles would be reversed. Reason itself was a determinant of identity by playing a central role in shaping human action and society, whereas divine providence was simply a vehicle through which to arrive at an understanding of one's place in the world. This reversal of roles carried with it profound implications.

The faculty of reason was accepted as being a common characteristic to all adults. Since reason was now viewed as being the prime determinant of one's identity, this commonality led to a radically different notion concerning the ordering of society: the proposition that all persons were created equally. This proposition thus seeks to destroy the central tenet of the Colonial Discourse: that maintaining a social hierarchy is vital to the promotion of social order and welfare. The above quote by George Washington to Brissot de Warville reflects this change underway in society. Consequently, when the Premodern Discourse gained ascendance, this leveling of status resulted in the common individual (who properly employed reason) being thrust into position as the ideal from which all would be measured. One implication flowing from this change was that it called for a radically different understanding of the role of democracy. During this period of transition between discourses, this new insight arising from the emerging Premodern discourse would influence the actions of our founding fathers when they boldly declared in the Declaration of Independence that "all men [sic] are created equal." However, the Colonial Discourse still exerted its dominance during this period; so, as we shall see presently, while boldly declaring the notion that all persons are created equal, the full implications of this concept were inadequately understood and applied by the founding fathers.

Attempting to Co-Opt Insights

This period of transition between discourses involved a competition in which each discourse vied for dominance. The Colonial Discourse would maintain its dominance to approximately 1820; yet, the Premodern discourse made steady gains in power and influence during this period, gains which eventually would lead to it supplanting the Colonial Discourse in the position of dominance. This competition sets up an interesting dynamic to examine during such a period of transition. The momentous event of the American Revolution took place during this period of transition and thus serves as an excellent illustration of the dynamics regarding these competing discourses. The new, emerging Premodern discourse was offering new insights, most notably the proposition that all persons are created equal.

What I would like to examine is the following dynamic: How does such an insight get incorporated and translated into the current dominant Discourse from which it did not spawn? Specifically, for this instance, how did the founding fathers incorporate this insight into their notion of a democratic government? Does this insight simply get cut and pasted into the existing dominant Discourse, creating a bifurcated understanding of the world working together side by side? Does this insight get co-opted by the dominant Discourse and utilized to serve its needs? Or does the incorporation of the insight somehow meld together the two discourses, creating a new, unique framework of understanding, an in-between state that gets replaced once the emerging discourse ascends to dominance?

Examining the case of the American Revolution, it appears that the second hypothesis is the one that occurs: The dominant Discourse of the time—in this case the Colonial Discourse—co-opts this insight to serve its needs, and in the process the most profound implications stemming from the insight get lost in translation, leaving a much weakened and watered-down version of the insight. Operating within the Colonial Discourse, the founding fathers embraced the notion that maintaining a social hierarchy is vital to the social order and the promotion of social welfare. They did not abandon this assumption. Consequently, they took the insight that all persons are created equally and attempted to apply it within a social hierarchy. One clear illustration of this from the get-go is the fact that they stated in the Declaration of Independence that "all *men* are created equal." Patriarchy was a firmly established part of the social hierarchy of this time; hence, from its inception, the application of this insight disenfranchised a whole class of people—women. This undercuts the most profound implication of this insight: that the faculty of reason is a commonality to all adult persons, creating an equality which levels any existing notions of a social hierarchy. In terms of democratic governance, this puts forward the concept of "one person, one vote" in which each individual has an equal voice.

Examining the Constitution of the United States provides further illustration of how this insight was co-opted to serve the needs of the Colonial Discourse in seeking to preserve the notion that a social hierarchy is a fundamental and vital component to society. Even working under the restricted notion that all men are created equal, not all men were given the right to vote. Those operating within the lower echelons of the social hierarchy were disenfranchised and denied this equal voice. Thus, the founding fathers did not grant the right to vote to any non-White males. In addition, those White males who did not own land were disenfranchised. Hence, the concept of equality was merely applied separately to each of the tiers of the social hierarchy; the separate tiers continued to denote different levels of status. Consequently, when George Washington was elected the nation's first president in 1789, only *6% of the population* was eligible to vote.[106] This fact serves to illustrate well the dynamic of how when a dominant Discourse attempts to incorporate a key insight from a competing discourse, the end result is a poor understanding and weakened application of the insight. We will see this same dynamic play out in future periods of transition covered in later chapters of the book as well.

While the full implications of the insight that all persons are created equally were not applied by the founding fathers, the aspects of it that were amenable to incorporation into a social hierarchy were embraced. Thus, the founding fathers embraced the notion of a strong social hierarchy supporting democracy and moved away from the stance that a strong social hierarchy naturally supports a monarchy. They also embraced the idea of individual rights, most notably those supporting the freedom to express one's opinion: freedom to peacefully assemble, freedom of religion, and freedom of the press. These freedoms mirrored well the freedom of the town hall meeting for any male to speak his mind, and thus were compatible with the central tenet of the Colonial Discourse—that a strong social hierarchy is what promoted social order and welfare. A number of elements of this new, democratic form of government clearly reflect this embrace of a strong social hierarchy.

The most telling element in this regard is that the founding fathers were able to enshrine slavery into the Constitution as an amenable aspect of a democratic form of government. Slavery dramatically illustrates the designation of a different status of person, one that is the very antithesis to the idea that all persons are created equally. The fact that slaves were counted as three-fifths of a person when computing population for determining representation in the House of Representatives illustrates this contradictory application of equality within a social hierarchy. On the one hand, slaves were recognized as de facto citizens deserving of representation just like everyone else, yet only being counted as three-fifths of a person quite clearly indicates their occupation below the lowest rung of the social hierarchy. As noted above, disenfranchisement of the majority of the population also reflects the importance placed upon the necessity of a social hierarchy for maintaining social order.

Yet beyond these already prominent deficiencies to the notion of equality, even those 6% of individuals allowed to vote were subjected to restrictions if they did not occupy the elite or aristocratic class at the top rung of the hierarchy. Thus, senators were not elected by the common people but rather appointed by those from the elite class—in the form of state legislators. In addition, the common people were not trusted to vote directly for the executive offices of president and vice president. Rather, an electoral college system was set up in which the common people voted for a person from the elite class, and then this person would cast a vote for president and vice president on behalf of these common people. Consequently, it is no surprise that historians conclude that the framing of the Constitution of the United States was more heavily influenced by Puritan thought than it was influenced by Enlightenment thought,[107] with historian Lord James Bryce aptly noting the following in 1888:

> Someone has said that the American government and Constitution are based on the theology of Calvin and the philosophy of Hobbes. This at least is true, that there is a hearty Puritanism in the view of human nature which pervades the instrument of 1787. It is the work of men who believed in original sin, and

were resolved to leave open for transgressors no door which they could possibly shut. Compare this spirit with the enthusiastic optimism of the Frenchmen of 1789. It is not merely a difference of race temperaments; it is a difference of fundamental ideas.[108]

The insight that all persons are created equally could only reach its full expression and understanding within the discourse that generated it (the soon to be dominant Premodern Discourse). This is because its full expression requires the destruction of a central tenet from the previous Discourse (in this case, the destruction of the tenet that a social hierarchy is the basis for social order); for this reason, this full expression remains incapable of occurring as long as the previous Discourse remains dominant. As we examine other transition periods in future chapters, we will discover this same dynamic reliably playing out among all such periods of transition.

The rise of Andrew Jackson in the 1820s and his election to the presidency in 1828 dramatically mark in the political arena the emergence of the Premodern Discourse in which the common person replaced the elite as the ideal. Jackson was the first president to be born in a log cabin—a symbol used to denote his status as a person of common origin. This symbol would be used by future presidential candidates throughout this era as a badge of honor, burnishing their credentials for assuming the presidency. This is in stark contrast to what came before in the Colonial Discourse, where being from the elite class is what denoted one as ready to assume the presidency.

The full realization of the insight that all persons are created equally would be the ongoing task of the Premodern Era in terms of suffrage. Enfranchisement would first be extended to all White men, the least threatening group to undermining past traditions and understandings on equality. However, racial prejudice put up stiff resistance to expressing this notion of equality, holding out until mid-century and requiring the violent struggle of a civil war before yielding to the idea that all men, of any race, are created equally. While racial prejudice continues to this day, the elimination of slavery dismantled an ignoble part of the previous social hierarchy for good and extended the right to vote to men of any race—in principle if not completely in practice.

Patriarchy, which had existed in the social consciousness for centuries, was the last element of an accepted social hierarchy to hold out against the insight of equality in terms of suffrage. It would not be until the end of the Premodern Era in 1920 that the Nineteenth Amendment to the Constitution would be passed, extending the right to vote to all women. Also toward the end of the Premodern Era, in 1913 citizens were given the right to directly elect senators rather than having them appointed by state legislators. The electoral college system remains with us today as an archaic holdover from a previous era; however, it is now commonly accepted that these electors are bound by popular will, with any historical instances to the contrary only arising after the elector realizes their vote will not affect the outcome already determined by the popular will.

This is not to say that the Premodern Discourse's embrace of the notion of the common person as the ideal translated on the ground to unfettered enfranchisement for all. To be sure, even at the close of this era, complete enfranchisement was a work in progress and remains so to this day. Whether it be from past Jim Crow laws to present attempts at voter suppression, various special interests have sought to undermine the spirit of enfranchisement. Yet these efforts involve the setting up of barriers for those seeking to exercise their right to vote—a right that is now fundamentally accepted as belonging to all adult citizens and which stems from the complete embrace of the insight that all persons are created equally.

Moral Blind Spots in the Colonial Discourse

In Chapter 1, it was discussed how a Discourse in exerting its dominance privileges some knowledge while subjugating other types of knowledge. Consequently, this dynamic necessarily creates various moral blind spots— areas of knowledge that are unable to find expression within the apparatus of the Discourse. One may visualize this dynamic as the apparatus of the Discourse casting a shadow, where, in these darkened spaces of shadow, subjugated knowledge never receives the light of understanding. When the Discourse organizes knowledge concerning the social welfare of society, these blind spots take on a moral character as they represent aspects of social welfare that the current Discourse is ill equipped to address.

The embrace of a social hierarchy, seen as essential for promoting social welfare, is what casts the main shadow in the Colonial Discourse. As just discussed concerning the transition period of 1700–1820, the Colonial Discourse was incapable of achieving a full understanding of equality and democracy, how the common humanity within all of us puts everyone on equal footing concerning the rights and responsibilities of participating in society.

Thus, various minority groups suffered significant oppression during this time period. Patriarchy, combined with the prominence of the family unit as an organizing feature of society, led to some women being treated as chattel. The colonists' belief in divine and supernatural forces at work in nature led them to persecute women by accusing of witchcraft those who refused to conform to patriarchal notions of a woman's role. The structure of a social hierarchy made room for a lower tier in which those of a different race were attributed an inferior status. The reliance upon a barter economy within which labor served as a commodity in the form of indentured servitude led them down the road toward the acceptance of slavery as a form of permanent indentured servitude for those attributed this inferior status. The dominance of Christian thought and belief alongside this hierarchy only allowed space for Native Americans to exist if they embraced Christianity and adopted the mores of the colonists; otherwise, they were viewed as heathens. Consequently, there were no moral qualms about forcing them off their land or massacring them if they refused to go.

It would take the emergence of a new dominant Discourse for the full expression of equality to take root concerning social welfare. And while significant oppression would continue to exist for these minority groups during the era comprising this new Discourse, over time, the egregious forms of oppression listed above would slowly become delegitimized and their practices disappear.

Reflections

The study of history represents an effort to learn about ourselves. By examining the human condition in the distant past, this distance offers one the opportunity to step out of one's cultural sphere and examine society's present human condition from a distant vantage point, similar in nature to the opportunity offered when one travels to a foreign country and immerses oneself in the local culture. Past Discourses serve this function by offering a culture of understanding much different than the Discourse operating today. Immersing oneself in this "foreign" culture of the past can help one to critically examine present taken-for-granted assumptions, and thus is one way the study of history is made relevant to present concerns. As the topic of this study is social welfare, I would like to offer two different reflections on how the understanding gained from the Colonial Discourse speaks to social welfare concerns of today.

Cultural Humility

Respect for diversity is a fundamental value for the field of social work today. Social workers today are tasked with developing an awareness of cultural differences and competently adjusting the planned intervention to account for these differences. However, somewhat at odds with the current application of this value is the goal of present social work to enhance the functioning of the client. This typically involves conducting an assessment which seeks to measure the level and quality of the client's deviance from a norm of functioning so that a pathway can be established to help move the client back toward this norm. The dangerous pitfall that social workers must avoid is when one mistakes a deviance in behavior arising from culture for a deviance in functioning that must be corrected. The term *cultural humility* represents social work's most recent eluci-dation seeking to capture the essence of this awareness needed to truly respect diversity.[109] Cultural humility seeks as its first step the letting go of all precon-ceived notions as to what proper functioning entails. Then, the next step is the attempt to "step into the shoes" of the client and seek to understand how the deviant behavior might make sense from the client's cultural viewpoint. To the extent that the behavior arises from cultural differences, the task of the social worker then becomes one of a cultural translator seeking to negotiate an under-standing between the client and those from the dominant culture who view the behavior as deviant and to whom the client must in some way account for their actions.

Confronting the colonial American approach to crime serves as an excellent vehicle through which to practice this skill of cultural humility. As presented in the beginning of Chapter 2, when the average person reads that over 20% of the laws in colonial America carried a maximum penalty of death, as well as the colonials' liberal use of corporal punishment in sentencing, there is typically a sense of shock and the immediate judgment of these practices as being bar-baric. This then easily leads to the privileging of one's present understanding and practices as being more humane and sophisticated, whereas we characterize the colonial Americans as not yet having achieved the level of enlightenment that we currently possess.

Yet, as one reads on and immerses oneself in the Colonial Discourse, a much different understanding arises; one learns that the colonists had a very tolerant and forgiving approach to crime. Similarly, due to the prominence given to orig-inal sin, once a convicted person displayed remorse via confession and pen-ance, they were welcomed back as full members of society, as going astray was seen as a natural part of the human condition. Contrast this approach toward criminal justice with our approach today. After convicts serve their time and are released back into society, they are stigmatized and treated as second-class citizens—being subjected to affronts such as having to check a box on all future job applications identifying themselves as convicted criminals, as well as losing some rights of citizenship such as the right to vote. In this regard, one could make a case that our present approach is the one that is barbaric when compared to the openness possessed by colonial Americans toward welcoming wayward members back into the community fold—in which case, the act of corporal pun-ishment loses its designation as deviating from traditional moral behavior.

The development of cultural humility is a critical skill for social workers to develop if they truly hope to meet the value of respecting diversity. As so-cial workers, the very reason we are brought into a helping situation is often that the client is exhibiting some type of strange behavior that deviates from the traditional norm. Consequently, seeking to advance the goal of enhancing functioning, we typically plan interventions to help the client move back toward this norm. Upon first encounter, the anecdotes at the beginning of Chapter 2 describing various practices in colonial America typically appear very strange and alien to the reader. Part of the reason behind this is that in judging a practice we bring with us the cultural experiences of our time. So, for example, upon reading of the practice of making those seeking poor relief wear a red letter "P" on their clothing, a typical reader will draw a connection to the practice in Nazi Germany of requiring those of the Jewish faith to wear a Star of David on their clothing—an event that quite obviously was not part of the colonial consciousness. Hence, our cultural experience of Nazi Germany interferes with our ability to correctly interpret the purpose and motives driving the colonial practice.

Thus, when seeking to practice cultural humility with a client, the first step is to reserve one's judgment concerning the client's behavior. Next, one attempts to "step into the shoes" of the client and to understand how that behavior might make sense to the client based upon their cultural context. Then, one is better positioned as to whether or not the behavior needs to be corrected or if some type of cultural translation between parties is needed. Confronting colonial practices in this manner allows the opportunity to practice this skill of cultural humility and thus hone its use when the social worker meets with clients of today. This argument so far regarding the transferability of engaging colonial practices in order to refine one's engagement with clients today for the most part remains at the abstract level. However, there is the opportunity to provide a more literal connection when it comes to encountering corporal punishment.

It is not unusual for social workers who work in the field of children and families to encounter parents who employ corporal punishment. The typical response to encountering this behavior that deviates from the accepted norm is to require or encourage the parents to attend parenting classes. The assumption behind this is that the parents are unenlightened to the more humane ways in which to discipline a child; thus, an effort is made to lift them out of their ignorance. Feeding into such an assumption is that social workers are mandated to report any suspicion of child abuse. Hence, corporal punishment is often conflated with child abuse, and thus all forms of corporal punishment are seen as dangerously deviant and in need of correction. Additionally, social workers may find scientific studies that indicate that corporal punishment is the least effective form of behavior modification. Hence, the cultural values that the social worker is bringing to the situation become cloaked in the guise of scientific fact, and thus are given privileged status.

Such a flaw in reasoning is illustrated by the earlier example of judging the practice of wearing a red letter "P" through the lens of one's knowledge of Nazi Germany. In this case, the flaw of reasoning lies in the assumption that the sole purpose behind disciplining a child is to achieve behavior modification—that is, to correct deviant behavior back to the accepted norm. However, as we learned in studying colonial America, discipline and the use of corporal punishment may have additional purposes as well. In the case of colonial America, it served primarily as a form of penance. The act of "stepping into the shoes" of the client helps the social worker uncover these additional purposes.

So, for example, if the family lives in a "tough" neighborhood, corporal punishment may be serving the purpose of "toughening up" the child—a necessary quality in helping the child navigate living in such a neighborhood. Or, in families that are very expressive emotionally, corporal punishment may serve the purpose of communicating the level at which the parents care for their child's welfare; behavior viewed as dangerous to the child's development is met by a stronger emotional response in disciplining the child to correct such behavior. In this instance, a more "humane" approach to disciplining severe behavior may mistakenly communicate to the child that the parent is not very invested in their future development. Additionally, it may be that the parents are simply repeating the style of discipline that they were subjected to as a child, and thus would welcome instruction on less severe forms of discipline. The point is, the social worker is not in a position to know which of the above applies until they have "stepped into the shoes" of the client and attempted to understand the perspective from their cultural viewpoint. To simply assume that the last scenario is always the case goes against the grain of good social work.

The Social Construction of Identity

The case of Nicolas Senison being brought up on charges of attempted sodomy serves as an excellent platform to illustrate the social construction of identity—in particular, the role sexual behavior plays in determining one's identity. It is now a well-established fact that the ancient societies in Greece and Rome not only tolerated men engaging in sexual relations with other men but, more so, embraced them as a normal and legitimate part of their cultural understanding. What makes the colonial experience so instructive toward understanding the social construction of identity is the very fact that the colonists adopted an intolerant attitude toward the practice—labeling it as mortal sin and open to criminal prosecution. Yet even in such a hostile environment—much more hostile than exists today—the colonists still did not consider the act of same-sex relations as a determinant of one's core identity. In fact, it was given so little consideration that the colonists did not even have the word *homosexual* in their lexicon as they had no conception of it as an identity feature. An equivalent attitude today would be that in present society we do not label people's sexual identity according to the color of the hair of one's partner. No such words existed during the Colonial Era that served to label individuals according to their sexual practices. Instead, they only used words such as *sodomy* that described the act itself; the term *sodomist* was used extremely rarely and would only apply to those individuals identified as an incorrigible sinner in this regard.[110]

Contrast this colonial attitude with the attitude of American society today. Those engaging in same-sex relations continue to experience institutionalized and societal oppression today, although improvement has occurred over time so that present circumstances are certainly less oppressive than existed in colonial times. Some hard-earned rights have been recently won, such as the 2015 Supreme Court case *Obergefell v. Hodges*, which legalized marriage between same-sex couples. Yet there has been a subversive cost to pay concerning these rights. The Discourse of our present time constructs cultural understanding through a scientific lens, with one significant trope being that of *nature versus nurture*. Consequently, a common argument made by those advocating for increasing the rights of these individuals is that it is in their nature, that they were born that way. Hence, since they are unable to change the nature with which they were born, they cannot be held accountable for their deviance from the heterosexual norm of society. Thus, society cannot reasonably expect them to change their nature, and consequently, it is society that must change by affording them the same rights enjoyed by heterosexuals.

Yet by making this argument, the position of individuals adopting this lifestyle in society is subverted. This is because, by doing so, one is reinforcing the notion that these individuals are fundamentally different than the heterosexual majority. Consequently, they are categorized as an *other*, with their sexual preference being solidified as a core component of their identity and with this accompanying label attaining a master status. By adopting this status of a minority *other*, the argument for rights then rests upon the theme of being separate but equal: that even though these individuals are fundamentally different than people comprising the conceived-of heterosexual norm, they are still human beings deserving of the same human rights as the majority heterosexuals.

The insidious nature of this subversion as *other* can be further illustrated if we were to apply this same line of reasoning to one's racial status—an area where American society has made significant progress since the 1960s in dismantling this notion of otherness. Suppose for a moment that a social worker, seeking to advocate for African Americans by supporting the Black Lives Matter movement, made the following argument: "African Americans can't help the fact that they have darker skin; they were born that way." The subversive nature contained within this line of reasoning—in this instance, that African American cannot be held accountable for their deviance from the accepted social norm of being Caucasian—becomes jarringly more apparent when applied to this context, even though racial characteristics and sexual orientation are both understood as having genetic origins. Now imagine a future society in which the concept of "race" was no longer present.

Or imagine for a second that we lived in a society where a sexual preference for blondes was considered the norm, while I happen to prefer brunettes. Consequently, I am denied certain rights enjoyed by those who prefer blondes. Someone arguing on my behalf makes the statement, "He deserves the same rights as those having preference for blondes. You can't fault him and hold him accountable for preferring brunettes; he was born that way, and so it is in his nature." While advocating for my rights, this argument at the same time classifies me as an *other*. This then prevents one from taking a step back, thereby allowing one to criticize the entire oppressive structure upon which this norm rests by instead making the argument, "Hair is hair. Why should the color of one's partner's hair matter when defining your core identity features? There is no difference between those who prefer blondes and those who prefer brunettes; we are all fundamentally the same in this regard, and any difference in preference of hair color simply represents one's personal taste."

Thus, the *nature versus nurture* trope within our present dominant Discourse impedes advocates' ability to critically examine the entire oppressive structure and make the argument, "Sex is sex. Why should the gender of whom one has sex with matter? We are all fundamentally the same in that we all possess a sex drive; any difference in preference for gender simply represents one's personal taste." Making such an argument puts the power back into the hands of the individual when deciding what weight to assign to this preference when constructing one's identity and sense of self, while also emphasizing the common connection that we all possess concerning sexuality and thus eliminating any classification of *other* in this regard.

Notes

1. Kelso, *History of Public Poor*, 138; Trattner, *From Poor Law*, 24.
2. Massachusetts Provincial Government (1693–94) as quoted in Kelso, 136–37; New York State Colonial Laws (1665) as quoted in Schneider, *History of Public Welfare*, 34, see also 81.
3. Massachusetts Provincial Government (1797) as quoted in Kelso, 137; Schneider, 81; Trattner, *From Poor Law*, 24–25.
4. Jernegan, *Laboring and Dependent Classes*, 209; Schneider, 81.
5. Abramovitz, *Regulating the Lives*, 85; Demos, *A Little Commonwealth*, 80; Jernegan, 207.
6. Abramovitz, 92; Demos, 73; Ulrich, *Good Wives*, 43–44.
7. Demos, 104; Rutman, "Mirror of Puritan Authority," 66.
8. Axinn and Levin, *Social Welfare*, 10–11; Trattner, *From Poor Law*, 17.

9. Kelso, *History of Public Poor*, 35–41; Schneider, *History of Public Welfare*, 45–60; Rothman, *Discovery of the Asylum*, 20–21.

10. Schneider, 36.

11. Quoted in Schneider, 36

12. Kelso, *History of Public Poor*, 65–66; Axinn and Levin, *Social Welfare*, 15; Rothman, *Discovery of the Asylum*, 20–25.

13. Rothman, 24–25.

14. Kelso, *History of Public Poor*, 65–66; Axinn and Levin, *Social Welfare*, 15; Rothman, 20–25.

15. Schneider, *History of Public Welfare*, 47–53; Rothman, 20–25.

16. Abramovitz, *Regulating the Lives*, 79; Rothman, 20–22.

17. Winthrop, "Model of Christian Charity," 27–28.

18. Winthrop, 27–28; Trattner, *From Poor Law*, 16.

19. Winthrop, 27–28.

20. Jernegan, *Laboring and Dependent Classes*, 209.

21. Bulkeley, "Willing and Voluntary Subjection," 34; Miller, "The Puritan State," 47; Morgan, *The Puritan Family*, 62.

22. Abramovitz, *Regulating the Lives*, 77.

23. Ulrich, *Good Wives*, 4, 59.

24. Abramovitz, *Regulating the Lives*, 79.

25. Abramovitz, 79; Jernegan, *Laboring and Dependent Classes*, 191–92.

26. Kelso, *History of Public Poor*, 37; Rothman, *Discovery of the Asylum*, 19.

27. Abramovitz, *Regulating the Lives*, 79; Schneider, *History of Public Welfare*, 47–48.

28. Kelso, *History of Public Poor*, 48–51; Schneider, 54; Rothman, *Discovery of the Asylum*, 12–13.

29. Axinn and Levin, *Social Welfare*, 15; Trattner, *From Poor Law*, 19.

30. Schneider, *History of Public Welfare*, 47–48, 148; Stansell, *City of Women*, 5–6.

31. Kelso, *History of Public Poor*, 42–43.

32. Axinn and Levin, *Social Welfare*, 15; Kelso, 49–60; Rothman, *Discovery of the Asylum*, 20–25.

33. Kelso, 10; Trattner, *From Poor Law*, 25; Rothman, 10.

34. Kelso, 97, 107; Rothman, 25, 32.

35. Boston Town Records (1674) as excerpted in Kelso, 104, see also 104–05; Schneider, *History of Public Welfare*, 47–48; Axinn and Levin, *Social Welfare*, 10–11.

36. Abramovitz, *Regulating the Lives*, 88.

37. Boston Town Records (1674) as excerpted in Kelso, *History of Public Poor*, 104, see also 104–05; Schneider, *History of Public Welfare*, 47–48; Axinn and Levin, *Social Welfare*, 10–11.

38. Boston Town Records (1635) as excerpted in Kelso, 103, see also 103–04; Boston Town Meeting (1656) as quoted in Trattner, *From Poor Law*, 18.

39. Ulrich, *Good Wives*, 37.

40. Abramovitz, *Regulating the Lives*, 85; Smith, *The Lower Sort*, 167; Ulrich, 148.

41. Smith, 170.

42. Moraley, *The Infortunate*, 52–53.

43. Abramovitz, *Regulating the Lives*, 85; Gardner Town Records (1789) as quoted in Kelso, *History of Public Poor*, 96–97; Trattner, *From Poor Law*, 22.

44. Bremner et al., *Children and Youth*, 262; Records of Fitchburg (1812) as quoted in Kelso, 109; Trattner, 18.

45. Morgan, *The Puritan Family*, 117.

46. Moraley, *The Infortunate*, 46.

47. Abramovitz, *Regulating the Lives*, 92; Demos, *A Little Commonwealth*, 73; Ulrich, *Good Wives*, 43–44.

48. Demos, 104.

49. Rutman, "Mirror of Puritan Authority," 66.

50. Bremner et al., *Children and Youth*, 263; Smith, *The Lower Sort*, 12, 166.

51. Bremner et al., 262.

52. Morgan, *The Puritan Family*, 109.

53. Abramovitz, *Regulating the Lives*, 88; Rothman, *Discovery of the Asylum*, 43; Schneider, *History of Public Welfare*, 63–64.

54. Abramovitz, 87; Kelso, *History of Public Poor*, 111; Rothman, 28.

55. Goodwin, *The Colonial Cavalier*, 245; Pennsylvania Statute (1718) as quoted in Axinn and Levin, *Social Welfare*, 14; New York Common Council (1707) as quoted in Schneider, *History of Public Welfare*, 64.

56. Schneider, 64; Axinn and Levin, 14.

57. Demos, *A Little Commonwealth*, 96.

58. Goodwin, *The Colonial Cavalier*, 245; Schneider, *History of Public Welfare*, 64.

59. Winthrop, "Authority and Liberty," as excerpted in Haskins, *Law and Authority*, 40, see also 52; Rothman, *Discovery of the Asylum*, 15, 51.

60. Oberholzer, *Delinquent Saints*, 13; Haskins, 28, 32, 43, 52; Erikson, *Wayward Puritans*, 56–57; Rothman, 15, 17.

61. Cotton, *Spiritual Milk*, 4; Demos, *A Little Commonwealth*, 100–04.

62. Cotton, 4; Miller, "The Puritan State," 42; Morgan, *The Puritan Family*, 19.

63. Rothman, *Discovery of the Asylum*, 51–52.

64. Ver Steeg, *The Formative Years*, 79; Zuckerman, *Peaceable Kingdoms*, 14.

65. Oberholzer, *Delinquent Saints*, 28–42; Haskins, *Law and Authority*, 210–11; Rothman, *Discovery of the Asylum*, 17–18.

66. Oberholzer, 30; Haskins, 175, 207; Zuckerman, *Peaceable Kingdoms*, 61; Rothman, 16.

67. Schneider, *History of Public Welfare*, 14, 60–61; Haskins, 175; Rothman, 15, 49–52.

68. Schneider, 60; Haskins, 82; Rothman, 18.

69. Bremner et al., *Children and Youth*, 307.

70. Oberholzer, *Delinquent Saints*, 30, 36–37; Haskins, *Law and Authority*, 83–84, 175; Zuckerman, *Peaceable Kingdoms*, 61–64.

71. Haskins, 204–05; Rothman, *Discovery of the Asylum*, 18, 49.

72. Oberholzer, *Delinquent Saints*, 36–37; Haskins, 61, 207; Zuckerman, *Peaceable Kingdoms*, 242; Rothman, 18.

73. Oberholzer, 30–31, 36; Haskins, 205–07; Zuckerman, 61; Rothman, 19.

74. Rothman, 52.

75. Oberholzer, *Delinquent Saints*, 169; Haskins, *Law and Authority*, 125; Rothman, 51.

76. Oberholzer, 193–96; Haskins, 153–54; Rothman, 51–52.
77. Demos, *A Little Commonwealth*, 70.
78. Morgan, *The Puritan Family*, 64.
79. Acts and Laws of Massachusetts Bay (1694) as excerpted in Rothman, *Discovery of the Asylum*, 52.
80. Johnson, *Reading the American Past*, 75; Rogers (1701) as quoted in Rothman, 15; Occom (1772) as cited in Rothman, 15.
81. Bridenbaugh, *Early Americans*, 184.
82. Bremner et al., *Children and Youth*, 307; Demos, *A Little Commonwealth*, 101.
83. Demos, 101.
84. Godbeer, *Sexual Revolution*, 104–11.
85. Godbeer, 46, 104–11.
86. Godbeer, 46.
87. Godbeer, 47, 50.
88. Godbeer, 47.
89. Godbeer, 104–11.
90. Godbeer, 104–11.
91. Godbeer, 104–11.
92. Godbeer, 104–11.
93. Rothman, *Discovery of the Asylum*, 50.
94. Bridenbaugh, *Early Americans*, 122; Jernegan, *Laboring and Dependent Classes*, 202; Morgan, "The Protestant Ethic," 184.
95. Jernegan, 202.
96. Godbeer, *The Salem Witch Hunt*, 5–6, 8, 30.
97. Godbeer, 5.
98. Godbeer, 30.
99. Godbeer, 9.
100. Godbeer, 12–13.
101. Goodman, *Essays in American Colonial*, 485.
102. Ulrich, *Good Wives*, 7; Morgan, *The Puritan Family*, 72.
103. Goodman, *Essays in American Colonial*, 144–45; Morgan, 71–72.
104. Goodman, 144–45; Miller, "The Puritan State," 47; Morgan, 88.
105. Miller, 42, 47; Morgan, 64–65; Ulrich, *Good Wives*, 59.
106. Northern California Citizen Project. "U.S. Voting Rights Timeline."
107. Bryce, *The American Commonwealth*, 271–73; McGiffert, "The Puritan Vision," 21.
108. Bryce, 271.
109. For example, Danson, "Cultural Competence"; Ross, "Notes from the Field."
110. Godbeer, *Sexual Revolution*, 46–50.

References

Abramovitz, Mimi. *Regulating the Lives of Women: Social Welfare Policy from Colonial Times to the Present*. Brooklyn: South End Press, 1988.

Axinn, June, and Herman Levin. *Social Welfare: A History of the American Response to Need*. New York: Harper & Row, 1975.

Bremner, Robert H., John Barnard, Temara K. Hareven, and Robert M. Mennel, eds. *Children and Youth in America*. Vol. 1, *1600–1865*. Cambridge, MA: Harvard University Press, 1970.

Bridenbaugh, Carl. *Early Americans*. New York: Oxford University Press, 1981.

Bryce, James. *The American Commonwealth*. Indianapolis, IN: Liberty Fund, 1888. https://oll.libertyfund.org/titles/bryce-the-american-commonwealth-vol-1#Bryce_0004-01_694.

Bulkeley, Peter. "Willing and Voluntary Subjection." In *Puritanism and the American Experience*, edited by Michael McGiffert, 33–37. Reading, MA: Addison-Wesley, 1969.

Cotton, Thomas. *Spiritual Milk for Boston Babes*. Cambridge: Samuel Green, 1656. https://digitalcommons.unl.edu/cgi/viewcontent.cgi?article=1018&context=etas.

Danson, Ransford. "Cultural Competence and Cultural Humility: A Critical Reflection on Key Cultural Diversity Concepts." *Social Work* 18 (2016): 410–30.

Demos, John. *A Little Commonwealth: Family Life in Plymouth Colony*. 2nd ed. New York: Oxford University Press, 1999.

Erikson, Kai. *Wayward Puritans: A Study in the Sociology of Deviance*. Rev. ed. Boston: Allyn Bacon, 2004.

Godbeer, Richard. *Sexual Revolution in Early America*. Gender Relations in the American Experience. Baltimore: John Hopkins University Press, 2002.

Godbeer, Richard. *The Salem Witch Hunt: A Brief History with Documents*. New York: Bedford/St. Martin's, 2011.

Goodman, Paul. *Essays in American Colonial History*. New York: Holt Rinehart and Winston, 1967.

Goodwin, Maud. *The Colonial Cavalier or Southern Life Before the Revolution*. Kindle ed. Seattle: Amazon Digital Services LLC, 2012. First published 1895.

Haskins, George. *Law and Authority in Early Massachusetts: A Study in Tradition and Design*. New York: Macmillan Company, 1960.

Jernegan, Marcus. *Laboring and Dependent Classes in Colonial America, 1607–1783: Studies of the Economic, Educational, and Social Significance of Slaves, Servants, Apprentices and Poor Folk*. Chicago: University of Chicago Press, 1931.

Johnson, Michael P. *Reading the American Past: Selected Historical Documents*. Vol. 1, *To 1877*. 5th ed. New York: Bedford/St. Martin's, 2012.

Kelso, R. W. *The History of Public Poor Relief in Massachusetts, 1620–1920*. New York: Houghton Mifflin, 1922.

McGiffert, Michael. "The Puritan Vision: 'A City upon a Hill.'" In *Puritanism and the American Experience*, 14–26. Reading, MA: Addison-Wesley, 1969.

Miller, Perry. "The Puritan State and Puritan Society." In *Puritanism and the American Experience*, edited by Michael McGiffert, 41–51. Reading, MA: Addison-Wesley, 1969.

Moraley, William. *The Infortunate: The Voyage and Adventures of William Moraley, an Indentured Servant*. Edited by Susan E. Klepp and Billy Gordon Smith. 2nd ed. University Park: Pennsylvania State University Press, 2005. First published 1743.

Morgan, Edmund S. *The Puritan Family: Essays on Religion and Domestic Relations in Seventeenth-Century New England*. Eastford, CT: Martino Fine Books, 1944.

Morgan, Edmund S. "The Protestant Ethic. The Puritan Ethic and the American Revolution." In *Puritanism and the American Experience*, edited by Michael McGiffert, 182–97. Reading, MA: Addison-Wesley, 1969.

Northern California Citizen Project. "U.S. Voting Rights Timeline." 2004. Accessed June 8, 2017, https://a.s.kqed.net/pdf/education/digitalmedia/us-voting-rights-timel ine.pdf.

Oberholzer, Emil. *Delinquent Saints: Disciplinary Action in the Early Congregational Churches of Massachusetts.* New York: Columbia University Press, 1956.

Ross, Laurie. "Notes from the Field: Learning Cultural Humility Through Critical Incidents and Central Challenges in Community-Based Participatory Research." *Journal of Community Practice* 18 (2010): 315–35.

Rothman, David J. *The Discovery of the Asylum: Social Order and Disorder in the New Republic.* 3rd ed. New York: Walter de Gruyter, 2002.

Rutman, Darrett. "The Mirror of Puritan Authority." In *Puritanism and the American Experience,* edited by Michael McGiffert, 64–76. Reading, MA: Addison-Wesley, 1969.

Schneider, David M. *The History of Public Welfare in New York State 1609–1866.* Chicago: University of Chicago Press, 1938.

Smith, Billy G. *The Lower Sort: Philadelphia's Laboring People, 1750–1800.* New York: Cornell University Press, 1994.

Stansell, Christine. *City of Women: Sex and Class in New York, 1789–1860.* New York: Knopf, 1986.

Trattner, Walter I. *From Poor Law to Welfare State: A History of Social Welfare in America.* 4th ed. New York: Free Press, 1989.

Ulrich, Laurel T. *Good Wives: Image and Reality in the Lives of Women in Northern New England, 1650–1750.* New York: Vintage, 1991.

Ver Steeg, Clarence L. *The Formative Years 1607–1763.* New York: Hill and Wang, 1964.

Winthrop, John. "A Model of Christian Charity." In *Puritanism and the American Experience,* edited by Michael McGiffert, 27–32. Reading, MA: Addison-Wesley, 1969. First published 1630.

Winthrop, John. "Authority and Liberty." In *Puritanism and the American Experience,* edited by Michael McGiffert, 38–40. Reading, MA: Addison-Wesley, 1969. First published 1645.

Zuckerman, Michael. *Peaceable Kingdoms: New England Towns in the Eighteenth Century.* New York: Alfred A. Knopf, 1970.

4

The Premodern Discourse
(c. 1820–1920)

The year is 1914. It is a beautiful spring night in St. Louis, and tens of thousands of individuals are gathering at Forest Park in a vast natural amphitheater. Civic leaders have organized a grand pageant and masque, a four-night event aimed at commemorating the 150th anniversary of the city's founding. An estimated 100,000 people would attend over these four nights. A truly grand spectacle, the pageant employed 1,500 cast members and a chorus of 750 voices. Its first offering, orchestrated by Thomas Wood Stevens, provided realistic historical re-enactments of key moments in the city's history. This was followed by Percy MacKaye's allegorical masque of this same history, with the city of St. Louis being personified in a story detailing its growth from a baby to a divine-like being. Within this story, Poverty personified enters the scene with her children in tow—Shame, Vice, Plague, Dumbness, Despair, Rebellion, and others. Troubled by their arrival and the pall of suffering cast by them, St. Louis appeals to his fellow cities for aid. Answering the call, figures representing the cities of Chicago, Washington, San Francisco, New York, Honolulu, Denver, and New Orleans enter the stage; and through their concerted effort, Poverty and her children arise from their decrepit state transformed. Ending in a spectacular display, the finale included fireworks, a flock of pigeons released into the air, and the chorus belting an anthem beginning with the words, "Out of the formless void, Beauty and Order are formed."[1] While a bit garish for present sensibilities, it is most likely not hard for the present reader to imagine such an event taking place. However, what may lie beyond one's imaginings is the fact that civic leaders organizing this event considered such performances as engaging in vital social work.

This next scene opens in the year 1826 in the town of Mount Pleasant, located in Westchester County, New York. Construction workers had recently erected a massive walled-in edifice sprawling over 130 acres of land: Sing Sing penitentiary. Government officials and social welfare agents gather to celebrate its opening. Yes, celebrate. These individuals did not look upon the creation of Sing Sing as we might with our present eyes—a necessary evil acting as a blight on the community. Rather, these government officials and social welfare agents took pride from their accomplishment. Not only did they view with unbounded optimism

A Genealogy of the Good and Critique of Hubris. Phillip Dybicz, Oxford University Press. © Oxford University Press 2023.
DOI: 10.1093/oso/9780197670071.003.0004

the potential for Sing Sing to reform criminals in a humanitarian manner, they sincerely believed that Sing Sing (and other penitentiaries like it) could serve as *a model for inspiration* for society as a whole to embrace and for communities across the nation to emulate regarding the proper fundamentals of social organization. To this end, much was written in popular journals of the time concerning these fundamentals. Foreign dignitaries from across Europe would come to view this marvel of innovation. Sing Sing and other penitentiaries even became tourist destinations for a curious population.[2]

Various evolutions of charity organization societies operated throughout the Premodern Era. These organizations assumed the main responsibility for providing direct relief to the poor in society. However, a common understanding throughout this era among these organizations was that poverty arose out of a defect of character. Thus, charity organization workers attempted to alleviate poverty by providing moral counseling; direct relief only came after this moral counseling took place and only to those deemed deserving (those who could demonstrate a clear inability to work). The slogan "not alms but a friend" adopted by the scientific charity movement succinctly captured this very judgmental approach toward helping the poor.

As was the case in Chapter 2 when first encountering colonial social welfare practices, upon first glance the above viewpoints and actions may appear quite bizarre. One is left scratching one's head as to how individuals could view a penitentiary as a model for society to emulate or how putting on a performance in the park could be considered social work. The "not alms but a friend" approach employed by scientific charity runs counter to core social work values that we embrace today. So, once again, we must examine the dominant Discourse operating during this era (which I have labeled the Premodern Discourse) to understand how the above viewpoints were arrived at by these social welfare agents.

By 1820 and beyond social welfare in the United States had clearly been reconceived; a new social order had been established placing self-discipline as the central element promoting social welfare rather than the deference to authority promoted during colonial times.[3] The scattered elements of this new discourse that began to arise after the Revolutionary War and early 1800s coalesced to become the dominant apparatus generating and legitimizing knowledge. A new, Premodern Discourse arose and the Colonial Discourse faded from dominance. The political, economic, and social landscapes of this era are prominently defined by the integration of the once "island communities" of the Colonial Era. This integration would proceed rapidly throughout this century, prompting social welfare efforts to tackle social welfare problems at ever greater levels of complexity: first being organization at the county level when various communities came together to build an almshouse, then occurring at the state level with the creation of state penitentiaries and insane asylums, and finally, at the end of the era, a modest effort at the national level mainly through regulatory laws for businesses to curb exploitation. Industrialization and urbanization served to fuel this process of integration. Revolutionary technological advances in communication (e.g., telegraph, telephone) and transportation (e.g., steamboat, railroad) further accelerated the rapid integration of America's once "island communities."

Conditions in Premodern America

Geographic Conditions

While the era dominated by the Colonial Discourse was marked by the various communities existing as islands unto themselves, this isolation would rapidly disappear in the nineteenth century. Beginning in the transition period between 1780 and 1820 and then continuing prominently in the era spanning roughly 1820 to 1920 that marks the dominance of the Premodern Discourse, there occurred a steady process of stitching together these communities into organic wholes at the county, state, and national levels. This physical integration on a geographic level was greatly fueled by revolutionary advances in transportation.

Population Demographics

Upon its formation as a country in 1781 with the Articles of Confederation, the United States comprised the previous thirteen existing colonies in an area of land confined along the eastern seaboard, although laying claim to territory extending to the Mississippi River.[4] This territory rapidly became settled, and by 1800 four more states had entered into the Union.[5] With the Louisiana Purchase in 1802, the geographic boundaries of the United States nearly doubled. By 1837, the number of states reached twenty-six, doubling in size from the thirteen original colonies. The addition of territory and the addition of states to the Union proceeded apace throughout the nineteenth century and into the early twentieth century. In 1890, the director of the census would declare that the frontier was no more.[6] And by 1912, the United States comprised forty-eight states representing a contiguous land mass stretching from the Atlantic to the Pacific.[7] Thus, the history of the United States in the nineteenth century is one of constant territorial expansion, the consequent settlement of this territory, and its establishment into political entities as states.

In addition to the expansive growth in territory, there was a corresponding expansive growth in population during this era. And with the onset of the Industrial Revolution, the United States experienced a long and steady stream of migration from country to city.[8] Much of the population growth was due to immigration, and thus, society was faced with the continuous challenge of integrating these recent arrivals into its midst. In 1820, the total population of the United States was just under 10 million, by 1920 the total population was over 106 million; during this same time span 33 million people immigrated to the United States.[9] Many of these immigrants would come to settle in cities, swelling the ranks of those already arriving from rural areas. A brief look at population statistics of this era reveals the striking nature of this urban growth:

In 1790, one-thirtieth of our population lived in cities of eight thousand inhabitants and over. In 1800, the proportion of urban population had become one twenty-fifth; in 1820, it was one-twentieth; in 1830, one-sixteenth; in 1840, one-twelfth; in 1850, one-eighth; in 1860, one-sixth; in 1870, one-fifth; in 1880, nearly one-fourth, i.e., 22.5 per cent; from 1790 to 1880 the population of the country increased twelvefold, that of the cities eighty-six fold.[10]

By 1900, 40% of the population was living in urban areas.[11] Also by 1900, New York City had reached a population of over 3 million, while Chicago's population reached 1,700,000.[12]

Transportation

This settlement of territory and its formation into states of the union was aided greatly by a technological revolution in transportation marking this era. The first of these innovations was the steamboat. The invention of the steamboat and its viability as an affordable mode of transportation in the early nineteenth century marks the first instance of machine power replacing human or animal power as the means of propelling a mode of transportation. The travel time between communities dropped precipitously; this served to strengthen connections between once disparate communities by breaking down the geographic barriers of distance that had previously led to their isolation.[13] One illustration of this is provided by Henry Fearon, who writes in his journal of his journey between New York and Boston aboard a steamboat in 1817, a journey of 140 miles which was completed in only two and a half hours.[14] The immense benefit to transportation and commerce offered by the steamboat prompted state legislators to appropriate money for public works projects in the form of building canals; the building of the Erie Canal in New York serves as a prominent example.[15] This marks a trend in which social welfare began moving away from primarily being a local concern to one in which the county and state began to take on a bigger and more active role.

The revolution that the steamboat brought to water travel was soon mirrored by a revolution to overland travel brought on by the invention and growth of the railroad.[16] Beginning by connecting the various communities along the Atlantic seaboard and inland to those in the Mississippi valley, 30,000 miles of track had been laid down between the years of 1831 and 1861.[17] After the Civil War, railroad construction increased exponentially. In 1869 the first transcontinental rail line was established, linking communities on the Atlantic seaboard to those as far away as the Pacific seaboard.[18] And by 1900 the American railway system consisted of 193,000 miles of track and effectively reached into every section of the country.[19]

The change arising from the breaking down of geographic barriers of distance separating communities was nothing short of dramatic. For example, during the pre-railroad era a trip from New York to San Francisco would have required months of overland travel or a lengthy sail around Cape Horn; by 1905, the travel time between New York and San Francisco had shrunk to eighty-two hours.[20] The railway and canal systems not only knitted together existing communities but also promoted the emergence and growth of communities along their routes. Benefiting from both canal systems and a railroad network, Chicago saw its population grow from less than one hundred in 1830 to 30,000 in 1850 and to an astounding 1,700,000 in 1900.[21] Not only was railroad construction subsidized at the state level as were canals but, in addition, it received federal subsidies as well as land grants.[22] The transportation revolution—in the establishment of the subway and trolley—also reached into the cities to connect their disparate communities, providing the means for the mass transit of people between them[23]—offering a stark contrast to the mere thirty-eight personal carriages that existed in Philadelphia in 1761 to move a few well-to-do individuals about.[24]

Communication

The revolution in transportation was accompanied by an equally dramatic revolution in communication, most particularly with the invention of the telegraph. Beginning with government funding first being appropriated in 1843 to establish a telegraph line between Washington, DC, and Baltimore,[25] by the end of the century Western Union alone had 22,900 offices nationwide and delivered 63 million messages a year.[26] The telegraph profoundly affected the integration of communities along economic, political, and social lines. Speaking on this integration toward the end of the nineteenth century, John L. O'Sullivan glowingly describes the railroads as providing "a vast skeletal framework" for the country, while the telegraph acted as its "infinitely ramified nervous system."[27]

One prominent example of this integration being brought on by the railroads was the standardization of time. During this era each community set its own standard. But in 1883, reflecting the national integration taking place, the railroads established four geographic time zones in alignment with England's use of Greenwich mean time.[28] Factories and major businesses soon fell in line with this proposed standardization, and by the end of the era in 1918, the US government imposed the standardization nationwide.[29]

Economic Conditions

During the Premodern Era, the United States remained a predominantly agrarian society. It would not be until the 1920 census when the percentage of people living in urban areas (defined by the census as towns with greater than 2,500 residents) would finally surpass the percentage of those living in a rural setting.[30] Yet the nature of farming changed considerably. Discounting the plantations established in the southern colonies, during the Colonial Era the vast majority of farming took place on family farms where its main goal was to provide sustenance for members of the household and contribute toward the sustenance of the community as a whole.[31] Beginning with the development of canals and the steamboat and extending to the growth of the railroads, the marketplace continuously grew in scope to operate regionally and ultimately nationally, with the establishment of the intercontinental railroad in 1869 prominently marking this transition.[32]

The profound effect brought on by such economic integration at an ever larger scale was that farming transformed into a commercial enterprise.[33] Farming quickly went from being a way of life to being a proprietary business of producing a crop for market, as illustrated by the creation of the Chicago Board of Trade in 1848.[34] The non-biologically related person providing extra help (such as that of persons like William Moraley described in Chapter 3) went from being conceptualized as a member of the family household to simply being hired labor.[35] Consequently, previously deeply embedded reciprocal obligations were reduced to relationships simply comprising an economic transaction, resulting in the dissolution of the rich harmony of interests binding the employer and employee.[36] Furthermore, mechanization (stemming from the Industrial Revolution taking place at this time) created less of a need for extra labor on the farm. The "vagabond," whose rootless nature was seen in colonial times as a threat to the social hierarchy of the community, and hence a threat to the social order, in this era became simply a common feature of the labor market. Advances in transportation greatly spurred the mobility of labor to meet the demands of a market that became national in scope. By the end of the nineteenth century, the time and labor needed to produce a harvest was one-tenth of what was needed at the beginning of this era.[37] This would serve to further spur the strong trend throughout this era of migration from rural to urban centers.[38]

While the United States remained predominantly an agrarian society during this era, the Industrial Revolution—which kicked into full gear during and after the Civil War[39]—spurred tremendous growth and development in the manufacturing sector and further strengthened proprietary capitalism as the defining feature of the American economy. Within such a model, no business achieves dominance to the point where it controls enough resources to unduly influence the market in its favor (i.e., achieve a monopoly); thus, proprietary capitalism calls for a more laissez-faire approach by government.[40] Coinciding with this steady integration of the economy at the national level were technological advances in manufacturing that allowed for large-scale production to produce items at a reduced cost per unit. Prior to the Civil War, there was no such competitive advantage enjoyed by large-scale production versus production by small local factories—per unit production costs were roughly equivalent.[41]

However, after the Civil War, technological advances in many sectors of manufacturing changed this dynamic: large factories now began to enjoy such a competitive advantage.[42] This, combined with a market reach now national in scope, led to the creation and tremendous growth of big business.[43] Furthermore, while throughout this era more people worked in the agricultural sector of the economy, for the year 1890 the total monetary value of manufactured goods in the United States exceeded the total value of agricultural products for the first time; by 1900, the total value of manufactured goods produced in the year was double that for agricultural products.[44] Thus, toward the end of the Premodern Era, a situation occurred in which a new style of capitalism—corporate capitalism (wherein big businesses could unduly influence the market in its favor)—began to operate in a laissez-faire political environment. This would lead to an ever-growing conflict between labor and management.

During colonial times, the family was the defining economic unit of production. As the marketplace steadily increased in scale, the economic role of the family transformed from being the defining unit of production into that of being the defining unit of consumption.[45] This transformation created some profound changes in the fabric of society. One such change was that one's labor was now viewed as a commodity to be traded in the marketplace.[46] As noted above, this change undercut the previously rich set of reciprocal obligations that existed between employer and employee, reducing the relationship to primarily that of an economic transaction. With the relationship between employer and employee now being reduced to that of an economic transaction, the antagonistic elements of the relationship became emphasized over the previous harmony of interests (i.e., increasing the value of labor results in a decrease in the employer's profitability and wealth).[47] In addition, the ever-increasing impersonal nature of these economic transactions between employer and employee seriously degraded the morality and ethics that previously held sway over them.[48] Consequently, numerous trade and labor unions were formed among the working class to protect their interests, which grew in size to match the growth of businesses into large corporations.[49]

Due in large part to the federal government's laissez-faire approach throughout the nineteenth century in regard to managing the economy, disputes over the value of labor were handled using conflict-oriented measures such as strikes and even labor riots as the members of the working class were forced to protect their own interests.[50] The Chicago Haymarket Square riot of 1886 serves as a prominent example of a long list of strikes and armed encounters resulting from labor unrest.[51] Beyond labor unrest, this laissez-faire approach also exerted no influence in taming the natural chaos of the marketplace's boom-and-bust cycles. Regularly occurring events such as bank failures or soaring bread prices led to riots.[52] And as a result of the periodic boom-and-bust cycles, masses of labor were regularly thrown out of work.[53]

Furthermore, this transition to a modern economy resulted in the creation of a distinct middle class and of a distinct working or lower class.[54] The immigrants flooding into the country were attracted to the cities and swelled the ranks of the working class.[55] As many of these immigrants were predominantly coming from countries such as Ireland, Italy, and Poland, the ranks of the working class began to heavily reflect a Roman Catholic orientation (German immigrants being the notable exception to this trend).[56] The middle class, by contrast, was predominantly represented by native-born White, Anglo-Saxon Protestants.[57] And a distinct feature of the middle class in this premodern economy was a household in which the wife was not responsible for earning money; instead, the wife's duty was circumscribed to maintaining the home and raising the children.[58] Important in their primary role of raising the children was providing moral guidance and instruction—a role that was filled by the father during the Colonial Era.[59] Consequently, women became the de facto moral guardians of society. And as middle-class women had time freed up from not having to be economically productive, they readily turned their attention to providing such guidance to the communities around them through various volunteer efforts—thus, it was middle-class women who comprised the front-line ranks of social welfare agents operating in this era.[60]

The wide adoption of Adam Smith's notion of proprietary capitalism contributed toward a further reweaving of the American culture fabric. Stemming from Enlightenment thought, the model of proprietary capitalism is based upon the premise that the workings of the market arise from the aggregate of individual decisions based upon one's rational self-interest: the "invisible hand" of the market at work. This same understanding was applied to the workings of society in general. In the political sphere, the notion that societal conditions arose from the aggregate of individual decisions based upon one's rational self-interest served to animate the various suffrage movements that occurred throughout the Premodern Era: as the aggregate of individual political decisions was seen as occurring through one's ability to vote. Both the wide adoption of proprietary capitalism and the suffrage movements contributed toward introducing a new weave to the American cultural fabric: a strong strain of individualism. This will be elaborated upon shortly under the section "Conceptions of the Self."

Political Conditions

While the economic infrastructure responsible for integration—in the form of canals, railroads, and telegraph lines—needed to be built from scratch during this era, the political infrastructure necessary for integration was created when the country was first formed. However, it would take the entire period of this era for social welfare to move from primarily being a local governmental concern to encompassing a concern of county, state, and then federal government. In fact, political integration would lag behind the rapid economic integration taking place. Combined with the traditional understanding of social welfare being a local responsibility, proprietary capitalism called for a laissez-faire approach toward managing the economy. Hence, the post office marked the only significant presence of the federal government in the everyday lives of its citizens.[61] It was not until 1887, with passage of the Interstate Commerce Act and extending into the trust-busting era of Teddy Roosevelt, that the federal government first took on a tentative but active role in promoting social welfare, through regulation of big business.[62] With the progressive era reforms that followed, capped by the ratification of the Sixteenth Amendment in 1913 creating a federal income tax, the groundwork for a federal welfare state had been laid—and would come to fruition in the following, Modern Era.

As the root causes of social problems began to transcend local boundaries and conditions, it would take the power of state government and, eventually, the federal government to step in and take responsibility for promoting social welfare. By far, the lion's share of legislation and policy addressing social problems took place at the state level. One consequence of the state assuming an ever-larger responsibility of social welfare, among a growing influx of immigrants and diversity, was that the state took on an ever-increasing secular nature. While the separation of church and state was enshrined in the Constitution, it wasn't until 1833 that the practice of using state tax monies to support religious enterprises was completely phased out.[63]

Social Conditions

As the country rapidly grew in size, so too did the social connectivity between individuals grow in scope and sophistication. While the telegraph primarily aided business communication, the post office primarily benefited social communication.[64] From the outset of our country's birth as a nation, the federal post office served as the primary vehicle connecting individuals across disparate communities. The advances in transportation described earlier served to increase the timeliness of such exchanges. Delivering the mail was easily the largest activity of the federal government and its most direct connection to the average individual; in 1820 there were more people working for the post office than all other aspects of the federal civilian bureaucracy combined.[65] And its effect in promoting social cohesion was nothing short of profound, with Alex de Tocqueville describing it as a "great link between minds" that reached into "the heart of the wilderness" and with the German scholar Francis Lieber labeling it as "one of the most effective elements of civilization."[66]

Technological advances in printing helped spur the development and growth of mass media, which served to disseminate current events and promote an American culture ultimately reaching national in scope. Newspapers and magazines proliferated in this era both in sheer numbers and in reach of circulation.[67] With the telegraph communicating important news as it happened and the post office delivering newspapers and magazines to persons' doorsteps, the consciousness of society steadily grew broader in scope.[68] In addition, these newspapers and magazines predominantly reported news stories at the state, national, and international levels rather than focusing upon local news.[69] Thus, individuals' primary identification as a member of a community shifted over this time. During colonial times, one's main affiliation was to one's local community, hence people primarily identified themselves in this manner, such as chiefly identifying oneself as a Bostonian. In the first half of the nineteenth century, this shifted to a primary identification at the state level, and thus people primarily identified themselves as a Tennessean, an Ohioan, etc. The secession of southern states prompting the Civil War serves as a strong illustration of this identification at the state level. The growth of mass media would fuel this transformation in civic culture. Writers of short stories and novels, such as Edgar Allen Poe and Mark Twain, gained a national repute. After the Civil War, the short story became hugely popular, and there were a number of writers offering the public a window into American culture across various regions of its landscape, helping to fuel the emergence of a national consciousness.[70]

Mass media also served as a useful vehicle for social reformers during the progressive era to deliver and promote their message of reform. The utopian novel gained popularity and was used as a vehicle in which to level criticisms of society as well as offer a path forward.[71] Muckrakers such as Upton Sinclair (e.g., *The Jungle*) and Hamlin Garland (e.g., *Main-Travelled Roads*) used the literary depth of the novel to expose corruption and injustices occurring in society.[72] And social reformers comprising the settlement house movement adopted the conducting of research and its dissemination through pamphlets and books as one of the three "R"s comprising the pillars of the movement (the other two being residency and reform).[73]

As was the case in the economic sphere wherein the integration of the economy was national in scope, and thus, consequently, resulted in a division of labor, the social and cultural integration of society into a national consciousness promoted the division of individuals into social groups sharing a similar characteristic, the most prominent being race, ethnicity, gender, and economic class.[74] Farmers joined the ranks of businessmen and thus eroded their traditional identification with the laboring class.[75] The infamous 1896 *Plessy v. Ferguson* decision enshrined the legitimacy of segregation based upon race.[76] Even those promoting social reform, such as the various settlement house leaders, were not immune to the driving influence of this social segregation, particularly around racial and ethnic lines.[77] They fell prey to this social segregation when acting as unwitting conspirators through their silence on racial injustices and when they actively worked to "Americanize" recent ethnic immigrants into the dominant White, Anglo-Saxon, Protestant culture. Yet, at the same time, throughout this era there was a strong moral reform movement aimed at righting the injustices being visited upon marginalized groups.[78]

Urgent Need

As mentioned in Chapter 1, Foucault's conception of an *urgent need* reflects society's viewpoint of what is most important to promote a robust society so that society can stave off existential threats to its survival. From the evidence presented thus far concerning the various conditions shaping the premodern experience, we are able to see a new urgent need arising for this era. As noted above, spurred on by technological advances in transportation and communication, throughout this era a rapid integration of society was taking place at many levels: political, economic, social. The lives of individuals at the beginning of this era were predominantly shaped by the influence of society operating at a local level; by the end of this era, society operating at the national and state levels would exert strong influence on the conditions of daily life. The once island communities were becoming integrated into a larger society. Population in the towns grew dramatically, transforming these towns into cities—cities that contained a patchwork of communities. Along with industrialization came the mobility of labor—the boundaries of communities had become much more permeable than they had once been. With the creation of these more permeable borders, responsibility for the poor and the deviant grew to encompass the county level and then the state level.

Social welfare agents of this era readily observed this rapid integration taking place at the political, economic, and social levels and grew concerned about the glaring exception to this trend: that of the moral integration of society. While political, economic, and social integration fed off each other, these same processes seemed to exert the opposite affect when it came to the moral integration of society—appearing to starve and weaken it. The growth of an industrial economy and the appearance of big business led to a quite literal class war—in which armed conflict routinely erupted in the streets between aggrieved workers and their employers.[79] As will be explored shortly below in the section on the main cultural feature of this Discourse, this class conflict served to fuel the prominence of: the wicked city stereotype, wherein cities were viewed as dens of vice, degradation, corruption, and violence. Such a stereotype contributed to the perception by social reformers of the steady moral decline of society.

As noted in Chapter 2, local communities in colonial America were typically founded by members of a single congregation. This structure helped to integrate members on a moral level as one's fellow community members were seen as part of one's "church" family. During this era, it was not the case that religion no longer played a central part in people's lives; rather, it was noted that the anonymity of the city made it easier for one to give into temptation to various vices and that working classes were less likely to maintain an active church life due to simple exhaustion arising from long working hours.[80] The structure of one's congregation comprising one's community had dissipated—and no alternative moral structure was seen as taking its place. To many of the middle and upper class—those comprising the ranks of social welfare agents—this lack of moral integration represented a grave peril to civilization and contained the real possibility of society falling into a state of anarchy if moral integration never arose.[81] The Civil War and the horrors that it spawned served as a grim example that the disintegration of society into anarchy and chaos was a very real possibility. In the years following the Civil War, apocalyptic warnings were routinely offered in newspapers and at the pulpit.[82] Loomis offered the following: " 'Is our civilization perishable?' To this startling question, which a recent writer answers in the affirmative. . . . So vast and complex a structure as that of modern civilization could only stand on the solid foundation of public integrity."[83]

Thus, the urgent need of this era was that of *attending to the moral integration of society*. Many different attempts were made at creating these alternative moral structures, the hope being that they would serve to promote a sense of fraternity with one's fellow citizens and appeal to one's moral nature in guiding one's behaviors.[84] As a noted revivalist once stated, "By bringing the rich man and poor together and associating them in public, the strong lines that exist in private life are softened, and, engaged in worshiping a common lord, different ranks meet as brothers."[85] And as summed up by Michael McGerr, "The progressive middle class wanted a 'moral revolution.' . . . In calling for 'association' and 'fellow-feeling,' the progressives and such political allies as Theodore Roosevelt wanted other Americans to transcend class differences."[86] The overarching goal of the social reformers of this era was that of bringing about what they termed the *great community*—a national moral community held together by fraternal bonds.[87] This overarching goal would be the driving force for all efforts at promoting social welfare.

Intellectual Thought

The Premodern Discourse would usher in the prominence of Enlightenment thought in understanding society and guiding social welfare efforts. Also referred to as the *age of reason* due to its promotion of reason as the main vehicle for navigating one's world, it sought to advance ideals such as liberty, fraternity, and progress. Exemplified first by René Descartes' elucidation of rationalism, it marked a clear break with the scholastic-Aristotelian philosophy that colonial Americans had embraced in the form of natural law theory. While natural law theory held a prominent role for reason, reason alone was seen as insufficient to guide one's moral actions. Rather, it was the operation of one's soul through its divine connection with God that served as the source of moral actions. Reason was employed to correctly interpret the messages coming through this connection. Hence, the operation of reason and the soul were intimately linked when guiding moral actions in the Colonial Discourse. In the Premodern Discourse this link would be severed. Reason was now viewed as being capable of operating on its own to guide one's moral actions. The operation of one's soul still played a prominent part as well, but now it also operated on its own. It served to promote a sense of fraternity among oneself and the rest of humankind and thus provided a foundation for a rationale to be built on how moral action served to advance one's self-interest.

However, the rationalist philosophy predominantly guiding social welfare efforts of this Premodern Discourse was much different than our current understanding and application of Enlightenment thought, which began early in the twentieth century to serve as the philosophical foundation for advancing scientific understanding of our world. Scientific thought would play a minor role in influencing the Premodern Discourse on social welfare; the social scientific disciplines would not arise until the latter part of the century. Scientific thought, in the form of specialized knowledge, would dominate the Modern Discourse arising in the twentieth century. The key contrast separating the two is the following. The Premodern Discourse's application of Enlightenment thought strongly embraced rationalist philosophy over empiricism. Information gleaned through one's senses was viewed as dubious, and thus served at the behest of reason. This resulted in a deductive approach to investigation when attempting to understand the causes of social ills and the consequent remedy needed. The modern application of Enlightenment thought does the reverse and strongly embraces empiricism over rationalist philosophy. In this scientific understanding of the world, the information gleaned through one's senses is viewed as the main route to truth/reality through the establishment of scientific facts, and thus reason serves at the behest of empirical data. Hence, this results in an inductive approach to investigation when attempting to understand the causes of social ills and the consequent remedy needed.

First, it will be useful to examine the broad movement in rationalist moral philosophy that shaped the understanding by Premodern-Era Americans of what moral actions were needed to achieve the good. Next, worthy of examination are some common broad intellectual concepts that existed, concepts that were pressed to the foreground within this Discourse on social welfare: These were concepts of the categorical imperative, the transcendental self, and utilitarianism.

Immanuel Kant: The Categorical Imperative

Enlightenment thought placed reason center stage concerning one's existence. Immanuel Kant, through his three critiques, exemplified this movement by grounding human existence in reason—in terms of both navigating the natural world and navigating the moral world. Kant's concept of the categorical imperative put reason center stage in guiding moral behavior. Kant surmised that through the proper use of one's faculty of reason, one was able to clearly understand that a moral act—even though it might work against one's material self-interest in the particular situation—ultimately benefited the individual's overall well-being by contributing to a sense of peace and fulfillment.

This notion would have a profound effect upon the social welfare agents of the time, dramatically changing their approach toward addressing poverty and deviant behavior. As discussed in the previous chapters on the Colonial Era, individuals suffering misfortune and poverty were not blamed for their condition; rather, as best illustrated by the parable of Job, their condition was seen as part of God's plan for the universe. Hence, help and support were generously offered. Similarly, deviant behavior was seen as arising from falling prey to original sin—a quality that all members of the community possessed—and hence simply required the remedy of proper atonement.

In this Premodern Discourse, adopting the notion of the categorical imperative served to individualize the blame for one's misfortune or deviant behavior as these conditions were now seen as arising from one's improper use of reason. Foils to this reason operating properly were unreason (i.e., insanity) and ignorance. But as every individual's existence was grounded upon the ability to reason, it was believed that this reason formed a potential in each individual. Thus, for example, it was confidently believed that the insane could be cured, if proper conditions were applied.[88] It was also believed that deviant moral behaviors (which were believed to contribute to poverty) resulted from moral ignorance: Properly employing one's reason in the form of the categorical imperative is what served as an inner check to giving in to one's base instincts and allowed one to see the benefits of qualities such as temperance and thrift. To be sure, social welfare agents of the time did recognize that forces outside of one's control might lead to the condition of poverty as well—such as becoming a widow or suffering a serious injury or disability which interfered with one's ability to work. Hence, it is in the Premodern Era that the distinction between deserving and undeserving poor arose[89]; the categorical imperative serves as the source for this distinction, not the Poor Laws of colonial America as is occasionally advanced by some historians. In this Premodern Discourse, both poverty and deviant behavior were seen as a result of moral ignorance, and hence, the remedy often turned to by social welfare agents was that of moral instruction to lift these individuals out of their ignorance.

We now gain a beginning of an understanding of why the scientific charity movement adopted the slogan "not alms but a friend." Charity workers were seeking to address the root cause of poverty, not simply looking to alleviate its symptoms. Material relief (i.e., alms) was seen as insufficient on its own because it merely alleviated the recipient's suffering and thus was simply a temporary fix. In order to help individuals escape from poverty, their defect in moral character had to be eliminated. The best route deemed to achieve this was through a "friend" offering moral counseling.

Revivalism and the Transcendental Self

As was the case in colonial times, religious thought continued to exert a prominent influence on the practices of social welfare. A widely held belief of this era was that religion served as the foundation of morality[90]; hence, social welfare agents turned to religious teachings of the Bible to provide the moral instruction needed to lift individuals out of their moral ignorance. In addition, the main concept undergirding the revivalist movement was the transcendental nature of the soul—that one was able to directly commune with God and did not need a preacher to act as an intermediary on one's behalf. These revivalist movements were referred to as *Great Awakenings*. As discussed in the previous chapter, the First Great Awakening occurred in the 1730s–1740s. However, the movement was quickly snuffed out as the idea of forming a direct communion with God was antithetical to the urgent need of the Colonial Discourse: that of maintaining the social hierarchy.

The Second Great Awakening started up around the turn of the nineteenth century and lasted well into mid-century, at which point the new denominations that it spawned had firmly established themselves in the social fabric of society.[91] With the urgent need of this Premodern Discourse being that of attending to the moral integration of society, the revivalists' conception of the transcendental nature of the soul gained traction.[92] Inherent in this notion was the understanding that one could also form a spiritual communion with others.[93] This great importance given to achieving spiritual communion with others is also reflected by the various communitarian movements that began to emerge mid-century, such as Brook Farm (in West Roxbury, Massachusetts), Fruitlands (also in Massachusetts), and Fountain Grove (in California).[94] Throughout the rest of the nineteenth century, numerous utopian communes (usually short-lived) would be established across the United States.[95]

The notion of a spiritual connection served to round out the understanding of the workings of the categorical imperative. The moral act became *imperative* due to one's spiritual connection to others; proper reasoning allowed one to see how an immoral act, while perhaps advancing one's material self-interest, poisoned this spiritual connection and thus created more harm than benefit for the individual. As Jerome Schneewind notes, "The social outgrowth of the idea that anyone could choose to be saved was that men and women, once they were transformed, could change society merely by choosing to do so."[96] Promoting this spiritual connection to others would be another strategy employed by social welfare agents to combat the ills of society.

And now we gain a glimmer of understanding as to how the Pageant and Masque of St Louis came into being as a vehicle to promote social welfare. Social welfare agents sought to utilize the natural beauty of the city park, along with a moral allegory conveyed through the beauty of art, to stir one's soul and thus foster a spiritual communion among the many citizens of St. Louis—helping to create the moral bonds necessary for the "great community" to emerge.

Utilitarianism

Jeremy Bentham

Utilitarianism, whose philosophy was broadly first laid out by Jeremy Bentham, offered a detailed elaboration marrying the concept of Kant's categorical imperative with the spiritual communion elucidated in the revivalist movement. Bentham's utilitarian doctrine united these two concepts of reason and spiritual communion, earning him the moniker of "the Newton of the moral world."[97] Viewing the individual as a rational self-interested actor, Bentham described a calculus of cause-and-effect mechanisms that led an individual to pursue their rational self-interest. Reason allowed one to enjoy moral pleasures (arising from one's spiritual communion with others), those behaviors that contributed to the good of the community.[98] Deviant behavior is conceived in this framework as occurring when—due to one's moral ignorance—individuals succumb to sensual pleasure and then promote this indulgence in simple pleasure over the interest of the community.[99] Bentham argued that this deviant behavior could be disciplined, through the imposition of an orderly routine and the separation from corrupting influences, toward a condition in which reason would once again prevail in guiding the offender's actions.[100] Bentham's notion of discipline found realization in the designs of the first institutional penitentiaries built during the Jacksonian era.[101] Social welfare agents now had a formula they could follow to address deviant behavior leading to social ills.

John Stuart Mill

John Stuart Mill built upon the principles of Bentham by introducing the concept of *sanctions*.[102] Sanctions act as a scaling ladder for one to make the transition from a desire to advance one's own happiness through satisfying simple pleasures to the realization that a greater level of individual happiness can be achieved through advancing the happiness of others. According to Mill, sanctions can be both external and internal. External sanctions take the form of laws and social approval or disapproval that serve to persuade or coerce an individual to adopt moral behavior.[103] So, for example, one refrains from stealing due to fear that being caught would carry the penalty of going to prison. External sanctions, however, are designed simply to act as a complement to self-directed moral behavior—which is the ultimate goal.[104] Self-directed moral behavior is represented by internal sanctions—a sense of pleasure derived from obeying a moral law and a sense of pain from violating one. As Mill wrote, "The deeply rooted conception which every individual even now has of himself as a social being tends to make him feel it one of his natural wants that there should be harmony between his feelings and aims and those of his fellow creatures."[105]

This notion of sanctions was reflected in the changing attitude toward the poor. As urbanization and modernization proceeded apace, many of the external sanctions of the colonial village dissipated. Through the eyes of the social agents, this made it all the more important for individuals to have a well-developed set of internal sanctions—for without them disorder would ensue. Social agents thought they viewed evidence of this disorder in the numerous taverns and brothels that were concentrated in the poor districts of the city,[106] the succumbing to sensual pleasures over moral pleasures. As these internal sanctions were thought to spring from a sense of spiritual communion, social welfare efforts turned toward interventions that would foster this spiritual integration and provide moral instruction.[107] Attempts to create external sanctions—reflected most strongly in the institutional movement that would arise in the Premodern Era (as exemplified by the creation of Sing Sing)—relied upon a heavy use of discipline to move individuals back to acceptable behavior.

Thus, we now have a bit of insight on why social welfare agents at first turned to the penitentiary as a model for the social organization of society. It was hoped that the fundamental principles of discipline and isolation from corrupting influences that the penitentiary embodied could somehow be applied to society as a whole as the means to replace the loss of the external sanctions present within the colonial village.

Defining Cultural Feature: The Wicked City Stereotype

As the external sanctions of the colonial village and town dissipated within the sheer size of the emerging cities, the city would be viewed throughout this century as a place of social disorder and moral licentiousness—concentrated in the poorer districts of the city.[108] By 1818, commentators were describing "the social indifference of New Yorkers" and how in Pittsburgh neighbors could pass months or years without ordinary exchanges of friendship.[109] Sermons and speeches of the 1820s began to issue somber warnings about the moral dangers prevalent in the city, such as gambling, sexual licentiousness, Sabbath breaking, and profanity.[110] And the cities' poor districts were seen as containing "a great mass of people beyond the restraints of religion."[111]

By the 1830s, cities were being described as "hotbeds of vice and immorality."[112] The concentrations of vice, crime, and drunkenness in the poor districts of the city became a stark and unpleasant reality by the 1840s; for example, one journalist described Dandy Hill in Philadelphia as "the rottenest and most villainous neighborhood ever peopled by human beings,"[113] while New York City would later be described as the modern Gomorrah.[114] In addition, the period including the 1830s to the 1850s contained numerous urban riots sparked by various incidents such as bank failures and soaring bread prices; numerous gang wars also perpetuated an ever-present air of lawlessness and violence.[115] Throughout this time period as well, the wicked city stereotype became a prominent theme in American fiction.[116] Adding even more to this stereotype were continuous waves of sensational stories appearing in newspapers, pulp novels, and popular magazines of this time.[117] In sum, social agents viewed poor neighborhoods as breeding pits for all manner of vices: drinking, prostitution, crime, and various other immoral behaviors.[118]

In the latter half of the century, added to the above concerns was the prominence of labor unrest spawned by abuses flowing from modernization and industrialization. The Chicago Haymarket Square riot of 1886 is a prominent example of a long list of strikes and armed encounters resulting from labor unrest.[119] This fueled concerns over the potential for anarchy. Finally, as Irish and other non-Protestant immigrants began to flood America's shores, concerns were heightened that they would upset the prevailing Protestant moral order.[120]

Social agents operating within the Premodern Discourse viewed the growth and development of the city through a moral lens: the dissipation of external sanctions coinciding with a distinct display of behaviors lacking inner sanctions. Material deprivation among poorer members of society remained a concern to be addressed, as the many relief societies of this era attest. But of even greater concern was moral deprivation—stemming from faulty moral reasoning interfering with one's ability to form a level of sympathy with one's fellow citizens; in addition, it was often viewed as the cause behind one's material deprivation.[121] Proper moral reasoning was seen as the key toward achieving this spiritual communion. The wicked city stereotype served as an ever-present grim example of the debasement of society and the anarchy that would occur if moral integration into a "great community" failed to arise.[122]

Paradigm of Understanding

As stated previously in Chapter 1, a paradigm consists of fundamental philosophical assertions concerning the nature of reality (ontology); how knowledge is captured by the human mind (epistemology), and the theory of causality used to explain human actions. The paradigmatic shift taking place in this transition from a Colonial Discourse to a Premodern Discourse is as follows.

Theory of Ontology: Coherence Theory of Truth

Immanuel Kant and Baruch Spinoza are the early architects of the coherence theory of truth. They viewed truth concerning objective reality as an interconnected network of propositions—the greater these propositions' coherence to each other, the closer one gets to grasping objective reality.[123] It is heavily axiomatic in nature and gets its inspiration from Euclidean geometry, in which an ever-increasing number of proofs of reality are established based upon a handful of fundamental assertions held to be true. Descartes' fundamental assertion of *Cogito ergo sum*, or "I think, therefore I am," is a prime example of such a fundamental assertion. It is a system heavily deductive in nature: Empirical observations play the role of pieces to a jigsaw puzzle in which the form of the puzzle itself already exists as interconnected propositions to which these "pieces" are added, contributing to a more complete picture of reality.[124] Its affiliation with Euclidean geometry leads to a mathematization of nature, and thus gives rise to the major criticism of Enlightenment thought that it offers an overly mechanistic view of human behavior. This mathematization of nature can be seen reflected in Bentham's offering of a moral calculus to behavior, and mechanization of human behavior is strongly reflected in Mill's offering of the role of internal and external sanctions in guiding human behavior.

Theory of Epistemology: Rationalism

One of the key elements of rationalism is the distrust in sensory experience (i.e., empiricism) to yield certainty that one's knowledge accurately reflects reality. René Descartes likened an individual's endeavor to achieve certainty of knowledge with an architect's endeavor at constructing a building. Before laying down the foundation for knowledge, one must remove any loose or shifting soil so that the foundation rests upon firm epistemological ground.[125] This loose or shifting epistemological soil came in the form of propositions whose certainty contained the least bit of doubt. Taking the position that one's senses can easily be deceived, Descartes placed empirical knowledge in this category of loose soil. Justifying factors for knowledge which comprised firm ground lay in innate ideas of the intellect. This methodological approach adopted by Descartes is often described as his method of doubt.[126] As stated above, the first step lies in the removal of doubtful propositions. The construction of an edifice of certain knowledge then takes place. This approach makes knowledge generation deductive in nature and relies heavily upon one employing solid reasoning in both the removal of doubt and the connecting of the propositions comprising one's edifice of knowledge.

Rationalists applied this method in the construction of moral knowledge; Descartes, for example, laid out four axioms concerning moral knowledge.[127] As certainty of knowledge relied upon rational insight, Descartes would describe its construction as arising from "a great light in the intellect."[128] When applied to moral behavior, social welfare agents operating within this Premodern Discourse likened it to a rational illumination taking place. This rational illumination is what they sought to foster among the poor and social deviants as the means to achieve the moral clarity comprising internal sanctions. They would use the term *moral uplift* to describe this effort.

Theory of Causality: Cause–Effect (Rational Mechanics)

The notion of cause and effect has been around since the time of Plato and Aristotle, if not longer. It is a concept that is so ingrained in our understanding of the world that it is often difficult for people to even conceive of a different, legitimate theory of causality. Its most recent elaboration within a scientific context can be attributed to Newton's laws of rational mechanics, formulated in terms of action–reaction. Vernacularly, this is understood as cause and effect: There is a cause (i.e., movement/change of physical properties of existence) that has an effect on the object(s) with which it interacts, producing a change in that object (i.e., movement/change of physical properties of existence). The classic example used to illustrate is that of a billiard ball hitting a group of other billiard balls. For social welfare agents of the Premodern Era, the various behaviors of concern (poverty, crime, etc.) were seen as arising from one's inability to employ proper moral reasoning, which was in turn attributed to a number of causal factors, with one primary example being the lack of a proper moral upbringing as a child.[129] Interventions then sought to compensate for past causes and to eliminate or ameliorate present causes contributing to the present behavior of concern.

Conceptions of Self

As was the case within the Colonial Discourse, individuals operating within the Premodern Discourse possessed a bifurcated sense of self. Society now viewed human beings as existing simultaneously in a natural world and a transcendental world; existence within the social world now became subsumed under these two dominant views. The soul continued to be a primary force motivating behavior, particularly moral behavior, and hence the notion of a transcendent self was widely embraced—as is reflected in the popularity during this era of both religious revivals and transcendental communes. However, different from the previous Colonial Discourse wherein one's soul and reason were intimately entwined, there was a definitive split between the two during the Premodern Discourse. Since we were now seen as in control of our own destiny, our soul was no longer seen as existing within a divine order, with reason serving as the aid in interpreting God's plan.

The soul was now primarily seen as the vehicle for forming a spiritual communion with God as well as with one's fellow citizens, one that did not rely upon the aid of reason whatsoever to establish. Spiritual communion with God occurred through being touched by the Holy Spirit, either through religious revelation or simply by communing with God's presence in nature. Achieving spiritual communion among one's fellow citizens promoted a sense of fraternity and sympathy with them. As stated earlier, establishing this spiritual communion was viewed by social welfare agents as the key factor in promoting the sorely needed moral integration of society; consequently, many intervention efforts strongly reflected this goal.

New on the scene was a sense of self that was heavily grounded in nature. Reason was viewed as the key player aiding one in navigating this natural world. Previously in the Colonial Discourse, Calvinist thought viewed the individual as being inherently depraved (through original sin) with the belief that one's impulses and urges sprang from this inner evil. Hence, colonists primarily situated themselves within a social world, belonging to the divinely ordered social hierarchy comprising society. This prompted a more communitarian approach toward addressing social ills.

The ascendancy of Enlightenment thought in the Premodern Discourse introduced a new thread into the fabric of American culture: individualism. Described as possessive individualism, persons were now viewed as autonomous rational units, with each being "essentially the proprietor of his own person or capacities, owing nothing to society for them."[130] Contrasted with Calvinist notions, transcendentalist thought in the Premodern Discourse offered the notion that the self was inherently good and that one's impulses and urges, guided by reason, represented moral intuition (as conceptualized by Kant's categorical imperative).

This idea of possessive individualism was articulated most strongly in Ralph Waldo Emerson's essay entitled "Self-Reliance," within which Emerson argues that society serves to dampen one's moral intuition:

> Society everywhere is in conspiracy against the manhood [i.e., personhood] of every one of its members. Society is a joint-stock company, in which the members agree, for the better securing of his bread to each shareholder, to surrender the liberty and culture of the eater. The virtue in most request is conformity. Self-reliance is its aversion.[131]

This resistance to society's attempted subjection of one's individuality resulted in a focus upon two fronts: the hewing of character and the embrace of self-reliance. Advancement in these areas would result in one's inner-directed, utilitarian moral intuition helping one to achieve salvation.[132] Unfortunately, one fallout from America's cultural embrace of individualism was that personal foibles often took center stage when examining social ills, leading to a strong proclivity in this era to blame individuals for the social ills under which they suffered. Hence, it was in the Premodern Era that being poor became a stigmatizing condition—being seen as primarily arising from one's own moral failings.

The notion of one's self situated within the natural world was exemplified strongly in the belief grounded in utilitarianism that human behavior was primarily guided by motivation to increase pleasure and to avoid pain. It was also reflected within Enlightenment thought as a whole adopting the position that behavior was motivated by one's rational self-interest. The realm of moral behavior is where these two separate senses of the self came together as opposite parts of the same coin. Spiritual communion was seen as necessary for one to feel the greater pleasure arising from moral acts than the pleasure arising from simply advancing one's material self-interests. Once this sympathy had been achieved, reason was responsible for providing the clarity of illumination that moral pleasure always trumped sensual pleasures. These two elements would form a common thread running through all social welfare efforts of this era.

Rules of Right

Having a clear understanding of the urgent need of this Discourse, along with the prominent intellectual thought guiding social welfare efforts, we are now positioned to decode the rules of right operating within this Discourse. Rules of right are the main organizing principles of knowledge production in service to the urgent need.[133] The embrace of Enlightenment thought's mathematization of human behavior in general, and its specific iteration in utilitarianism as a formulaic calculus guiding moral behavior, speak to a quest for certainty in the mechanics of moral behavior. Inspired by the successes of Newton in the realm of physics and his ability to describe the motion of objects with mathematical precision, a similar precision in describing moral behavior would prove invaluable in efficiently directing efforts to promote the moral integration of society.

The end goal of moral integration served as the sought-after ideal or "answer" to the moral equation being applied to human behavior. With social welfare agents regularly observing chaos and violence erupting as a result of integration happening at the social, economic, and political levels, it was quite apparent to their eyes that many people in society were falling short and deviating from this ideal. Consequently, the first rule of right for this era was that of *measuring deviance from the ideal*. And the second rule of right was that of *seeking causal mechanisms*.

Measuring Deviance from the Ideal

This precise measurement would provide the essential first step in directing efforts to move the individual toward achieving this ideal. Such certainty of measurement would reveal the levers of power available to affect change in this regard. Having a clear understanding of the variables operating in the first half of the equation would allow one to manipulate these variables in order to produce the desired "answer": moral integration.

Seeking Causal Mechanisms

One must keep in mind that this effort at determining causality was approached deductively. The moral calculus was a product of rationalism, its genesis arising from innate ideas of the intellect. Observational data was plugged into the appropriate variables within this calculus to achieve an understanding of human behavior. So, for example, the observation that an individual experiencing a social ill (e.g., poverty) regularly drank alcohol, when plugged into the moral calculus, would be interpreted as the individual giving in to sensual pleasures over moral pleasures. Consequently, moral counseling would be needed to correct the individual's ignorance of the greater pleasure that resulted from adopting moral behavior in this area (i.e., temperance). The money saved as well as the sharpening of intellect occurring through adopting temperance would now position the individual to begin moving out of their condition of poverty.

Theme of the Discourse: The Common Person as the Ideal

While people in society continued to categorize themselves along different levels of social status within this era, such a hierarchical structure was no longer viewed as the glue holding society together. Due to the influence of Enlightenment thought responding to the changing conditions of society, for the Premodern Discourse one factor acting as glue holding society together was individuals' ability to properly employ their faculty of reason. A second factor acting as glue holding society together was the ability of one's soul to form a sympathetic bond with one's fellow citizens. Acting as a form of epoxy, these two factors working together were seen as the means to cement the social order in place through meeting the urgent need of moral integration.

Since reason and a soul were seen as properties common to all individuals, properly employing both to achieve moral clarity and pleasure was seen as an ideal within the grasp of every individual. In terms of promoting social welfare, this new view had a profound leveling effect. It demolished the previous notion of each person's contribution to societal welfare being determined by their position in the social hierarchy and replaced it with a deep sense of equality regarding each person's contribution. This deep sense of equality resulted in the flowering of democratic freedom at the political and spiritual levels.

In terms of political freedom, this was the era of suffrage movements. Kicking off this era, beginning with Kentucky in 1792 and ending with North Carolina in 1856, the various states began abolishing property requirements and religious requirements for White males to vote.[134] Marking the middle of this era, the Fifteenth Amendment was adopted, which abolished race criteria for voting. Lastly, marking the very end of this era, the Nineteenth Amendment was adopted, abolishing gender requirements for voting. In addition, the Seventeenth Amendment was passed, allowing for the direct election of senators. The electoral college for the election of president—which is still in use today—represents the sole vestige of democracy as interpreted through the Colonial Discourse's emphasis on social hierarchy as opposed to the Premodern Discourse's emphasis on equality.

In terms of spiritual freedom, the revivalist movement fostered a democratic stance concerning one's relationship with God in two very important ways. First, a more democratic stance now determined who could become a preacher—with race, gender, class, or education no longer representing qualifying criteria. This type of democratic change mainly swept through the Protestant faiths, with a few new denominations being created. The second reflection of this democracy— which encompassed not only Protestantism but also the more tradition-bound religions of Catholicism and Judaism—was that the preacher/priest/rabbi was no longer seen as the necessary intermediary for one's communication with God. One could send one's prayers to God directly.

This deep sense of equality permeating society consequently affected the relationship between social welfare agents and those they sought to help. Social welfare agents now viewed the difference between themselves and those they served as a difference in degree (those being helped fell short of the ideal employment of reason and sympathy, an ideal embodied by the social welfare agents) rather than a difference in kind (those being helped occupying a different position in the social hierarchy than the social welfare agents themselves). This is reflected in the rule of right for this era of measuring deviance from this ideal—hence, by embodying this ideal, social welfare agents sought to encourage clients to be more like them. This difference of degree, within the new cultural dynamic of possessive individualism, also had the effect of blaming the clients for their condition. Yes, as the spirit of the St. Louis pageant outlined at the beginning of this chapter attests, environmental factors were considered. But the far more numerous approaches, as reflected by scientific charity's slogan "not alms but a friend," saw this degree of difference arising from an individual's poor choices and actions.

However, tainting this flowering of democratic equality was the fact that the various demographic characteristics of the dominant group—White, Anglo-Saxon, Protestant, male, heterosexual—were baked into this notion of what the ideal represented. This only had a moderate impact in curbing the spiritual freedom taking place, mainly resulting in various congregations naturally segregating themselves along racial lines. However, the flowering of political freedom taking place was severely undermined. It took the entire span of this era to finally recognize a woman's right to vote. And numerous laws were passed, particularly in the Deep South, that set up massive barriers for those seeking to exercise their right to vote, guaranteed by the Fifteenth Amendment, laws that would remain in effect well into the twentieth century.

Unfortunately, no such flowering of democratic equality occurred within the economic and social spheres. Rather, the reverse occurred—the continuance of structural oppression on many fronts. The inherent contradiction between demographic qualities of the dominant group being baked into the flowering of democratic equality among all individuals resolved itself through embracing the bizarre notion of "separate but equal." The demographic characteristics of race and gender were viewed as being rooted in biology; this reflected a clear separation into various demographic groups wherein each held a different inherited potential. Yet, all individuals comprising a particular demographic group were viewed as being equal. In addition, the notion of the ideal being within the grasp of every individual in these various subgroups supported the growth of the eugenics movement—wherein genetic defects were seen as biologically barring individuals from reaching this ideal, and thus future such individuals needed to be culled from society through a process of reproductive sterilization of any present individuals possessing such genetic defects.

Lasting well into the twentieth century before beginning to be challenged, many laws and customs acted to severely restrict economic opportunity for women, non-Whites, non-heterosexuals, and to some extent non-Protestants. This structural oppression also took many forms on the social front, again with no significant challenges to it until well into the twentieth century; what follows are but a few examples. Society's wide embrace of the scientific claim of racial superiority (i.e., polygenism) resulted in racial segregation in housing and various forms of social participation, with the Deep South taking it to its extreme limits. It also took the form of anti-miscegenation laws banning interracial marriage. Patriarchy continued to be extensively diffused throughout society. Within the household, women were primarily confined to the role of domestic servant and caretaker of children. Common law legitimized a moderate form of domestic violence. And while minor gains were made in granting women access to higher education, such participation was highly restricted. Sodomy laws were passed criminalizing sexual relations between individuals of the same sex, while the medical community viewed such behavior as mental illness. Prejudice against non-Protestants nurtured the growth of such groups as the Know Nothing Party, which sought restrictions on the immigration of non-Protestant groups, and the Ku Klux Klan, which visited reigns of terror upon non-Protestants and non-Whites. And in the realm of social work, being motivated by the goal of helping clients to be more like them, social welfare agents followed a strong program of cultural assimilation when working with immigrants. Also, the US government actively followed a strong program of the forced cultural assimilation of

Native Americans, encouraging activities such as the removal of children from reservations to be placed in religious boarding schools.

Notes

1. Stevens and MacKaye, *The Book of Words*.
2. Rothman, *Discovery of the Asylum*, xix, 79–81.
3. Gilkeson, *Middle-Class Providence*, 13.
4. Gates, *History of Public Land*, 49–50.
5. "List of U.S. States."
6. McGerr, *A Fierce Discontent*, 9.
7. "List of U.S. States."
8. Davis, *Homicide in American Fiction*, 63; Hofstadter, *The Age of Reform*, 32.
9. Ward, *Cities and Immigrants*, 52.
10. Loomis, *Modern Cities*, 27.
11. Davis, *Homicide in American Fiction*, 63; Edwards, *New Spirits*, 39.
12. De Santis, *Shaping of Modern America*, 97–98.
13. Andrews, "The Andrews Report," 303–06.
14. Fearon, *Sketches of America*, 90.
15. Andrews, "The Andrews Report," 303–06; Howe, *What Hath God Wrought*, 216.
16. Edwards, *New Spirits*, 36; Howe, 217.
17. De Santis, *Shaping of Modern America*, 6.
18. Howe, *What Hath God Wrought*, 697.
19. De Santis, *Shaping of Modern America*, 6; Link and Link, *The Gilded Age*, 3–4.
20. Edwards, *New Spirits*, 36.
21. De Santis, *Shaping of Modern America*, 97–98; Howe, *What Hath God Wrought*, 701.
22. De Santis, 3, 23.
23. Glaab, *The American City*, 178–79.
24. Channing, *A Students' History*, 529; "Colonial Travel," 1st paragraph.
25. Howe, *What Hath God Wrought*, 691.
26. Edwards, *New Spirits*, 49.
27. Howe, *What Hath God Wrought*, 697.
28. Link and Link, *The Gilded Age*, 3–4; "When the Standardization."
29. "When the Standardization."
30. Edwards, *New Spirits*, 39; Ward, *Cities and Immigrants*, 7.
31. Bremner, *From the Depths*, 103; Demos, *A Little Commonwealth*, 183; Howe, *What Hath God Wrought*, 201.
32. De Santis, *Shaping of Modern America*, 1; Howe, 217; Link and Link, *The Gilded Age*, 5.
33. Hofstadter, *The Age of Reform*, 38; Howe, 217.
34. Howe, 567; Lears, *Rebirth of a Nation*, 55.
35. Hofstadter, *The Age of Reform*, 121.
36. Gilkeson, *Middle-Class Providence*, 132.

37. Edwards, *New Spirits*, 39; Loomis, *Modern Cities*, 49.
38. Edwards, 39; Tucker, "On Cities and Towns," 173; Hofstadter, *The Age of Reform*, 32.
39. De Santis, *Shaping of Modern America*, 2; Tucker, 173.
40. "Forms of Capitalism," subheading "Proprietary Capitalism."
41. Porter, *Rise of Big Business*, 58–59.
42. Porter, 58–59.
43. Link and Link, *The Gilded Age*, 5; Loomis, *Modern Cities*, 49; Porter, 100.
44. De Santis, *Shaping of Modern America*, 1.
45. Howe, *What Hath God Wrought*, 556.
46. De Santis, *Shaping of Modern America*, 1; McGerr, *A Fierce Discontent*, 15.
47. De Santis, 2; Gilkeson, *Middle-Class Providence*, 132.
48. De Santis, 8.
49. Loomis, *Modern Cities*, 98.
50. Headley, *The Great Riots*; Loomis, 98.
51. Miller, *Urbanization of Modern America*, 47–48; Boyer, *Urban Masses*, 15; Wiebe, *The Search for Order*, 10.
52. Headley, *The Great Riots*; Asbury, *Gangs of New York*; Geffen, "Violence in Philadelphia."
53. Lears, *Rebirth of a Nation*, 75.
54. Howe, *What Hath God Wrought*, 556; Loomis, *Modern Cities*, 58, 78.
55. De Santis, *Shaping of Modern America*, 99; Ward, *Cities and Immigrants*, 3.
56. Loomis, *Modern Cities*, 78.
57. Loomis, 78.
58. Howe, *What Hath God Wrought*, 556.
59. Hankins, *The Second Great Awakening*, 111; Sennet, *Families Against the City*, 59.
60. Edwards, *New Spirits*, 208.
61. van der Linden, *Airlines and Air Mail*, 4.
62. Hofstadter, *The Age of Reform*, 233; De Santis, *Shaping of Modern America*, 15.
63. Hankins, *The Second Great Awakening*, 4.
64. Edwards, *New Spirits*, 49.
65. Edwards, 49; Howe, *What Hath God Wrought*, 225.
66. Howe, 225–26.
67. Hofstadter, *The Age of Reform*, 188–92.
68. Howe, *What Hath God Wrought*, 226–27; McGerr, *A Fierce Discontent*, 233–34.
69. Howe, 227.
70. De Santis, *Shaping of Modern America*, 91.
71. Glaab, *The American City*, 318.
72. De Santis, *Shaping of Modern America*, 92.
73. Kalberg, "Commitment to Career Reform," 612; Trolander, *Professionalism and Social Change*, 16.
74. Edwards, *New Spirits*, 10–11.
75. Hofstadter, *The Age of Reform*, 121.
76. McGerr, *A Fierce Discontent*, 194.
77. McGerr, 183–84.

78. Stewart, *A Half Century*, 50–102; Burnett, *Five for Freedom*, 45–57; Herbert, *The Abolition Crusade*, 22–48.

79. Davis, *Homicide in American Fiction*, 158; Edwards, *New Spirits*, 71; Lears, *Rebirth of a Nation*, 79.

80. Ward, *Cities and Immigrants*, 117.

81. Hofstadter, *The Age of Reform*, 70; Loomis, *Modern Cities*, 80–81.

82. Edwards, *New Spirits*, 219.

83. Loomis, *Modern Cities*, 79.

84. Hankins, *The Second Great Awakening*, 51; Hofstadter, *The Age of Reform*, 62; Quandt, *From Small Town*, 1, 23–24.

85. Hankins, 55.

86. McGerr, *A Fierce Discontent*, 122.

87. Gilkeson, *Middle-Class Providence*, 10; Quandt, *From Small Town*.

88. Earle, *The Curability of Insanity*, 23, 27–29; Rothman, *Discovery of the Asylum*, 129–31.

89. Lears, *Rebirth of a Nation*, 173.

90. Schneewind, *Moral Philosophy from Montaigne*, 20.

91. Hankins, *The Second Great Awakening*, 50–55; Schneewind, *Sidgwick's Ethics and Victorian*, 4, 13–15.

92. Schneewind, 53–54.

93. Miller, *Urbanization of Modern America*, 3–10.

94. Hine, *California's Utopian Colonies*, 12–32; Francis, *Transcendental Utopias*, 35–66, 140–73.

95. Hine, 3–11; Francis, 1–34.

96. Schneewind, *Sidgwick's Ethics and Victorian*, 87.

97. Mack, Introduction, viii.

98. Shaw, *Public Relief*, 37–39.

99. Flower, *Boston's Democracy of Darkness*, 303.

100. Foucault, *Discipline and Punish*.

101. Smith, *The Norton History*, 376; Rothman, *Discovery of the Asylum*, 82.

102. Mill, *Utilitarianism*, 41.

103. Mill, 41–42.

104. Mill, 42.

105. Shaw, *Contemporary Ethics*, 71.

106. Cole, *The Social Ideas*, 100; Beecher, *The Autobiography*, 192–94; Handy, *A Christian America*, 45.

107. Shaw, *Contemporary Ethics*, 75.

108. Strong, "Urban Problems," 330.

109. Fearon, *Sketches of America*, 11; Wade, *The Urban Frontier*, 310.

110. Boyer, *Urban Masses*, 5.

111. Stafford (1817) as quoted in Boyer, 9.

112. Asbury, *Gangs of New York*, 44–45; Kelly, "William Kelly on San Francisco," 197; "Town and Country," 537–39.

113. Blumin (c. 1840s) as quoted in Boyer, *Urban Masses*, 69.

114. Asbury, *Gangs of New York*, 158.
115. Headley, *The Great Riots*; Asbury, *Gangs of New York*; Geffen, "Violence in Philadelphia."
116. Dunlap, *The City*, 14, 68–69; Arden, "The Evil City."
117. Davis, *Homicide in American Fiction*, 161–63, 262–63; Crouthamel, "James Gordon Bennett," 303.
118. Thernstrom, *Poverty and Progress*, 41–43; Modell, "The Peopling," 77; Ward, *Cities and Immigrants*, 105–21.
119. Boyer, *Urban Masses*, 15; Miller, *Urbanization of Modern America*, 47–48; Wiebe, *The Search for Order*, 10.
120. Loomis, *Modern Cities*, 86–87, 182–83; Abell, *The Urban Impact*, 91–93.
121. Loomis, 103.
122. Flower, "The Slums of Boston," 279; Loomis, 103.
123. Young, "Coherence Theory of Truth," heading 2.1.
124. Spinoza, *The Collected Works*, 41.
125. Newman, "Descartes' Epistemology," heading 2.
126. Skirry, "René Descartes 1596–1650," 2nd paragraph.
127. Descartes, *Discourse on Method*, AT VI 23–28: CSM I 122–25.
128. Newman, "Descartes' Epistemology," subheading 1.1.
129. Strong, "Urban Problems," 328.
130. MacPherson, *The Political Theory*, 3.
131. Emerson, "Self-Reliance," 6th paragraph.
132. Seiler, *Republic of Drivers*, 33.
133. Foucault, *The Order of Things*.
134. "Timeline of Voting Rights."

References

Abell, Aaron. *The Urban Impact on American Protestantism, 1865–1900.* Cambridge, MA: Harvard University Press, 1943.

Andrews, Israel. "The Andrews Report on Transportation and Cities." In *The American City: A Documentary History,* edited by Charles Glaab, 303–06. Homewood, IL: Dorsey Press, 1963. First published 1853.

Arden, Eugene. "The Evil City in American Fiction." *New York History* 52 (1954): 259–79.

Asbury, Herbert. *The Gangs of New York.* New York: Capricorn Books, 1970. First published 1928.

Beecher, Lyman. *The Autobiography of Lyman Beecher.* Edited by Barbara Cross. 2 vols. Cambridge, MA: Harvard University Press, 1961.

Boyer, Paul S. *Urban Masses and Moral Order in America, 1820–1920.* Cambridge, MA: Harvard University Press. 1978.

Bremner, Robert. *From the Depths: The Discovery of Poverty in the United States.* New York: New York University Press, 1956.

Burnett, Constance. *Five for Freedom: Lucretia Mott, Elizabeth Cady Station, Lucy Stone, Susan B. Anthony, Carrie Chapman Catt.* New York: Greenwood Press, 1968.

Channing, Edward. *A Students' History of the United States*. New York: Macmillan Company, 1908.

Cole, Charles. *The Social Ideas of the Northern Evangelists, 1826–1860*. New York: Columbia University Press, 1954.

"Colonial Travel." ConstitutionFacts.com. Accessed May 22, 2019, https://www.constituti onfacts.com/founders-library/colonial-travel/.

Crouthamel, James. "James Gordon Bennett, the *New York Herald*, and the Development of Newspaper Sensationalism." *New York History* 54 (1973): 294–316.

Davis, David B. *Homicide in American Fiction, 1798–1860*. Ithaca, NY: Cornell University Press, 1957.

Demos, John. *A Little Commonwealth: Family Life in Plymouth Colony*. 2nd ed. New York: Oxford University Press, 1999.

De Santis, Vincent P. *The Shaping of Modern America: 1877–1920*. Hoboken, NJ: Wiley-Blackwell, 1973.

Dunlap, George. *The City in the American Novel, 1789–1900*. Philadelphia: University of Pennsylvania Press, 1934.

Earle, Pliny. *The Curability of Insanity: A Series of Studies*. Philadelphia: J. B. Lippincott, 1886. https://books.google.com/books/about/The_Curability_of_Insanity.html?id= qfERAAAAYAAJ.

Edwards, Rebecca. *New Spirits: Americans in the Gilded Age: 1865–1905*. Oxford: Oxford University Press, 2006.

Emerson, Ralph Waldo. "Self-Reliance." In *Essays: First Series*. Project Gutenberg. First published 1841. https://www.gutenberg.org/files/2944/2944-h/2944-h.htm.

Fearon, Henry Bradshaw. *Sketches of America: A Narrative of a Journey of Five Thousand Miles Through the Eastern and Western States*. New York: Benjamin Bloom, 1969. First published 1819.

Flower, Benjamin. "The Slums of Boston." In *The American City: A Documentary History*, edited by Charles Glaab, 278–85. Homewood, IL: Dorsey Press, 1963. First published 1893.

Flower, Benjamin. "Boston's Democracy of Darkness." In *The American City: A Documentary History*, edited by Charles Glaab, 303–06. Homewood, IL: Dorsey Press. 1963. First published 1893.

"Forms of Capitalism—Current and Past." Ebrary.net. Accessed April 25, 2017, https://ebr ary.net/3625/management/forms_capitalism-current_past.

Foucault, Michel. *Discipline and Punish: The Birth of the Prison*. New York: Vintage Books, 1991.

Foucault, Michel. *The Order of Things: An Archaeology of the Human Sciences*. New York: Vintage Books, 1994.

Francis, Richard. *Transcendental Utopias: Individual and Community at Brook Farm, Fruitlands, and Walden*. Ithaca, NY: Cornell University Press, 1997.

Gates, Paul W. *History of Public Land Law Development*. Washington DC: Public Land Law Review Commission, 1968.

Geffen, Elizabeth. "Violence in Philadelphia in the 1840s and 1850s." *Pennsylvania History* 36 (1969): 381–410.

Gilkeson, John S. *Middle-Class Providence, 1820–1940*. Princeton: Princeton University Press, 2014.

Glaab, Charles. *The American City: A Documentary History*. Homewood, IL: Dorsey Press, 1963.

Handy, Robert. *A Christian America: Protestant Hopes and Historical Realities*. New York: Oxford University Press, 1971.

Hankins, Barry. *The Second Great Awakening and the Transcendentalists*. Greenwood Guides to Historic Events 1500–1900. Santa Barbara: Greenwood, 2004.

Headley, Joel Tyler. *The Great Riots of New York, 1712–1873*. New York: Dover, 1971. First published 1873.

Herbert, Hilary. *The Abolition Crusade and Its Consequences: Four Periods of American History*. New York: AMS Press, 1912.

Hine, Robert. *California's Utopian Colonies*. Berkeley: University of California Press, 1953.

Hofstadter, Richard. *The Age of Reform: From Bryan to F.D.R.* New York: Knopf, 1960.

Howe, Daniel W. *What Hath God Wrought: The Transformation of America, 1815–1848*. Oxford: Oxford University Press, 2007.

Kalberg, Stephen. "Commitment to Career Reform: The Settlement House Leaders." *Social Service Review* 49 (1975): 608–28.

Kelly, William. "William Kelly on San Francisco." In *The American City: A Documentary History*, edited by Charles Glaab, 196–98. Homewood, IL: Dorsey Press, 1963. First published 1851.

Lears, Jackson. *Rebirth of a Nation: The Making of Modern America, 1877–1920*. New York: Harper Perennial, 2010.

Link, Susannah J., and William A. Link. *The Gilded Age and Progressive Era: A Documentary Reader*. Hoboken, NJ: Wiley-Blackwell, 2012.

"List of U.S. States by Date of Admission to the Union." Wikipedia. Accessed May 15, 2019, https://en.wikipedia.org/wiki/List_of_U.S._states_by_date_of_admission_to_ the_Union.

Loomis, Samuel L. *Modern Cities and Their Religious Problems*. New York: Arno Press, 1970. First published 1887.

Mack, Mary. Introduction to *A Bentham Reader: The Essential Texts and Key Ideas of the Great Architect and Inventor of a Whole New Social Order*. Edited by Mary Mack, iii–xix. Cambridge: Pegasus, 1969.

MacPherson, Crawford. *The Political Theory of Possessive Individualism: Hobbes to Locke*. Oxford: Oxford University Press, 1962.

McGerr, Michael. *A Fierce Discontent: The Rise and Fall of the Progressive Movement in America, 1870–1920*. Oxford: Oxford University Press, 2003.

Mill, John Stuart. *Utilitarianism*. Pinnacle Press, 2017. First published 1863.

Miller, Zane. *Urbanization of Modern America: A Brief History*. New York: Harcourt Brace Jovanovich, 1973.

Modell, John. "The Peopling of a Working-Class Ward: Reading, Pennsylvania, 1850." *Journal of Social History* 5 (1971): 71–95.

Newman, Lex. "Descartes' Epistemology." In *Stanford Encyclopedia of Philosophy*. Last modified February 15, 2019, https://plato.stanford.edu/entries/descartes-epist emology/.

Porter, Glenn. *The Rise of Big Business, 1860–1920*. Hoboken, NJ: Wiley-Blackwell, 1973.

Quandt, Jean. *From Small Town to Great Community: The Social Thought of Progressive Intellectuals*. New Brunswick, NJ: Rutgers University Press, 1970.

Rothman, David. *The Discovery of the Asylum: Social Order and Disorder in the New Republic*. 3rd ed. New York: Walter de Gruyter, 1971.

Schneewind, Jerome B. *Sidgwick's Ethics and Victorian Moral Philosophy*. Oxford: Oxford University Press, 1977.

Schneewind, Jerome B. *Moral Philosophy from Montaigne to Kant*. Cambridge: Cambridge University Press, 2002.

Seiler, Cotton. *Republic of Drivers: A Cultural History of Automobility in America*. Chicago: University of Chicago Press, 2008.

Sennet, Richard. *Families Against the City: Middle-Class Homes of Industrial Chicago*. New York: Vintage Books, 1947.

Shaw, Josephine. *Public Relief and Private Charity*. New York: G. P. Putnam's Sons, 1884.

Shaw, William. *Contemporary Ethics: Taking Account of Utilitarianism*. Hoboken, NJ: Wiley-Blackwell, 1999.

Smith, Roger. *The Norton History of the Human Sciences*. New York: HarperCollins, 1997.

Spinoza, Baruch. *The Collected Works of Spinoza*. Vol. 1. Translated and edited by Edwin Curley, 1661–65. Princeton: Princeton University Press, 1985.

Stevens, Thomas Wood, and Percy MacKaye. *The Book of Words of the Pageant and Masque of St. Louis*. St. Louis: The Book Committee St. Louis Pageant Drama Association, 1914. https://ia902701.us.archive.org/26/items/bookofwordsofpag00stevrich/bookofword sofpag00stevrich_bw.pdf.

Stewart, Frank. *A Half Century of Municipal Reform: The History of the National Municipal League*. Los Angeles: University of California Press, 1950.

Strong, Josiah. "Urban Problems." In *The American City: A Documentary History*, edited by Charles Glaab, 330–36. Homewood, IL: Dorsey Press, 1963. First published 1885.

Thernstrom, Stephan. *Poverty and Progress: Social Mobility in a Nineteenth Century City*. Cambridge, MA: Harvard University Press, 1969.

"Timeline of Voting Rights in the United States." Wikipedia. Accessed May 22, 2019, https://en.wikipedia.org/wiki/Timeline_of_voting_rights_in_the_United_States.

"Town and Country." *The Knickerbocker*. November 8, 1836, 537–39. Accessed May 22, 2019, https://babel.hathitrust.org/cgi/pt?id=mdp.39015011269829;view=1up;seq=13.

Trolander, Judith A. *Professionalism and Social Change: From the Settlement House Movement to Neighborhood Centers, 1886 to the Present*. New York: Columbia University Press, 1987.

Tucker, George. "On Cities and Towns." In *The American City: A Documentary History*, edited by Charles Glaab, 170–72. Homewood, IL: Dorsey Press, 1963. First published 1843.

van der Linden, Robert. *Airlines and Air Mail: The Post Office and the Birth of the Commercial Aviation Industry*. Lexington: University Press of Kentucky, 2002.

Wade, Richard. *The Urban Frontier: The Rise of Western Cities, 1790–1830*. Cambridge, MA: Harvard University Press, 1959.

Ward, David. *Cities and Immigrants: A Geography of Change in Nineteenth-Century America*. New York: Oxford University Press, 1971.

"When the Standardization of Time Arrived in America." Smithsonian.com. Last modified December, 19, 2016, https://www.smithsonianmag.com/smithsonian-institution/ how-standardization-time-changed-american-society-180961503/.

Wiebe, Robert. *The Search for Order: 1877–1920*. New York: Hill and Wang, 1967.

Young, James O. "The Coherence Theory of Truth." Stanford Encyclopedia of Philosophy. Accessed May 22, 2019, https://plato.stanford.edu/entries/truth-coherence/.

5

Social Welfare Practices in the Premodern Era (c. 1820–1920)

By 1820 and beyond, social welfare in the United States had clearly been reconceived. The scattered elements of a new discourse that began to arise after the Revolutionary War and early 1800s coalesced to become the dominant apparatus generating and legitimizing knowledge. A new urgent need arose outside the bounds of the Colonial Discourse. The island communities were becoming integrated into a society. Population in the towns grew dramatically, transforming these towns into cities—cities that contained a patchwork of communities. Along with industrialization came the mobility of labor—the boundaries of communities had become much more permeable than they had once been. With the creation of these more permeable borders, responsibility for the poor and the deviant grew to encompass the county level and then the state level. The stability of society depended upon the successful moral integration of these once separate communities into that of a *great community*.

The associative network described in this chapter—that of power responding to an urgent need through the formation of rules of right—represents the Premodern Discourse on social welfare operating in the United States from roughly 1820 until 1920. The sheer size of society as a great community, the increased organizational complexity of community institutions, and the specialization of labor within an industrial economy all served to create layers of separation between individuals that did not exist within the colonial town and village. The fraternal connection and community identity that seemed to naturally arise among members of the colonial community became problematic within society of the nineteenth century—especially in the cities, where these dynamics where particularly concentrated.

Seeking moral integration on a rational and transcendental level, knowledge generation bent its efforts—and its translation into social welfare practices—toward measuring deviance from an ideal of moral behavior and then seeking causal mechanisms as the means to correct this deviance back to the ideal. Hence, within this Premodern Discourse a new center of power arose. Human beings now existed in the natural world as rational creatures that controlled their destiny. Rather than simply letting society unfold according to God's plan, a measure

A Genealogy of the Good and Critique of Hubris. Phillip Dybicz, Oxford University Press. © Oxford University Press 2023.
DOI: 10.1093/oso/9780197670071.003.0005

of control was needed to stem the mounting moral degradation occurring in society. By grounding moral action upon reason, the ideas of the Enlightenment served to address the need for exerting this control concerning moral integration to a much greater degree than could be done by any Protestant doctrine.

Human beings were also still seen as simultaneously existing in a transcendental world via possessing a soul. But since we were now seen as in control of our own destiny, our soul was no longer seen primarily as existing within a divine order. Rather, it too responded to the urgent need for successful integration: The main quality of one's soul was now seen as its capability to form bonds of sympathy. Human beings were seen as possessing a soul that could achieve a spiritual communion, and thus integration, with all other souls in society.[a] These changes would result in profound ramifications concerning the notion of behavioral deviance that threatened the social order.

In colonial communities, the bawdy tavern wench or the miller who was fond of drink were not behavioral deviances that threatened their place within the hierarchy of the community and the divine order—and thus, while their actions were frowned upon, they were not seen as threats to the social order. Being poor or suffering from mental illness also did not threaten one's placement within these hierarchies as they were accepted as a part of God's plan. There was no place for criminal deviance in this hierarchy, and thus infractions were met with harshly. Thus, in the Colonial Discourse, deviances seen as threatening the social order were much more narrowly conceived, restricted to the incorrigible sinner and outsiders such as vagabonds.

In the Premodern Era the list of deviances threatening the social order expanded greatly to include any behavior not founded upon reason: poverty, licentiousness, intemperance, mental illness, etc. All of these many deviances would be lumped together under the same problematization: failure to employ reason properly and failure to form bonds of sympathy with one's fellow human beings. They were seen as emblematic of a soul that was not in spiritual communion with other souls and/or a mind not using its rational capacities to achieve integration at the various levels of society. In addition, the notion that one is in control of one's own destiny via one's use of reason—especially in America, where there existed a wealth of opportunities—led to the common perception that the poor were to blame for their condition. It would be up to the upstanding members of the community to instruct them of their errors and to attempt to create environments that fostered their moral development. As human beings

---

[a] Note, my argument is *not* that before 1820 human beings were never thought of as rational creatures or possessing a soul that could achieve spiritual communion. Rather, I am arguing that after 1820 these became the dominant facets of viewing individuals on the natural and transcendental level in American society.

were now seen primarily as rational creatures capable of sympathy, it was viewed with hope that these deviances could be corrected back to an ideal of proper behavior and a level of spiritual communion affected.

Consequently, social welfare efforts in this era would follow one of three broad approaches to combat this threat to social stability. The first approach to arise consisted of moral education. Moral deprivation was seen as arising from ignorance; this approach embraced education as the method to correct this ignorance. Its focus was to stimulate a latent capacity for moral reasoning. The second approach to arise was that of institutionalization. This approach was reserved for those individuals whose ability to reason had seriously degraded: the criminally deviant (severe lack of moral reasoning), the insane, and the chronic poor (severe lack of moral reasoning due to giving in to base instincts) to name a few. Its focus was to create an artificial environment of order and routine that would separate individuals from corrupting influences and then condition and discipline them back to the proper use of reason. The third approach was that of environmentalism. As with the above approaches, environmentalism viewed the lack of spiritual communion arising among the poor as a result of the unwholesome environments in which they were forced to live; but rather than blame the poor for creating the environments in which they lived, they blamed society. Its focus was to create wholesome spaces within the city, places where citizens could interact (interaction among the different economic classes was viewed as especially important) upon a level that was conducive to building social harmony. The institutionalization movement can be classified as the most coercive of these approaches and the environmentalist approach the least so.

Moral Education—Combating Ignorance

Moral Uplift Societies

Early efforts at moral education reflected nostalgia for the moral order of the colonial village and were attempts to recapture that moral order. The moral uplift societies that arose in the early 1800s were one such effort, and they embraced a definitely coercive strategy. The first of these societies that gained prominence was formed in 1812 by a revivalist preacher named Lyman Beecher.[1] Named "The Connecticut Society for the Suppression of Vice and the Promotion of Good Morals," it sought to address what it viewed as a disturbingly large catalog of immoral trends.[2] By the 1820s and 1830s moral uplift societies were a common feature within numerous American cities and across the rural landscape.[3]

By acting as a disciplined moral militia, individuals who made up these societies sought to reassert the external sanctions of social disapproval prevalent within earlier colonial communities concerning deviant behavior.[4] Relying upon the power of shame to address immoral tendencies, these societies would usually target a specific issue (such as Boston's Association of Young Men targeting liquor sales on the Common) and seek to draw up a petition containing signatures of city notables and dignitaries which they would present to the offending business or to the city legislature.[5] Some, such as the New York Female Moral Reform Society formed in New York in 1834, sought to establish sidewalk patrols that would monitor places of ill repute (such as a brothel) and then publish in the newspaper the names of the individuals partaking in the immoral behavior.[6] When such efforts proved ineffectual, some individuals resorted to more drastic measures by engaging in moral vigilantism.[7] For example, during the 1840s and 1850s in cities such as Detroit, St. Louis, Boston, and Philadelphia, brothels were burned to the ground by irate citizens.[8] Yet this vigilantism simply reflected pent-up frustrations and were not part of any society's declared agenda; it was soon realized that such actions contributed to the very social disorder that they were trying to prevent.

Bible Tract Societies

Another early effort, reflecting a more subtle approach, was that taken by the Bible tract societies. A spin-off of the Bible society movement and its effort to spread the word of God via the production and distribution of Bibles, Bible tract societies turned to the tract to accomplish this same purpose as a strategy to better reach the uneducated poor. In 1825, local societies came together and formed the American Tract Society (ATS), based in New York City.[9] Written in simple vernacular, the typical tract was comprised of a short narrative exemplifying a particular moral behavior.[10] Their nostalgia for the moral order of the village is reflected by the fact that these narratives were always placed in a pastoral setting. The purpose of these tracts was clear: "to awaken inner checks on behavior to replace external checks that had been left behind."[11] By 1850, the ATS had established a list of over 500 titles and was printing over 5 million tracts a year.[12] These tracts were distributed by local tract societies via volunteers who visited the poor in their homes[13]—marking the first home visits by social agents of this era. These volunteers each had an assigned section of the city; they were to visit each household on a monthly basis.[14] Besides delivering a tract, these volunteers were also expected to provide moral counseling and collect data, which was then filed at the district tract society office.[15] In addition, bulk shipments of these tracts were sent to various institutions such as prisons, poorhouses, and orphanages[16]— indicating a level of cross-fertilization that would commonly appear among the moral education, institutionalization, and environmentalist movements.

Sunday School Movement

Lastly, one of the early efforts turned its attention toward children: the Sunday school movement. In 1824, the American Sunday School Union (ASSU) was founded in Philadelphia, providing sponsorship to over 700 Sunday schools in various states.[17] By the 1830s, enrollment in ASSU-affiliated schools topped 350,000.[18] The Sunday school movement, targeting the children of the poor, represented a hybrid between the institutional movement and the moral education movement. For a short block of time every Sunday, volunteers sought to immerse children in a highly hierarchical and orderly environment (through the school's physical layout, rule structure, and routine) in which moral education was delivered.[19] The moral education, as well as the modeling of behavior by teachers, was geared toward bringing about a transformation of character,[20] the rationally planned environment was deemed important in disciplining the children "to train them to control themselves" by serving "to touch inward springs."[21] The Sunday school also sought to serve as a site in the city where parents from differing social stations would come together and thus capture a lost feature of village life that helped facilitate spiritual communion[22]—incorporating an environmentalist perspective, and thus attesting to another incidence of cross-fertilization among movements. While the Sunday school movement would never die out, by the 1860s it was no longer seen as an effective intervention in reforming the children of the poor. Abandoning outreach efforts into poor neighborhoods, Sunday schools turned inward and solely provided instruction to children of parishioners.[23] A brief revival would occur at the end of the century, only to turn inward once again.[24]

Charity Relief Societies

Another effort at moral education was that which became incorporated into the work of charity relief societies. Charity societies that contained a strong moral reform element appeared as early as the 1790s, and many merchant-led anti-pauperism societies sprang up in response to the financial panic of 1819.[25] However, charity societies that combined relief with moral education did not come into prominence until the 1840s and beyond.[26] These efforts were reflected in societies such as the New York Association for Improving the Condition of the Poor (AICP). Unlike the earlier efforts at moral education, the leaders of these organizations were drawn from the ranks of business leaders and professionals rather than the clergy.[27] Another divergence from early efforts is that instead of relying heavily upon part-time volunteers, these organizations depended upon full-time, salaried staff[28]—laying the groundwork for social work to arise as a profession.

As the slum areas that arose in cities became a permanent fixture of the city landscape, social reform agents were taken aback by the mores—such as public inebriation, sexual promiscuity, and Sabbath breaking—that residents of these communities readily embraced.[29] It was a common viewpoint among the middle class that poverty resulted from a defect of character[30]—for example, the New York Society for the Prevention of Pauperism listed six such defects as leading to poverty (intemperance, extravagance, consorting with prostitutes, idleness, gambling, and early and imprudent marriage), and even two of the three environmental factors (pawnshops and lack of education) reflected the notions of reason falling prey to instincts.[31] The final factor (indiscriminate almsgiving) was seen as merely reinforcing the six character defects.[32] Hence, since these societies viewed the causes of poverty to be chiefly moral, their view was that they needed moral remedies.[33] Robert Hartley, first head of the New York AICP, saw as its mission "not merely to alleviate wretchedness, but to reform character" by enlightening the poor to "the true origins of their suffering" via "encouragement and counsel along the path to rehabilitation."[34] And as the Baltimore AICP framed it, the visitor's goal was to help the poor reform "from sources within themselves."[35] Home visitations became a central element to this approach.[36]

The AICP and other relief societies gave way to the charity organization societies (COS) of the latter part of the nineteenth century. COS saw the failings of these early societies to reform the character of the poor as resulting from inefficient and uncoordinated almsgiving. Their solution, which they termed *scientific charity*, lay in organizing the various relief societies under the umbrella of a single society, which would then be able to coordinate a more rational and systematic method for the disbursement of alms.[37] They also created the casework method as a rational and systematic method for separating the worthy poor from the unworthy.[38] By creating the casework method, a method currently in use in the practice of social work today, the COS are viewed by many historians as one of two foundational movements (the second being the settlement house movement) from which the profession of social work was born. Adopting the slogan "not alms but a friend," the COS continued to view poverty as mostly arising from a defect in character.[39] Home visitations, in the form of friendly visitors, were seen as attempts to re-establish neighborly ties between the poor and the middle and upper classes—not simply as a venue to provide material relief but rather to counsel and model the type of moral behavior that led to proper use of one's reason and to affect spiritual communion.[40]

During the 1890s, most likely in response to the catastrophic depression that hit, the COS began to be influenced by the growing prominence of the environmentalist movement. The environmentalist movement emphasized the role that society played in determining the moral and physical health of the poor. While not completely abandoning the view that moral defect caused poverty,[41] they accepted the idea that environment played a large role as well and sought, in the words of Mary Richmond, to understand "the family life as a whole."[42] Casework turned toward documenting environmental as well as personal information affecting the family.

City Missions

Occurring also at the latter half of the nineteenth century was the development of city missions. Not only were hefty sums collected to establish missions in existing cities[b] but also the major railroads donated parcels of land for the construction of churches in places where they expected cities to spring up.[43] City mission work was directed toward poor immigrants, its aim being to inculcate them in the benefits of a Protestant moral order.[44] Yet, like the COS, city mission workers found that a moral message alone was not enough for their purpose, and they too began to incorporate environmentalist elements. They began to offer programs and activities such as boys' clubs, recreational facilities, congregational choirs, and job training programs[45]—they sought to present the city mission as a wholesome space for social interaction. The mission movement most successful in combining this stance of moral rehabilitation with social awareness was the Salvation Army. Established in the United States in the 1880s, by 1900 the Salvation Army had 700 corps (i.e., congregations) carrying a total staff of 3,000 officers.[46]

The Moral Crusade

Of final note, deriving its genesis in the moral uplift societies at the beginning of the century was the notion of the moral crusade. These efforts at moral education sought to change the political landscape through moral reform. Taking a different tack, these crusades were directed not at the lower classes but rather at the upper and middle classes; moral crusades were based on the notion that if upstanding citizens were simply made aware of immoral conditions, they would take actions to eradicate them.[47] The moral uplift societies targeted specific vices, and this trend would continue throughout the century, culminating in the successful prohibition and anti-prostitution crusades of the progressive era.[48] But

---

[b] Davis, *Immigrants, Baptists*, 97–112. For example, in 1883 the American Home Missionary Society collected $200,000 for the creation of city missions and churches.

these moral crusades also targeted other causes within their scope of oppressive practices, such as the abolition of slavery, municipal government reform, and female suffrage.[49] Lastly, during the progressive era they also targeted inhumane labor and social conditions as moral blights. Organizations bent their efforts toward ending child labor and sweatshop labor,[c] as well as inhumane and unhealthy conditions in the slums.[50] What all these endeavors had in common was that their arguments for change rested upon moral grounds[d]—not impartial scientific evidence, a condition more common in the next century's Discourse.

Summary

Among all these many efforts, two elements stand out. First is the overriding concern and importance placed upon moral behavior. Yet, while specific behaviors were often highlighted, one can see a more general concern arise: a concern "to awaken inner checks on behavior," "to touch inward springs," and "to reform character." Efforts were aimed at stimulating inner sanctions to behavior. In addition, they aimed at creating new external sanctions (such as sidewalk patrols and early casework investigations) to face new community realities. Second is the importance placed upon neighborly interaction between lower-income citizens and upper- and middle-class citizens.

An explanation that justifies both these overriding concerns is that social welfare agents viewed interdependence on two levels: the natural and the transcendental. Cooperation in the economic and political sphere was not enough by itself; communion on the transcendental level was necessary as well to preserve social order. This concern is further reflected in the language of these times. The poor were predominantly referred to as paupers: a definition that emphasizes one's *dependency* upon charity. Social welfare was referred to as charity: a definition that emphasizes performing *benevolent* actions to the needy. Benevolence arises from a condition of sympathy—or spiritual communion—with a fellow human being. A pauper is one who is dependent upon material relief arising from this condition of spiritual communion. In this nineteenth-century Premodern Discourse, what is emphasized is how spiritual communion serves as the linchpin of this relationship between charity and pauperism.[e]

---

[c] Storrs, *Civilizing Capitalism*, 2. For example, the National Consumer League led by Florence Kelly—whose motto became "investigate, agitate, and legislate."

[d] Boyer, *Urban Masses*, 196–97. For example, appearing before the US Supreme Court in 1908, Louis D. Brandeis argued that long working hours for women, and the physical and mental fatigue that resulted, served to undermine their moral fiber.

[e] In the Colonial Discourse, both *charity* and *pauperism* were used. Within that Discourse, the hierarchical nature of the relationship between charity and pauperism was emphasized in terms of rights and responsibilities of each station.

These social welfare agents were faced with an apparent paradox: The more individuals became interdependent in the natural world via modernization, urbanization, and specialization of labor, the more they began to live separate lives—making interdependence on a transcendental level more and more difficult. They viewed this imbalance with alarm; thus, they bent their efforts toward correcting it.

The Birth of the Institution—Creating a Protected Environment

The institutional movement represents the government response to social welfare for this era. In addition, the ascendancy of institutions to remedy numerous forms of behavioral deviance represents social welfare interventions of this era at their most coercive. When institutions began to arise in great numbers during the Jacksonian era,[51] they were hailed as models for the community in their ability to provide external sanctions through a disciplined and orderly environment.[52] An institution arose to address each form of deviance: the penitentiary for criminal behavior, the asylum for insanity, the almshouse for pauperism, the house of refuge for the juvenile delinquent, and the orphanage for the child pauper.

The Penitentiary

While the practice of confinement gained acceptance toward the end of the Colonial Discourse, it is only with the emergence of the Premodern Discourse that attention began to focus on the internal routine of those confined. No longer simply viewed as sin, criminal behavior was now attributed to causal mechanisms.[53] These causal mechanisms were two. First, social welfare agents traced criminal behavior back to one's childhood—that of living in a morally destitute environment in which parents failed to exercise proper parental control.[54] As one group of social agents noted, "The mass of criminals is composed of persons whose childhood and youth were spent in the uncontrolled exercise of vicious instincts."[55] Thus, as children these convicts were never modeled or taught the inner sanctions necessary to combat one's base instincts. Second, cities and towns now offered a multitude of temptations toward vice, temptations that, due to their upbringing, these convicts were unprepared to handle.[56]

Despite their morally dissolute upbringing, social welfare agents were confident that these criminals could be reformed.[57] The first step in this process was removal from the community and all its corrupting influences.[58] This attention to isolation from corrupting influences was maintained within the penitentiary walls as well. Penitentiaries followed one of two models.[59] Under the system known as the Pennsylvania model, inmates faced total isolation for their entire period of confinement; this was seen as conducive to promoting the development of inner sanctions by being left to one's own conscience.[60] Under the system known as the Auburn model, prisoners were isolated in cells at night but put to work together during the day, yet forbidden to communicate with their fellow inmates.[61]

Merely isolating the individual from corrupting influences was not enough; a regular and orderly routine was at the core of both systems.[62] Obedience to rules became paramount[63]—obeying the rules indicated one's ability to employ inner sanctions. Consequently, rule breaking was met with serious discipline—and was viewed as a means of instruction toward employing these inner sanctions.[64] More subtle means of moral education were present in the form of a chaplain assigned to the prison and a Bible that was placed in every cell.[65] Finally, idleness was viewed as both a symptom and a cause of criminal behavior—if one was unwilling to work to earn one's bread, then one was prone to turn to criminal means to secure it.[66] Thus, the prison routine required a rigorous schedule of daily labor on the part of the convicts.[67]

The Almshouse

Within the Premodern Discourse, poverty too was seen as the result of a failure to abide by inner sanctions. Again, the community was seen as possessing great temptations toward vice, temptations that led the poor to cultivate the reckless behaviors responsible for their condition.[68] Within this Discourse, the distinctions between criminal deviance and economic dependency all but disappeared—both were seen as resulting from a lack of applying inner sanctions and thus the embracing of immoral practices.[69] With poverty now being linked to attributable causes resulting from individual choice, the poor no longer were viewed as occupying a predetermined place in the social hierarchy; consequently, the poor were no longer viewed as full members of the community.[70]

Rather than leave individuals idle within a community that provided a vast array of temptations, public aid for the poor embraced institutionalization as the necessary measure to combat pauperism.[71] Like the penitentiary, emphasis was placed upon reforming the individual.[72] Again, separation from the community was seen as the crucial first step.[73] Also, while not as successful as the penitentiary, almshouses sought to impose a regimen of order, discipline, and routine.[74] Workhouses were created for the able-bodied poor.[75] Even though they often fell far short of achieving an orderly regimen, and producing reformed individuals, almshouses continued to dominate public relief efforts toward the poor throughout the nineteenth century.[76]

The Insane Asylum

The institutionalization of the insane is particularly interesting in that, unlike inmates at other institutions, the insane were not perceived as mainly lacking a sense of spiritual communion and the improper use of reason to guide moral behavior. Rather, their failure to successfully integrate into society was viewed as stemming from the improper use of reason occurring on the natural level of human nature: that of adapting to the demands of society.[77] Insanity was viewed as conjoined with the progress of civilization: It was believed that as greater intellectual demands began being placed upon individuals from a progressively more fluid and open society, the incidence of insanity rose.[78] As was the case with other forms of behavioral deviance, blame was placed upon the family environment. In the case of insanity, it was the family's failure to properly buffer the susceptible individual from the frantic demands of a society seeking integration at a rapid pace.[79]

Treatment, interestingly enough, called for many of the same prescriptions as applied in the penitentiary. As always was the case, separation from the community was the crucial first step.[80] The idea was to create a protected environment where the pressures of the outside world would not interfere with one's reform.[81] This extended to the facilities themselves being placed outside community boundaries and included the discouragement of contact with family members.[82] Next, an orderly daily routine was deemed necessary as a means to impose a level of stability—a necessary countermeasure to the openness and fluidity of the community.[83] This led to the creation of a system of discipline to enforce adherence to the daily routine.[84] Finally, daily labor was prized as a way to inculcate regular habits—a trait deemed necessary as a buffer to the chaotic nature of the community.[85]

Institutions for Children—Orphanages and Houses of Refuge

With deviant and dependent behaviors being perceived as having their roots in childhood, children naturally became a prime target for intervention efforts. As poor children were equally exposed to the corrupt environment shaping their parents' behavior, poverty was seen as creating "moral orphans"; thus, poverty itself was viewed as an adequate reason to place a child in an orphanage.[86] It was a given that the parents would not provide any defense against the corruption in which they themselves wallowed.[87] As was the case with the almshouses, a strict orderly routine was seen as necessary to reforming the child.[88]

Institutionalization also created a venue to reform the disobedient child. Houses of refuge were built as places where children could be "sheltered from the perils of want and the contamination of evil example."[89] As with all of the above institutions, the first step involved separation of the individual from society and from their family—both being viewed as sources of corruption.[90] Parents were encouraged to transfer legal guardianship to the reformatory, and visits were highly restricted.[91] An orderly routine emphasizing obedience was deemed necessary as the means to promote adherence to inner sanctions: As one spokesperson declared, "The object is not alone to make the boys behave well while in our charge; that is not difficult. . . . [But] any discipline . . . which does not enable the boy to *resist temptation* wherever and whenever he finds it, is ineffectual, and the whole object of houses of refuge is a failure."[92] Taking a strong stance on the benefits of corporal punishment, numerous references were made to Solomon's admonishment not to "spare the rod."[93] This strong emphasis on obedience was even reflected in the wave of child guidance books that appeared throughout the 1830s to 1850s.[94]

And as was the case with penitentiaries and workhouses, strong emphasis was placed upon the reformatory benefits of labor.[95] As deviant behavior was also attributed to ignorance, both secular education and moral education were emphasized.[96] The child's ability to become a productive worker was the standard for release from the reformatory. Those who had responded reasonably well to the regimen of hard work and obedience were placed in apprenticeships within various city businesses; more difficult cases were sent off to work on ships—a stricter and more isolative environment.[97]

From Reformatories to Custodianships

By the 1850s and beyond, the ability of all of the above institutions to reform individuals began to be seriously questioned, as did the humaneness of their treatment.[98] Yet, despite being ineffectual, social welfare agents never called for their elimination; instead, cries for improvement were circumscribed to measures to promote better administration and more humane treatment.[99] Dorothea Dix's efforts on behalf of the mentally ill are just one prominent example.[100] In addition, no alternative measures were even offered for dealing with the criminally deviant or mentally insane.[101] Caretakers of the insane asylums readily acknowledged the custodial function of their institutions.[102] The penitentiary, the house of refuge, and, to a lesser degree, the poorhouse all turned their attention to maintaining obedience—letting the specter of the institution serve as a form of dissuasion to those who might enter.[103]

Summary

The common feature that stands out among all of the types of institutions described above is the emphasis upon separating undesirables from the community. These undesirables were seen as being unable to effectively employ inner sanctions to their behavior—leading them to engage in deviant acts. For the mentally insane, their inability occurred on the rational level; for all others, their inability occurred on the moral level. These deviants targeted for institutionalization were judged as failing to measure up to society's ideal: integration on a spiritual and a rational level.

Efforts were bent toward seeking causal mechanisms to explain and correct this deviant behavior. Working deductively from an accepted ideal of moral and rational behavior, causes of deviant behavior were easily attributable to failures of both the family and the community. One's family upbringing was seen as the time and space where one learned to develop inner sanctions and gain insight into their merits. An inferior family upbringing would deprive one of this proper development. In addition, the community was now seen as holding out a vast array of temptations—temptations that one could easily fall prey to if one did not have a well-developed set of inner sanctions. Little investigation beyond common sense was needed to see these causal forces at work.

These identified causal mechanisms pointed the way toward correcting this deviant behavior. Institutions were seen as protected environments where external sanctions could be imposed upon the deviant individuals. Little more was thought needed than isolation from corrupting influences, an orderly routine emphasizing daily labor, and a bit of moral education. Finally, even when institutions failed in their promise to reform deviant individuals and thus devolved into mere custodial operations, they did not lose prominence in this Discourse. Deviant individuals were no longer viewed as full members of the community. By performing the function of removing deviant individuals from the community, institutionalization still responded to the Premodern Discourse's urgent need for promoting integration among the remaining members of the community.

Environmentalism—Creating Wholesome Spaces

While institutionalization sought to create protected environments designed to provide external sanctions to behavior, environmentalist concerns about creating environments were much different. The interventions falling under this category sought to create wholesome spaces within the city that would nurture feelings of sympathy with one's fellow citizens. Environmentalist approaches include the following: the child saving efforts of the children's aid societies; the Young Men's Christian Association (YMCA) and other recreation-based associations; settlement houses, parks and playgrounds; and civic idealism.

Child Saving

Child saving, a self-adopted moniker by the social agents performing this work, straddled both institutionalization and environmentalism. The focus of child saving efforts was to remove children from corrupt environments. This often involved placing dependent children in orphanages or residency-based state schools.[104] Yet in the latter half of the century, these efforts also involved placing children (mainly infants) within adoptive families.[105]

By mid-century, many child saving agents began to become critical of institutionalization. Charles Loring Brace, founder of the New York Children's Aid Society, serves as a prominent example.[106] He often expounded upon the many positive qualities—such as independence, initiative, and individualism—that many street urchins possessed.[107] In addition, he "clearly saw that the children of the outcast poor must be removed from their debasing surroundings."[108] The goal of the New York Children's Aid Society, as well as for all the other children's aid societies that sprang up in numerous cities, was to harness these positive qualities by placing children within environments where these qualities could be put toward positive ends.[109] The accomplishment of this goal was sought via two approaches.

One was the creation of lodging houses, reading rooms, and industrial schools in the slum districts to which vagrant street youth could retreat when not plying the streets,[110] the aim being that these would be a "moral and physical disinfectant, a seed of reform and improvement amid the wilderness of vice and degradation."[111] While each of these entities had a set of rules one must follow—as opposed to the institutions—attendance was voluntary.[112] In order to appeal to the youths' independence, occupancy was treated more like a business exchange—a nominal fee was charged.[113] In addition to providing a comfortable place to sleep, good food, and job training, these places sought to shape these children "to be honest and industrious citizens; here taught economy, good order, cleanliness, and morality."[114] This was to be accomplished not through direct moral education but rather through the influence of a wholesome environment created by the middle- and upper-class volunteers working at these places, the aim being "to connect the two extremes of society in sympathy, and carry the forces of one class down to lift up another."[115]

But their "best remedy for juvenile pauperism"[116] lay in completely removing these children from the vice-ridden temptations of the city and the baleful influence of their debased parents by sending them to live with farm families along the western frontier[117]—a practice that later came be to referred to as the *orphan trains*. While referred to as an orphan train, approximately 40% of the children sent aboard these trains had either one or both parents living.[118] Due to their lack of a moral upbringing by their parents, these children were looked upon as moral orphans. Parental permission was never strenuously sought for these children as the parents were often seen as negatively influencing the child's moral development.[119] As with the lodging houses, placement with a farm family was presented as a voluntary contract: The child could leave the family any time that they wanted, and the family was given the right to dismiss the boy any time that they chose.[120] Of course, with no supervision being conducted after placement, such contracts were left open to abuse.

The YMCA and Other Associations

The founding in 1951 of the YMCA in Boston represents an early American effort of social welfare agents to target a population above the poverty line.[121] Young men's associations had existed in American cities since the 1820s, yet these were organizations that were founded by the members themselves along the lines of a common interest.[122] The emergence of the YMCA marks the transition to social welfare agents taking an active involvement in the creation, recruitment, and development of an association.[123] YMCAs targeted young middle-class men new to the city: "We shall meet the young stranger as he enters our city, take him by the hand . . . and in every way throw around him good influences."[124] By creating a wholesome environment for these men to gather and associate, it hoped to shield them from the vice-ridden amusements in the city that might lead them down the path to moral degradation.[125]

As was the case with all interventions based within the environmentalist approach, participation was voluntary.[126] Yet, if one joined, one agreed to abide by the YMCA's moral guidelines for behavior.[127] Programs varied among numerous local chapters, yet their purpose was the same: to create an association "which links hearts to hearts, and man to man, each doing something to keep the other from slipping."[128] The facilities often contained a reading room as a place for congregating, stocked with numerous small-town newspapers to help individuals keep apprised of events back home. Soon recreational programs were added.[129] Also, all members were expected to lend their time to one of many YMCA-sponsored charitable endeavors geared toward moral uplift—endeavors that depended upon the interaction between lower-class individuals and their moral betters.[130]

By 1860, the YMCA had 200 local chapters nationally serving 25,000 members. By 1900 the number had grown to 1,500 local chapters and 250,000 members.[131] The model of providing wholesome recreational activities within a framework of moral cultivation quickly gained wide appeal as a way to inculcate individuals against the temptations of the vice-ridden forms of entertainment dominating the city landscape: The Young Women's Christian Association formed to address the needs of women; Young Men's and Young Women' s Hebrew Associations formed to address the needs of Jewish Americans; and Boys Clubs, Boy Scouts of America, Girl Scouts, and Camp Fire Girls formed to address the needs of children.[132]

Parks and Playgrounds

The movement to create parks and playgrounds in the city was also motivated by the desire to create wholesome spaces in the city in which to foster the human spirit. The creation of city parks was based upon a faith in the elevating power of nature.[133] When it first appeared on the scene in 1851, the park movement rested simply on the goal of providing a pleasant space for the classes to intermingle, a space wherein the natural environs would exert a "harmonizing and refining influence . . . favorable to courtesy, self-control, and temperance."[134] The creation of Central Park in New York City serves as a prime example of this movement's goal. In this capacity, the park was seen as a place serving to counteract the erosion of the social bond perceived to be a problematic feature in city life.[135] However, as recreation-based associations grew in prominence, the parks were seen as a perfect setting for wholesome city-sponsored recreational activities.[136] The parks began to be used as a site to promote the cultural development of residents through the presentation of musical and dramatic performances.[137] These and other community events were seen as serving to promote a "spirit of neighborliness . . . the spirit which made earlier life in America wholesome and desirable."[138]

The playground/recreation center movement did not begin until the end of the century, but it remained strong throughout the progressive era.[139] From the start playgrounds/recreation centers echoed the prevailing notion of wholesome recreation facilitating the development of a child's moral nature and the promotion of civic unity.[140] They were seen as one of the "wholesome counterinfluences to the saloon, street gang, and similar evils."[141] Intermingling of the classes was to take place through the person of a trained supervisor who could exert the level of moral leadership necessary to guide the children to a greater level of social consciousness through their play.[142] The fact that this supervisor needed to be trained speaks to the growing presence during the progressive era of expertise being a valued trait in social welfare agents.[143]

Settlement Houses

The settlement house movement represented the environmentalist approach at its most sophisticated. Arising during the progressive era, settlement houses sought to carve out a wholesome household/community center environment directly in the midst of the poorest city wards.[144] By 1910, approximately 400 settlement houses had been established across the United States.[145] Containing play spaces, large kitchens, and a living room with library and fireplace, they served as a household extension to one's cramped tenement apartment.[146] As the settlement house movement grew, so did the settlement houses: They began to include gymnasiums, music halls, and meeting halls in which classes were held, making them part recreation center as well.[147] Lastly, they often established within themselves such services as a penny-savings bank, a dispensary, an employment bureau, a legal aid office, and a loan office.[148]

Jane Addams succinctly described the core features of the settlement house movement as consisting of three "R"s: residency, research, and reform.[149] The first of these, residency, was required for all settlement house workers: They had to reside at the settlement house and thus join the local community being served. An important feature of settlement house life was that the settlement house would serve as a place to help bridge the gap between classes and promote a level of fraternity.[150] As Jane Addams put it, "Certain it is that spiritual force is found in the Settlement movement, and it is also true that this force must be evoked and must be called into play before the success of any Settlement is assured."[151] While this interaction was seen as promoting a sense of moral uplift through democratic association,[f] this association had its practical benefits as well.[152] It was a way to connect the poor to those who might later have political[g] or business

---

[f] Addams, "The Subjective Necessity," 19–21. Jane Addams described this emphasis on fellowship, a fellowship that was based upon the idea of seeking the good in every individual, as indicative of a renaissance of early Christian humanitarianism.

[g] Trolander, *Professionalism and Social Change*, 16. The most prominent example is Eleanor Roosevelt, who worked as a dance instructor at University Settlement in New York. Other examples include Frances Perkins and Robert C. Weaver (the first woman and the first African American to hold a US cabinet position).

influence.[153] Also, settlement house workers and volunteers were looked to for the education that they possessed, often acting as teachers for the many classes offered at the settlement house.[154]

Settlement house workers' environmentalism did not stop at simply providing the wholesome space of the settlement house in which to promote fraternity. Research (the second "R") was also a central feature of a settlement house worker's activity. Relying upon the notion of spiritual communion operating among the better-off members of society, settlement house leaders sought to publicize the conditions of the poor as a means to draw upon that sympathy and thus mobilize citizens to affect needed change.[155] Settlement house leaders published an impressive output of literature during the progressive era,[156] including over forty-five books as well as numerous pamphlets and articles.[h] Settlement house workers also turned their efforts toward documenting substandard working and living conditions through conducting research in the form of social surveys.[157]

The settlement house workers did not conduct research as neutral observers. The purpose of research was to promote the third "R": reform. They turned their attention to improving the industrial environment of the neighborhoods themselves; they viewed these reform efforts also as a means toward bettering the moral environment of the city.[158] Settlement house workers joined others pressing for tenement house reform.[159] They allied themselves with those fighting for fair labor[i] standards.[160] And, albeit unsuccessful in this era, they also advocated for social insurance programs.[161]

Civic Idealism

Beginning in the 1890s, the movement to arouse civic loyalty and pride looked to dispel notions of the city as inherently wicked. The wholesome environment it looked to create was not physical in nature but rather in the imagination. Thus, it turned to the city itself to become a font of moral influence.[162] As one proponent exclaimed, "social workers should idealize and purify" the city in the same manner that the family is sanctified as a source of moral development.[163] The means offered to accomplish this were the city pageant, city beautification, and city planning.

---

[h] Gilman, "Catheryne Cooke Gilman," 206. Catherine Cooke Gilman, who headed the Northeast Neighborhood House in Minneapolis, herself wrote over 200 pamphlets and articles.

[i] Storrs, *Civilizing Capitalism*, 1–3. For example, Florence Kelley, a former resident at Hull House, later became head of the National Consumer's League and campaigned heavily to improve working conditions for women and end child labor.

The city pageant used allegorical expression to attempt to put the abstract notion of civic idealism into tangible form.[164] The goal of the pageant was to transform "estrangement and conflict . . . into harmony"[165] and to "foster community spirit."[166] The city beautification movement based its efforts on the premise that a city's physical appearance was intimately connected to its moral state: A more pleasant and attractive urban environment would promote sympathetic feelings of civic loyalty and pride[167] Architectural artworks such as domes, fountains, and statuary were seen as means to beautify the city "not merely in appearance, but in that higher sense . . . that demands the devotion, loyalty, and pride of its citizens."[168] By 1905, over 2,400 improvement societies existed across the United States.[169] The city planning movement complemented the city beautification movement. What city beautification attempted through domes, statuary, and fountains, the city planning movement would accomplish through monuments and public buildings.[170] As one advocate stated, "A proper city plan has a powerful influence for good upon the mental and moral development of the people."[171] City planners believed that creating a visual and aesthetic harmony—through the imposition of a rationally ordered city design—would actively contribute toward the development of a harmonious social order among its residents.[172]

Summary

There are a couple of elements of the environmentalist movement shared by the two previous movements discussed. One was the emphasis placed upon the interaction of individuals from different economic classes. This interaction was seen as an important dynamic in fostering the spiritual communion so desperately sought in the Premodern Discourse. While the development of spiritual communion was given a highly secular face—explicated in terms such as democratic spirit, community spirit, or civic unity—its goal was the same: integration of individuals on a transcendental level.

Another common feature is the importance placed upon the environment in shaping one's behavior and moral character. Yet it is in this area as well that the environmentalist movement differed markedly from previous movements. Environmentalists saw society as responsible for creating the unwholesome environments in which the poor lived. Thus, the poor were no longer blamed for creating their condition of poverty. The measuring of deviance consequently shifted from the individual to the environment—as represented by the social survey, city planning documents, and city improvement measures. With the environment being seen as causally connected to promoting spiritual communion among society's members, efforts naturally were directed toward creating a proper and wholesome environment for this to occur.[j]

This subtle influence of environment in directing one toward knowledge of the Good briefly opened up a prominent space for knowledge of the Beautiful. Whether it manifested itself within arts and recreation programs, communing with nature, or physical artworks and architecture—knowledge of the Beautiful was seen as leading one directly to knowledge of the Good. Such an intimate connection between knowledge of the Beautiful and knowledge of the Good would not survive the coming shift into the Modern Discourse; consequently, knowledge of the Beautiful, shortly, would once again fall within the dominant Discourse's darkened spaces when it came to advancing social welfare.

c. 1880–1920: A Discourse in Transition

In these days of specialization, when we train our cooks, our apothecaries, our engineers, our librarians, our nurses,—when, in fact, there is a training school for almost every form of skilled service,— we have yet to establish our first training school for charity workers, or, as I prefer to call it, "Training School in Applied Philanthropy."

—Mary Richmond, 1898[173]

Scientific thought would play a minor role in influencing the Premodern Discourse on social welfare; the social scientific disciplines would not arise until the latter part of the nineteenth century. Scientific thought, in the form of specialized knowledge, would dominate the coming Modern Discourse of the twentieth century. Yet, similar to the transition period between the Colonial Discourse and the Premodern Discourse, the Premodern Discourse attempted to co-opt the major insight being articulated by its succeeding Discourse: the Modern Discourse. As enumerated in Chapter 3, the transition period at the end of the Colonial Discourse resulted in an attempt to apply the concept of democratic *equality*, which resulted in its very watered-down application in establishing democratic governance. The key insight being offered by the emerging Modern discourse was that of *science* and its role in knowledge building. However, as was the case with the colonial transition period, attempts to apply this new insight— in this case scientific investigation—were by default done through the lens of

---

[j] The most extreme example of this notion in operation is provided by the various communitarian movements described in Chapter 4, such as Brooks Farm, which became popular in the latter half of the nineteenth century.

the Premodern Discourse, a Discourse from which this insight did not originate, and hence resulted in a very watered-down version in its application.

Scientific Charity and the Social Survey

One approach that attempted to employ the insights of scientific investigation was that of the scientific charity movement employed by the COS at the end of the nineteenth century. The scientific charity movement spawned the casework method: a systematic, organized means in which to collect empirical information on the lives of the clients being served. This information was then used to advance the aims of moral instruction, which COS workers viewed as the primary remedy for eliminating poverty. As noted earlier, the COS of this period adopted the slogan "not alms but a friend [providing moral instruction]" as their main conceptual model directing their interventions. Thus, this systematic data was used to prevent individuals from "double dipping," thus enabling them to more efficiently disburse the alms that they decided to give. This systematic data was also used to separate the worthy from the unworthy poor: Through the eyes of COS workers both groups were in need of moral instruction; however, efforts in this vein for the latter group would actually be undermined if alms were disbursed.

The other attempt to apply the key insights concerning scientific investigation was the use of the social survey. The survey gained its greatest prominence during the progressive era.[174] Conducted by settlement house workers and other urban reform leaders,[175] observations were turned toward documenting unsanitary and harmful conditions existing in the poor neighborhoods. Thus, the social survey consisted of the collection and statistical organization of empirical observations concerning deviance from a sought-after ideal. This systematic data was then employed to advance efforts at moral reform aimed at improving conditions in the environment. This hard data was used to buttress the weight of their arguments for legislative change when lobbying elected officials.[k]

Rationalism over Empiricism

The social survey and the casework method of investigation were noteworthy for two reasons. First, for all practical purposes these were research endeavors that were unique to social work—no other disciplines seriously conducted this type of research.[176] Second, neither would survive the shift into the Modern Discourse

---

[k] Zimbalist, *Historic Themes*, 129. Zimbalist notes that the primary emphasis of the social survey was to "bring about change, rather than obtain answers," making the process "closer to education or crusading or propagandizing than it is to research."

that would occur during the twentieth century. The social survey would die out as a research methodology altogether.[177] The casework method of investigation would survive the transition to the Modern Discourse, but it would considerably evolve from its simple origins within the scientific charity movement.

So the question becomes, "How do the social survey and the casework method of investigation employed by these early social workers represent a watering down of insights concerning the role of scientific investigation?" The key insight lost upon the social workers of this Premodern Era was the ability of scientific investigation to test hypotheses, and hence assess truth claims. The scientific method consists of three broad steps: obtaining empirical observations, forming a hypothesis based upon these observations, and then testing the hypothesis through some type of experiment. The COS casework method and the social survey only employed the first of these three steps: the systematic gathering of empirical observations.

The Premodern Discourse these social workers lived within prevented them from seeing the relevance or importance of the final two steps of the scientific method. Understanding this Premodern Discourse yields insights as to why this was so. As discussed in Chapter 4, the Premodern Discourse was heavily embedded in rationalism for its understanding of truth. Within rationalism, empirical observations represent a lesser form of knowledge; empirical knowledge is viewed as less trustworthy than rational insight and carries within it the potential to mislead one from the truth. Such an understanding blocked these social workers from ever being able to fully exploit the power of scientific investigation. This dynamic mirrors that which occurred with our founding fathers' inability to fully exploit the power of democracy due to filtering Enlightenment insight on equality through their understanding of the importance of maintaining the social hierarchy.

As we will see in the next chapter, scientific investigation would come to dominate the social work landscape in the Modern Discourse. Within the Modern Discourse, research is still used to aid efforts at advocacy; however, it lends it weight through the truth claims it is able to assert. Similar to casework, social workers do not simply stop short after data collection and use it to aid a predetermined intervention. Rather, caseworkers form an assessment (i.e., hypothesis) based upon the data they collect, with the intervention to be employed arising from this assessment (i.e., testing one's hypothesis).

Moral Blind Spots in the Premodern Discourse

Since the main feature of a dominant Discourse is to privilege some types of knowledge over others, as was elaborated in Chapter 3 regarding the Colonial

Discourse, we can envision the dominant Discourse as casting a shadow—creating darkened spaces wherein lie moral blind spots. For the Premodern Discourse, the notion of measuring deviance from an ideal looms large, and hence correspondingly casts a huge shadow over this era. The thing about measuring deviance is that one needs a reference point from which to do so: In this case, it is a clear conceptualization of what comprises the ideal. While the end result of avoiding poverty, criminal activity, and mental instability was taken as an indication that a person was properly employing their ability to reason, the fact that these social ills existed in society illustrated that many people were not. Consequently, an effort was made to enumerate the qualities of those succeeding at avoiding these social ills. Most of those avoiding poverty naturally came from the dominant cultural group as this dominance best positioned them to succeed economically. Therefore, the ideal came to embody the various cultural features of the dominant cultural group: White, middle class, male, Anglo-Saxon, Protestant, and heterosexual. This left the door open for the continued oppression of women, homosexuals, and the various racial, religious, and ethnic minorities. The more one deviated from matching the characteristics of the dominant group, the greater the oppression that was visited upon the individual.

At one end of the spectrum fall groups such as European immigrants from Germany, Ireland, Italy, etc. They were not Anglo-Saxon, and most were not Protestant. Thus, males from these groups only deviated from the ideal in one or two areas. This minor deviance was still sufficient to spawn nativist movements such as the Know Nothing Party, which sought to severely restrict immigration, exclude foreign-born individuals from voting or holding public office, and require twenty-one years of residency before qualifying for citizenship.[178] Fortunately, provisions such as these were never codified into law. However, oppression still was visited upon these groups via the informal channels of society acting to restrict their participation and inclusion at various levels: socially (Protestant preachers discouraged intermarriage between Protestants and Catholics and often refused to marry couples who broached this prohibition),[179] economically (through blatant discrimination in hiring practices, most visibly reflected by the frequent inclusion of the phrase "no Irish need apply" in job advertisements),[180] and politically (opportunities to hold public office were often restricted to the local level where these groups comprised a majority of the voters). In addition, violence was periodically visited upon these groups in the form of anti-Catholic riots—such as that which occurred in Philadelphia in 1844 resulting in sixteen dead and over forty buildings being demolished[181]—or through terror campaigns by the Ku Klux Klan, most prominently in the 1920s and 1930s.[182]

At the other end of the spectrum were groups such as the Native Americans; they were neither White, Anglo-Saxon, nor Protestant. The various forms of

oppression and violence visited upon Native Americans are too numerous to catalog fully here: a few examples include the brutal massacres and confiscation of
lands, forced internment on reservations, and forced acculturation through the
removal of children from families so that they could be educated in boarding
schools.

Deviance from the ideal categories of race, gender, and sexual orientation
carried with it the strongest backlash. As with the Native Americans, the forms
of oppression and violence visited upon these groups are too numerous to fully
catalog. With sexual orientation being viewed as comprising moral behavior, homosexuality was criminalized well into the twentieth century; the only remedy
open to such individuals was to hide their status and attempt to pass as heterosexual. Fueled by the misappropriation of Darwin's theory of evolution, deviance
in terms of either race or one's biological sex—as both were seen as inherited
characteristics—consigned racial minorities and women to have their deviance
viewed as indicative of a biologically determined inferior status. Such thinking
would serve to spawn the eugenics movement in the United States and give
rise to such organizations as the Ku Klux Klan. It also resulted in various forms
of institutionalized oppression, such as the Supreme Court's ruling in *Plessy
v. Ferguson* enshrining racial discrimination into law by offering a warped interpretation of the notion of equality through the idea of "separate but equal."
This inferior status led to severe restrictions to participation and inclusion in
society: economically (through very limited available career paths, difficulty in
obtaining loans, etc.), socially (through anti-miscegenation laws prohibiting interracial marriage, the various forms of segregation in the South, etc.), and politically (through the inability to seriously be considered for elected office, in the
case of racial minorities—particularly African Americans—outright voter suppression, etc.).

In addition, extreme forms of violence would be visited upon these groups
with very little or no punishment of the perpetrators. Throughout much of
the nineteenth century husbands had the ability to involuntarily commit their
wives to a mental institution. Domestic violence against one's wife was legal in
some states up until 1920, and even afterward, little in the way of punishment
was given to perpetrators. Lynching was technically illegal but still occurred
with frightening regularity, especially in the South. And racial riots periodically
occurred, resulting in multiple deaths, the most extreme being the Colfax riot of
1873 which resulted in the murder of approximately 150 African Americans.[183]
Again, perpetrators of these various lynchings and mass murders notoriously
escaped justice with regularity. Hate crimes resulting in the death of LGBTQ+
individuals occurred with disturbing regularity throughout the nineteenth and
well into the twentieth centuries, again with perpetrators often escaping justice or facing minimal consequences—illustrated most notably in 1978 by the

"twinkie defense" employed by lawyers of Dan White, who was being tried for the murder of Harvey Milk, an openly gay elected official.[184] Only recently have perpetrators of these hate crimes begun receiving the full measure of justice.

It would become the task of the Modern Discourse in the twentieth century to begin turning the abstract ideal of equality into a functioning reality in society. The lengthy struggle of the various civil right movements born in the Modern Era would act as a shining light slowly causing this shadow to recede. And as was the case with the suffrage movement's elucidation of democracy extending to the very end of the Premodern Era with women not being granted the right to vote until 1920, we can point to the significant progress the United States has made in terms of civil rights while still recognizing that there is much left to do.

Reflections

When encountering the social welfare practices of colonial America in Chapters 2 and 3, the historical distance separating these practices from those of today made them appear bizarre and somewhat barbaric upon first glance. Consequently, this offered an excellent educational opportunity for social workers to practice applying the concept of cultural humility when encountering strange behaviors. This same educational opportunity exists when studying social welfare in the Premodern Era and should be exploited.

However, another educational opportunity arises as well. Due to the Premodern Era being distinct from our present Modern Era, the historical distance is still great enough to create a safe space for social workers to critically examine these practices in such a way that any weaknesses or flaws revealed do not act as an indictment against themselves. Yet at the same time, being only once removed from our present era, the closeness in historical distance allows for similarities to be discovered from which parallels can be drawn to present practices engaged in by social workers. The insights being drawn from the critical examination of the Premodern Era thus serve as a starting point from which to begin the challenging journey of examining current biases, flaws, and moral blind spots in one's efforts to serve clients.

Not Alms but a Friend: A Case Study

Critical examination of scientific charity's notion of "not alms but a friend" offers an excellent opportunity for creating such a starting point. The COS of the late 1800s are commonly recognized as one of the two main springs from which modern social work arose (the second being the settlement house movement). As mentioned, social workers today continue to employ the casework method, albeit at a more sophisticated and scientific level. Thus, the basis of similarity is there from which to take insights drawn from the critical examination of casework employed as "not alms but a friend" and apply them to casework as it is practiced today.

Good Intentions

The major flaws and potential to do harm to the client through employing "not alms but a friend" as one's planned intervention are readily apparent when viewed from the vantage of our present era. Interventions easily devolved into simple proselytizing, and undue suffering was visited upon clients when material aid was either delayed or denied, all in the name of helping the client. Now these COS workers, while plagued by the various cultural and class biases of the time, can be assumed to have possessed good intentions. As is the case with charity work today, an individual volunteers due to a desire to help other people and give back to the community. So the first insight to arise from this critical examination of "not alms but a friend" is that good intentions, by themselves, are not sufficient to ensure good practice and the avoidance of visiting harm upon the client. While such an insight should come as no surprise to most social workers, it is nonetheless an important one to recognize. We cannot allow ourselves to be lulled into complacency by our good intentions into believing that, just because we are there to help the client, in fact we will indeed help the client rather than causing harm. We must remain constantly vigilant against becoming unwitting accomplices in abetting social control elements to oppress those who deviate from expected behavior. Such vigilance challenges us to bring more than merely good intentions to the helping situation.

Expertise

The response to this challenge was the recognition that, in addition to bringing good intentions, one must bring some form of expertise. Through understanding the Premodern Discourse, we can determine that social welfare agents of this era viewed their expertise—and thus their authority base for intervening—as arising from their moral knowledge. As their status as an economically successful and morally upstanding citizen testified to the fact that they possessed this moral expertise, no further extensive training was deemed necessary. Yet, despite being armed with both expertise and good intentions, through adopting "not alms but a friend" as their approach, COS workers still visited harm upon some of the clients they served.

In the present day, social workers base their authority for intervening upon a scientific understanding of human behavior; thus, expertise in this scientific knowledge arises from being professionally trained. Does this professional expertise based upon scientific knowledge somehow shed the pitfalls of social control inherent in employing moral expertise? I and many others would argue that it does not, and as social workers we need to be further vigilant and challenge ourselves even more. Some common elements to expertise are found in both moral expertise and scientific expertise. Expertise is derived from some type of authority base; hence, social workers are vested with this authority when they bring their expertise to the helping situation. This is what makes them ably qualified to intervene as opposed to someone just off the street. Yet, unless clients have been professionally trained themselves, they lack such authority in the helping situation when determining the direction of treatment. This power imbalance opens the door for the social worker to potentially impose their understanding of the helping situation upon the client. In fact, one's expertise acts as a siren's call luring one down this path—as it promises that your understanding is in fact the correct understanding of the helping situation.

We can easily imagine that there were some clients being served by COS workers who falsely responded favorably to the COS workers' ministrations on the value of thrift and temperance while they were visiting. Yet, once these COS workers left, these clients—seeing little or no relevance of these ministrations to their current situation—simply continued on with their lives as before. In essence, they were simply telling the COS workers what they wanted to hear. This is not to say that all clients did this. It is conceivable that some clients responded well to the "tough love" approach being offered by COS workers. Yet it is more than reasonable to assume (and made easily apparent by the distant vantage offered by our present times) that some, if not many, clients viewed the ministrations being offered by COS workers as overly coercive and nothing more than proselytizing.

It is not an uncommon experience of social workers practicing today to find themselves with a client who is resistant in some measure to the treatment plan being offered. For those clients who agree to the plan anyway, can social workers be confident and rest assured that such clients are not simply telling them what they want to hear? While employing expertise helps one to avoid the pitfall of ignorance that accompanies interventions based solely upon good intentions, the insight to be drawn from here is that expertise carries within it pitfalls of its own. Hence, to maintain vigilance against unwittingly visiting harm upon the client, social workers must challenge themselves to bring more than just good intentions and expertise to the helping situation. In the twentieth century, the social work profession responded to this challenge through the creation of a strong and vibrant code of ethics; it is understood that the application of social work values serves to keep our expertise from running amok and visiting harm upon the client. This is the area wherein most social workers today have been trained: that when we bring to the helping situation our good intentions, our well-honed expertise, and a strong commitment to social work values, good practice will follow. But are these three qualities enough to completely avoid the pitfall of exerting social control?

The Relativity of Absolute Morals

While the COS of the nineteenth century did not possess ethical guidelines in codified form, it is not unreasonable to assume that such guidelines existed. The very fact that they based their expertise in moral knowledge would lead one to assume that values played a significant part in guiding their actions. Yet, as is made clear from our present vantage, COS workers—even when armed with good intentions, solid expertise, and firm values to guide their actions—still developed an approach such as "not alms but a friend" which most surely visited harm upon some clients. So the question becomes, "How may the application of values lead one astray?" The answer to this question, I believe, lies in understanding the notion of what I like to describe as the relativity of absolute morals.

To be absolute, the moral needs to be timeless. No matter what the context or time period, the rightness and goodness of the moral shines brightly, acting as a guiding star in directing one's actions. Within social work, examples of such values are as follows: empowerment, respecting the dignity and worth of the individual, and self-determination, to name but a few. Such values are defining features of social work; no matter what the time period, it is impossible to conceive of social welfare agents embracing the opposite of these values to guide their actions. So, for example, even though the word *empowerment* may not have existed during the Colonial Era, social welfare agents sought to promote the self-sufficiency of those they helped through providing the necessary support and skill training. It is antithetical to conceive of a social welfare agent who actively seeks to disempower those they are purported to serve. So, for example, even within the context of forcibly committing someone to a behavioral health hospital over concerns for harm to self or others, this action is guided by the understanding that in doing so the client will become stabilized and will be receiving aid and services aimed at arming them with the awareness and the tools to achieve and maintain healthy functioning into the future. Thus, it is understood that the temporary sacrifice of the client's freedom sets the table for empowering the individual to succeed on their own.

The relativity of such absolute values such as empowerment arises from the various contexts within which they are applied. Let's now turn back to the context of poverty relief in the late 1800s. COS workers adopted the practice "not alms but a friend" as their form of intervention. Through one's understanding of the Premodern Discourse, it is possible to conceive that COS workers drew their inspiration for fostering empowerment from sources such as the common biblically inspired proverb of teaching a person to fish: "Give a man a fish and you feed him for a day. Teach a man how to fish and you feed him for a lifetime." Teaching a person to fish is definitely the more empowering approach. Applying this understanding to their situation, COS workers would have viewed their efforts at moral counseling as equivalent to teaching a person to fish, and thus fostering empowerment. Moral counseling was seen as educating the client in moral reasoning and was undertaken due to the understanding that lacking such moral reasoning was the underlying cause of poverty.

The COS position against indiscriminate almsgiving (i.e., merely giving a person a fish) is well documented. And whether or not leaders of the movement drew inspiration from this particular proverb, they clearly viewed their approach as fostering empowerment—likening "not alms but a friend" metaphorically as acting as God's hand in "lifting up the poor and helpless out of the gutter."[185] Continuing this metaphor further, during their early rivalry with the settlement house movement (whose many activities closely match our present understanding of empowerment), COS workers derided the efforts of settlement house workers to help the poor as choosing to sit down in the gutter with them[186]— thus merely offering consolation rather than empowerment.

So clearly, despite coming with good intentions, being armed with expertise, and applying the social work value of empowerment, COS workers still managed to visit harm upon the clients they served. I am arguing not that COS workers' efforts did not achieve any good whatsoever but, rather, that in their efforts to do good they unwittingly visited harm upon the client. This insight should give present social workers pause as it indicates that even when we bring our good intentions, expertise, and social work values to the helping situation, we still face the pitfall of unwittingly visiting harm upon the client.

How is it that settlement house workers mostly avoided this pitfall, whereas COS workers predominantly fell into it? I would argue that it is because the COS workers ran afoul of a major moral blind spot cast by the Premodern Discourse. In so doing, they hubristically attributed undue importance to their expertise and operated under a warped understanding of empowerment. This leads us to the final insight to be drawn from examining the practice of "not alms but a friend," that in order to avoid the pitfall of becoming an unwitting accomplice to the social control elements in society, social workers must bring a critical consciousness to the helping situation in the form of cultural humility, a critical consciousness arising from an awareness that moral blind spots exist within the dominant Discourse shaping our present understanding of social work. One such aspect entailing a critical consciousness is illustrated next: the examination of power.

Social Control

In the twentieth century, the adoption of professional expertise based within scientific knowledge did not rid the social work profession of this pitfall to potentially act as an unwitting agent for societal forces of social control; the tendency for unsuspecting social workers to get trapped by this pitfall is a common critique offered by many social work academics over the years.[187] The Modern Discourse—which we will turn to in the next chapter—casts darkened spaces of its own making, which hides its own share of pitfalls. The propensity to inadvertently act as a social control agent is one such pitfall.

One aspect to employing a critical consciousness to avoid such a pitfall is vigilance in the examination of power operating in the helping relationship. As noted earlier, there is typically a power imbalance that exists between the client and the social worker. Expertise is what positions the social worker as being qualified to enter the helping situation. This expertise that a social worker brings to the helping situation derives from a base of authority; in our present era, this authority base is that of scientific understanding which a social worker gains through undergoing a rigorous program of study leading to a degree and then, when combined with experience, possibly some form of licensure. Hence, social workers are vested with the power of this authority, while the clients with whom they work are not.

Social workers employ their expertise to gain an understanding of the helping situation; they use it to evaluate what is problematic behavior, what the causes might be of this behavior, and possible remedies for moving toward more healthy or positive behavior. Social workers today move from being agents of social change and cross into the territory of being agents of social control when they begin to impose their scientific understanding of the helping situation upon the client. The siren's call of scientific expertise is that it is based in evidence, and thus gives the social worker a privileged view into the truth of the helping situation: In short, we begin to view our scientific understanding as scientific fact. Consequently, we assume an air of superiority in determining the parameters of the helping situation.

Turning back to the examples of the COS and settlement house workers, we can see perhaps how such a line is crossed from social change to social control. Both COS workers and settlement house workers brought moral expertise to bear on their understanding of the helping situation. However, settlement house workers (while not achieving a perfect track record) for the most part were able to avoid the pitfall of becoming an agent for social control. Adopting a stance of cultural humility, they entered into a more cooperative stance toward the client when determining the parameters of the helping situation. On the other hand, for COS workers, their moral expertise transformed into moral superiority as they sought to impose their understanding of the helping situation upon the clients they served.

A similar dynamic occurs today regarding social workers' employment of scientific expertise. Scientific expertise can be effectively employed in efforts at social change when the social worker adopts a cooperative stance with the client when determining the parameters of the helping situation. When we quickly jump to evaluating the situation based upon our scientific understanding, scientific expertise transforms into scientific superiority, and social control then ensues. However, social workers have tools at their disposal to aid them in maintaining an awareness of where lies this line demarcating the boundary into social control.

One such tool is that of cultural humility, as elaborated upon in Chapter 3. Cultural humility teaches us to pause in our rush to evaluate and dissect strange behavior. It encourages us to first attempt to "step into the shoes" of the client and try to understand how this strange behavior may make sense to them. Then, rather than seeking to impose our scientific understanding as the "truth" of the situation, we enter into a dialogue with the client to which we bring our scientific understanding. One's cultural humility (in this case, humility regarding our professional culture) encourages one to make this dialogue into a cooperative endeavor, an endeavor that captures the spirit of a Socratic dialogue. In a Socratic dialogue, while one brings one's knowledge and experience into the dialogue, one adopts a stance of "not knowing": that one does not already know the answer to the question being posed (e.g., "What is the problematic behavior?" or "What is the best remedy?"). Working answers to one's questions arise through this process of engaging in an honest dialogue with the client. Thus, rather than employing one's scientific understanding to impose a scientific truth onto the helping situation, one employs one's scientific understanding within a Socratic dialogue in order to arrive at a philosophical truth of the helping situation. This and other tools that aid one in bringing a critical consciousness to the helping situation will be elaborated upon more fully in the chapters to follow.

Notes

1. Beecher, *The Autobiography*, v. 1 85–91; Purcell, *Connecticut in Transition*, 182.
2. Krout, *The Origins of Prohibition*, 87; Beecher, v. 1 192, 194, 255.
3. Wade, *The Urban Frontier*, 220; Handy, *A Christian America*, 57–58; Heale, "Patterns of Benevolence," 334–36.
4. Handy, 45; Cole, *The Social Ideas*, 100.
5. Beecher, *The Autobiography*, v. 2 107–08; Boyer, *Urban Masses*, 14.
6. Cole, *The Social Ideas*, 125–29; Melder, "Ladies Bountiful," 245; Smith-Rosenberg, *Religion and the Rise*, 562–84.
7. Wade, *The Urban Frontier*, 145; Boyer, *Urban Masses*, 83.
8. Wade, 145; Boyer, 83.
9. Thompson, "The Printing and Publishing," 84–85; Boyer, 25.
10. Boyer, 29.
11. Boyer, 30.

12. Thompson, "The Printing and Publishing," 83, 90–97, 102–06.
13. Thompson, 83, 90–97, 102–06; Melder, "Ladies Bountiful," 236; Smith-Rosenberg, *Religion and the Rise*, 79–83.
14. Thompson, 83, 90–97, 102–06; Melder, 236; Smith-Rosenberg, 79–83.
15. Thompson, 83, 90–97, 102–06; Melder, 236; Smith-Rosenberg, 79–83.
16. Thompson, 83, 90–97, 102–06; Melder, 236; Smith-Rosenberg, 79–83.
17. Rice, *The Sunday-School Movement*, 66; Boyer, *Urban Masses*, 34.
18. Rice, 66; Boyer, 34.
19. Boyer, 43–53.
20. Tyng, *Forty Years' Experience*, 60; Boyer, 306.
21. Channing, *A Students' History*, 361–62; Boyer, 51.
22. Boyer, 45.
23. Boyer, 83.
24. Boyer, 133.
25. Coll, "The Baltimore Society"; Mohl, "Humanitarianism in the Preindustrial"; Heale, "The New York Society."
26. Lubove, "The New York Association," 308; Boyer, *Urban Masses*, 88.
27. Lubove, 313; Boyer, 88–89.
28. Boyer, 86.
29. Chapin, *Moral Aspects*, 18, 146–47; Boyer, 317–18; Griscom, *The Sanitary Condition*, 23.
30. Mohl, "Humanitarianism in the Preindustrial," 583; Trattner, *From Poor Law*, 52–55, 63.
31. Mohl, 583; Boyer, *Urban Masses*, 90.
32. Mohl, 583; Boyer, 90.
33. Watson, *The Charity Organization*, 84; Boyer, 90.
34. Boyer, 318.
35. Becker, "The Visitor," 385; Boyer, 91.
36. Boyer, 91.
37. Watson *The Charity Organization*, 218.
38. Richmond, *Social Diagnosis*; Sheffield, *The Social Case History*, 5–18.
39. Boyer, *Urban Masses*, 146–47; Trattner, *From Poor Law*, 89–90.
40. Boyer, 151–52; Richmond, *Friendly Visiting*, 179–95.
41. Richmond, 9, 45, 47, 73, 86, 109; Sennet, *Families Against the City*, 42–43, 237.
42. Richmond, 45.
43. Oliphant and Saricks, "Baptists and Other," 132; Boyer, *Urban Masses*, 134.
44. Clark, *Leavening the Nation*, 267–68; Abell, *The Urban Impact*, 35–43; Davis, *Immigrants, Baptists*, 97–112.
45. Calkins, *Substitutes for the Saloon*, 128; Abell, 151–61; Weeks, "Oscar C. McCulloch."
46. Abell, 118–35; Wisbey, *Soldiers Without Swords*, 1–31.
47. Quandt, *From Small Town*, 1, 23–24.
48. Odegard, *Pressure Politics*, 30–32, 181–218; Pivar, *Purity Crusade*, 18, 32, 83–85.
49. Stewart, *A Half Century*, 50–102; Burnett, *Five for Freedom*, 45–57; Herbert, *The Abolition Crusade*, 22–48.
50. Axinn and Levin, *Social Welfare*, 126–28; Zimbalist, *Historic Themes*, 123–26; Storrs, *Civilizing Capitalism*, 2–7.

51. McKelvey, *American Prisons*, 16–21, 29–33; Rothman, *Discovery of the Asylum*, 80–81, 130, 180.

52. Rothman, xxxiv.

53. Dr. Charles Caldwell (1833) as quoted in Lewis, *Development of American Prisons*, 200; George Combe (1863) as quoted in Lewis, 199; McKelvey, *American Prisons*, 61.

54. Rothman, *Discovery of the Asylum*, 65.

55. Inspectors of Eastern State Penitentiary (c. 1830) as quoted in Rothman, 72.

56. Gerrish Barrett (1837) as quoted in Lewis, *Development of American Prisons*, 184–85; George Combe (1863) as quoted in Lewis, 199; Rothman, 76.

57. Gershom Powers (1828) as quoted in Lewis, 103; Chas. Robbins (1843) as quoted in Lewis, 169; Brinkerhoff, "The Convict Contract," 110–11.

58. Gershom Powers (1829) as quoted in Lewis, 114–15; Lewis, 85–86; Rothman, *Discovery of the Asylum*, 97.

59. Lewis, 77–129; McKelvey, *American Prisons*, 8–12; Rothman, 82.

60. Lewis, 118–29; McKelvey, 8–12.

61. Lewis, 77–106; McKelvey, 8–12; Lewis, *From Newgate to Dannemora*, 81–110.

62. Prison Discipline Society of Boston (1826) as quoted in Lewis, *Development of American Prisons*, 87; Dorothea Dix (1845) as quoted in Lewis, 171.

63. Samuel Hopkins (1830) as quoted in Lewis, 114; Captain Basil Hall (1829) as quoted in Lewis, 116; McKelvey, *American Prisons*, 42.

64. Judge Walworth (1826) as quoted in Lewis, 93; Dorothea Dix (1845) as quoted in Lewis, 98; Wines and Dwight (1867) as cited in McKelvey, 39.

65. Prison Discipline Society of Boston (1826) as quoted in Lewis, 87; McKelvey, 9–10, 38–39.

66. Gustave de Beaumont and Alexis de Tocqueville (1832) as quoted in Lewis, 231; Dorothea Dix (1845) as quoted in Lewis, 203; McKelvey, 10.

67. Shaler-Wharton-King (1827) as quoted in Lewis, 122; George Combe (1863) as quoted in Lewis, 220; Brinkerhoff, "The Convict Contract," 106–09; Lewis, 85.

68. Quincy (1822) in Pumphrey and Pumphrey, *The Heritage of American*, 67; Johnson, *The Almshouse*, 49; Gillin, *Poverty and Dependency*, 46–47.

69. Quincy (1822) in Pumphrey and Pumphrey, 67.

70. Johnson, *The Almshouse*, 5–6; Rothman, *Discovery of the Asylum*, 156–61.

71. Quincy (1821) in Pumphrey and Pumphrey, *The Heritage of American*, 65–66; Johnson, 3.

72. Gillan, *Poverty and Dependency*, 184–85.

73. Rothman, *Discovery of the Asylum*, 187–89.

74. Johnson, *The Almshouse*, 5, 60–61, 69–72; Rothman, 188–93.

75. Rothman, 293–94.

76. Johnson, *The Almshouse*, 5–6; Gillan, *Poverty and Dependency*, 172–77.

77. Dain, *Concepts of Insanity*, 84–86; Rothman, *Discovery of the Asylum*, 114–15.

78. Dain, 88–90; Rothman, 115, 119.

79. Dain, 95–97; Rothman, 121, 125.

80. Dix, "Memorial," 16; Rothman, 137–39.

81. Kirkbride *On the Construction*, 17–18; Deutsch, *The Mentally Ill*, 186–87.

82. Rothman, *Discovery of the Asylum*, 143; Kirkbride, 282–87.

83. Kirkbride, 271–82; Dain, *Concepts of Insanity*, 117.

84. Kirkbride, 254–56; Deutsch, *The Mentally Ill*, 213–28; Dain, 122–24.

85. Dix, "Memorial," 20–22; Kirkbride, 269–72; Dain, 117.

86. Dudley, "Saving the Children," 112–13; Folks, *The Care of Destitute*, 84–85.

87. Folks, 72–78; Thurston, *The Dependent Child*, 40.

88. Merill, "State Public Schools," 211; Thurston, 46–50.

89. Boston Children's Friend Society (1851) as quoted in Rothman, *Discovery of the Asylum*, 210.

90. Pickett, *House of Refuge*, 103–09.

91. Pickett, 175–76; Rothman, *Discovery of the Asylum*, 221–24.

92. Hastings (1843) as quoted in Rothman, 212.

93. Pickett, *House of Refuge*, 68–69; Rothman, 231.

94. Rothman, 216.

95. Folks, *The Care of Destitute*, 227; Pickett, *House of Refuge*, 123–24.

96. Evans, "Statement from the Trustees," 227–50; Pickett, 121–23.

97. Folks, *The Care of Destitute*, 39–42; Pickett, 126–27.

98. Rothman, *Discovery of the Asylum*, 227; Gillan, *Poverty and Dependency*, 173.

99. Kirkbride *On the Construction*, 293–94; Rothman, 204–05, 265–68, 285–87.

100. Deutsch, *The Mentally Ill*, 158–85; Lightner, *Asylum, Prison, and Poorhouse*, 109–10.

101. Deutsch, 237–38; McKelvey, *American Prisons*, 107–12.

102. McKelvey, 107–12; Deutsch, 237.

103. Johnson, *The Almshouse*, 2–3; Rothman, *Discovery of the Asylum*, 294.

104. Dudley, "Saving the Children," 99; Alden, "Non-Sectarian Endowed"; Folks, *The Care of Destitute*, 52–60, 82–86.

105. Merill, "State Public Schools," 204; Minton, "Family Life," 37–53.

106. Brace, *The Dangerous Classes*, 76–77, 223–25; Brace, "The Children's Aid Society," 24.

107. Brace, *The Dangerous Classes*, 97–113; Brace, "The Children's Aid Society," 9.

108. Brace, "The Children's Aid Society," 23–24.

109. Brace, *The Dangerous Classes*, 246–70; Brace, "The Children's Aid Society," 15–16, 23–24.

110. Brace, *The Dangerous Classes*, 97–113, 132–46; Brace, "The Children's Aid Society," 9–23.

111. Brace, "The Children's Aid Society," 8.

112. Brace, *The Dangerous Classes*, 100–01; Brace, "The Children's Aid Society," 9.

113. Brace, *The Dangerous Classes*, 100–01, 146; Brace, "The Children's Aid Society," 9.

114. Brace, "The Children's Aid Society," 12.

115. Brace, 18.

116. Brace, 23.

117. Brace, *The Dangerous Classes*, 246–70; Brace, "The Children's Aid Society," 23–26.

118. Boyer, *Urban Masses*, 102.

119. Brace, *The Dangerous Classes*, 234–35; Brace, "The Children's Aid Society," 1–3, 7–8.

120. Brace, *The Dangerous Classes*, 243; Brace, "The Children's Aid Society," 25.

121. Williamson, *The Social Worker*, 10.

122. Wade, *The Urban Frontier*, 106, 255; Horlick, *Country Boys*, 252–59.

123. Hopkins, *History of the YMCA*, 22–24; Zald, *Organizational Change*, 31.
124. Doggett, *A Brief History*, 12.
125. Hopkins, *History of the YMCA*, 44–46; Boyer, *Urban Masses*, 116–17.
126. Boyer, 118–19.
127. Morse, *An Analytical Sketch*, 49–55; Horlick, *Country Boys*, 229–31.
128. Roe (1901) as quoted in Boyer, *Urban Masses*, 117.
129. Boyer, 116.
130. Morse, *An Analytical Sketch*, 57–61; Hopkins, *History of the YMCA*, 383–84.
131. Hopkins, 22–24; Zald, *Organizational Change*, 31.
132. Williamson, *The Social Worker*, 9.
133. Fein, *Fredrick Law Olmstead*, 16; Boyer, *Urban Masses*, 238.
134. Olmstead, "Public Parks," 75.
135. Kessler (1893) as excerpted in Glaab, *The American City*, 260; Eliot (1893) as excerpted in Lubove, *The Urban Community* 167.
136. Weir, *Parks*, 1–11.
137. Weir, 1–11; Boyer, *Urban Masses*, 240.
138. Weir, 7, 11.
139. Curtis, *The Play Movement*, 15–18; Mero, *American Playgrounds*, 240.
140. Addams, "Public Recreation," 494; Lubove, *Twentieth Century Pittsburgh*, 51.
141. Riis (1903) as quoted in Lubove, *The Progressives*, 72.
142. Curtis, *The Play Movement*, 28–31; Jerome, "The Playground," 35.
143. Baker, "Expression versus Suppression," 312; Rainwater, *The Play Movement*, 232–33.
144. Woods, *The City Wilderness*, 1–9; Wald, *The House*, 1–25; Simkhovitch, *Neighborhood*, 90–103.
145. Trattner, *From Poor Law*, 158.
146. Taylor, *Chicago Commons*, 41–42; Simkhovitch, *Neighborhood*, 70; Trolander, *Professionalism and Social Change*, 21.
147. Wald, *The House*, 82–87; Taylor, 61–64; Simkhovitch, 153–54; Trolander, 8.
148. Wald, 26–43; Trattner, *From Poor Law*, 158; Trolander, 8.
149. Wade, "The Heritage from Chicago's," 414.
150. Woods, *The City Wilderness*, 273–74; Trattner, *From Poor Law*, 147, 150; Trolander, *Professionalism and Social Change*, 15, 18.
151. Addams, "The Subjective Necessity," 20.
152. Woods, "The University Settlement Idea," 65–67; Trattner, *From Poor Law*, 151; Trolander, *Professionalism and Social Change*, 17.
153. Trolander, 16.
154. Addams, "The Objective Value," 39–41; Wald, *The House*, 106–08; Trattner, *From Poor Law*, 151–52.
155. Quandt, *From Small Town*, 65.
156. Kalberg, "Commitment to Career Reform," 612; Trolander, *Professionalism and Social Change*, 16.
157. Woods, "The University Settlement Idea," 70; Taylor, *Chicago Commons*, 150–52; Zimbalist, *Historic Themes*, 121–28.
158. Addams, "The Settlement," 29–40; Taylor, 65–84; Boyer, *Urban Masses*, 156.

159. Trolander, *Professionalism and Social Change*, 16.
160. Woods, *The City Wilderness*, 275–77; Taylor, *Chicago Commons*, 125–41; Trattner, *From Poor Law*, 165; Trolander, 14.
161. Trattner, 165; Trolander, 18.
162. Ely, *The Coming City*, 72–74; Hall, *Civic Righteousness*, 4–10.
163. Patten, *The New Basis*, 214.
164. MacKaye, *The Civic Theatre*, 161–71; MacKaye, *Community Drama*, 45–47.
165. MacKaye, *The Civic Theatre*, 87.
166. Gundlach (1914) as quoted in Boyer, *Urban Masses*, 259.
167. Peterson, "The City Beautiful," 416–20; Boyer, 262.
168. Robinson, *The Improvement*, 219.
169. Peterson, "The City Beautiful," 416–17.
170. Burnham and Bennett, *Plan of Chicago*, 1–12; Moody, *What of the City*, 40–49; Hines, *Burnham of Chicago*, 175–78.
171. McAneny (1915) as quoted in Lewis, *The Planning*, 9.
172. Burnham and Bennett, *Plan of Chicago*, 111–21; Hines, *Burnham of Chicago*, 315.
173. Richmond, "The Need," 181.
174. Young, *Scientific Social Surveys*, 22; Zimbalist, *Historic Themes*, 174–75.
175. Young, 22; Zimbalist, 121.
176. Young, 34; Zimbalist, 128.
177. Eaton and Harrison, *A Bibliography*, xxvii; Zimbalist, 136–39.
178. "Know-Nothing Party."
179. *Wikipedia* "Anti-Irish Sentiment," subheading " '19th Century.' "
180. "Irish and German Immigration," 4th paragraph.
181. "Irish and German Immigration," 5th paragraph.
182. Zeitz, "When America Hated Catholics," subheading "In the Early 20th Century, the Backlash."
183. Lane, *The Day Freedom Died*.
184. Hincle, *Gayslayer*.
185. Ashworth, Untitled address, 61.
186. Davis, *Spearheads for Reform*, 20.
187. For example, Greenwood, "Social Science," 25; Taylor, "The Social Control," 18; Leonard, "Social Control," 10; Toren, *Social Work*, 96.

References

Abell, Aaron. *The Urban Impact on American Protestantism, 1865–1900*. Cambridge, MA: Harvard University Press, 1943.

Addams, Jane. "The Objective Value of a Social Settlement." In *Philanthropy and Social Progress: Seven Essays*, edited by Henry C. Adams, 27–56. New York: Thomas Y. Crowell, 1893. https://books.google.com/books?id=vTEiMYNkwioC&pg=PR3&lpg.

Addams, Jane. "The Subjective Necessity for Social Settlements." In *Philanthropy and Social Progress*, edited by Henry C. Adams, 1–26. New York: Thomas Y. Crowell, 1893. https://books.google.com/books?id=vTEiMYNkwioC&pg=PR3&lpg.

Addams, Jane. "Public Recreation and Social Morality." *Charities and Commons* 18 (1907): 492–94.

Addams, Jane. "The Settlement as a Factor in the Labor Movement." In *Readings in the Development of Settlement Work*, edited by Lorene Pacey, 57–97. New York: Association Press, 1950. First published 1895.

Alden, Lyman. "Non-Sectarian Endowed Child-Saving Institutions." In *The History of Child Saving in the United States: At the Twentieth National Conference of Charities and Correction in Chicago, June, 1893*. Report of the Committee on the History of Child-Saving Work, 68–88. Boston: Geo H. Ellis, 1893. https://books.google.com/books?id= 6KIzAQAAMAAJ&printsec=frontcover&dq#v=onepage&q&f=false.

"Anti-Irish Sentiment." Wikipedia. Accessed November 13, 2018, https://en.wikipedia. org/wiki/Anti-Irish_sentiment.

Ashworth, John. Untitled address in *Proceedings of the Friends' General Conference*, 61. Mountain Lake Park, MD, September, 1906. https://books.google.com/books?id= RYw4AQAAMAAJ.

Axinn, June, and Herman Levin. *Social Welfare: A History of the American Response to Need*. New York: Harper & Row, 1975.

Baker, Newton. "Expression versus Suppression." *Social Hygiene* 4 (1918): 310–17.

Becker, Dorothy. "The Visitor to the New York City Poor, 1843–1920." *Social Service Review* 35 (1961): 372–87.

Beecher, Lyman. *The Autobiography of Lyman Beecher*. Edited by Barbara Cross, 2 vols. Cambridge, MA: Harvard University Press, 1961.

Boyer, Paul S. *Urban Masses and Moral Order in America, 1820–1920*. Cambridge, MA: Harvard University Press, 1978.

Brace, Charles Loring. *The Dangerous Classes of New York and Twenty Years' Work among Them*. New York: Wynkoop and Hallenbeck, 1872.

Brace, Charles Loring. "The Children's Aid Society of New York: Its History, Plans, and Results." In *The History of Child Saving in the United States: At the Twentieth National Conference of Charities and Correction in Chicago, June, 1893*. Report of the Committee on the History of Child-Saving Work, 1–36. Boston: Geo H. Ellis, 1893. https:// books.google.com/books?id=6KIzAQAAMAAJ&printsec=frontcover&dq#v=onep age&q&f=false.

Brinkerhoff, "The Convict Contract"

Burnett, Constance. *Five for Freedom: Lucretia Mott, Elizabeth Cady Station, Lucy Stone, Susan B. Anthony, Carrie Chapman Catt*. New York: Greenwood Press, 1968.

Burnham, Daniel, and Edward Bennett. *Plan of Chicago*. New York: Da Capo Press, 1970. First published 1909.

Calkins, Raymond. *Substitutes for the Saloon*. Boston: Houghton-Mifflin, 1901.

Channing, Edward. *A Students' History of the United States*. New York: The Macmillan Company, 1908.

Chapin, Edwin. *Moral Aspects of City Life*. New York: Kiggins, 1843.

Clark, Joseph. *Leavening the Nation: The Story of American Home Missions*. New York: Baker and Taylor, 1903.

Cole, Charles. *The Social Ideas of the Northern Evangelists, 1826–1860*. New York: Columbia University Press, 1954.

Coll, Blanche. "The Baltimore Society for the Prevention of Pauperism, 1820–1822." *American Historical Review* 61 (1955): 77–87.

Curtis, Henry. *The Play Movement and Its Significance*. New York: Macmillan, 1917.

Dain, Norman. *Concepts of Insanity in the United States, 1789–1865*. New Brunswick, NJ: Rutgers University Press, 1964.

Davis, Allen F. *Spearheads for Reform: The Social Settlements and the Progressive Movement, 1890–1914*. New Brunswick, NJ: Rutgers University Press, 1967.

Davis, Lawrence. *Immigrants, Baptists, and the Protestant Mind in America*. Urbana: University of Illinois Press, 1973.

Deutsch, Albert. *The Mentally Ill in America: A History of Their Care and Treatment*. New York: Doubleday, Doran & Company, 1937.

Dix, Dorothea. "Memorial." In *Asylum, Prison, and Poorhouse: The Writings and Reform Work of Dorothea Dix in Illinois*, edited by David Lightner, 13–30. Carbondale: Southern Illinois University Press, 1999. First published 1847.

Doggett, Laurence L. *A Brief History of the Boston's Young Men's Christian Association*. Boston: Young Men's Christian Association, 1901. https://ia902607.us.archive.org/13/items/historyofyoungmemca00dogg/historyofyoungmemca00dogg_bw.pdf.

Dudley, Oscar. "Saving the Children: Sixteen Years' Work among the Dependent Youth of Chicago." In *The History of Child Saving in the United States: At the Twentieth National Conference of Charities and Correction in Chicago, June, 1893*. Report of the Committee on the History of Child-Saving Work, 99–115. Boston: Geo H. Ellis, 1893. https://books.google.com/books?id=6KIzAQAAMAAJ&printsec=frontcover&dq#v=onepage&q&f=false.

Eaton, Allen, and Shelby Harrison. *A Bibliography of Social Surveys*. New York: Russell Sage Foundation, 1930.

Ely, Richard. *The Coming City*. New York: T. Y. Crowell, 1902.

Evans, Glendower. "Statement from the Trustees of the State Primary and Reform Schools for Massachusetts." In *The History of Child Saving in the United States: At the Twentieth National Conference of Charities and Correction in Chicago, June, 1893*. Report of the Committee on the History of Child-Saving Work, 227–56. Boston: Geo H. Ellis, 1893. https://books.google.com/books?id=6KIzAQAAMAAJ&printsec=frontcover&dq#v=onepage&q&f=false.

Fein, Albert. *Fredrick Law Olmstead and the American Environmental Tradition*. New York: Braziller, 1972.

Folks, Homer. *The Care of Destitute, Neglected, and Delinquent Children*. New York: Johnson Reprint Corporation, 1970. First published 1900.

Gillin, Jon. *Poverty and Dependency: Their Relief and Prevention*. New York: The Century Co., 1922.

Gilman, "Catheryne Cooke Gilman."

Glaab, Charles. *The American City: A Documentary History*. Homewood, IL: Dorsey Press, 1963.

Greenwood, Ernest. "Social Science and Social Work: A Theory of Their Relationship." *Social Service Review* 29 (1955): 20–33.

Griscom, John. *The Sanitary Condition of the Laboring Population of New York, with Suggestions for Its Improvement*. New York: Harper, 1845.

Hall, Newton. *Civic Righteousness and Civic Pride*. Boston: Sherman and French, 1914.

Handy, Robert. *A Christian America: Protestant Hopes and Historical Realities*. New York: Oxford University Press, 1971.

Heale, Mathew. "The New York Society for the Prevention of Pauperism, 1817–1823." *New-York Historical Society Quarterly* 55 (1971): 153–76.

Heale, Mathew. "Patterns of Benevolence: Charity and Morality in Rural and Urban New York, 1783–1830." *Societas* 3 (1973): 339–46.

Herbert, Hilary. *The Abolition Crusade and Its Consequences: Four Periods of American History*. New York: AMS Press, 1912.

Hincle, Warren. *Gayslayer! The Story of How Dan White Killed Harvey Milk and George Moscone & Got Away with Murder*. Park City: Silver Dollar Books, 1979.

Hines, Thomas. *Burnham of Chicago: Architect and Planner*. New York: Oxford University Press, 1974.

Hopkins, C. Howard. *History of the YMCA in North America*. New York: Association Press, 1951.

Horlick, Allan. *Country Boys and Merchant Princes: The Social Control of Young Men in New York*. Lewisburg, PA: Bucknell University Press, 1975.

"Irish and German Immigration." U.S. History. Accessed November 13, 2018, http://www.ushistory.org/us/25f.asp.

Jerome, Amalia. "The Playground as a Social Center." *American City* 5 (1911): 30–36.

Johnson, Alexander. *The Almshouse: Construction and Management*. New York: Russell Sage Foundation, 1911.

Kalberg, Stephen. "Commitment to Career Reform: The Settlement House Leaders." *Social Service Review* 49 (1975): 608–28.

Kirkbride, Thomas. *On the Construction, Organization, and General Arrangements of Hospitals for the Insane*. New York: Arno Press, 1880.

"Know-Nothing Party." Encyclopaedia Britannica. Accessed May 24, 2019, https://www.britannica.com/topic/Know-Nothing-party.

Krout, John. *The Origins of Prohibition*. New York: Alfred A. Knopf, 1925.

Lane, Charles. *The Day Freedom Died: The Colfax Massacre, the Supreme Court, and the Betrayal of Reconstruction*. New York: Henry Holt and Company, 2008.

Leonard, Peter. "Social Control, Class Values and Social Practice." *Social Work* 22 (1965): 7–22.

Lewis, David. *From Newgate to Dannemora: The Rise of the Penitentiary in New York, 1796–1848*. Ithaca, NY: Cornell University Press, 1965.

Lewis, Nelson. *The Planning of the Modern City*. New York: John Wiley and Sons, 1916.

Lewis, Orlando. *The Development of American Prisons and Prison Customs, 1776–1845*. Montclair, NJ: Patterson Smith, 1967. First published 1922.

Lightner, David. *Asylum, Prison, and Poorhouse: The Writings and Reform Work of Dorothea Dix in Illinois*. Carbondale: Southern Illinois University Press, 1971.

Lubove, Roy. "The New York Association for Improving the Condition of the Poor: The Formative Years." *New-York Historical Society Quarterly* 43 (1959): 306–17.

Lubove, Roy. *The Progressives and the Slums: Tenement House Reform in New York City, 1890–1917*. Pittsburgh: University of Pittsburgh Press, 1962.

Lubove, Roy. *The Urban Community: Housing and Planning in the Progressive Era*. Englewood Cliffs, NJ: Prentice-Hall, 1967.

Lubove, Roy. *Twentieth Century Pittsburgh: Government, Business, and Environmental Change*. New York: John Wiley and Sons, 1969.

MacKaye, Percy. *The Civic Theatre in Relation to the Redemption of Leisure*. New York: Mitchell Kennerley, 1912.

MacKaye, Percy. *Community Drama: Its Motive and Method of Neighborliness*. Boston: Houghton Mifflin, 1917.

McKelvey, Blake. *American Prisons: A Study in American Social History Prior to 1915*. Chicago: University of Chicago Press, 1936.

Melder, Keith. "Ladies Bountiful: Organized Women's Benevolence in Early Nineteenth-Century America." *New York History* 48 (1967): 231–54.

Merrill, Gildea. "State Public Schools for Dependent and Neglected Children." In *The History of Child Saving in the United States: At the Twentieth National Conference of Charities and Correction in Chicago, June, 1893*. Report of the Committee on the History of Child-Saving Work, 204–26. Boston: Geo H. Ellis, 1893. https://books.google.com/books?id=6KIzAQAAMAAJ&printsec=frontcover&dq#v=onepage&q&f=false.

Mero, Everett. *American Playgrounds: Their Construction, Equipment, Maintenance and Utility*. Boston: American Gymnasia, 1908.

Minton, Sophie. "Family Life versus Institution Life." In *The History of Child Saving in the United States: At the Twentieth National Conference of Charities and Correction in Chicago, June, 1893*. Report of the Committee on the History of Child-Saving Work, 37–53. Boston: Geo H. Ellis, 1893. https://books.google.com/books?id=6KIzAQAAMAAJ&printsec=frontcover&dq#v=onepage&q&f=false.

Mohl, Raymond. "Humanitarianism in the Preindustrial City: The New York Society for the Prevention of Pauperism, 1817–1823." *Journal of American History* 57 (1970): 576–99.

Moody, Walter. *What of the City? America's Greatest Issue—City Planning*. Chicago: A. C. McClurg, 1919.

Morse, Verranus. *An Analytical Sketch of the Young Men's Christian Association in North America from 1851–1876*. New York: International Committee of Young Men's Christian Associations, 1901.

Odegard, Peter. *Pressure Politics: The Story of the Anti-Saloon League*. New York: Oxford University Press, 1928.

Oliphant, J. Orin, and Ambrose Saricks. "Baptists and Other Home Missionaries Labors in the Pacific Northwest, 1865–1890." *Pacific Northwest Quarterly* 41 (1950): 125–38.

Olmstead, Frederick. "Public Parks and the Enlargement of Towns." In *Civilizing American Cities: A Selection of Frederick Law Olmstead's Writings on City Landscapes*, edited by Stephanne Sutton, 52–100. Cambridge, MA: MIT Press, 1971.

Patten, Simon. *The New Basis of Civilization*. New York: Macmillan, 1907.

Peterson, Jon. "The City Beautiful Movement: Forgotten Origins and Lost Meanings." *Journal of Urban History* 2 (1976): 415–34.

Pickett, Robert. *House of Refuge: Origins of Juvenile Reform in New York State, 1815–1857*. Syracuse, NY: Syracuse University Press, 1969.

Pivar, David. *Purity Crusade: Sexual Morality and Social Control, 1868–1900*. Westport, CT: Greenwood Press, 1973.

Pumphrey, Ralph, and Muriel Pumphrey, eds. *The Heritage of American Social Work: Readings in Its Philosophical and Institutional Development*. New York: Columbia University Press, 1961.

Purcell, Richard. *Connecticut in Transition, 1775–1818*. Middletown, CT: Wesleyan University Press, 1963.

Quandt, Jean. *From Small Town to Great Community: The Social Thought of Progressive Intellectuals*. New Brunswick, NJ: Rutgers University Press, 1970.

Rainwater, Clarence. *The Play Movement in the United States*. Chicago: Chicago University Press, 1922.

Rice, Edwin. *The Sunday-School Movement, 1780–1917*. Philadelphia: American Sunday-School Union, 1917.

Richmond, Mary. "The Need of a Training School in Applied Philanthropy." *The Social Welfare Forum: Official Proceedings [of the] Annual Meeting* 24 (1898): 181–87. https://books.google.com/books?id=rAEpAQAAIAAJ&pg=.

Richmond, Mary. *Friendly Visiting among the Poor.* New York: Macmillan, 1916.

Richmond, Mary. *Social Diagnosis.* New York: Russell Sage Foundation, 1917.

Robinson, Charles M. *The Improvement of Towns and Cities.* New York: G. P. Putnam's Sons, 1901.

Rothman, David. *The Discovery of the Asylum: Social Order and Disorder in the New Republic.* 3rd ed. New York: Walter de Gruyter, 1971.

Sennet, Richard. *Families Against the City: Middle-Class Homes of Industrial Chicago.* New York: Vintage Books, 1947.

Sheffield, Ada. *The Social Case History: Its Construction and Content.* New York: Russell Sage Foundation, 1924.

Simkhovitch, Mary. *Neighborhood: My Story of Greenwich House.* New York: W. W. Norton, 1938.

Smith-Rosenberg, Carroll. *Religion and the Rise of the American City: The New York City Mission Movement, 1812–1870.* Ithaca, NY: Cornell University Press, 1971.

Stewart, Frank. *A Half Century of Municipal Reform: The History of the National Municipal League.* Los Angeles: University of California Press, 1950.

Storrs, Landon. *Civilizing Capitalism: The National Consumer's League, Women's Activism, and Labor Standards in the New Deal Era.* Chapel Hill: University of North Carolina Press, 2002.

Taylor, Graham. *Chicago Commons Through Forty Years.* Chicago: Chicago Commons Association, 1936.

Taylor, Robert. "The Social Control Function in Casework." *Social Casework* 1 (1958): 17–21.

Thompson, Lawrence. "The Printing and Publishing Activities of the American Tract Society from 1825 to 1850." *The Papers of the Bibliographical Society of America* 35 (1941): 83–106.

Thurston, Henry. *The Dependent Child.* New York: Columbia University Press, 1930.

Toren, Nina. *Social Work: The Case of a Semi-Profession.* Beverly Hills: Sage Publications, 1972.

Trattner, Walter I. *From Poor Law to Welfare State: A History of Social Welfare in America.* 4th ed. New York: Free Press, 1989.

Trolander, Judith A. *Professionalism and Social Change: From the Settlement House Movement to Neighborhood Centers, 1886 to the Present.* New York: Columbia University Press, 1987.

Tyng, Stephen. *Forty Years' Experience in Sunday-Schools.* New York: Sheldon, 1860.

Wade, Louise C. "The Heritage from Chicago's Early Settlement Houses." *Journal of the Illinois State Historical Society* 60 (1967): 411–41.

Wade, Richard. *The Urban Frontier: The Rise of Western Cities, 1790–1830.* Cambridge, MA: Harvard University Press, 1959.

Wald, Lillian. *The House on Henry Street.* New York: Henry Holt, 1915.

Watson, Frank. *The Charity Organization Movement in the United States.* New York: Macmillan, 1922.

Weeks, Genevieve. "Oscar C. McCulloch Transforms Plymouth Church, Indianapolis, into an 'Institutional' Church." *Indiana Magazine of History* 64 (1968): 87–108.

Weir, Lawrence H. *Parks: A Manual of Municipal and County Parks.* New York: A. S. Barnes, 1928.

Williamson, Margaretta. *The Social Worker in Group Work.* New York: Harper Brothers, 1929.

Wisbey, Herbert. *Soldiers Without Swords: A History of the Salvation Army in the United States.* New York: Macmillan, 1955.

Woods, Robert. *The City Wilderness: A Settlement Study.* Boston: Houghton Mifflin, 1899.

Woods, Robert. "The University Settlement Idea." In *Readings in the Development of Settlement Work,* edited by Lorene Pacey, 57–97. New York: Association Press, 1950. First published 1893.

Young, Pauline. *Scientific Social Surveys and Research.* 2nd ed. New York: Prentice-Hall, 1949.

Zald, Mayer. *Organizational Change: The Political Economy of the YMCA.* Chicago: University of Chicago Press, 1970.

Zeitz, Josh. "When America Hated Catholics." *PolicticoMagazine.* Last modified September, 23, 2015, https://www.politico.com/magazine/story/2015/09/when-amer ica-hated-catholics-213177.

Zimbalist, Sidney. *Historic Themes and Landmarks in Social Welfare Research.* New York: Harper & Row, 1977.

6

The Modern Discourse
(c. 1920–Present)

In 1955, Walter Friedlander offered the following definition of social welfare:

> Social Welfare is the organized system of social services and institutions, designed to aid individuals and groups to attain satisfying standards of life and health. It aims at personal and social relationships which permit individuals the development of their full capacities and promotion of their well-being in harmony with the needs of the community.[1]

In 1981, Martin and Zald offered a more streamlined definition: "Social welfare attempts to enable people in need to attain a minimum level of social and personal functioning."[2] In 1990, Popple and Leighninger gave their definition of social welfare as follows:

> For society to survive, individuals must function as interdependent units, each carrying out the full range of his or her roles and responsibilities. A society cannot survive if it contains too many individuals who cannot function in an interdependent manner (who are dependent). On the other hand, the social system cannot endure if it contains too many dysfunctional culture patterns and inefficient structures that inhibit people's ability to function in an interdependent manner.[3]

The present chapter examines the elements of the Discourse on social welfare that currently holds a position of dominance in American society—and thus is labeled as the *Modern Discourse*. Unlike the case from previous chapters, as the Modern Discourse directs present efforts of social work, there are no strange or incomprehensible practices to highlight. Rather, above I offer various definitions of social welfare that have remained remarkably consistent over the decades comprising the Modern Era. Thus, the task of this chapter in describing the elements of the Modern Discourse will be to illustrate why the above definitions of social work appear so comprehensible to our present understanding of social welfare.

A Genealogy of the Good and Critique of Hubris. Phillip Dybicz, Oxford University Press. © Oxford University Press 2023.
DOI: 10.1093/oso/9780197670071.003.0006

As described in Chapter 4, during the Premodern Era the federal government adopted a predominantly laissez-faire approach to promoting the general welfare. This would change in the twentieth century; the political, economic, and social landscapes of the Modern Era would be marked by an ever-increasing federal presence in their management, resulting in its deeper penetration into the everyday lives of its citizens. One of the prominent features of these landscapes would be their contribution toward the creation of a strong national identity and culture. This development of a strong national identity went hand in hand with the ever-greater acceptance and expectation of an increased federal presence in the promotion of the general welfare.

Conditions in Modern America

Geographic Conditions

Following the ascendancy of the Modern Discourse in social welfare in 1920, the rapid territorial expansion and geographic growth of the country slowed to a trickle as Alaska and Hawaii would be the only two states added to the Union during this era. And unlike its many European counterparts, the United States did not pursue an agenda of overseas expansion leading to the establishment of an empire—in the territorial sense. Furthermore, with the United States no longer rapidly expanding its territory, gone were the days of an open-border immigration policy—letting all who wished to enter the United States.

By 1920 as well, a vast national network of railroad lines had been established and served to link the various disparate parts of the country. Technological innovation in transportation would continue with the mass production of the automobile and the development of a commercial aviation industry; however, rather than stitching together rapidly expanding territory into a network, they would instead serve the purpose of creating a deeper penetration of this network into disparate communities by not only linking up every single community in the country but ultimately directly reaching every single citizen. This would greatly enhance the mobility of the average American.

A similar development happened in the arena of communication as well. By 1920 a vast network of telegraph lines linked the various disparate parts of the country. Yet technological innovation would continue with the creation of a vast network of telephone lines and the consequent mass marketing of the telephone. Achieving a similar deep penetration into the disparate communities across the country, this communications network would eventually lead to every single citizen being directly plugged into it. The managerial approach adopted by the federal government would extend to each of the above areas (immigration, transportation, and communication).

Population Demographics
With the disappearance of the frontier and the United States no longer rapidly expanding its territory, the demand for people to occupy and settle untapped wilderness in the United States precipitously dropped. This would deeply impact policy on immigration. Gone would be the laissez-faire open-borders policy of the Premodern Era, most notably captured by the poet Emma Lazarus' words inscribed on the base of the Statue of Liberty: "Give me your tired, your poor, Your huddled masses yearning to breathe free, The wretched refuse of your teeming shore." Rather, similar to their actions in regard to regulating the growth of transportation networks, in the Modern Era the federal government would adopt a managerial role when it came to the growth of its population via immigration. In 1921 and 1924 the federal government passed immigration acts that severely limited immigration, establishing quotas based upon national origin. The quotas for persons from eastern, central, and southern Europe were sharply restrictive, slowing immigration from these areas to a trickle, whereas immigration from Asia was stopped altogether.[4] The rationale supporting such restrictions was that they were an attempt to maintain the social cohesion of the country by preventing further dilution of the White, Protestant majority that was viewed (by this same majority) as embodying the cultural ethos of US society.[5] The intervening Great Depression and World War II would serve to exacerbate this decline. In 1924, 707,000 immigrants came to our shores; by 1929 the number had dropped to 280,000, and in 1936 it had dropped to 36,000.[6]

In 1965, Congress passed the Immigration Act, which dispensed with quotas based upon race and ethnicity. The promotion of economic development and family cohesion were given preference with new admission standards—still active to this day—which now are based upon family relationship or one's skill and occupation.[7] While immigration was being curtailed by federal regulation, the trend toward urbanization continued. By 1950 two-thirds of the population lived in urban/suburban centers; by 1970 three-quarters of the population did so.[8] By the end of the century, 80% of the population lived in urban/suburban areas (which comprise only 3% of the country's total land mass).[9] And the 20% living in rural areas no longer do so on isolated, self-sufficient farms. Thus, in our Modern Era, individuals live within a highly differentiated and interdependent economic, social, political, and cultural network that now comprises society.

Transportation
Prior to the Modern Era, the responsibility fell to local government when it came to building and maintaining roads.[10] The few paved roads that did exist

were located in cities and would stop at the city line.[11] And more than 90% of roads in the United States were simple dirt paths.[12] This led them often to degrade into a pathetic condition: turning muddy after a rain, often becoming washed out to passage after a heavy rain, becoming rutted after minimal use, and sometimes becoming overgrown as nature attempted to claim back the land.[13] In 1918 Herbert Hoover—then acting as the US food administrator—declared that approximately 50% of all farm produce in the United States failed to make it to market before spoiling; he cited the woefully unkempt roads as the chief cause.[14] Also at this time began the mass marketing of the automobile. This led to a growing clamor for the building of regional highways to promote long-distance travel; Virtually no such routes existed at the time.[15]

Propelled by the Good Roads movement established in the 1890s, the public citizenry began to view free-of-charge paved roads and highways as a public good.[16] This movement led to the passage in 1916 of the Federal-Aid Highway Act,[a] which would serve to launch the most expensive and largest public works project in human history.[17] Followed by the additional passage of major highway acts in the decades that followed (1921, 1944, and 1956), an explosive period in the building of paved roads, highways, and interstates began in 1916 and continued on uninterrupted up to 1973.[18] In the period from 1956 to 1975 alone, over 42,500 miles of paved roads, highways, and interstates were added to the nation's road network.[19] Thereafter, the federal government assumed responsibility for their maintenance, providing monies for resurfacing, restoring, and rehabilitating the road network where needed.[20]

Yet the passage of the 1916 Federal-Aid Highway Act did more than simply give the federal government primary responsibility for the funding of this public works project. It also entailed federal regulations, ensuring that the federal government would exert a strong hand in the management of the roads program. The US Bureau of Public Roads (BPR) was created; acting as an independent bureaucracy of expert engineers, the BPR managed the granting of federal aid.[21] This included a formal mandate for the states to create a highway department along the lines of a prescribed format which would administer the federal grant monies according to the technical regulations of the BPR and congressionally legislated formulas.[22] In addition, the BPR held veto power over any state maps of planned roads created by their highway departments, typically resulting in final maps that conformed to the internal maps created by the BPR staff.[23] This strong regulatory role adopted by the federal government to manage the building of public roads stood in stark contrast to the laissez-faire stance adopted in the

---

[a] Goddard, *Getting There*, 118. Thomas Harris MacDonald, chief of the Bureau of Public Roads from 1919 to 1939, grandiosely opined that only three immense road building programs occurred in all of human history: that of the Roman Empire, France during the Napoleonic era, and the current US effort.

Premodern Era of simply granting land to railroad companies when supporting railroad construction.

Accompanying the explosive growth in road building was the explosive growth of the automobile industry and the mass marketing of cars. In 1916, President Woodrow Wilson was the last elected president to arrive at his inauguration by a horse-drawn vehicle, symbolically marking the end of an era in terms of ground transportation.[24] By the time Warren G. Harding was elected president in 1920, 8 million cars (plus over a million trucks) were on the road, representing one car for every 13.3 people.[25] By the end of the twentieth century, over 220 million cars were on the road, marking one car for every 1.3 people.[26] At century's end, 90% of US households owned at least one car, with non-owning households concentrated in urban areas wherein easy access to public transportation existed by motor vehicle (e.g., bus, taxi) or by subway.[27] Clearly, the use of a motorized vehicle for ground transportation had become ubiquitous.

Whereas the railroad in the Premodern Era connected disparate communities across the country into a national network, the deeper penetration achieved by the US road network—in which a paved road literally reaches to practically every person's doorstep—serves to directly connect each individual citizen to its national network. Economic growth, technological progress, and the promotion of public health, national unity, and/or defense were all commonly cited to justify the investment in building such a vast network.[28] One example is that by the end of the twentieth century, 78% of US freight was moved by trucks and accounted for 15% of the gross national product.[29] And during its height, highway building and the various industries connected to the motor vehicle employed one out of every six workers.[30] Also, the boon that a mobile labor force confers upon a capitalist economy has long been recognized.[31]

Beyond the economic benefits arising from mobility, the automobile exerted an influence on social customs and culture.[32] The freedom that mobility confers upon each individual to travel to and from work resulted in the expansion of choice as to where to live—establishing a new type of community: the suburb. Hence, in today's mobile society, the average citizen enjoys the freedom and opportunity to work, play, and live each in separate communities. This freedom offered by the automobile and vast road system has become ingrained in American culture; throughout the decades of the Modern Era, such freedom was regularly extolled by advertisement, television shows, and popular songs.[33] A new sense of oneself as an autonomous agent arose. Whereas within the Premodern Discourse it was one's faculty of reason that positioned oneself as an autonomous agent, within the Modern Discourse mobility offers autonomy in self-expression—and, in the process, enhances one's adaptability in response to societal changes that would seek to constrict this autonomy.[34] This autonomy in self-expression would further cement the quality of individualism as a strong component that marks US culture.[35] First introduced in the Premodern Discourse, American individualism promoted the idea that the nature of existing societal systems (economic, social, political) could be attributed to "the aggregate of innumerable acts of choice and consent on the part of free individuals."[36]

The other technological innovation in transportation occurring during the Modern Era was the development of the aviation industry. Passenger air service modestly began in the 1920s, selling a few thousand tickets annually.[37] Yet the demand quickly grew; by 1930 over 400,000 passenger air tickets were sold.[38] By the end of the twentieth century, America's passenger airlines would carry over a half a billion people annually.[39] Earlier aircraft, such as the DC-3 of the 1930s and 1940s, achieved cruising speeds of 180 miles per hour (mph).[40] By mid-century cruising speeds of passenger planes reached 480 mph.[41] And today, cruising speeds of up to 600 mph are achieved by most passenger aircraft.[42] This has exponentially increased the mobility of the average citizen—and the freedom conferred by this mobility. One can now easily travel thousands of miles across country on a business trip, move anywhere in the United States and still visit family and relatives, and vacation in distant parts of the country.[43]

As had been the case for railroad companies of the Premodern Era, the aviation industry was offered substantial federal financial assistance to promote its growth and development.[44] And due to its military applications, technological improvements would consistently be spurred by defense spending.[45] But as was the case for the country's public roads project, this financial assistance was accompanied by a heavy dose of federal regulation. The Airmail Act of 1925 created the financial mechanism for supporting the creation of a private commercial airlines industry; however, this was quickly followed in 1926 by the Air Commerce Act, which put the secretary of commerce in charge of creating and enforcing air traffic rules, certifying aircraft and the licensing of pilots, establishing air routes, and the operation and maintenance of ground-based navigation aids.[46] The Civil Aeronautics Act of 1938 created the Civil Aeronautics Authority (CAA) and granted it the power to determine which routes were given to the individual airlines, as well as to regulate fares.[47] And in 1958 the Federal Aviation Act created the Federal Aviation Agency (FAA) to replace the CAA and additionally tasked it with maintaining the safety of air traffic through a system of federal air traffic controllers directing traffic.[48] Soon after, while keeping the aviation industry in private hands, the federal government would eventually claim ownership of all airspace between 18,000 and 60,000 feet.[49]

Communication
The introduction of the telephone spurred advancements in telecommunications which mirrored those taking place in transportation with the building of paved roads. Society moved from having each of its various communities

integrated into a vast communications network via the telegraph to having individuals themselves plugged into this network directly via the telephone. After its patent in 1876, the reach of the telephone quickly grew so that by the start of the Modern Era of social welfare in 1920 35% of all households were connected by telephone.[50] By 1950 this coverage almost doubled as 68% of all households had a telephone.[51] By the end of the twentieth century a vast network of telephone lines had been laid which connected 98% of all households in the United States.[52] As was the case with the deep penetration of paved roads eventually reaching to practically every doorstep in the United States, telephone lines—which numbered over 100 million by century's end—connected practically every household. And with the recent innovation of the cell phone, this connection has become mobile so that individuals have the option to always be connected.

The ability to speak with another individual in real time despite being separated by a vast distance would have profound effects on how we conduct business, foster governmental responsiveness to public safety, and maintain social ties. The advent of the 911 emergency call network in 1968 to accelerate the response time for police, firefighters, and ambulance drivers is but one example of the value of immediate communication in our present highly integrated and interdependent society. And as was the case with the automotive and aviation industries, while the federal government allowed the telecommunication industry to remain in private hands, it assumed a strong role in regulating it. Similar to the BPR for roads and the FAA for aviation, the Communications Act of 1934 created an independent government agency—the Federal Communications Commission (FCC)—to regulate all forms of wired and wireless communications: telephone, radio, television, and later the internet.

Regarding the telephone industry, for most of the twentieth century the FCC treated telephone service as a public utility; as such, it granted private companies (such as AT&T) monopoly power over their coverage area, to be kept in check through federal regulation of the rates that they could charge.[53] In addition, the FCC sets various standards regarding infrastructure and accessibility, as well as the policing of services.[54] The Telecommunications Act of 1996, along with the advent of the cell phone, served to break up the previously held monopoly power of the various companies; but the regulation of standards continues. Some prime examples are mandating the offering of 911 service, truth in billing (charges must be clear and factual), accessibility for those who are deaf or hard of hearing, and the creation of a do-not-call registry to shield consumers from unwanted telemarketers.[55] Thus, in the areas of transportation, immigration, and communication, the Modern Discourse is marked by the federal government assuming a strong responsibility for managing the proper growth and functioning for each.

Economic Conditions

Economically, the Modern Discourse marked the transition from economic activity heavily based within proprietary capitalism to one heavily based within corporate capitalism. Proprietary capitalism—which dominated during the Premodern Era—is marked by a situation in which the market is primarily comprised of interactions involving small, sole-proprietary businesses. It should be noted that in the area of agriculture these proprietary businesses take the form of the family farm.

As was noted in Chapter 4, toward the end of the nineteenth century technological innovation in business finally reached a point where production of items in bulk resulted in a lower cost per unit. This spurred the rise of big business, led by the likes of Carnegie's Steel Company, Rockefeller's Standard Oil Company, and the American Tobacco Company, each of which soon dominated its respective market. Through the passage of the Sherman Antitrust Act of 1890, the federal government took its first step toward adopting a more active role in the management of the economy. By 1920 the economic landscape would change to the point where corporate entities primarily defined market interactions.[56] This new era, which is described as *corporate capitalism*, would require a more active role by the federal government to ensure the free and fair exchange of goods and to curb abuses visited by corporations upon labor and the consumer.

This more active role by the federal government would occur on three fronts: single-industry regulation (such as the FCC and FAA), cross-industry regulation through the establishment of rules which all businesses must follow (such as the forty-hour workweek and unemployment insurance), and governmental actions which served to indirectly influence the national business environment (such as the building of paved roads or the establishment of federally protected lands).[57] Various major events would influence the extent of this federal involvement: Events such as the Great Depression and World War II spurred on a stronger, more active role, while events such as the stagflation of the 1970s led to a retreating from this role through the wave of deregulation that followed. Yet throughout the Modern Era, the need of the federal government to exert control over the economy and to check potential abuses by corporate entities has always been widely recognized; rather, debate centers upon the extent to which the federal government should do so.[58]

One prime example of the federal government's check on corporate power was the passage of the National Labor Relations Act of 1935 (which made unions legal and created the National Labor Relations Board to arbitrate disputes between labor and management) along with the passage of the Fair Labor Standards Act of 1938 (which created a minimum wage as well as the forty-hour workweek). These labor regulations proved highly successful in terms of managing industrial conflict; while the number of strikes actually increased in the following decades,[b] the labor riots common to the Premodern Era disappeared so that these labor conflicts now rarely resulted in violence.[59] Next came the passage of civil rights legislation in the 1960s and 1970s: guaranteeing nondiscrimination in hiring, minimum standards of occupational health and safety, and minimum standards for health and retirement plans.[c] The resolution of conflict surrounding these concerns moved from the shop floor to the courtroom, further sanitizing industrial conflict of its potential for violence.[60] Meanwhile, through the mechanisms of collective bargaining and grievance arbitration, industrial conflict outside the courtroom followed a non-violent jurisprudential model in its resolution.[61]

Yet the pacification of industrial conflict and the reigning in of corporate abuse simply marked a portion of the much broader effort of the federal government to scientifically manage the national economy.[62] As part of the Employment Act of 1946, the Council of Economic Advisors (CEA) was created, wherein notable economists advise the president concerning fiscal policy and submit an annual report to Congress as well as monthly updates. Keynesianism was the first broad policy framework produced by the CEA to guide the federal government's efforts at scientifically managing the economy.[63] Later, this approach would be replaced by the supply-side philosophy of Reaganomics.[64] However, throughout the Modern Era, the federal government's effort has been primarily aimed at maintaining and enhancing the capitalist elements of the economy; consequently, the various macroeconomic policies produced over the decades would inevitably possess a conservative bent: concentrating on issues such as stabilizing aggregate demand, price stability, balance of payments, and tax cuts to stimulate growth.[65] Such a conservative bent to policies would serve to hobble the federal government's transformation toward a more vibrant welfare state and oftentimes work in opposition to the gains being made with civil rights legislation and the support of labor.

Yet despite this conservative bent in managing the economy guided by scientific expertise, substantial gains were achieved in the standard of living for the average individual. Critical to such gains was the strong counterpoint offered by organized labor—by 1953 more than one-third of non-farmworkers belonged to a trade union.[66] It was commonly observed, such as by *Fortune* magazine in 1951, that the "worker is to a remarkable extent a middle class member of a middle class society."[67] Real wages for the average worker doubled from 1940 to

---

[b] Lichtenstein, *State of the Union*, 136. Union power would face a precipitous decline beginning in the late 1970s; yet, while this resulted in a corresponding decline in the number of strikes per year, violence still rarely arises from industrial conflict.

[c] Civil rights legislation for the workplace included the Civil Rights Act of 1964, the Mine Safety Act of 1969, the Occupational Safety and Health Act of 1970, the Rehabilitation Act of 1973, and the Employee Retirement Income Security Act of 1974.

1967.[68] This in turn bolstered the already burgeoning consumer-driven nature of the national economy.

Gains in later years to real wages, however, would be tempered considerably by the diminishing power of organized labor. From 1979 to 2015, growth in real wages remained remarkably flat; those wage earners in the 95th percentile did well in seeing a 41% increase to real wages, but those workers in the 50th percentile saw only a 6% increase to their real wages, while those workers in the 10th percentile saw their real wages actually decline by 5%.[69] Meanwhile, union membership began to plummet. By 1983 only 20% of the workforce belonged to a union, and by 2015 this number was down to 11%.[70] Thus, over this time span, decline in union membership negatively mirrored the income gains of the top 10% of wage earners.[71] This trend stands in stark contrast to the Scandinavian countries of Denmark, Sweden, and Finland—well known for being vibrant welfare states which possess stronger income equality—wherein, despite facing the same global economic pressures, union membership continues to hover around 65% of the workforce.[72] This is twice the rate achieved by the United States at its height in 1953. Thus, in summary, for a better part of the twentieth century, the federal government's scientific management of the national economy along with its modest support of labor resulted in steady economic growth and the steady increase of the average individual's economic power. However, this scientific management approach appears less adept in responding to recent economic challenges and forces. These recent economic pressures and forces will be more thoroughly discussed in Chapter 8.

The transition to corporate capitalism at the beginning of the twentieth century and its subsequent regulation by the federal government, beyond that of simply increasing economic prosperity, also introduced changes in the social and cultural fabric of the United States. To be sure, proprietary businesses continue to coexist with corporations, but in the age of corporate capitalism these proprietary businesses are confined to a minor role in the overall economy—such as that of filling niches eschewed by corporations or experimenting with innovation.[73] Even in the area of agriculture, the corporation dominates. Family-owned farms declined precipitously during the twentieth century, with those remaining typically filling the role of a contract worker to a corporation or adopting the minor role of occupying a niche market.[74]

Yet while businesses began to grow in size during the end of the nineteenth century, it would not be until decades later that fundamental shifts in their organization would become widely adopted.[75] Similar to the federal government, the corporation looked to harness the organizational power of the bureaucracy to aid in their management.[76] The hierarchical structure of the bureaucracy led to the specialization of function among workers, replacing their previous autonomous artisanal status in manufacturing and their autonomous yeoman status as independent farmer.[77] Businesses subsequently began creating new tiers of workers, with specialized technicians and engineers becoming commonplace.[78] Added to this was the centralization of authority, with decision-making confined to the top of the hierarchy and the authority of the chief executive officer rarely challenged.[79] Observing these changes taking place as early as 1891, the economist Sydney Webb noted the loss of individualism occurring in the workplace when he opined that the contemporary laborer transformed "from a self-governing producing unit" to "a mere item in a vast industrial army over the organization and direction of which he had no control."[80] Bureaucracy's need to place workers in a highly hierarchical structure wherein decision-making power was concentrated at the top, along with its need to reduce the scope of the worker's creativity through specialization, severely undercut the Premodern Discourse's Emersonian understanding of individualism as representing an autonomous, rugged self as public citizen.

One of the key events marking this cultural shift in the understanding of individualism was Fredrick Taylor's introduction of scientific management principles to business and their subsequent adoption by corporate entities.[81] First developed in the final decades of the nineteenth century, they would become widely embraced by 1920 and greatly influence the shape of management practices and factory organization well into the 1970s.[82] The overall essence of Taylor's method is captured by the following sentence taken from his work *The Principles of Scientific Management* (1911): "In the past, man has been first; in the future the system must be first."[83] Under Taylor's approach, an increase in productivity was achieved through the monitoring and enforcement of workers' activities according to precisely delineated and measurable standards.[84] He advocated the use of these rationally determined standards to replace the previous regulating structures of guild codes; consequently, workers' adherence to these scientific standards now required monitoring by specialized workers university-trained in bureaucratic management—resulting in managers who were now firmly allied with ownership rather than an outside guild organization.[85] Henry Ford's introduction of the assembly line in 1913 is an iconic example illustrating this organizational approach.

The loss of personal agency in the workplace was deeply felt by the average worker. Many of the strikes that occurred in the beginning of the twentieth century were less over wage demands and more to do with complaints over the adoption of Taylor's management principles.[86] This dehumanizing effect resulting from subsuming one's individuality to the system of the corporate enterprise would later be eloquently captured by Sloan Wilson's 1955 novel *The Man in the Gray Flannel Suit*. The Emersonian understanding from the Premodern Discourse—that of the individual as an autonomous, rational actor as public citizen—no longer fit the demands of the corporate age. A new understanding of individualism was called for and soon emerged. Echoing themes from Taylorism, Herbert Hoover's 1922 treatise *American Individualism* called for the subsumption of the individual as citizen in the service to the common enterprise of community.[87] And in a 1949 commencement speech at Columbia University, Eisenhower also voiced this new understanding of individualism when stating, "there is no limit to the temporal goals we set ourselves—as free individuals joined in a team with our fellows."[88]

Thus, in the Modern Era, it would appear on the surface that Emerson's warning in "Self-Reliance"—that the surrendering of one's individual freedom to the demands of a "joint-stock company" form of society—had indeed come true. Yet the Modern Discourse's understanding of individualism put forth a different vision of freedom. Rather than society being "in conspiracy against the manhood [personhood] of its members" as Emerson described,[89] this new vision proposed that society actually conferred identity upon the individual through their act of subsumption.[90] Thus, achieving freedom was now arrived at through cooperation (rather than through fiercely maintaining autonomy), and independence now derived from the creative self-expression of an inner self (rather than the acts of an autonomous public citizen).[91]

Yet the new regimented work spaces of the shop floor and bureaucratic office no longer provided an outlet in which to creatively express one's individualism; hence, the full realization of one's humanity now required some form of escape from work.[92] Responding to this change, corporate capitalism offered a route to creative self-expression through commodified leisure and consumption.[93] Hence, early advertisers promoted the notion of the *sovereign consumer* as the means to express one's self-cultivation through the freedom to choose "among already selected brands of goods."[94] The mobility offered by the automobile would offer freedom of choice in pursuing leisure activities, ultimately leading to the automobile's glorification in American culture as the means for achieving freedom and creative self-expression. In the Modern Discourse, one's "outer" world in the public sphere demands that one subsume one's individuality to the functioning of the system; the unique expression of one's individuality—and the freedom and fulfillment this engenders—is now to be found in one's private inner world. As will be elaborated fully in Chapter 7, social work in the Modern Era would lean heavily on the field of psychology in its effort at understanding the workings of the client's inner world.

Political Conditions

As noted in Chapter 4, progressive era reforms and the ratification of the Sixteenth Amendment in 1913 creating a federal income tax laid the groundwork for a federal welfare state to be born. Thus, when the country fell into the Great Depression in the 1930s, the federal government easily stepped into the role of assuming the primary responsibility for the health and welfare of its citizens. Prior to this event, responsibility was shared equally between state governments (which were primarily responsible for building and maintaining corrective institutions) and private sector charities (which were primarily responsible for the dispensation of direct relief).

However, when the Great Depression first hit, state and local governments as well as private relief agencies were overwhelmed with requests for aid; it soon became clear that the existing system for relief aid was ill equipped to deal with the demands brought on by this tragic event.[95] Under President Franklin D. Roosevelt, the federal government began to assume the primary responsibility for meeting the burgeoning general welfare needs. The rapid pace with which this occurred led one conservative columnist to write in 1933, "There is a country-wide dumping of responsibility on the Federal Government . . . Mr. Roosevelt goes on collecting mandates, one after another, until their sum is startling."[96]

Once started, there was no turning back; in the decades that followed, a plethora of legislation was passed, placing the federal government firmly in the role of guarantor of the general welfare of its citizens.[d] Another high point was reached in the 1960s with President Lyndon B. Johnson's War on Poverty initiative. There would follow a period of retrenchment toward the end of the twentieth century—marked by President Bill Clinton in 1996 signing into law the Personal Responsibility and Work Opportunity Reconciliation Act. Yet, while this act would devolve some power back to the states, what lies unquestioned even during this period of retrenchment is that the federal government holds the primary responsibility for attending to the general welfare of its citizens.[97]

However, as has been the case with the federal government's regulation of the economy throughout the Modern Era, in promoting the general welfare the federal government has adopted a scientific management approach. This managerial approach inserts a conservative bias in its efforts, with welfare legislation aimed at patching up the weaknesses of the existing system rather than offering

---

[d] The following is but a brief list of the variety of significant welfare legislation passed: the 1933 Federal Emergency Relief Act; the 1934 Home Owners Loan Act; the 1935 Social Security Act; the 1937 National Housing Act; the 1938 Fair Labor Standards Act; the 1946 National School Lunch Program; the 1949 Housing Act; the 1954 special Milk Program; the 1954 Indian Health Service Act; the 1960 Kerr-Mills Act; the 1963 Community Mental Health Act; the 1964 Economic Opportunity Act; the 1965 Elementary and Secondary Education Act; the establishment of Medicare and Medicaid in the 1965 Social Security Act Amendments; the 1970 Occupational Safety and Health Act; the 1972 Supplemental Security Income program; the 1974 Family Planning Services and Population Act; the 1975 Earned Income Tax Credit; the Social Security Amendments of 1977; the 1988 Family Support Act; the 1997 creation of the Children's Health Insurance Program; the 2003 Medicare Prescription Drug, Improvement, and Modernization Act; and the 2010 Affordable Care Act.

any type of fundamental change to the system.[98] This has resulted in the establishment of a fairly modest welfare state, one which stands in contrast to those which have arisen within the various developed countries of Europe.

Yet by adopting the mantle of a welfare state, the federal government's welfare focus shifted from one that had been primarily concerned with respecting property rights to one now that is primarily concerned with the advancement of individual rights.[99] The passage of the Social Security Act in 1935 would mark the first step down this road by seeking to guarantee minimal financial security as the right of its citizens;[100] progress down this legislative road would lead to passage of the landmark 1964 Civil Rights Act. Throughout the Modern Era, the power of the executive branch was also harnessed to advance individual rights. Early examples include President Franklin D. Roosevelt's 1941 executive order 8802 banning ethnic and racial discrimination in the defense industry and Truman's issue of an executive order in 1948 committing to end segregation in the armed forces. Furthermore, the Supreme Court weighed in prominently in 1954 with *Brown v. Board of Education*, starting a period in which the judicial branch would act as guarantor of individual rights—the most recent example being the *Obergefell v. Hodges* decision in 2015 legalizing same-sex marriage. In the creation of a welfare state, the Modern Era in social welfare is one marked by the steady advancement of civil rights.

This strong strain of individualism in American culture, and the Modern Discourse's new understanding of it, can be seen as one of the primary influences propelling this drive toward advancing civil rights. Earlier, I iterated the influence of economic factors on shaping the Modern Discourse's understanding of individualism. One of the primary political factors was that of the Cold War: the US response to the threat of Soviet-style communism. In 1950, the National Security Council would write in its *United States Objectives and Programs for National Security* (better known as NSC 68) that "the system of values which animates our society—the principles of freedom, tolerance, the importance of the individual, and the supremacy of reason over will—are valid and more vital than the ideology which is the fuel of Soviet dynamism."[101] Recognizing the importance of the individual was viewed as one of the defining features of American society.

Many politicians of this era were thus faced with the task of merging the concepts of freedom and independence with that of cooperation and its requirement of subsuming one's individuality to the system (i.e., society); this would entail what Herbert Croly described as using "statist means to individualist ends."[102] One of the contributing factors to this effort of using statist means to promote individualist ends is that of glorifying the Premodern Discourse's rhetoric of republican self-reliance as an essential feature of one's identity as an American.[103] Consequently, while the Modern Discourse continues to demand the subsumption of individuality to the cooperative effort, the spirit of this cooperative effort gets de-emphasized in the crafting of American identity. This stands in stark contrast to what occurred within the Colonial Discourse, when this spirit of cooperation and communal effort toward ensuring social welfare was highly ensconced in the identity of what it meant to be a colonist—and resulted in individuals viewing other members of the community as de facto family members.

This trumpeting of republican self-reliance in the Modern Discourse thus acts to reinforce the already conservative elements arising from the federal government's scientific management of social welfare—which has served to produce a very modest US welfare state. As one prominent author on social welfare noted, "Poverty in America is profoundly individual; like popular economics, it is supply-side";[104] thus, the Modern Discourse continues the trope that was started in the Premodern Discourse of blaming the individual for their condition—whereas before it was attributed to lack of moral fiber, now it is attributed to lack of coping mechanisms to adequately function in the economic or social system.

Due to the Cold War's clash of ideologies, socialism became a dirty word in the American lexicon—often equated with communism. Thus, even though there are and always have been socialist elements within the government's efforts to promote social welfare—free public education until the twelfth grade being a prime example—efforts to apply this approach in other areas have met strong resistance, being characterized as guarding against "creeping socialism."[105] Starting in 2016 with his run in the democratic primary for president, Senator Bernie Sanders has gained some traction in reappropriating the meaning of socialism in the American lexicon by aligning it with the democratic socialism practiced by most developed countries. This will be touched upon in Chapter 9 as it is more representative of the Postmodern discourse.

But the Modern Discourse's understanding of individualism—that of the individual being the primary unit within the system comprising the cooperative effort—has strongly promoted the advancement of civil rights. Under scientific management aimed toward enhancing the functioning of the system (i.e., society), inequality arising not from differences in skill and talent but rather from socially imposed criteria interferes with the proper functioning of the system/ society and thus eventually must be corrected. Yet, as we shall see in Chapter 7, while the advancement of human rights is seen as a core value of the social work profession, social workers in the Modern Era have adopted a much more modest role in spearheading reform to advance civil rights, passing the mantle of leadership to advocates from other professions and walks of life: such as Martin Luther King, Jr., in regard to racial inclusion; Betty Friedan and Gloria Steinem in regard to feminism and inclusion of both sexes; and Sylvia Rivera and Harvey Milk in regard to the gay rights movement and inclusion of LGBTQ+ individuals.

On a more direct level, with the federal government assuming primary responsibility for promoting the welfare of its citizens, social welfare had become a public endeavor. This undercut one of the prime raisons d'être for private welfare agencies and the social workers that they employed.[106] Previously, private agencies in the form of the various charity organization societies assumed the primary responsibility for dispensing direct relief, and thus served to shape the government's contribution to this effort. The transformation to a welfare state meant that a new alignment was called for between public and private social welfare and, by extension, reconsideration of the primary endeavor of professional social work.[107]

The passage of the Social Security Act in 1935 would lay out the primary framework for this realignment. Influenced by the strong strain of individualism within American culture, the poor continued to be thought of as falling into two broad categories: the "worthy" poor and the "unworthy."[108] The federal government assumed a direct role in dispensing relief to the worthy poor, falling into the subcategories of the temporarily unemployed,[e] the disabled, and the retired worker. In addition, the federal government provided grants-in-aid for state-administered relief (the acceptance of which required adherence to federal standards) to the remaining worthy poor, such as those falling into the subcategory of widows and dependent children. The states were also tasked with attending to those classified as the unworthy poor, though without the benefit of much federal aid.[109]

Comments by the Committee on Economic Security (from which the Social Security Act arose) in their report to President Franklin D. Roosevelt illustrate the nature of this realignment:

With the Federal Government carrying so much burden for pure unemployment, the State and local governments . . . should resume responsibility for relief. The families that have always been partially or wholly dependent on others for support can best be assisted through the tried procedures of social casework, with its individualized treatment.[110]

Recognition by the social work profession soon followed. In February 1936, heated debates occurred at the annual conference of the American Association of Social Workers concerning this need for realignment, which resulted in a growing "perception that professional social work practices and relief giving were separate entities, however overlapping their concerns."[111] This was shortly confirmed when in March of 1936 the Family Welfare Association of America—whose member family agency workers at the time were seen as the primary

---

[e] While the individual states administer unemployment relief to individuals, the money comes from a federal payroll tax, and the US Department of Labor is tasked with oversight of collected tax monies.

representation of social work—published a report stemming from their survey of over ninety agencies in which they took the position "to hold firmly to the principle that intensive casework treatment is the primary function of a family service organization."[112]

This change in orientation resulted in social workers occupying three broad areas of the workforce: as a public employee (such as a worker within a state's Department of Children and Family Services), as a de facto public employee in an private agency that is dependent upon public funds and thus subject to governmental standards (such as foster care and community mental health agencies), and as a private employee in agencies that rely upon their case management or counseling expertise (such as hospitals). Consequently, this realignment kicked off an era in which now social work and social workers are primarily identified by the professional services they provide toward advancing social welfare, rather than as was the case in the Premodern Era wherein they were primarily defined by the ends of social justice they wished to achieve.

Social Conditions

Just as technological advancements in transportation (building of roads) and communication (telephone) represented a deeper penetration of connectivity—literally extending to each person's residence—technological advancements in media, in the form of radio and television, produced this same deep penetration of connectivity between American households. As early as 1953, 96% of American families had a radio in their homes; and in this same year, television—still in its infancy—reached into 44% of American homes.[113] By the twentieth century's end, television had also achieved this deep penetration by reaching into 99% of American homes; and radio became a standard feature in cars, adding a level of mobility to its reach on par with that later achieved by the cell phone.[114] And as was the case in the economic and political realms, these social innovations and the industries they spawned were viewed as in need of scientific management by the federal government to maintain their proper and healthy functioning within American society.[f]

Similar to the telephone, this deeper connectivity brought on by radio and television occurred in real time—adding a temporal dynamic to this connectivity. Serving as a "social lubricant," radio and television helped people to feel present at news and sporting events and part of a large audience for the various

---

[f] Most notably this was through the creation of the FCC via the Communications Act of 1934, along with many subsequent amendments that addressed issues such as customer privacy, aiding law enforcement, nondiscrimination, and access for individuals with disabilities. The Supreme Court ruling of *Roth v. United States* in 1957 outlined the parameters for obscenity.

theatrical shows broadcast—creating a shared experience.[115] One early example illustrating this dynamic was the popular radio show *Amos 'n Andy*, which in 1930 had already attracted a following of over 40 million listeners.[116] Thus, it is no surprise that radio and television, along with the development of the cinematic and phonographic record industries, are seen as significant contributors to the development of a strong national identity in the twentieth century and the promotion of an American culture comprised of a shared set of values and beliefs.[117]

Consequently, television, radio, and cinema played a prominent role in disseminating cultural norms—both serving to reflect changes occurring and helping to shape change in this area.[118] Many saw this dissemination as promoting national unity through de-emphasizing class differences.[119] As NBC's president in 1930 opined, broadcasting was ideally suited "to preserve our now vast population from disintegrating into classes. . . . We must know and honor the same heroes, love the same songs, enjoy the same sports, realize our common interest in our national problems."[120] And it appears that such predictions have come true, with surveys in the first two decades of the twenty-first century finding that approximately 70% of individuals identify themselves as belonging to the middle class.[121] Hence, within the Modern Discourse the United States has been markedly resistant to the development of a strong class consciousness; this has acted as a major contributor toward the development of a relatively modest welfare state in the United States as compared to the more vibrant welfare states that have developed in its many European counterparts.

One of the major social movements promoted by the Modern Discourse has been the advancement of civil rights. This can be seen as a further articulation of the notion of equality within a democratic society that was begun in the Premodern Discourse. As noted previously, the Premodern Era was marked by the gradual advancement of suffrage extending the right to vote to heretofore excluded groups. Yet the suffrage movement represented a quite literal articulation of democratic equality, and thus notions of equality were limited to the narrow band of political participation as a voter. Mirroring the deeper penetration and connectivity occurring in transportation and communication, the advancement of civil rights in the Modern Era represents a richer articulation of democratic equality, extending it to the broad area of equal opportunity to participate in all aspects of society as a whole, not just in the political process.

The new forms of media in this era—primarily television and radio—contributed to the steady advancement of these civil rights. News of the various civil rights struggles was brought into the living rooms of all Americans, often in real time, creating a shared experience of witnessing the various atrocities arising from such struggles.[122] This shared experience in turn mobilized broad public support for change.[123] The ability of television and radio to place the individual listener within a national audience gave particular emphasis to the individual as a consumer of this information and entertainment. Hence, this relationship also fits the *sovereign consumer* aspect of expressive individualism—one's creative self-expression was formulated as a choice from already selected brands (i.e., networks and programs). By making an appeal to individuality, radio (and television after the advent of cable tv) began to target specific population groups to better garner market share: rock 'n' roll for youth, religious broadcasting, and racial and ethnic cultural programs are but a few examples.[124] Meanwhile, National Public Radio was able to offer inclusion to groups—such as programs broadcast in Eskimo or Navajo—who would be ignored in the private marketplace due to being economically unproductive.[125]

As noted previously, the thematic trope of scientific management facilitated this advancement of civil rights as discrimination and oppression were viewed as systemic dysfunction. In addition, the new understanding of individualism as expressive individualism facilitated the advancement of civil rights. In the social arena of identity, the subsumption of one's individuality to the system took the form of de-emphasizing one's uniqueness and conversely emphasizing oneself as a member of a population group; thus, the particular circumstances of oppression being visited upon various individuals could be extended to represent a grievance of inequality for the population group as a whole. This new understanding of individualism arising from the Modern Discourse results in an emphasis upon individuality being understood as the individual as the basic unit in a broader system—over that of the individual as a unique, autonomous unit. The scientific management by social workers of the social ills being experienced by individuals also reflects this dynamic between scientific understanding and individuality. The social work profession in the Modern Era relies upon knowledge generated by social science investigations. To generate such knowledge, the individual is viewed as the basic unit of study, yet what is emphasized is individuals' membership in a population group. This is what allows for the extension of this knowledge to a broader population and its application to said individuals through scientific management.

Urgent Need

By 1920, the national integration of US society in terms of political engagement, economic trade, and social interconnectedness was solidly established. The questions and concerns over whether this rapid integration would produce an accompanying moral integration in the form of a "great community" or whether society would devolve into moral anarchy could now be answered. The answer, it appeared, was that US society had reached a sort of middle ground regarding addressing the social ills that plagued it. There was no longer any fear that the very foundations of society would collapse into anarchy under the weight of these social ills. Yet, at the same time, there was recognition that these social ills had an intractable quality to them: Gone was the earlier optimism that a great community would arise and produce wholesale reform of criminal deviance, cure mental illness, and eliminate poverty. Thus, as noted by Cotton Seiler, "many social scientists turned their attention to inefficiencies or 'deviance' within an existing social system that they increasingly regarded as more or less sound."[126] Hence, a more pragmatic and managerial approach toward addressing social ills would arise. And the many social scientific models generated to guide this managerial approach would contain a conservative bias against fundamental structural change (as the existing system was assumed to be functionally sound).

By the time president Franklin D. Roosevelt entered office and began proposing various aspects of the New Deal, most Americans both accepted and expected governmental intervention on the federal level in an effort to promote social welfare.[127] Social welfare efforts under the Modern Discourse—now led and directed primarily by the federal government—were directed toward management of social ills, the goal now being that of keeping them from metastasizing into greater problems while at the same time seeking to slowly whittle away at their foundations to lessen their impact on the health of society.[128] A new understanding of individualism directed this scientific managerial approach. Hence, the urgent need of the Modern Discourse on social welfare is that of *maintaining and enhancing the functioning of society (with the individual as the basic unit in the various systems comprising society).*

Broadly understood, meeting this urgent need would involve "the scrutiny, classification, and management of populations with an eye to their improvement."[129] The American social sciences at the dawn of the twentieth century— now embracing an "engineering–reformatory–managerial" focus in knowledge generation—would provide the tools with which to accomplish this scrutiny, classification, and management.[130] So, for example, in the economics sphere the federal government created the CEA, relying upon their advice in its effort "to develop control mechanisms to moderate the ups and downs of business cycles and the continued vigor of the economy."[131] Keynesian economic policy and Reaganomics represent two examples of attempts at engineering, the various labor laws and civil rights legislation represent examples of the reformatory impulse, and social welfare programs created by the Social Security Act and its subsequent amendments represent examples of a managerial approach in dealing with individual misfortune.

In the broader sphere of social welfare in general, social workers offered their expertise in working with the individual and family units comprising the broader system of society. As noted, during Roosevelt's rollout of the New Deal the profession of social work underwent a realignment in which social workers now primarily identified their expertise as lying in the delivery of intensive case-work services. Social work programs had recently ensconced themselves in universities and boasted of producing social workers educated in understanding the structure and functioning of society.[132] This professional identification as experts in the structure and functioning of society—and the individual and family units comprising this system—was reaffirmed in the 1950s with the creation of the Council on Social Work Education as an accrediting body to oversee the training of this expertise. And in the 1960s it was reaffirmed once again when President John F. Kennedy tasked a committee—comprised primarily of social workers—to recommend measures to improve the functioning of welfare programs. The committee offered recommendations "designed to reinforce and support family life through rehabilitation, prevention and protection"; however, rehabilitation services were attributed foremost importance.[133]

As aptly observed by Porter Lee at the beginning of this new era, social workers moved from primarily being moral reformers advancing a cause to primarily being social engineers tending to the functioning of society.[134] As will be elaborated upon more in Chapter 7, social work did not abandon its social reform impulse in our present era; however, the Modern Discourse has operated to significantly mute it. Agitating for reform has been retained as part of our professional ethic. But, as such, it is something that we as social workers are tasked to bring to situations we encounter in the course of our work rather than something demanded by our role in responding to the urgent need of society. Instead, the Modern Discourse's urgent need demands an army of social experts to engage in social engineering at the individual/family level (through the development of various concept models designed to enhance functioning) and to provide scientific management of the interventions designed from these conceptual models.

Intellectual Thought

While the Premodern Discourse strongly embraced rationalism, the Modern Discourse has strongly embraced empiricism as the source for all knowledge. This has led to the ascendency of scientific knowledge as the driving force guiding social work intervention models and understanding in the Modern Discourse. As stated above, social workers operating in the Modern Discourse engage in social engineering in order to scientifically manage social ills. The various specific psychological and sociological theories that social workers have drawn upon in this era will be fully explored in Chapter 7 as they represent the blueprints for these various engineering attempts. Here, we will examine the foundational scientific theories broadly informing the development of these various psychological and sociological theories embraced by social work. As science represents the study of the natural world and human beings as living organisms are the subject for social welfare concerns, these foundational theories all relate to the field of biology in some manner.

Empiricism

Empiricism serves as a foundational theory for all scientific investigation. It proposes that the source of all knowledge/truth is derived from one's biological senses (sometimes enhanced by tools) encountering the natural world in which one lives. These sense experiences—when appropriately verified—serve as the building blocks of truth claims. Reason is employed in the form of theory to organize the various building blocks into a coherent whole. Logical positivism—which serves as the theory of epistemology for the Modern Discourse—represents a particular application of empiricism's premise. Hence, all logical positivists are necessarily empiricists as well, whereas being an empiricist does not necessarily entail also being a logical positivist.

By denying any validity to metaphysical claims, moral knowledge lies outside the grasp of science. Science can legitimately describe what is; it is unable, however, to morally comment upon what should be. Rather, scientific investigation—which is driven by empiricism—can only offer a "what is" in the form of a normative model of functioning when seeking to comment upon "what should be" in terms of social welfare. This conflation of a "what is" with a "what should be" combined with attempts to socially engineer and manage this "what should be" is what has kept alive the risk of social workers operating in the Modern Discourse of turning into social control agents.

This risk first arose in the Premodern Discourse with its embrace of rationalism; rationalism offered definitive moral ideals of "what should be." The charity organization societies' employment of "not alms but a friend" is but one of the prominent notorious examples of social control arising from this application of rationalism. The reason such practices of social control arise is that the operation of reason is susceptible to be unduly influenced by the culture within which it operates. Within the Premodern Discourse, this led to cultural ideals being mistaken for absolute moral ideals.

Unfortunately, the embrace of empiricism in the Modern Discourse has done little to correct this flaw as it has simply replaced a definitive moral ideal of "what should be" with a functional norm of "what should be." This is because these functional norms are the product of reason attempting to organize various empirical observations into a coherent "story" of what is occurring. Consequently, reason is still open to be unduly influenced by culture; in this case, cultural norms can easily get mistaken for scientific descriptions of normal functioning. The earlier editions of the *Diagnostic and Statistical Manual of Mental Disorders* classified homosexuality as a mental illness, which serves as one of the most notorious examples that has occurred in the Modern Era of mistaking a cultural norm for a scientific norm.[135]

This is why social work in the Modern Era has developed a vibrant set of professional values. Social work values act as a check against the Modern Discourse's predilection to lead social workers down the path of social control. When awareness of this predilection is met with a firm employment of these values, good social work practices ensue. However, when this awareness is either muted or absent, social control elements begin to seep into social work practices. In these instances, while technical efficiency may be achieved in the scientific management of the targeted social ill, it comes at the price of moral lapse.

Immanuel Kant: Organisms as Purposes

In his critique of teleological judgment, Immanuel Kant weighs in on the science of biology by seeking to distinguish organisms from inorganic objects in nature. He does this by claiming that organisms are the only objects in the natural world "which, even when regarded in themselves and without relation to other things, must still be thought of as possible only as purposes of nature."[136] This argument rests upon the premise that mechanical laws alone are insufficient to adequately explain the actions of organic matter (which includes the organism as a whole as well as the various biological parts comprising the organism). Yet, scientific understanding of organic matter requires that the various regularities of behavior that are noted through empirical observation must follow some type of law-like behavior. Kant states that this is accomplished by assuming that organic matter conforms to various normative laws in addition to following mechanical laws.[137] Thus, the empirically observed regularity in which a caterpillar metamorphoses into a butterfly is thus conceived of as following a normative law that caterpillars *ought to* metamorphose into a butterfly; similarly, we can examine an organic part of the butterfly—such as its wings—and from the empirically observed regularity of seeing butterflies using their wings to fly, we come up with the normative expectation that a butterfly's wings *ought to* provide the capability of flight. This further illustrates the comment made earlier when discussing empiricism on how science offers a "what is" (in terms of normative functioning) as its what *ought to be*.

When human beings are the organic objects of study (such as in the field of medicine), these philosophical principles can be directly applied to describe their biological functioning (i.e., how the heart *ought to* function, how the lungs *ought to* function, etc.). And looking back at the many amazing medical advances that have occurred since the dawn of the twentieth century, it is not difficult to argue that they rest upon Kant's fundamental philosophical understanding of organisms containing purposes (i.e., following normative laws of functioning).

Yet the concerns of social welfare entail more than just biological functioning. Consequently, the various social sciences were turned to in an attempt to scientifically understand the various other aspects of the human condition—with psychology and sociology being given the most prominent attention in the field of social work. The various social sciences have also relied upon this philosophical understanding of organisms as purposes; however, as their topics of concern lie outside the field of biology, this philosophical understanding and the various biological theories that arise from it are used by way of analogy when attempting to make social scientific truth claims.[138] This reliance upon applying scientific principles via analogy is the main feature contrasting the categorization of scientific fields as being either hard (i.e., very rigorous) or soft (i.e., less rigorous). The hard sciences (e.g., physics, chemistry, biology) seek to describe the workings of physical matter, and when offering hypotheses or theories, their truth claims rest directly upon empirical observations and controlled experimentation. By contrast, the soft sciences (e.g., the various social sciences—psychology, sociology, etc.) primarily have human beings as their locus of study. Before advancing social scientific theories based upon empirical observation, social scientists must first adopt via analogy foundational truth claims established in the hard sciences as their starting point.

The various social sciences are considered "soft" because of their reliance upon analogy as their connection to foundational scientific premises justifying truth claims, whereas truth claims in the "hard" sciences—such as biology—draw direct lineage to empirically established foundational premises. So, for example, very broadly the field of psychology seeks to scientifically explain the inner workings of human thought (in terms of emotional responses, logical thought, moral reasoning, etc.) utilizing Kant's notion of the component parts of an organism containing purposes, while some theories (such as Freud's elaboration of the ego, id, and superego) go as far as hypothesizing actual psychological components. In viewing the component parts of organisms as purposive, the field of psychology in turn offers many different theories on the normative functioning of these psychological components. In addition, psychological theories will draw upon biological theories which rest upon Kant's principle and—by way of analogy—seek to apply to the psychological sphere the insights stemming from these firmly established biological theories.[g] For example,

---

[g] The notable exception to this is classical behaviorism, which is firmly rooted in empirical observation.

drawing upon cell theory's understanding of differentiation and growth (rigorously established through empirical observation), a number of psychological theories from the Modern Discourse offer stage-of-growth models of psychological functioning.

The same holds true for sociological theory. Sociology looks at organisms as a whole as being purposive. Thus, sociology offers normative models of functioning in regard to social relations. Similarly, sociological theory will draw upon biological theories of organisms as a whole which rest upon Kant's principle and, by way of analogy, seek to apply their insights. The most prominent example in the United States is that of ecological systems theory (rigorously established through empirical observation and investigation) from the field of ecology, in which various organisms in a defined environment are viewed as having interdependent relationships. Through use of analogy, Carel Germain (at times, with various collaborators) applied these ecological insights to human social relations and developed the person-in-environment model, which has since become the defining conceptual model of practice for American social work. Germain herself did not conduct controlled experimentation to develop this model. Germain's reliance upon analogy can be readily observed in her earlier writings where she often uses the term *organism* when describing human beings:[h] doing this to make more explicit the application of insights arising from (rigorously established) ecological theory to that of human relations.[139] Germain's person-in-environment model—and its consequent ubiquitous acceptance in defining American social work—reflects the overall trend in the social sciences marking the Modern Discourse of drawing upon the use of analogy from biology and other hard sciences as the means to advance truth claims.

There are two important implications for social welfare that stem from the proposition that organisms contain purposes. First, the field of medicine has relied upon Kant's proposition (and various biological theories that rest upon it) in order to inform the practice of medicine along the lines of promoting and enhancing the physical health of individuals according to empirically established norms of function. As the practice of medicine represents the practical application of knowledge created in this fashion, it is described as a medical model of practice. Thus, within the Modern Discourse, the practice of social work relies upon this same proposition by Kant (along with various biological theories that rest upon it) in order to inform the practice of social work along the lines of promoting and enhancing the mental health and social welfare of individuals according to empirically established norms of functioning. Hence, social work

---

[h] See Gordon, "Basic Constructs." William E. Gordon is one of a number of additional system theorists who readily used the term *organism* for human beings when applying systems concepts to human social systems.

operating in the Modern Discourse has also been historically described as following a medical model of practice.

Due to recent postmodern critiques of this approach, the term *medical model* has recently developed a negative connotation in the field of social work as representing an overly focused attention on pathology. Hence, many social workers currently practicing will not describe their approach as following the medical model. However, if one understands the medical model as representing the practical application of knowledge seeking to promote and enhance the mental health and social welfare functioning of individuals according to normative models—derived from adopting Kant's proposition that organisms contain purposes—then any social work practice which is conceptualized as the promotion and enhancement of client functioning can accurately be described as following a medical model. We may call it a problem-solving approach or even strengths-based practice,[i] but doing so does not escape the fact that practices based upon models of normative functioning represent a medical approach in their application of scientific insights. The numerous examples in the social work lexicon—such as referring to counseling as psycho*therapy*—serve to reveal this ongoing connection to the medical model. Thus, practices based within the Modern Discourse are still subject to these critiques of the medical model (which will be more fully elaborated in Chapters 7, 8, and 9).

The other important implication has to do with scientific rigor in the social sciences. When scientific conclusions/theories are grounded within an analogy, rather than arising from controlled experimentation applying Karl Popper's standard of falsification, their acceptance rests not upon scientific claims of validity but, rather, upon their utility.[140] Again, we can turn to the person-in-environment model to illustrate this dynamic. Germain and her various collaborators did not employ controlled experimentation as the means to develop the person-in-environment model for social work. Rather, Germain relied upon Ludwig von Bertalanffy's (a biologist) systematic observations revealing the interdependence of a living system. Then, through use of analogy, Germain applied these insights to human living systems. Consequently, its wide acceptance in American social work is not due to its uncontestable scientific rigor, as is the case of theories arising from the hard sciences. Rather, person-in-environment owes its wide acceptance to it aligning well with various elements of the Modern Discourse, by offering the means to focus upon the individual as a basic unit of a greater system as demanded by expressive individualism, to meet

---

[i] In Chapters 7, 8, and 9, I will articulate the difference between the strengths perspective (which is firmly grounded in the Postmodern discourse) and its misapplication as strengths-based practice (which is firmly grounded in the Modern Discourse).

the urgent need of maintaining and enhancing the functioning of society and its component parts (i.e., individuals), and to explain interdependence in a society with a muted class consciousness.

We only need to contrast this with the case of the United Kingdom—which has a more sharply developed societal class consciousness—to illustrate the power of utility in regard to acceptance. After the person-in-environment model was introduced to the United Kingdom in the 1970s, it never strongly took root and was quickly relegated to a minor status in guiding social work endeavors.[141] Its inability to speak to class conflict made it less useful to social workers in the United Kingdom, and hence diminished the acceptance of its truth claims, whereas if the person-in-environment model represented a rigorous scientifically established truth, then the implications flowing from this theory could not be so easily ignored by UK social workers.

Mathematical Statistics

In addition to conceiving of organisms as purposes, Kant offered one other prerequisite for a science of organic matter to exist: mathematizability. Similar to Newton's development of calculus as the means to mathematize the principles of rational mechanics, a science of organic matter would need a branch of mathematics that could explain regularities occurring along a normative mean. This occurred in the nineteenth century with the synthesis of probability theory and inferential statistics, which led to the development of mathematical statistics as it is understood today. Through its ability to measure standards of deviation from a normative mean, mathematical statistics fulfilled the requirement of mathematizing observations of functional regularities in terms of normative law-like behavior.

The impact that the development of statistics has had on the social sciences in the Modern Era has truly been profound. While not relying exclusively upon statistics, the advancement of truth claims in the social sciences heavily rests upon statistical models. Thus, statistics is what undergirds our present notion of evidence-based practice. The ability of statistics to describe with mathematical certainty various observed regularities of behavior allows for these observations to count as evidence; thus, the description of a "what is" (i.e., evidence) with mathematical accuracy lends power to the move of offering the regulative norm of "what is" as a "what ought to be." Statistics' natural tendency of offering a "what is" as a scientifically established fact of "what ought to be" serves as another component operating in the Modern Discourse on social welfare which directs social welfare interventions along the path of social control through the means of social engineering.

Darwin: Adaptation

Described by some as the Newton of biology and the Galileo of psychology, Darwin and his theory of evolution is recognized as having a profound impact on legitimizing the science of biology and influencing the development of the social sciences.[142] Similar to what Newton accomplished for physics through his laws of rational mechanics is what Darwin accomplished for biology through his theory of evolution: Darwin met the necessary preconditions for science,[j] laid down by Kant, to legitimize biology (i.e., the study of living organisms) as a true science by providing a regulative principle in describing the actions of living organisms.[143] Galileo utilized extensive and detailed empirical evidence to prove Copernicus' theory that the earth revolved around the sun, thus placing the sun at the center of our universe; this resulted in a fundamental and dramatic shift in society's understanding of the universe. Similarly, Darwin utilized extensive and detailed empirical evidence to propose his theory of evolution, which in turn resulted in a fundamental and dramatic shift in society's understanding of the human condition.

Darwin detailed the main principles of his theory of evolution in his book *On the Origin of Species* (1859); his next two books—*The Descent of Man, and Selection in Relation to Sex* (1871) and *The Expression of the Emotions in Man and Animals* (1872)—sought to apply evolutionary theory as a means to explain human behavior and development.[144] This application to human beings entails viewing people as *Homo sapiens*—that is, viewing humankind as one species out of many occupying the animal kingdom. Drawing this continuity between humans and animals is what allows for the transfer of evolutionary principles to human beings.[145] Yet Darwin does not stop at drawing this continuity solely at the level of physical characteristics; he goes on to claim that human reason, human behavior, human morality, and human emotions[k] also share this continuity.[146]

For example, while human beings possess reason, human reason is viewed merely as a more sophisticated form of what is possessed by lower animals.[147] Hence, it is a difference of degree along a continuum, with human beings located at the furthest end. By placing human psychology on a continuum with animal psychology, human behavior was no longer viewed as simply stemming from personal preference, beliefs, and morals.[148] Rather, via the concept of adaptation, Darwin offers explanations of cause–effect origins for these preferences, beliefs, and morals; and thus, by extension, he opens the door for those seeking

---

[j] These conditions are systematicity, objective grounding, and apodictic certainty.
[k] Reason, behavior, morality, and emotions together comprise the concerns of psychology—hence the Galileo of psychology reference.

cause–effect explanations of human behavior.[149] This view of all human behavior as ultimately rooted in biology represents the fundamental shift of Galilean magnitude that occurred in how society would understand the human condition.

Darwin writes in *On the Origin of Species* that human being, "are called 'creatures of reason,' more appropriately they would be creatures of habit."[150] The concept of adaptation provides the framework for social scientists to describe these human habits in terms of cause–effect explanations that follow normative law-like behavior.[151] Darwin articulates two biological sources for determining behavior: instinct and habit. As animals move up the continuum toward *Homo sapiens*, instincts play a decreasing role in determining behavior, while habit plays an increasing role.[152] This interplay between instinct and habit sets the parameters for debate in the social sciences operating within the Modern Discourse as explaining human behavior in terms of nature versus nurture. Keeping in line with the Modern Discourse's conception of expressive individualism, social scientists were able to explain adaptive behavior as promoting cooperation and cohesion in society (as opposed to the social Darwinists of the Premodern Era who emphasized conflict).[153]

Two significant implications flow from Darwin's theory as understood in the Modern Discourse. First, in order to have a science of human behavior, one must be able to explain and predict this behavior in a cause–effect manner. Darwin accomplishes this by depicting human behavior as the interplay between instinct and habit. Consequently, there is no prominent role or recognition of free will in explaining human behavior; rather, a deterministic view of human behavior is emphasized.[154] As Kant famously noted, free will is antithetical to cause–effect explanations and predictions.[155] Thus, social work in the Modern Discourse is necessarily deterministic in its outlook. By relying upon scientific understanding of human behavior and evidence-based practice to develop interventions, it has little to say about the role that personal agency plays in human action. Again, social work must turn to its value base (e.g., recognizing the importance of human relationships, self-determination) to overcome this deficit and speak to qualities of the helping process such as belief in the client's capacities or nurturing hope.

The second significant implication pertains to the emphasis placed upon humans as being simply one species on a continuum with other animal species. This continuity is essential to justifying the move of applying scientifically grounded theory in biology, via analogy, to develop theory in the social sciences as they relate to social welfare—as the analogy is based upon simply a difference of *degree*. What is lost is an appreciation for how the human condition is different in *kind* from that of animals, such as in possessing free will. Consequently, personal agency in the form of free will—and the role that belief and hope play in fostering this personal agency—gets de-emphasized within the Modern

Discourse's efforts at social engineering, and overshadowed by its deterministic elements provided by evidence-based practice and normative theory.

Defining Cultural Feature: Faith in Science (Scientism)

The Modern Discourse marks a time period wherein scientific knowledge gained ascendancy as the premier arbiter of truth. Ever since Martin Luther nailed his 95 Theses to the Church of Wittenberg's door, the certainty of knowledge of the True had been cast in doubt in the Western world. As knowledge of the True at that time was firmly rooted in religious thought, the various sects of Christianity that arose each offered their own version of truth—thus eroding the certainty that had existed up to this time. Enlightenment thought would begin the project of anchoring knowledge of the True on solid ground. While the Premodern Discourse made gains in this regard, it was not until the Modern Discourse's full embrace of the scientific method that society once again granted a high level of certainty to knowledge of the True.

Technological innovation spurred on by scientific investigation has proceeded rapidly within the Modern Era—introducing numerous modern conveniences to the everyday experience of the average person. Numerous advancements in the field of medicine throughout the twentieth century and into the twenty-first century have dramatically improved the health and well-being of the average person. The combination of technological and medical advancement has continuously rewarded a strong public faith in the certainty of scientific knowledge generated in the fields of medicine and the natural sciences. In turn, this strong public faith in the certainty of scientific knowledge has buoyed the profession of social work's embrace of the scientific method for knowledge generation; its application via the medical model is then used to promote social welfare through social engineering and scientific management.

Yet this certainty has not come without cost. The certainty offered by scientific investigation under logical positivism comes with the proposition that scientific knowledge is the sole arbiter of truth (with a capital "T"); other forms of inquiry—such as the dialectic method or the comparative method—are seen as weaker and less trustworthy as they offer pathways toward truth that pass through subjective knowledge. While it is now widely recognized that even scientific inquiry cannot totally avoid subjective knowledge when advancing its truth claims, scientific inquiry bases its confidence and validity of these truth claims solely within the objective knowledge it has to offer. This delegitimizes all forms of subjective knowledge (such as that generated by belief and hope) when designing social work interventions as scientific inquiry seeks to monopolize the generation of truth claims.

In practical terms, truth is equated with scientific fact (while other forms of truth such as philosophical truth, poetic truth, and historical truth) go mostly unrecognized when it comes to designing a social work intervention. In addition, while subjective knowledge is able to speak directly to knowledge of the Good (the concern of social welfare), objective knowledge produced by science only speaks to knowledge of the True. Consequently, in the Modern Discourse, an understanding of knowledge of the Good can only be accessed through knowledge of the True. This makes social workers more willing to accept the scientific offering of "what is" as a "what ought to be." It also positions the social worker as an expert in human functioning, and thus a broker for the client in accessing knowledge of the Good. As noted earlier, both can easily lead social workers down the path of social control—something that must be vigilantly guarded against and constantly countered through a solid application of social work values guided by cultural humility.

There is another cost that comes from the general public equating truth with scientific fact. The typical social work student—untrained in the probability theory that undergirds scientific claims of truth—graduates with a naivety concerning the limitations of scientific truth claims as they pertain to human beings. As a result, social workers often confuse pseudoscience with science—which has led to the adoption of questionable social work practices throughout the Modern Era. A prime example of this can be found in the early years of professionalization in social work. Psychodynamic theory by Freud and his disciples was heavily employed to direct social work practice well into the 1960s—with highly questionable results.[1]

The current understanding of pseudoscience traces its origin to Karl Popper's concept of falsification.[156] In his work *The Logic of Scientific Discovery* (1959), Popper uses Freud's theory to illustrate the defining characteristics of pseudoscience: a reliance upon confirmation (which is easily biased) to justify truth claims rather than falsification. Hence, the first few decades of professional social work practice were primarily directed by the pseudoscientific claims made by Freud. This embrace of pseudoscience was not an isolated incident in the history of social work during the Modern Era. When social scientific theory is based upon an analogy to biological theory, the drawing out of this analogy rests upon confirmatory observations as the means to justify its truth claims. The current dominant conceptual model directing American social work practice—person-in-environment—rests upon an analogy to Ludwig von Bertalanffy's theory of ecological systems. Its application of Bertalanffy's principles to human social

---

[1] Joel Fischer's article "Is Casework Effective" marks a seminal point in the critical examination of the effectiveness of social work practice based in Freudian thought. It concluded that these claims were based on shoddy science. The movement spawned by this critique would call into question the effectiveness of social casework under this model.

systems occurs through an exercise in confirmation, not through a rigid program of experimentation based on falsification. Thus, even today, pseudoscientific truth claims continue to be conflated with scientific fact when directing social work practice.

Paradigm of Understanding

With the main cultural feature operating during the Modern Discourse being a strong embrace of and faith in science, it will come as no surprise that the philosophical theories providing our fundamental understanding of the world are heavily scientific in nature. With scientific fact being given a higher status of truth than other forms of knowledge generation, prime importance is given to objective knowledge in forming our understanding of the natural world, and thus our understanding of human behavior.

Theory of Ontology: Correspondence Theory of Truth

The history of the correspondence theory of truth can trace its origins back to Aristotle[m] and Plato.[157] However, its elaboration as utilized within the Modern Discourse is offered by the philosophers Bertrand Russell[n] and George Edward Moore.[158] Their formulations are described as *fact-based* in that truth arises through its correspondence to an established fact; and in this Modern Discourse, facts concerning human behavior are established through scientific investigation and produce objective knowledge of reality. Hence, it is easy to see how in the Modern Discourse scientific fact does not simply represent one form of truth but, rather, represents truth in its most pure form (with a capital "T").

As the name implies, *objective* knowledge takes the stance that knowledge of reality lies within the *object* of study—it is what philosophers' term *mind-independent* in that the brain simply acts as an organ in which to record reality: It does not play an active role in creating the reality of the object.[159] Reality is understood to the extent that the image one forms in one's mind (through accurate observation) corresponds to the actual properties of existence for the object— hence why this ontological stance is named the *correspondence theory of truth*. For social work, the human properties of existence are conceived as comprising biological, psychological, and social elements—and hence the reason many

---

[m] Aristotle states in his work *Metaphysics* (1011b25), "To say of what is that it is not, or of what is not that it is, is false, while to say of what is that it is, and of what is not that it is not, is true."

[n] Russell, *Problems of Philosophy*, 129: "Thus a belief is true when there is a corresponding fact, and is false when there is no corresponding fact."

social workers perform a bio-psycho-social assessment as a standard part of their practice. Also, all of the human behavior theories we employ to guide our practice of social work have their roots in the scientific investigation of these properties of existence.

There are three important implications that flow from this privileging of objectivism. First, subjective knowledge gets translated as representing one's point of view (the point at which one observes objective reality). Hence, it is attributed a lesser status, being seen as comprising an incomplete or partial truth—capturing only those properties of existence observable from one's present vantage. Second, objective knowledge does not require one to apply value or judgment to understand reality—rather, it aims for a value-free stance: The reality of gravity does not depend upon my judgments of its usefulness to me. And third, objective knowledge is not bound by time; it is eternal. Thus, gravity is recognized as always having existed and operated in nature, operating well before Newton discovered the formula to describe it. We can see this dynamic at work when considering mental health diagnoses captured by the various editions of the *Diagnostic and Statistical Manual of Mental Disorders*. So, for example, our present understanding of mental health diagnoses such as schizophrenia leads us to believe that schizophrenia is comprised of objectively observed properties of existence, and hence does not owe any of its basic reality to subjective knowledge in the form of cultural beliefs. Additionally, it is viewed as an illness that has occurred throughout human history. While the diagnostic description of it did not arise until the twentieth century, we perceive its existence in the past even though previous generations did not recognize it as such.

Theory of Epistemology: Positivism

Objective knowledge in one's mind is validated via an appeal to other minds achieving the same image of reality. This appeal is made via careful and accurate observation. Positivism is the theory that informs the modernist paradigm in this regard. Briefly, positivism states that the truth claims of objective knowledge are validated via positive verification by others.[160] This verification takes place through observation—by duplicating the observation of others, a truth claim is validated when the same image (i.e., knowledge) is created in the additional person's mind. As others' observations begin to consistently yield the same result, the truth claim grows in strength (from hypothesis to theory to natural law—e.g., the law of gravity).

As noted earlier, the use of one's senses (i.e., observation) to obtain and verify knowledge is known as empiricism. This is how theories of human behavior, and the various norms of functioning they propose, are understood to be created. In addition, it explains the value and importance placed upon evidence-based practice: These are practice approaches that—through repeated observations of their effectiveness in manipulating the properties of concern for a particular population group—lay claim to the status of an objective (i.e., timeless) truth (at the level of hypothesis or theory).

The implications for social work which stem from positivism are twofold. Evidence-based practice relies upon the social worker primarily viewing the client as a member of a population group—thus, the uniqueness of the individual is de-emphasized. When this membership is defined by one's dysfunction in a particular life domain—which is often the case in social work—pathology gets emphasized as an identity feature of the client.[161] In addition, primarily viewing the client as a member of a population group can easily lead the social worker to apply a template-based intervention approach, rather than one reflecting the unique needs of the client. In fact, this is what comprises the whole claim of evidence-based practice: that a particular intervention should be effective for any member of the requisite population group.

Theory of Causality: Cause–Effect (Rational Mechanics)

This is one area in which the Modern Discourse shares a similarity with the Premodern Discourse: There is a cause (i.e., movement of physical properties of existence) that has an effect on the object(s) with which it interacts, producing a change in that object (i.e., movement/change of physical properties of existence). Two important implications—concerning free will and one's orientation to time—flow from this conception of causality.

First, by its very definition it cannot capture human action arising from free will.° Free will is not a property of existence and, as such, cannot be a subject of scientific investigation. It can be marshaled only as a cause, never as an effect. And to explain effects as arising from free will erodes any predictive claims upon which scientific understanding is based. Hence, there is a dependency upon deterministic explanations to describe human behavior. This allows scientific understanding to lay out the pathway needed to be taken in order to achieve desired change; then the social worker appeals to the client's free will to traverse this pathway in the form of the treatment plan (following the *sovereign consumer* ideology described earlier—that of the consumer exercising freedom to choose

---

° Kant, *Groundwork of the Metaphysics*, 52: "As will is a kind of causality of living beings so far as they are rational, *freedom* would be that property of this causality by which it can be effective independent of external causes *determining* it, just as *natural necessity* is the property of the causality of all non-rational beings, by which they are determined in their activity by the influence of external causes."

among already selected brands). If the client chooses not to traverse this pathway or to only partially do so, this is then interpreted as client resistance (to the acknowledged truth of what will improve client functioning as determined by the scientific investigation of the social worker).

Second, the premise that a cause must always precede its effect results in an orientation to the past when it comes to knowledge gathering. So, for example, the social worker views the client's current problematic behavior as an effect; next, the social worker conducts a bio-psycho-social assessment to collect observations pertaining to cause-and-effect linkages. Thus, indubitably, the social worker's knowledge gathering efforts are directed toward events of the past. Solutions to presenting problems arise via this investigation of cause–effect linkages in the past and highlight the pathway that must be traversed to achieve the desired effect. By adopting the premise that solutions to client problems arise from an understanding of their causes, social workers are susceptible to overly focusing upon client pathology (i.e., causes leading to the dysfunction) during the process of developing treatment plans.

Conceptions of Self

In the examination of the previous two Discourses on social welfare, individuals operating within the Colonial Discourse and individuals operating within the Premodern Discourse each had a bifurcated sense of self. As a result of the scientific gaze gaining primacy in knowledge generation, the Modern Discourse on social welfare marks the first instance when conceptualizations of one's self in the world are monolithic. When it comes to social welfare in the Modern Era, individuals view themselves as existing solely in the natural world. We view ourselves as human beings in terms of existing as a living organism, one which contains biological, psychological, and social properties. The various social sciences have arisen in an attempt to understand the workings of psychological and social properties of our existence, and the science of biology (with some crossover from chemistry) has arisen to understand the organic physical properties of our existence.

This reductionism from a conceptualization of a dual existence to a single existence is what I like to melodramatically describe as "the fall of the human soul." In both the Colonial and Premodern Discourses, individuals viewed themselves as possessing a transcendental self. Filtered through a religious gaze that held primacy in these eras, this transcendental self took the conceptual form of human beings possessing a soul. The lack of a similar conceptualization of a transcendental self gaining prominence within the Modern Discourse serves as an excellent example for how a Discourse acts to privilege some forms of knowledge while subjugating others. According to recent polling, the vast majority of Americans continue to hold the belief that human beings possess a soul.[162] So conceptualization of a transcendental self in the form of a soul is not knowledge that has disappeared from American society. Rather, what has disappeared is the relevance of this knowledge in directing efforts at social welfare.[P]

In both the Colonial and the Premodern Discourses, the soul was viewed as an animating force driving human interaction. As such, social welfare practices of these eras targeted the soul as a vehicle for producing change. This is no longer the case in the Modern Era. This change in relevance is illustrated by the prominence achieved by four famous theorists of the nineteenth century: Karl Marx, Friedrich Nietzsche, Charles Darwin, and Sigmund Freud. Marx famously stated that religion served as "the opium of the people," thus delegitimizing its role in guiding political and economic activity. In declaring "God is dead," Nietzsche delegitimized the role of a transcendental self in directing culture and social activity. While Darwin's theory of evolution leaves open the door for considerations of intelligent design directing life processes, it is by no means a recognized or essential element of his theory. And Freud's conceptualization of the unconscious posited a transcendental self as an illusion, instead grounding human action as solely arising from inner biological and psychological drives.

Putting aside any considerations concerning the role of religion in society, I would like to examine the implications that this reductionism from a bifurcated sense of self to a monolithic sense of self has had in the practice of social welfare in the Modern Era. By conceptualizing ourselves as solely existing in the natural world, we posit ourselves as human organisms living in an environment. As outlined earlier, we share an affiliation with other organisms living in the environment; hence, our relationship to animals becomes one of *degree* rather than *kind*. While still being unique within the animal kingdom, human beings are simply conceived as being a more sophisticated form of animal. This is why theorists such as Ivan Pavlov experimented upon dogs, or B.F. Skinner on pigeons, in order to better understand human behavior. By contrast, colonial Americans would have viewed as incredulous the proposition that studying a pigeon could somehow yield knowledge concerning the actions of a human being.

This is not to say that conceptualizing our existence as a difference in *degree* with animals is inherently wrong or unproductive. As elucidated earlier, the most widely embraced conceptual model in American social work—person-in-environment—arose through drawing an affiliation with ecological systems. However, the monolithic view of humans existing solely in the natural world is

---

[P] Social work did not significantly explore issues of spirituality until the late 1980s, most prominently reflected in the works of Edward Canda who offers a more holistic conceptualization influenced by postmodern thought. This topic will be addressed further in Chapter 7.

unnecessarily limiting. Within the Modern Discourse, we have lost any consideration of human beings existing as different in *kind* when planning social welfare interventions. Whether conceived as some type of spiritual force or, more simply, possessing an indomitable human spirit as an animating force to our actions (each stemming from free will), this difference in *kind* from animals that we as human beings possess is no longer a target to be exploited by social welfare interventions. Science involves the study of the physical, natural world; hence, it is ill equipped to speak to this difference in *kind*. It will take a new discourse to return to such considerations.

This monolithic view of the self as solely existing in nature also reflects the move from the notion of possessive individualism in the Premodern Discourse to one of expressive individualism in the Modern Discourse. The Premodern Discourse's bifurcated understanding of the self—as subject to both natural impulses and one's spiritual connection to others—privileged an Emersonian view of the individual as a public citizen in pursuit of a communal end; this resulted in problematic behavior being evaluated against a moral ideal.[163] The Modern Discourse's monolithic view of the self—as subject to natural impulses which are then shaped by one's environment—privileges a Taylorized view of persons not as public citizens, but rather, as individual units comprising a social system (i.e., organisms in an environment); thus, problematic behavior is evaluated against normative standards of functioning for this system.[164]

Rules of Right

As the Enlightenment view of causality (action–reaction) in the Modern Discourse remained unchanged from the Premodern Discourse, a rule of right that it heavily supported also remained unchanged: *seeking causal mechanisms*. In addition, the second rule of right— *measuring deviance from the norm*— simply marks a subtle shift from its predecessor, the Premodern Discourse's *measuring deviance from an ideal*.

Seeking Causal Mechanisms

A main premise guiding social work interventions in the Modern Discourse is that solutions to client problems arise from a thorough understanding of the various causal mechanisms contributing to the problem. Hence, this is described as the *problem-solving approach* and has become the definitive model for how social work is practiced in the Modern Discourse. Three basic steps comprise this approach. The first step is to accurately describe the nature and characteristics of the problem which brings the client in for services; this is referred to as the *presenting problem*. The second step is to diagnose the causal mechanisms contributing to and maintaining the presenting problem. The third step is to employ this knowledge to develop a treatment plan which disrupts or counteracts these causal mechanisms (a process often described as fostering coping skills) so that the problem is minimized or eliminated and normative, healthy functioning is restored.

Measuring Deviance from the Norm

Similarly, the Modern Discourse continues to emphasize the mathematizability of human behavior that was started in the Premodern Discourse. Within the Premodern Discourse, this occurred through employing the utilitarian calculus of pleasure and pain in relation to a moral ideal. Within the Modern Discourse, this mathematization occurs through the employment of statistics to measure deviance from a norm of functioning.. While social workers themselves do not engage in mathematical calculations when describing a client's presenting problem, the description references social scientific norms of functioning that have been established through the use of statistics. Thus, the helping process in the Modern Discourse is conceived of as an effort at correcting client dysfunction through moving them back to a norm of healthy functioning. The route to do this is laid down by a thorough understanding of the causal mechanisms responsible for the dysfunction.

Theme of the Discourse: Professionalization

As noted earlier, the urgent need of the Modern Discourse demanded an army of social experts to engage in social engineering and scientific management. Hence, the professionalization of social work was simply one manifestation of a broader movement in society toward establishing expertise. Born out of the civil service reform movement of the progressive era, in 1923 Congress passed the Classification Act; it represented an effort at aligning the federal merit system with scientific management principles.[165] Through establishing the principle of rank in position, wages and salary would now be determined by the level of expertise one brought to the position. These levels of expertise were linked directly to the level of education (in terms of training in the area of concern) and experience one brought to the position.

The state did not stop at solely seeking to scientifically manage federal employees; it also turned its eye to regulating practices in the private marketplace.

As formal training (typically university-based) began to define practitioners of a craft as belonging to a profession, the various states applied scientific management principles—in the form of licensure—to regulate who gained entrance into a respective profession. As licensure now signified a unique realm of expertise for a particular craft, it served to reserve jobs in practicing this craft solely for members of the profession. Consequently, social work practitioners readily embraced licensure as the means to carve out their territory in the marketplace. While in 1950 positions in the US workforce subject to a licensing requirement rested between 4% and 5%, sixty years later it would expand to 25% of the workforce and include positions such as cat groomers, bartenders, and florists.[166]

In 1917, Mary Richmond would offer *Social Diagnosis* as the first definitive textbook on social casework theory and method—helping to kick off social work's drive for legitimization as a profession. This served to carve out for social work an expertise in the structure and functioning of social systems (and the individual units that comprise them). As the title's use of the term *diagnosis* implies, Richmond's work introduced the medical model to social work. It introduces the steps of gathering data, forming a diagnosis (now commonly referred to as an *assessment*), and administering treatment as the foundational elements comprising social work practice.[167] These three steps to social work practice have remained to this day as basic steps to the helping process.[168] In the social worker–client relationship, this positioning of the social worker as the professional expert is one more element operating in the Modern Discourse naturally prodding social workers to travel down a pathway whereon interventions may also serve as exercises in social control.

Notes

1. Friedlander, "Introduction," 4.
2. Martin and Zald, *Social Welfare in Society*, 4.
3. Popple and Leighninger, *Social Work*, 33.
4. Axinn and Stern, *Social Welfare*, 224; Nicholson, *Labor's Story*, 191.
5. Degler, *In Search of Human*, 54.
6. Axinn and Stern, *Social Welfare*, 223.
7. Axinn and Stern, 224.
8. Axinn and Stern, 225.
9. US Census Bureau, "New Census Data," paragraph 6.
10. Gutfreund, *Twentieth-Century Sprawl*, 7.
11. Goddard, *Getting There*, 1.
12. Goddard, 2.
13. Goddard, 2; Gutfreund, *Twentieth-Century Sprawl*, 8.
14. Gutfreund, 17.

15. Gutfreund, 14.
16. Gutfreund, 8.
17. Goddard, *Getting There*, 116; Seiler, *Republic of Drivers*, 71.
18. Goddard, 223; Seiler, 71.
19. Seiler, 71.
20. Goddard, *Getting There*, 225.
21. Gutfreund, *Twentieth-Century Sprawl*, 16.
22. Gutfreund, 16.
23. Seeley, *Building the American*, 75.
24. Goddard, *Getting There*, 3.
25. Gutfreund, *Twentieth-Century Sprawl*, 20.
26. "Number of Motor Vehicles," 1st graph.
27. Gershgorn, "After Decades," 2nd graph.
28. Seiler, *Republic of Drivers*, 90.
29. Goddard, *Getting There*, 239.
30. Goddard, 1.
31. Seiler, *Republic of Drivers*, 22.
32. Seiler, 1.
33. Seiler, 84.
34. Seiler, 84.
35. Seiler, 12–13, 32.
36. Seiler, 4.
37. Heppenheimer, *Turbulent Skies*, 22.
38. Heppenheimer, 22.
39. Heppenheimer, 1.
40. Heppenheimer, 152.
41. Heppenheimer, 152.
42. "Cruising Speeds," 1st graph.
43. van der Linden, *Airlines and Air Mail*, 2.
44. van der Linden, 11–12; Heppenheimer, *Turbulent Skies*, 1–2.
45. Heppenheimer, 225.
46. "A Brief History of the FAA," subheading "Origins of the FAA"; Heppenheimer, 12.
47. "A Brief History of the FAA," subheading "Origins of the FAA."
48. "A Brief History of the FAA," subheading "Birth of Federal Aviation Agency"; Heppenheimer, *Turbulent Skies*, 3; Hudson and Pettifer, *Diamonds in the Sky*, 43.
49. Heppenheimer, 269.
50. "Percentage of Housing."
51. "Percentage of Housing."
52. US Census Bureau, "Historical Census of Housing"; "Percentage of Housing."
53. Brooks, *Telephone*, 5–7.
54. Foster, "The FCC."
55. Foster, "The FCC."
56. Lichtenstein, *State of the Union*, 62.
57. Galambos and Pratt, *Rise of the Corporate*, 2.
58. Galambos and Pratt, 142–43.

59. Lichtenstein, *State of the Union*, 13, 136.
60. Lichtenstein, 201.
61. Lichtenstein, 62–63, 149.
62. Berstein, *A Perilous Progress*, 118; Galambos and Pratt; *Rise of the Corporate*, 133–35.
63. Berstein, 108; Galambos and Pratt, 136.
64. "Reaganomics."
65. Galambos and Pratt, *Rise of the Corporate*, 180; "Reaganomics."
66. Lichtenstein, *State of the Union*, 56.
67. Lichtenstein, 56.
68. Lichtenstein, 56.
69. Mishel, Gould, and Bivens, "Wage Stagnation," figure 4.
70. Dunn and Walker, "Union Membership," 2.
71. Mishel, Gould, and Bivens, "Wage Stagnation," figure 9.
72. Gunn, "What Caused the Decline," 2nd paragraph.
73. Galambos and Pratt, *Rise of the Corporate*, 175.
74. Axinn and Stern, *Social Welfare*, 225; Mooney and Majka, *Farmers' and Farm Workers'*, 90.
75. Galambos and Pratt, *Rise of the Corporate*, 76.
76. Galambos and Pratt, 76.
77. Galambos and Pratt, 73–74; Seiler, *Republic of Drivers*, 12.
78. Nicholson, *Labor's Story*, 193.
79. Galambos and Pratt, *Rise of the Corporate*, 12.
80. Webb, "The Difficulties of Individualism," 373.
81. Seiler, *Republic of Drivers*, 12.
82. Lichtenstein, *State of the Union*, 62.
83. Taylor, *Principles of Scientific Management*, 2.
84. Seiler, *Republic of Drivers*, 25–26.
85. Seiler, 26.
86. Nicholson, *Labor's Story*, 178.
87. Seiler, *Republic of Drivers*, 32–33.
88. Seiler, 91.
89. Emerson, "Self-Reliance," 2.
90. Seiler, *Republic of Drivers*, 91.
91. Cushman, *Constructing the Self*, 67; Seiler, 12–13.
92. Wiebe, *Self-Rule*, 187.
93. Seiler, *Republic of Drivers*, 13.
94. McGovern, *Sold American*, 77.
95. Axinn and Stern, *Social Welfare*, 183–84, 198; Popple and Leighninger, *Social Work*, 235.
96. McCormick, "Vast Tides."
97. Axinn and Stern, *Social Welfare*, 269–70; Katz, *The Undeserving Poor*, 125; Trattner, *From Poor Law*, 362.
98. Axinn and Stern, 201; Trattner, 239.
99. Axinn and Stern, 188.

100. Axinn and Stern, 201.
101. As quoted in Seiler, *Republic of Drivers*, 70.
102. Seiler, 91.
103. Hamby, *Liberalism and Its Challengers*, 120.
104. Katz, *The Undeserving Poor*, 236–37.
105. Seiler, *Republic of Drivers*, 96.
106. Axinn and Stern, *Social Welfare*, 198.
107. Axinn and Stern, 198.
108. Axinn and Stern, 192.
109. Axinn and Stern, 192.
110. Committee on Economic Security (1935) as quoted in Axinn and Stern, 189.
111. American Association of Social Workers (1936) as quoted in Axinn and Stern, 198.
112. Family Welfare Association of America (1936) as quoted in Axinn and Stern, 198.
113. Fornatale and Mills, *Radio*, 21.
114. Berry and Woodward, "Average Number of Televisions," 1st graph; Fornatale and Mills, xv.
115. Fornatale and Mills, xvii; Keith, *Talking Radio*, 89.
116. Hilmes, *Radio Voices*, 86.
117. Boddy, *New Media*, 4; Hartley, *Television Truths*, 5–6; Hilmes, 1.
118. Hartley, 1; Hilmes, 5.
119. Boddy, *New Media*, 25, 29.
120. Sarnoff (1930) as quoted in Boddy, 19.
121. *Planning & Progress*, paragraph "The Makings of the Middle Class"; Martin, "70% of Americans."
122. Ponce de Leon, *That's the Way*, 72.
123. Boddy, *New Media*, 4; Keith, *Talking Radio*, 183.
124. Fornatale and Mills, *Radio*, 61.
125. Fornatale and Mills, 184.
126. Seiler, *Republic of Drivers*, 73.
127. Axinn and Stern, *Social Welfare*, 172.
128. Cushman, *Constructing the Self*, 73.
129. Seiler, *Republic of Drivers*, 14.
130. Seiler, 73.
131. Axinn and Stern, *Social Welfare*, 228.
132. Trattner, *From Poor Law*, 243.
133. Axinn and Stern, *Social Welfare*, 240.
134. Lee, "Social Work as Cause," 5; Trattner, *From Poor Law*, 267.
135. Baughey-Gill, "When Gay," 8–10.
136. Kant, *Groundwork of the Metaphysics*, §65, 5:375.
137. Ginsborg, "Kant on Understanding," 233, 248–50.
138. Cohen, "An Analysis of Interactions," 35.
139. Germain, "An Ecological Perspective"; Germain and Gitterman, *The Life Model*.
140. Cohen, "An Analysis of Interactions," 35–37.
141. Payne, "The Politics of Systems," 278–79.

142. Degler, *In Search of Human*, 6; Heyer, *Nature, Human Nature*, 97.
143. Van den Berg, "Kant's Conception," 8–18.
144. Degler, *In Search of Human*, 7; Heyer, *Nature, Human Nature*, 101.
145. Degler, 329; Heyer, 102.
146. Degler, 8–10; Heyer, 101.
147. Heyer, 105–06.
148. Hodgson and Knudsen, *Darwin's Conjecture*, 42.
149. Hodgson and Knudsen, 34.
150. As quoted in Hodgson and Knudsen, 42.
151. Degler, *In Search of Human*, 315.
152. Heyer, *Nature, Human Nature*, 107.
153. Degler, *In Search of Human*, 14.
154. Degler, 315.
155. Kant, *Groundwork of the Metaphysics*, 52.
156. Popper, *Logic of Scientific Discovery*.
157. Plato, *Cratylus*, 385b2.
158. Moore, *Some Main Problems*, chapter 15.
159. Popper, *Objective Knowledge*.
160. Popper, *Conjectures and Refutations*.
161. Cushman, *Constructing the Self*, 278.
162. Murphy, "Most Americans Believe"; Weldon, "Paradise Polled."
163. Cushman, *Constructing the Self*, 67.
164. Cushman, 67; Seiler, *Republic of Drivers*, 33–34.
165. National Research Council, *Pay for Performance*, 15.
166. Larkin, "A Brief History," 2.
167. Trattner, *From Poor Law*, 255.
168. Hepworth et al., *Direct Social Work Practice*, 37–41.

References

"A Brief History of the FAA." Federal Aviation Administration. Last modified January 4, 2017, https://www.faa.gov/about/history/brief_history/.

Axinn, June, and Mark J. Stern. *Social Welfare: A History of the American Response to Need*. Boston: Allyn and Bacon, 2001.

Baughey-Gill, Sarah. "When Gay Was not Okay with the APA: A Historical Overview of Homosexuality and Its Status as Mental Disorder." *Ocam's Razor* 1 (2011): 5–16.

Berry, Chip, and Maggie Woodward. "Average Number of Televisions in U.S. Homes Declining." US Energy Information Administration. Last modified February 28, 2017, https://www.eia.gov/todayinenergy/detail.php?id=30132#.

Berstein, Michael A. *A Perilous Progress: Economists and Public Purpose in Twentieth-Century America*. Princeton, NJ: Princeton University Press, 2001.

Boddy, William. *New Media and Popular Imagination: Launching Radio, Television, and Digital Media in the United States*. New York: Oxford University Press, 2004.

Brooks, John. *Telephone: The First Hundred Years*. New York: Harper & Row, 1975.

Cohen, Bernard. "An Analysis of Interactions Between the Natural Sciences and the Social Sciences." In *The Natural Sciences and the Social Sciences: Some Critical and Historical Perspectives*, edited by Bernard Cohen, 1–99. Boston Studies in the Philosophy of Science, vol. 150. Boston: Kluwer Academic, 1994.

"Cruising Speeds of the Most Common Types of Commercial Airliners," Statista. Accessed May, 24, 2019, https://www.statista.com/statistics/614178/cruising-speed-of-most-common-airliners/.

Cushman, Phillip. *Constructing the Self, Constructing America: A Cultural History of Psychotherapy*. New York: Addison-Wesley, 1995.

Degler, Carl. *In Search of Human Nature: The Decline and Revival of Darwinism in American Social Thought*. New York: Oxford University Press, 1991.

Dunn, Megan, and James Walker. "Union Membership in the United States." US Bureau of Labor Statistics. Last modified September, 2016, https://www.bls.gov/spotlight/2016/union-membership-in-the-united-states/pdf/union-membership-in-the-united-states.pdf.

Emerson, Ralph Waldo. "Self-Reliance." In *Essays: First Series*. Project Gutenberg. First published 1841. https://www.gutenberg.org/files/2944/2944-h/2944-h.htm.

Fischer, Joel. "Is Casework Effective? A Review." *Social Work* 18 (1973): 5–21.

Fornatale, Peter, and Joshua E. Mills. *Radio in the Television Age*. New York: Overlook Press, 1980.

Foster, Patrick. "The FCC and Your Phone Service: What You Need to Know." Talkroute. Accessed May 28, 2019, https://talkroute.com/the-fcc-and-your-phone-service-what-you-need-to-know/.

Friedlander, Walter. "Introduction: Generic Principles of Social Work." In *Concepts and Methods of Social Work*, edited by Walter Friedlander, 1–14. Englewood Cliffs, NJ: Prentice-Hall, 1958.

Galambos, Louis, and Joseph Pratt. *The Rise of the Corporate Commonwealth: U.S. Business and Public Policy in the Twentieth Century*. New York: Basic Books, 1988.

Germain, Carel. "An Ecological Perspective in Casework Practice." *Social Casework* 54 (1973): 323–30.

Germain, Carel, and Alex Gitterman. *The Life Model of Social Work Practice*. New York: Columbia University Press, 1980.

Gershgorn, Dave. "After Decades of Decline, No-Car Households Are Becoming More Common in the US." Quartz. Last modified December 28, 2016, https://qz.com/873704/no-car-households-are-becoming-more-common-in-the-us-after-decades-of-decline/.

Ginsborg, Hannah. "Kant on Understanding Organisms as Natural Purposes." In *Kant and the· Sciences*, edited by Eric Watkins, 231–58. New York: Oxford University Press, 2001.

Goddard, Stephen. *Getting There: The Epic Struggle Between Road and Rail in the American Century*. Chicago: Chicago University Press, 1996.

Gordon, William E. "Basic Constructs for an Integrative and Generative Conception of Social Work." In *The General Systems Approach: Contributions Toward an Holistic Conception of Social Work*, edited by Gordon Hearn, 5–11. New York: Council on Social Work Education, 1969.

Gunn, Dwyer. "What Caused the Decline of Unions in America?" *Pacific Standard*, April 24, 2018. Accessed May 28, 2019, https://psmag.com/economics/what-caused-the-decline-of-unions-in-america.

Gutfreund, Owen. *Twentieth-Century Sprawl: Highways and the Reshaping of the American Landscape*. New York: Oxford University Press, 2004.

Hamby, Alonzo L. *Liberalism and Its Challengers: FDR to Reagan*. Oxford: Oxford University Press, 1985.

Hartley, John. *Television Truths: Forms of Knowledge in Popular Culture*. Malden, MA: Blackwell Publishing, 2008.

Heppenheimer, Thomas A. *Turbulent Skies: The History of Commercial Aviation*. New York: John Wiley & Sons, 1986.

Hepworth, Dean, Ronald Rooney, Glenda Rooney, and Kim Strom-Gottfried. *Direct Social Work Practice: Theory and Skills*. 9th ed. Brooks/Cole Empowerment Series. Chicago: Brooks/Cole, 2012.

Heyer, Paul. *Nature, Human Nature, and Society: Marx, Darwin, Biology, and the Human Sciences*. Contributions in Sociology. Westport, CT: Greenwood Press, 1982.

Hilmes, Michele. *Radio Voices: American Broadcasting, 1922–1952*. Minneapolis: University of Minnesota Press, 1997.

Hodgson, Geoffrey M., and Thorbjørn Knudsen. *Darwin's Conjecture: The Search for General Principles of Social and Economic Evolution*. Chicago: University of Chicago Press, 2010.

Hudson, Kenneth, and Julian Pettifer. *Diamonds in the Sky: A Social History of Air Travel*. London: British Broadcasting Corporation, 1979.

Kant, Immanuel. *Groundwork of the Metaphysics of Morals*. Edited and translated by Allen W. Wood. New Haven: Yale University Press, 2002. First published 1785.

Katz, Michael B. *The Undeserving Poor: From the War on Poverty to the War on Welfare*. New York: Pantheon Books, 1989.

Keith, Michael C. *Talking Radio: An Oral History of American Radio in the Television Age*. Armonk, NY: M. E. Sharpe, 2000.

Larkin, Paul J., Jr. "A Brief History of Occupational Licensing." The Heritage Foundation. Last modified May 23, 2017, https://www.heritage.org/sites/default/files/2017-05/LM-204.pdf.

Lee, Porter. "Social Work as Cause and Function: Presidential Address, National Conference of Social Work 1929." In *Social Work as Cause and Function and Other Papers*. New York: Columbia University Press, 1937.

Lichtenstein, Nelson. *State of the Union: A Century of American Labor*. Princeton, NJ: Princeton University Press, 2002.

Martin, Emmie. "70% of Americans Consider Themselves Middle Class—but Only 50% Are." CNBC: Make It. Last modified June 30, 2017, https://www.cnbc.com/2017/06/30/70-percent-of-americans-consider-themselves-middle-class-but-only-50-percent-are.html.

Martin, George, and Mayer Zald, eds. *Social Welfare in Society*. New York: Columbia University Press, 1981.

McCormick, Anne O'Hare. "Vast Tides That Stir the Capital." *New York Times*, May 7, 1933.

McGovern, Charles. *Sold American: Consumption and Citizenship, 1890–1945*. Chapel Hill: University of North Carolina Press, 2006.

Mishel, Lawrence, Elise Gould, and Josh Bivens. "Wage Stagnation in Nine Charts." Economic Policy Institute. Last modified January 6, 2015, https://www.epi.org/publication/charting-wage-stagnation/.

Mooney, Patrick, and Theo Majka. *Farmers' and Farm Workers' Movements: Social Protest in American Agriculture.* New York: Twayne Publishers, 1995.

Moore, George Edward. *Some Main Problems of Philosophy.* London: George Allen & Unwin, 1953. First published 1910.

Murphy, Caryle. "Most Americans Believe in Heaven . . . and Hell." Pew Research Center. Last modified November 10, 2015, https://www.pewresearch.org/fact-tank/2015/11/10/most-americans-believe-in-heaven-and-hell/.

National Research Council. *Pay for Performance: Evaluating Performance Appraisal and Merit Pay.* Washington, DC: National Academies Press, 1991.

Nicholson, Philip Yale. *Labor's Story in the United States.* Philadelphia: Temple University Press, 2004.

"Number of Motor Vehicles Registered in the United States from 1990 to 2016." Statista. Acecessed May 28, 2019, https://www.statista.com/statistics/183505/number-of-vehicles-in-the-united-states-since-1990/.

Payne, Malcolm. "The Politics of Systems Theory Within Social Work." *Journal of Social Work* 2 (2002): 269–92.

"Percentage of Housing Units with Telephones in the United States from 1920 to 2008." Statista. Accessed May 8, 2019, https://www.statista.com/statistics/189959/housing-units-with-telephones-in-the-united-states-since-1920/.

Planning & Progress Study 2018. Milwaukee: Northwestern Mutual Life Insurance Company. Accessed May 28, 2019, https://news.northwesternmutual.com/planning-and-progress-2018.

Plato. *Cratylus.* Translated by C. D. C. Reeve. Indianapolis: Hackett Publishing Company, 1998.

Ponce de Leon, Charles L. *That's the Way It Is: A History of Television News in America.* Chicago: University of Chicago Press, 2015.

Popper, Karl. *Conjectures and Refutations.* London: Routledge, 1963.

Popper, Karl. *Objective Knowledge: An Evolutionary Approach.* New York: Oxford University Press, 1972.

Popper, Karl. *The Logic of Scientific Discovery.* Eastford, CT: Martino Fine Books, 2014. First published 1959.

Popple, Phillip, and Leslie Leighninger. *Social Work, Social Welfare, and American Society.* Needham Heights, MA: Allyn & Bacon, 1990.

"Reaganomics." UShistory.org. Accessed May, 24, 2019, http://www.ushistory.org/us/59b.asp.

Richmond, Mary. *Social Diagnosis.* New York: Russell Sage Foundation, 1917.

Seeley, *Building the American.*

Seiler, Cotton. *Republic of Drivers: A Cultural History of Automobility in America.* Chicago: University of Chicago Press, 2008.

Taylor, Fredrick W. *The Principles of Scientific Management.* First published 1911. Accessed May, 24, 2019, https://wwnorton.com/college/history/america-essential-learning/docs/FWTaylor-Scientific_Mgmt-1911.pdf.

Trattner, Walter I. *From Poor Law to Welfare State: A History of Social Welfare in America.* 4th ed. New York: Free Press, 1989.

US Census Bureau. "Historical Census of Housing Tables: Telephones." Last modified October 31, 2011, https://www.census.gov/hhes/www/housing/census/historic/phone.html.

US Census Bureau. "New Census Data Show Differences Between Urban and Rural Populations." Last modified December 8, 2016, https://www.census.gov/newsroom/press-releases/2016/cb16-210.html.

Van den Berg, Hein. "Kant's Conception of Proper Science." *Synthese* 183 (2011): 7–26.

van der Linden, Robert. *Airlines and Air Mail: The Post Office and the Birth of the Commercial Aviation Industry*. Lexington: University Press of Kentucky, 2002.

Webb, Sydney. "The Difficulties of Individualism." *Economic Journal* 1 (1891): 370–81.

Weldon, Kathleen. "Paradise Polled: Americans and the Afterlife." HuffPost. Last modified December 6, 2017, https://www.huffingtonpost.com/kathleen-weldon/paradise-polled-americans_b_7587538.html.

Wiebe, Robert. *Self-Rule*. Chicago: University of Chicago Press, 1995.

7

Social Welfare Practices in the Modern Era (c. 1920–Present)

The Modern Discourse within which we operate today gained its dominance near the start of the twentieth century. While this resulted in radically different approaches to providing social work, this shift in dominance to a new Discourse was less dramatic, less revolutionary, than that which took place when the Premodern Discourse replaced the Colonial Discourse. This is because the rules of right for the Modern Discourse remained largely unchanged from those operating during the Premodern Discourse. Seeking mechanisms of causality and then bringing about change remained as a central rule of right of this Modern Discourse. Its companion rule of right, measuring deviance from a particular norm of behavior so that change involves movement back toward this norm, represents a minor alteration to the Premodern Discourse's rule of right of measuring deviance from an ideal. This would result in some elements of practice having an eerie similarity to the Premodern Era. However, the urgent need to which the Modern Discourse responded—maintaining and enhancing the functioning of the individual/society—did represent a dramatic shift from the Premodern Discourse, and hence the dynamics of power operating within the Modern Discourse did significantly change from those of its predecessor. As will be shown in this chapter, this shift was of a great enough degree to substantially change approaches to social welfare knowledge generation and the application of this knowledge in the form of social welfare practice.

By 1920 the US economy had considerably matured from its early days of industrialization. Also, the city began to be viewed in a much more positive light than it had in the past. The country had become connected nationally on the economic, political, and social levels to an unprecedented degree, now led by a federal government taking a lead role in promoting social welfare efforts. Integration of individuals into society began to be seen more and more as an established fact rather than a process in doubt. Attention was now directed toward maintaining the functionality of this interdependence: This became the urgent need of the twentieth-century Modern Discourse.

A Genealogy of the Good and Critique of Hubris. Phillip Dybicz, Oxford University Press. © Oxford University Press 2023.
DOI: 10.1093/oso/9780197670071.003.0007

Concerns over spiritual communion withered. Technical expertise replaced moral superiority as the source of authority for knowledge generation. The main source of power supporting moral authority—viewing an individual as part of a transcendental world—lost prominence and faded from the Discourse. Human beings were now seen as existing solely in one world—the natural world. Greater attention was now given to the potential of impersonal forces in the environment acting upon the individual. Consequently, the view of individuals as public citizens in the form of rational, self-interested actors within a world of human beings (i.e., society) was no longer the primary lens through which to view clients. The power shaping our current Modern Discourse gives rise to a primary lens through which individuals exist as interdependent organisms in a social environment, and hence, clients are viewed as needing assistance to adapt or conform (i.e., to subsume one's individuality to the greater functioning of the system).

This shift to the natural world created a new power relationship within the existing central elements of causality and deviance and, thus, has led to the production of a distinctly different cast of knowledge. The mechanisms of causality are now sought within a reality that solely encompasses the natural world. Under the scientific gaze, this reality brooks no other; and thus, this reality becomes Reality with a capital "R," and truths uncovered are Truth with a capital "T." The manner by which to measure deviance also underwent a change. It was no longer deviance from the ideal of the morally and civically responsible citizen. As human beings are now viewed as organisms existing in an environment, a norm of the healthily functioning organism has become the standard to which deviance is measured. Social welfare thus became translated into efforts to promote healthy functioning. These new dynamics operating within the Modern Discourse will be elaborated upon in greater detail in the sections below.

The forces directing this shift are most clearly illustrated via their crystallization in the emergence of the thought of Sigmund Freud, his development of psychodynamic theory, and its ready embrace by social work. Note, I am declaring not that Freud was the cause for this shift in the Discourse but, rather, that his thought acts as a prominent milestone marking this shift. First, his theory marks a schism occurring between psychology and religion (reflective of the schism occurring between all of the social sciences and religion). Second, his concept of the *unconscious* not only opened the door for the discovery of internal psychological components (and thus the further objectification of the individual) but also signaled knowledge of the True as being hidden from both the client and the social worker (and thus something that must be uncovered). Furthermore, it also offered an answer to the conundrum of trying to seek causal mechanisms operating upon human beings possessing free will by offering the concept of the unconscious as an operating mechanism in directing human behavior absent this free will.

Within the nineteenth-century Premodern Discourse, human beings were viewed as existing equally in a transcendent world as well as a natural world. The schism marked by Sigmund Freud resulted in a distinct shift toward the natural world and the disappearance of the transcendental—attention was given to biology, not inner sanctions. Individuals were now seen as natural organisms possessing biological, psychological, and social components and interacting with an environment: The associations flowing from this view represent the main power circulating within the current Modern Discourse.

Freud's concept of the unconscious and his subsequent development of the psychological components of the id, ego, and superego resulted in further objectification of the individual. Throughout the Modern Era, psychological components were added onto biological components. As with their biological counterparts, these psychological components represented real sites that could be the target of an intervention—that is, acted upon in order to produce a reaction. In terms of seeking causality, a whole new category of objects could now be placed within a causal chain. In terms of deviance, another level (psychological) was added to the new norm of the healthily functioning organism in an environment.

This objectification occurred on the sociological level as well. Within the Premodern Discourse, the objectification of the natural world was already present in terms of finding resources within an environment to meet physical (i.e., biological) needs. With the turn toward science, social relations became objectified as well. Relationships with neighbors, family, friends, etcetera could now be described as resources: Rather than being referred to in terms emphasizing their human qualities (e.g., fellow citizen), such terminology grants them the status of an object (i.e., they are a "resource"). Systems theory would place these relations as objects within a system. This dynamic is reflected in the bio-psycho-social assessment that is still with us today. Thus, social components took their place alongside psychological and biological components in terms of becoming items within a causal chain and in terms of creating another level to the norm of healthy functioning. Human residence in an objective, natural world was now firmly established.

Lastly, Freud's concept of the unconscious relegated causal knowledge and deviance from the norm to hidden areas. Concomitant with humankind taking up residence in the natural world was the shift that authority regarding knowledge of the Good (and thus the promotion of social welfare) resides within the natural world. Hence, this created the dynamic that is now operating in our current Modern Discourse: Knowledge of the True is necessary in order to achieve knowledge of the Good. The scientific authority of the natural world has replaced the moral authority of the transcendental world of the Premodern Discourse as the means for uncovering causal mechanisms and measuring deviance, now from a norm of healthy functioning.

In the following sections, I will explore in greater detail how these shifts into the Modern Discourse played out in the field of social work. The first section explores how social work's approach toward knowledge generation changed. The final section explores how this shift into the Modern Discourse transformed the settlement house movement and the scientific charity movement into the social work practices we are familiar with today.

Knowledge Generation

Theory

Psychological Theory

For social work, it was Sigmund Freud's psychodynamic theory, and later theorists' transformation of it into ego psychology, which first took root in this newly tilled epistemological soil of human beings as organisms living in an environment. As mentioned, Freud introduced the psychic components of the id, ego, and superego, all of which interacted upon each other to produce certain behaviors. According to Freud, every behavior—from a slip of the tongue to hysterical paralysis—had an underlying cause traceable to the interaction of these psychic components: a cause that could be identified by a professional with the appropriate expert knowledge. Freud also introduced five stages of psychosexual development, thereby extending the metaphor of growth and development of an organism to the psychological sphere. Under Freud, the norm of development was predominantly characterized by intrapsychic conflict, and thus he advanced a picture of normal functioning that was quite grim.

Ego psychology, ushered in by Heinz Hartmann, gave greater prominence to the psychic structure of the ego and its role in conscious determination.[1] In this broader role, greater emphasis was given to the ego's ability to interact with the psychic components of other individuals, as well as with objects in its environment (which would include social components when wedded with sociological theory). Causal relationships were sought between these various components, and the source for change lay in influencing their interaction. Again, expert knowledge was required to uncover these causal relationships. The other prominent contributor to the development of ego psychology was Robert White. Through his work *The Abnormal Personality* (1948), he moved psychopathology from being prominently situated in the unconscious and a conflict-driven id to being prominently situated in personality and the ego's striving for adaptation.[2] This new understanding of measuring deviance from a norm of functioning laid the theoretical foundation for the development of *The Diagnostic and Statistical Manual of Mental Disorders*, which would rapidly gain hegemony within the field of mental health in defining the nature of deviance from a norm of mental functioning.

Through drawing upon Charles Darwin's theory of evolution, ego psychology brought the concept of adaptation into the psychological sphere. Hartmann's language describing this process baldly reflects the Modern Discourse's view of humankind—that of an organism living in an environment: "Thus, adaptation is a reciprocal relationship between the *organism* and its *environment* [my emphasis]"[3] and "The processes of adaptation are influenced both by constitution and external *environment*, and more directly determined by the ontogenetic phase of the *organism* [my emphasis]."[4] The norm of functioning under this outlook was now set as successful adaptation to one's environment. Deviation from this norm was described as maladaptation or maladjustment. The actions an individual took to psychologically adapt to their environment (i.e., the causal mechanisms employed to achieve successful adaptation/homeostasis) were called *coping skills*.[5]

The pioneering work of Erik Erikson gave greater prominence to the social nature of being human so that personality was now seen in terms of psychosocial development.[6] Building upon ego theory, Erikson further shifted emphasis away from instincts of the id as reflected in Freudian psychodynamic theory to a conflict-free ego engaged in reality orientation.[7] Erikson helped usher in a number of life cycle perspectives during the remaining half of the twentieth century.[8] In terms of seeking causal relationships, the individual continued to be viewed as an organism within an environment.[9] Erikson is the only life-span theorist to use the term *organism* when referring to human beings.[10]

Yet, later theorists, while not using the term *organism*, all state that they are building upon Erikson's work and the notion of growth and development (i.e., of an organism).[11] This dynamic illustrates how an analogy (i.e., organism in environment) gets pushed into the subconscious with its continued use through the power of the dominant discourse. As described in the previous chapter, social scientists make liberal use of drawing analogies to empirically validated theories in biology in order to advance truth claims in a social scientific context. Thus, even though the term *person-in-environment* has been widely adopted, the validity of its concept lies upon humans' continuity with animals, and thus in viewing persons as organisms in an environment.

And while Erikson also explored spiritual development,[12] by consigning it to the natural world of scientific investigation, spirituality within the Modern Discourse becomes conceptualized merely as another trait—albeit unique to the human organism—that can act upon its functioning. As was stated in Chapter 6, social work in the Modern Era did not significantly explore issues of spirituality until the late 1980s, most prominently reflected in the works of Edward Canda, who offers a more holistic conceptualization influenced by postmodern thought.

Like the concept of strengths, this conceptualization of spirituality gets watered down in its application within the Modern Discourse; it too is typically tacked on to a bio-psycho-social assessment, with social work practitioners seeking to explore issues of client spirituality by rebranding the assessment as a bio-psycho-social-spiritual assessment. In terms of the norm of healthy functioning, life-span theories added a further characteristic. It was no longer merely viewed as achieving homeostasis through successful adaptation/adjustment with one's environment. As noted earlier, psychodynamic theory introduced the notion of psychological stages of growth, but these were limited to development in childhood. Now, healthy functioning also encompassed the positive growth and development of the organism throughout adulthood.[13]

Alongside the rise of theories concerning personality development, there appeared theories of cognitive development and theories of moral development. Jean Piaget is recognized as the father of cognitive development theory.[14] As is the case with personality development, Piaget, and many who followed in his wake,[15] linked cognitive development to biological development; Piaget did so by offering four stages of cognitive development coinciding with various age spans in childhood.[16] Piaget's theory as a product of this Modern Discourse which places humankind squarely within the natural world is quite clear: "For Piaget, human intelligence is a type of evolutionary biological adaptation that enables people to interact successfully with the environment."[17]

Piaget linked one's ability to employ cognitive reason with one's ability to employ moral reason.[18] This resulted in the creation of a psychological structure governing moral thought.[a] Lawrence Kohlberg and Carol Gilligan each built upon the foundations laid by Piaget to advance theories of their own,[19] both of which perpetuated the objectification of moral reasoning. Thus, unique qualities of being human—personality, intellectual reasoning, and even moral reasoning—were all objectified as structures acting within cognitive processes: processes that are intimately linked to our biological growth and processes that are acted upon and in turn act upon one's environment. Within this Modern Discourse, these structures follow the model of a natural organism in that, along with the individual's physical growth and development, they are seen as something that grows and develops as well.

This objectification of human beings, and their placement within a natural world, is most baldly illustrated via behaviorist theory. Behaviorist theory emerged in the early 1900s as an attempt to ground psychology as a natural

---

[a] Kanjiranthinkal, *A Sociological Critique*, 50. Kanjiranthinkal provides an excellent critique of this objectification through emphasizing Piaget's connection to Kant. By linking moral reason to the biological structure and growth of the brain, Piaget provided a psychological structure governing moral reason that existed in the natural world: "In contrast to Kant's transcendental turn, Piaget takes a biological turn via psychology to answer both the origin and nature of the *a priori*."

science through strict employment of empirical observation and the scientific method (John Watson, Edward Thorndike, and Ivan Pavlov are recognized as the prominent authors of early behaviorist thought—now referred to as *classical behaviorism*). As human behavior could be directly observed, these behaviors received the focus and attention of study as the means to indirectly observe psychological conditions in action. In its search for causality, behaviorism focuses on environmental conditions that shape behavior. While avoiding the creation of psychological components, the individual becomes the object—which can lead to a radical environmental determinism. B. F. Skinner drew upon Darwin in order to describe this environmental conditioning as a process of natural selection[b]—and posited that the primary motivation for human behavior was the drive to survive.[20]

In its reduction of the individual to an object to be acted upon, classic and neo-behaviorism represent the most extreme consequences of the objectification that takes place with humankind's residence in a natural world: By considering as irrelevant the many inner qualities that make us human (such as free will), within both classical and neo-behaviorism there is little that differentiates human being from animal—continuity becomes equality. Thus, it is no surprise that behaviorist researchers turned to experimentation on animals—for example, Ivan Pavlov (dogs), Edward Thorndike (cats), and B.F. Skinner (pigeons)—as the means to elucidate how human behavior is shaped.

Social learning theory built upon behaviorism by including internal processes such as cognition and emotions as factors conditioning behavior (John Dollard and Neal Miller, as well as Albert Bandura and Richard Walters, are all noted theorist representing social learning theory). Exchange theory builds upon social learning theory by substituting profit seeking for survival as one's prime motivation guiding behavior (George Homas and Peter Blau are noted exchange theorists). Yet while this evolution of behaviorism into cognitive-behavioral theory attempts to move away from a strict equality with animals by considering cognitive reasoning as an element in shaping behavior, it maintains the scientific gaze of viewing human beings as existing solely in the natural world. Within cognitive-behavioral theory, objectification and the elements of causality and deviance from a norm remain prominent. Identifying and employing causal mechanisms in order to condition behavior is the prime focus—hence among the theories so far discussed, behaviorist-oriented theories respond most strongly to the power exerted by the rules of right of this Modern Discourse. These theories see all behavior as coping mechanisms resulting from efforts at adaptation.

---

[b] Skinner's employment of Darwinian concepts in behaviorist thought is known as *neo-behaviorism*.

While this avoids the path of labeling behaviors as abnormal, it does provide a ready tool for shaping undesirable behavior toward a desired norm—thus finding great resonance with aims of scientific management being employed in the economic, political, and social spheres. With its strong adherence to causal mechanisms and its ability to condition behavior toward a norm, it is no surprise that behaviorist-oriented theories have found many applications within social work practice: These include the use of token-economy systems by institutions through which residents earn privileges; relapse prevention in areas of substance abuse, violent aggression, and other behaviors; contingency contracting; social skills training and assertiveness training; exposure therapy for anxiety; and cognitive restructuring for depression.[21]

Sociological Theory

Sociological theory embraced by social work also contributed to the further objectification of humankind and the placing of us solely within a natural world. Systems theories have gained wide acceptance in social work courses and textbooks from the 1970s to the present, and the person-in-environment perspective advanced by ecological systems theory has gained wide currency as a meta-theory for practice.[22] As is the case with the psychological theories discussed above, as a consequence of viewing human beings as existing in a natural world, system theories embrace biology when depicting the human condition. Thus, human social systems are seen as analogous to biological systems—as when Gordon Hearn states, "Finally, it is assumed that human behavior is always the result of the interaction between the *natural organism and its environment* [my emphasis]."[23] The human being is seen as a system onto itself containing biological, psychological, and sociological components. This human being as a system is viewed as an organism,[24] one that seeks to grow and develop[25] as well as one that seeks to maintain a level of homeostasis[26]; it engages in adaptation to do so,[27] and it exists within an environment[28]—further differentiated in ecosystems theory by the terms *habitat* and *niche*.[29] In terms of their relation to causality, the objectification of humankind is advanced through the conceptualization of components that can act as sites of intervention, as described by Hearn:

> Each system consists of *objects* which are simply the parts or components of the system; there are *attributes* which are properties of the objects; and there are *relationships* among the objects and their attributes which tie the system together.[30]

A multiplicity of social components is created—from family to leisure groups to work groups and to society in the form of local community, nation, and world, to name but a few examples. Each can be viewed as a system of its own. The individual is even viewed as a system, as are their inner cognitive, emotional, and spiritual qualities. The norm of healthy functioning becomes quite literally the healthy functioning of the system as evidenced by a state of homeostasis or goodness-of-fit. This has led to a very conservative approach to social change efforts; as the individual is most often the site of intervention, adaptation to the present system gets emphasized.[31] As Susan P. Robbins, Pranab Chatterjee, and Edward R. Canda aptly note, "in most textbooks the prevailing version of systems theory implicitly overemphasizes the functionalist concepts of adaptation and system maintenance."[32] Dynamic systems theory, through addressing creative system transformation, attempts to avoid the dehumanizing implication of referring to humans as objects. However, it retains the view of humans possessing components and interacting as part of a system—analogous to a natural organism in an environment.[33] In terms of deviance from the norm of healthy functioning, it is from systems theory that we get the word *dysfunctional.*

Even social work's application of symbolic interactionism in the form of role theory reflects this pattern of objectification.[34] Symbolic interactionism stresses human beings' capacity for interpretation and ascribing meaning to interactions within a social situation. However, even though this school of theory has the least connection to biological processes of the individual, symbolic interactionism cannot escape the process of objectification resulting from the Modern Discourse's placement of humankind within a natural world. The individual's social world is seen as comprised of objects with which the individual interacts: "The social world is comprised of objects that are physical (such as buildings), social (such as rules), and abstract (such as customs)."[35] Within this mode of interaction, the individual becomes an object, and the world they inhabit is a social environment filled with objects.

The profession of social work has mainly employed symbolic interactionism in the form of role theory. Role theory is unique in that it does not propose an abstract or ideal norm of functioning but creates a particular norm based upon the client's situation.[c] Yet, roles become sociological objects that can be acted upon to produce change. Casework employing role theory is viewed as a form of treatment for a client,[36] who lives in an environment,[37] and who is experiencing social dysfunction.[38] While the social work helping situation centers upon combating such things as stigmatization or role conflict, it is still viewed as an effort to achieve individual adjustment through the alleviation of problems and/or an effort to achieve individual growth.[39]

---

[c] Strean, *Clinical Social Work*, 210. As Strean notes, "The utilization of role theory, with its emphasis on interaction and transaction and its respect for the client's and 'significant others' own definitions of appropriate behavior, truly meets the client where he is and accepts him as he is."

One can easily see the various elements of the Modern Discourse finding expression through the generation of psychological and sociological theory. The *two rules of right*—seeking causal mechanisms and measuring deviance from the norm—reinforce *the paradigm of understanding* and its privileging of objective knowledge, and hence the objectification of human beings. The shift in *conception of the self* which places humankind solely within a natural world privileges biology. Biology takes on great importance, for it serves as humankind's anchor in the natural world. The *intellectual thought* of Charles Darwin's theory of evolution, Immanuel Kant's understanding of organisms as purposes, and empiricism all combine to offer an organizing principle for biology in the true Kantian sense that stresses humankind's continuity between nature and human nature. Undergirding all these efforts at knowledge generation is the *defining cultural feature* promoting a faith in science as the sole arbiter of knowledge of the True—in the form of objective knowledge and its consequent objectification of humankind—and thus the primary means to arrive at knowledge of the Good. Consequently, all efforts at knowledge generation are bent toward serving the *urgent need* of maintaining and enhancing the functioning of the individual/ society.

Society, while being social in character, has its social qualities objectified. Culture, customs, human relationships, etcetera all become objects that comprise a social environment—objects which can act upon or be acted upon by the individual, resources that may be tapped and used. The individual is seen as a natural organism possessing biological, psychological, and social components, which interacts with an environment. The focus of the helping relationship centers upon achieving healthy growth and development as well as successful adaptation and adjustment to one's environment, or proper functioning of the system to which one belongs. Inner qualities of being human—such as personality, cognition, and even moral reasoning—are objectified as components of a human organism and seen as having a growth and development of their own, intimately tied to one's biological growth and development.

The wide embrace of systems theory—and the hegemonic acceptance of person-in-environment as the definitive conceptual model for social work— serves as an excellent example of the power operating in the Modern Discourse to privilege certain knowledge as being the most useful and valid. First, the notion of the individual being enmeshed within interdependent systems mirrors the deep penetration of integration that has occurred in transportation, communication, and media. Next, the intellectual thought of Darwin and Kant adds a strong biological component undergirding the social interaction of this interdependence. Combined, these two elements serve to advance the Modern Discourse's understanding of individualism as expressive individualism; within expressive individualism, subsuming one's individuality to the system is the route to enhanced functioning and growth. Within social work practice, this occurs through the classification of individuals as belonging to a particular population group. The expertise of the social work professional in employing this conceptual model promotes a scientific management approach in helping clients resolve their problems.

Research

As just shown, the power of this Discourse and its sole placement of humankind within a natural world work to stress the continuity between nature and human nature concerning knowledge formation in the realm of theory; its effect in research endeavors—knowledge formation through investigation—has been to stress the continuity between the natural sciences and the social sciences. The social survey discussed in the previous chapter—the methodology unique to social work and the tool of the moral reformer—would fade from the social work research landscape. During the 1920s a negative reaction had set in against the survey, and its popularity as a research tool precipitously dropped. The last prominent social survey was conducted in 1938, the *Social Study of Pittsburgh*—a follow-up to its 1907 predecessor which served to initiate the social survey movement. Lastly, in 1952 the journal *Survey*—which had helped spawn the survey movement and served as its flagship—ceased publication due to lack of support.[40] Social work would embrace the research methodologies of the social sciences—methodologies most effective for measuring and describing individuals residing within a natural world.

Thus, the search for causality would rely heavily upon the scientific method,[41] with textbooks privileging the scientific method as the only reliable route to truth.[d] Ideally, this would involve the use of a control group, yet the practicality of implementing such a study oftentimes lies outside the bounds of an agency's or researcher's resources. The quasi-experiment offers the next best alternative.[42] Adapted to an individual, the quasi-experiment spawned the single-organism design,[e] now known as the single-system design.[43] Yet even the quasi-experiment faces obstacles concerning implementation in a real-life setting.[44] Consequently, when attempting to sketch a causal connection, much use is made of descriptive

---

[d] For example, Engel and Schutt, *Fundamentals*; Krysik, *Research for Effective*. Research texts contrast the scientific method with authority, common sense, tradition, and personal experience as vehicles for truth. The latter are all depicted as generators of subjective knowledge, and thus as being unreliable, whereas the scientific method generates objective knowledge.

[e] Zimbalist, *Historic Themes*, 245. Designated as such by Donald Campbell and associates in their development and refinement of the time-series design.

statistics:[45] such as analysis of variance, factor analysis, path analysis, multiple regression, and other techniques.

These techniques all rely upon the measurement and description of objects (referred to as *variables*); the descriptions of how these objects interact represent notions of causality. With humankind's shift in residence to the natural world, these objects now represented components of a human organism or components of society as an environment. On the individual level, this shift in objectification began with the transformation of the concept of personality as well as with the measurement of intelligence. At the beginning of the twentieth century, the term *personality* lost its spiritual connotation and became a purely psychological term; by the 1930s, it was common to view personality as possessing components[46]— components that could be observed in behavior and thus measured. Scales were developed that sought to measure both a battery of personality components[f] as well as individual components such as extroversion–introversion and adjustment.[47] What fell under the scope of the measurable soon expanded[g] and would encompass emotional and moral qualities[48]—such as honesty,[49] empathy,[50] and temperament[51]—and qualities of the human spirit—such as humor,[52] resiliency,[53] and even love.[54] In this purely natural world that humankind now occupies—humor, resilience, and even love have been transformed into components of a human organism, variables within a causal equation.

With the arrival in this Discourse's epistemological space of personality components (as natural objects) that could be measured in attempts to determine causality, these measurement tools could be also turned upon the individual and used diagnostically—to measure deviance from the norm. The most codified and enduring example of this dynamic found expression in psychologists' efforts at measuring deviance in the area of mental health with the development of the *Diagnostic and Statistical Manual of Mental Disorders*—a tool prominently embraced and used by the social work profession.[55] Needing a much more general instrument in the practice setting applicable to many different populations and helping situations, social work employed Mary Richmond's (1917) diagnostic approach outlined in her work *Social Diagnosis* to create the psychosocial assessment, commonly referred to today as the bio-psycho-social assessment— reflecting the importance given by the Modern Discourse to the biological

---

[f] Early versions include the following: Bernreuter's (1935) *Personality Inventory*; Rorschach's (1921) *Rorschach Psychodiagnostic Test*; Tyron's (1934) *Tyron Personality Inventory*, Conklin's (1927), *Extroversion–Introversion Test*; Hayes' (1927), *Minnesota Personal Traits Rating Scales: Introversion-Extroversion and Inferiority Attitudes*. Examples of personality tests that have stood the test of time include the following: Briggs and Myers' (1963) *The Myers-Briggs Inventory*; Rorschach's (1921) *The Rorschach Test*; and *The Minnesota Multiphasic Personality Inventory*.

[g] Buros Institute of Mental Measurements, *Twentieth Mental Measurements Yearbook*. The Buros Institute of Mental Measurements has compiled measurement scales into a database since 1939. Its 2017 database compilation, entitled *The Twentieth Mental Measurements Yearbook*, lists over 2,500 measurement tests.

root of human behavior. This approach is used to diagnose the etiology of the presenting problem (i.e., disruption in normal functioning) as well as identify potential resources to alleviate the problem.[56]

Social work employed these research techniques upon objects in society as well. With society now viewed as a social environment, social relations themselves became objectified and viewed as resources. Thus, measurement instruments placed social relations among one's family, friends, and community within this realm of resources, in addition to the existing list of material resources such as food and shelter.[57] Placed within a causal chain, the lack of these resources could be shown to lead to abnormal functioning within the individual. Societal measurement tools also came to be used diagnostically—to measure deviance from the norm—in the form of indexes of social need.[h] The most recent development of this approach involves the quantification of concepts (such as poverty) in the form of social indicators,[i] defined as a "statistic of direct, normative interest which facilitates concise, comprehensive and balanced judgments about the condition of major aspects of society."[58] This occurs despite the fact that social concepts such as poverty are highly difficult to operationalize.[59]

With humankind's shift in residence to a purely natural world came an accompanying shift in the base of authority of the social change agent. It was no longer moral knowledge of human character that was needed but rather scientific knowledge of humans' place within a natural world: Scientific authority replaced moral authority. As the historian Leslie Leighninger aptly notes, "The appeal of science as a foundation for a bona fide profession was a strong one. Porter Lee, Edith Abbott, and others stressed the development of social work as a profession based on the scientific knowledge and technique gained through special training."[60] After World War I, "Conscious social change was seen more and more as the prerogative of the expert or the efficient social engineer."[61] Hence, proof of one's authority no longer lay in demonstrating the fact that one was an exemplary and upstanding citizen; it now lay in demonstrating professional expertise as a social engineer.

Beginning in the early 1900s, calls were made first for training programs and then for professional schools of social work.[62] By 1939 there were thirty-nine schools of social work;[63] as of 2019 they number in the hundreds. Debate ensued

---

[h] Zimbalist, *Historic Themes*, 204–05. I. M. Rubinow is looked upon as the pioneer in social work index making, devising the first major index of dependency in 1917 for New York City. The next evolution in social index making occurred in 1939 with the publication of *Social Breakdown: A Plan for Measurement and Control* by Community Chests and Councils Incorporated and its development of the Social Breakdown Index. This approach was soon replaced in the late 1940s by the development of indexes measuring social need—which could take many different forms, such as health needs, recreation needs, welfare needs, youth service needs, and others.

[i] Zimbalist, *Historic Themes*, 208. Published in 1969 by the US Department of Health, Education, and Welfare, *Toward a Social Report* introduced the concept of the social indicator.

concerning where this professional expertise lie and if there existed a foundational body of knowledge applicable to all areas of social work. This debate was resolved in the 1950s when the various associations governing curriculum merged into the Council on Social Work Education (CSWE).[64]

Yet the need to adopt the uniform of professional expertise was felt in all areas of social work, as testified by the numerous social work professional organizations that were founded around this time. Hospital social workers in 1918 would form the first professional association for social workers, the American Association of Hospital Social Workers. They were joined in 1922 by the psychiatric social workers, who splintered off and formed their own organization in 1926, the American Association of Psychiatric Social Workers. Social workers involved with group work were the last to organize under a professional banner, forming the American Association for the Study of Group Work in 1936.[65] In 1955 all the disparate professional groups united to form the National Association of Social Workers (NASW), an organization that is still with us today. This embrace of professionalism has remained strong throughout the ensuing years under the Modern Discourse, intensifying even further with the introduction of licensing procedures for general and clinical social work practice.

Social workers no longer presented themselves as moral reformers; they have become service providers. Their service is ensconced within their unique professional expertise. Consequently, in the area of knowledge generation a new need arose: the need to demonstrate the effectiveness of one's expertise (through the demonstration of a cause–effect linkage). This was especially so once social workers began to receive money (both federal and through community chests) based upon their declared expertise.[66] In 1923, the newly formed American Association of Social Workers established a "Sub-Committee on Evaluation." The subcommittee found that there "had been almost no attempt, either by organizations or individual workers, to evaluate the results of social casework."[67] Just a few short years later, June Purcell-Guild would optimistically state, "the day when a clear and precise evaluation of social work should be available is approaching if it has not already arrived. The extensive adoption of the community fund method of financing social work has apparently precipitated the issue."[68]

Hence, evaluative research in social work was born. From its inception, this evaluative research has relied upon the objectification of various qualities of the individual, such as personality. In 1926 Walter Whitson would note, "Social case workers cannot indefinitely excuse their lack of accuracy, when asked to state results, by answering that they are dealing with the intangible. Personality is a *reality* [my emphasis]";[69] and in 1927 Edward Wilcox would state, "Those intangibles of personality held but yesterday to be sacred mysteries beyond our ken are now the *quantitative materials* [my emphasis] of the new psychology."[70]

A number of attempts were made to quantify the linkage between the social worker's interventions and change in a client's behavior, invariably measuring this change in terms of adjustment: In 1931, Ellery F. Reed developed a formula for rating and scoring numerous factors involved in the casework process; in 1944, John Dollard and O. Hobart Mowrer developed the Discomfort Relief Quotient as a way to measure changes in overall adjustment; and in 1947, Joseph McVicker Hunt and Leonard Kogan developed the Community Service Society Movement Scale as a way to measure change in adaptive efficiency of the client or environmental situation.[71]

Drawing upon the metaphor discussed in Chapter 1 of a discourse acting as a chess game, the following can be stated. Standing in counterpoint to this tremendous movement toward the scientization of the profession was a lone chess piece: the moral base for action. Humankind's shift to the natural world divested this moral base from its anchor in religion—it would now be viewed as a professional ethic. Yet ironically, and more importantly, this moral base was freed from its previous mooring to the nineteenth-century Discourse's main rules of right: explanations of causality and deviance from the norm. Consequently, while no longer being drawn upon to generate knowledge in the form of a treatment plan, social work values would serve to circumscribe the boundaries within which scientific knowledge could be generated. While the power that this piece exerted would be sometimes muted, it was never completely diminished. For example, the "working definition of social work" gives equal weight to social work values guiding interventions as it does to expert knowledge and skills.[72]

It was not uncommon that the difficulty in demonstrating the effectiveness of social work interventions would be met over the years by calls for more scientific rigor.[73] The most prominent example in this vein occurred in 1973, when Joel Fischer surveyed the various evaluative research studies on casework that had occurred up to that point and concluded that all such studies failed to meet minimal standards for scientific rigor[74]—thus casting doubt upon any claims that casework was indeed effective in significantly contributing to client change and growth. His critique dealt a decisive blow to the approach of casework guided by ego theory and created an opening exploited by the newly emerging influence of systems theory, resulting in ecological systems theory soon thereafter supplanting ego theory as the definitive model guiding social work practice.

Regarding evaluative research, Fischer's critique served to spawn the single-systems design movement—a movement that promoted the idea of social workers as "scientist-practitioners" diligently conducting evaluative research in the field to better hone their practice.[75] However, by the late 1990s it was clear that this dream never materialized.[76] The vast majority of social work practitioners (between 88% and 94% in various studies) did not employ single-system design to hone their practice and continually reported finding little relevance in evaluative research to guide their practice.[77] As concluded in one study, due to the lack of any empirical evidence, current claims that employing scientific investigation serves to improve one's practice did not rest upon the merit of proven results; rather, they rested upon an indoctrinated authority: "It seems that social work students (and faculty) remain in a position to accept *on authority* [my emphasis] that research is good for them and, hence, good for practice."[78]

This prompted a shift in the profession's dream of social work practitioners diligently embracing scientific investigation to guide their practice; transforming it from a practice of social workers as scientist-practitioners to one of social workers as educated consumers of evaluative research. This shift is reflected in the currently prominent evidence-based practice movement that arose at the dawn of the twenty-first century. The jury is still out as to whether or not social work practitioners readily or predominantly incorporate evidence-based practice research to guide their intervention efforts. Yet signs are not promising. Indicative of the neurotic paradox to be described below, standing in counterpoint to calls by academics for scientific rigor to guide practice, the literature repeatedly finds over the years that social work students and practitioners find minimal usefulness in engaging and employing social work research in practice.[79] As noted by one scholar, "no other part of the social work curriculum has been so consistently received by students with as much groaning, moaning, eye rolling, hyperventilation and waiver strategizing as the research course."[80]

Summary

Hence, this estranged chess piece—the moral base for action—throughout the Modern Era serves to constantly prick the conscience of the social work profession in its pursuit of scientific rigor—never allowing a complete embrace of the scientific approach. In the area of knowledge generation, it would find voice over the years in critiques repeatedly pointing out the neurotic paradox (a term coined by the Dutch psychologist Johan T. Barendregt) inherent in social scientific investigation: the fact that rigor works in opposition to relevance or, more plainly, "a methodologically correct project is irrelevant to life; a project relevant to life is methodologically incorrect."[81] This is due to the fact that for a study to obtain sufficient scientific rigor, it must control for all variables not being tested; the greater the control of variables that occurs, the more artificial of an environment is created—creating ever greater distance from the real-life environment wherein findings are applied.

Noted scholars such as David Holbrook, Alfred Kahn, and Donald Schon represent three such critiques among those occurring regularly throughout the

Modern Era. Holbrook stated in 1931, "Any hint of setting up a final quantitative goal for evaluating an art increases the hazards of practicing the art, whether it be in the field of music, painting, or human relations."[82] Kahn expounded in 1958, "The social worker who is on the front line of service finds the social scientist somewhat silent on subjects of major concern, and also inclined to conceptualize the obvious and complicate the simple."[83] And Schon wrote in 1983,

> In the varied topography of professional practice, there is a high hard ground where practitioners can make effective use of research-based theory and technique, and there is a swampy lowland where situations are confusing "messes" incapable of technical solution. The difficulty is that the problems of the high ground, however great their technical interest, are often relatively unimportant to clients or to the larger society, while in the swamp are the problems of greatest concern.[84]

The Modern Discourse advances the idea that knowledge of the True (in the form of objective knowledge produced by scientific investigation) provides the necessary route by which to arrive at knowledge of the Good (positive outcomes for clients). Yet the underlying tension between rigor and relevance continually exerts pressure in opposition to this premise, creating cracks in the philosophical foundation upon which the Modern Discourse rests. Once a new urgent need arises to replace that currently supporting the Modern Discourse, this tension will most likely be a primary cause leading to the crumbling of this foundation—clearing the way for the rise in dominance of an emerging discourse to supplant it.

The Transformation of the Scientific Charity and Settlement House Movements

Roughly between the years 1880 and 1920, the scientific charity movement and the settlement house movement represented the two most prominent factions of social work. As the term *social work* arose at this time period, most social work histories point to these two movements as serving as the foundation from which social work in the Modern Era arose. Yet the rise of the Modern Discourse in the early twentieth century opened up new epistemological possibilities for casework and settlement house work, while at the same time closing off others. The scientific charity movement and the settlement house movement would both expire after the Modern Discourse ascended to dominance—they were home to a now darkened, moral-laden epistemological landscape of humankind existing in both a transcendental and a natural world. Within the Modern Discourse, knowledge of the True was now seen as the necessary precursor to arriving at knowledge of the Good; and a valid, rigorous methodology was seen as the means to uncover knowledge of the True. Thus, the casework approach introduced by charity organization societies (COS) in their pursuit of scientific charity—being a systematic method of information gathering—found fertile epistemological soil in which to grow and flourish within the new scientific landscape of humankind existing in a purely natural world. By contrast, settlement house efforts were directed toward creating healthy environments that promoted a community consciousness, not upon establishing a clearly defined method to their approach. Consequently, the Modern Discourse would fracture and transform the settlement house movement into entirely different entities—that of group work and community organizing.

Casework

Scientific charity, as practiced by the COS, used casework as its method to efficiently dispense relief.[85] With the shift into the Modern Discourse, authority for knowledge development was granted to scientific expertise.[86] The term *charity* was no longer vested with moral authority. Consequently, charity workers became known as *caseworkers*.[87] Authority was now vested in technical expertise, and thus social workers became known by the method that they employed. Thus, by the 1940s, it was well recognized that the field of social work consisted of three broad areas: casework, group work, and community organizing.[88] By the same token, charity organizations became known as *service* organizations or agencies.[89] Social work under the rubric of charity was a moral obligation; social work under the rubric of scientific expertise was now a service.[90] Social work rapidly became a profession, offering expert service in the administration of social welfare.

The casework method, as most richly elaborated by Mary Richmond,[91] provided a rational and systematic method for information gathering concerning an individual. In their new role as service providers, early social workers employed the casework method to determine client need, then followed it with appropriate referrals to aid agencies.[92] With the incorporation of Freudian thought, this limited role of casework greatly expanded. And as psychodynamic theory expanded, evolved, and spawned variations—such as ego theory and life-span theory— casework would continue to incorporate its ideas. The casework method, being based heavily upon the medical model approach to inquiry,[93] already offered a framework for diagnosis—married with Freudian thought, it now offered a way to diagnose intrapsychic conflict as a (heretofore unknown) cause behind an individual's welfare ills.[94] In addition, it offered something that previously the casework method did not offer:[95] treatment.[j] Casework was no longer merely a method of investigation used to determine what services were needed; it was now viewed as a form of treatment.[96]

The casework approach resonated well with the rules of right of this Discourse: Deviance from the norm was assessed and causation sought for this deviance. Within psychodynamic theory, this norm was viewed in terms of adjustment. Life-span theory added notions of growth; systems theory added notions of healthy functioning. Causes were sought that led to maladjustment, stagnant growth, or dysfunction. As all these norms related to the overall *health* of individual organisms, casework adopted terminology from the medical field. Interventions were seen as *therapeutic*[97]—with psychological counseling getting the signifier of psycho*therapy*.[k] Achieving healthy adjustment or functioning was the focus of treatment—the Modern Discourse's understanding of knowledge of the Good. Knowledge of the True—in the form of measuring deviance and determining causality—was the pathway needed to be traveled to reach knowledge of the Good.

Casework arising in the 1920s, which incorporated psychodynamic theory, saw treatment in terms of individual adjustment.[98] This approach would later become known as the *diagnostic school* of casework due to its emphasis on diagnosing the extent and reason for deviance (i.e., maladjustment). The name *diagnostic school* arose from an article by one of this approach's main proponents, Gordon Hamilton, and served to differentiate this approach from its main rival, the functionalist school.[99] The diagnostic approach, which viewed the individual as in need of social adjustment back to a healthy status, resonated strongly within the Modern Discourse: It sought, unique to each individual, causality within the natural world and a measurable deviance from a norm. Treatment—in the form of casework services—relied on scientific expertise in diagnosing causality and deviance. As the expert knower of truth, the caseworker acted upon the client to produce change. The diagnostic approach, later known as the *psychosocial approach*,[l] came to dominate the casework field by the 1940s and into the 1950s.[100] The three phases emphasized in this approach—*study, diagnose, treatment*[101]—became the definitive elements of casework.

---

[j] The signifier *treatment* encapsulates a medical notion of intervention as well as concern for the health of an organism—a stance not present in the casework method under scientific charity, which concerned itself with the moral reform of individuals and their material relief.

[k] *Merriam Webster Dictionary*, s.v., "therapy" and "therapeutic," accessed July 2, 2019 at https://www.merriam-webster.com/dictionary/therapy. Merriam Webster defines *therapy* as "therapeutic medical treatment of impairment, injury, disease, or disorder" and *therapeutic* as "of or relating to the treatment of disease or disorders by remedial agents or methods."

[l] Hamilton, "The Underlying Philosophy." In 1941 Gordon Hamilton chose the phrase *diagnosing psychosocial need* as the definitive term for this approach.

The early rival to the diagnostic school of casework was the functional school of casework, developed in the early 1930s at the University of Pennsylvania by Otto Rank and other faculty members such as Jessie Taft, Kenneth Pray, and Virginia Robinson.[102] It operated from a psychology of growth rather than that of addressing illness. It also placed the center for change within the client, to be released through a relational process with the caseworker. This psychological growth was viewed in terms of the growth of an organism, an organism that is "purposeful" and thus is the source of its own change.[103] Rather than seeking causal mechanisms, the functional approach sought to "understand the phenomenon" of the client in their particular situation,[104] which would then lead to some type of action toward growth. To a much greater degree than the diagnostic approach, the functional approach was aligned with the value base of social work: for example, concepts that would later be elaborated as self-determination and empowerment. Yet, while the functional approach aligned itself with some of the elements of the Modern Discourse (intellectual thought and conception of self as solely in a natural world), it did not resonate well with the main rules of right: seeking causality and measuring deviance from a norm. By the 1950s, the functional approach began to fade from the social work scene.[105]

In the 1950s, life-span theory would serve to introduce the notion of psychological growth to the psychosocial approach—yet the notion of adjustment would remain, leaving it to the individual caseworker how much emphasis was given to each. Also in the 1950s, ideas from systems theory began to enter the social work literature.[106] With its focus on the human organism as part of an environmental (social) system, systems theory was seen as a way to bring the "social" back into social work.[107] Emerging strongly in 1957 with Helen Harris Perlman's *Social Casework: A Problem-Solving Process*, the problem-solving method of casework became the new rival to the psychosocial approach.

The problem-solving method offered an alternative that was more eclectic in its use of theory than the psychosocial approach,[m] which drew solely upon psychodynamic theory. As with the psychosocial approach, the problem-solving approach leaves much room open to view the client as either ill or seeking growth. In addition, it professes to not be a method for manipulating the client— emphasizing that the goal is to release the client's motivation for change.[108] Yet, it again leaves much room open to the individual caseworker regarding who determines the norm to which this change is directed, as when Perlman states, "Our first concern with every client is that we reach the most immediate goal: that

---

[m] The problem-solving method draws upon psychodynamic theory, behaviorism, and various systems theory, which, as discussed in the previous section, all view individuals as organisms in an environment.

he engage himself as feelingly and as understandingly as he can in wanting to take and use our help."[109]

The problem-solving approach utilizes the same main elements of casework established by the psychosocial approach: study (interview the client), diagnose (the etiology of the problem), and treatment (develop a plan for achieving chosen goal). It resonates well within the Modern Discourse in that it seeks causality[n] and movement toward a norm.[o] With its eclectic use of theory, the problem-solving approach is more open to discovering causal factors in the environment. Its introduction in the 1960s—a decade containing much social strife—served to enhance its acceptance within social work. At the same time, the psychosocial approach came under attack due to its firm association with psychodynamic theory and resulting strong focus on intrapsychic factors.[110]

Yet the psychosocial approach resonated too strongly with the Modern Discourse to be completely snuffed out. Rather, it was divested of its strict allegiance to psychodynamic theory and transformed—into clinical social work. Clinical social work arose in the 1960s as a specialized form of casework that concentrates on addressing the intrapsychic conflict of an individual or system.[111] Furthermore, in 1976 the NASW created the *Register of Clinical Social Workers.* This register defined clinical social work as consisting of a psychosocial orientation; it also listed requirements for inclusion on the list.[112] At first, clinical social workers engaged in psychotherapy with a client, usually within an office setting, to address issues of psychosocial impairment or dysfunction.[113] Psychotherapy remains a prominent form of intervention of this approach today.[114] Yet social work soon expanded the reach of the psychosocial approach represented by clinical social work and its strong embrace of the model of study, diagnose, and treatment. In 1987 the following definition was offered for clinical social work:[p]

Clinical social work practice is the professional application of social work theory and methods to the treatment and prevention of psychosocial dysfunction, disability, or impairment, including emotional and mental disorders. . . . It includes but is not limited to individual, marital, family, and

---

[n] Perlman, *Social Casework*, 175–76. For example, "The purposes of establishing recent or precipitating causation have already been discussed in chapter 9 (pp. 126–29) mainly as these: to clarify whether the problem lies chiefly in the client himself or in his life-situation; to deal with causal factors so as to nullify them or modify their impact; or conversely, to take into account such causal factors as are immutable."

[o] Perlman, *Social Casework*, 197. For example, "Whichever diagnostic data are used, the purpose is to give guidance to the caseworker's ongoing work of promoting and rewarding the client's adaptive efforts."

[p] Northen, *Clinical Social Work*, 8. "the Board of Directors of NASW, the Board of the National Registry of Health Care Providers, which had been established by the Federation of Societies of Clinical Social Work, and the American Board of Examiners in Clinical Social Work" all voted to accept the above definition (quoted here in part).

group psychotherapy. Clinical social work services consist of assessment; diagnosis; treatment, including psychotherapy and counseling; client-centered advocacy; consultation; and evaluation.[115]

Psychotherapy has become a specialized approach in need of a higher level of expertise; as such, social workers are now required to possess a clinical licensure in order to bill their treatment as clinical service.

Meanwhile the problem-solving approach has become the dominant approach in what has been traditionally known as casework; this is due to its ability to be flexible to all types of theory and its ability to easily incorporate many traditional social work functions such as servicing welfare recipients, servicing children in foster care, and servicing the mentally ill. While no longer commonly identified as the problem-solving approach, practice textbooks speak of identifying the client's problem situation or problems of living and then matching them with an effective intervention.[116] Thus, casework is now often referred to as *direct practice*.[117] Direct practice in social work continues to offer the main three elements of study, diagnose, and treatment as the means for providing social work service.[118]

Upon the fading of the Premodern Discourse, the shift to the twentieth-century Modern Discourse produced a scientific gaze of humankind residing in the natural world. Knowledge of the Good was hidden within this natural world, hidden within natural mechanisms unique to each individual; knowledge of the True—to be provided by scientific and technical expertise—was now needed to reach the knowledge of the Good. This would be accomplished through treatment.

The prominent casework approaches developed within the Modern Discourse have viewed humankind as existing in a natural world, and thus view individuals as human organisms living in an environment. The approaches that have endured have also resonated closely to the Modern Discourse's rules of right: seeking causality and measuring deviance from a norm. Until recently,[q] there had been only one approach that contested these main rules of right and their subsequent objectification of the individual—the functionalist school of casework. It was unable to maintain its challenge and thus became sidelined by the workings of the Modern Discourse.

The major debates over the casework method during the twentieth century are fully a product of the Modern Discourse and illustrate its influence: They do not contest these main elements of the Modern Discourse but rather center upon the form taken by them. One major debate involved how the individual organism is viewed when beginning casework treatment: The organism is ill and needs

---

q The strengths perspective, solution-focused therapy, and narrative therapy all challenge the main elements of this Discourse and will be discussed in Chapter 9.

correction back to a healthy status versus the organism is healthy and needs support in its growth and development. This debate did not have a side which advocated an illness approach; rather, it centered around whether a particular approach (e.g., psychosocial approach) inherently contained such a stance, with one side charging that it did and the other that it did not.[119] A second major debate involved how change takes place: the caseworker acting upon the organism versus the organism acting upon itself via support from the caseworker. Again, this debate did not have a side which advocated the social worker as exerting social control as the agent of change but rather centered around whether a particular approach (e.g., the psychosocial approach) inherently contained such a stance, with one side charging that it did and the other that it did not.[120]

Group Work

The settlement house movement emphasized promoting the moral and civic integration of disadvantaged individuals into society. One of the avenues used to promote this mission was the organizing of cultural and recreational events for groups of individuals. As the twentieth-century Modern Discourse arose with its scientific gaze, methodology acted as the main signifier for social welfare interventions and the workers who administered them. Thus, this type of activity became known as *group work*, and the social worker became known as a *group worker*. What group work signified became abstracted into method, divorcing its identity from being derived from its setting in any way (i.e., the settlement house). The settlement house merely became a location, one of a number of possible locations,[r] where group work took place.

At first, group work consisted solely of organizing recreational activities. As noted in the previous chapter on the Premodern Discourse, recreational activities for youth were seen as promoting their character and spiritual development. As the central rules of right of the Modern Discourse remained relatively unchanged from those of the Premodern Discourse (causality and change toward a norm/ideal), it was relatively easy for this work to now be described within the Modern Discourse's scientific gaze. Instead of character building and spiritual development, group work was now said to help develop a richer personality and emotional growth, thus promoting one's effectiveness in social adjustment.[121] Hence, group work was accepted into the new and developing field of social work and the social work profession.

---

[r] Williamson, *The Social Worker*. As part of the job analysis series that the American Association of Social Workers conducted in the 1920s, Williamson lists group work as taking place in settlement houses, recreation centers, religious centers (e.g., the YMCA, Jewish centers), national organizations (e.g., Boys Scouts, Girl Scouts), and playgrounds.

Unlike casework, group work did not entail a systematic method and thus was looked upon as requiring little or no expertise. The rise of the Modern Discourse now supported the need for technical expertise: The building of a scientific base of knowledge and a unique methodology became the main project for group workers.[122] Group workers formed a professional organization in 1936,[123] the last social work subfield specialty to do so.[s] With its efforts to build this scientific knowledge base, combined with its new focus on the development of personality, group work began to incorporate elements of psychodynamic theory. Group work began to see itself as combining understanding of individual dynamics with the understanding of group dynamics.[124] This translated into the use of group work to treat psychosocial problems common to the individuals comprising the group[125]—what is now known as *group therapy*.

During the 1950s, the profession of social work focused on developing a common base of knowledge and skills applicable to all fields of social work. The core conceptual orientation to arise from this effort concerning method was the notion of study, diagnose, treatment as common phases to all social work practice.[126] With the Modern Discourse's power acting to promote technical expertise, group work began to embrace more and more of a psychosocial orientation. This psychosocial orientation is what began to be signified by social group work,[127] as opposed to "merely" recreational group work—whose low-level of expertise allowed it to be conducted by a volunteer, under the auspices of a social worker.[128] The alignment of this new conceptualization of social group work with the Modern Discourse's agenda of maintaining and enhancing functioning through scientific management is quite clear. Gisela Konopka, an early pioneer in the development of social group work, defined it as follows: "a method of social work which helps individuals to enhance their social functioning through purposeful group experiences and to cope more effectively with their personal, group or community problems."[129]

What was still lacking was a distinct systematic method for social group work practice. In the 1960s and 1970s these began to arrive in the form of the following: the interactionist approach,[130] the preventative and rehabilitative approach,[131] and the developmental approach.[132] Group work was now clearly seen as a method to promote therapeutic change:[133] Group therapy was now the primary component of group work.

While group work had become more psychosocial in orientation, casework during the 1960s and 1970s (as stated above) began to heavily incorporate systems theory and started adopting a problem-solving approach. The differences separating casework from group work were now not as vast. They came to

---

[s] Leighninger, *Social Work*, 155–56. Except for community organizers, who never founded a social work professional association.

commonly share the same therapeutic modalities, such as systems therapy and cognitive-behavioral therapy. With the rise of systems theory, the main distinguishing feature for categorizing social work interventions became the site of the intervention: micro-/mezzo-system and macro-system. With both having as their site of intervention the micro-/mezzo-system, by the 1970s casework and group work were no longer seen as broadly distinct and were folded together in practice textbooks under the signifier of *direct practice*.[134]

Community Organizing

With the Modern Discourse exerting a scientific gaze, one in which rigorous methodology and technical expertise were promoted in an effort at scientific management of social problems, community organizing would undergo the least smooth transition and most radical transformation. In the Premodern Era as part of the settlement house work and national organizations like the National Consumers League, social workers had organized community members to protest social inequalities and advance social reform. Yet these efforts did not employ a systematic methodology: They were viewed as political, rather than scientific, activity.[135] Consequently, this type of intervention did not require a strong measure of technical expertise. And finally, these efforts sought predetermined objectives: Knowledge of the Good was assumed, rather than arising from knowledge of the True. Thus, while community organizing in this mold sought causality, it did not require expert knowledge to reveal these causal mechanisms. And while it sought correction to an ideal, it was a predetermined good, not one arising through the investigation of the true. For these reasons, community organizing fell outside of this new, scientific gaze resulting from the rise of the Modern Discourse. In the early part of the Modern Era, this put the status of community organizing in doubt as to whether it still merited the designation of social work.

Porter Lee in his 1929 presidential address to the National Conference of Social Work, "Social Work as Cause and Function," advocated for the new role of the social worker as technical expert efficiently administering the functions of social welfare in community life over that of the reformer fighting for a cause.[136] This shift in understanding arising from the Modern Discourse and its influence of a scientific gaze is clearly seen in the following comparisons made by Lee during his 1929 speech:

> Zeal is perhaps the most conspicuous trait in adherents to a cause, while intelligence is perhaps most essential to those who administer a function. The emblazoned banner and the shibboleth for the cause, the program and manual

for the function; devoted sacrifice and the flaming spirit for the cause, fidelity, standards and methods for the function; an embattled host for the cause, an efficient personnel for the function.[137]

Intelligence, program and manual, fidelity (as professional ethic), standards and methods, and efficient personnel all clearly align with the role of the professional expert, whereas zeal, emblazoned banner and shibboleth, flaming spirit, and embattled host all can be attributed to the political activist. Consequently, in a 1935 address delivered before the New York State Conference on Social Work, Lee would state that social work community organizing faced the challenge of providing leadership in social action which fell within the professional competence of the social worker and that did not fall prey to "unintelligent intrusive methods of radical propaganda."[138]

During the 1920s and 1930s the search for this professional competence of the community organizer took place. Prevalent among caseworkers of the time, such as Miriam Van Waters in her 1930 presidential address to the National Conference of Social Work, was the attitude "that reform activity was not 'genuine' social work."[139] This attitude was further buttressed by the prevailing opinion, voiced by notables in the field such as Grace Abbott, that professional social work required an objective, nonpartisan stance.[140] Furthermore, around this same time, more than two-thirds of the Chicago members of the American Association of Social Workers responded to an ethics survey by stating that "social agencies should not take an active part in any political activity."[141] What did fall within the realm of the professional expert was scientific research into social policy. Hence, as described in the earlier subsection titled "Research," the stance toward advancing social reform—coalescing under the scientific gaze of the Modern Discourse—was becoming one of providing expert testimony.[142]

The rank and file movement (c. 1931–1936) would represent the last gasp of the field of social work attempting to grasp the leadership mantle in the arena of social reform through protest. Arising in response to the economic upheaval of the Great Depression, the rank and file movement represented a group of social workers who sought broad social and economic change through a conflict strategy of community organizing based upon using the organized group (social workers, labor, etc.) as a source of power to press for change.[143] A prominent member of the rank and file movement, Harry Lurie, chided the 1934 Delegate Conference of the American Association of Social Workers over their concern for a professional model of action, arguing instead that social action was not an issue "of expertness but of politics."[144] Yet this model for action advanced by the rank and file movement now fell within the darkened spaces of the Modern Discourse. By the end of the decade, social work community organizing would be seen as work done by the professional expert, not the political activist.[145]

In 1939, questions of whether or not community organizing was social work would be put to rest with the Lane Committee Report—concluding that community organizing did in fact share a conceptual base with other social work methods.[146] Community organizing had now been officially welcomed into the fold of social work, yet it had undergone an incarnation that had left it much transformed. Social work community organizing of the 1940s and beyond would emphasize "process, method, and skill."[147] It would place greater emphasis on strengthening the intergroup process among community members and promoting fruitful and satisfying social relationships over protest and the achievement of pre-established goals.[148] As Genevieve Carter prominently noted in 1958, "When it becomes manipulative, when pressure or 'political' techniques are employed, it is beyond the limit of the social work method."[149]

During the 1950s and that decade's push for social work skills based in a generic method, social work community organizing—in stark contrast to the watchwords *investigate, agitate, legislate* embraced by the National Consumers League of the Premodern Era—would fall in line with casework and group work through its alignment with study, diagnose, treatment as the defining conceptual mode of practice.[†] Social work community organizers relegated themselves to working in positions such as health and welfare planning, social service exchange administration, promotion of programs in specialized fields, and public relations.[150] Current understanding conceptualizes efforts in this area more broadly as community social work, of which community organizing is simply a subfield. As one organization notes in words clearly in line with the Modern Discourse's urgent need of maintaining and enhancing functioning through scientific management, "Community social workers help communities function. Some work directly with individuals, conducting needs assessments and making referrals to resources in the community. Others assess needs on a larger scale. They may plan and administer programs."[151]

After the 1930s, community organizing under a conflict model—that of seeking social reform through protest—would continue throughout the twentieth century to the present day, albeit without any significant leadership from the social work profession. The social reform efforts of neighborhood councils of the 1940s and 1950s such as the Back of the Yards and the Alinsky-style of organizing that it spawned, the civil rights movement of the 1960s and the various style of protests it employed, and the community organizing efforts of the now defunct Association of Community Organizations for Reform Now (ACORN) all

---

[†] Carter, "Social Work Community Organization," 224–25. Carter describes these phases for community organizing as the *reconnaissance phase*, the *diagnostic phase*, and the *treatment phase*.

derived their leadership from outside the field of social work.[u] The social upheaval of the 1960s provides a good backdrop to illustrate the shift in roles of the
social worker—from moral reformer to technical expert—that had taken place
under the scientific management promoted by the Modern Discourse: Moving
from a role of leading a cause to that of performing a function, social work community organizers during the 1960s were not among the ranks of civil rights
leaders organizing protests (as was the case for the likes of Jane Addams and
Mary Parker Follet in the Premodern Era);[v] rather, they were called upon for
their technical expertise in community organizing to administer community social programs such as Community Action Programs.[152]

Yet social work has not abandoned its efforts at promoting social reform. In
fact, *advancing human rights* is one of the nine competencies under CSWE's *2015
Educational Policy and Accreditation Standards*; this continues a long tradition
set by CSWE throughout its various iterations of accreditation standards over
the years.[153] However, under the scientific gaze of the Modern Discourse, social
reform is redirected along a different path—the path of the expert. Starting with
the New Deal in the 1930s, a number of prominent social workers were called
upon for their expertise in matters of social welfare to help draft and implement
policy initiatives.[w] While the New Deal era may have represented a high point
in terms of direct involvement in federal or state governmental committees, the
pathway of the expert remains as social work's avenue toward advancing reform.
This is accomplished today through state and federal funding of social work
researchers, who through their expert analyses provide testimony regarding necessary reforms.

Summary

In the Modern Era scientific expertise in both knowledge and method is required for casework, group work, and community organizing. This stems from

---

[u] As a personal anecdote, upon obtaining my M.S.W. in the late 1990s, I briefly worked at ACORN
in its Chicago chapter. Of over a dozen community organizers working for ACORN and its affiliates
in Chicago, I was the only social worker.

[v] This is not to say that social workers were not involved in civil rights protests. The point that I am
arguing is that social workers who were employed as community organizers did not prominently
incorporate into their job responsibilities the organizing of civil rights protests. Social workers who
engaged in civil rights protests commonly did so outside of their job responsibilities.

[w] Trattner, *From Poor Law*, 271. These included the likes of Frances Perkins (secretary of labor),
Harry Hopkins (head of the Federal Emergency Relief Administration), "Molly" Dewson (of the
Women's Division for the Democratic National Committee), Aubrey Williams (director of the
National Youth Association), Katherine Lenroot and Martha Eliot (of the U.S. Children's Bureau),
Jane Hoey (of the Social Security Administration), Ellen Woodward (of the Federal Emergency
Relief Administration and the Works Progress Administration), and numerous others."

the Modern Discourse's notion that knowledge of the True must be uncovered to reach knowledge of the Good (now seen as healthy functioning). The social worker thus became the technical expert. Porter Lee's 1929 presidential address to the National Conference of Social Work marked the rise of this new, more prominent role—from moral reformer to technical expert, from fighting for a cause to providing a service. The ensuing years marked a time in which the profession of social work struggled to determine exactly where this technical expertise lay. The diagnostic and functionalist schools of casework that arose placed this expertise heavily within the psychological sphere. But under the leadership of Harriet Bartlett and William Gordon in the 1950s and onward, sociological concerns began to be given equal weight. A working definition of social work was created that placed this expertise within the area of social functioning[154]— which would be elaborated as the transaction between the individual and their environment.[155] The domain of technical expertise of the social worker was now firmly elaborated.

c. 1990–Present: The Emergence of a Postmodern discourse

The perspective taken in this book asserts that the adaptive point of view has provided an inadequate foundation for clinical social work theory. A theory of meaning in which psychological health is indicated by a constructed personal meaning system (or identity) that is highly differentiated, articulated, and integrated is proposed to take the place of conceptualizations about adaptation.
—Carolyn Saari, 1991[156]

The Modern Discourse on social welfare continues to dominate to the present day. Yet in recent decades it has faced a serious challenger in the emergence of a Postmodern discourse. This challenge has been strong enough that it has forced the Modern Discourse to attempt to co-opt and incorporate key insights from social work practices informed by this Postmodern discourse, the most prominent example being the insight of focusing upon client strengths that arose as a core element of the strengths perspective. Hence, the transition periods examined in previous chapters serve as a useful guide on how the co-opting of insights from a different discourse inevitably lead to a watered-down version that gets incorporated into the existing discourse. We saw how this occurred with the Colonial Discourse's attempts to incorporate the insight of democratic equality and with the Premodern Discourse's attempts to incorporate scientific investigation. The same result occurs with the Modern Discourse's attempt to incorporate the insight of client strengths.

It is not uncommon to find social workers today who declare that they follow a strengths-based approach to practice. However, there is much difference between declaring that one adopts a strengths-based approach and employing the strengths perspective. This co-opting of a name mirrors what took place when the COS of the Premodern Era adopted the self-moniker *scientific charity*, as described in Chapter 5, while falling far short of applying true scientific investigation principles. Similarly, a strengths-based approach in this vein operates within the Modern Discourse, and thus, it is guided by the various elements of this dominant Discourse. So, for example, a strengths-based approach continues to view the helping situation as being an effort at maintaining or enhancing functioning. It continues to follow the rules of right in seeking to measure deviance from a norm of functioning and to understand the root causes of the dysfunction. There remains a faith in science that it will serve to uncover this root cause, and the social worker brings to bear their professional expertise in human functioning to do so. The client continues to be viewed as existing in an environment (i.e., the natural world); hence, the concomitant objectification of human qualities continues to take place. Thus, *strengths* get translated as a resource—an object upon which clients are able to draw as an aid in their attempt to enhance their functioning.

A typical way in which such strengths-based practitioners search for strengths as a resource happens by including an inquiry into strengths as part of conducting a bio-psycho-social assessment. The bio-psycho-social assessment directs the study phase of the generic scientific management model of study, diagnose, treatment, which comprises the Modern Discourse's understanding of the helping process by delineating which information is valuable and relevant to collect. The information obtained from a bio-psycho-social assessment is used to diagnose the etiology of the client's presenting problem and to identify causal factors that may serve to enhance functioning. How this application of strengths represents a water-downed version of its articulation in the Postmodern discourse may at present be unclear to the reader—as it requires a thorough understanding of how the Postmodern discourse operates. This thorough understanding will hopefully come after reading the subsequent chapters, which cover the Postmodern discourse. However, for now, the bio-psycho-social assessment serves as a good litmus test as to which side you may fall on concerning identifying client strengths. If conducting a bio-psycho-social assessment represents a standard part of one's practice—as opposed to conducting a strengths assessment—then you are applying this watered-down version of the insight on strengths.

The inherent limitation of the Modern Discourse which handicaps its ability to incorporate insights from the Postmodern discourse is that by placing human beings solely within the natural world, a scientific understanding of what it means to be human privileges objective knowledge while delegitimizing subjective knowledge. The various insights generated from the Postmodern discourse (such as the role strengths play) happen to arise from employing subjective knowledge, and within the Postmodern discourse subjective knowledge is understood as being an equal contributor (along with objective knowledge) to discovering knowledge of the True (i.e., reality). Again, the full import of the Modern Discourse's limitation in this regard will only become apparent once we have thoroughly examined the Postmodern discourse. However, for now, a brief example will serve to illustrate the process by which this delegitimization occurs.

Social constructionism (which will be described more fully in Chapter 8) is an epistemological theory which takes the position that true knowledge of reality is socially constructed; social constructions represent subjective knowledge that has been wedded to objective knowledge concerning the existence of a phenomenon. Both subjective knowledge and objective knowledge contribute equally to defining the phenomenon, and it is their synthesis that defines its reality. The objective knowledge (e.g., size, shape, color, etc.) concerning the phenomenon remains constant across contexts. Thus, for example, if you place a chair at your dining room table and then place the chair out on your front lawn, the physical properties of the chair don't change. On the other hand, subjective knowledge (e.g., the meaning that is imbued in the chair) can change across contexts. If I place the chair at my dining room table, I am imbuing it with the meaning that it is a useful item, as I would use it to sit upon when I ate meals. Others would view it that way as well, and by its placement in my house it would be viewed as property that I value. Hence, someone visiting my house would not look to pick up the chair and take it to their home.

However, if I take the same chair and place it on my front lawn next to my garbage can, I am imbuing it with the meaning that it is not something useful to me, and thus not something I value. Hence, it is quite possible that someone walking by would feel free to pick up the chair and take it home with them if they found it useful when placed in the context of their home. Thus, social constructionism purports that there are multiple truths of the reality of a phenomenon due to the variation of subjective knowledge across different contexts. Social constructionists will use a small "t" when describing truth claims—signifying the position that multiple truths can be equally valid for the same phenomenon; they will use a capital "T" to describe the truth claims made by positivism (the dominant epistemological theory within the Modern Discourse)—signifying how scientific fact is seen as representing a single underlying truth.

In a popular social work research textbook put out by prominent scholars in this area (Allan Rubin and Earl Babbie), the authors attempt to explain social constructionism.[157] In their textbook, they provide four different illustrations of a book: One view is from the vantage of looking directly at the front cover, another is a vantage from the side looking directly at the open pages, another is a vantage from the opposite side looking directly at the spine, and lastly they provide an illustration from the vantage of looking at the open book from above.[158] By operating within the Modern Discourse which delegitimizes subjective knowledge, they are only able to conceive of social constructions as being equivalent to one's point of view. Within this understanding, subjective knowledge is not synthesizing with objective knowledge to constitute a distinct reality. Rather, subjective knowledge represents an incomplete grasp (a particular viewpoint of the book) of the underlying truth arising from objective knowledge (the book as a whole).

Thus, returning to the example earlier, a social worker who is inquiring about strengths while conducting a bio-psycho-social assessment is viewing strengths as representing a particular vantage that comprises the person as a whole. By combining this vantage with the biological, psychological, and social aspects of the person, a more complete grasp of the underlying truth of the person is arrived at. By being trapped within the Modern Discourse, it never occurs to the social worker to explore the meaning-making elements of strengths and their role in the helping process.

Moral Blind Spots in the Modern Discourse

In the previous chapters, we benefited from historical distance, placing ourselves outside the dominant Discourse being examined, thus positioning ourselves to readily examine how individuals operating in that dominant Discourse were blind to certain failings and flaws of that Discourse. Here, we face the challenge of attempting to identify moral blind spots of the dominant Discourse within which we are currently operating. As was noted in Chapter 1, power circulating in a dominant Discourse operates below the conscious awareness of those individuals operating within it. So, for example, the average individual in today's society is not familiar with the correspondence theory of truth and would be unable to articulate its foundational premises if asked; nevertheless, their everyday actions and understandings are based upon its foundational premises. Furthermore, it would never occur to the individual that they would have the option to choose a different ontological theory in which to conceive of reality and thus base their actions and understanding upon it.

And even for intellectual thought of which the individual is aware, such as Charles Darwin's theory of evolution, the power exerted by this element of the Modern Discourse goes unexamined. So, for example, one may be able to attribute the concept of adaptation to Darwin's theory, as well as the notion of conceiving of human behavior in terms of nature versus nurture; however, what is typically unexamined is that Darwin's theory fosters the conception of human beings existing solely in the natural world. And, once again, it would never occur to the individual that even while accepting Darwin's theory as valid, one has the option to choose a different conception of how human beings exist in their world and thus base their actions and understanding upon it. Hence, this is why Michel Foucault describes the power circulating within a dominant Discourse as acting like "a machine in which everyone is caught."[159]

It takes a critical consciousness to break free of one's enmeshment in the dominant Discourse. As stated above, historical distance served to place the reader outside any enmeshment in a dominant Discourse from a previous era, thus positioning one to critically examine the moral blind spots arising from acceptance of those dominant Discourses. The process in the previous chapter of deliberately identifying and articulating the various elements comprising the Modern Discourse serves as a good first step toward achieving this critical consciousness. An additional step is to mimic the effects granted by historical distance.

This now will be attempted in two ways. The first involves revisiting the critique of social work practices from the previous Premodern Era. While the Modern Discourse represents a distinct break from the Premodern Discourse, the two rules of right remained relatively unchanged. Thus, even though on one level much has changed in how we conceive of social work practice, on another level much has remained the same. And it is at this level that the critiques readily apparent in the Premodern Discourse would continue to be valid for the Modern Discourse as well. The second way is to position oneself in an alternate future discourse and then, from this position, turn back to critique the Modern Discourse. The emerging Postmodern discourse offers such an opportunity. As the Postmodern discourse will be fully elaborated in the next two chapters, this aspect of critiquing the Modern Discourse will be picked up again in Chapter 9. For now, we will examine the ways in which social work practices within the Modern Discourse have remained relatively unchanged from the Premodern Discourse.

Over the years both historians and social work scholars have commented upon parallels between practices from the Premodern Era with those from the Modern Era. William Trattner summarizes a few historians' analyses attesting to the commonality that this new type of social work arising in the 1920s had with its premodern era counterpart:

> The new professionalism, however, may not have been as far removed from the old moralism as many social workers would have liked to believe. As David and Sheila Rothman have pointed out, the net result of the new approach, "was to couch in modern terminology some very traditional ideas." Or as an equally perceptive person put it: "Substituting expertise for moral superiority as the basis of the relationship, social workers perpetuated the charity organization

ideal of personal contact and influence in place of material relief, but avoided the fiction that such contact was one of friends and peers bound in neighborhood association." Or in the words of John Ehrenreich, yet another commentator on this return to a theory of client culpability in a new guise, "It was a matter of St. Sigmund [Freud] rather than St. Peter . . . it was certainly not a matter of St. Karl [Marx]."[160]

So one of the aspects of social work practice that has remained unchanged from the previous to the present era is the positioning of the social worker as the expert knower while the client is positioned as operating under a veil of ignorance. Under the Premodern Discourse, this expertise lay in moral reasoning and the client was seen as lacking such reasoning. Under the Modern Discourse, this expertise lies in scientific knowledge of human functioning and the client is viewed as not possessing such knowledge.

Consequently, the helping relationship is structured in such a way that what the client is seen as possessing is local knowledge of their symptomology as it relates to the presenting problem. However, the client is in a state of ignorance as to the causal connections behind and between this symptomology; and hence, the client reports this symptomology to the social worker and then relies upon the social worker to indicate the direction that treatment should take. This structure of the helping relationship falls in line with the medical model approach. By way of comparison, when you visit a medical doctor upon suffering an illness or injury, you report your symptoms to the doctor. While you may have some suspicions or hypotheses as to what may be the underlying problem or what the best treatment may be, you rely upon the doctor's expertise to make a diagnosis and suggest the best treatment. And if the doctor made a diagnosis different than yours or suggested a different form of treatment, you would be inclined to bow to their expertise on the matter. You would not expect the doctor to turn to you and say, "You're in a much better position than me to diagnose your illness and determine the best course in treatment. I will follow your lead." The doctor's expertise in medical knowledge, just as the social worker's expertise in human functioning, is one of the primary attributes one brings to the helping relationship as a professional. Yet, by taking up the mantle of expert knower, the professional creates a power imbalance in the helping relationship. And under certain conditions, this power imbalance can provide corrupted ground in which the seeds of good intentions grow into efforts at social control.

Let's take a look at another commentary on the similarity between social work practices from the Premodern Era with those of the Modern Era to examine what these conditions might be that interact with this power imbalance to produce efforts at social control. As late as 1958 in social work literature, parallels were still being drawn between current practices and nineteenth-century social welfare interventions. The basis of similarities in practice between these two eras lies in the fact that the rules of right influencing practice—measuring deviance from an ideal/norm and seeking causality regarding this deviance—remained relatively unchanged in the transition from the Premodern Discourse to the Modern Discourse. The following observation serves to illustrate one of the ways that this dynamic played out:

> It is not true that "no one talks of sin anymore," but social workers rarely talk of sin. Today a new language has evolved. . . . Whether jargon or scientific terminology, the new language has a strong emotional content. Behavior is still labeled as "good" or "bad." "Good" may be termed "wholesome personality," "adjustment," or "normal"; "bad" may be termed "maladjustment," "neurotic," or "abnormal." . . . In other words, "bad" behavior is behavior that does not conform with the community models. Sin is now "deviant behavior."[161]

This author makes the argument that social workers' focus upon identifying and diagnosing problematic behaviors continued unabated into the Modern Era; what changed was simply the jargon used to label such behaviors—from moralistic to scientific. Measuring deviance requires the use of judgment, whether it be moralistic or scientific, and efforts at correcting that deviance toward conformity with community models open the door to the danger of such efforts simply becoming exercises in social control.

The Modern Discourse's turn toward science did not mitigate this danger; rather, I would argue that it served to increase it. This is because scientific knowledge is understood as arising from impartial observations. This dulls the social worker's awareness of the fact that a judgment is being made as it is passed off in the social worker's mind as simply being the application of an impartial, scientific fact. So, for example, the social worker may suggest an evidence-based treatment modality as the means to mitigate the client's presenting problem. Rather than being clearly aware that this represents a judgment on the part of the social worker as to what is best for the client, the social worker treats it as an impartial fact. When this dulling of awareness occurs within a helping relationship containing a power imbalance, you have a recipe for social control. This is why a term such as *resistant client* has arisen in our nomenclature. When the expert knower's judgment is questioned by the client, the resistance of the client to the proposed treatment is viewed as refusal to recognize an impartial, scientific fact.

Now the profession of social work takes comfort in the accomplishment of articulating a strong professional ethic in the form of social work values. In particular, the social work value of self-determination is viewed as the check against falling into a stance of exerting social control. But is this always the case? This is a question worth exploring. Turning back to Chapter 5 and the case study examination of the COS employment of the practice approach "not alms but a friend," it was concluded that good intentions by themselves are not a guarantee against a predilection toward social control. Furthermore, combining good intentions with expertise did not prevent the COS workers from engaging in the practice of social control. As the analysis above revealed, embracing the mantle of expert knower actually feeds this predilection toward social control rather than combating it. Lastly, the role of values was examined, in particular the value of empowerment. For some situations (e.g., settlement house work), employing the value of empowerment did serve as an effective check against settlement house workers engaging in the practice of social control. However, for the situation of employing "not alms but a friend," embracing the value of empowerment did not serve to prevent COS workers from engaging in social control efforts. Describing this discrepancy as arising from the relativity of absolute morals, the value of empowerment was absolute in that all social workers embraced it; however, it was relative in that the context of the situation determined its application and interpretation. Thus, simply possessing the value of empowerment (along with good intentions and expertise) was not sufficient to eradicate practices of social control in the Premodern Era.

Does this analysis remain unchanged for the Modern Era? I believe it is safe to assume that no one would argue the position that good intentions by themselves are enough to guard against inadvertently exerting social control. Furthermore, following the above analysis, I believe most would agree that positioning oneself as the expert knower does not protect against inadvertently exerting social control. Embracing the value of self-determination certainly has the potential to prevent one from inadvertently exerting social control, but has it done so across all situations? We only have to turn to the social work literature to come to the conclusion that it has not. Over various decades, social work scholars have repeatedly voiced the alarm that practices in the Modern Era can easily devolve into efforts at social control. The following represent a few examples:

> 1955: Social work along with the other practices, is concerned with action and change; it therefore belongs among the controlling agencies of society. Social workers, committed as they are to the principle of self-determination in the social relationship, may conceivably resist this characterization of their profession. However, the plain fact is that social workers, by virtue of their technical knowledge and community sanctioned status, possess a form of power which they exercise to reach certain ends.[162]

> 1958: Our definition points to a distinction between "coercive" and "persuasive" control, but aside from the function of the agency, this distinction, in most casework situations, may be one of degree. . . . Implicit, therefore, in the counselor–client relationship is the presence of power which induces the client to modify his behavior, since he requires what the counselor has to give.[163]

1965: This view of social control elements in the casework relationship puts one further nail into the coffin of the myth of client self-determination. This has been a powerful and valuable myth, playing an important part in the ideological superstructure of social work, but its continuation unmodified may prevent a realistic appraisal of what actually happens in interviews.[164]

1972: Ensuring conformity of individuals to social norms entails the activation of social control mechanisms. It is interesting, though not surprising, that until quite recently social workers and social work writings tended to deny the social control function of their profession.[165]

1981: The reasoned perception by theorists and social workers of non-conforming people as pathological, the proliferation of organizations to "help" them to conform, and the overwhelming message given through mass media and social institutions in support of non-deviance through mental health leave little room for those who do not "fit in." Worse, not "fitting in," being harmlessly different, is often seen as deviance by the people so labeled. . . . They become more stressed when they cannot meet the expectations of those people who "know" what good behaviors and good emotions are, and may be lost as whole persons in the process of diagnosis, labeling, treatment, and conformation.[166]

Robert Taylor's 1958 comment drawing a distinction between coercive power and persuasive power is particularly instructive toward illustrating the dynamic of the relativity of absolute morals at play as it pertains to the value of self-determination practiced in the Modern Discourse. Typically, self-determination in the Modern Discourse is understood as "the freedom to choose" one's direction in life or course of action. With this understanding, very few social workers inadvertently exert coercive power. Even when working with mandated clients, while the terms of the mandate are non-negotiable, there is much within the helping relationship open for negotiation. The most likely scenario for coercive power to be exerted is when the client exhibits diminished mental capacity—that is, with individuals suffering from a mental illness and children. Within these helping relationships, short-sighted social workers may stumble to the conclusion that these clients are handicapped in their ability to effectively employ this freedom of choice—that due to their diminished mental capacity, they are unable to fully grasp the import of the knowledge of the True as determined by the social worker. As knowledge of the True is viewed as a necessary precondition for making an informed choice, the social worker consequently steps in and makes the choice for them.

However, the more insidious and often unexamined occurrences of social control involve the use of persuasive power. The insidious aspect of persuasive power arises when the social worker takes the position that the client *is* in a position to make an informed choice as to the direction of treatment; as the social worker believes that they are employing self-determination in this scenario, it is quite easy for the operation of persuasive power to go unexamined. In the previous chapter, it was described how a new understanding of individualism arose in the Modern Discourse: that of expressive individualism. As scientific management began to permeate the workplace, opportunities there for creative self-expression quickly disappeared. Consequently, one's outlet for creative self-expression was redirected away from being a producer of goods/knowledge to one of being a consumer of goods/knowledge. Thus, the notion of the *sovereign consumer* arose, wherein one expresses one's self-cultivation and growth through the freedom to choose "among already selected brands of goods."[167] What the marketplace achieved in this regard concerning the purveying of goods, the mass media—as reflective in the rise of television and radio—achieved regarding the purveying of knowledge/entertainment: the freedom of the individual to choose from already selected channels and programs.

Hence, within the Modern Discourse on social welfare, it is quite common for the helping relationship to place the social worker in the role of expert knower producing selected treatment options, while the client is placed in the role of sovereign consumer of social work services who selects from these options. Turning back to the case study of the COS workers' employment of "not alms but a friend," it was observed that those social workers truly believed that they were empowering the clients with whom they worked. However, benefiting from the vantage of viewing this practice from outside the confines of the Premodern Discourse, we are able to easily see that the practice of "not alms but a friend" represented a misguided application of empowerment and inadvertently led these social workers down the path of social control.

Similarly, social workers practicing today who apply self-determination within the confines of the client as sovereign consumer of services most likely believe that they are faithfully applying the value of self-determination, and thus avoiding any predilections for exerting social control. However, those social workers who have stepped out of the Modern Discourse and now operate within the Postmodern discourse are able to easily see how this application represents a very weak and limited application of self-determination and, consequently, does not prevent them from being inadvertently led down the path of social control. The rationale informing this critique will be taken up again within Chapter 9's discussion of postmodern practices.

Reflections

The profession of social work in the Modern Era has a long and dubious history in its embrace of the medical model; this history, along with how the medical model contributes to social work's predilection toward social control under the Modern Discourse is worthy of closer examination. Currently, the term *medical model* has a negative connotation within social work literature, born from critiques that this approach fosters an undue focus on describing pathology.[168] As a result, few social workers practicing today will declare a preference for employing the medical model approach to practice. But this was not always the case. Social workers practicing at the advent of the Modern Era readily embraced the medical model. And the field of medicine—the place where the medical model was born—continues to this day to highly prize this approach. For the first part of this examination, let's inquire as to why the medical model has been so successful for the field of medicine.

History of the Medical Model in the Field of Medicine

In surveying the advances in medicine over the past 100+ years the medical model has been employed, while there certainly have been various missteps along the way (most notably the Tuskegee syphilis study), one cannot begrudge the amazing advances that have occurred—from the eradication of smallpox and other fatal diseases to organ transplant surgery to the various treatments developed to fight cancer. For the field of medicine, few would refute that embracing scientific inquiry to drive knowledge generation and practice has been an unqualified and tremendous success. Yet, as examined earlier, a purely scientific investigation of the human condition (i.e., placing human beings as existing solely in the natural world) is based upon the pursuit of objective knowledge, and hence inevitably leads to objectifying the human condition. So why is this not problematic for the field of medicine, whose concern is with the physical health and biological functioning of the individual? I would argue that it is because it is quite easy for one to divest one's sense of self from one's physical body. Thus, both doctor and patient can easily view the patient's body as an object to be acted upon. The amazing successes achieved by the field of medicine this past century have served to confirm the usefulness of this approach and to increase the willingness of both patient and doctor to adopt this process of objectification.

This understanding falls in line with what is described in the medical field as the biomedical model, which is "characterized by a reductionist approach that attributes illness to a single cause located within the body."[169] Furthermore, the biomedical model "assumes disease to be fully accounted for by deviations from the norm of measurable biological (somatic) variables."[170] This understanding and approach have worked tremendously well for both illnesses and injuries. So, for example, if one should break one's arm, it is easy to view the arm simply as a part of one's body, to separate and isolate it from one's sense of self, and thus reduce it to an object to be acted upon. The deviance in functioning can be easily measured (via X-ray) and the scientifically tested remedy confidently applied. The merit of such a reductionist approach to illness and injury is illustrated by the fact that if I happen to live in the United States and I break my arm, compared to if I happen to live in Ethiopia and break my arm, the recognized method of diagnosis (using X-ray) and treatment is the same for both. Culture only plays a superficial role in terms of administering treatment.

However, even though the biomedical model in the field of medicine has achieved a tremendous track record since its inception, in the past few decades there have been calls for improvement.[171] This critique has been led by the subfield of psychiatry, whose concern regarding both the biochemical functioning of the brain and neurophysiological processes most clearly illustrates some of the limitations of the biomedical model. Comparing diabetes to schizophrenia serves as a useful example illustrating these limitations. During the Modern Era, a disease such as diabetes has been the subject of much scientific investigation. Eventually, this cumulative investigation resulted in successfully reducing our understanding of diabetes from that of a general cluster of functional abnormalities to that of specific biochemical abnormalities.[172] This in turn has led to specific and targeted treatment. Schizophrenia has also been the subject of much scientific investigation in the Modern Era. Yet, while biochemical abnormalities have been identified (and hence treatment with psychotropic medication developed), schizophrenia remains stubbornly resistant to reduction as a disease of purely biochemical processes; and thus, our understanding remains at the level of conceiving it as a general cluster of functional abnormalities.[173]

Since its inception, psychiatry recognized the role that psychological factors could play concerning the manifestation of symptoms and their amelioration. Both Sigmund Freud and Adolf Meyer contributed to the development of psychosomatic medicine—an effort to provide frames of reference wherein psychological and biological factors could be combined as a means to diagnose and treat disease and injury. However, in order to combine with biological factors on an equal footing, psychological factors needed to fall within the realm of objective knowledge and hence required objectification; Freud's conception of the id, ego, and superego as psychological components is a prime example. While Freud and Meyer recognized that social factors could play a part as well, the field of sociology had not yet elaborated a prominent theory to account for social factors in this manner.

This would not occur until the 1950s with sociology's application of systems theory to social systems. This final development now provided the foundation for the noted psychiatrist George Engel in 1977 to propose an evolved version of the biomedical model, which he termed the *bio-psycho-social medical model*. As he stated, "For medicine, systems theory provides a conceptual approach suitable not only for the proposed bio-psycho-social concept of disease but also for studying disease and medical care as interrelated processes."[174] Systems theory's ability to objectify social factors along with various psychological theories' ability to objectify psychological factors opened the door for considerations of how psychological and social factors contribute to patients reporting symptoms of their disease, serve to either exacerbate or ameliorate symptoms based upon their interaction with life stresses, determine when the individual views themselves as sick and thus seeks medical aid, and explain how the therapeutic relationship between doctor and patient can influence outcomes.[175]

As the bio-psycho-social medical model merely represents an evolution of the biomedical model, the similarities shared by the two models far outweigh any distinguishing differences. These similarities include the following: (1) both rely upon objective knowledge and hence result in the objectification of the human condition; (2) the physician is poised as the expert knower, with their expertise lying in this objectified knowledge of human functioning; (3) both rely upon the generation of knowledge concerning the patient arising from application of the basic precepts to scientific investigation, these being study (observe), diagnose (hypothesize), and treatment (test the hypothesis); (4) both conceive of self-determination within the rubric of the sovereign consumer, where the patient is free to choose among selected treatment options (including no treatment); and (5) both follow the Modern Discourse's rules of right, that of proposing a norm of human function against which deviance can be measured and the notion that biological, psychological, and social "objects" interact in a causal manner. The main difference between the bio-psycho-social medical model and the biomedical model entails the following: (1) by examining a constellation of biological, psychological, and social factors, the bio-psycho-social medical model avoids the reductionism inherent in the biomedical model. In addition, it can be said that, due to its holistic approach, (2) the bio-psycho-social medical model is better poised to explore aspects of human growth and development in the healing process rather than being primarily focused upon identifying and correcting pathology.

History of the Medical Model in Social Work

Abraham Flexner's 1915 speech to the National Conference of Charities and Correction, which questioned the legitimacy of social work as a profession due to its lack of a knowledge base, serves as a convenient bookend to mark our profession's turn toward enshrining scientific inquiry as the sole means for generating knowledge and guiding practice.[176] Taking a look at the state of various other professions, social work leaders of that time discovered that the field of medicine had experienced some impressive advancements—such as surgical anesthetic and antisepsis—arising from their recent embrace of scientific inquiry. As outlined above, through their wholesale adoption of the steps involved in scientific inductive inquiry, leaders in medicine developed what is now referred to as the medical model: gathering data through observations of patient symptoms, diagnosing (i.e., hypothesizing) the cause of said symptoms, and then testing the validity of this diagnoses through employing a treatment designed to eradicate or counteract the underlying cause. An integral component necessary to support such an approach is that one must employ a normative model of what healthy functioning looks like; problematic functioning is thus identified through its deviance from this healthy norm, and the successful testing of one's hypothesis/diagnosis is measured by one's ability to move the patient back toward this healthy norm.

Mary Richmond's publication of *Social Diagnosis* in 1917 marked the first attempt to apply the medical model to social work practice. She advised paying equal attention to both psychological and social factors impacting client functioning; however, beyond adopting the basic steps of scientific investigation, she offered little in the way of scientific theory concerning how the various psychological and social factors interacted. So her work can be said to offer a prototype of the medical model as she was still burdened by the Premodern Discourse's overemphasis on accurate data collection.

In a period known as the *psychiatric deluge* occurring during the 1920s and 1930s, social workers heavily relied upon the "scientific"[x] theories of Freud to provide hypotheses for client dysfunction, and thus a direction for treatment as the means to test said hypotheses. Sociological theory at the time was viewed by social workers as inadequate and underdeveloped as an aid to diagnosing the various problems and life struggles that were brought to them by clients. Hence, this gave rise to the diagnostic school—an approach that focused upon diagnosing and treating psychological causes of client dysfunction. As Freud's theories were deterministic and heavily focused upon pathology, social work practice under the diagnostic school can be viewed as embracing a mirror image of the biomedical model being practiced in the field of medicine. It contained an undue focus upon pathology and sought reductionist explanations for behavior, the only difference being that this reductionism took place in the area of psychology rather than biology. Thus, it may be described as a psychomedical model for practice.

---

[x] Popper, *Logic of Scientific Discovery*. I am putting the word "scientific" in quotes stemming from Karl Popper's definition of science being based upon falsification. Popper specifically uses Sigmund Freud's theory to exemplify his definition of pseudoscience as being scientific investigation based upon confirmation.

With the addition of ego theory pioneered by Heinz Hartmann and later the various life-span theories arising from humanistic psychology, the notion of attending to healthy growth and enhancement of functioning was added to the diagnostic school's approach. Soon after, this spawned the problem-solving approach. While this approach offered a move away from a sole focus upon pathology, it retained the reductionist leanings in psychology present in the psychomedical model. While the problem-solving approach was open to the inclusion of sociological theory, social work was still waiting for the firm articulation of sociological theory to the concerns of social welfare.

Hence, it can be stated that up until the early 1970s, social work followed a psychomedical model of practice. However, in these first fifty years of practice social work's employment of the psychomedical model achieved a starkly different track record than that achieved by the medical field's use of the biomedical model. Not only are there no major or startling advances to speak of arising during this time but, as was pointed out by the critique led by Joel Fischer and cohorts, social work practice up to this point was unable to scientifically claim that its interventions were effective at all.

What is to account for such a stark difference of results between the field of medicine and the field of social work in their employment of the medical model? I believe the answer lies in examining scientific inquiry's sole pursuit of objective knowledge. As described earlier, it is relatively easy to divest one's sense of self from one's physical body and then look upon the various components comprising the physical body as objects to be acted upon. However, it is quite difficult to divest one's sense of self from one's personality, and hence to look upon the various psychological components of one's personality as objects to be acted upon. The same can be said for social factors. It is quite difficult to divest one's sense of self from one's various social roles (as father, sister, student, etc.), and hence to look upon the various social dimensions of these roles as objects to be acted upon. Both seem to call out for the addition of subjective knowledge to yield a much fuller picture concerning the interaction of psychological and social aspects present in a client's life struggles.

Picking back up at the 1970s and the examination of social work practice, it was at this time that systems theory was articulated and applied to social work by Carel Germain (at times, with various collaborators) in the form of ecological systems theory. This gave rise to the person-in-environment perspective which, wedded to the problem-solving approach, dominates our understanding of social work practice to this day. By adding sociological factors to the mix of objects to be acted upon, ecological systems theory enabled social work to take a more holistic approach to confronting client problems by using a bio-psycho-social analysis, and thus avoid the reductionism inherent within a psychomedical model.

This latest divergence from the psychomedical model often fosters claims that ecological systems theory applied within a problem-solving method marks a clean break from the medical model. Yet this claim is only partially true, for, as was the case in the field of medicine, the inclusion of objectified biological, psychological, and now social factors in one's analysis simply represents an evolution of the medical model to that of a bio-psycho-social medical model. To be sure, both reductionism and an overt focus on pathology may be avoided when employing the bio-psycho-social medical model. However, the five elements defining the model remain the same: (1) the objectification of the client by pursuing objective knowledge; (2) the social worker positioned as the expert knower; (3) the primacy of study, diagnose, and treatment as steps comprising the helping process; (4) the narrow application of client self-determination as sovereign consumer; and (5) the Modern Discourse's rules of right emphasizing correcting deviance and searching for causal factors. As was determined previously, the combination of these five elements operating within the Modern Discourse is what leads to a predilection toward social control.

Consequently, this predilection toward social control requires social workers to actively guard against it in order to prevent its expression. As stated earlier, due to the negative connotations now associated with the medical model (born from critiques of the psychomedical model's reductionism and overt focus upon pathology), many social workers take the principled stance that they will not employ the medical model in their practice. And this is where the real danger now lies: By utilizing systems theory to provide a more holistic understanding of the client situation in objectified terms and by employing a problem-solving approach that avoids an overt focus upon pathology and recognizes strengths, the social worker may easily be led to believe that they are no longer operating within a medical model—whereas in reality the social worker has simply moved away from employing a psychomedical model to employing a bio-psycho-social medical model.

Both systems theory and the problem-solving approach are products of the Modern Discourse. When a social worker employs them, while at the same time no longer remaining cognizant that they are operating within a bio-psycho-social medical model, they are no longer actively guarding against its predilection toward social control. The test that practitioners can give themselves in this regard is quite simple: If one employs person-in-environment as one's main conceptual framework for the helping situation, if one conducts or utilizes bio-psycho-social assessments as an integral part of the helping process, and/or if one employs scientific investigation (encapsulated in the steps study, diagnose, treatment) as the primary form of knowledge generation in the helping process, then one is operating within a bio-psycho-social medical model. Consequently, one must be on guard against one's endeavors inadvertently transforming into efforts at social control.

Evaluating the Medical Model in Social Work

As described above, for the first fifty years of the Modern Era, social work practice under a psychomedical model generated nothing in terms of the development of groundbreaking treatment interventions that were proven to yield dramatic and reliable results. Furthermore, it has been called into question whether or not social work practice during this time period could lay claim to having had any effectiveness at all. Furthermore, it is clear that social workers periodically lapsed into practicing social control. Not only is this attested to by the evidence outline above, wherein over decades social work scholars of this time period regularly commented upon its occurrence, but also we have a bit of historical distance allowing us to clearly and dispassionately identify practices that occurred in this vein. One prominent example is that of child welfare social workers in the 1950s who readily embraced the role of social police by conducting midnight "raids" into the homes of single mothers on welfare in order to ensure that there was no man in the house (which would disqualify the mothers from receiving welfare payments).[177]

Now let's turn to the most recent fifty years and examine the track record of social work practice under a bio-psycho-social medical model. This will be a bit more difficult in that we will be attempting to critique a time period within which we are currently living, and hence we do not derive benefit from the vantage of historical distance. I would argue that, as a profession, social work has made moderate progress under the bio-psycho-social medical model. On the plus side, there is no longer any doubt being expressed in the literature as to whether or not social work practice is at all effective in helping clients. Admittedly, this is a pretty low bar, but it does mark an improvement from where we started. We can also look at the great demand in the job market for social workers, along with predictions of this demand continuing to grow. This certainly attests to the value society now places upon social workers as professionals. However, what is indeterminate is the nature of the usefulness being valued as society may value social workers as agents of social change, but society may also value the usefulness of social workers as agents of social control.

Lastly, we can look at the established body of evidence–based practice literature that has steadily accumulated and which attests to the effectiveness of various treatment interventions. However, we must proceed with caution before vesting too much importance in the claims of evidence-based practice literature. First, there is the issue of the neurotic paradox inherent in social scientific investigation; most of these claims of validity rest upon a subpar foundation of rigor due to the unavoidable limitations involved in attempting to conduct a controlled study in a live environment. But even with putting such skepticisms aside, there also exist claims regarding the effectiveness of interventions operating outside the Modern Discourse—such as the strengths perspective and solution-focused therapy, both of which are informed by the Postmodern discourse.[178] While this observation does not detract from the claims of effectiveness for interventions practiced within the bio-psycho-social medical model (e.g., cognitive-behavioral therapy, family systems therapy, problem-solving case management, etc.), it does speak to the issue of cost and benefit. If the costs in operating within a bio-psycho-social medical model are judged to be steeper than those for approaches operating within the Postmodern discourse, why would one pay the higher price for equal results?

Let's continue this analysis of cost/benefit as we begin to examine the negative side of employing a bio-psycho-social medical model. First let's look at benefits. Once again, in comparison to the field of medicine, social work lags far behind. The field of medicine has continued to make incredible advances, such as gene therapy, minimally invasive surgery, and angioplasty along with the development of statins to treat heart disease, to name but a few. While one may argue that moderate progress has been made within social work's various areas of concern—such as mental health, child welfare, hospice and medical social work, administering to the poor and homeless, etc.—in not a single area can social work point to the development of a treatment/intervention that produces a dramatic and profound improvement in the client's functioning on par with what continues to be accomplished in the field of medicine. The closest that comes to mind is the development of psychotropic medication in helping individuals to manage mental illness; and, of course, this development has arisen from the field of medicine's employment of a medical model. The yield from employing a medical model continues to be great for the field of medicine yet has only resulted in meager improvement for the field of social work.

While meager or moderate improvement is certainly better than no improvement at all, we must consider this improvement in relation to the costs that are being paid in using the bio-psycho-social medical model. One of the major costs that has been thoroughly explored in this chapter is the predilection of the model to steer social workers toward practices of social control. Granted, under ideal circumstances this predilection can be counteracted through insightful application of social work values, such as when adopting a stance of cultural humility (a postmodern insight). I would like to think that the majority of social work today occurs in such a vein—similar to the responsive approach of settlement house workers of the Premodern Era.

However, it is also deeply disturbing that the vast majority of social workers are most likely unaware that they are practicing within a medical model—in the form of the bio-psycho-social medical model. While this evolution of the medical model, when employed properly, effectively sidelines an overt focus upon pathology and the tendency toward reductionism, it still retains the various elements which foment a predilection toward social control. It is much more difficult to guard against this predilection when one is unaware of its operation. During the Premodern Era, this resulted in COS workers believing that they were empowering clients by providing moral counseling in place of material relief, a practice we now clearly understand as being an effort at social control. Indubitably, this lack of awareness continues within the Modern Discourse. Hence, it is reasonable to assume that there is a fair number of social workers practicing today who believe that they are supporting a client's self-determination, when in fact they are merely placing the client in the role of sovereign consumer: free to choose among socially engineered treatments.

Furthermore, we must consider circumstances when the bio-psycho-social medical model is poorly employed, resulting in less than ideal outcomes. Under such circumstances, the bio-psycho-social medical model will devolve back into its reductionist, pathology-oriented roots across its various disparate parts. Thus, there are occurrences of it devolving back to a biomedical model, one example being when attempts to improve the lives of those suffering from mental illness devolve into efforts at mere medication monitoring. There are also the occurrences of it devolving back into a psychomedical model, a good illustration being when minority youth in the school system exhibit behavioral conflict, with the consequent psychological assessment and socially engineered solution resulting in the overrepresentation of minority children in special education programs. And finally, there are occurrences when it devolves back to a social–medical model, such as when in child welfare the birth mother is given only two choices as sovereign consumer—accepting a single plan of scientific management or opting out of participation in the plan (and thus losing the opportunity to be reunited with her child). In each of these circumstances the client is disempowered rather than empowered, with some experiencing real harm as a result of the intervention.

So the bio-psycho-social medical model comes with a high cost in the form of its predilection toward social control. Another cost not to be overlooked is that of the profession's steady retreat from the field of community organizing and grassroots advocacy. During the Premodern Era, community organizing in the form of grassroots advocacy comprised one of three central pillars of social work (along with casework and group work). As a result, social workers were among the leaders of reform. Beginning with the psychomedical model and continuing on with the bio-psycho-social medical model, the professional education and training of social workers has effectively sidelined community organizing as a prominent feature of social work. It is the rare, if there are any, CSWE-accredited school that offers a specific concentration in community organizing. Rather, its influence has been diluted through its inclusion into the broader area of macro social work—being mixed in with the concerns from public administration and policy analysis. And even in this diluted form, a cursory examination of CSWE-accredited schools reveals that a distinct minority offer a concentration in macro social work. Social engineering works at cross purposes to social reform.

This brings our examination to one final consideration. Earlier, it was pointed out that social scientific investigation contains an inherent dissonance between rigor and relevance, which was described as a neurotic paradox. I would like to propose that a similar dissonance is inherent in social work practice within the Modern Discourse: that between technical efficiency (as represented by scientific management and social engineering) and ethic (as represented by social work values). The main elements of the Modern Discourse, through their objectification of the individual, promote interventions that treat the client as an object to be acted upon.

This causes tension with social work values. The Modern Discourse, which promotes technical expertise on how intrapsychic and social objects interact, supports an approach in which social workers use their expertise to manipulate these objects or promote insight within clients to manipulate these objects themselves, along a course that achieves healthy functioning. This is then paired with the Modern Discourse's support of the notion that knowledge of the True must be attained in order to reach knowledge of the Good. Their technical expertise makes social workers arbiters of this truth, facilitating their role as agents of this change: either directly, through behavior modification or "attitude change," or indirectly, through helping the client discover this Truth and then act accordingly. This is where scientific management and social engineering enter the scene. Under such a rubric, it is easy to understand how the social control of behavior occurring within casework can confusedly be seen as liberating (the social worker leads the client to knowledge of the Good by facilitating enlightenment of the true), while a community organizer as leader advancing a cause is seen as controlling (knowledge of the particular good in terms of confronting injustice is a predetermined political activity that is imposed upon the client; no truths arise from the process).

Yet social work values remain a prominent element in guiding practice. The rise of the Modern Discourse occurring early in the twentieth century freed values from their mooring to causality. They now work in opposition to it, striking a discordant note in the Modern Discourse. Values such as self-determination, empowerment, and the dignity and worth of the individual all work against the forces of objectification, social engineering, and scientific management. Consequently, the Modern Discourse on social welfare contains an inherent dissonance in the practice of social work between the application of values and the application of knowledge—what may be called a second neurotic paradox. For practice interventions—in the area of bringing about change—this dissonance takes the form of technical knowledge seeking to be applied to an object while humanitarian values seek to emphasize the human qualities of the client. This may be described as a dissonance of efficiency versus ethic, *efficiency* in this case referring to the design of the intervention and *ethic* referring to its adherence to social work values.

Social work practice in the Modern Discourse—taking the form of employing knowledge of the True to achieve knowledge of the Good—expresses itself as employing social scientific expertise in human functioning to design and implement a desired change. Yet the more one seeks to apply this expertise to an intervention (i.e., efficiently designing a change in reality), the more one emphasizes the manipulation of objects (and the potential for social control) while consequently de-emphasizing social work values that respect the human condition of the client—such as self-determination and empowerment in designing one's own treatment plan despite lacking this professional expertise. This inherent dissonance, I believe, is what may lead to the Modern Discourse's eventual collapse and replacement by a new dominant Discourse. History tells us that this collapse will occur; it is simply a question of when.

Notes

1. Hartmann, *Ego Psychology*.
2. White, *The Abnormal Personality*.
3. Hartmann, *Ego Psychology*, 24.
4. Hartmann, 30.
5. Barker, *Social Work Dictionary*, 34.
6. Erikson, *Childhood and Society*; Erikson, *Life History*.
7. Erikson, *Childhood and Society*.
8. For example, Gould, *Transformations*; Levinson et al., *The Seasons*; Oldham and Liebert, *The Middle Years*, to name but a few.
9. Erikson, *Life History*, 45, 46; Greene, *Human Behavior Theory*, 108–09, 111, 115; Robbins, Chatterjee, and Canda, *Contemporary Human Behavior Theory*, 208–09, 255.
10. Erikson, *Childhood and Society*, 30, 32, 40–41; Erikson, *Life History*, 46.
11. Levinson et al., *The Seasons*, 5; Oldham and Liebert, *The Middle Years*, 2.
12. Erikson, *Identity and the Life Cycle*.

13. Greene, *Human Behavior Theory*, 107, 114–16, 118; Robbins, Chatterjee, and Canda, *Contemporary Human Behavior Theory*, 254–55.

14. Siegler, *Children's Thinking*.

15. Gardner, *Frames of Mind*; Papalia and Olds, *Human Development*; Sternberg, "Mental Self-Government," to name a few.

16. Piaget, *The Origins of Intelligence*.

17. Robbins, Chatterjee, and Canda, *Contemporary Human Behavior Theory*, 260.

18. Piaget, *The Moral Judgment*.

19. Gilligan, *In a Different Voice*; Kohlberg, "The Child."

20. Robbins, Chatterjee, and Canda, *Contemporary Human Behavior Theory*, 353.

21. Robbins, Chatterjee, and Canda, 72.

22. Greene, *Human Behavior Theory*, 1.

23. Hearn, *Theory Building*, 36.

24. Germain and Gitterman, *The Life Model*, 3–6, 28; Gordon, "Basic Constructs," 6–9, 11; Greene, *Human Behavior Theory*, 268, 278, 281; Hearn, *Theory Building*, 43–44, 49–50, 56–57.

25. Germain and Gitterman, 7, 13, 28, 79; Gordon, 7, 9–11; Greene, 230, 259, 271, 274, 280; Hearn, 43, 44.

26. Germain and Gitterman, 5, 28, 137, 297; Gordon, 6, 11; Greene, 232–33, 259, 269.

27. Germain and Gitterman, 5, 9, 12, 28, 80; Greene, 233, 260, 275–77, 280; Hearn, *Theory Building*, 43, 45, 47.

28. Germain and Gitterman, 3, 5, 7, 12, 28; Gordon, "Basic Constructs," 6–9, 11; Greene, 253, 259, 274–75, 278; Hearn, 40, 43–44.

29. Greene, 271, 274; Robbins, Chatterjee, and Canda, *Contemporary Human Behavior Theory*, 36.

30. Hearn, *Theory Building*, 39.

31. Robbins, Chatterjee, and Canda, *Contemporary Human Behavior Theory*, 50.

32. Robbins, Chatterjee, and Canda, 50.

33. Robbins, Chatterjee, and Canda, 54.

34. For example, Davis, "Role Theory"; Perlman, *Persona*; Strean, *Clinical Social Work*.

35. Robbins, Chatterjee, and Canda, *Contemporary Human Behavior Theory*, 304.

36. Davis, "Role Theory," 550, 553, 556–57; Perlman, *Persona*, 177–92; Strean, *Clinical Social Work*, 212, 214–15, 221.

37. Davis, 542, 548–49, 555; Perlman, 3, 26, 27; Strean, 212–13.

38. Davis, 547, 551, 553, 557; Perlman, 3, 4, 63; Strean, 212, 221.

39. Perlman, 11, 14, 27, 55; Strean, 216, 218, 221; Davis, 549, 553, 555.

40. Zimbalist, *Historic Themes*.

41. Germain, "Casework and Science," 25–32; Zimbalist, 244–46.

42. Zimbalist, 245.

43. Engel and Schutt, *Fundamentals*; Krysik, *Research for Effective*.

44. Zimbalist, *Historic Themes*, 246–47.

45. Zimbalist, 245.

46. Smith, *The Norton History*.

47. Hildreth, *Bibliography of Mental Tests*, 199–205; Kline, *Personality*.

48. Buros Institute of Mental Measurements, *Twentieth Mental Measurements Yearbook*; Hildreth, 190–98, 215–17; Tzeng, *Measurement of Love*, 190.

49. Buros Institute of Mental Measurements: for example, Bathurst (1920), *Test of Honesty* (disguised); Chambers (1926), *Tests of Honesty*; and James (1933), *Honesty Tests*.

50. Buros Institute of Mental Measurements: for example, La Monica (2005), *La Monica Empathy Profile*; Mehrabin (2005), *The Balanced Emotional Empathy Scale*; Noland (2005), *Personalysis*.

51. Buros Institute of Mental Measurements: for example, Allen (1928), *Temperament Tests*; Bathurst (1929), *The Diagnostic Temperament Test*; and Humm and Wadsworth (1935), *Humm-Wadsworth Temperament Scale*.

52. Buros Institute of Mental Measurements: for example, Giese (1925), *Test of Humor*; Almack (1928), *Almack Humor Test*; Landis (1932), *Landis Sense of Humor Test*.

53. Buros Institute of Mental Measurements: for example, Kenneth and Tymon (2005), *Stress Resiliency Profile*; Epstein (2005), *Behavioral and Emotional Rating Scale*.

54. Buros Institute of Mental Measurements: for example, Hendrick and Hendrick (1970), *Love Styles*; Hatfield and Sprecher (1986), *Passion Love Scale*; and Spanier (1976), *Dyadic Adjustment Scale*.

55. Abramovitz, Williams, and Mattaini, "The Pros and Cons"; Keefe, Smith, and McPeak, "What's in a Label?" 79–82; McQuaide, "A Social Worker's Use."

56. Hamilton, "Basic Concepts"; Hamilton, "The Underlying Philosophy"; Hollis, "The Psychosocial Approach."

57. Bowling, *Measuring Health*, 98–103; Hildreth, *Bibliography of Mental Tests*, 246–47.

58. *Toward a Social Report*, p. 97, quoted in Zimbalist, *Historic Themes*, 208.

59. Sheldon and Freeman, "Social Indicators."

60. Leighninger, *Social Work*, 16

61. Leighninger, 9.

62. Leighninger, 15.

63. Leighninger, 15.

64. Leighninger, 185–202.

65. Leighninger, 185–202.

66. Zimbalist, *Historic Themes*, 234.

67. Blackman, "Some Tests," 132.

68. Purcell-Guild, "But What Good," 515.

69. Whitson, "What Measures," 142.

70. Wilcox, "The Measurement of Achievement," 46.

71. Zimbalist, *Historic Themes*, 253–64.

72. Bartlett, "Toward Clarification."

73. Fischer, "Is Casework Effective?"; Kadushin, "The Knowledge Base"; Segal, "Research on the Outcome"; Wood, "Casework Effectiveness"; Wotton, *Social Science*.

74. Fischer, "Is Casework Effective?"

75. Bloom and Fischer, *Evaluating Practice*; Howe, "Casework Evaluation"; Jayaratne and Levy, *Empirical Clinical Practice*.

76. Marino, Green, and Young, "Beyond the Scientist-Practitioner"; Rosen, "The Scientific Practitioner Revisited"; Wakefield and Kirk, "Un-Scientific Thinking."

77. Baker, Stephens, and Hitchcock, "Social Work Practitioners"; MacEachron and Gustavsson, "Reframing Practitioner Research"; Richey, Blythe, and Berlin, "Do Social Workers Evaluate."

78. Adam, Zosky, and Unrau, "Improving the Research Climate."

79. Epstein, "Pedagogy of the Perturbed": Forte, "Teaching Statistics Without Sadistics"; Green et al., "Research Learning Attributes"; Montcalm, "Applying Bandura's Theory"; Wainstock, "Swimming Against the Current."

80. Epstein, 71.

81. Smith, *The Norton History*, 770.

82. Holbrook, "Relativity of Casework Measurement," 523.

83. Leighninger, *Social Work*, 168.

84. Schon, *The Reflective Practitioner*, 42.

85. Cannon, "Where the Changes," 110–11; Glenn, "Growth of Social Casework," 70; Pumphrey and Pumphrey *The Heritage of American*, 168–69.

86. Pumphrey and Pumphrey, 278.

87. Germain, "Casework and Science," 12.

88. Friedlander, *Introduction: Generic Principles*, 13; Pray, *Social Work*, 274.

89. Axinn and Levin, *Social Welfare*, 141.

90. Trattner, *From Poor Law*, 222.

91. Richmond, *Social Diagnosis*.

92. Garrett, "Historical Survey," 220–22; Robinson, *A Changing Psychology*, 110.

93. Aptekar, "Diagnosis," 249; Bartlett, *The Common Base*, 33; Germain, "Casework and Science," 13; Trattner, *From Poor Law*, 233.

94. Garrett, "Historical Survey," 220–21; Marcus, "The Status," 126–35; Robinson, *A Changing Psychology*, xiv, 28–37, 81–93.

95. Pumphrey and Pumphrey, *The Heritage of American*, 168–69; Robinson, 40.

96. Finlayson, "The Diagnostic Process"; Garrett, "Historical Survey," 221–23; Merrill, "The Case Worker's Role"; Moorhead, "What Is Involved"; Robinson, 9, 106–14.

97. Garrett, 223; Hollis, "Some Contributions of Therapy"; Merrill, 281.

98. Queen, *Social Work*, 415; Rich, *Current Trends*, 3; Robinson, *A Changing Psychology*, 80; Watson, *The Charity Organization Movement*, 415.

99. Hamilton, "Basic Concepts."

100. Hepworth, Rooney, and Larson, *Direct Social Work Practice*, 17.

101. Aptekar, "The Continuity of Intake," 222; Germain, "Casework and Science," 13; Hamilton, "The Underlying Philosophy," 141; Kadushin, "The Knowledge Base," 52; Maas, "Social Casework," 12; Wallerstein, "Purposeful Investigation," 225–28.

102. Smalley, "The Functional Approach."

103. Pray, *Social Work*, 72–73; Smalley, 86–87; Taft, "A Conception," 250–53.

104. Pray, 76–78; Robinson, *The Development*, 352–57; Smalley, 108–12.

105. Strean, *Clinical Social Work*, 16.

106. Kadushin, "The Knowledge Base," 58–65.

107. Kadushin, 62; Mathews, *The Social Work Mystique*, 89–96; Strean, *Clinical Social Work*, 12.

108. Perlman, "The Problem-Solving Model," 131.

109. Perlman, *Social Casework*.

110. Eyseneck, *The Effects of Psychotherapy*, 5–7; Kadushin, "Two Problems," 41–46; Mathews, *The Social Work Mystique*, 36, 40–41.

111. Carlton, *Clinical Social Work*, 5; Northen, *Clinical Social Work*, 2.

112. National Association of Social Workers, *Register of Clinical Social Workers*, xi.

113. Carlton, *Clinical Social Work*, 5; Northen, *Clinical Social Work*, 2.

114. Barker, *Social Work Dictionary*, 62; Lieberman, *Clinical Social Workers*, 17; Northen, 8.

115. Northen, 8–9.

116. Boyle et al., *Direct Practice*, 40–41; Hepworth, Rooney, and Larson, *Direct Social Work Practice*, 17; Johnson and Yanca, *Social Work Practice*, 60–61; Wood and Middleman, *The Structural Approach*, 9–10.

117. Boyle et al., 3–27; Hepworth, Rooney, and Larson, 24–25; Johnson and Yanca, 253–92; Wood and Middleman, 10–15.

118. Boyle et al., 30: Hepworth, Rooney, and Larson, 33–42; Johnson and Yanca, 164–292.

119. Aptekar, "Diagnosis"; Giovanonni, "Prevention of Child Abuse"; Kaufman & Poulman, "Coherency among Substance"; Miller, "Casework and the Medical"; Wellman, "From Evil to Illness."

120. Austin, "The Political Economy"; McLaughlin, "Social Work's Legacy"; Patti, Poertner, and Rapp, "Managing for Service"; Smith, "Black Adolescent Fathers"; Stadum, "A Critique."

121. Newstetter, "What Is Social Group"; Williamson, *The Social Worker*, 7.

122. Leighninger, *Social Work*, 155; Pumphrey and Pumphrey, *The Heritage of American*, 362; Schwartz, "Group Work," 122.

123. Leighninger, 155.

124. Konopka, "Method of Social Group," 141; Newstetter, "What Is Social Group," 368.

125. Konopka, 140, 195; Slavson, "Meaningful Personal Relations," 369–70; Smalley, *Theory for Social Work*, 210.

126. Konopka, 132; Schwartz, "Group Work," 131–33; Strean, *Clinical Social Work*, 17.

127. Doverman, "Letter to the Editor"; Konopka, 195; Schwartz, 122; Wilson, "Social Group Work," 143–59.

128. Konopka, 195; Schwartz, 123.

129. Konopka, *Social Group Work*, 34.

130. Schwartz, "The Social Worker."

131. Vinter, "The Essential Components."

132. Tropp, "Expectation, Performance, and Accountability."

133. Konopka, *Therapeutic Group Work*, vi; Strean, *Clinical Social Work*, 17.

134. Hepworth, Rooney, and Larson, *Direct Social Work Practice*, 16; Wood and Middleman, *The Structural Approach*, 91–154.

135. Leighninger, *Social Work*, 68; Trattner, *From Poor Law*, 153, 161–65.

136. Lee, "Social Work as Cause."

137. Lee, 5.
138. Lee, "The Social Worker," 267.
139. Leighninger, *Social Work*, 56.
140. Leighninger, 56.
141. Leighninger, 56.
142. Leighninger, 59, 68.
143. Leighninger, 60–65; Spano, *Rank and File Movement*, 50–52.
144. Leighninger, 61.
145. Carter, "Social Work Community Organization," 227–78; Fisher, *Let the People Decide*, 15; Leighninger, 68; Spano, *Rank and File Movement*, 258–60.
146. Morales and Sheafor, *Social Work*, 19.
147. Carter, "Social Work Community Organization," 253–60; Pray, *Social Work*, 283.
148. Carter, 278–82; Pray, 283–86; Strean, *Clinical Social Work*, 19.
149. Carter, 278.
150. Carter, 210; Strean, 20.
151. "Community Social Workers," 1st sentence.
152. Fisher, *Let the People Decide*, 215.
153. Council on Social Work Education, *2015 Educational Policy*.
154. Bartlett, "Toward Clarification," 3–9; Gordon, "A Critique," 3–7.
155. Bartlett, *The Common Base*; Gordon, "Basic Constructs," 5–11.
156. Saari, *The Creation of Meaning*, 4.
157. Rubin and Babbie, *Research Methods*, 16–19.
158. Rubin and Babbie, 17.
159. Foucault, *Power–Knowledge*, 156.
160. Trattner, *From Poor Law*, 239.
161. Taylor, "The Social Control," 19.
162. Greenwood, "Social Science," 25
163. Taylor, "The Social Control," 18.
164. Leonard, "Social Control," 10.
165. Toren, *Social Work*, 96.
166. Day, "Social Welfare," 37
167. McGovern, *Sold American*, 77.
168. Casstevens, "Social Work Education"; Weick, "Issues in Overturning," for example.
169. Wade and Halligan, "The Biopsychosocial Model," 996.
170. Engel, "The Need for," 130.
171. Engel, 130; Wade and Halligan, "The Biopsychosocial Model."
172. Engel, 131.
173. Engel, 131.
174. Engel, 134.
175. Engel, 132.
176. Flexner, "Is Social Work."
177. Margolin, *Under the Cover*, 92–94.
178. De Jong and Kim Berg, *Interviewing for Solutions*, 245–51; Rapp and Goscha, *The Strengths Model*, 71.

References

Abramovitz, Robert, Janet Williams, and Mark Mattaini. "The Pros and Cons of the Diagnostic and Statistical Manual for Social Work Practice and Research." *Research on Social Work Practice* 2 (1992): 338–49.

Adam, Najma, Diane Zosky, and Yvonne Unrau. "Improving the Research Climate in Social Work Curricula: Clarifying Learning Expectations Across BSW and MSW Research Courses." *Journal of Teaching in Social Work* 24 (2004): 1–18.

Aptekar, Herbert. "The Continuity of Intake and Treatment Processes." In *Readings in Social Case Work 1920–1938: Selected Reprints for the Case Work Practitioner*, edited by Fern Lowry, 217–23. New York: Columbia University Press, 1939.

Aptekar, Herbert. "Diagnosis: A Changing Concept." In *Readings in Social Case Work 1920–1938: Selected Reprints for the Case Work Practitioner*, edited by Fern Lowry, 249–57. New York: Columbia University Press, 1939.

Austin, David. "The Political Economy of Human Services." *Policy and Politics* 11 (1983): 343–59.

Axinn, June, and Herman Levin. *Social Welfare: A History of the American Response to Need*. New York: Harper & Row, 1975.

Baker, Lisa, Fredrick Stephens, and Laurel Hitchcock. "Social Work Practitioners and Practice Evaluation: How Are We Doing?" *Journal of Human Behavior in the Social Environment* 20 (2010): 963–73.

Barker, Robert, ed. *The Social Work Dictionary*. 3rd ed. Washington, DC: NASW Press, 1995.

Bartlett, "Toward Clarification."

Bartlett, Harriet. *The Common Base of Social Work Practice*. Washington, DC: NASW Press, 1970.

Blackman, Edward. "Some Tests for the Evaluation of Case Work Methods." *The Family* 6 (1925): 132–37.

Bloom, Martin, and Joel Fischer. *Evaluating Practice: Guidelines for the Accountable Professional*. Englewood Cliffs, NJ: Prentice-Hall, 1982.

Bowling, Ann. *Measuring Health: A Review of Quality of Life Measurement Scales*. 2nd ed. Philadelphia: Open University Press, 1997.

Boyle, Scott, Larry Smith, O. William Farley, Grafton H. Hull, and Jannah Hurn Mather. *Direct Practice in Social Work*. New York: Pearson, 2006.

Buros Institute of Mental Measurements. *The Twentieth Mental Measurements Yearbook*. Edited by Janet F. Carlson, Kurt F. Geisinger, and Jessica L. Jonson. Lincoln: University of Nebraska Press, 2017.

Cannon, M. Antoinette. "Where the Changes in Social Case Work Have Brought Us." In *Readings in Social Case Work 1920–1938: Selected Reprints for the Case Work Practitioner*, edited by Fern Lowry, 109–21. New York: Columbia University Press, 1939.

Carlton, Thomas. *Clinical Social Work in Health Settings: A Guide to Professional Practice with Exemplars*. New York: Springer, 1984.

Carter, Genevieve. "Social Work Community Organization Methods and Processes." In *Concepts and Methods of Social Work*, edited by Walter Friedlander, 210–82. Englewood Cliffs, NJ: Prentice-Hall, 1958.

Casstevens, Willa. "Social Work Education on Mental Health: Postmodern Discourse and the Medical Model." *Journal of Teaching in Social Work* 30 (2010): 385–98.

"Community Social Workers." SocialWorkLicensure.org. Accessed July 5, 2019, https://socialworklicensure.org/types-of-social-workers/community-social-workers/.

Council on Social Work Education. *2015 Educational Policy and Accreditation Standards.* Washington, DC: CSWE, 2015. https://www.cswe.org/getattachment/Accreditation/Standards-and-Policies/2015-EPAS/2015EPASandGlossary.pdf.aspx.

Davis, Liane. "Role Theory." In *Social Work Treatment: Interlocking Theoretical Approaches,* edited Francis J. Turner, 541–63. New York: Free Press, 1986.

Day, Phyllis J. "Social Welfare: Context for Social Control." *Journal of Sociology and Social Welfare* 8 (1981): 29–44.

De Jong, Peter, and Insoo Kim Berg. *Interviewing for Solutions.* 4th ed. Belmont, CA: Brooks/Cole, 2013.

Doverman, Max. "Letter to the Editor." *Social Work* 3 (1958): 127–28.

Engel, George. "The Need for a New Medical Model: A Challenge for Biomedicine." *Science* 196 (1977): 129–35.

Engel, Rafael, and Russel Schutt. *Fundamentals of Social Work Research.* 2nd ed. Thousand Oaks, CA: Sage Publications, 2014.

Epstein, Irwin. "Pedagogy of the Perturbed: Teaching Research to the Reluctants." *Journal of Teaching in Social Work* 1 (1987): 71–89.

Erikson, Erik. *Childhood and Society.* New York: W. W. Norton & Company, 1950.

Erkison, Erik. *Identity and the Life Cycle.* New York: International Universities Press, 1959.

Erkison, Erik. *Life History and the Historical Moment.* New York: Norton, 1975.

Eysenck, Hans. *The Effects of Psychotherapy.* New York: International Science Press, 1966.

Finlayson, Alan. "The Diagnostic Process in Continuing Treatment." In *Readings in Social Case Work 1920–1938: Selected Reprints for the Case Work Practitioner,* edited by Fern Lowry, 268–79. New York: Columbia University Press, 1939.

Fischer, Joel. "Is Casework Effective? A Review." *Social Work* 18 (1973): 5–21.

Fisher, Robert. *Let the People Decide: Neighborhood Organizing In America.* Boston: Twayne, 1994.

Flexner, Abraham. "Is Social Work a Profession?" Virginia Commonwealth University Social Welfare History Project. First published 1915. http://socialwelfare.library.vcu.edu/social-work/is-social-work-a-profession-1915/

Forte, James. "Teaching Statistics Without Sadistics." *Journal of Social Work Education* 31 (1995): 204–18.

Foucault, Michel. *Power–Knowledge: Selected Interviews & Other Writings 1972–1977.* Edited by Colin Gordon. New York: Pantheon Books, 1981.

Friedlander, Walter. *Introduction to Social Welfare.* New York: Prentice-Hall, 1955.

Gardner, Howard. *Frames of Mind: The Theory of Multiple Intelligences.* New York: Basic Books, 1983.

Garrett, Annette. "Historical Survey of the Evolution of Casework." *Casework* 30 (1949): 219–29.

Germain, Carel. "Casework and Science."

Germain, Carel, and Alex Gitterman. *The Life Model of Social Work Practice.* New York: Columbia University Press, 1980.

Gilligan, Carol. *In a Different Voice.* Cambridge, MA: Harvard University Press, 1982.

Giovannoni, Jeanne. "Prevention of Child Abuse and Neglect: Research and Policy Issues." *Social Work Research and Abstracts* 18 (1982): 23–31.

Glenn, Mary. "The Growth of Social Casework in the United States." In *Readings in Social Case Work 1920–1938: Selected Reprints for the Case Work Practitioner*, edited by Fern Lowry, 67–80. New York: Columbia University Press, 1939.

Gordon, William. "A Critique of the Working Definition." *Social Work* 7 (1963): 3–13.

Gordon, William E. "Basic Constructs for an Integrative and Generative Conception of Social Work." In *The General Systems Approach: Contributions Toward an Holistic Conception of Social Work*, edited by Gordon Hearn, 5–11. New York: Council on Social Work Education, 1969.

Gould, Robert. *Transformations: Growth and Change in Adult Life*. Oxford: Simon & Schuster, 1978.

Green, Robert, Antoinette Bretzin, Christine Leininger, and Rose Stauffer. "Research Learning Attributes of Graduate Students in Social Work, Psychology, and Business." *Journal of Social Work Education* 37 (2001): 333–41.

Greene, Roberta. *Human Behavior Theory and Social Work Practice*. 2nd ed. New York: Aldine De Gruyter, 1999.

Greenwood, Ernest. "Social Science and Social Work: A Theory of Their Relationship." *Social Service Review* 29 (1955): 20–33.

Hamilton, Gordon. "Basic Concepts in Social Casework." *Family* 18 (1937): 147–56.

Hamilton, Gordon. "The Underlying Philosophy of Social Casework." *Family* 23 (1941): 139–48.

Hartmann, Heinz. *Ego Psychology and the Problem of Adaptation*. New York: International Universities Press, 1939.

Hearn, Gordon. *Theory Building in Social Work*. Toronto: University of Toronto Press, 1958.

Hepworth, Rooney, and Larson, *Direct Social Work Practice*.

Hildreth, Gertrude. *A Bibliography of Mental Tests and Rating Scales*. 2nd ed. New York: Psychological Corporation, 1939.

Holbrook, David. "The Relativity of Casework Measurement: Discussion." In *Proceedings of the National Conference of Social Work*, 520–25. Chicago: University of Chicago Press, 1931.

Hollis, Florence. "Some Contributions of Therapy to Generalized Case Work Practice." In *Readings in Social Case Work 1920–1938: Selected Reprints for the Case Work Practitioner*, edited by Fern Lowry, 305–18. New York: Columbia University Press, 1939.

Hollis, Florence. "The Psychosocial Approach to the Practice of Casework." In *Theories of Social Casework*, edited by Robert Roberts and Robert Nee, 35–75. Chicago: University of Chicago Press, 1970.

Howe, Michael. "Casework Evaluation: A Single-Subject Approach." *Social Service Review* 48 (1974): 1–23.

Jayaratne, Srinika, and Rona L. Levy. *Empirical Clinical Practice*. New York: Columbia University Press, 1979.

Johnson, Louise, and Stephen Yanca. *Social Work Practice: A Generalist Approach*. 8th ed. Boston: Allyn & Bacon, 2004.

Kadushin, Alfred. "The Knowledge Base of Social Work." In *Issues in American Social Work*, edited by Alfred Kahn, 39–79. New York: Columbia University Press, 1959.

Kadushin, Alfred. "Two Problems of the Graduate Program: Level and Content." *Journal of Education for Social Work* 1 (1965): 33–46.

Kanjirathinkal, Mathew. *A Sociological Critique of Theories of Cognitive Development: The Limitations of Piaget and Kohlberg*. Lewiston, NY: Edwin Mellen Press, 1990.

Kauffman, Stephen, and John Poulin. "Coherency among Substance Abuse Models." *Journal of Sociology and Social Welfare* 23 (1996): 163–74.

Keefe, Robert, Carrie Smith, and William McPeak. "What's in a Label? Helping Undergraduates Become Familiar with the DSM in Preparation for Their Senior Year Fieldwork Practice." *Journal of Baccalaureate Social Work* 9 (2003): 79–92.

Kline, Paul. *Personality: Measurement and Theory*. London: Hutchinson, 1983.

Kohlberg, Lawrence. "The Child as a Moral Philosopher." *Psychology Today* 58 (1968): 24–31.

Konopka, Gisela. *Social Group Work: A Helping Process*. New York: Pearson, 1963.

Konopka, Gisela. *Therapeutic Group Work with Children*. Minneapolis: University of Minnesota Press, 1963.

Konopka, "Method of Social Group."

Krysik, Judy. *Research for Effective Social Work Practice*. 4th ed. New York: Routledge, 2018.

Lee, Porter. "Social Work as Cause and Function: Presidential Address, National Conference of Social Work 1929." In *Social Work as Cause and Function and Other Papers*. New York: Columbia University Press, 1937. First published 1929.

Lee, Porter. "The Social Worker and Social Action." In *Social Work as Cause and Function and Other Papers*. New York: Columbia University Press, 1937. First published 1935.

Leighninger, Leslie. *Social Work: Search for Identity*. New York: Greenwood Press, 1987.

Leonard, Peter. "Social Control, Class Values and Social Practice." *Social Work* 22 (1965): 7–21.

Levinson, Daniel, Charlotte Darrow, Edward Klein, Maria Levinson, and Braxton McKee. *The Seasons of a Man's Life*. New York: Knopf, 1989.

Lieberman, Florence. *Clinical Social Workers as Psychotherapists*. New York: Gardner Press, 1982.

Maas, Henry. "Social Casework." In *Concepts and Methods of Social Work*, edited by Walter Friedlander, 1–14. Englewood Cliffs, NJ: Prentice-Hall, 1958.

MacEachron, Ann, and Nora Gustavsson. "Reframing Practitioner Research." *Families in Society: The Journal of Contemporary Human Services* 78 (1997): 651–56.

Marcus, Grace. "The Status of Social Case Work Today." In *Readings in Social Case Work 1920–1938: Selected Reprints for the Case Work Practitioner*, edited by Fern Lowry, 122–35. New York: Columbia University Press, 1939.

Margolin, Leslie. *Under the Cover of Kindness: The Invention of Social Work*. Charlottesville: University Press of Virginia, 1997.

Marino, Robert, Robert Green, and Ellen Young. "Beyond the Scientist-Practitioner Model's Failure to Thrive: Social Workers' Participation in Agency-Based Research Activities." *Social Work Research* 22 (1998): 188–92.

Mathews, Marie. *The Social Work Mystique: Toward a Sociology of Social Work*. Washington, DC: University Press of America, 1981.

McGovern, Charles. *Sold American: Consumption and Citizenship, 1890–1945*. Chapel Hill: University of North Carolina Press, 2006.

McLaughlin, Anne. "Social Work's Legacy: Irreconcilable Differences?" *Clinical Social Work Journal* 30 (2002): 187–98.

McQuaide, Sharon. "A Social Worker's Use of the Diagnostic and Statistical Manual." *Families in Society* 80 (1999): 410–16.

Merrill, Laura. "The Case Worker's Role in Treatment." In *Readings in Social Case Work 1920–1938: Selected Reprints for the Case Work Practitioner*, edited by Fern Lowry, 281–85. New York: Columbia University Press, 1939.

Miller, Walter. "Casework and the Medical Metaphor." *Social Work* 25 (1980): 281–85.

Montcalm, Denise. "Applying Bandura's Theory of Self-Efficacy to the Teaching of Research." *Journal of Teaching in Social Work* 19 (1999): 93–107.

Moorhead, Muriel. "What Is Involved in Simplicity of Treatment?" In *Readings in Social Case Work 1920–1938: Selected Reprints for the Case Work Practitioner*, edited by Fern Lowry, 258–67. New York: Columbia University Press, 1939.

Morales, Armando, and Bradford W. Sheafor. *Social Work: A Profession of Many Faces*. Boston: Allyn & Bacon, 1977.

National Association of Social Workers. *Register of Clinical Social Workers*. Washington, DC: NASW, 1976.

Newstetter, W. I. "What Is Social Group Work?" In *The Heritage of American Social Work: Readings in Its Philosophical and Institutional Development*, edited by Ralph Pumphrey and Muriel Pumphrey, 365–68. New York: Columbia University Press, 1961. First published 1935.

Northen, Helen. *Clinical Social Work: Knowledge and Skill*. 2nd ed. New York: Columbia University Press, 1995.

Oldham, John, and Robert Liebert. *The Middle Years*. New Haven: Yale University Press, 1989.

Papalia, Diane, and Sally Olds. *Human Development*. New York: McGraw-Hill, 1992.

Patti, Rino, John Poertner, and Charles Rapp. "Managing for Service Effectiveness in Social Welfare Organizations, Section Seven: Constraints and Dilemmas." *Administration in Social Work* 11 (1987): 255–84.

Perlman, Helen. *Social Casework: A Problem-Solving Process*. Chicago: University of Chicago Press, 1957.

Perlman, Helen. *Persona: Social Role and Personality*. Chicago: University of Chicago Press, 1968.

Perlman, Helen. "The Problem-Solving Model in Social Casework." In *Theories of Social Casework*, edited by Robert W. Roberts and Robert H. Nee, 129–80. Chicago: University of Chicago Press, 1970.

Piaget, Jean. *The Moral Judgment of the Child*. London: Kegan Paul, Trench, Trübner & Co., 1932. Originally published as *Le Jugement Moral Chez l'Enfant*.

Piaget, Jean. *The Origins of Intelligence in Children*. Translated by Margaret Cook. New York: International Universities Press, 1952. Originally published 1936 as *La Naissance de l'Intelligence Chez l'Enfant*.

Popper, Karl. *The Logic of Scientific Discovery*. Eastford, CT: Martino Fine Books, 2014. First published 1959.

Pray, Kenneth. *Social Work in a Revolutionary Age: And Other Papers*. Edited by Jessie Taft, 274–87. Philadelphia: University of Pennsylvania Press, 1949.

Pumphrey, Ralph, and Muriel Pumphrey. *The Heritage of American Social Work: Readings in Its Philosophical and Institutional Development*. New York: Columbia University Press, 1961.

Purcell-Guild, June. "But What Good Came of It at Last?" *The Survey* 59 (1928): 515–17.

Queen, Stuart. *Social Work in the Light of History*. New York: Russell Sage Foundation, 1922.

Rapp, Charles, and Richard Goscha. *The Strengths Model: Case Management with People Suffering from Severe and Persistent Mental Illness*. 2nd ed. New York: Oxford University Press, 2006.

Rich, Margaret. *Current Trends in Social Adjustment Through Individualized Treatment*. New York: International Universities Press, 1936.

Richey, Cheryl, Betty Blythe, and Sharon Berlin. "Do Social Workers Evaluate Their Practice?" *Social Work Research & Abstracts* 23 (1987): 14–20.

Richmond, Mary. *Social Diagnosis*. New York: Russell Sage Foundation, 1917.

Robbins, Susan, Pranab Chatterjee, and Edward Canda. *Contemporary Human Behavior Theory: A Critical Perspective for Social Work*. 2nd ed. Boston: Allyn & Bacon, 2006.

Robinson, Virginia. *A Changing Psychology in Social Casework*. Chapel Hill: University of North Carolina Press, 1930.

Robinson, Virginia. *The Development of a Professional Self: Teaching and Learning in Professional Helping Processes. Selected Writings 1930-1968*. New York: Ames Press, 1978.

Rosen, Aaron. "The Scientific Practitioner Revisited: Some Obstacles and Prerequisites for Fuller Implementation in Practice." *Social Work Research* 20 (1996): 105–11.

Rubin, Allan, and Earl Babbie. *Research Methods for Social Work*. 3rd ed. Pacific Grove, CA: Brooks/Cole, 1997.

Saari, Carolyn. *The Creation of Meaning in Clinical Social Work*. New York: Guilford Press, 1991.

Schon, Donald. *The Reflective Practitioner*. New York: Basic Books, 1983.

Schwartz, William. "Group Work and the Social Scene." In *Issues in American Social Work*, edited by Alfred Kahn, 110-37. New York: Columbia University Press, 1959.

Schwartz, William. "The Social Worker in the Group." In *The Social Welfare Forum—1961: Official Proceedings, 88th Annual Forum, National Conference on Social Welfare*. 1962.

Segal, Steven. "Research on the Outcome of Social Work Therapeutic Interventions: A Review of the Literature." *Journal of Health and Social Behavior* 13 (1972): 3–17.

Sheldon, Elenaore, and Howard Freeman. "Social Indicators." In *Encyclopedia of Social Work*, edited by John Turner, 1350-54. 2nd ed. Washington, DC: NASW, 1971.

Siegler, Robert. *Children's Thinking*. Upper Saddle River, NJ: Prentice-Hall, 1968.

Slavson, Samuel. "Meaningful Personal Relations." In *The Heritage of American Social Work: Readings in Its Philosophical and Institutional Development*, edited by Ralph Pumphrey and Muriel Pumphrey, 368-70. New York: Columbia University Press, 1961. First published 1938.

Smalley, Ruth. *Theory for Social Work Practice*. New York: Columbia University Press, 1967.

Smalley, Ruth. "The Functional Approach to Casework Practice." In *Theories of Social Casework*, edited by Robert W. Roberts and Robert H. Nee, 77-128. Chicago: University of Chicago Press, 1970.

Smith, Linda. "Black Adolescent Fathers: Issues for Service Provision." *Social Work* 33 (1988): 269–71.

Smith, Roger. *The Norton History of the Human Sciences*. Norton History of Science. New York: W. W. Norton, 1997.

Spano, Rick. *The Rank and File Movement in Social Work*. Washington, DC: University Press of America, 1982.

Stadum, Beverly. "A Critique of Family Case Workers 1900-1930: Women Working with Women." *Journal of Sociology and Social Welfare* 17 (1990): 73–100.

Sternberg, Robert. "Mental Self-Government: A Theory of Intellectual Styles and Their Development." *Human Development* 31 (1988): 197–224.

Strean, Herbert. *Clinical Social Work: Theory and Practice.* New York: Free Press, 1978.

Taft, Jessie. "A Conception of the Growth Process Underlying Social Casework Practice." In *Principles and Techniques in Social Casework: Selected Articles, 1940–1950*, edited by Cora Kasius, 247–59. New York: Family Association of America, 1950.

Taylor, Robert. "The Social Control Function in Casework." *Social Casework* 1 (1958): 17–21.

Toren, Nina. *Social Work: The Case of a Semi-Profession.* Beverly Hills: Sage Publications, 1972.

Trattner, Walter I. *From Poor Law to Welfare State: A History of Social Welfare in America.* 4th ed. New York: Free Press, 1989.

Tropp, Emmanuel. "Expectation, Performance, and Accountability." *Social Work* 19 (1974): 139–49.

Tzeng, Oliver. *Measurement of Love and Intimate Relations: Theories, Scales and Applications for Love Development, Maintenance, and Dissolution.* Westport, CT: Praeger, 1993.

Vinter, Robert. "The Essential Components of Social Group Work Practice." In *Readings in Group Work Practice*, edited by Robert Vinter, 8–38. Ann Arbor, MI: Campus Publishers, 1967.

Wade, Derick, and Peter Halligan. "The Biopsychosocial Model of Illness: A Model Whose Time Has Come." *Clinical Rehabilitation* 8 (2017): 995–1004.

Wainstock, Susan. "Swimming Against the Current: Teaching Research Methodology to Reluctant Social Work Students." *Journal of Teaching in Social Work* 9 (1994): 3–16.

Wakefield, Jerome, and Stuart Kirk. "Un-Scientific Thinking about Scientific Practice: Evaluating the Scientist-Practitioner Model." *Social Work Research* 20 (1996): 83–95.

Wallerstein, Helen. "Purposeful Investigation." In *Readings in Social Case Work 1920–1938: Selected Reprints for the Case Work Practitioner*, edited by Fern Lowry, 225–28. New York: Columbia University Press, 1939.

Watson, Frank. *The Charity Organization Movement in the United States: A Study in American Philanthropy.* New York: Lippincott, 1922.

Weick, Ann. "Issues in Overturning a Medical Model of Social Work Practice." *Social Work* 28 (1983): 467–71.

Wellman, David. "From Evil to Illness: Medicalizing Racism." *American Journal of Orthopsychiatry* 70 (2000): 28–32.

White, Robert. *The Abnormal Personality: A Textbook.* New York: Ronald Press, 1948.

Whitson, Walter. "What Measures Do We Have for Growth in Personality?" *The Family* 7 (1926): 139–43.

Wilcox, Edward. "The Measurement of Achievement in Family Case Work." *The Family* 8 (1927): 46–49.

Williamson, Margaretta. *The Social Worker in Group Work.* New York: Harper Brothers, 1929.

Wilson, Gertrude. "Social Group Work Theory and Practice." In *The Social Welfare Forum—1956: Official Proceedings, 83rd Annual Forum, National Conference on Social Welfare.* New York: Columbia University Press, 1957.

Wood, Gale, and Ruth Middleman. *The Structural Approach to Direct Practice in Social Work.* New York: Columbia University Press, 1989.

Wood, Katherine. "Casework Effectiveness: A New Look at the Research Evidence." *Social Work* 23 (1978): 437–58.

Wotton, Barbara. *Social Science and Social Pathology.* London: George Allen and Unwin, 1959.

Zimbalist, Sidney. *Historic Themes and Landmarks in Social Welfare Research.* New York: Harper & Row, 1977.

8

The Emerging Postmodern discourse (c. 1990–Present)

A number of postmodern practice approaches have arisen within the emerging Postmodern discourse.[a] I believe the three most prominent to be the following: the strengths perspective, narrative therapy, and solution-focused therapy/case management. The quotes below represent a sample of excerpts taken from the progenitors of these approaches (I have taken the liberty to place in bold font key concepts that will be discussed in this and the subsequent chapter):

If, as a practitioner, you wish to put **clients in the position of being the experts** about their own lives, you will have to know how to set aside your own frame of reference as much as possible and explore those of your clients. In other words, you will have to **learn to adopt the posture of** *not knowing.*[1]

We think that it makes a difference whether or not the therapist assumes that clients have the capacity to create meaningful descriptions of what they want their lives to look like and **how they want to be in the world.** Asking the miracle question both implies and demands **faith** in the client's capacity to do this and the question needs to be asked in a manner that **communicates this faith.**[2]

In a sense, what is happening at this point is the writing of **a better "text."** Reframing is a part of this, not the reframing of so many family therapies, but adding to the picture already painted, brush strokes that depict capacity and ingenuity, and that provide a different coloration to the substance of one's life. . . . Last it is wise to carefully lay out with an individual what might be possible in her or his life—big or small things, it doesn't matter. And all of this must **ring true** to the person and be grounded in the dailiness of life.[3]

I would go so far as to say that the central dynamic of the strengths perspective is precisely the rousing of **hope**, of tapping into the visions and the promise of that individual, family, or community. Circumstances, bad luck, unfortunate decisions, the harshness of life lived on the edge of need and vulnerability, of

---

[a] Note: I am using a small letter "d" when discussing the Postmodern discourse as it has yet to achieve dominance in society.

A Genealogy of the Good and Critique of Hubris. Phillip Dybicz, Oxford University Press. © Oxford University Press 2023. DOI: 10.1093/oso/9780197670071.003.0008

course may smother these. Nonetheless, it is the flicker of possibility that can **ignite the fire of hope.**[4]

Concluding that we cannot have direct knowledge of the world, social scientists proposed that what persons know of life they know through "lived expe-rience." . . . Those social scientists embracing the text analogy responded by arguing that, in order to make sense of our lives and to express ourselves, ex-perience must be **"storied"** and it is this storying that determines the meaning ascribed to experience.[5]

"Externalizing" is an approach to therapy that encourages persons to objectify and, at times, to personify the problems that they experience as **oppressive**. In this process, the problem becomes a separate entity and thus external to the person or relationship that was ascribed as the problem. Those problems that are considered to be inherent, as well as those relatively fixed qualities that we attributed to per-sons and to relationships, are rendered less fixed and less restricting.[6]

The above statements may or may not appear strange or odd to the reader, depending upon the amount of one's exposure to these practices and to post-modern thought. Since the 1990s, a Postmodern discourse has arisen within the field of social work, acting as a counterpoint and challenge to the existing dominant Modern Discourse. As was the case with Chapter 6 in describing the Modern Discourse, the goal of this chapter in describing the Postmodern dis-course will be to provide the reader a deeper understanding of the true import of the above statements and thus the ability to find answers to questions stem-ming from their key insights, such as the following. How exactly is the client considered an expert? Where does this expertise lie? What does it mean to adopt a not-knowing approach, and how does it differ from the modernist approach, positioning the social worker as the expert in human functioning? How is it that communicating faith in the client's abilities centers practice? Why is inspiring hope in the client a key dynamic (rather than problem solving), and conse-quently, how does it change the role of the social worker in the helping process? What does it mean to conceive of human behavior within the framework of a *text* of one's life wherein how these events being *storied* becomes the main focus in the helping process? And, within a therapeutic[b] context, how is it that the helping

---

[b] For ease of understanding in regard to the helping relationship—which entails assisting the client to resolve disturbing emotional and psychological aspects stemming from their current life struggle—I have chosen to use the words *therapeutic* and *therapy* despite their incongruence with a postmodern understanding of the helping relationship as a political endeavor to confront oppres-sion. Obviously, the etymology of *therapy* stems from medical practice and the Modern Discourse's understanding of the social work helping situation as a scientific endeavor to promote healing and enhance functioning. For now, rather than confusing readers by adopting an appropriate new term, I have elected to continue to use *therapy* and *therapeutic* to capture this aspect of what is familiarly considered clinical social work practice.

process is conceived as an endeavor at confronting oppression rather than an effort at enhancing functioning?

Describing the Postmodern discourse poses a greater challenge than that faced when describing the various other dominant Discourses that precede it. This is due to the fact that the Postmodern discourse is newly emergent and has not yet achieved dominance; hence, it has not yet fully established a historical record. Some elements of the Postmodern discourse can be described with a high level of confidence—such as its paradigmatic philosophical foundation and key intellectual thought—as these elements are typically laid down decades before the discourse begins to emerge. Others, such as the various geographic, economic, political, and social conditions and conceptions of the self, typically make themselves known during the transition period when the discourse begins to emerge but has not yet achieved dominance, so there is a modicum of historical evidence pointing to these elements. However, other elements of the discourse—such as the urgent need, rules of right, defining cultural event, and broad theme—don't truly make themselves known until after the Discourse achieves dominance. The description of these elements forces me to switch from the role of historian to that of prognosticator drawing upon recent historical trends. Thus, my efforts in this area simply represent educated guesses rather than firm conclusions drawn from substantive historical facts. Hopefully, history will be kind to me and prove these educated guesses to be for the most part correct. With that said, I now turn to describing the Postmodern discourse.

Conditions in Postmodern America

Geographic Conditions

Population Demographics
During the Modern Era, technological innovations in transportation and communication led to a deeper penetration of these elements across society, resulting in a highly integrative transportation and communication network permeating society. However, the same cannot be said regarding the ethnic and racial cultural dimension to society. During the Modern Era, immigration has been curtailed. And throughout the Modern Era up to the present, Whites of European ancestry continue to represent a majority of the population. Thus, the cultural values of this group have often been assumed and recognized as comprising the values that make up American society; in other words, core values defining what it means to be an American have been heavily ethnocentric in nature throughout our nation's history, including up to the present. In addition, the White majority continues to exert a dominant hold on the political

and economic levers of society, levers which serve to shape and support these core values.

Yet also, the Modern Era marked the advancement of civil rights. Civil rights seek to assert equality across difference. Building upon this foundation, I believe that the cultural project taken up in the Postmodern Era will be that of building an integrative network across cultural lines, what is referred to in the literature as *normative cultural relativism*. Seeking linkage among multiple cultures through the deconstruction of objective knowledge, normative cultural relativism aims at the creation of a shared value system comprised from the input of multiple cultures, while at the same time respecting the uniqueness of the various cultures comprising this network concerning how these shared values are expressed.[7] Thus, if such a project comes to pass, what it means to be an American, and the core values seen as defining American society, will undergo a transformation in an emergent Postmodern Era.

Demographic trends seem to point toward such a project as being in the works. While the United States continues to grow in population, the rate of this growth has steadily declined. During the Premodern Era, the US population increased an astounding average of approximately 30% each decade; during most of the Modern Era (1920–1990), this growth slowed to an average of 15% each decade; and from 1990 to the present the growth rate has averaged 10% each decade.[8] However, recent waves of immigration have primarily been from Asia and Latin America. Along with higher birth rates among ethnic and racial minorities already settled in the United States, these groups account for more than 75% of the population growth since the beginning of the twenty-first century.[9] Illustrating this trend, 2011 marked the first year in US history when more babies were born to ethnic and racial minorities than were born to the White majority population.[10] Another illustration of this trend is that in 1990 only five of the nation's largest one hundred metropolitan areas contained more people representing ethnic and racial minorities than those representing the White majority; by 2010, this number had jumped to twenty-two out of one hundred.[11] Furthermore, as these same ethnic and racial minorities have entered the middle class in greater numbers over the past few decades, they have begun to disperse themselves into suburban and rural areas as they respond to the demands of the labor market.[12]

As can be expected, these trends have caused a demographic rift generationally. More than 70% of the baby boom generation (born 1946–1964) and seniors are comprised of the White majority population; this can be contrasted to the generation Xers and subsequent groups who followed the baby boomers, wherein the White majority as of 2015 accounts for a little over 50%.[13] Consequently, as members of this younger and more diverse generation enter adulthood and begin assuming political and economic positions of power, it is not unlikely that their social and economic interests will differ from those of the older, White majority population.[14]

This will likely result in a clash of ideals and values chosen to define American society. One indicator of such a clash comes from a 2011 Pew Research poll wherein only 23% of baby boomers and seniors were of the opinion that the growing population of immigrants represented a change for the better; furthermore, more than half of the White majority baby boomers and seniors considered the growing number of immigrants as a "threat to traditional U.S. values and customs"[15]—indicative of a stance aimed at preserving the ethnocentric nature of American values and customs. This cultural clash might be in retrospect (once some historical distance is achieved) considered an example of the dynamic that occurs during transition periods between the eras marking the reign of dominant Discourses, in which the heretofore dominant Discourse seeks to preserve traditional forms of understanding, while the emerging discourse seeks to assume dominance by advancing a new paradigm of understanding.

Transportation

The Modern Era experienced a major technological revolution in the massive production and wide dissemination of the automobile and the invention of the jet airplane. It is difficult to imagine that a new mode of transportation will arise in the Postmodern Era that will further transcend the connectivity established by these two innovations. If a major transformation were to take place in transportation, the only likely scenario that I see possibly occurring would be that of a precipitous drop in the cost of transporting goods and people. There are two potential scenarios where this might come to pass, both heavily weighted toward the automobile: a precipitous drop in the price of fuel or the development and widespread use of driverless vehicles.

It is quite possible that the development of alternative energy sources may result in prices of electricity plummeting from the current national average of 13.19 cents per kilowatt hour[16] to less than a penny per kilowatt hour. This combined with innovations that increase the efficiency and range of electric automotive vehicles would result not so much in greater levels of integration than already established via our nation's network of roads but, rather, in an increase in the frequency of people traversing this network as well as wider access to such routes for those of limited economic means. Such a scenario would produce a spillover effect to the aviation industry. With the vast majority of automotive vehicles no longer requiring gasoline, the demand for petroleum would be greatly reduced, thus making the cost of jet fuel much cheaper. The other potential innovation acting to reduce transportation costs would be the development and widespread use of driverless vehicles. Such a development could greatly reduce the cost of shipping goods across the nation. Consequently, both scenarios would easily serve to expand the experience of encountering different cultures (ethnic, regional, etc.)—either through personal travel or access to goods—to a much broader portion of the population.

Communication

Whereas technological innovation in vehicles and energy would represent a moderate transformation in the area of transportation, technological innovation in communication has a much different story. The development of the internet[c] has resulted in a revolutionary transformation in how we communicate, radically reshaping societal communication and interaction. Much of this profound change will be explored in the subsection *Social Conditions*, wherein the development and growth of social networking sites will be examined. Yet there is still a bit left to explore in terms of profound change arising from internet use in general.

Digital universe is a term used to describe the transformation in society ushered in by the internet as "a global human environment saturated with intelligent devices (increasingly, wireless ones) that enhance our ability to collect, process, and distribute information."[17] Particularly in the United States (as well as in other developed societies), these intelligent devices are ubiquitous. While the advent of the telephone eliminated geographic distance as a barrier to communication through instant communication (although cost would remain a barrier for much of the twentieth century), the sharing of information could only occur between the parties on each side of the line (whether it be verbal or written record via fax). In addition, such communication is time-bound to within the period that the connection is maintained.

The internet has opened up many more possibilities. Written communication as well as attached documentation, in the form of an electronic document attached to an email, for example, can be easily shared with multiple parties simultaneously without the constraint of everyone having to be present at the same time, as would be the case with a conference call. Thus, email is able to eliminate barriers of both time and distance. Furthermore, the internet stores this communication as a written record that can be accessed at a future date. Another innovation is videoconferencing; it not only opens up the visual element of verbal communication but also has eliminated cost as a barrier arising from geographic distance. Social networking sites, such as Facebook, open up possibilities for indirect communication as information about one's life and interests can be posted; however, rather than being directed at specific parties, this information acts as

---

[c] Technically, the internet solely refers to the global network of computers, whereas the World Wide Web acts as a software program to aid in finding items in this global network. This distinction is irrelevant to our discussion here, so I have adopted the cruder but simpler understanding of the internet representing a combination of both, as is frequently used in common parlance.

an open invitation to respond by anyone who belongs to this person's network. Lastly, information can be shared indirectly, anonymously if preferred, to society as a whole by posting it on a website accessible to all. WikiLeaks is a prominent example; how-to videos or recipes are more innocuous examples.

The ability offered by the internet to easily and effortlessly disseminate information is what marks this as a revolutionary change in the area of communication. The vision of this revolutionary transformation was first laid out in 1964 by Marshall McLuhan, a prominent social philosopher and media theorist (who also coined the term *global village*), when he stated, "Rapidly, we approach the final phase of the extensions of man—the technological simulation of consciousness, when the creative process of knowing will be collectively and corporately extended to the whole of society."[18] Since its inception around 1990, the internet has considerably advanced the collective sharing of this societal creative process of knowing.[19] And while this vision has not yet been reached as barriers to this process have been imposed by more closed societies, the internet has already provided the technological solution necessary for McLuhan's vision to be realized. What is currently lacking is the necessary political solution.

There is no doubt that the internet is not simply a technological fad. In only a few decades its growth in permeating society has been nothing less than astounding. Some brief examples are as follows. In 1994, there existed a mere 3,000 websites that an individual could easily access. By 2001, this number had risen to 30 million; and by 2004, the number had grown to 4.2 billion.[20] As mentioned, social media networking sites have opened up a new mode of communication. A Pew Research poll taken in 2012 examined the percentage of people, by age group, who regularly used social networking sites to communicate. The results are as follows: 92% of those aged 18–29, 73% of those aged 30–49, 57% of those aged 50–64, and 38% of those aged 65 or older.[21]

Now, in order to explore the influence the internet's revolutionary form of communication may have in shaping the Postmodern discourse on social welfare, a brief digression is necessary—into political philosophy. As examined previously in the chapters on the Premodern Discourse as well as the Modern Discourse, US society has embraced a form of liberal individualism from the early 1800s to the present; this embrace can be attributed to the influence of Enlightenment thought and its proposition that the individual is a rational actor who seeks to promote their own self-interest. Within the Premodern Discourse, this took the form of possessive individualism wherein individuals were seen as autonomous rational units whose aggregate actions represented the movements of society. Within the Modern Discourse, one is seen as an individual within a greater societal unit, which requires the subsumption of a fair degree of one's independence and freedom in order to advance the goals of the greater unit to which one belongs. Consequently, independence and freedom were now relegated to the creative self-expression of one's inner self—one aspect of which was taking on the role as sovereign consumer.

Postmodern thought supports a move away from extreme individualism and back toward communitarianism. Exemplified most notably by the writings of Charles Taylor (a Canadian philosopher) and Michael Sandel (an American political theorist), this school of thought has come to be known as *responsive communitarianism*.[22] One of the main contrasts between individualism and communitarianism relevant to our discussion here is the following. While both seek to advance individual rights as well as the common good, the priority given to each differs. Individualism, as reflected in the writings of John Rawls and Alasdair MacIntyre, prioritizes the advancement of individual rights, which then lays down the pathway by which to reach the common good.[23] The birth of the civil rights struggle in the 1960s serves as a prominent example illustrating this focus on promoting individual rights. This position mirrors that of the Modern Discourse's more comprehensive position that knowledge of the True lays down the pathway for one to achieve knowledge of the Good. Paradoxically, one gains access to individual rights through one's membership in a community. Thus, it is because I belong to the human race that I am afforded human rights, not because of personally who I am. Similarly, it is my membership as a citizen which affords me civil rights. Again, we can see this dynamic mirrored more broadly throughout the Modern Discourse, one example being that what legitimizes a social welfare intervention based within evidence-based practice is not who I am personally but, rather, my membership in a population group. This propensity for society to view one as a generic individual, rather than a unique person, is described as being "radically situated."[24]

Communitarianism, on the other hand, seeks to prioritize the common good before that of individual rights. Yet, responsive communitarianism stakes out a middle ground, seeking to draw society back to an equal balance in the center in response to periods when one is overly emphasized versus the other.[25] In a similarly paradoxical manner, communitarianism's emphasis upon advancing the common good requires individual choices and preferences that arise from one's uniqueness as an individual; these take the form of the personal expression of values that are commonly esteemed in society.[26]

Now both individualism and communitarianism possess a negative or darker side which may infect society. For individualism, it is anomie, as elaborated by Émile Durkheim. Being radically situated as a generic individual serves to handicap one's ability to form the communal bonds that give life meaning. Relationships and bonds are built upon the interaction of unique individuals. Communitarianism's dark side appears in the form of totalitarianism wherein individual rights are unduly sacrificed to the common good as determined by an authority apparatus. The communist former Soviet Union and China are two prime examples. However, even liberal democracies contain currents of totalitarianism wherein government officials will seek to circumvent the democratic process, requiring the public at large to maintain a constant vigilance.

Now we are ready to turn back to examination of the internet and its influence in shaping and supporting the Postmodern discourse on social welfare. Sometime around the middle of the twentieth century sociologists began documenting a disturbing trend in American society: the degradation of communal bonds, as measured by a steep decline of 25%–50% in membership of voluntary associations.[27] This trend was famously highlighted by Robert Putnam in his classic study on social capital wherein he observed that from 1980 to 1993, while the number of people bowling in the United States increased by 10%, the number of bowling leagues decreased by 40%.[28] Such changes in part could be attributed to the increasing mobility of American society arising from the proliferation of roads and automobile ownership during this time period.[29] The meaningfulness of communal participation can be seen as being undercut by such mobility; thus, this increased mobility can be seen as conducive to the growth of radical individualism, as described above. This erosion of communal bonds works contrary to the Modern Discourse's urgent need of enhancing and maintaining the functioning of society—as the subsumption of one's individuality to the greater system requires the spirit of cooperation. Thus, it represents a fault line in the Modern Discourse, one that could undermine its dominance.

The introduction of the internet to society, it has been noted, tends predominantly to further reinforce a move toward radical individualism.[30] By enhancing this negative side to individualism, the growth of anomie in society increases (while social capital decreases), thus deepening the fault line developing in this regard within the Modern Discourse. To clarify this further, the philosopher Gordon Graham makes a distinction between belonging to a community and belonging to an interest group.[31] An interest group is formed around the shared interests of its members, whether they be subjective interests (members are interested in the same things) or objective interests (members who are affected by the same things, whether they be beneficial or harmful). A community, he argues, not only consists of shared interests among its members but also has a moral component of accepted values which determines "what their objective interests *are* and what their *subjective interests* ought to be."[32] This moral component arises from the communal bonds that are established through interaction among its members.

While the internet contains the potential to enhance and maintain these communal bonds, it is not conducive to creating them. A good portion of the average person's time spent on the internet involves no social interaction whatsoever, as when one seeks information or entertainment. Socializing online typically takes the form of an interest group, such as with massively multiplayer online games.

Social networking sites such as Facebook allow one to maintain, and perhaps enhance, the socializing of an already established community of friends; however, they do a poor job of creating communal bonds among friends met purely online—as is the case when one has hundreds of such "friends" attached to one's account.

As noted earlier, the global network which comprises the internet is extremely conducive toward extending the "creative process of knowing" that forms McLuhan's vision of a global village. It acts as a powerful tool in the free and open dissemination of information by providing speed, ease of access, and reach to the breadth and depth of information available. In this manner, its effect on communitarianism is the exact opposite of its effect on individualism: Rather than feeding the negative side, as it does for individualism, it works toward undercutting the negative side of communitarianism, which is totalitarianism. Totalitarianism relies heavily upon total control in the dissemination of information as the means to advance its propaganda and keep the citizenry in the dark regarding the abuses of its power. By offering a platform for easily and rapidly disseminating information, the internet acts to support the move toward a more open society[33]—as was most keenly illustrated during the Arab Spring[d] in the early 2010s.

Thus, after this quite lengthy digression, we are now able to make the following observations. The internet marks a revolutionary change in how we communicate. It works to further radicalize the individualism inherent within the Modern Discourse, thus handicapping efforts to advance its urgent need (which relies upon the spirit of cooperation): that of enhancing and maintaining the functioning of society. Conversely, it works to undercut the negative aspect of communitarianism inherent in the Postmodern discourse, thus working to promote its urgent need—that of promoting social cohesiveness via fostering a more open society. Hence, the internet's introduction in the 1990s may mark the beginning of a transition period between dominant Discourses. The emergence of the Postmodern discourse in social welfare at this same time further speaks to this view.

Furthermore, interestingly enough, various activities that people engage in utilizing the internet actually mirror some of the key insights offered by the postmodern social welfare practitioners/scholars quoted at the beginning of this chapter. For example, home pages—such as one creates in a Facebook account—serve as sites where one places visual and textual material of one's lived

---

[d] The Arab Spring refers to the wave of anti-government protests that swept across many Arab countries in the early 2010s. People made ready use of social media to coordinate these protests centered upon governmental corruption and economic stagnation.

experiences. As is the case in literature and cinema, this *storied* self-presentation offers a vision of one's identity, one to which others add visual and textual material of their own in response—thus legitimizing and strengthening its construction.[34] The individual does not rely upon an expert for this vision of identity but, rather, situates themselves as the one best positioned to elaborate its essence. Also, by exploring various constructions of one's identity across numerous sites that the internet has to offer, the process of interacting with others that this entails fosters a greater understanding of other people's realities.[35] In terms of direct application to social welfare practices, this allows for community "spaces" to be created wherein those identifying with a particular marginalized group (e.g., women Vietnam veterans) can come together to share their lived experiences and have them honored, as the means to educate and raise consciousness to effect change.[36]

Economic Conditions

Economic globalization marks a recent and significant change in US economic conditions, a change worthy of examination. Economic globalization is widely recognized as arising in the latter part of the twentieth century, approximately from the 1980s onward.[37] Now it should be noted that multinational corporations have existed since the late 1800s with the rise of big business.[38] So, international trade is not the defining feature of economic globalization. Rather, the change that marks the rise of economic globalization—spurred on by innovations in communication and information technologies—is the free movement of capital.[39] The ability to rapidly and nimbly employ capital and information to promote entrepreneurship is what has led to the deepening of economic integration at the global level.[40]

The operation of the US economy in a deeply integrated global network has resulted in an imbalance in the functioning of the political economy as the main political institution tasked with regulating such an economy remains at the level of the nation-state.[41] Yes, the Bretton Woods agreement post–World War II established various international organizations for managing the economy; however, these institutions were designed for a world in which the movement of capital was not freely and readily transmitted at the global level.[42] This imbalance puts the United States in a situation parallel to what occurred at the end of the Premodern Era, wherein due to the rise of big business the economy was operating at the national level, whereas political regulation remained at the state and local levels. Consequently, many of the same social problems that arose then due to this imbalance—such as an ever-growing disparity in wealth—have risen anew in present society.

To be sure, capitalism has proven itself to ably yield many benefits for society. As one author notes, "business is good because it creates value, it is ethical because it is based on voluntary exchange, it is noble because it can elevate our existence, and it is heroic because it lifts people out of poverty and creates prosperity."[43] Yet this moral logic to capitalism—which is built upon the values of free choice and voluntary exchange—gets subverted when market failures lead to situations of impaired choice, slavish working conditions, and the degradation of the environment.[44] Capitalism's only rival in recent history—communism in the form of a command economy—has been tried and discredited. However, the criticisms leveled by Karl Marx of unregulated capitalism (arising from an imbalance in the political economy) remain valid. When highly unregulated, capitalism leads to the following: a concentration of wealth among the richest, the exploitation of workers and their subsequent alienation from society, the degradation of the environment, and the avoidance of social responsibility (such as in the form of taxes used to promote the public good).

The rise of the nation-state in the Modern Era and the United States' evolution into a welfare state in the 1930s served to minimize the impact of the above-mentioned abuses. Thus, for example, during the time period extending from the 1940s to 1980, the share of income going to the top 10% of earners remained steady at 35%.[45] With the advent of economic globalization in the 1980s, and with it the decline of unions as well as generous tax breaks for the wealthy, the top 10% earners' share of income has steadily grown, reaching and then surpassing its previous peak of 45% in the late 1920s.[46] And by 2005, the richest 1% of households annually earned the equivalent of the bottom 60% of earners, whereas in terms of amassed wealth, this same 1% possessed an amount equal to that of the bottom 90%.[47] As noted in Chapter 6, growth in real wages for the average worker remained remarkably flat from 1979 to 2015;[48] and union membership fell by approximately 50% during this same time span.[49] Beginning with President Ronald Reagan in 1981 and extending to President Donald Trump in 2017, the United States has enacted various tax cuts that favor the wealthy and corporations—the argument being that such breaks would stimulate the economy and thus wealth would "trickle down" to lower-wage earners.

Beyond overcoming the political ideology behind such policy, economic globalization presents some real challenges for effectively taxing the wealthy and corporations. Just as corporations in the Premodern Era due to the imbalance in the political economy were able to effectively pit US states against each other, threatening to move their operations to another state if not given a break on taxes, economic globalization in the Modern Era has led corporations to effectively pit nations against each other.[50] As George Soros aptly notes, "When capital is free to move around, it can be taxed and regulated only at the risk of driving it away."[51] Thus, corporations and billionaires are able to avoid what they view as onerous taxes and regulations because of the mobility of financial capital.[52] Hence, it is not uncommon to come across a news item declaring a multibillion-dollar company paying no taxes whatsoever, with Amazon in 2018 being one of the most recent examples.[53] Similarly, individuals with vast fortunes can easily move assets to another country and thus avoid having to report their total wealth to the Internal Revenue Service.[54] These handicaps arising from an imbalance in the political economy severely limit the nation-state's ability to promote social welfare as social problems such as alienation and economic injustice get exacerbated, while the ability of the nation-state to render social services to its citizens to ameliorate such problems gets hampered by the difficulty in effectively taxing capital accumulation.[55]

In brief, capitalism in the form of economic globalization can act as both a positive force and a negative force in society. As was the case for the development of the internet, economic globalization may also represent a major fault line between the Modern Discourse and the Postmodern discourse as they vie for dominance. Notably, economic globalization and the communication prowess of the internet are intertwined and mutually reinforcing. Thus, similar to the internet, it appears that the Modern Discourse seems to feed the darker side of economic globalization's expression of capitalism, whereas the Postmodern discourse appears to promote its nobler side.

The Modern Discourse's Influence on Economic Globalization

When it comes to judging value in the marketplace, the following basic premise is offered regarding the understanding of value: "to judge that something is good is to judge that it is properly valued. And to judge that it is bad is to judge that it is properly disvalued."[56] The quest for objective knowledge versus the quest for subjective knowledge in determining value is what distinguishes a modern versus a postmodern understanding of economic activity. The Modern Discourse represents a quest for objective knowledge. This quest spawns what can be described as consequentialist theories of value and action. Deriving from a long tradition in Western philosophy, consequentialism seeks to contrast reason with more subjective ways of knowing such as emotions and social norms as the means to achieve an independent, or "objective," perspective.[57] Thus, this quest for objective knowledge leads to the following broad understandings of economic activity: that value is intrinsically located in the activity (i.e., the market exchange); that rational action is directed toward a single end, the production of consequences, and thus is evaluated in these terms (i.e., the results obtained through market exchange); that the rational action producing these consequences follows a single norm of value (i.e., the profit motive); and that this rational action is justified through showing that it maximizes this intrinsic value (i.e., profit).[58]

Very broadly, the political economy is comprised of two major components: There is policy which determines the rules by which the "game" is played (i.e., the political component) and the actual market exchanges made by participants (the economic component). Within capitalism, market participation is heavily grounded upon individualism—in particular, the individual's right to freedom of choice—whereas political policy guiding economic activity is more of a communitarian endeavor in that its goal is to promote the common good by seeking to advance fairness and economic justice through a collective decision-making process.[59] When the economic component expands beyond the reach of the political component, the individualism driving market participation gets overly emphasized and is less likely to be held in check by the communitarian impulse of the policymaking process to promote fairness and advance economic justice.

The Modern Discourse, and the Enlightenment thought it draws upon, heavily supports a strain of individualism. As individualism in the form of market participation is already being overemphasized due to the imbalance resulting from economic globalization, further emphasis of individualism by the Modern Discourse only serves to exacerbate this imbalance, thereby contributing further to the market failures described above that result in economic injustice and decreasing fairness. Thus, similar to the case of the internet, economic globalization's expression in the Modern Discourse results in its individualism becoming radically situated—in terms of market participation, this takes the form of embracing market fundamentalism.[60]

Market fundamentalism embraces objective knowledge. Within science, objective knowledge arises from empirical observations that when properly tested reveal truths that cannot be denied even when they fly in the face of common sense. When specifically applied to market participation, objective knowledge reveals itself in the form of profit—the ultimate arbiter to objectively measure successful market participation.[61] This overemphasis on profit as the sole criterion for measuring success naturally leads to a moral insensitivity infusing market participation, for a number of reasons.[62] First, the very nature of individualism itself, which seeks to advance the person's/corporation's right to freely choose, relies upon being unconstrained by the needs and interests of others in order to maximally exercise this right.[63] Second, market fundamentalism is averse to any type of collective decision-making in regard to imposing social values to infringe upon this individual right; rather, it relies upon such values to arise through the automatic error-correcting mechanism of market exchange.[64] This results in the argument that the common good is best advanced politically through a laissez-faire approach—in the era of economic globalization, this has found expression through massive deregulation and the wide adoption of free trade agreements. However, as was examined in Chapter 6, while such an argument may hold some merit for proprietary capitalism, a laissez-faire approach has proven itself ill equipped to advance the common good when it comes to corporate capitalism. Third, reminiscent of the efficiency versus ethic dynamic elaborated upon in Chapter 7, efficiency in the pursuit of profit increases when moral constraints are decreased.[65] So, for example, consumers may maximize their profit from an exchange (i.e., getting high-quality goods/services for a low price) through purchasing stolen merchandise or engaging in theft themselves. Corporations are able to maximize profit through fully exploiting labor and shirking all caretaking responsibility for the environment. Consequently, market fundamentalism exerts pressure toward seeking the least moral environment.

The main method to push back against this pressure toward an amoral environment is through the creation of policy which advances economic justice by placing constraints upon the individual's right to choose. Within the Modern Discourse, this takes the form of scientific management of the economy. This approach worked reasonably well for the Modern Era pre–economic globalization, with the assumption by the federal government of attending to social welfare needs offering an effective counterbalance to the individualism inherent in market activity. However, in regard to economic globalization, as stated above, the state's ability to scientifically manage the economy is greatly reduced due to the imbalance created by the economy operating at a global level, while political institutions remain at the level of the nation-state.

To overcome this limitation, what is called for is a political consciousness to directly find expression within the market exchange. However, scientific management's reliance upon objective knowledge in the form of expertise makes it ill equipped to stimulate such a political consciousness. Rather, scientific management has employed deregulation and free trade as the means to extend its reach to the global level and, in the process, rely upon the promotion of market values into the role that social values serve: to advance the common good.[66] Such faith in market values contains two major flaws: "First, markets are not designed to address issues of distributive justice; they take the existing distribution of wealth as given. Second, the common interest does not find expression in market behavior. Corporations do not aim at creating employment; they employ people (as few and as cheaply as possible) to make profits."[67] These flaws are illustrated in the widening of income inequality described above as well as the periodic news stories uncovering a corporation's efforts at exploiting labor (e.g., Nike[68]) and/or degrading the environment and resulting harm to the local population (e.g., the Bhopal disaster[69]).

The Postmodern discourse's Influence on Economic Globalization

While the Modern Discourse currently reigns supreme when it comes to understanding economic activity in the era of economic globalization, what might a postmodern understanding of economic activity look like in terms of subjective knowledge? The economist/philosopher Elizabeth Anderson offers one such illustration with her *pluralistic rational attitude theory*. This theory embraces the view that there is a plurality of ways in which to value goods within the market exchange. Market fundamentalism seeks only to assess goods within the market exchange by asking "how much we should value them" (i.e., price + demand equating to profit); Anderson's theory seeks not only to assess how *much* we should value goods (an objective assessment) but also to assess "*how* we should value them" (a subjective assessment).[70] Thus, her theory is built upon the premise that beyond the empirical observation of intrinsic value (the objective assessment), more fundamental to understanding overall value is the subjective assessment of how we value and care about things; or, in simpler terms, we are able to know that goods/services are appropriately valued when the valuation makes sense to us.[71] As Anderson notes, "The link between self-understanding and justification is provided by the fact that valuations are expressive states. They are bearers of meanings and subject to interpretation. Since meanings are public, I can understand my own attitudes only in terms that make sense to others."[72]

The source of *pluralism* in Anderson's theory lies within the variety of ways in which to care about things: "we need a plurality of standards to make sense of the plurality of emotional responses and attitudes we have to things."[73] Thus, beyond profit, value in the market exchange can be assessed in terms of trust, respect, honesty, promoting the good, etc. In addition, for each of these evaluative criteria there exists a plurality of forms to consider; for example, there is trust in the workmanship of the product/service, trust in honoring the exchange as agreed upon, trust in claims made about the product/service, etc.

The *rational attitude* aspect of Anderson's theory embraces a postmodern understanding of rationality as being socially grounded and thus anti-individualistic. It takes the stance that individuals are not autonomous bearers of practical reason. Rather, a context of social norms is required for individuals to express their attitudes adequately so that others may grasp their intelligibility in action.[74] Individuals view themselves in terms of an ideal that they would like to emulate; thus, it is constitutive of a person's identity and governs one's self-assessments and valuations when framing one's choices.[75] Hence, Anderson states, "An ideal-based pluralistic theory of goods does not concern itself exclusively with the qualities of the goods people enjoy. It also focuses on the realization of distinct ideals of the person and community, and it views goods as mediating these relations among people."[76] Since the expression of the market exchange represents an activity that is meaning-making, it relies upon a publicly intelligible vehicle to achieve its valuation. This vehicle comes in the form of social norms, and these norms are constitutive of *rational attitudes.* Consequently, in order to have an evaluative attitude toward something (i.e., valuation), one's deliberations and actions are governed by social norms which in turn communicate distinctive meanings to others.[77]

Anderson's theory can be classified as an expressive theory. In contrast to consequentialist theory, described earlier, expressive theory of valuation embraces subjective knowledge of meaning-making. This quest for subjective knowledge leads to the following broad understandings of economic activity: that value is located within individual desires, preferences, and choices, which are derived from social norms for expressing evaluative attitudes; that rational action is directed toward two ends—the production of consequences as the final end as well as an end for the sake of which these consequences are sought (in the form of people, animals, things one cares about); that rational action is evaluated in terms of its expressive meanings and the relevance of consequences as informed through social norms; that rational action is justified by a plurality of appropriate norms;[e] and that this justification conforms to one's rational valuations constituting the expressive social norms.[78]

One prime example of what these features may look like within the market activity taking place under economic globalization is illustrated by the rise of social entrepreneurship. Building upon a business trend in the early 1980s called *cause-related marketing,* "social entrepreneurs develop innovative business models to address specific social challenges."[79] Social entrepreneurship embraces the viewpoint that rational action is directed not only toward the end consequence of profit but also toward social responsibility. In such an effort, profit no longer serves as the defining motive but, rather, serves as a means to a socially responsible end determined by the mission and ideals comprising the raison d'être of the company's existence.[80] Warby Parker, GoldieBlox, and Lush are a few companies that model this approach. Warby Parker sells eyeglasses and not only seeks to offer high quality at low prices but also adopts a company policy that for each pair of eyeglasses sold, one will be donated to those in need. GoldieBlox is a toy company whose mission is to create toys related to engineering and technology—specifically designed and marketed to inspire girls to pursue careers in these fields. Lush is a cosmetic company which offers "naked" packaging (solid products free from any packaging) in order to promote sustainability of the environment; in addition, it uses the platform of its ecommerce website to promote charitable giving and advance social causes that fit its mission. These three companies also serve to illustrate a sample of the plurality of

---

[e] Anderson, *Value in Ethics,* 33. The variety of appropriate norms is often quite puzzling to those adopting a consequentialist view as they can be intentional, backward-looking, distributive, and non-instrumental.

norms possible as Warby Parker promotes charitable giving to address human need, GoldieBlox promotes the empowerment of girls, and Lush promotes sustainability of the environment.

Consumers motivated to purchase products from these companies do so not only with the intent of seeking to maximize quality gained versus price paid but also as a rational act to support the mission of the company. Thus, the individual's decision to purchase the product is partly derived from the effort to adhere to socially responsible norms, and one's action in doing so is justified when it conforms to one's rational valuations constituting the expressive social norms. Consequently, evaluating the value of this market exchange requires more than just empirical observation as to how well the product serves its intended function (objective knowledge). It also relies upon expressive meanings and the relevance of consequences as informed through the socially responsible norms promoted by the company (subjective knowledge). While the objective knowledge contributing to one's assessment of value relies upon one's own empirical observations, the subjective knowledge contributing to one's assessment relies upon trust in the relationship between consumer and producer—trust that the company is both authentic and honest in its claims of advancing social causes. The building of this trust—and by extension confidence in the accuracy of one's subjective assessment—requires transparency and the free flow of information concerning the company's actions in advancing its stated socially responsible mission. This transparency and free flow of information thus serve to help regulate the market.[81]

Transparency and the free flow of information indicative of an open society are not limited to simply regulating the behavior of social entrepreneurs. They also serve to curb company malfeasance and the exploitation of labor and the environment.[82] The development of the internet has provided a platform to make transparency and the free flow of information readily accessible to the average consumer, thus invigorating the contribution of subjective knowledge to assessment of valuation. Consequently, companies are entering an era in which they cannot solely focus upon the delivery of a quality product; they must also demonstrate a social consciousness as the means to gain the trust of the consumer. As Mark Zuckerberg, CEO of Facebook, states, "You need to be good in order to get people's trust. In the past people just didn't expect goodness from companies. I think that's changing now."[83] Within an open society, "being good" can grant companies a competitive advantage; this market demand for goodness thus serves to "raise their consciousness level and recognize a higher purpose which addresses the contribution they intend to make to society."[84] By clarifying their original purpose for coming into existence and thus the contribution they intend to make to society, these companies serve to promote the nobler aspects of capitalism.[85]

Additionally, the internet has offered a specific tool by which to promote the free flow of information concerning the market exchange: the microblog. Again, in seeking a competitive advantage, numerous businesses now solicit customers' opinions in the public forum created by the microblog. These opinions can take the form of sharing one's judgments based upon one's empirical observations of the product—such as when people leave opinions reviewing a restaurant and the meal that they ate there or, as commonly found on ecommerce sites, when customers leave reviews on how well a product functioned for them. Additionally, these reviews can also speak to subjective valuations—such as how well the customer was treated. This marks a significant change in the producer–consumer relationship. In the past, companies through their advertising controlled close to 100% of the messaging of their product; the microblog now makes this messaging a shared endeavor with the consumer. Consequently, this serves to move the customer out of the passive role of sovereign consumer—simply free to choose from "among already selected brands of goods"[86]—to that of an active consumer whose participation is solicited as the means to increase the authenticity of the messaging, which in turn promotes trust.

Bringing this back to the concerns of social welfare, we now have identified a second force operating in society to shape the nature of the social welfare discourse. The internet and economic globalization offer two loci of power, recently manifested, which serve to delegitimize the Modern Discourse's understanding (in areas such as the scientific management of problems or the role of expertise in determining meaning) of how to address social ills, while at the same time serving to legitimize the Postmodern discourse's understanding (in areas such as meaning-making and the development of trust) of how to address social ills. Many parallels can now be drawn between the use of these two forces and the postmodern social welfare interventions described at the beginning of this chapter. So, for example, the microblog's influence in yielding a bit of power by companies to consumers regarding the messaging of the product mirrors that of postmodern practitioners yielding their power of expertise to clients (aka *the client is the expert*) regarding defining the helping situation.

Trust then arises as a key component to this shared decision-making. While the building of trust within the social worker–client relationship is prominently recognized as being important in both the Modern Discourse and the Postmodern discourse, its expression in each differs. Within the Modern Discourse trust serves to advance objective knowledge. Hence, there is the social worker's trust in the client that they are being open and forthcoming concerning the nature and symptoms of the problem so that an accurate diagnosis can be made. Then there is the client's trust in the social worker that their expertise will yield an accurate diagnosis and thus offer effective treatment plans from which the client may select in the role of sovereign consumer.

In contrast, within the Postmodern discourse trust serves to advance subjective knowledge. The social worker's trust in the client takes the form of having faith in the client's ability to meaningfully describe *how they want to be in the world*, and thus be an equal partner in the shared decision-making process concerning how the helping relationship is defined. In addition, the client trusts the social worker to recognize and believe in the client's vision of *how they want to be in the world*, thus rousing *hope* for achieving the desired change. Hence, within the Postmodern discourse, trust serves to promote the shared endeavor of meaning-making as the social worker assists the client in *storying* the client's experience in order to *write a better text* concerning how they want to be in the world.

Political Conditions

The most prominent political trend from the 1980s to the present has been the rise of neoliberalism.[87] Neoliberalism is the political partner to market fundamentalism. It is the ideological stance that the mechanisms and principles behind free market exchange are the most efficient means for addressing social issues.[88] As described above, when applied to economic policy, this has resulted in the rise of deregulation and the growth of free trade agreements. Consequently, as was also noted, this has led to a strong embrace of market fundamentalism and the growing inequity in wealth. Its influence on social welfare policy has marked a retreat from the hearty embrace of the liberal welfare state that occurred for a good portion of the twentieth century. While marking a retreat from the liberal welfare state, neoliberalism is still firmly rooted within the Modern Discourse. It simply represents a more hands-off approach to scientific management as opposed to the more active hands-on approach of the welfare state. Scholars have begun to use the label *new managerialism* to describe the present incarnation of scientific management within the philosophy of neoliberalism.[89]

Some prominent illustrations of this are as follows. The first prime example of this retreat is the passage of the Personal Responsibility and Work Opportunity Reconciliation Act (PRWORA) of 1996. PRWORA marked a decisive shift away from the unconditional support of single mothers in poverty who qualified for meager benefits to a stance of conditional support in the form of a five-year lifetime limit to benefits along with a number of regulations circumscribing the behavior of recipients. The second prime example occurs in the area of criminal justice, where neoliberalism has led to the mass incarceration of the poor,[90] while at the same time allowing the privatization of prisons which serve to profit the wealthy and provide a bit of employment to the middle class.[91] And a third prime example is that of the privatization of the health care industry, with 21%

of hospitals now operating on a for-profit basis.[92] This has led to various limitations in coverage (somewhat corrected with the passage of the Affordable Care Act in 2010), which serve to fuel inequities in treatment as the wealthy and those with generous employer-sponsored plans are afforded easier access to available treatments. A fourth prime example is comprised of the wave of deregulation brought on by neoliberalism which has impacted environmental policy, yielding a strong resistance among many in the United States to even recognizing global warming as a social problem. And lastly, this retreat toward less government has resulted in the considerable scaling back of investment monies devoted to building and maintaining infrastructure.

Neoliberalism has not been received well by the social work academic community. Just as market fundamentalism radicalizes individualism and thus serves to exacerbate the negative side to globalization, neoliberalism radicalizes individualism as well in the form of overemphasizing the role of personal responsibility (and embracing disciplinary techniques toward those deemed as failing in that responsibility), thereby undercutting attempts to focus upon promoting social justice through addressing structural oppression.[93] While the vast majority of this critique is delivered by social work academics outside the United States, there exist a few who attempt to apply the critique specific to the context of social welfare and social welfare education in the United States.

As stated previously, radical individualism comprises the stance of primarily viewing people as generic individuals rather than unique persons. Neoliberalism is seen by social work scholars as contributing toward radical individualism in the following manner. First, neoliberalism is viewed as encouraging the uncritical embrace of evidence-based practice as the means to promote scientific management.[94] It is worth noting that the evidence generated (i.e., objective knowledge) is built upon the premise of viewing subjects as belonging to a population group, rather than emphasizing the uniqueness of the person and the cultural/environmental context in which they are embedded. As evidence-based research more easily lends itself to studies at the micro level, greater emphasis is given to interventions that target the individual.[95] Consequently, evidence-based intervention is predominantly directed toward the development of human capital over the development of social capital; this further emphasizes social work's role in social engineering as aimed at seeking to enhance functioning, while de-emphasizing its role as a political activity aimed at confronting oppression.[96]

Second, neoliberalism encourages the acceptance of the globalization of society under market fundamentalism as a given.[97] Combined with person-in-environment as the defining conceptual model along with the neutral stance toward the environment typical in evidence-based research, neoliberalism further pushes the focus of social work interventions toward facilitating adaptation to the environment in the form of personal transformation while de-emphasizing confronting social injustices.[98] This further situates social workers as agents who monitor and facilitate client compliance to the disciplinary regime under neoliberalism—with welfare-to-work requirements and the technically oriented therapeutic goals predominant in behavioral health serving as two prominent examples.[99]

Lastly, neoliberalism has resulted in an ideological change in the mission of academic institutions and, consequently, departments of social work. With an ever-decreasing share of state revenue allocated for its operating budget (now commonly below 50%), public universities have had to move further away from the operating model of the university as acting as a public good seeking to promote informed public citizens and more heavily toward operating under a business model seeking profit and whose main goal is to arm graduates with the technical knowledge/skill to effectively adapt to the demands of the market-place.[100] This trend in turn has led social work departments to overemphasize acquisition of the technical knowledge/skill reflective of the social engineer, while limiting exposure to critical theory necessary for the activist for social justice.[101] This is prominently illustrated in the noted increasing marginalization of macro–social work's place in social work education during the neoliberal era.[102] Thus, while the rhetoric of advancing social justice, confronting oppression, and fostering empowerment still holds a prominent place in the vision of social work education, neoliberalism sanitizes these values by diverting one's attention away from their deeper political and ideological significance in addressing structural inequities.[103]

While social entrepreneurism merely represents a minor current in present economic activity, postmodern theory has more substantively churned the political waters with the growth of identity politics. Steven Best and Douglas Kellner offer the following definition of identity politics: " 'Identity politics' refers to a politics in which individuals construct their cultural and political identities through engaging in struggles or associations that advance the interests of the groups with which they identify."[104] Social justice is achieved by advancing the interests of identity-based groups who are suffering oppression, focused around a particular issue.[105] The #MeToo movement[f] serves as one prominent example of identity politics in action. Identity politics seeks to build upon the objective, universalistic principles used to advance the struggle for human and civil rights that arose during the Modern Era.[106] Postmodern theorists' critique of this

---

[f] The #MeToo movement is a movement that utilizes social media to speak out against sexual abuse and sexual harassment in the workplace by providing a platform where victims post allegations of their own experiences of sexual abuse and harassment in support of individuals who are making a public claim in the courts. Since prominently breaking upon the American scene in 2017, the #MeToo movement has gained an international reach and now has evolved into a broader movement seeking justice for marginalized people.

Enlightenment project is not that these universalistic principles are unnecessary but, rather, that, when pursued as a sole strategy for promoting social justice, they also serve to suppress differences which in turn privilege certain groups over others.[107]

Let's refer back to the #MeToo movement to illustrate. As initially started, the #MeToo movement can be seen as embracing the universalistic principle of respect for the dignity and worth of the individual in regard to personal boundaries, specifically that those in power (stemming either from position or male privilege) should not seek to coerce another into having sexual relations. The fact that sexual harassment laws exist speaks to the universal acceptance of this principle in society. However, what the #MeToo movement seeks to contest is the subjective meaning applied by the dominant male culture *to the violation of this principle*: that various transgressions are relatively harmless, part of human nature, the folly of youth, the price of doing business, etc. This postmodern form of contestation is described as *micropolitics*. In contrast to macropolitics, where structural change is sought to the economy and the state, micropolitics contests the power and hierarchy of privileged groups who seek to exert inordinate control over the construction of narratives about the universalistic principles comprising society.[108] The consciousness-raising of society that occurs through this contestation then in turn inspires structural policy change at the state and federal levels. Some examples of this for the #MeToo movement are as follows: states beginning to ban nondisclosure agreements that encompass sexual harassment, states seeking to extend federal sexual harassment laws' protection to independent contractors (e.g., Uber drivers) and to employees working for small businesses consisting of fewer than fifteen employees (e.g., many domestic and farm laborers), and the US Congress having passed legislation that reforms the process governing staffers' efforts to report sexual harassment.[109]

This same postmodern understanding informing identity politics, in turn, informs the postmodern social work practices described at the beginning of this chapter. Thus, client problems are looked at as comprising more than simply structural dysfunction within a system. In addition, client problems are viewed *as acting in an oppressive manner* in regard to client identity: This manifests itself in the dominant cultural narrative commonly depicting the client as abnormal, "broken," a failure, or in some other disempowering manner. In fact, within the Modern Discourse, societal legitimization as to why someone needs social work services in the first place is based upon the client embracing such a disempowering identity; in other words, normal, functional individuals are not seen as needing social work services. Mirroring the approach taken by micropolitics, postmodern practitioners do not look to directly target the structural symptomology of the client problem but rather target the disempowering subjective meaning being applied to client identity by the dominant cultural Discourse concerning the problem. Once the client's consciousness has been raised, in turn, leading to the embrace of a more empowering identity, the client is inspired to take action to address the symptomology of the presenting problem.

The role of the social worker thus becomes that of assisting the client in constructing an empowering identity in relation to the problem. One way this occurs is through the social worker helping the client identify experiences of resistance and resilience in the face of the problem and then helping the client explore how the same qualities responsible for these acts of resistance and resilience are reflected in experiences from other facets of the client's life. This empowering identity then fosters *hope* in the client's ability to change the structural symptomology of the presenting problem so that it no longer interferes with the client's dreams and vision for a better future. Thus, this process of constructing an empowering identity in relation to the presenting problem is described as *storying experiences* with the goal of *creating a better text* in the form of an empowered identity.

Micropolitics marks a decided move toward a greater level of participatory democracy; citizens take a more active role in shaping policy through joining social movements. And as was the case with the microblog empowering consumers to greater levels of participation in determining the nature of the market exchange, the internet—with its ability to offer rapid, free flow of information—has been highly conducive to promoting micropolitics. In the case of micropolitics, it is the platform of social media that has greatly enhanced its efforts. Again, we need simply to look at the #MeToo movement to see the crucial role that social media has played in promoting its cause.

The internet has also been highly conducive to promoting greater participation in other facets of the political process. In the area of fundraising, the internet has enabled candidates to easily connect to the multitude of their supporters to make direct appeals for donations, most notably illustrated in the 2020 primary presidential campaign of Elizabeth Warren, who pledged to seek no donations from big donors, relying 100% on the support from the multitude of her supporters representing the average voter.[110] The enhanced connectivity and rapid communication offered by the internet have also increased citizen participation in making direct change at the macropolitical level. Most states and local entities provide the option for voters to put policy measures directly on the ballot; the ability to garner the requisite number of signatures to do so is greatly aided by the internet. Furthermore, with a majority of states experimenting with allowing online voting as of the 2018 elections (primarily for service personnel and citizens living overseas),[111] once security issues are worked out, the ability of the average citizen to engage in participatory democracy of this sort will be even more greatly enhanced.

Lastly, the internet serves to enhance connectivity between average citizens and their elected officials, thus facilitating greater interaction in the relationship rather than elected officials simply broadcasting information to constituents through the television, radio, and print media. This is most notably illustrated by elected officials' use of social media.[112] In addition, the We the People website[g] initiated by President Barack Obama greatly enhanced the average citizen's ability to petition the government (a right guaranteed by the First Amendment to the Constitution); if a person was able to gather 100,000 signatures in thirty days, the White House would officially respond to the petition by sending an email to all the signatories.[113] This broad theme of enhancing participatory democracy reflected by the above measures finds resonance within postmodern social work practices. Rather than use the power inherent in their professional expertise to define (i.e., diagnose) and shape (i.e., offer a selection of possible treatments) the helping situation, postmodern practitioners invite greater participation on the part of the client in regard to meaning-making serving to define and shape the helping situation through adopting a *not-knowing approach* and recognizing the *expertise of the client* in this regard.

Social Conditions

As stated previously, the development of the internet has introduced a profound change in the dynamic of social communication and interaction. Additionally, it has marked a revolutionary change in the nature of media and the role it plays in communicating and shaping society's cultural mores and understandings.[114] The advent of mass circulation newspapers and books in the Premodern Era and the arrival of radio, television, and that of movies in the Modern Era are reflective of a category of media referred to as *mass media*; this is due to the ability of these types of media to reach the broad mass of people comprising society. One of the prime characteristics of mass media is that the economic and political levers used to produce content are limited to a select few in society. Consequently, this constrains the participation of the broad mass of individuals in society to acting in the role of sovereign consumer—choosing from a variety of preselected content that is broadcast to them.

However, echoing the theme of participatory democracy described above, the development of the internet and its related technology has expanded access to the production of media content, placing it within the grasp of the average individual.[115] Digital ebooks have opened the door for first-time authors to self-publish, while blogs offer a new platform for self-publishing material that one

---

[g] The We the People website closed down in December 2016.

normally would find in a magazine or newspaper. Podcasts (for radio) and video platforms such as YouTube (for television) have opened the door for the average individual to develop programming content and broadcast it to the masses. Everything ranging from market analysis to political commentary to music to informational how-to and self-improvement tips all now lie within the grasp of the average individual to produce programming content on if they should so desire.

Media serves to stimulate the exchange of ideas in society; society's cultural mores then arise from this exchange. Thus, this is how our understanding of American values, and what it means to be an American, takes shape. The development of the internet has greatly democratized the process for contributing to this social exchange of ideas. This creates a new challenge as there is now a multiplicity of voices participating in the forging of culture mores, a challenge that requires society to find unity among diversity, while at the same time respecting and valuing difference.

In addition, the development of the internet has created a new form of media, called *social media* (e.g., Facebook, Twitter, and Instagram, to name a few). As the name *social* implies, social media represents a form of media that relies upon the social exchange of content between participants in an interactive milieu. Social media marks a dramatic departure from the previous experience of mass media in which the mass of individuals in society are limited to the role of sovereign consumer of content that is broadcast or transmitted by a limited cadre of producers. Rather, the interactive nature of social media dissolves the distinction between producer and consumer as each individual participating in social exchange acts simultaneously in the roles of both.[116]

Let's use the example of Facebook to illustrate. To participate in the social exchange occurring within the platform of Facebook, first I would need to create a home page. This involves the addition of personal content (e.g., personal information, photos, thoughts/comments), which serves as the "face" that I present to the community, the identity I choose to embrace. Once created, this affords me the opportunity to visit the home pages of others in the network who are open to my desire to visit, and thus allows me to enter into a social exchange. As part of this social exchange, I am able to add content (typically in the form of comments) to the page of the person/entity I am visiting. This addition of content in turn (which may act in either an affirming or a disaffirming manner) contributes toward the identity formation process occurring on the home page. While a good portion of the content posted on one's web page is actual content produced by the individuals themselves (e.g., photos or the reporting of one's experiences, such as a recent vacation), there also occurs the "repackaging" of mass media content. This often takes the form of sharing news items.[117]

John Potter uses the term *curator* to describe this facet of the identity formation process. He likens this action to what a museum curator might do when selecting various items to create a display.[118] The curator's selection of the items to be placed together in the display serves to highlight particular qualities of the items which contribute to an overall theme; this theme then emphasizes various identity features of the item. So, for example, if paintings are placed together from various impressionist painters, the theme that arises is impressionism, while the topics and brushwork of the different artists are highlighted in terms of illustrating various approaches. However, if one of those impressionist paintings is placed with a cubist painting by Pablo Picasso and a pop art picture by Andy Warhol, the theme may speak to the historical progression of styles, with the conceptual premise of each style now serving as the main identity feature being emphasized. Thus, while the curator does not produce the various artworks, the curator's selection and arrangement of pieces creates a contextual meaning that overlays the pieces; this contextual meaning acts as a sort of lens to bring prominence to certain identity features over others. This same dynamic occurs when individuals post news stories or other media content on their Facebook home page. The selection of such content, in concert with content already on the page, serves to highlight various identity features of the individual (such as political leanings, sports team affiliation, or musical taste).

This dynamic of curatorship is mirrored in the approach adopted by postmodern social work practitioners in assisting clients in the curating of their lived experiences, helping them to craft an empowering identity in relation to the client problem which triggered services. The client's life experiences are seen as comprising behavioral texts.[119] The postmodern social worker encourages the client to select life experiences in which the problem was absent or less severe.[120] The curation of these life experiences alongside the client problem gives rise to a theme of strengths in the face of adversity. This serves to highlight qualities of capacity and ingenuity within the client—which are then drawn upon to help ameliorate the problem. Thus, referring to the quotes at the beginning of the chapter, this curatorship is what is meant by the *storying* of experiences, which then serves as a *better text*, one which helps the client to craft an empowering identity. This empowering identity is looked to as the source from which to promote client change.

Social media has proven itself to be an information system that is highly democratized and more open to the sharing of information than any other form of media preceding it.[121] However, this very democratization and openness poses some real challenges to the promotion of social cohesiveness in society. One thing that is not present in this form of media compared to others is an authority acting as gatekeeper for the validity of information.[122] Consequently, misinformation is easily circulated within the network. This erodes the ability for citizens to engage in fruitful debates on matters of concern. Furthermore, social media often places people in a network of like-minded individuals, which can lead to a steady diet of one-sided information and the avoidance of experiencing cognitive dissonance, an important element for a healthy debate.[123] Similarly, there is the common tendency among individuals to seek information that matches their preference, and hence does not challenge their predispositions—another important element for a healthy debate.[124] Thus, it is not surprising that the twenty-first century has experienced a dramatic rise in polarization within American politics.[125]

Urgent Need

Describing the urgent need for the emerging Postmodern discourse is a bit of a challenge in that urgent needs make themselves clearly apparent only after a discourse has achieved dominance. Thus, the description of the urgent need being offered in this section will be that of an educated guess. Now, it is possible to examine past patterns and evidence to provide the "educated" aspect of the guess. In terms of past patterns, we can note a broad commonality between the urgent need of the Colonial Discourse and that of the Modern Discourse. During both of these eras, while there was plenty of change occurring, overall the social welfare agents of these eras viewed the social structures of society as being relatively stable. Hence, both of these Discourses seek to maintain and enhance the existing social structures of society: the social hierarchy in the case of the Colonial Discourse and the structural functioning of society in the case of the Modern Discourse. The Premodern Discourse stands in contrast as the social welfare agents of this time period viewed a particular aspect of society (moral cohesiveness) as disintegrating, and thus in need of mending and transformative change. The growth and change occurring during this era were highly uneven, placing many aspects of society out of balance. Most notable of this unevenness was the imbalance in the political economy that occurred as growth of the economic marketplace moved beyond the political sphere of influence operating at that time.

Thus, one can easily note that the Postmodern discourse shares an affinity with the Premodern Discourse in this regard: Various aspects of society, most notably the political economy, are out of balance. In the Premodern Era, this occurred due to the transformative economic change brought on by the Industrial Revolution; various technological revolutions enabled big businesses to achieve a lower cost of production per unit. Along with technological advances in transportation and communication, this allowed the marketplace to quickly become national in scope. In the emergent Postmodern Era, there is economic globalization.

Globalization has come about through revolutionary change in communications technology; with the advent of computers and the internet, this has enabled capital to quickly and easily circulate on a global level, while its regulation remains primarily at the national level. Social concerns regarding the cohesiveness of society have begun to be noted by scholars.

Various sociologists have commented upon the dramatic decline in social capital occurring during the era of globalization.[126] These communal ties have come under attack by a wave of radical individualism—spurred on by the Modern Discourse's response to globalization in the form of market fundamentalism and neoliberalism, both of which are exacerbated by the technological innovation of the internet. This has fed a growing inequity in the distribution of wealth which serves to erode the cohesiveness of the socioeconomic classes of society. In addition, the twenty-first century thus far has seen a marked increase in the level of political polarization infecting American society. Social media provides the platform for a multiplicity of voices from previously subjugated groups to have their say and begin to demand recognition for various microaggressions being perpetrated against them; this has led to a backlash from various dominant groups in society to negatively label such demands as *political correctness* in an effort delegitimize these demands by painting them as being extreme, and thus seek to dismiss and subjugate them once more. The sum total of these observations leads me to believe that the urgent need of the Postmodern discourse (i.e., once it achieves dominance) will be that of *attending to the social cohesiveness of society.*

Intellectual Thought

Immanuel Kant: Phenomena and Aesthetic Judgment

Once again, Immanuel Kant offers a foundational concept which underpins the formation of a discourse. From his work *Groundwork of the Metaphysic of Morals*, the Premodern Discourse granted prominence to his concept of the categorical imperative, which served to guide social welfare's moral reform efforts of that era. From the second part of his work *The Critique of Judgement*, which deals with teleological judgment, the Modern Discourse granted prominence to his concept of organisms as natural purposes. This concept served to set the foundation for the scientific study of human beings, and thus guides social welfare's social engineering efforts adopted in the Modern Era. Turning once again to *The Critique of Judgement*, this time from the first part which deals with aesthetic judgment, Kant elaborates upon the concept of *phenomena* as a product of a discursive intellect, which has been taken up and given prominence by the Postmodern discourse. While much of Kant's works contributed to the further articulation of Enlightenment thought, his concept of phenomena in regard to aesthetic judgment marks the first major step toward a postmodern understanding of our world.[127]

Phenomena are the human mind's attempt to perceive objects; they are the representations of objects in the human mind. However, rather than simply acting as a tabula rasa upon which to record sense perceptions, when the mind perceives objects Kant argues that the mind exercises judgment as to the organization and assigning of importance to the various observed properties.[128] Furthermore, Kant distinguishes this judgment as being aesthetic in character in its effort to organize and assign value to knowledge. Kant's takeaway from making this distinction is that the human mind, through its employment of aesthetic judgment, sets the terms for knowledge of reality. Consequently, he asserts that reality conforms to aesthetic judgment and not the other way around (which is the assertion of the correspondence theory of truth).[129]

The major significance in this shift of understanding is that by accepting that knowledge of reality is created in the human mind, there is a privileging of subjective knowledge when attempting to perceive reality.[130] This privileging of subjective knowledge is what defines postmodern thought in general, as well as the social welfare interventions that derive from postmodern thought. With his concept of phenomena as a product of a discursive intellect, Kant opened the door to exploring the role of subjective knowledge in constructing reality. Edmund Husserl and Martin Heidegger would later walk through that door in their development of a new conceptualization of phenomenology based in language[131]— which in turn now serves as the theory of ontology for the Postmodern discourse (which will be discussed later, in this chapter's section describing the postmodern paradigm of understanding).

When examining the quotes made by postmodern practitioners at the beginning of this chapter, one can easily intuit the privileging of subjective knowledge by these practitioners. Thus, when Dennis Saleebey speaks of "the writing of *a better text*," one which promotes depictions of "capacity and ingenuity," he is calling on the social worker to help clients employ aesthetic judgment when attempting to understand their life struggles and identity. Similarly, when Michael White and David Epston speak of the *storying* of lived experiences when ascribing meaning to one's life situation and identity, they too are calling upon the social worker to help clients employ aesthetic judgment in this endeavor. In this manner, similar to the environmentalist movement in the Premodern Discourse, the Postmodern discourse opens anew a doorway once more for the prospect of knowledge of the Beautiful to lead to understanding knowledge of the Good.

Michel Foucault: Power/Knowledge

By accepting Kant's proposition that reality is partly based in language through the application of aesthetic judgment, Michel Foucault was able to offer a new conceptualization of power in which power operates within language, circulating within discourses and acting to privilege some knowledges over others.[132] With the social work helping situation now being conceptualized as an endeavor at helping clients to employ their aesthetic judgment (when organizing their life experiences surrounding their current experience of distress), Foucault's conception of power/knowledge arms the social worker with the means to examine how power acts to shape or warp the client's employment of aesthetic judgment. Foucault emphasizes the productive capacity of power, that by legitimizing particular knowledges it produces "regimes of truth";[133] these regimes of truth then provide the standards upon which one's aesthetic judgment of reality is based. This dynamic is what Foucault is referring to when he describes the operation of power not as being held by some and exercised over others but, rather, as "a machine in which everyone is caught" and which no one owns.[134] When a regime of truth's standards work against the best interests of clients (e.g., depicting them as dysfunctional, abnormal, or deficient in basic skills), they begin to act in an oppressive manner by deflating clients' ability to meet the challenges of their current struggle. Hence, clients' self-worth may be overshadowed by an overidentification with the problem, thus disempowering clients when they seek to promote positive change.

When Michael White and David Epston write about their technique of externalizing the problem (as captured in the quote at the beginning of this chapter), it represents an effort "to personify the problems that they experience as *oppressive*."[135] Consequently, the first step entails confronting the regime of truth's standards acting in this oppressive manner by bringing to bear a critical consciousness. Once the current regime of truth is critically examined in this manner, and thus its legitimacy questioned, the client can begin to construct a new regime of truth whose standards are empowering rather than oppressive. Foucault states that regimes of truth arise from local conditions and particular needs;[136] for example, the various dominant Discourses examined in this book have arisen from local conditions throughout society in response to an overarching urgent need. Thus, when a client seeks to construct a new regime of truth to guide their aesthetic judgment, it will arise from the uniqueness of the client's lived experiences and the particular nature of the client's needs. This dynamic will be examined in greater depth in Chapter 9 when examining the case study of Nick.

But for now, there are two important implications that arise from Foucault's conception of power being applied to the social work helping situation that dramatically differentiate practice within a Postmodern discourse with that of practice within the Modern Discourse. First, the Postmodern discourse conceptualizes the helping situation primarily as a political endeavor at confronting oppression, not merely a technical endeavor at enhancing functioning.[137] Second, the uniqueness of the client and the client's situation is emphasized,[138] rather than the categorization of the client into a population group and the placing of the client's situation into a common diagnostic category.

Paulo Freire: Praxis

Paulo Freire has written extensively on the topic of oppression, most notably in his seminal work *Pedagogy of the Oppressed* (1968). And by focusing upon pedagogy and knowledge generation within oppressive regimes, Freire's examinations resonate strongly with Foucault's notion of power/knowledge and its role in creating oppressive regimes of truth. Using Foucault's understanding of power as a starting point, one can see how Freire seeks to elucidate the means to confront this oppression and, in doing so, liberate oneself from its influence. As is the case for every postmodernist who accepts the Kantian premise that aesthetic judgment plays a role in the construction of reality, Freire first emphasizes how human beings are different *in kind* from animals;[h] as where both animals and human beings act in the world, only human beings employ their aesthetic judgment to transform their world.[139] Or, in other words, animals can only act toward adapting to their environment, whereas human beings can employ their aesthetic judgment to imagine a better world and then act to help make this transformation to a better world possible.

In the *Poetics*, Aristotle introduces the term *praxis*, which involves the marrying of reflection and action. Freire takes up Aristotle's formulation and emphasizes the ethical component to this reflection through his concept of *conscientization*.[140] This is so because the critical insights derived from reflection on oppressive structures *compel* one to act toward transforming said oppressive structures. Once such a critical consciousness is achieved, there is no turning back as one's critical consciousness increasingly begins to organize

---

[h] Recall that this stance is quite different than what occurs in the Modern Discourse. The Modern Discourse only contains a conception of self as existing in nature. As such, while human beings are still considered unique creatures, what is emphasized is that it is a difference in *degree* (i.e., human beings are the most sophisticated form of animal). This is why biology classifies human beings as belonging to the animal kingdom, why psychologists such as Pavlov and Skinner did experiments upon animals and then applied the principles to human beings, and why a biological model such as ecological systems theory—which examines the interdependence of plants and animals in an ecosystem—gets transformed into a sociological theory which is subsequently adopted by the field of social work as its defining model: person-in-environment.

one's thinking.[141] So even though it may take some time to transform societal structures of oppression, simply acting in an attempt to transform these structures sets one on the transformative path to becoming more fully human and empowered.[142] Freire describes this process of employing praxis as a dialogical cultural action,[i] which becomes a cultural revolution once power is taken.[143]

Prior to achieving such a critical consciousness, Freire notes that it is not uncommon for one to adopt a self-disparaging understanding of oneself as one internalizes the oppressive regime of truth setting the standards for one's aesthetic judgment.[144] This is reflected in the social work helping situation when clients become so beaten down by the problem they are struggling with that they internalize an overpathologized view of themselves, which then serves to sap motivation and hope for change. When the educator (or social worker) is confronted with such a situation, Freire states that it is important for the helper to have trust in the ability of the oppressed to achieve the critical consciousness necessary to free themselves of oppression; hence, communicating one's *faith* in their ability to do so becomes an important aspect of this process.[145] This notion is reflected in the solution-focused quote by Steve DeShazer at the beginning of this chapter, wherein he states that asking the miracle question (a therapeutic technique) "demands *faith* in the client's capacity" to engage in critical thought and that the question must "be asked in a manner that *communicates this faith.*"[146]

This sets the stage for the oppressed to begin engaging in a dialogical relationship with the oppressive regime of truth, which up until this point has presented itself in an anti-dialogical manner as the one and only truth.[147] Freire states that entering this dialogical process fosters belief: The oppressed start to believe in themselves—the consideration of new standards for their aesthetic judgment enlightens them to heretofore hidden positive and empowering qualities they possess—and thus they begin down the path of praxis.[148] This journey is aided further by the educator (or social worker) sharing and reinforcing this *belief.*

Furthermore, this growing belief in themselves engenders *hope*, which serves as the fuel for action in the transformative change process of praxis. Freire describes hope as being "based on the need for truth as an ethical quality of the struggle" and that, while hope alone is insufficient, without hope one can never achieve praxis.[149] This importance placed upon hope is reflected in Dennis Saleebey's quote at the beginning of this chapter, when he writes "the central dynamic of the strengths perspective is precisely the rousing of *hope.*"[150] Hence, in summary, Freire clearly lays out how faith, belief, and hope—human

---

[i] This is what serves to differentiate Freire's use of praxis from someone like Marx. By placing praxis within a dialogical relationship, Freire is emphasizing the role of language, thus putting him squarely in the postmodern camp. Marx, by contrast, places praxis within a dialectic of historical materialism, giving it a more modernist, scientific grounding.

qualities that distinguish us as different in *kind* from animals—form the tripartite elements that comprise praxis, and thus, conscientization. Lastly, Freire points out that bearing witness to the struggle, accomplished when others are brought in to the dialogical cultural action, is indispensable to bringing about a cultural revolution.[151] This dynamic of bearing witness will be explored further in Chapter 9 through techniques such as Michael White's use of outsider witnesses in the therapeutic process.

Defining Cultural Feature: The Playful Construction of Multiple Identities

The defining cultural feature of a discourse is another element that typically reveals itself only after the discourse has achieved dominance. Hence, the description of the Postmodern discourse's defining cultural feature requires an educated guess. Once again, building upon the similarities the Postmodern discourse shares with the Premodern Discourse, we can turn back to the Premodern Discourse for some insights and guidance on how the postmodern defining cultural feature will arise. One of the momentous changes that occurred in the Premodern Era was the Industrial Revolution, which dramatically changed social relations and how society was organized. The Industrial Revolution led to urbanization as workers were drawn to factories. As a result of this urbanization, the defining cultural feature of the wicked city stereotype arose.

In the emergent Postmodern Era, there has also been a momentous change leading to a revolution in social relations and how society is organized. Currently, we are experiencing a technological revolution or, more specifically, a digital revolution. Advancements in computer technology have led to revolutionary change in the processing and sharing of information, which has fundamentally changed the nature of social relations (e.g., the emergence of social media) and how society is organized (e.g., enabling the globalization of capital).[152] This revolutionary change in the processing and sharing of information is leading us down the road toward achieving a truly open society.[153] An open society promotes transparency, which relies upon trust over expertise.[154] The implications of this demand for transparency will be explored in more detail at the end of this chapter when discussing the overall theme of the Postmodern discourse.

In regard to trying to hypothesize what defining cultural feature will arise for the Postmodern discourse on social welfare, this societal embrace of transparency is leading toward a reconceptualization of privacy as it is now commonplace in the (online) environment for individuals to readily post photos, videos, thoughts, and opinions about themselves and their daily activities.[155] Consequently, as Mia Consalvo and Susanna Paasonen aptly note, "the Internet allows for multiple identities that are easily shuffled by individuals and . . . for the exploration of different identities."[156] As described previously, this playful curating of these daily activities serves to provide markers of identity within a narrative.[157]

In addition, the construction of these identities is relational in nature, aptly reflected by Gordon Graham's statement, "the story of my life is always embedded in the story of those communities from which I derive my identity"; hence, there is both a historical and a social component.[158] This playful construction of multiple identities, I believe, will arise as the defining cultural feature for the Postmodern discourse on social welfare. As we shall see in Chapter 9, this resonates strongly with the various postmodern approaches to social work practice as they form a common project of confronting negative identity conclusions arising from oppressive standards of aesthetic judgment, leading to the construction of a more empowering identity arising from adopting new standards of aesthetic judgment. Having already experienced this process of embracing and constructing multiple identities in their daily lives, clients will enter the helping situation already equipped with the tools and experience to construct a new identity within the therapeutic context of the helping situation.

Paradigm of Understanding

Of the three fundamental philosophical theories comprising the postmodern paradigm of understanding—phenomenology (theory of ontology), social constructionism (theory of epistemology), and mimesis (theory of causality)—social constructionism has by a large margin received the most press in social work academic journals. However, despite the prominence of social constructionism in the social work literature, I would argue that each of these theories is equally important. Each can be thought of as comprising a leg on a three-legged stool. Working in a mutually reinforcing fashion, each theory both informs and is informed by the other two. Working in this concerted fashion, they lend a deeper understanding to postmodern social work practice.

Theory of Ontology: Hermeneutic Phenomenology

As a philosophical theory, phenomenology has been around since the time of Plato. However, Martin Heidegger's mentor Edmund Husserl would be the first to take up Kant's concept of aesthetic judgment and apply it to phenomenology and, in so doing, provide the first postmodern articulation of phenomenology. The basic premise of phenomenology is that reality is comprised of both properties of existence and an essence. Husserl dubbed prior articulations of phenomenology as the "natural standpoint" due to their assumption that the essence of a phenomenon was hidden within the nature of the object itself.[j] Husserl marks his departure from the natural standpoint by first giving prominence to the temporal quality of existence. For Husserl, what gives an object existence is its persisting presence in time: the fact that when one's current present or "now" becomes past and the following present occurs, one is still able to observe the object.[159] Flowing from this conception of existence, the essence of a phenomenon is the rule operating to organize the empirical properties of the entity as it passes through time and is observed by humans.[160] This places the essence of an object within the human consciousness, thus making it a product of subjective knowledge. By emphasizing that an essence arises from the temporal quality of the phenomenon, he advances the notion that an essence may be unique to a particular entity rather than an ideal form.

Heidegger, in his seminal work *Being and Time* (1927), would fully elaborate this notion when understanding human beings as phenomena. When examining the essence of being human, Heidegger creates the word *Da-sein* to capture this notion of a unique individual revealing oneself temporally, rather than the general term "human" (a categorization based upon normative qualities).[161] Furthermore, Heidegger's analysis argues that the essence of being—and thus the rule for ordering contents (i.e., physical properties and actions) of existence—is located in our use of language and culture, rather than in one's consciousness as Husserl proposed, thus embedding it in a social context.[162]

A few important implications arise from Heidegger's move. In regard to uniqueness, Heidegger asserts that human beings are unique in that we are the only creatures that have foreknowledge of the inevitability of our death.[163] Consequently, we do not simply pass through time, but rather we journey through it; we retain experiences and imagine future possibilities to define our essence and thus being. In short, one understands one's life as being comprised of a beginning, a middle, and an end. That journey grants uniqueness to each individual life. It also sets the stage for understanding one's life (i.e., one's being) in a narrative framework entailing the storying of experiences. Additionally, when considering objects as phenomena, the essence that we infuse on outside objects is time-bound for the duration we interact with the particular phenomenon.

Taking the example of conceiving of a chair as a phenomenon will serve as a simple illustration of how existence and essence combine to form reality. When observing the various chairs (all typically from the same factory) contained within a classroom and then observing the properties of existence of a particular

---

j This "natural standpoint" view is what informs philosophical essentialism. By contrast, Husserl's and Heidegger's placing of essence in the subject's mind marks a dramatic departure from the natural standpoint view and undercuts the premise of essentialism.

chair, one will conclude that its properties are relatively the same as any other chair in the classroom. Next, take the scenario where students leave the classroom during a break. Now imagine that one student, let's call her Susan, comes back to the classroom and finds that one of her classmates, let's call her Heidi, is sitting in the chair in which Susan was previously sitting. What might be Susan's reaction upon seeing Heidi? If Susan truly viewed the world through the Modern Discourse's scientific understanding of reality as being comprised solely of properties of existence, then Susan would easily observe that the other chairs in the room are exactly the same as the one she was previously sitting in, and thus she would simply sit in an unoccupied chair. However, if Susan views the world phenomenologically, her response would be to tell Heidi, "Hey, you're sitting in *my* chair!" While the properties of existence of that particular chair are the same as all of the others, the essence of the chair is unique in that it is understood by Susan to be "*my* chair." Thus, one way to conceive of essence is that it equates with identity (e.g., *my* chair). In addition, this scenario illustrates the time-bound nature of this reality. When class is dismissed, the chair loses its designation as Susan's chair; once other students enter the classroom for the next class, the chair takes on a new essence stemming from a new student laying claim to it.

Social work practice informed by a phenomenological understanding of reality marks a dramatic departure from practice informed by a scientific understanding of reality. Within the Modern Discourse's understanding of reality as being solely comprised of properties of existence, interventions are aimed at manipulating these properties of existence (i.e., biological, psychological, and social functioning) in order to produce the desired change. Whereas within the Postmodern discourse's phenomenological understanding of reality as comprised of both existence and essence, interventions target the *essence* (i.e., identity) of the client in an effort to liberate the client from oppressive narratives. Client problems in functioning only gain their relevance through this liberating process—oftentimes conceived as impediments to one's transformation, and thus they are overcome as the means for the client to claim a more empowered identity.

We can see this targeting of the client's essence implied in three of the quotes found at the beginning of this chapter. First, Steve DeShazer in describing the solution-focused approach states, "the therapist assumes that clients have the capacity to create meaningful descriptions of what they want their lives to look like."[164] Second, Dennis Saleebey in describing the strengths perspective states, "adding to the picture already painted, brush strokes that depict capacity and ingenuity, and that provide a different coloration to the substance of one's life."[165] And third, Michael White and David Epston in describing narrative therapy state, "those relatively fixed qualities that we attributed to persons and to relationships, are rendered less fixed and less restricting."[166]

Theory of Epistemology: Social Constructionism

Theories of epistemology seek to address the question, "How do I know that my knowledge of reality (ontological knowledge) is in fact accurate?" Continuing with the previous scenario of viewing a chair phenomenologically, the question becomes, "How does Susan know that her knowledge of the chair's essence as *her* chair is in fact accurate?" She seeks confirmation through her social context. The organizing principle of the chair's essence that Susan employs in claiming the chair as hers runs along the lines of the cultural understanding of "first come, first served." This understanding is a social custom commonly understood and accepted in today's society. Heidi has put into question the accuracy of applying this social custom to the present situation by advancing one of her own, perhaps along the lines of "shuffle your feet, lose your seat." Susan's (or Heidi's) truth claim of the chair being hers (for the present context) will get reinforced only if it makes sense to the other individuals in the classroom; this agreement does not necessarily require verbal confirmation by other students but, rather, is tacitly communicated by their reactions to the social interchange between Susan and Heidi. Hence, it is the application of a cultural custom as the organizing principle for the chair's essence that gives the construction of this reality its social character; in other words, the reality of the chair is socially constructed. In addition, agreement by others to the correctness of applying this cultural custom to the present situation serves the epistemological function of confirming the accuracy of Susan's (or Heidi's) ontological knowledge of the chair for the present situation.

Through the further articulation of the chair example, we can now begin to see how phenomenology informs social constructionism: What is being constructed is the essence of a phenomenon. Physical properties of existence are not socially constructed; rather, the organizing principle for understanding these properties of existence is what is constructed. Furthermore, we can begin to see how social constructionism informs phenomenology: Through social construction, multiple essences (i.e., multiple realities) can exist for the same object when it makes its presence known in different situations. This may involve applying the same social customs to different situations, such as when successive classes enter the classroom. In each successive situation, the chair takes on the identity of a different student. And it may involve applying different social customs to a different situation. Let's now place the chair in the airport. While waiting for your plane at the gate, you sit in the chair. Then imagine the scenario that you get up and leave for about fifteen minutes as you visit the restroom and get something to eat. When you return, someone else is sitting in the chair that you were sitting in previously. Laying claim to the chair as *my* chair typically is not supported in such a situation. Rather, by the chair being placed in a public area where there may be limited seating capacity and which experiences heavy foot traffic, the social custom akin to "shuffle your feet, lose your seat" commonly applies. In each of these scenarios, it is the time-bound nature of phenomena that allows for multiple realities.

Additionally, by applying a different theory of ontology, one can easily see how it will misinform and pervert the understanding of social constructionism. By way of example, in Chapter 7, I described Allen Rubin and Earl Babbie's attempt to explain social constructionism in their textbook *Research Methods for Social Work* (1997). To illustrate the notion of multiple realities being constructed, they provide various illustrations of a book from different vantage points.[167] By positioning themselves within the correspondence theory of truth wherein objects are solely comprised of properties of existence, the only way to conceive of multiple realities for the same object is through observations of its properties from different points of view. However, different than the case for phenomenology, the subjective knowledge of the book in terms of one's point of view represents incomplete knowledge—as it only partially captures the underlying properties of the object that comprise its true (i.e., complete) reality. By positioning oneself ontologically in this manner, one naturally assigns subjective knowledge a lesser status. Consequently, I would argue that much of the dismissiveness and many of the criticisms of social constructionism by hard-hat scientists in our profession stem from this misinformed view that arises when ontologically positioning oneself within the correspondence theory of truth.

The concept of multiple possible constructions of one's essence (and thus being) undergirds much of postmodern social work practice. As Paulo Freire notes in his elaboration of praxis, an oppressive regime of truth presents itself as anti-dialogical. Accepting the idea of multiple realities of existence is the key to effectively questioning the oppressive regime of truth as the one and only truth; viewing it as simply one of a possible number of regimes of truth represents the beginning stage of praxis. Furthermore, when creating an alternative, more empowering construction of one's being, belief in this alternate construction by others who play an important role in one's life serves to strengthen its truth claim—which in turn fosters hope.

Theory of Causality: Mimesis

The theory of causality plays a particularly prominent role in a discourse on social welfare as causality speaks to how change occurs, and transformative change for the client is the goal of the helping relationship. For the Postmodern discourse, Aristotle's theory of mimesis—which he articulates in the *Poetics*—serves as the theory of causality guiding postmodern social work interventions.

Aristotle's formulation of *mimesis* stands in stark contrast to Sir Isaac Newton's third law of rational mechanics: action/reaction. When formulating his theory, Newton was attempting to articulate a theory that would apply to all objects in the universe, with human beings as simply one of many such objects that adhere to action/reaction. By placing human beings within the category of "all objects in the universe," objective knowledge gets privileged when attempting to describe human behavior in any of the social or natural sciences. This scientific attempt to understand human behavior carries with it a major, inherent flaw: It is unable to account for free will. As Immanuel Kant poignantly points out in his *Groundwork of the Metaphysics of Morals* (1785), the very definition of free will entails that it is not subject to the laws of action/reaction.[168] Hence, while social workers attempt to facilitate and inspire change in the client, within the Modern Discourse, these social workers have no scientific theory of change that speaks to engaging the client's free will to take action—despite the fact that clients exercising their free will is an essential component to producing change. Rather, social workers operating within the Modern Discourse attempt to engage the client's free will through application of the value of self-determination.

By contrast, Aristotle had far less grand ambitions when formulating his theory of causality as mimesis. He restricted himself to simply attempting to explain human behavior. In viewing human beings as subjects who comprise their own unique category, Aristotle's theory of mimesis privileges subjective knowledge. In brief, Aristotle's concept of mimesis can be summed up in the following manner. Each of us has both an image of "who I am" and an image of "who I would like to be": The image of "who I would like to be" is what motivates our present actions. Two extremely important implications arise from Aristotle's formulation. First, by placing the process of causality within subjective knowledge, Aristotle's theory is able to account for the operation of free will—in fact, his theory is built upon it. This puts it in line with Martin Heidegger's definition of freedom—which posits freedom as "the ground of the possibility of existence."[169] Second, as present actions arise from the image of "who I would like to be," attempts to harness the insights of causality in producing change are future-focused. These implications are in stark contrast to social work practice within the Modern Discourse as its theory of causality fails to capture the operation of free will. And with causality understood as action/reaction, the *reaction* represents the present, while the *actions* lie in the past; hence, attempts to harness the insights of causality in producing change are focused in the past. These implications stemming from mimesis (future focus and personal agency), when added to the one discussed above in phenomenology—that the client's essence becomes the primary target for change rather than the client's properties of existence—make social work practices informed by the Postmodern discourse starkly different than those from the Modern Discourse.

There is one important caveat to Aristotle's formulation of mimesis: One must have hope that the "image of who I would like to be" is attainable; otherwise, one will not act upon it. Now we are ready to examine how phenomenology and social constructionism inform mimesis. Heidegger's concept of *Da-sein* provides a rich formulation of what "the image of who I am" encompasses, whereas the image of "who I want to be" reflects Da-sein's process of becoming. Social constructionism provides instruction on how hope in attaining the "image of who I want to be" is fostered: through the positive verification by others that one's empowering social construction of Da-sein is accurate. In more common parlance, when others who are important to you and respected by you communicate their affirmation in terms of "yes, I see you that way too" (e.g., "yes, I recognize that you possess the qualities of a good mother, and hence if you act upon those qualities and improve your skills, you can get your children back"), your empowering construction of Da-sein is strengthened, achieving greater verisimilitude. This process of having one's social construction of Da-sein affirmed by significant others lends deeper understanding to Freire's conceptualization of the role and importance of bearing witness to one's struggle to become more fully human. In Chapter 9, we will explore more fully how this plays out in the social work helping situation.

In his seminal work *Time and Narrative* (1984, 1985, 1988), Paul Ricœur takes up Aristotle's concept of mimesis and gives it a deeper and richer elaboration by dividing mimesis into three parts: *prefiguration, configuration,* and *refiguration.* Ricœur's framework matches up nicely with Freire's elaboration of praxis. *Prefiguration* represents a state of consciousness in which one has internalized the social construction guiding one's action to the extent that action takes place without the need for much reflection.[170] Building upon the previous example of phenomenologically interacting with a chair, students will typically return from break and sit in the chair that they were sitting in previously. For the vast majority of social interactions, operating in a *prefigurative* state works extremely well, as reflecting upon every single action one takes during the day would be overly burdensome and time-consuming. The social construction serves as an organizing principle for ordering one's understanding of one's actions into a narrative, which in turn speaks to the construction of one's essence. However, as Freire points out, operating in this *prefigurative* state works to the detriment of the individual when the internalized social construction acts in an oppressive manner to disempower the individual by getting them to accept negative identity conclusions.[171]

In such cases, it is both important and useful to reflect upon such social constructions and confront them. This is what occurs during configuration. *Configuration* is a state of consciousness wherein one is actively attempting to create a new social construction to replace the social construction that one had been operating under previously.[172] The metaphor of an author is often used to describe the individual engaged in this process: In creating a new social construction to organize one's actions, a new narrative is created, which in turn leads to a new, more empowering identity conclusion. Freire emphasizes the importance of having faith in the individual's ability to enter this configurative state.[173]

During this process of forming a new social construction to guide one's actions, one will periodically switch between a configurative state and a refigurative state of consciousness. *Refiguration* represents the state of consciousness wherein one adopts the position of audience member to the recently crafted narrative and evaluates its verisimilitude.[174] This begins the process of positive verification that occurs when presenting a social construction. Thus, Freire points out that it is essential that one believes in oneself;[175] this belief arises when one's new social construction makes sense to oneself and thus achieves a level of verisimilitude. This dynamic is echoed in Dennis Saleebey's comment at the beginning of the chapter that the narrative created through this reframing process must *ring true* for the client.

Next, as "author" one begins to present one's narrative to other important individuals in one's life wherein they act as audience members. Their belief in the verisimilitude of this new social construction serves to further strengthen its reality. In addition, their reactions to the narrative provide feedback to the "author," allowing one to refine the narrative so as to make it stronger. This providing of feedback is the role adopted by the social worker in the helping situation, and the metaphor of "editor" is used to describe it. Beginning with one believing in oneself, hope is kindled. The more that significant people in one's life affirm this newly configured narrative, the stronger this hope becomes. This final step is where praxis is achieved as one then begins to base one's actions on this newly configured narrative which has achieved a strong level of verisimilitude in one's eyes. Ultimately, this new social construction is internalized, and one falls back into a *prefigurative* state,[176] wherein one's empowered actions become second nature and no longer require a heightened level of reflection.

In Ricœur's elaboration of mimesis, he makes a distinction between clock time and human time. Clock time is how we typically conceive of time: as the progression of discrete measurable units such as seconds, minutes, and hours.[177] Clock time is what we employ when reflecting upon changes to properties of existence, such as when I bake lasagna in the oven for forty-five minutes. Thus, clock time matches up with the theory of causality as action/reaction. However, Ricœur argues that mimesis relies upon human time, that we employ human time when reflecting upon changes to the essence of a phenomenon; human time refers to the expansion or contraction of time within a narrative structure.[178] For example, if someone were to ask me how my day went, I would not respond utilizing clock time—that is, by providing a second-by-second account of what happened during my day. Rather, I would selectively choose events that capture the essence of my day in terms of its quality. Similarly, if I happened to be in a harrowing accident, the essence of "harrowing accident" might cause me to report in exacting detail all that happened during the accident such that I take twenty minutes to describe an event that occurred over a span of one minute in clock time.

Ricœur's conception of human time serves to further inform phenomenology and social constructionism. Concerning phenomenology, we simply need to look at the titles of the seminal works of Martin Heidegger—*Being and Time*—and Ricœur—*Time and Narrative*—to see how Ricœur's formulation of mimesis serves as a continuation of the phenomenological project begun by Heidegger. Placing these titles (which capture the key insight of each work) into an equation yields us Being = Time = Narrative; thus, when *Time* represents human time, this yields us the concept of narrative identity: A phenomenon's process of becoming occurs within a narrative framework.

Earlier, it was stated that the essence of a phenomenon serves as the organizing principle in which to view/understand a phenomenon's properties of existence. Additionally, it was later stated that this organizing principle arises as a social construction. As this social construction organizes actions (i.e., the progression of these properties of existence occurring in the "persisting presence" of time), it places these actions into a narrative. Hence the essence (i.e., identity) of a phenomenon lies within this narrative framework. In a mutually reinforcing fashion, the essence organizes actions into a narrative, while the addition of events (i.e., actions) to the narrative serves to strengthen and shape the essence.

This is the dynamic employed by postmodern practitioners when adopting the role of "editor" in the helping relationship. The social worker appeals to the client's use of aesthetic judgment by encouraging the client to consider adding actions to the client's narrative of the presenting problem—actions that depict *capacity and ingenuity*—which in turn give a new shape to the client's essence in relation to the problem. Consequently, hope is kindled, and the client is empowered to act based upon this more capable image of "who I am" and its proximity to "who I would like to be." This in turn diminishes the significance of the problem and leads to positive changes in the client's properties of existence (i.e., functioning). In Chapter 9, the therapeutic techniques of the miracle question and externalizing the problem will be examined as the means to more fully illustrate this dynamic.

Conceptions of the Self

Within the Postmodern discourse, individuals return once again to viewing themselves as possessing a bifurcated sense of self: partly existing in the natural world and partly existing in a social world. The distinction between the two falls right in line with the understanding of being promoted by phenomenology. Within the natural world—which emphasizes how human beings' relation to animals is that of a difference in degree—resides an individual's properties of existence (e.g., biological, psychological, and social functioning). In this manner, it remains unchanged from the view within the Modern Discourse of how human beings exist in the natural world. However, now within the Postmodern discourse, this view of a difference in degree merely represents the first half of the phenomenological understanding of being as comprised of an existence plus an essence.

The essence of one's being is understood to reside in a social world. Jerome Bruner is a major proponent of this view, and his work has contributed much to the articulation of this viewpoint.[179] John Potter succinctly sums it up as follows: "in storying the self we are simultaneously making the self."[180] This aspect of the self is relational in nature, as one's essence is socially constructed. Hence, this aspect captures the notion of how human beings are different in kind from animals. Qualities such as free will and imagination—the ability to imagine a different world and a different state of being—are given prominence. As a result of this prominence, qualities such as faith, belief, and hope (the tripartite elements that comprise praxis) are turned to when attempting to explain, and motivate, human behavior. This idea of a relational self operating in a social world marks a dramatic shift in how social work interventions are conceived. The client's essence becomes the focus of change; engaging the client's free will and imagination leads to a more empowering and liberating experience for the client. Change in the client's essence prompts changes in the client's functioning (i.e., properties of existence), particularly the problematic area of functioning that prompted the client to engage social work services, as they are now seen by the client as barriers to their process of authentically becoming.

Rules of Right

Rules of right are broad organizing principles for knowledge generation that are widely embraced due to their ability to effectively attend to the urgent need of the dominant Discourse that they serve. Consequently, the "educated" part of guessing the rules of right for the Postmodern discourse builds upon the information used to prognosticate the urgent need. I have proposed that the urgent need for the Postmodern discourse is that of *attending to the social cohesion of society*. With our newly acquired understanding of phenomenological essence, we can further refine this conceptualization of the urgent need to that of *attending to the social cohesion of society (among various unique individual essences)*. Working under the assumption that this is in fact the soon-to-be urgent need, likely rules of right are as follows.

Promoting Unity Within Diversity

The forming of a social construction involves a process of mutual consensus: As more people embrace the particular social construction, the stronger its verisimilitude becomes. Hence, the forming of a social construction itself represents an act of unity. However, at the same time, there is a level of recognition in this act that it represents only one out of a number of possible social constructions that serve to capture the reality of one's particular situation; or, in other words, there exist a diversity of social constructions to fit each particular situation.

Consequently, achieving unity across a diverse set of social constructions represents the next layer to achieving unity, which in turn promotes social cohesion. This next layer of unity is sought through appeals to commonly held values. For example, one such value—respect for difference—promotes unity by allowing one to fully embrace a social construction that facilitates one's process of becoming within a commonly occurring situation (e.g., parenting), while at the same time accepting that a different social construction may be more fitting for another's process of becoming within this same commonly occurring situation (e.g., parenting). Thus, inquiry into what type of social construction is most fitting for another's process of becoming—which is the role wherein social workers are placed within the postmodern helping situation—requires a genuine curiosity in the Socratic sense, to discover and learn. Hence, rather than adopting a stance that one's expertise in human functioning positions one to advance/impose a social construction to fit another's process of becoming, the social worker embraces a genuine curiosity to learn by *adopting the posture of not knowing*—as is reflected in the quote by Peter DeJong and Insoo Kim Berg at the beginning of this chapter.[181]

It is for this reason that postmodern practitioners describe their approach as value-based practice. It is to distinguish it from evidence-based practice, which is an attempt to find and implement reliable methods for facilitating change in client functioning that apply to all individuals finding themselves within a commonly defined situation. As can be readily surmised, evidence-based practice is not positioned to attend to the urgent need of attending to the social cohesiveness of society (among unique individual essences); this is because evidence-based practice does not attend to a client's process of becoming and, in fact, may even act in a counterproductive manner. Unity (in the form of mutual consensus) within evidence-based practice arises through logical argumentation based upon empirical observations that human properties of existence act and react in a certain way—for all or most individuals finding themselves in a commonly defined situation. Therefore, evidence-based practice seeks a single common understanding for the functioning of human properties of existence in various situations. The mutual consensus, or unity, achieved by evidence-based practice thus offers aid to efforts of social engineering, while offering little or nothing toward promoting social cohesion. In fact, there is the distinct possibility that evidence-based practice may at times even act in a counterproductive manner toward promoting social cohesion; this occurs when the normative social construction begins to act in an oppressive manner within a particular client's situation by imposing a pathology-oriented focus to the client's process of becoming. This dynamic is further elaborated upon below.

Confronting Oppression

Social constructions rely upon mutual consensus. In forming a social construction, when the focus is upon a particular individual's process of becoming, the individual in question (i.e., Da-sein) acts as the ultimate arbiter around which consensus is built. That is because no one can speak more authoritatively than myself on "who I would like to be." Hence, the embrace of various social work values during the process of forming this social construction—values such as respect for diversity, self-determination, and respecting the dignity and worth of the individual—serves to empower the individual in their role as ultimate arbiter. As was illustrated with the #MeToo movement, this process of consensus building mirrors that of participatory democracy as the individual contributes input as "author" while others provide input as "audience member/editor." And it is for this reason that social cohesion is advanced.

Social scientific inquiry into human properties of existence (biological, psychological, and social functioning) also relies upon establishing a mutual consensus. The mutual consensus of scientific inquiry, however, is not the result of a political endeavor at participatory democracy. Rather, it arises from a form of argumentation which seeks to establish reliable and valid proof that the properties of existence in question act and react in a certain manner. Evidence acts as the ultimate arbiter around which consensus is built. Now if we are located in the Modern Discourse which views reality as only consisting of properties of existence, then reality has been fully captured, and nothing more needs to be investigated.

Yet the Postmodern discourse entails a phenomenological understanding of reality: Properties of existence are linked to the essence of a phenomenon. Consequently, it is recognized that comments upon properties of existence give birth to social constructions about the essence. Thus, when we locate ourselves within the Postmodern discourse as social workers, we begin to consider how scientific understanding of normative functioning contributes toward the forming of a normative social construction. By employing Immanuel Kant's concept of *organisms as purposes* in the above scientific understanding, clients privilege this scientific understanding when organizing their lived experiences, thus forming a normative social construction which yields negative identity conclusions depicting them as weak, abnormal, and/or dysfunctional. This aligns with the quote from Michael White and David Epston at the beginning of the chapter, wherein they state that clients often experience their problem as *oppressive*. In such situations, the goal of the social worker is to initiate and support client movement toward achieving praxis. As described earlier, the first step in moving toward praxis entails confronting the oppressive social construction that has been internalized. A more thorough illustration of this process will be undertaken in Chapter 9 when examining the case study of Nick.

This postmodern approach to understanding leads to a much different conceptualization of the helping relationship and the implications that it has on client identity. As stated earlier, the very act of a client seeking social work services within the Modern Discourse's conception of the helping relationship as an effort to enhance functioning signifies that the client is not functioning properly, and thus is a failure in this regard. Only when they complete treatment will they be deemed "normal" and thus no longer in the need of services. Conversely, within the Postmodern discourse's conception of social work as a political activity aimed at confronting oppression, the seeking of services marks the very first step in that fight, and thus positions the client as one who possesses courage. Thus, from the start, positive identity features of the client are emphasized.

As can be seen in Freire's work, this process plays out similarly when the client is facing oppressive structures in society. The first step remains the same: to confront any internalized oppressive social constructions that were spawned by the oppressive structure. Once praxis is achieved, the client is liberated from the influence of the oppressive social constructions. Additionally, even though the client may continue to experience material forms of oppression from these structures, once liberated, the client is no longer subject to negative internalizations. This is a key point, for enacting change by achieving the dismantling of these oppressive societal structures may take a good deal of time. But commitment to the struggle to confront and end oppression leads to a situation wherein one's authentic process of becoming (i.e., one's essence) is no longer influenced by the material problems arising from the oppression.

Theme of discourse: The Open Society

As stated previously, the digital revolution ushered in by the internet has created a structural grid that has greatly enhanced the ability and ease of disseminating information. In addition, with the advent of social media, cultural mores have shifted concerning the free sharing of personal information. These two developments have served to fuel greater demands and expectations by everyday individuals for transparency from sources of authority: a process reflective of an open society. First articulated by Henri Bergson in *The Two Sources of Religion and Morality* (1932), the articulation of an open society originally served as a point of contrast to the extreme form of totalitarianism modeled by the Soviet Union. At its core, an open society acts as a safeguard against totalitarian impulses by those in authority. The concept was then further developed by Karl Popper in his two-volume work *The Open Society and Its Enemies* (1945). With Popper being grounded in critical realism, he provided the concept of an open society with an epistemological foundation (the critical realist's stance of imperfect understanding inherent to the human condition), thus expanding it from its purely political roots to encompass more broadly the idea that an open society serves as a safeguard against all universalist ideologies that would lay claim to being the sole possessor and arbiter of ultimate truth.[182] Thus, an open society in Popper's formulation acts as a safeguard to deter authoritarian impulses not only from governments but also from all sources of authority, such as professions or the scientific community.[183]

And it is with the latter two of these sources of authority—in the form of expertise—where postmodern social work scholars and practitioners seek to employ critical thought to "open up" the process of knowledge generation and truth claims in the helping process to greater participation by clients. In residing in the ontological position of phenomenology, these postmodern scholars and practitioners do not dispute the claim made by modernist scholars and practitioners that expertise is needed to advance truth claims concerning properties of existence (e.g., diagnosis of symptomology); however, the postmodern scholars' and practitioners' critical stance allows them to recognize that truth claims are comprised not only of properties of existence but also of the essence being granted to the phenomenon. Thus, there is a situation that arises wherein modernist scholars and practitioners of social welfare believe that they are embracing the spirit of the open society in regard to knowledge generation as truth claims are open to debate among the community of scholars and practitioners possessing the requisite expertise to enter the debate. When change is believed to occur through the manipulation of properties of existence, the expertise of social engineering is seen as the appropriate route to achieve this change. However, postmodern scholars and practitioners of social welfare seek change through the alteration of the essence of the phenomenon. As such, clients not only are eminently positioned to enter a debate concerning identity truth claims of their life experiences but, in fact, possess the premier position in directing such a debate.

If we look over the previous dominant Discourses, we can trace the trajectory of the intellectual thought informing them. Starting with the Colonial Discourse, we are able to observe the dominance of religious thought. One dynamic at play during the dominant era of religious thought in America (and Europe, from which most American settlers came) was the fact that even though most individuals embraced Christianity, there existed a multitude of various denominations, each of which claimed to be the ultimate arbiter of truth. This dynamic was not problematic for the Colonial Era, wherein a community was its own island and members typically belonged to a single congregation. However, this dynamic became problematic once the country began to rapidly integrate.

In Europe, where communities were already fairly integrated, this dynamic became highly problematic. European scholars witnessed the vast destruction that occurred from numerous religious wars and the clashing of ideologies. In response to this chaos, there arose an intellectual movement commonly known as Enlightenment thought. And the subsequent eras that embraced Enlightenment thought are often referred to as the "age of reason." At its heart, Enlightenment thought represented a quest for certainty, something that was lacking during the clash of religious ideologies that occurred previously. Rather than simply accepting on faith the word of religious scholars as to what comprised the truth, Enlightenment scholars viewed individuals as creatures of reason. We each possessed the ability to apply reason in navigating our natural, social, and moral worlds. And these scholars believed that through the pure application of reason, certainty of knowledge of the True could be attained. Interestingly, Immanuel Kant played a central role in advancing not only Enlightenment thought but also the postmodern thought that has followed. Tracing the arc of his contributions can give us a better understanding of how the concept of an open society has gained particular significance in the emergent Postmodern Era.

A Brief Digression into Kant, Evidence-Based Practice, and Value-Based Practice

Within the Premodern Discourse, social welfare agents embraced Kant's formulation of the categorical imperative, which provided them with a level of moral certitude to guide their actions. The knowledge generated from this moral certitude shaped the nature and design of social welfare interventions from the moral uplift and Bible tract efforts at the beginning of the era to the settlement house movement, charity organization societies, and city missions at the end of the era. This moral certitude helped address the urgent need of moral integration in a society that was rapidly integrating at all other levels.

Porter Lee's "Social Work as Cause and Function" speech in 1929 served to mark the transition that had taken place away from the Premodern Discourse and into the Modern Discourse. Rather than seeking the moral certitude necessary to take up and advance a cause, social workers now turned their focus upon a newly emergent urgent need: maintaining and enhancing the functioning of individuals and society. In doing so, they embraced Kant's concept of organisms as purposes, which provides a level of scientific certitude regarding the functioning of individuals and society. The knowledge generated from this scientific certitude is what has shaped the nature and design of social welfare interventions for this era: from the adoption of the medical model to the application of person-in-environment to the recent embrace of evidence-based practice.

Certitude, whether moral or scientific, arises from expertise. Hence, social welfare agents from these two eras positioned themselves as experts in the helping relationship—thus placing themselves in the role of directing the debate concerning the nature and design of social welfare interventions. This mirrors a broader trend in society which has occurred during the Modern Era in which the professional—by virtue of expertise and sanctioned autonomy in setting the standards for one's craft—assumes the right to define what success and failure look like, as well as the ability to assert power in defining the client's needs.[184] This results in the notion that knowledge of the True (reachable by the expert) is a necessary prerequisite for obtaining knowledge of the Good.

By contrast, social workers operating within the Postmodern discourse have embraced Kant's formulation of aesthetic judgment. This marks a distinct move away from the stance that one's expertise provides one with a level of certitude as to what correct functioning looks like and, by extension, what ought to be done to efficiently socially engineer an enhancement of client functioning. By accepting the stance that multiple socially constructed realities are possible, postmodern practitioners and scholars view the application of Kant's formulation of aesthetic judgment as the key determinant in achieving knowledge of the Good. This is due to their keen awareness of the limitations of professional expertise and knowledge in obtaining certitude, and hence the importance placed upon employing cultural humility as the key driver in generating knowledge concerning the nature and shape of the social welfare intervention.

Thus, by way of contrast to the age of reason that preceded it, the emergent Postmodern Era can be described as the "age of fallibility."[185] Hence, rather than employing the instrumental rationality of the social engineer as to what should be done to enhance client functioning, postmodern practitioners' employment

of cultural humility represents a form of procedural ethics wherein one stead-
fastly maintains an awareness of the fallibility of one's instrumental rationality
to determine proper ends, leading one instead to emphasize the consensual nature in constructing authentic ends with the client. Adopting the premise of "do
no harm" when it comes to knowledge generation, cultural humility follows a
procedural ethic seeking to ensure that one's power of expertise does not unduly
influence the generation of knowledge comprising the nature and design of the
social welfare intervention. This holding in check of one's power of expertise to
define the helping situation is what is captured by adopting a *not-knowing* stance,
as described in the Peter De Jong and Insoo Kim Berg quote at the beginning of
this chapter and is reflective of the penetrating curiosity modeled in the early
dialogues by Socrates—famous for his quote on wisdom, "I know that I do not
know." This not-knowing stance advocated by postmodern practitioners is dependent upon maintaining a state of genuine curiosity.

In addition, the procedural ethics required to employ cultural humility is
the reason postmodern social work scholars and practitioners define their approach as being value-based practice. This definition is not meant to imply that
modernist social work practitioners employing evidence-based practice are
somehow lacking or weak in their application of social work values. Nor is it
meant to imply that postmodern practitioners employing value-based practice
are somehow lacking or weak in their application of the instrumental rationality
of science. The distinction between the two approaches is more subtle yet still
profound: It centers on the difference in how knowledge of the planned intervention is generated and then carried out.

Within the Modern Discourse, social workers developed a strong value base
in the form of a professional code of ethics. And it can be arguably stated that,
when compared to most other professions, social work grants the highest prominence to its code of ethics in directing professional behavior when helping the
client. Yet, it is the instrumental rationality of science in the form of evidence
that directs the knowledge generation of what shape the social welfare intervention should take, not this strong professional ethic. Rather, once this intervention is formed, the code of ethics establishes the parameters within which the
social work intervention takes place. Thus, for example, the social worker will
employ the conceptual model of person-in-environment to diagnose possible
causes of dysfunction and strengths of resistance and then use that information
to develop an intervention plan with the client. This places the social worker in
the role of professional expert primarily responsible for engineering possible
solutions, while placing the client in the role of sovereign consumer selecting
from said options. After these options are generated, the social worker applies
values such as self-determination to respect the needs and wants of the clients so
that if they dislike a particular option, then that wish is respected and another is

offered (which also was generated through employing the instrumental rationality of science).

Conversely, postmodern scholars and practitioners in adopting the *not-knowing* stance of cultural humility adopt the premise not only that one's employment of knowledge of the Beautiful (in terms of aesthetic judgment) can lead one to knowledge of the Good but that the client is best positioned to grasp this in the helping relationship. This stance demands that the social worker have *faith* in the client's ability to employ their aesthetic judgment regarding knowledge of the Beautiful to grasp and articulate the knowledge of the Good for the particular social matrix comprising their life experiences. The authenticity of the client's particular knowledge of the good then gets affirmed (i.e., refigured) by their family, friends, and the social worker. This newly socially constructed knowledge of the client's particular good, in an empowering fashion, gives new meaning to the client's previous actions; consequently, it then provides direction to their future actions—which take the form of a plan for the social welfare intervention.

By emphasizing a procedural ethics, the social worker turns to the application of values to generate knowledge of the shape and design of the treatment plan, hence adopting a value-based practice. This is complemented by the use of the instrumental rationality of science to form the parameters within which the planned intervention should take place. Thus, when contrasted to evidence-based practice, in value-based practice the roles played by the instrumental rationality of science and the application of values become reversed, with values generating the knowledge of the intervention plan and instrumental rationality guiding its implementation.

The Current Evolution of the Open Society

Sociologists have recognized as a social fact that in recent decades there has been a rise in the expectation and demand for transparency from centers of authority.[186] Transparency is particularly important in the establishment of trust between strangers in a contractual relationship.[187] The act of transparency—in following a procedural ethics—operates heavily upon trust rather than expertise.[188] This dynamic is reflected in the postmodern helping relationship wherein the social construction of knowledge of the Good arises from the established trust within the processes of configuration and refiguration. Many elements comprising the open society are mirrored in the postmodern helping relationship, thus its selection as the probable theme for the Postmodern discourse.

By contrast, many elements of the Modern Discourse in their attempts to address present societal conditions effectively work toward undermining or subverting the spirit and meaning of the open society. The importance placed upon privileged, expert knowledge when designing the social welfare intervention serves to close off debate from the non-expert clients, limiting their participation to that of a sovereign consumer.[189] True to the medical model, clients are seen as possessing the intimate knowledge of their symptomology and strengths, which when shared is used by the professional social worker to diagnose the problematic areas of functioning and to design appropriate remedies.

This type of exchange of knowledge does not comprise the framework of an open debate leading to cooperative decision-making among equals. Rather, cooperative decision-making takes the form of clients as sovereign consumers making their needs and wants known and then the professional social worker producing various intervention plans from which the clients are free to choose. The very premise of evidence-based practice is that the debate which generates appropriate interventions has already taken place (among experts); these finished products—which are stamped with the approval that they are "scientifically" proven—are then offered to clients as selections from which to choose and perhaps tweaked or tailored to fit their particular situation.[190] This reliance on the cognitive authority of experts works in direct opposition to promoting the spirit of an open society within the helping relationship.[191]

Early in the Modern Era when Henri Bergson first articulated the notion of the open society, it stood in direct contrasted to the closed society operating within the Soviet Union. Communism under Soviet rule placed priority on the common interests of society high above that of individual freedom and rights, whereas the liberal democracies of the West adopted a more equal balance in the form of the welfare state. In the 1980s, the fall of the Soviet Union resulted in the discrediting of the communist model as a viable alternative ideology for the structure of a political economy. However, this victory of liberal democracy did not automatically result in the triumph of the open society.[192] This is because during this same time period the rise of globalization occurred. As stated previously, the Modern Discourse's response to the era of globalization has resulted in radically situating individualism within America's liberal democracy in the form of market fundamentalism and neoliberalism. This radicalization of individualism has disrupted the previous existing balance achieved between that of the common interests of society and that of individual freedom and rights and has placed a much higher priority upon promoting individual freedom and rights as the means to promote the common interest.[193]

Thus, rather than the stark contrast to and rejection of the open society that communism offered, radical individualism serves to distort it by subverting the spirit and meaning of the open society by undermining the promotion of common interests through the process of cooperative decision-making.[194] Market fundamentalism and neoliberalism elevate unbridled self-interest through emphasizing competition and profit motive at the expense of the cooperative decision-making representative of the open society.[195] The common good is seen as naturally arising from the numerous individual decisions advancing one's self-interest that take place within the marketplace and democratic governance. Hence, there is no need to engage in cooperative decision-making; rather, those in authority simply need to provide a selection of finished products from which the individual has the freedom to choose. And by the Modern Discourse embracing the stance that knowledge of the True is a necessary perquisite step for obtaining knowledge of the Good, it is the expert who is positioned to utilize the knowledge of the True to craft these finished products embodying knowledge of the Good. This is the distortion taking place to the value of cooperative decision-making that forms the basis of the open society: The generation of knowledge arising from open debate is restricted solely to the expert (as is the case with the development of evidence-based interventions), whereas the client's contribution to the decision-making process is relegated to that of the sovereign consumer.

Notes

1. De Jong and Kim Berg, *Interviewing for Solutions*, 20.
2. De Shazer and Dolan, *More than Miracles*, 39.
3. Saleebey, "The Strengths Approach," 88–89.
4. Saleebey, "Introduction," 8.
5. White and Epston, *Narrative Means*, 9–10.
6. White and Epston, 38.
7. Spinello, *Global Capitalism, Culture*, 67–72.
8. "Demographic History."
9. Frey, *Diversity Explosion*, 3.
10. Frey, 1.
11. Frey, 4
12. Frey, 51.
13. Frey, 32.
14. Frey, 21.
15. Frey, 32.
16. Electric Choice, "See Electricity Rates," 1st sentence.
17. Seel, *Digital Universe*, 1.
18. Kirkpatrick, *The Facebook Effect*, 332.
19. Kirkpatrick, 332.
20. Hillstrom, *Defining Moments*, 31.
21. Wagner, *Tweeting to Power*, 1.
22. Etzioni, "Communitarianism," subheading "Varieties of Communitarianism."
23. Graham, *The Internet*, 131.
24. Graham, 137.
25. Etzioni, "Communitarianism," subheading "Varieties of Communitarianism."

26. Graham, *The Internet*, 139.
27. Graham, 128–29.
28. Putnam, *Bowling Alone*, 111–13.
29. Graham, *The Internet*, 130.
30. Graham, 141.
31. Graham, 133.
32. Graham, 133.
33. Interrogate the Internet, "Contradiction in Cyberspace," 129; Soros, *Open Society*, 180.
34. Paasonen, "Gender, Identity," 33.
35. Consalvo and Paasonen, "Introduction," 11.
36. Tiernan, "Women Veterans," 226.
37. Panitch and Gindin, *Making of Global Capitalism*, 187–91; Soros, *Open Society*, 176; Sweet and Meiksins, *Changing Contours of Work*, 192.
38. Panitch and Gindin, 113.
39. Soros, *Open Society*, 162.
40. Soros, 173–74.
41. Soros, 168.
42. Panitch and Gindin, *Making of Global Capital*, 123; Soros, xiv.
43. Spinello, *Global Capitalism, Culture*, 38.
44. Spinello, 10.
45. Pressman, *Understanding Piketty's Capital*, 67.
46. Pressman, 67; Smil, *Made in the USA*, 171.
47. Smil, 172.
48. Mishel, Gould, and Bivens, "Wage Stagnation," figure 4; Panitch and Gindin, *Making of Global Capital*, 20.
49. Dunn and Walker, "Union Membership," 2.
50. Pressman, *Understanding Piketty's Capital*, 173; Spinello, *Global Capitalism, Culture*, 19; Sweet and Meiksins, *Changing Contours of Work*, 21.
51. Soros, *Open Society*, xii.
52. Soros, 174.
53. Shannon, "Amazon Pays No Federal," 1st sentence.
54. Pressman, *Understanding Piketty's Capital*, 139.
55. Soros, *Open Society*, xii, 168.
56. Anderson, *Value in Ethics*, 2.
57. Anderson, 44.
58. Anderson, 32–33.
59. Soros, *Open Society*, 143.
60. Soros, 117, 196.
61. Soros, 145.
62. Spinello, *Global Capitalism, Culture*, 24.
63. Spinello, 24.
64. Soros, *Open Society*, 151.
65. Soros, 141.
66. Soros, 149.

67. Soros, 151.

68. Lemon, "Nike Called Out."

69. Taylor, "Bhopal."

70. Anderson, *Value in Ethics*, xii–xiii.

71. Anderson, 2–3.

72. Anderson, 3.

73. Anderson, 5.

74. Anderson, 18.

75. Anderson, 6–7.

76. Anderson, 14.

77. Anderson, 18.

78. Anderson, 32–33.

79. "What Is Social Entrepreneurship?," 5th paragraph.

80. Soros, *Open Society*, 162.

81. Holzner and Holzner, *Transparency in Global Change*, 67.

82. Holzner and Holzner, 52.

83. Kirkpatrick, *The Facebook Effect*, 329.

84. Spinello, *Global Capitalism, Culture*, 38.

85. Spinello, 38.

86. McGovern, *Sold American*, 77.

87. Monbiot, "Neoliberalism"; Navarro, "Neoliberalism as a Class."

88. Smith, "Neoliberalism."

89. Entemen, *Managerialism*; Jones, *Social Work*; Lawler, *The Rise of Managerialism*.

90. Gottschalk, *Caught*, 10; Jaffee, "Real Reason Behind."

91. Campbell, "Neoliberalism's Penal and Debtor."

92. "Fast Facts on U.S. Hospitals."

93. Hanesworth, "Neoliberal Influences," 43; Reisch, "Social Work Education," 717.

94. Hanesworth, 43; Reisch, 716.

95. Hanesworth, 43–44; Reisch 717.

96. Hanesworth, 43; Reisch, 717.

97. Hanesworth, 50; Reisch, 716–17.

98. Hanesworth, 51; Reisch, 718.

99. Reisch, 719.

100. Hanesworth, "Neoliberal Influences," 42; Reisch, 726.

101. Fook, *Social Work*, 22–24; Hanesworth, 52; Reisch, 717.

102. Hanesworth, 51; MacKinnon, "Social Work Intellectuals," 514; Reisch, 718.

103. Hanesworth, 51; Reisch, 718.

104. Best and Kellner, "Postmodern Politics," subheading "Forms of Postmodern Politics."

105. Best and Kellner, subheadings "Forms of Postmodern Politics" and "Leftist Politics."

106. Best and Kellner, subheading "Forms of Postmodern Politics."

107. Best and Kellner, subheading "Concluding Comments."

108. Best and Kellner, subheading "Contributions and Limitations of Postmodern Politics."

109. North, "7 Positive Changes."

110. Godfrey, "Elizabeth Warren's New Fundraising"; Wilson, "Warren's Fundraising Pledge."

111. Horwitz, "More than 30 States"; Montellaro, "Why You (Still) Can't."

112. Parmelee and Bichard, *Politics & the Twitter*, 2–3; Wagner, *Tweeting to Power*, 3.

113. "We the People," subheading "Step-by-Step Guide."

114. Consalvo and Paasonen, "Introduction," 18–19; Potter, *Digital Media*, 3.

115. Seel, *Digital Universe*, 95.

116. Potter, *Digital Media*, 3; Wagner, *Tweeting to Power*, 2.

117. Kirkpatrick, *The Facebook Effect*, 8, 295.

118. Potter, *Digital Media*, 15–16.

119. White and Epston, *Narrative Means*, 9–10.

120. De Jong and Kim Berg, 109–13; White and Epston, 55–63.

121. Seel, *Digital Universe*, 95; Wagner, *Tweeting to Power*, 51.

122. Wagner, 51.

123. Wagner, 14.

124. Wagner, 14–15.

125. "Political Polarization, 1994–2017."

126. Graham, *The Internet*, 130; Putnam, *Bowling Alone*, 111–13.

127. Hicks, *Explaining Postmodernism*, 40.

128. Kant *Critique of Judgement*, 17.

129. Hicks, *Explaining Postmodernism*, 39–41.

130. Hicks, 39–41.

131. Hicks, 65–66.

132. Foucault, *Power–Knowledge*, 113.

133. Foucault, 119, 131–33.

134. Foucault, 156.

135. White and Epston, *Narrative Means*, 38.

136. Foucault, *Power–Knowledge*, 159.

137. Dybicz, "Confronting Oppression," 35–38.

138. Dybicz, 28–31.

139. Freire, *Pedagogy of the Oppressed*, 53, 100–01, 125.

140. Freire, 160–61.

141. Freire, 131.

142. Freire 47–48.

143. Freire, 160–67.

144. Freire, 63–64.

145. Freire, 66–67.

146. De Shazer and Dolan, *More than Miracles*, 39.

147. Freire, *Pedagogy of the Oppressed*, 140–41.

148. Freire, 65.

149. Freire, *Pedagogy of Hope*, 1.

150. Saleebey, "Introduction," 8.

151. Freire, *Pedagogy of the Oppressed*, 176.

152. Kirkpatrick, *The Facebook Effect*, 332–33; Seel, *Digital Universe*, 1–4.

153. Holzner and Holzner, *Transparency in Global Change,* 5–7; Seel, 323.

154. Holzner and Holzner, 81–84; Notturno, "The Open Society," 44–47.

155. Seel, *Digital Universe,* 190.

156. Consalvo and Paasonen, "Introduction," 11.

157. Potter, *Digital Media,* 15–16, 34, 45.

158. Graham, *The Internet,* 137.

159. Mensch, "Existence and Essence," 72.

160. Mensch, 72.

161. Heidegger, *Being and Time,* 143–45, 250–87.

162. Heidegger, 160–67.

163. Heidegger, 235–67.

164. De Shazer and Dolan, *More than Miracles,* 39.

165. Saleebey, "The Strengths Approach," 88–89.

166. White and Epston, *Narrative Means,* 38.

167. Rubin and Babbie, *Research Methods,* 17–18.

168. Kant, *Groundwork of the Metaphysics,* 52.

169. Heidegger, *Essence of Human Freedom,* 93–94.

170. Ricœur, *Time and Narrative* (Vol. 1), 54–64.

171. Freire, *Pedagogy of the Oppressed,* 63–64.

172. Ricœur, *Time and Narrative* (Vol. 1), 64–70.

173. Freire, *Pedagogy of the Oppressed,* 66–67.

174. Ricœur, *Time and Narrative* (Vol. 1), 70–71.

175. Freire, *Pedagogy of the Oppressed,* 65.

176. Ricœur, *Time and Narrative* (Vol. 1), 72.

177. Ricœur, 8, 30.

178. Ricœur, 6, 52.

179. Bruner, "Life as Narrative"; Bruner, *Acts of Meaning*; Potter, *Digital Media,* 43–44.

180. Potter, 43.

181. De Jong and Kim Berg, *Interviewing for Solutions,* 20.

182. Soros, *Open Society,* xx–xxi.

183. Notturno, "The Open Society," 44–46; Soros, xx–xxi.

184. Lieberman, *The Tyranny of Experts,* 58–60.

185. Soros, *Open Society,* 345.

186. Holzner and Holzner, *Transparency in Global Change,* 81; Kirkpatrick, *The Facebook Effect,* 323.

187. Holzner and Holzner, 84.

188. Holzner and Holzner, 1–3.

189. Lieberman, *The Tyranny of Experts,* 58–60; Notturno, "The Open Society," 51.

190. Lieberman, 60.

191. Notturno, "The Open Society," 44–47.

192. Pralong, "Minima Moralia," 129; Soros, *Open Society,* xxi.

193. Pralong, 130.

194. Soros, *Open Society,* 167.

195. Pralong, "Minima Moralia," 132; Soros, xxi.

References

Anderson, Elizabeth. *Value in Ethics and Economics.* Cambridge, MA: Harvard University Press, 1993.

Bergson, Henri. *The Two Sources of Morality and Religion.* Translated by Ashley Audra. Notre Dame, IN: University of Notre Dame Press, 1977. First published 1932.

Best, Steven, and Douglas Kellner. "Postmodern Politics and the Battle for the Future." *Illuminations: The Critical Theory Project.* Accessed January 23, 2020.

Bruner, Jerome. "Life as Narrative." *Social Research* 54 (1987): 11–31.

Bruner, Jerome. *Acts of Meaning.* Cambridge, MA: Harvard University Press, 1990.

Campbell, John L. "Neoliberalism's Penal and Debtor States." *Theoretical Criminology* 14 (2010): 59–73.

Consalvo, Mia, and Susanna Paasonen. "Introduction: On the Internet, Women Matter." In *Women and Everyday Uses of the Internet: Agency and Identity*, edited by Mia Consalvo and Susanna Paasonen, 1–20. New York: Peter Lang, 2002.

De Jong, Peter, and Insoo Kim Berg. *Interviewing for Solutions.* 4th ed. Belmont, CA: Brooks/Cole, 2013.

"Demographic History of the United States." Wikipedia. Accessed September 13, 2019, https://en.wikipedia.org/wiki/Demographic_history_of_the_United_States.

De Shazer, Steve, and Yvonne Dolan. *More than Miracles.* New York: Routledge, 2007.

Dunn, Megan, and James Walker. "Union Membership in the United States." US Bureau of Labor Statistics. Last modified September 2016, https://www.bls.gov/spotlight/2016/union-membership-in-the-united-states/pdf/union-membership-in-the-united-states.pdf.

Dybicz, Phillip. "Confronting Oppression not Enhancing Functioning: The Role of Social Workers Within Postmodern Practice." *Journal of Sociology and Social Welfare* 37 (2010): 23–47.

Electric Choice. "See Electric Rates Available to Your Home/Business." Accessed June 19, 2020, https://www.electricchoice.com/electricity-prices-by-state/.

Entemen, Willard F. *Managerialism: The Emergence of a New Ideology.* Madison: University of Wisconsin Press, 1993.

Etzioni, Amitai. "Communitarianism." *Encyclopaedia Britannica.* Accessed September 19, 2019, https://www.britannica.com/topic/communitarianism

"Fast Facts on U.S. Hospitals, 2019." *The American Hospital Association.* Last updated January 2019. https://www.aha.org/statistics/fast-facts-us-hospitals.

Fook, Jan. *Social Work: A Critical Approach to Practice.* 2nd ed. Thousand Oaks, CA: Sage Publications, 2012.

Foucault, Michel. *Power–Knowledge: Selected Interviews & Other Writings 1972–1977.* Edited by Colin Gordon. New York: Pantheon Books, 1981.

Freire, Paulo. *Pedagogy of the Oppressed.* Translated by Myra Bergman Ramos. New York: Continuum International Publishing, 2000. First published 1968.

Freire, Paulo. *Pedagogy of Hope: Reliving Pedagogy of the Oppressed.* Translated by Robert Barr. London: Bloomsbury Academic, 2014. First published 1992.

Frey, William H. *Diversity Explosion: How New Demographics Are Remaking America.* Washington, DC: Brookings Institution Press, 2015.

Godfrey, Elaine. "Elizabeth Warren's New Fundraising Rule Is More Than a Gimmick." *The Atlantic*, March 5, 2019. https://www.theatlantic.com/politics/archive/2019/03/elizabeth-warren-rejects-big-donor-events-2020-bid/583951/.

Gottschalk, Marie. *Caught: The Prison State and the Lockdown of American Politics.* Princeton, NJ: Princeton University Press, 2014.

Graham, Gordon. *The Internet: A Philosophical Inquiry.* New York: Routledge, 1999.

Hanesworth, Carolyn. "Neoliberal Influences on American Higher Education and the Consequence for Social Work Programs." *Critical and Radical Social Work* 5 (2017): 41–57.

Heidegger, Martin. *Being and Time.* Translated by John Macquarrie and Edward Robinson. New York: Harper and Row, 1962. First published 1927.

Heidegger, Martin. *The Essence of Human Freedom.* Translated by Ted Sadler. New York: Continuum, 2002. First published 1930.

Hicks, Stephen. *Explaining Postmodernism: Skepticism and Socialism from Rousseau to Foucault.* Milwaukee: Scholargy Publishing, 2004.

Hillstrom, Kevin. *Defining Moments: The Internet Revolution.* Detroit: Omnigraphics, 2005.

Holzner, Burkart, and Leslie Holzner. *Transparency in Global Change: The Vanguard of the Open Society.* Pittsburgh: Pittsburgh University Press, 2006.

Horwitz, Sari. "More Than 30 States Offer Online Voting, but Experts Warn It Isn't Secure." *Washington Post,* May 17, 2016. https://www.washingtonpost.com/news/post-nation/wp/2016/05/17/more-than-30-states-offer-online-voting-but-experts-warn-it-isnt-secure/.

Interrogate the Internet. "Contradiction in Cyberspace: Collective Response." In *Cultures of the Internet,* edited by Rob Shields, 125–32. London: Sage, 1996.

Jaffee, David. "Real Reason Behind Prison Explosion." *Florida Times-Union,* December 29, 2014.

Jones, Chris. "Social Work: Regulation and Managerialism." In *Professionals and the New Managerialism in the Public Sector,* edited by Mark Exworthy and Susan Halford, 37–49. Philadelphia: Open University Press, 1999.

Kant, Immanuel. *The Critique of Judgement.* Translated by James Meredith. New York: Oxford University Press, 1952. First published 1790.

Kant, Immanuel. *Groundwork of the Metaphysics of Morals.* Edited and translated by Mary Gregor. New York: Cambridge University Press, 1997. First published 1785.

Kirkpatrick, David. *The Facebook Effect: The Inside Story of the Company That Is Connecting the World.* New York: Simon & Schuster Paperbacks, 2010.

Lawler, John. "The Rise of Managerialism in Social Work." In *Management, Social Work, and Change,* edited by Elizabeth Harlow and John Lawler, 29–52. Philadelphia: Routledge, 2000.

Lemon, Jason. "Nike Called Out for Low Wages in Asia Amid Colin Kaepernick Ad Promotion." *Newsweek,* September 6. 2018, https://www.newsweek.com/nike-factory-workers-still-work-long-days-low-wages-asia-1110129

Lieberman, Jethro. *The Tyranny of Experts: How Professionals Are Closing the Open Society.* New York: Walker and Company, 1970.

MacKinnon, Shauna T. "Social Work Intellectuals in the Twenty-First Century: Critical Social Theory, Critical Social Work and Public Engagement." *Social Work Education* 28 (2009): 512–27.

McGovern, Charles. *Sold American: Consumption and Citizenship, 1890–1945.* Chapel Hill: University of North Carolina Press, 2006.

Mensch, James. "Existence and Essence in Thomas and Husserl." In *Horizons of Continental Philosophy: Essays on Husserl, Heidegger, and Merleau-Ponty,* edited by Hugh Silverman, 62–92. Dordrecht, the Netherlands: Kluwer Academic Publishers, 1988.

Mishel, Lawrence, Elise Gould, and Josh Bivens. "Wage Stagnation in Nine Charts." Economic Policy Institute, January 6, 2015, https://www.epi.org/publication/charting-wage-stagnation/.

Monbiot, George. "Neoliberalism—The Ideology at the Root of All Our Problems." *The Guardian*, April 15, 2016, https://www.theguardian.com/books/2016/apr/15/neolib eralism-ideology-problem-george-monbiot.

Montellaro, Zach. "Why You (Still) Can't Vote Online." *The Atlantic*, January 16, 2018, https://www.theatlantic.com/politics/archive/2016/01/why-you-still-cant-vote-onl ine/459183/.

Navarro, Vicente. "Neoliberalism as a Class Ideology; Or, the Political Causes of the Growth of Inequalities." *International Journal of Health Services* 37 (2007): 47–62.

North, Anna. "7 Positive Changes That Have Come from the #MeToo Movement." Vox, October 4, 2019, https://www.vox.com/identities/2019/10/4/20852639/me-too-movement-sexual-harassment-law-2019

Notturno, Mark A. "The Open Society and Its Enemies: Authority, Community, and Bureaucracy." In *Popper's Open Society after Fifty Years*, edited by Ian Jarvie and Sandra Pralong, 41–55. New York: Routledge, 1999.

Paasonen, Susanna. "Gender, Identity, and (the Limits of) Play on the Internet." In *Feministische Theorie und Kritische Medienkulturanalyse*, edited by Tanja Thomas and Ulla Wischermann, 547–56. Berlin: Transcript Verlag, 2020.

Panitich, Leo, and Sam Gindin. *The Making of Global Capitalism: The Political Economy of American Empire*. New York: Verso, 2013.

Parmelee, John, and Shannon Bichard. *Politics & the Twitter Revolution: How Tweets Influence the Relationship Between Political Leaders and the Public*. Lanham, MD: Lexington Books, 2012.

"Political Polarization, 1994–2017." Pew Research Center, October 20, 2017. https://www.people-press.org/interactives/political-polarization-1994-2017/.

Popper, Karl. *The Open Society and Its Enemies*. Vol. 1, *The Spell of Plato*. London: Routledge, 1945.

Popper, Karl. *The Open Society and Its Enemies*. Vol. 2, *Hegel, Marx, and the Aftermath*. London: Routledge, 1945.

"Postmodern Politics." All about Worldview. Accessed January 23, 2020, https://www.allaboutworldview.org/postmodern-politics.htm.

Potter, John. *Digital Media and Learner Identity*. New York: Palgrave and Macmillan, 2012.

Pralong, Sandra. "Minima Moralia: Is There an Ethics of the Open Society?" in *Popper's Open Society after Fifty Years*, edited by Ian Jarvie and Sandra Pralong, 128–45. New York: Routledge, 1999.

Pressman, Steven. *Understanding Piketty's Capital in the Twenty-First Century*. New York: Routledge, 2016.

Putnam, Robert. *Bowling Alone: The Collapse and Revival of American Community*. New York: Simon and Schuster, 2001.

Reisch, Michael. "Social Work Education and the Neo-Liberal Challenge: The U.S. Response to Increasing Global Inequity." *Social Work Education* 32 (2013): 715–33.

Ricœur, Paul. *Time and Narrative*. Vol. 1. Chicago: University of Chicago Press, 1984.

Ricœur, Paul. *Time and Narrative*. Vol. 2. Chicago: University of Chicago Press, 1985.

Ricœur, Paul. *Time and Narrative*. Vol. 3. Chicago: University of Chicago Press, 1988.

Rubin, Allen, and Earl Babbie. *Research Methods for Social Work*. 3rd ed. Boston: Cengage Learning, 1996.

Saleebey, Dennis. "Introduction: Power to the People." In *The Strengths Perspective*, edited by Dennis Saleeey, 1–23. 4th ed. Boston: Pearson, 2005.

Saleebey, Dennis. "The Strengths Approach to Practice." In *The Strengths Perspective*, edited by Dennis Saleeey, 77–91. 4th ed. Boston: Pearson, 2005.

Seel, Peter B. *Digital Universe: The Telecommunication Revolution*. Malden, MA: Wiley-Blackwell, 2012.

Shannon, Joel. "Amazon Pays No Federal Income Tax for 2018, Despite Soaring Profits, Report Says." *USA Today*, updated February 16, 2019, https://www.usatoday.com/story/money/2019/02/15/amazon-pays-no-2018-federal-income-tax-report-says/2886639002/.

Smil, Vaclav. *Made in the USA: The Rise and Retreat of American Manufacturing*. Cambridge, MA: MIT Press, 2013.

Smith, Nicola. "Neoliberalism." *Encyclopaedia Britannica*. Accessed November 21, 2019, https://www.britannica.com/topic/neoliberalism.

Soros, George. *Open Society: Reforming Global Capitalism*. London: Little Brown, 2000.

Spinello, Richard A. *Global Capitalism, Culture, and Ethics*. New York: Routledge, 2014.

Sweet, Stephen A., and Peter F. Meiksins. *Changing Contours of Work: Jobs and Opportunities in the New Economy*. 2nd ed. Sociology for a New Century Series. London: Sage, 2012.

Taylor, Ann. "Bhopal: The World's Worst Industrial Disaster, 30 Years Later." *The Atlantic*, December 2, 2014, https://www.theatlantic.com/photo/2014/12/bhopal-the-worlds-worst-industrial-disaster-30-years-later/100864/.

Tiernan, Jennifer M. "Women Veterans and the Net: Using Internet Technology to Network and Reconnect." In *Women and Everyday Uses of the Internet: Agency and Identity*, edited by Mia Consalvo and Susanna Paasonen, 211–27. New York: Peter Lang, 2002.

Wagner, Kevin. *Tweeting to Power: The Social Media Revolution in American Politics*. New York: Oxford University Press, 2014.

"We the People." Accessed January 23, 2020, https://petitions.whitehouse.gov/about.

"What Is Social Entrepreneurship?" *International Relations*, November 14, 2017, https://ironline.american.edu/blog/social-entrepreneurship-degree/.

White, Michael, and David Epston. *Narrative Means to Therapeutic Ends*. New York: Norton, 1990.

Wilson, Reid. "Warren's Fundraising Pledge Scares Some Democrats." *The Hill*, October 11, 2019. https://thehill.com/homenews/campaign/465255-warrens-fundraising-pledge-scares-some-democrats.

9

Solutions, Narrative, and Strengths

The three postmodern practice approaches to be examined in this chapter—solution-focused therapy (SFT), narrative therapy (NT), and the strengths perspective (SP)[a]—all share a similar timeline in terms of their development. Progenitors of these approaches began working out key concepts comprising their approaches through various published works in the 1980s (SFT,[1] NT,[2] and SP[3]). Seminal treatises were published for each of the approaches in the 1990s (SFT[4], NT[5], SP[6]), which thoroughly outlined the recently emergent approach and which progressive new editions continue to this day to serve as prominent sources for those wishing to learn the approach. Solution-focused therapy, originally called *solution-focused brief therapy*, originated in the 1980s through the work of Steve de Shazer, Insoo Kim Berg, and their colleagues and clients at the Milwaukee Brief Family Therapy Center.[7] Thus, these scholars were practitioners as well, constantly honing and refining their ideas with experiences in the field. Similarly, narrative therapy originated in the 1980s; the most prominent and prolific developments occurred through the work of Michael White, David Epston, and their colleagues and clients at the Dulwich Centre in Australia.[8] Thus, they too were practitioners as well as scholars, constantly honing and refining their ideas with experiences in the field. The strengths perspective differs a bit from the other two in that it represents a model/perspective toward the delivery of case management services rather than psychotherapy. The strengths perspective arose through the collaboration of scholars belonging to the Study Group for Philosophical Issues,[9] a core group of which resided at the University of Kansas. They honed the concepts comprising the strengths perspective through the work done via various state and national grants aimed at promoting case management services.

While each of these three approaches is distinct in its own right, it was noted by these early authors that they all shared a common conceptual base.[10] Each of these three approaches employs the concepts of solutions, narrative, and strengths. Their distinction lies within their chosen entry point of focus. Solution-focused therapy chooses as its entry point of focus the articulation of solutions over that of the investigation of problems. While the strengths perspective and

---

[a] The abbreviations for these three approaches—SFT, NT, and SP—will be used when citing sources to support commonly shared concepts and conclusions.

A Genealogy of the Good and Critique of Hubris. Phillip Dybicz, Oxford University Press. © Oxford University Press 2023.
DOI: 10.1093/oso/9780197670071.003.0009

narrative therapy do not give prominence to the term *solution*, these approaches employ the concept through their efforts at getting the client to describe their goals, dreams, and aspirations.[11] Narrative therapy chooses its entry point as the co-construction of a narrative framework upon which to reorder clients' life experiences. Again, while solution-focused therapy and the strengths perspective do not give prominence to the term *narrative*, they both employ the concept of narrative through their efforts at the co-construction of the storying of these experiences.[12] And lastly, the strengths perspective chooses the articulation of clients' strengths as its entry point of focus. Whereas narrative therapy and solution-focused therapy do not heavily utilize the term *strengths*, they mine for such strengths when exploring for unique outcomes and exceptions to the problem.[13]

With the brief origins history of these approaches concluded, I will now turn toward examining how various elements of the Postmodern discourse described in Chapter 8 inform these approaches. As the Postmodern discourse represents a shared base of understanding, what follows will be an examination and articulation of the various broad commonalities among these three approaches reflective of their shared base. Part of the challenge of offering an approach born from a new discourse is that early efforts by those seeking to understand it, adopt it, or critique it inevitably occur through the prism of attempting to understand and interpret it through the current dominant Discourse in which they are enmeshed. This leads to many misunderstandings and misinterpretations, provoking comments of frustration by progenitors of these approaches as they attempt to clear up these misunderstandings; this dynamic has indeed occurred again in the case of these postmodern practices.[14] And as was illustrated by the case of the charity organization societies in the late 1800s and their attempt to employ science in the form of scientific charity, the application, while perhaps serving as an improvement to their then current way of practice, fell woefully short in incorporating the major key insights that scientific practice had to offer.

Thus, the goal of this chapter is to help students and practitioners avoid such misunderstanding when attempting to employ the strengths perspective, narrative therapy, and solution-focused therapy. Reflecting upon the chapters on the Colonial Discourse and the Premodern Discourse, the practices offered at the beginning of each were chosen so that upon first encounter they would most likely be easily misunderstood and appear strange to our present eyes. However, once a thorough description of the underlying Discourse supporting these practices was given, these practices were hopefully rendered more intelligible. The two main elements from the Postmodern discourse to be elaborated upon in this manner, the concepts of *praxis* and *mimesis*, were chosen as they both directly speak to the underlying theory of change being sought by practitioners of the strengths perspective, narrative therapy, and solution-focused therapy. At the heart of every social work intervention is the goal of facilitating some type of change in the client, so these two elements—*praxis* and *mimesis*—serve as an effective bridge to assist one in understanding these three approaches.

Praxis (Faith, Belief, and Hope)

As explicated in Chapter 8, Paulo Freire's concept of *conscientization* involves the operation of praxis within a moral framework—comprised of such values as maintaining the dignity and worth of the individual, self-determination, and empowerment. Praxis is more than just the of achieving of intellectual insight. It occurs when the achievement of this insight is so strong or dramatic that it prompts one to action. As Freire's focus is upon achieving praxis in the face of oppression, there arises an additional moral component driving one to action.

For narrative therapy, Michael White embraces the concept of praxis through his articulation of *katharsis*.[15] He intentionally spells it with a "k" to distinguish it from the current, modern understanding of catharsis as the purging of repressed emotions. White chooses the classical Greek understanding of *katharsis* as that of being so moved by one's "witnessing powerful expressions of life's dramas" (for the Greeks, most notably at the theater in the form of tragedy) that a deep reflection upon one's life ensues in such forms as gaining "a new perspective on one's life and identity," re-engaging with "neglected aspects of one's own history," or reconnecting with "revered values and purposes for one's life."[16] Praxis is achieved when such reflection spurs one to action. Typically within the therapeutic context, this conscientization is a gradual process which unfolds over a few sessions with the therapist. However, this spurring to action can unfold in quite the dramatic fashion, as David Epston's case study of Carol illustrates. Plagued by guilt over her perceived inadequacies as a single mother, Carol had allowed her adult son to manipulate her and to take advantage of her. With the help of therapy, Carol's conscientization arrives in dramatic fashion:

> Tony was looking pleased with himself, beer cans everywhere. I didn't know what happened but it felt like something had snapped. I felt like I was outside my body. I was screaming and crying at the same time: "I've given, given, given and I've got no more to give." I saw a big deep hole: "Get out or I'll call the police." All my fear went . . . everything went out of me. I even had him physically up against the wall. He went on in his usual way. He tried all his ways: "So you want a hug?" He then threatened to smash my car, break my windows, kill me. I felt terrific—I'm not afraid anymore. "You can do nothing to me." I was surprised it was happening.

... Kicking him out—that was the solution in the back of my mind. It happened just like you said it would. It's wonderful. .... A whole new life can start for me. There was no room for compromise once I started.

... I hope one day the "hole" will fill up again and I will be able to give, but I know I won't ever lose my self-respect again.[17]

There are two items of note in the above case study illustration. First, the level of empowerment that accompanies conscientization, as reflected in Carol stating, "You can do nothing to me." This signals her throwing off the yoke of the oppressive narrative (i.e., I need to let Tony's transgressions slide as a form of penance for being an inadequate mother) that had up until this point guided her actions. Second, the point that once conscientization is achieved there is no going back to one's previous worldview, as reflected in Carol stating, "There was no room for compromise once I started" and "I know I won't ever lose my self-respect again." Within the therapeutic context, postmodern practitioners have recognized how this process of conscientization serves as a powerful antidote in resolving a client's issues and life struggles. It is no wonder that even when faced with profound issues of abuse and trauma, clients have been able to achieve dramatic improvement in merely six sessions or less.[18]

Furthermore, it is clear that this powerful employment of conscientization is one of the elements that gets lost when practitioners within the Modern Discourse attempt to interpret the notions of *strengths* and *solutions*. This loss of key insights occurs because these modernist practitioners attempt to interpret these key insights within the modern paradigm of understanding which privileges objective knowledge. Within the postmodern paradigm of understanding wherein these approaches were born, phenomenology conceptualizes reality as consisting of both an existence and an essence. Whereas knowledge of existence is objective in nature, knowledge of essence is subjective. And postmodern approaches seek to target change in the client's (i.e., the phenomenon's) essence as the means to promote positive change as reflected by the fact that conscientization arises from critical reflection upon this subjective knowledge of one's essence.

By contrast, within the modernist paradigm of understanding, the correspondence theory of truth conceives of reality as merely comprising an existence and thus searches for objective knowledge to promote change. Thus, when practitioners follow the phases of "study, diagnosis, treatment" within the Modern Discourse, simply inquiring about strengths when conducting a bio-psycho-social assessment during the "study" phase does not lead to conscientization. By not incorporating strengths into a narrative framework of client empowerment, the understanding and the power that client strengths bring get pared down simply to the objective knowledge of being a resource.

Similarly, during the "treatment" phase, inviting greater participation by the client in offering input on solutions when planning an intervention does not lead to conscientization as the diagnosis of the problem serves as the framework to organize such input. Not incorporating solutions within a narrative framework of client empowerment that speaks directly to their essence divests the notion of solutions of much of its power; client solutions simply become a product of brainstorming when seeking to set goals. Thus, this dynamic mirrors that which occurred when premodern practitioners attempted to employ the notion of scientific management in the form of scientific charity. Key insights are lost (such as conscientization), as is the tremendous power they bring to initiate change, resulting in a very watered-down and weak application.

Confronting Oppression

Conscientization is aimed at throwing off the yoke of oppression. And each of these three approaches conceptualizes its efforts in this manner (SFT,[19] NT,[20] SP[21]). The exercise of power is an integral part of oppression. Therefore, to fully appreciate postmodern practices as endeavors at confronting oppression, we must refer back to Foucault's conceptualization of power described in Chapter 8. Foucault conceives of power as embedded in language and circulating within a discourse. This power acts to privilege some knowledges as being correct or common sense while subjugating others as being incorrect or dubious. Soon the privileged knowledges coalesce into what he terms a "regime of truth," which acts to delegitimize alternative knowledges.

Thus, among adherents of postmodern practice, the oppression conducted by this regime of truth takes the form of cultural imperialism;[22] it seeks to advance its understandings as the norm and widely accepted truth.[23] The insidious nature of the oppression perpetrated by this regime of truth is that it convinces individuals to police themselves according to the norms of the regime of truth.[24] It does this by imposing a framework of understanding which restricts individuals in their efforts to employ their aesthetic judgment (as defined by Kant) when determining their personal good, thus limiting the possible conceptions of one's personal good to those sanctioned by the regime of truth.[25] This dynamic was illustrated above in the case study of Carol when, prior to her conscientization, her self-imposed perceived failures as a single mother diminished her self-respect and led her to excuse her son's outrageous transgressions as a form of penance for these said failures.

This postmodern conceptualization of oppression is what informs the critique offered by these postmodern scholars concerning scientific management and the bio-psycho-social medical model being employed within the Modern Discourse.

Relying upon a theory of causality as action/reaction, modernist practitioners give importance to diagnosing the problem as the means to uncover solutions, as reflected in the adoption of the phases of study, diagnose, and treatment. The study phase focuses upon the information needed to make an accurate diagnosis (i.e., dysfunctional behavior leading to symptomology). According to postmodern practitioners, such an approach inevitably leads to supporting, or lending power to, a problem-focused organizing of the client's life experiences (SP,[26] NT,[27] SFT[28]). The power lent to this problem-saturated description allows it to assume the role of an unquestioned master narrative;[29] it undisputedly offers itself as the scientifically established truth which points to the most technically efficient means in which to counter the problem (e.g., evidenced-based practice). Since an accurate diagnosis and subsequent treatment options rely upon the technical expertise of the social worker,[30] the client's role in this process gets diminished to that of a sovereign consumer. Thus, clients are put into the disempowering position in which external forces seem to be organizing their life experiences.[31]

Oppression takes hold in the form of the negative identity conclusions that arise from these problem-saturated descriptions of the client's life (SFT,[32] NT,[33] SP[34]). Clients thus internalize these oppressive notions, which in turn diminishes their self-worth.[35] In the recounting of their symptoms and experiences to the social worker, a plot or theme of failure and incompetence takes shape.[36] Clients begin to view themselves as helpless and impotent in the face of their problems, and thus lose hope that they will be able to effect change on their own.[37] Hearkening back to the wisdom of Paulo Freire, for the postmodern practitioner the remedy to facilitate positive change in clients is to liberate them from the oppression of these master narratives and the negative identity conclusions that they breed.[38] Postmodern practitioners do this by encouraging clients to articulate their implicit understandings of their situation and resulting identity conclusions produced by the master narrative.[39] Once these understandings are made explicit, the postmodern practitioner seeks to assist the client in questioning the power producing these master narratives by undermining the requirements for their survival.[40] As will be discussed in further detail in the section on mimesis, undermining these requirements opens the door for clients to begin configuring alternative understandings of their issues, understandings that lead to empowering identity conclusions.

This postmodern focus upon confronting oppression as the means to engender conscientization translates what we know as therapy into a political activity.[41] This leads to a bit of a misnomer for the two postmodern clinical approaches that have been named narrative therapy and solution-focused therapy. The term *therapy* quite clearly arises from the medical lexicon. For modernist approaches such as cognitive-behavioral therapy or family systems therapy this terminology fits as they are both a product of the Modern Discourse, which envisions clinical social welfare as an effort in scientific management or social engineering. It is understandable that the progenitors of these postmodern "clinical"[b] approaches labeled them as a form of therapy when first introducing them; this served as the means to make them recognizable to the vast majority of their peers who remained enmeshed in the Modern Discourse. However, in so doing, this misnomer can easily lead one to the misunderstanding that these approaches are equivalent to traditional approaches to psychotherapy, and lead one to simply being categorize them as a different variety of the same approach. This can lead to the medicalization of these postmodern approaches wherein the focus upon confronting oppression and spurring conscientization gets lost. Thus, I would argue that more apropos designations of these approaches are *narrative conscientization* and *solution-focused conscientization*, to better capture their conceptualization as a political activity. It should be noted that the strengths perspective also conceives of the helping situation as a political activity geared toward empowerment.[42]

This quibbling over nomenclature may seem trivial; however, the difference implied by it is anything but. To illustrate, we can examine how this difference plays out when initial contact is made with the client. Let's envision the scenario in which two individuals, Mr. A and Mr. B, both experienced a loss, and thus are currently suffering from depression. Mr. A, along with mental health professionals, determines that he is not in need of psychotherapy, whereas Mr. B seeks psychotherapy, and mental health professionals concur that he is in need of such services. Within the Modern Discourse that gives primacy to concerns over functioning, wherein lies the difference between Mr. A and Mr. B? Both are experiencing dysfunction in the form of depression. Yet, by it being determined that Mr. A is not in need of psychotherapy services, there is implicit recognition that he possesses adequate coping mechanisms to return himself to healthy functioning. Such self-reliance is the hoped-for norm for all individuals. By extension, there is implicit recognition that Mr. B possesses inadequate coping mechanisms. Thus, by the very act of seeking psychotherapy services, before even a single word is said, Mr. B is forced to embrace a negative identity conclusion that he is inadequate in this regard and has fallen below the hoped-for norm.[43] Psychotherapists hold out the promise that, with their guidance, they can help the client to return to the hoped-for norm of functioning and self-reliance. This promised return is seen as the end result of therapy—as indicated by termination: the client no longer being in need of services.

---

[b] The word "clinical" is put in quotes as it too is a medical term not fitting to activities seeking to confront oppression.

Now contrast this to postmodern practitioners who assess Mr. A's and Mr. B's need for services in terms of a political activity geared at confronting oppression and awakening conscientization. Mr. A does not seek services and is not seen as in need of them because he has not internalized and thus he currently is not being oppressed by a master narrative that depicts him as inadequate. Consequently, Mr. B's need for services indicates that he currently is experiencing oppression. Consequently, the act of seeking services represents the first step in confronting this oppression: fostering a positive identity conclusion of the client as heroically taking a stand to end the oppression.[44] So rather than occurring at the end of therapy, the return to normalcy in terms of a positive identity conclusion occurs at the start of therapy. This echoes Paulo Freire's insight that even though it may take some time to transform structures of oppression, simply acting in an attempt to transform these structures sets one on the transformative path to becoming more fully human and empowered.[45] This dynamic will be further illustrated when discussing the case study of Nick in the section on mimesis.

Now returning to the three key elements that comprise praxis, Freire identifies them as follows: faith, belief, and hope. Each of these elements will be given extensive treatment in the subsections that follow. I define these terms as follows: (a) faith is trust and confidence in someone or something—this may extend to either another's knowledge or ability; (b) belief is the acceptance of something on principle, as opposed to acceptance due to empirical proof; and (c) hope is the expectation that one will achieve one's desires—an expectation that is not mainly dependent on evidence gathered from empirical observations but rather upon belief and faith.

For now, it is simply worth noting the recognition of these elements, and by extension the operation of praxis, in the writings comprising the strengths perspective, narrative therapy/conscientization and solution-focused therapy/conscientization. Thus, for the strengths perspective, Kisthardt describes these elements as comprising a healing power which "ignites the fire of potentials and possibilities for another."[46] As noted above, the concept of katharsis captures the elements of praxis for narrative therapy/conscientization. And for solution-focused therapy/conscientization, these elements are reflected in John L. Walter and Jane E. Peller's conceptualization of the three primary tools used in therapeutic conversations: frames of goals, exceptions, and hypothetical solutions.[47] The goal frame relies upon faith in clients' ability to determine their personal good, articulated in the form of goals. The exceptions frame relies upon belief in the existence of these exceptions and, by extension, belief in client strengths responsible for the exceptions. And the hypothetical solutions frame relies upon hope that steps can be taken in order to reach one's personal goal.

Faith

Faith in the client comes in the form of the postmodern practitioner's unquestioned faith that every client has the ability to determine their own personal good. In other words, it is an absolute faith in clients' ability: to determine how they want to be in the world (SFT,[48] NT,[49] SP[50]), to direct the helping process (SFT,[51] NT,[52] SP[53]), and to determine what is best for themselves (SFT,[54] NT,[55] SP[56]). As commonly is the case upon initial meeting, even when clients do not recognize that they already possess this knowledge of their personal good,[57] this faith in their ability to articulate it remains. Hence, there is faith in clients' ability to describe what "better" looks like for their unique situation.[58] Yet articulation of one's personal good faces challenges for the client, particularly when the client views the social worker as an agent of the state. For clients, their personal good often falls under the category of subjugated knowledge (as stated above, being oppressed is understood as the trigger for one's need for services). Thus, this absolute faith plays a critical role in the building of trust within the helping relationship:[59] It is from this trust between client and social worker that clients begin to articulate their personal good.

Each of these postmodern approaches embraces the notion that "the client is the expert" (SP,[60] NT,[61] SFT[62]). Yet wherein does this client expertise lie? When viewed through the prism of the Modern Discourse, client expertise lies in their local knowledge of the problem; or, in other words, clients are best positioned to share the nature and occurrences of symptoms being experienced and possible resources available. Social workers then take this local knowledge and translate it by filtering it through their expert knowledge on human biological, psychological, and social functioning. Solutions are recommended by the social worker, placing the client in the role of sovereign consumer when deciding upon a treatment plan.

By contrast, postmodern social work practitioners see client expertise existing as the clients' ability to determine their own personal good. Relying upon mimesis as their theory of change (i.e., theory of causality) in which to direct interventions, postmodern practitioners view the client as having images of "who I am" and "who I would like to be." Practitioners then take the position that the client is best positioned to articulate "who I would like to be." To argue that practitioners are better suited to tell the client "who they would like to be" becomes ludicrous; and thus, therein lies the need for faith in the client. As Rapp notes concerning the strengths perspective, "In the strengths model, the long-term goal is rarely a subject of negotiation." These goals are not rejected by the case manager as "unrealistic" but, rather, are treated as sincere aspirations of the person.[63] So clients are viewed as being expertly positioned in the following ways: to know the type of change they would like to see,[64] to describe what this change will look like when applied to their own unique context,[65] to identify steps toward this change that are already taking place,[66] and to determine what they would like to work upon.[67] The focus of the practitioners' efforts thus becomes that of helping clients to articulate these items, all of which serve to depict their personal good.

With clients donning the role of expert in treatment planning, the question now becomes what role does the practitioner play as the non-expert in helping clients to articulate their personal good? Each of these three postmodern approaches urges the practitioner to adopt a not-knowing stance as the means to help clients articulate their personal good (SFT,[68] NT,[69] SP[70]). First coined by Anderson and Goolishian,[71] the term *not-knowing* seeks to capture the process used by Socrates in his early dialogues. Due to his pronouncement "One thing only I know and that is that I know nothing," Socrates was famously dubbed "the wisest man in all of Greece" by the oracle of Delphi.[72] Such cultural humility by Socrates enabled him to put aside any biases and preconceived notions that he might have concerning a topic of interest. However, this cultivated ignorance of not-knowing does not speak to incapacity of knowing truth or to the blind acceptance of another's truth claim. Rather, "It is the bite or sting that wakes us from our complacency, arouses us to excellence, to learn and discover and inquire."[73] Adopting the role of questioner, one embraces an attitude of genuine curiosity in one's pursuit toward understanding the particular truth of the client's personal good.

Thus, in seeking to understand a client's personal good, practitioners are advised to adopt this attitude of genuine curiosity (SFT,[74] NT,[75] SP[76]). Solution-focused therapy/conscientization describes this process of not-knowing as "leading from one step behind."[77] It involves putting aside one's own and the profession's frame of reference for understanding client struggles.[78] And it actively encourages practitioners to refrain from offering suggestions concerning what clients need or what they should strive for as their preferred solution.[79] Narrative therapy/conscientization describes this process of not-knowing as adopting an editorial stance wherein one's questions act as a catalyst for the client to confront oppressive narratives and then reauthor a more empowering truth.[80] The confronting of oppressive narratives takes place through the deconstruction of these narratives.[81] Genuine curiosity on the part of the editor/therapist serves to clarify the practitioner's confusion and invites the client and practitioner to wrestle with ambiguity, which then serves to empower the client to take control over the organization of their life experiences.[82] The strengths perspective describes this process of not-knowing as adopting the role of collaborator seeking to dialogue with clients concerning their aspirations and perceptions of their experience and their strengths.[83]

To better illustrate these notions of client expertise and adopting a not-knowing stance, the following case study of Mrs. J taken from the strengths perspective is offered.

Mrs. J. was due to be discharged into the community after several years of hospital residence. When faced with her compulsory discharge, she was considerably panicked. She stated her wants in terms of residence in a nursing home with no responsibility plus daily care activities. Everyone agreed that her likely self-care skills and anxiety levels seemed to indicate that this would be the best plan. Once *a trusting relationship had been established* [my emphasis], Mrs. J. divulged that she hated the idea of living in a home and going to day centers, and that she really wanted to be the Queen [of England]. She challenged the Practitioner to work toward that aim. Without promising too much, the Practitioner began to work out with Mrs. J. what she felt the Queen did that was worth aiming for. It emerged that Mrs. J. believed that the Queen did not have financial or administrative worries, she always knew where she was going to live, people respected her because she helped them, and most importantly, she had "companions" and "ladies in waiting" who helped her and kept her company. The subsequent assessment stated that Mrs. J. needed a strong sense of financial security and the guarantee of help with day-to-day organization, she needed to move to one location and be promised that she need never move again, she needed to feel that she was helping people and feel respected for it, and she needed some "old-fashioned" companionship. Mrs. J eventually began considering sharing a house with another person being discharged who was already a firm friend and an effective organizer both of good works and administration.[84]

First of note, we can see the self-policing taking place by Mrs. J when she initially aligns her wants and needs to those produced by a functional assessment: residence in a nursing home with daily care activities. Next, the social worker practicing the strengths perspective successfully communicates to Mrs. J that he has faith in her ability to know what is best for her. This creates a high level of trust between the social worker and Mrs. J to the point where she feels safe enough to truly share her knowledge of personal good: to be the queen of England. Now at this point, we can clearly see the divergent paths offered by modernist and postmodernist approaches to treatment planning. Within a modernist approach solely embracing objective knowledge of existence, Mrs. J's statement desiring to be the queen of England would translate as being a symptom of her dysfunction: an impossible existence and hence a detachment from reality. Thus, at best, it would be ignored, and at worst, this knowledge of her personal good would be further subjugated by stressing the impossibility of its achievement.

The postmodern practitioner, however, targeting the essence of Mrs. J's statement (i.e., "who I would like to be"), adopts a not-knowing stance which encourages Mrs. J to share her subjective knowledge as to what it means for her to be queenly. The social worker's faith in Mrs. J to know her personal good leads the social worker to exhibit genuine curiosity as to what such a personal good looks like for Mrs. J. This in turn prompts Mrs. J to further articulate the details of her personal good: no financial or administrative worries, having a permanent residence, helping people and thus earning their respect, and "companions" and "ladies in waiting" who provide friendship and assistance. Adopting the role of collaborator, the social worker then works with the client in trying to achieve the essence of this personal good within Mrs. J's unique context of being discharged from the behavioral health hospital. This then produces the goals for her treatment plan: financial security, the guarantee of help with daily administrative tasks and organization, a permanent home, the opportunity to help people as the means to garner their respect, and companionship. Drawing upon existing resources in the community (i.e., objective knowledge), this collaboration results in the formation of a treatment plan: sharing a house with a good friend who is able to provide Mrs. J both with volunteer opportunities and with help in daily organizational concerns.

Belief

Belief represents an ideological stance for solution-focused therapy/conscientization, narrative therapy/conscientization, and the strengths perspective. Flowing from the strong sense of faith articulated above, each of these approaches embraces the belief that clients (along with their environment) already possess the strengths, skills, and capacities necessary to help them throw off the yoke of their oppressive narratives and begin moving toward achieving their personal good. Now, recognizing that clients possess strengths and that environments contain resources certainly is nothing new to the field of social work. However, by embracing this belief as an ideological stance, each of these approaches *deliberately* chooses to make the focus of the investigation into the client's problem one of uncovering these strengths, skills, and resources (SP,[85] NT,[86] SFT[87]).

As Dennis Saleebey noted, "if you want to find strengths, you have to assume that they are there."[88] By extension, this engenders a further belief in clients' capacity to draw upon these strengths, skills, and resources to effect desired change (SP,[89] NT[90], SFT[91]). This is understandable when one considers that mimesis is the theory of causality that they are working under, and thus, the uncovering of these strengths, skills, and capacities is essential to moving the client toward confirming an empowering "who I am" and the capacity to employ them to attain "who I want to be." Contrast this to the scientific management approach operating within the Modern Discourse. Working under the theory of causality as cause–effect, practitioners direct their investigation into the various occurrences and symptoms of the problem in the quest for an accurate diagnosis. Thus, the uncovering of strengths, rather than being the primary focus, instead plays a supporting role. The search for strengths is temporarily put aside, to be returned to once an accurate diagnosis points the way forward toward resolution of the problem.

Postmodern practitioners readily admit that they do not embrace cause–effect as their guiding theory of causality, and hence spend very little time and attention on the pursuit of causes to the problem.[92] Rather, their belief that clients (and their environment) already possess the strengths, skills, and capacities to enact positive change leads these practitioners to focus their inquiry on helping the client to articulate examples of their personal agency (i.e., free will) at work in confronting aspects of the problem (SP,[93] NT,[94] SFT[95]). Solution-focused therapy/conscientization refers to these client achievements as *exceptions*.[96] Narrative therapy/conscientization refers to them as *unique outcomes*,[97] and the strengths perspective simply refers to them as *successes*. Again, we can contrast this approach to that of scientific management and its use of cause–effect as its guiding theory of causality. As was examined in Chapter 6, the theory of cause–effect holds no explanatory power for the operation of free will. Consequently, these acts of personal agency by the client get sidelined to a supporting role in the same manner as their strengths.

As stated previously, the postmodern practitioner's working assumption is that clients—by reason of needing services—are each suffering under an oppressive narrative; this results in the subjugation of client knowledges concerning their strengths, skills, and resources as well as the subjugation of client knowledges concerning instances of their personal agency at work in achieving various successes in confronting their problems. Consequently, knowledge of these strengths and successes fades to the background, rendering them invisible and thinly known to the client.[98] Faced with the challenge of liberating these knowledges, postmodern practitioners see their role as highlighting these strengths and successes with the client so as to render them more visible and better known.[99] The not-knowing stance epitomized by Socrates is ideally suited for such an endeavor. Through genuine curiosity for learning more about the nature of these client strengths and successes, postmodern practitioners encourage clients to more richly describe them in detail (SP,[100] NT,[101] SFT[102]). This greater attention to these strengths and successes serves to lend more weight to their importance.[103] Postmodern practitioners will also skillfully offer compliments in order to underscore the client personal agency driving such successes.[104]

To illustrate many of the aspects of belief described above, this time I will draw upon the case study of Jane from solution-focused therapy/conscientization.[105] Jane came for therapy seeking help to break her cocaine habit, where almost every night she used about $400 worth of cocaine. A sample of the dialogue follows. For the first session, *exceptions* were sought; thus, the focus was placed on describing the situations when she chose not to do coke and to underscore her personal agency at work behind this choice. I have added my comments in brackets.

THERAPIST: So tell me about the times where you do not do coke. [exceptions]
CLIENT: Oh, there are lots of times when I don't do it. I never do coke when I'm going to work or when I am at work.
THERAPIST: Really, how is it you decide not to do coke then? [personal agency]
CLIENT: I would never do that. I am a responsible person [who I am]. My mother did not bring me up to be a coke head.
THERAPIST: Yes, but how do you decide not to do it? [greater detail]
CLIENT: I just tell myself that my mother did not bring me up to be a coke head and I don't do it.
THERAPIST: Are there other times when you do not do coke? [exceptions]
CLIENT: Yes, I never do coke when I am going to see my lover. She would kill me if she saw me high and she always knows.[106]

As can be seen, at no time in this initial session is there the discussion of triggers or causes explaining the times that Jane elects to do coke. Rather, the focus is upon seeking exceptions—times when she deliberately decides not to do coke. The therapist then underscores her personal agency at work during these exceptions and shows genuine curiosity as means to elicit greater detail from the client. Jane clearly affirms an empowering "who I am": a responsible person. This empowering feature of her identity will then be drawn upon to help her attain her "who I want to be."

Jane's second session occurred two and a half weeks later due to her having been on vacation. At this stage, her subjugated knowledge of how she is able to decide not to do coke is still thinly known. Thus, the emphasis of the session is upon eliciting greater details behind her motivation and choices not to do coke.

THERAPIST: So what is different or better since I saw you? [exceptions]
CLIENT: I have not done any coke. Can you believe that!
THERAPIST: That's really great! How did you do that? [detail]
CLIENT: I just don't want to feel bad anymore.
THERAPIST: Of course you don't. But how do you do that? [detail]

CLIENT: Well, some of the time I was on vacation with my lover, so that helped a lot, but I could have gotten some coke. Mostly, I just put it out of my mind.

THERAPIST: Really, what were you thinking instead? [detail]

CLIENT: Well, I was just thinking of myself more and I was sleeping better. Just generally calmer.[107]

For the rest of the session, the focus turned to exploring the "who I want to be." This was accomplished through questions about what things she would be doing instead of coke and encouraging a greater articulation of her "who I want to be," which led to her describing her dreams of changing careers by opening a store. Note how the articulation of her "who I want to be" is not stated in terms of the absence of the problem (i.e., a person who does not do coke). There are two reasons for this. First, to do so grants an undue importance to coke in defining her identity. Rather, her dream of becoming an entrepreneur serves as a future goal defining an empowering identity for Jane. Cocaine only gets its relevance by serving as an obstacle to achieving such a goal. Second, there is never any completion to maintaining the absence of something; it can only be in terms of "up until now." Thus, the problem is granted lifelong importance in defining her identity.

By the end of the second session, the articulation of her personal agency is still thinly known by Jane. The therapist ends the session by providing a compliment to underscore her personal agency at work and a task to promote greater awareness as to what strengths and skills she is drawing upon to motivate her not to do coke.

THERAPIST: I am really excited and impressed that you have not done coke in over three weeks now. . . . I am also very impressed that you have decided to be thinking of yourself more.

THERAPIST: Therefore, I want you between now and the next time to watch closely for how you overcome the temptation to do coke—in other words, the way you say "No" to coke.[108]

By the third session, the client was able to articulate in greater detail the various methods she employed to refrain from using coke. These included picturing herself engaging in buying the coke, cooking it, getting high, then realizing how it would never be enough; hanging around more with friends who were non-drug users, and giving all her money to her lover so that she could be put on an allowance. These actions can then be linked to the strengths she is drawing upon: her sense of responsibility, her imagination, and her sociability. In-between the third and fourth sessions, as typically occurs with those seeking to break a drug habit, Jane had a relapse. Yet, rather than place undue focus on the circumstances leading her to decide to do coke, the therapist uses the relapse as an opportunity to explore more instances of her personal agency at work motivating her to refrain from doing coke.

THERAPIST: How is it that you stopped at $50.00 worth?
CLIENT: Well, once I got high, I freaked out. I got paranoid. I was looking in the bathroom mirror and my eyes were jumping out of my head, sweat was pouring down my face, and I freaked. And I thought, "Something is wrong here," what would my mother say if I died of coke?[109]

The rest of the session was spent exploring the other six days when she successfully refrained from using coke. This yielded a description of a plethora of changes that occurred in her life since starting therapy, which became for her "all the positives of not doing coke." The therapist once again concludes by offering a compliment as well as a task aimed at increasing awareness of the importance and influence of the positive changes she identified as the means to underscore her personal agency at work.

THERAPIST: I am sorry to hear how painful this episode was for you, yet I am very impressed that you stopped at 50 dollars worth. Other people would have continued.
THERAPIST: Continue to do and practice the positives and notice what happens.[110]

Due to her greater articulation of her personal agency at work over these past four sessions, along with a greater awareness of her empowering "who I am" and clear goals of "who I want to be," and with the greater realization of the strengths that she possessed to attain her goals, Jane had achieved conscientization before her fifth session, so there was no turning back for her. She happily conveyed that she had not done coke over the past three weeks and expressed confidence in her ability to continue the changes in her life that helped her refrain from using coke.

The sixth session was scheduled for four weeks later, she described continued abstinence and the solidifying of the positive changes in her life. At this point, both therapist and client agreed that Jane was ready for termination, and a follow-up appointment was set for three months later. At the follow-up appointment Jane reported continued progress, and her case was effectively closed, with the practitioner assuring her that she could call if she ever felt that she needed another session. Thus, this case study reveals the power of conscientization described earlier. Despite dealing with a drug habit, oftentimes viewed as an intractable problem, the client only needed *six sessions* to move past her drug habit for good. The power of conscientization is truly noteworthy.

Hope

By way of recap, Paulo Freire identified three key elements to praxis: faith, belief, and hope. Within postmodern practice, faith sets the stage for the social work helping situation by directing efforts to help clients articulate their personal good. Stemming from this faith, belief directs efforts toward identifying client strengths and successes, thus further empowering the client through the reinforcement of positive identity conclusions. By examining how these strengths have been drawn upon already to effect some positive change, even if just a little bit, focus is placed upon the client's personal agency in bringing about this change. This brings attention to their capacity for change, and thus rouses hope that future steps toward their personal good are achievable.

Each of these approaches places much importance on the rousing of hope to propel the helping process (SFT,[111] NT,[112] SP[113]). Just as Paulo Freire noted that while hope alone is insufficient, without hope one can never achieve praxis,[114] William Sullivan and Charles Rapp state, "hope is an indispensable ingredient for success."[115] This makes sense, again, if we reflect upon the theory of mimesis. In mimesis, the "who I want to be" is what propels present actions—geared toward reaching this desired state. One must have hope that one's "who I want to be" is achievable; otherwise, being seen as impossible, it will not motivate present actions to move toward achieving it. Additionally, client ownership of the helping process is stressed[116] as clients must strongly identify with their "who I want to be" to act upon it. If made to feel as if a "who I want to be" was thrust upon them, clients will be much less motivated to act upon it.

Now, as is the case of the social work profession's long history of recognizing strengths and resources, the importance of hope to the helping process has long been recognized in the social work profession. Similar to free will, hope represents a difference *in kind* between us and animals. Therefore, within the Modern Discourse, it lies beyond the explanatory reach of modernist psychological theories, which are all grounded in naturalism and the causal theory of cause–effect. Consequently, none of the modernist psychological schools that inform psychotherapy approaches have ever contributed toward the development of specific skills or techniques that speak directly to how to rouse hope; rather, they target improvements in functioning.

Conversely, solution-focused therapy/conscientization, narrative therapy/conscientization, and the strengths perspective each has developed techniques on how to rouse hope in clients. Solution-focused therapy/conscientization starts with the miracle question as the means to communicate the practitioner's faith in clients to articulate their personal good.[117] Once this ultimate goal is well articulated, it informs nested subgoals that will lead the client toward this ultimate outcome. Next, the practitioner assumes that clients already possess the strengths, skills, and resources to begin moving toward their goal; and they communicate this belief to clients through questions aimed at searching for *exception* times.[118] Furthermore, these questions serve to awaken clients' belief in themselves. This sets the stage for the rousing of hope. Developing with clients a task for them to perform in-between the present and the next session, practitioners encourage clients to do "more of the same" of what they have been doing during *exception* times.[119] By basing this task upon their previous (even if partial) successes, a spark of hope is ignited that they can begin to move toward problem resolution. When clients return for subsequent sessions, compliments are used to affirm recent successes,[120] and scaling questions are used to numerically mark clients' progress toward their ultimate goal.[121] The attention given to these successes and progress serves to fan the flames of hope even further. As one client notes concerning her experience with solution-focused therapy/conscientization, "They [the therapists] tell you that you have the abilities to change. They don't specifically tell you how that change will come about. But, in time, you begin to see a good change and you come to believe that you do have the ability to change on your own."[122]

Narrative therapy/conscientization commonly starts with externalizing the problem as the means to communicate the practitioner's faith in clients to determine their personal good. By excising the problem from their identity conclusions, clients are freed to immediately embrace empowering identity conclusions reflective of their efforts in combatting the problem.[123] This focus on personal agency at work communicates the practitioner's belief that clients already possess various strengths, skills, and resources to begin combatting the problem and awakens clients' belief in themselves to do so. This occurs through relative influence questioning in which mapping client influence on the problem leads to a search for *unique outcomes*—times when clients were at least partially successful in combatting the problem.[124] Furthermore, even if a client is unable to recall a single unique outcome, the relative influence questioning directs attention toward client strengths that can be used to produce a unique outcome.[125] As in the case above, the attention given to clients' personal agency at work serves to spark hope that they can begin moving toward their desired outcome. This leads to techniques such as bringing in outsider witnesses to affirm the importance of the client's personal agency and progress;[126] the celebration of accomplishments via verbal praise, letters to the client, and certificates of achievement;[127] and the performance of new meaning around unique outcomes that allows clients to restory their relationship to the problem.[128] These techniques further fan the flames of hope within the client. Ultimately, conscientization serves to create an eternal flame of hope.

The strengths perspective uses the strengths assessment as the means to communicate faith in the client, to awaken belief in strengths, and to rouse hope.

Unlike traditional assessments, the strengths assessment represents a collaborative endeavor wherein both parties—practitioner and client—receive a copy.[129] Rather than being a one-and-done assessment, the strengths assessment acts as a living document being continually added to as new developments in the client's life take shape.[130] First, client dreams or aspirations are discussed and recorded.[131] Clients' choice of their ultimate goal is non-negotiable,[132] thus communicating the practitioner's faith in clients that they are capable of determining their personal good. Next, strengths and resources are assumed and looked for, then are added to the assessment.[133] As above, this process communicates belief in clients' possession of strengths as well as awakens this belief in the clients themselves. This belief sparks hope in clients that they can begin moving toward their aspirations. Client priorities are recorded, and these serve as short-term goals for clients.[134] In subsequent sessions, new developments concerning client strengths and successes are added to the strengths assessment, fanning these nascent flames of hope that clients' "who I want to be" is achievable. The purposeful celebration of client accomplishments along the way affirms their progress,[135] feeding the flames of hope even further.

The case study of Ah Yan from solution-focused therapy/conscientization serves as an excellent example to illustrate the rousing of hope within the client as an integral part of the helping process. Ah Yan seeks therapy because she suffers from bouts of severe anxiety. The therapist, Peter De Jong, communicates his faith in Ah Yan to describe her personal good by asking her the miracle question. Peter follows up with questions asking Ah Yan to elaborate various details of this miracle picture in terms of observable behaviors:

PETER: So when the miracle happens, what would be there instead of fear?
AH YAN: Oh, I don't know . . .
[They continue to explore further details]
PETER: So when this miracle happens, you'd be happier? [she nods] So what would he [her husband] notice about you that would tell him that you were happier—on the inside as well as the outside?
AH YAN: I'd talk to him. . . . He'd see I was happier. I wouldn't be crying. I'd have something to eat. I'd do more around the house.
[They continue to explore further details]
PETER: Well, that's OK. You've already mentioned several things that might be different. Let me ask you this: If you were to decide to do just one part of this miracle tomorrow morning, which part would it be the easiest to do?
AH YAN: Oh, I'm not sure. Maybe I could talk to my husband more.
PETER: What might you say to him?
AH YAN: Oh, you know, nothing special. Just say "Good morning, it's a beautiful day. What are you going to do today?" Things like that. That's all.

PETER: So you can do that? [she nods] What would it take for that to happen?

AH YAN: Just doing it, I guess.

PETER: Really, is that true? If you decide to do something, you can make it happen, just by putting your mind to it?

AH YAN: [nodding] Yes, but it's hard because I can still feel really scared inside and . . .

PETER: Yes, I know. From what you have told me, it's going to take a lot of hard work for you to do that.[136]

By asking the miracle question and inquiring about specific details, Peter encourages Ah Yan to begin articulating her personal good. Note how Peter directs Ah Yan away from conceptualizing her personal good in negative terms as the absence of fear. And even when Ah Yan frames her personal good in positive terms—the presence of happiness—Peter encourages her even further to describe observable behaviors that reflect the presence of her personal good and to emphasize her personal agency in making it happen. This sets the stage for the creation of subgoals, beginning with the "easiest to do." This proposed first step provides the spark of hope for Ah Yan that she can act to improve things. Peter then moves into inquiring about exception times. Ah Yan is able to identify that these exception times do occur, but at this point she is unable to articulate her personal agency at work during these exception times.

To start their second session, Peter inquires about exceptions that have occurred between the previous session and now:

PETER: Well, what have you noticed that tells you that things are better?

AH YAN: I'm back to work. I didn't go to work all week last week.

PETER: [wondering if returning to work might somehow represent an exception] Oh, you went back to work this week?

AH YAN: Yeah, this week I went back to work.

PETER: [noticing that she seemed pleased with herself and complimenting her apparent success] Well, good for you!

[Continuing to explore for exceptions]

PETER: [affirming her perception and asking Ah Yan to begin amplifying her exception] Yeah, it sounds very difficult. But sometime during the weekend, you said, you felt better?

AH YAN: Yeah, and this weekend, I fought it. Me and my husband went to a dance. We went to a wedding dance Saturday, and I got kind of sick there in the middle of the dance. And he, my husband, asked me, "Are you OK?" And I says, "No, I don't think so. I want to get out." You know. And he says, "Well, let's go outside." And we went outside for a walk, you know. We went walking for 10 minutes. And he says, "Are you OK? Do you want to go home?" And I says, "No! We're not going home."

Peter [exploring for what was different about the exception and indirectly complimenting] Really? Was that different for you—saying no to leaving like that.

AH YAN: Yeah, it was, and I said, you know, "We're not going to stop." You know, I just—I have to keep going.

[They continue to explore further details]

PETER: Yeah. And then you went back to the dance, and did it come back?

AH YAN: Like it wanted to, but I'd just ignore it. Something like . . .

PETER: [amplifying by explicitly asking for her role in making the exception happen] How do you do that—ignore it?

AH YAN: Because it's like, when it starts, and my mind goes to what's happening to me, it gets worse. It gets worse. And if I just, like brush it off, you know, like they say, brush it off, just forget it, I, like, start talking, you know, paying attention to the people that are talking to me and just . . . I forget about it. You know.[137]

The focus of this second session is upon exploring exceptions. Due to this focused attention placed upon exception times and Ah Yan's personal agency in bringing them about, Ah Yan has moved from responding "I don't know" in the first session when asked about why these exceptions occur to fully embracing and recognizing her role in bringing them about by the end of the second session. This recognition of her successes, further affirmed through Peter's use of compliments, fans her initial spark of hope into a bright flame.

In their further explorations of exceptions, Ah Yan herself identifies the importance of hope in continuing these successes:

PETER: [asking once again for amplification] I can see that you are. Seems like you've already learned a lot. OK. Is there anything else you do differently to put yourself in charge?

AH YAN: Faith. I got to have faith in myself before I do anything. And deep breathe, saying, "OK, you know, stop thinking about what's wrong," you know, 'cause I'm that type. I get a little panicky, "Oh no, what's wrong with me?" You know. Now I says, "No, that's the way I was before," and then, I think back to the way that I used to get, really bad, I'm thinking, "At the time that was happening, what was I thinking then?" I was thinking to myself, I would think more things wrong—you know, "This is going to happen to me, what if this, or what if . . . ?" It just—my mind was going and going and going, you know, and it's like . . .

PETER: So instead of that, now you're doing what?

AH YAN: I'm trying to, you know—how do you say this? [she takes a deep breath][138]

Ah Yan explicitly recognizes the importance of having faith in herself. This confidence, born from her hope that she can act to achieve her "who I want to be," is viewed by Ah Yan as essential to her continued success. She also recognizes that maintaining hope is simply the first step; she must act on that hope by drawing upon her strengths to develop successful strategies that lead her to successes in confronting her anxiety.

Next, Peter begins to employ the technique of scaling as the means to help Ah Yan measure her progress and further affirm her personal agency contributing to her progress. As success builds upon success, reflection upon these successes feeds the flames of hope to even greater heights:

PETER: OK, great. So, let me ask you a question using my numbers again. OK? Let's say that 10 equals the miracle and 0 was where you were at when you decided that you were going to come in and talk with me about this. Where would you say you are at this week?

AH YAN: Now?

PETER: Yeah, now.

AH YAN: Seven, maybe 8.

PETER: Oh wow, 7 or 8! OK. Sure that makes sense. You've been telling me about feeling better and all the things you do to make that happen. Like you're back to work, and you're smiling more, and even when it comes on, you come up with ways to handle it . . .

AH YAN: Yeah, yeah, that's right. I'm doing that.[139]

Not only has the scaling question fanned her flames of hope even higher, but Ah Yan now has taken full ownership of her successes, as indicated by her response "I'm doing that." As was illustrated by the case study of Jane and her experience of a relapse, it is important to note that continuous progress is not necessary for scaling questions to fan hope. If Ah Yan were to return next session and report that she was at a 5 in her progress toward her miracle, Peter would continue to respond in ways that emphasize her personal agency at work in combatting the problem. So he could ask questions such as, "What were you doing that prevented you from falling down to a 4 or a 3?"

In addition to using scaling questions to measure Ah Yan's progress and instill greater hope, Peter then turns to using scaling questions to directly measure the growth of her hope. This direct attention to hope as an essential ingredient for success adds further fuel to its growth:

PETER: Ok. So you're at a 7 or 8 . . . umm, and I've been asking you about all the things that you do to keep them at a 7 or 8. Now, if I were to ask you, "on a scale from 1 to 10, where 1 means that you have no confidence and 10 means you have every confidence, how confident are you that you can keep them at a 7 or 8?" What would you say?

AH YAN: I think a 9.

PETER: Is that right?

AH YAN: Yeah, and I can tell because some things just, I don't know . . .

PETER: Where does that confidence come from? What tells you that you can be that confident, that sure?

AH YAN: I want to be that way . . . to repeat it

PETER: [complimenting an apparent strength] So you're determined.

AH YAN: Yeah, I am. I want to be . . .

PETER: So where does this determination come from?

AH YAN: I don't know. You know, it's just the way I feel right now. It just feels good to feel like this. I just want to keep quiet, so it doesn't come back anymore. I just want to keep going. I know how positive it feels, you know. It's very good.[140]

Peter uses a scaling question to measure her level of confidence, the extent of her hope that she will achieve "who I want to be." He is then able to use this measure as the means to explore the source of her hope. Similar to when they were first exploring her exception times and Ah Yan had difficulty recognizing her personal agency at work, at this point in time she is unable to articulate the source of her hope. However, continued inquiry will bring further attention to her strengths and those strengths in her environment, as well as her personal agency, and thus raise Ah Yan's awareness into the source of her confidence/hope.

The case study of Ah Yan serves as a marvelous example illustrating the various elements to praxis: faith, belief, hope, and conscientization. The miracle question communicates Peter's faith in Ah Yan to articulate her personal good, from which arise various concrete goals Ah Yan feels to be within her reach. The search for exceptions already occurring communicates Peter's belief that Ah Yan possesses the necessary strengths and skills, and this in turn begins to foster Ah Yan's belief in herself in the same manner. Continued exploration of exceptions occurring between sessions, the strategic use of compliments, and use of scaling questions all serve to fan the flames of Ah Yan's hope that she can achieve "who I want to be." The steady inquiry into her personal agency at work bringing about these positive changes leads Ah Yan down the path toward achieving conscientization. After just two sessions, her progress has already been quite significant, to the point that at the end of the second session Peter and Ah Yan begin discussing the parameters for termination. This takes the form of discussing what it will look like to her once she has achieved full conscientization, that is, even though her symptoms may never disappear completely, when she will know that she will never go back to feeling helpless and incapable in the face of her problem, thus ending its oppression over her.

Mimesis

As was covered in Chapter 8, mimesis is the theory of causality defining the post-modern paradigm. As such, it acts as the theory of change which informs social work practices developed within the Postmodern discourse. In a number of important ways, it marks a dramatic departure from how change is conceived in the Modern Discourse. First, there is a shift in focus of the conversation comprising the helping situation. When clients first meet with the social worker, the first step is always to discuss the presenting problem that led them to seek services. For the Modern Discourse's theory of change as action/reaction, the presenting problem represents the reaction. Thus, this first step is followed up by an assessment—such as a bio-psycho-social assessment—which concerns itself with systemic interaction of past experiences of functioning as the means to understand the present condition of dysfunction. Thus, the conversation moves from present concerns to past experiences. This examination of action/reaction yields insights into causes contributing to the problem; at this point, the social worker turns the focus of the conversation to future actions in the form of developing goals with the client.

By contrast, postmodern approaches privilege a future focus.[141] The conversation comprising the helping situation begins the same, with the client discussing present concerns. Within the theory of mimesis these present concerns speak to the "who I am." Following this step, social workers employing postmodern approaches also seek to make an assessment—such as a strengths assessment; however, this assessment turns the focus of the conversation to that of articulating client future goals and aspirations as these represent the "who I want to be."[142] Once the connection between "who I am" and "who I want to be" yields actionable insights, only then do postmodern social workers turn the helping conversation back to the past in the form of exploring for strengths and successes already experienced that can serve to move the client toward their future goal and to "who I want to be."[143]

The second departure from a modernist approach is that greater focus is placed upon client behaviors in the form of successes, as opposed to the problem-solving approach wherein diagnosis requires a careful examination of client failures in functioning. Furthermore, emphasis is placed upon getting the client to articulate their personal agency (i.e., free will) contributing to these successes.[144] The reason there is such a strong emphasis on recognizing personal agency is that within mimesis actions define the person. For example, it is by doing kind acts that I am able to demonstrate (to myself and others) that I am a kind person. Within the helping situation, emphasizing client successes serves to construct their phenomenological essence as one who is empowered.[145]

This process begins by deconstructing with clients the problem-saturated narrative which they are using to organize their current life struggles. In so doing, this helps them to extricate themselves from a "passengerhood" understanding in which they are subject to cause–effect forces acting upon them to embracing an understanding in which they are active participants in the creation of their successes.[146] This serves to change their notion of "who I am" from that of someone who is weak, less than normal, or dysfunctional to an empowered notion of "who I am" which arises from this depiction of the various actions they have already taken to influence the problem to some degree.[147] And as was explained under the section on praxis, this movement to a more empowered "who I am" acts to spur the growth of hope in achieving one's "who I want to be."

Thus, through mimesis, postmodern practitioners focus upon the interaction between action and meaning.[148] A text analogy to human behavior is used to frame this interaction: Client actions and lived experiences take the form of events in a story.[149] Mimesis is the mechanism for how the client's lived experiences are organized and structured into the format of a story.[150] The goal then is to move the client away from an organization of their lived experiences around a problem-saturated plot that depicts the client as a "passenger" in life to the construction of an alternative story around a solution-oriented plot that depicts the client as empowered.

In the construction of this alternative story—a story depicting ingenuity and capacity—future actions in the form of goals also play a role in the construction of this empowering identity.[151] This occurs through examining the various values underlying such goals; these values further define the main "character" in the story (i.e., the client) in terms of their likelihood to perform future actions based upon these values.[152] Consequently, great attention is given to helping the client to articulate what they will be doing as future actions that will be indicative that the hoped-for change has occurred.[153] As stated previously, once client goals and future actions are clearly articulated, attention is turned to examining present and past experiences that depict this ingenuity and capacity already at work.[154] Hence, the plot of this alternative story moves away from one of "(failed) attempts at solving a befuddling problem" to one of "keeping this ingenuity and capacity going."[155] This alternative plot clearly places the client in an empowering light. Lastly, as explained earlier, skillful use of compliments concerning the client's accomplishments of these future actions serves to further strengthen the client's empowering identity that is being socially constructed.[156]

The case study of Mr. H. from the strengths perspective will now be turned to as an example illustrating the above and earlier concepts.[157] Mr. H. had increasing physical health problems. These problems were greatly exacerbated by his frequently not having enough money to pay for his heating and other necessities. If the situation were allowed to deteriorate further, he would probably have to be taken into a nursing home at great expense. And once there, he would probably recover simply as a result of receiving proper care. As far as the practitioner and everyone else (except Mr. H.) was concerned, he needed help in learning to budget properly so that he could heat the house, thus avoiding physical deterioration and being taken into care.

Mr. H. actually preferred to spend his money on gambling. As far as he was concerned, he wanted to feel he was earning his money, and he needed all the money to make enough winnings to be able to make his life easier by going to the pub a lot. He was not concerned about his ill health as long as he could keep meeting his friends in the pub and the betting shop. Since Mr. H. did not feel that he needed to reorganize his financial approach to budget for heating, it would not truly be part of a User-led plan if the Practitioner were to record this as a need. There might be a temptation to nag Mr. H. ("for his own good") into agreeing to put "don't gamble and drink less in order to save money for heating" in his plan. At this point it would not be Mr. H.'s plan but someone else's—no matter how sensible it might be. It would be less likely to succeed than a plan truly based on what he wanted, and intended, to do. The chances are that he would cheat and show signs of low motivation and try and return to the behavior he was actually motivated to do.

Mr. H. was helped to make the connection between his damp house and the likelihood that he would become so ill that he could not carry on his preferred pattern of life. It was pointed out that he would probably have to go to a nursing home some miles away, and would lose contact with his friends. He began to accept that he needed to reconsider his priorities to avoid losing everything. His idea was to work out how much money was needed to be sure that just enough heating was paid for. He would then save half the necessary money and bet the rest on safer "dead certainties" to earn the money. Whilst this was not the Practitioner's original idea of what needed to be done, Mr. H. had at least accepted that he needed to do something. His solution still gave him the opportunity to meet his other social needs and provided motivational challenges whilst taking on board his, and everyone else's, wish to keep him out of a nursing home.[158]

This case study provides a clear contrast to the social engineering approach taken when social workers operate within the Modern Discourse. Under such an approach, the client's presenting problem would be viewed as a deviation from normal functioning: not setting aside sufficient funds to meet his basic needs in maintaining his physical health. A socially engineered solution would seek to convince the client to eliminate or reduce those factors contributing to not having the funds to adequately supply his basic needs: namely his gambling and drinking. It would be unthinkable to adopt a stance of helping the client to find ways to continue to pursue the "dysfunctional" behaviors of gambling and drinking.

By contrast, the postmodern practitioner employing the strengths perspective in this anecdote views the client actions of gambling and drinking in terms of how they speak to the client's essence (i.e., identity) in the forms of "who I am" and "who I want to be." Viewing these actions with genuine curiosity as to why they hold such importance for the client, the social worker gains the understanding that the client values the traits of independence and sociability. By possessing these traits the client will come to know himself as a person who contributes to his own financial independence and who is a good and gregarious friend to others. This is the way that the client views himself now, and he wishes to maintain that view of himself. By gambling, the client exerts his personal agency toward earning income, thus contributing toward maintaining the valued aspect of independence within his preferred image of himself. For the client, exerting his personal agency in deciding to drink alcohol simply provides him the opportunity to socialize at the pub, thus contributing toward maintaining this aspect of his preferred identity.

Once the social worker gains this understanding of the client's preferred essence and, by extension, the client learns that his desire to gamble and to drink at the pub does not come under threat, the social worker and client can begin examining the presenting problem that triggered services: the client not having sufficient funds to meet his basic health needs. First, by not judging or attacking the client's desire to gamble and drink, a truly collaborative partnership is established between the client and social worker, one which is built upon a high degree of trust. Second, by first seeking a clear understanding of the client's preferred essence/identity, the presenting problem no longer takes center stage as the main focus driving the intervention plan. Rather, the presenting problem gains relevance from its relationship to the client's preferred identity (i.e., essence). Based on this preferred essence, the focus of the intervention plan becomes that of helping the client to maintain a modicum of financial independence and to maintain the vibrant social life that he has created for himself. So the presenting problem of the client not having adequate funds to take care of his basic needs becomes viewed in terms of how it may threaten the client's ability to maintain his preferred essence.

It is pointed out to Mr. H. that simply ignoring the presenting problem would most likely result in placing him for a short-term stay in a nursing home. Such an outcome would severely undercut his ability to contribute to his financial independence as well as to continue socializing among his friends. Mr. H. agrees that such an outcome would be highly undesirable; thus, in collaboration with the social worker, Mr. H. begins exploring options as to how he may counter this threat. This leads Mr. H. to agree to "save half the necessary money and bet the rest on safer 'dead certainties' to earn the money." By placing focus upon his personal agency at work in the implementation of this strategy, a new positive trait can be added to the client's preferred essence/identity: being a savvy individual. This will provide further motivation for Mr. H. to take the necessary actions to preserve his preferred essence/identity and, by extension, everyone's preferred outcome of maintaining adequate functioning of his physical health.

As was stated in Chapter 8, the philosopher Paul Ricœur took Aristotle's concept of mimesis and gave it a richer elaboration, describing it as comprising three parts: prefiguration, configuration, and refiguration. Jerome Bruner's concepts of *landscape of action* and *landscape of consciousness* as dual elements to comprise a story serve to further elaborate this mechanism of mimesis. The *landscape of action* centers on organizing these events around a certain plot.[159] The *landscape of consciousness* involves reflecting upon this plot as means to reveal the qualities of the main character (i.e., the client) via the substantiation of the values they embraced to fuel their motivation to perform the said events in the story.[160] Each of Ricœur's three elements to mimesis will now be examined separately regarding their application to postmodern social work practice. By way of illustrating the movement along these three elements, the case study of Nick from narrative therapy/conscientization will be used in each of the sections to follow.

Prefiguration: Default Understanding

As was stated in Chapter 8 when describing the postmodern paradigm, the ontological theory of phenomenology and the epistemological theory of social constructionism both serve to inform mimesis (the postmodern theory of causality). Phenomenology conceptualizes the reality of phenomena as being comprised of both an existence and an essence. Let's use the example of a stop sign to illustrate this conceptualization as well as how it informs our understanding of prefiguration. The physical properties of existence of the typical stop sign found in the United States include that it is octagonal in shape, roughly thirty inches in diameter, colored bright red with the word "STOP" written in white capital letters, and mounted on a pole approximately seven feet off the ground. Its essence, or the meaning we attribute to the stop sign, is that when approaching with a vehicle, one is to make a full stop before continuing one's journey.

Note that while I retain the free will as to whether or not I will bring my vehicle to a complete stop, the meaning attributed to the stop sign—that one is to make a full stop—is not simply my opinion of what I believe the stop sign to represent; rather, its essence is a social construction. This social construction of the stop sign's essence is extremely solid; it has gained universal acceptance as the dominant narrative for understanding the meaning of a stop sign. Well before one learns to drive a car, or even ride a bike, one learns the meaning of the stop sign from one's experience being a passenger in a vehicle as well as when being specifically instructed in driving a motor vehicle.

By the time one learns to drive, this understanding of the meaning of a stop sign is so ingrained in one's psyche that upon approaching a stop sign, little mental energy is needed to grasp what it requires one to do. This natural "default" as to the understanding of a phenomenon's essence is what is represented by prefiguration. And in this example, we can see how useful it is having this default understanding when navigating one's world. Imagine, for example, the scenario of someone who suffers a brain injury that affects their long-term memory concerning reading signs, and thus they have lost the ability to form a prefigurative understanding of stop signs. Each time they approached the stop sign anew, they would have to take the time and energy to decode its meaning. This would make driving a vehicle extremely difficult.

Yet, while necessary and useful in decoding phenomena, prefiguration can have a negative side as well. Just as we all become indoctrinated as to the meaning of the stop sign, within the realm of concerns addressed by social welfare, the people comprising our society get indoctrinated as to the meaning and acceptance of what normal functioning looks like for a plethora of conditions. Now, for the vast majority of people, this is not problematic as many fall within the boundaries of normal functioning. Thus, having this prefigurative understanding confirms their status as normal and promotes an image of themselves as competent. However, social work clients receive services because they need assistance with their life struggles. By being enmeshed within the Modern Discourse, the very existence of this need signifies that they failed to achieve the status of normal functioning. Hence, for these individuals seeking social work services, this prefigurative understanding concerning normal functioning results in the formation of negative identity conclusions, and thus begins to exert an oppressive influence on the person's essence, depicting them as abnormal, dysfunctional, maladaptive, etc.

This negative influence of prefiguration on social work clients is noted by the progenitors of narrative therapy/conscientization, solution-focused therapy/conscientization, and the strengths perspective. They recognize that, similar to the example given above wherein we learn the meaning of the stop sign simply by being passengers in a car, clients come to view their understanding of their problems and life struggles as the natural state of the world.[161] Furthermore, due to the nature of this indoctrination of understanding, they typically remain unaware of the underlying assumptions supporting their understanding.[162]

This becomes problematic in a number of ways. First, clients become inured to the restrictive nature of this dominant narrative underlying their understanding of their problem.[163] Just like when one approaches a stop sign, critical thinking no longer arises when clients begin to examine their life struggles. The default or prefigurative understanding they employ consequently is heavily problem-focused;[164] this is because of the underlying assumptions that place value and importance on norms of functioning as well as on the use of cause–effect as the modality to resolve the client's problem. This then lends an oppressive air to the prefigurative understanding, as was described in detail under the earlier section on praxis. A clear understanding behind the causes of the client's failures drives the investigation into the client's current life struggles as such an understanding is seen as necessary to remedy them. This in turn leads the client to draw negative identity conclusions about themselves.[165]

The second way this prefigurative understanding becomes problematic is that it serves to disempower clients. Rather than taking an active and lead role in authoring the social construction of meaning to their life struggles, clients yield that power by metaphorically adopting the role of passenger to their life struggles.[166] For postmodern practitioners seeking to empower clients in their efforts at social construction, rather than viewing clients' life struggles as simply problems in functioning, they more importantly view them as products of discursive conditions.[167] Ludwig Wittgenstein, a prominent philosopher of language, is turned to for help in framing this understanding of client problems as products of discursive conditions.[168] Prefigurative understanding which leads to negative identity conclusions is seen as arising from traps or knots inherent in language which lead to an uncritical acceptance of the "rules of the game" for generating meaning to the client's lived experiences.[169]

Armed with this understanding of the nature of client problems provided by Wittgenstein, the postmodern practitioner approaches the helping situation as an endeavor at helping the client deconstruct the problem-saturated understanding of their life experiences.[170] The goal of such an approach is to help the client liberate themselves from the oppressive self-imposed constraints and language traps that result in impoverished views of their situation and to thus empower them to take greater authorship in defining both "who I am" and "who I can be."[171] Consequently, when seeking to develop an assessment of the client's life struggles, postmodern practitioners concentrate upon exploring the nature and strength of the grip that the dominant story holds over the client's understanding of themselves.[172]

This type of assessment (as any assessment lays the groundwork for an intervention plan) directs the postmodern practitioner on how to help the client construct an alternative and more empowering understanding of themselves amid their life struggles;[173] this approach is captured by the next stage of mimesis—configuration—which will be explored presently. It is important to note that the transition from prefiguration to configuration does not occur as a clear break: Deconstruction of the dominant narrative opens up space for the configuration of an alternative, more empowering narrative, while the process of configuring an alternative narrative opens space for further deconstruction.[174]

Now let us turn to applying the above aspects of prefiguration to a case study. As mentioned previously, I will be drawing upon a relatively famous case study by Michael White involving a six-year-old boy, Nick, who was experiencing the life struggle of encopresis.

Nick, aged six years, was brought to see me by his parents, Sue and Ron. Nick had a very long history of encopresis, which had resisted all attempts to resolve it, including those instituted by various therapists. Rarely did a day go by without an "accident" or "incident," which usually meant the "full works" in his underwear.

To make matters worse, Nick had befriended the "poo." The poo had become his playmate. He would "streak" it down walls, smear it in drawers, roll it into balls and flick it behind cupboards and wardrobes, and had even taken to plastering it under the kitchen table. In addition, it was not uncommon for Ron and Sue to find soiled clothes that had been hidden in different locations around the house, and to discover poo pushed into various corners and squeezed into the shower and sink drains. The poo had even developed the habit of accompanying Nick in the bath.[175]

The first thing we may note about Nick's case is the connection between prefiguration and praxis. Suffering under a particularly oppressive prefigurative understanding of himself, Nick has experienced the utter destruction of hope in being able to resolve his problem. This results in Nick accepting and embracing his encopresis by befriending the poo.

As mentioned previously, people who seek social work services typically enter the helping situation with a prefigurative understanding of their life struggle prominently anchored in the Modern Discourse and its rules of right which center on norms of functioning. In Nick's case, the norm of functioning being violated is quite clear: normal six-year-olds do not defecate in their pants. When examining the properties of existence (which the Modern Discourse solely does) of six-year-olds, developmentally they are quite capable of controlling their bowel movements. Thus, when Michael White phenomenologically seeks to help Nick and his family to deconstruct their understanding of their life struggle, he does not view the above norm as doubtful or incorrect. Rather, White's concern is the value and importance this property of existence is granted by them (i.e., the power it exerts) in defining Nick as a unique individual (i.e., his essence).

In what White describes as *mapping the influence of the problem*, he begins the deconstructive process by helping the clients examine how their present pre-figurative understanding of their essence in relation to the life struggle they are experiencing has negatively impacted their lives and relationships. White helps them discover the following:

1. The poo was making a mess of Nick's life by isolating him from other children and by interfering with his school work. By coating his life, the poo was taking the shine off his future and was making it impossible for him and others to see what he was really like as a person. For example, this coating of poo dulled the picture of him as a person, making it difficult for other people to see what an interesting and intelligent person he was.

2. The poo was driving Sue into misery, forcing her to question her capacity to be a good parent and her general capability as a person. It was overwhelming her to the extent that she felt quite desperate and on the verge of "giving up." She believed her future as a parent to be clouded with despair.

3. The ongoing intransigence of the poo was deeply embarrassing to Ron. This embarrassment had the effect of isolating him from friends and family.... Ron had always regarded himself as an open person, and it was diffi-cult for him to share his thoughts and feelings with others and at the same time keep the "terrible" secret.

4. The poo was affecting all the relationships in the family in various ways. For example, it was wedged between Nick and his parents. The relationship between him and Sue had become somewhat stressed, and much of the fun had been driven out of it. And the relationship between Nick and Ron had suffered considerably under the reign of tyranny perpetuated by the poo. Also, since their frustrations with Nick's problems always took center stage in their discussions, the poo had been highly influential in the relationship between Sue and Ron, making it difficult for them to focus their attention on each other.[176]

Notice how this above assessment does not focus upon the cause–effect mechanisms leading to the incidents of encopresis in an attempt to problem-solve but, rather, concentrates on the power being exerted by the problem-saturated narrative (i.e., prefigurative understanding) in defining each of the family member's essence and, consequently, the impact the resulting negative identity conclusions have on their relationships with others.

This case study illustrates quite prominently the particularly insidious nature of oppression as it occurs within the postmodern context of circulating within the discourse. It is put further into relief when contrasted to the nature of oppression as understood within the Modern Discourse. By concentrating upon properties of existence, the Modern Discourse views oppression as being structural in nature. For example, the Jim Crow laws of the Old South were an expression of structural oppression. The power being exerted by structural oppression seeks to restrict the actions or freedom of a target population. It does this in a blanketed fashion; all members of the target population suffer under the oppression, and its operation is readily visible.

The oppression circulating within a discourse is much more hidden in nature. Clearly visible is the existence of a biological or social norm; in Nick's case this norm is that developmentally six-year-olds are quite capable of controlling their bowel movements. What often goes undetected, slipping under one's conscious awareness as a default understanding (i.e., prefiguration), is the dominant implicit meaning that naturally flows from one's recognition of the norm and that speaks to one's essence. In this example, it is the following: Normal six-year-olds do not defecate in their pants. Or, as it might be interpreted through a child's eyes, good boys don't defecate in their pants. Thus, Nick begins to view himself as a bad boy, undeserving of his parents' love. This in turn saps his hope that he can achieve his "who I want to be": a good boy who makes his parents proud.

And here we can see the insidious nature of this form of oppression. Unlike structural oppression, the social construction of "normal/good six-year-olds do not defecate in their pants" in and of itself is not oppressive. In fact, for upward of 99% of the population—those who have adequate control of their bowel movements at six years of age—it serves a positive function in that it reinforces their view of themselves as a normal and competent person. It is only when this social construction is applied to the unique context of Nick's life that it becomes oppressive. Thus, this also serves as specific illustration of one of the broad distinctions between the Modern Discourse and the Postmodern discourse. With its focus on properties of existence, the Modern Discourse primarily views individuals as members of a population group, whether it be a targeted group for structural oppression or a targeted treatment group in the form of evidence-based practice. With postmodern practitioners' focus upon one's essence as the vehicle to promote change, it is the uniqueness of the client and the context of their life situation that gets emphasized. Thus, treatment is directed toward assisting clients in confronting their oppressive prefigurative understanding of their life situation and helping them to generate an alternative, more empowering understanding of their life situation. Generating this more empowering alternative narrative serves to rob the oppressive narrative of its power. This in turn renews hope and frees the individual to begin taking positive actions toward change. This process of generating an alternative social construction is what takes place in the next phase of mimesis: configuration.

Configuration: The Personal Is Political

I have argued previously that one of the key aspects informing postmodern practice is Paulo Freire's concept of *conscientization* and that attempting to apply various insights from these approaches while continuing to operate within the Modern Discourse and its paradigm of understanding naturally leads to this crucial aspect being completely overlooked. Furthermore, I have gone as far as to argue that narrative therapy and solution-focused therapy are misnomers for what is actually taking place; that these approaches more appropriately should be described as *narrative conscientization* and *solution-focused conscientization*. Paul Ricœur's concept of *configuration* as applied within these approaches clearly represents a process of conscientization. Consequently, postmodern practitioners describe their approach as a form of consciousness-raising.[177]

Before proceeding to examine in detail the configuration process captured by these postmodern approaches, it may be useful to tease out some of the nuances between traditional forms of therapy and these postmodern efforts at conscientization. An excellent historical example illustrative of this dynamic is provided to us by the women's liberation movement in the form of women's consciousness-raising groups that formed in the late 1960s and early 1970s. Similar to the misnomer of narrative and solution-focused efforts as narrative therapy and solution-focused therapy, these women's consciousness-raising groups were often touted by the less informed as simply representing a form of personal therapy.[178] It wasn't until Carol Hanisch pushed backed in her now famous and seminal essay "The Personal Is Political" that the discussions being held in these groups were described as a political activity seeking to confront structural oppression in society in the form of patriarchy.[179] The main goal of these groups was to confront taken-for-granted norms concerning the role of women in society and to take back control over defining what it meant to be a woman:[180] succinctly summarized by Hanisch when stating, "women are messed over, not messed up!"[181] We now describe this process of confronting taken-for-granted normative social constructions as *deconstruction*. The first step in deconstruction is to bring into conscious awareness these taken-for-granted social constructions, with the next step involving their examination and critique.

The parallels between these consciousness-raising groups and the postmodern approaches discussed in this chapter are numerous. Both conceive of the oppression being experienced as insidious in nature by being so deeply embedded into the social mores and customs of society that they are all-pervasive and thus typically unnoticed and unexamined.[182] And by advancing the propaganda of undisputable interpretations of social norms, this insidious oppression indoctrinates individuals into policing themselves.[183] All confront these taken-for-granted social constructions in the form of consciousness-raising.[184] The raising of one's consciousness results in making the previous implicit assumptions explicit and the new understanding that the oppressive norms were not of their making.[185]

Admittedly, for both the women's consciousness-raising groups of the 1960s and 1970s and present efforts at postmodern social work practice, this revelation provides a therapeutic element naturally arising from their newly empowered understanding of their life struggles and of themselves. One way it does this is that when examining one's life struggles, it helps individuals move away from self-blame and the negative identity conclusions engendered by it.[186] Realization occurs that feelings of inadequacy in the face of one's problems are not personal failings but, in fact, products of an oppressive narrative of accepted social norms and mores.[187] Thus, in the face of one's life struggles this newly empowered understanding of oneself begins to engender positive identity conclusions that embolden hope in one's capacity to successfully resolve said life struggles.[188] And the second therapeutic benefit is the level of freedom that occurs when liberated from the old oppressive understandings;[189] people begin to think for themselves and move from being simply a passenger to being an active driver in the process of socially constructing the meaning of their life struggles.[190] Yet the political activity of confronting oppression remains the core of both approaches;[191] as Hanisch emphasized, "I prefer to call even this aspect 'political therapy' as opposed to personal therapy."[192]

Such "political therapy," or what Freire terms conscientization, involves the examination of power supporting the experienced oppression. By ending one's isolation,[193] both seek to undercut the power and survival of one's afflicting personal problems.[194] Within the realm of narrative conscientization and solution-focused conscientization, this ending of isolation begins with the therapist joining with the client in dialogue; and then, in time, significant others are brought into the dialogue as well (which will be discussed further in the next section on refiguration). For both, the ending of isolation frees individuals to begin verbalizing feelings and alternative knowledges that previously were dismissed as unimportant.[195] As a final note of comparison, similar to the laments of the progenitors of the postmodern practice approaches,[196] Hanisch would later lament how her concept of "personal is political" has been misunderstood and misused by many who followed her, and thus must be defended against revisionism by those still trapped in an old way of thinking.[197]

Hopefully, the above comparison to women's consciousness-raising groups has yielded a deeper understanding as to why postmodern social work approaches are conceived of primarily as a political activity by those who practice them.[198] However, there is one contrast worth noting as well. Women in the consciousness-raising groups sought to confront an oppression that was structural in nature in the form of patriarchy. The social constructions arising from these old, patriarchal customs granted privileges across clearly demarcated gender lines, making them a bit easier to examine, whereas the oppression being confronted by clients receiving postmodern social work services is much subtler in nature. Circulating within a discourse, oppression takes the form of norms of functioning, the objective knowledge of which often arises from scientific observation, not societal customs or traditions. Thus, as was stated earlier, no one will dispute the fact that six-year-old children have the developmental capability to control their bowel movements.

But for those children who fall outside this norm of behavior, this objective statement advances the implicit meaning that such outliers are dysfunctional, abnormal, etc. This is subjective knowledge that speaks to the phenomenon's essence, and thus can be confronted; this confrontation is not aimed at attacking the objective knowledge of the client's functioning but, rather, attacking the weight and importance granted to it in defining the individual. The challenge then becomes one in which the incidents of encopresis are not ignored but, rather, surrounded by events depicting the valiant efforts by these children to overcome the problem they are struggling against. In such a move, the valiant efforts of the child take on greatest importance in defining who they are. This is the shape that configuration takes within the postmodern helping situation: the process of seeking heretofore neglected experiences of client triumphs and success and plotting them into a narrative in such a way as to promote an empowering image of the client in the face of the problem.

Before configuration can take place, the client must break free of the prefigurative understanding and narrative under which they are operating. Each approach uses a specific technique by which to confront this prefigurative understanding. For solution-focused conscientization it is the miracle question: "Furthermore, the miracle question requires an alteration in both the therapist's and the client's everyday way of thinking. And this is a rather rapid paradigmatic shift from the way most people conceptualize and talk about problems both in therapy and everyday life."[199] The choice to evoke an image of a miracle taking place as the means to stimulate the client's imagination to describe life absent the problem is quite deliberate. Doing so provides two important means by which the prefigurative understanding is confronted. First, describing the hoped-for change as a miracle frees up the client's imagination to consider "an unlimited range of possibilities" and encourages the client to "think big."[200] This opens the client's mind to exploring multiple possible realities, which serves as a powerful driver for change. Second, aligning with mimesis concerning how change occurs, it prompts the client to be future-focused. This moves clients away from their prefigurative understanding and its focus on current and past problems and toward describing a "preferred future" in which their identity (i.e., "who I am") is no longer definitively tainted by the presence of the problem.[201]

Narrative conscientization relies upon *externalizing the problem* as its technique to confront prefigurative understanding, "the externalization of the problem helps persons identify and separate from unitary knowledges and 'truth' discourses that are subjugating of them."[202] Externalization of the problem confronts one's prefigurative understanding in a number of important ways. It does so by creating a narrative framework in which the problematic behavior is painted as an antagonist—an outside force acting against the best interests of the client.[203] This serves to deconstruct the essence being depicted by prefiguration by directly targeting it,[204] thus loosening the grip of its power.[205] Externalization effectively excises the problematic behavior from the client's identity,[206] thus undercutting the negative identity conclusions that derive from association with the problematic behavior.[207] This narrative framework of externalization creates opportunities for clients to redefine their identity in a more empowering manner by freeing up space in which to identify partial successes in confronting the problem.[208] This is important for with mimesis one is defined by one's actions; the identification of partial successes serves to invite examination as to the client's personal agency in bringing them about,[209] resulting in more empowering identity conclusions.[210]

The strengths perspective uses the strengths assessment to aid clients in confronting their prefigurative understanding, "The creative practitioner does not see the strengths assessment as paperwork, but rather a canvas on which to create a portrait of the unique person that is before them."[211] Similar to narrative conscientization's use of the miracle question, the strengths assessment directs the client to think in terms of preferred futures. It does this by seeking to capture that client's aspirations and dreams across seven life domains.[212] The strengths assessment is viewed as a tool that is used to record and organize multiple strengths of the client.[213] The very act of recording these multiple strengths serves to confront one's prefigurative understanding of oneself as a failure, incompetent, dysfunctional, etc. In turn, client strengths form the building blocks of the new, empowering narrative identity that arise as the product of the configuration process. Hence, the goal of a strengths assessment is to amplify the well part of the client,[214] which serves to help them reclaim a sense of who they are removed from the oppressive yoke of a disempowering narrative of failure.[215] In line with a phenomenological understanding of individuals, it seeks to highlight the uniqueness of the client.[216] Client problems are not ignored; rather, a more holistic view of the client is sought.[217]

With the grip of prefigurative understanding now loosened, clients' minds are opened to the possibility of multiple realities; hence, these postmodern approaches turn next to developing an alternative social construction of their lived experiences.[218] By its very nature of being a *social* construction, the collaborative nature of the configuration process is emphasized,[219] a process in which the metaphor of author/editor is evoked to describe the client/social worker roles.[220] As "author," the client is the ultimate arbiter as to what lived experiences are to comprise the alternative social construction,[221] whereas, as editor, the social worker's responsibility is to ask questions which invite the client to consider new possibilities.[222]

Based upon Ricœur's concept of human time (i.e., the temporal unfolding that occurs within a narrative framework), configuration involves the careful selection of events that align themselves to a particular theme.[223] Within the postmodern social work helping situation, the existence of the presenting problem that triggered services comprises the core elements to the client's narrative. Within literary theory, such core elements to a story are known as *constituent events*—they constitute the core elements to the plot of the story (which for the social work helping situation is the client's currently experienced life struggle with their presenting problem) and, hence, cannot be removed from the narrative without making the story into something different.[224] This understanding of constituent events resonates with the claim by postmodern practitioners that they are not simply putting on rose-colored glasses and conveniently ignoring the problem.[225]

However, the majority of events comprising a narrative are known as *supplementary events*. Supplementary events are not essential to the plot of the story; they can easily be removed and replaced by another event.[226] Yet, supplementary events contribute to the theme that arises from the story.[227] And when a narrative takes the form of a biography, as is the case for the client in the helping situation, the theme that arises speaks directly to the client's identity (as it is defined by the client's actions in their life story).[228] Under the modernist problem-solving approach wherein information gathering involves the hunt for cause–effect linkages to the problem, the supplementary events being added to the narrative primarily speak to failures in functioning; hence, a theme arises of failure and dysfunction.[229] Postmodern practitioners, seeking to help the client configure an empowering theme, seek supplementary events that speak to client successes in the face of the problem.

Solution-focused practitioners describe these supplementary events as *exceptions*.[230] Narrative practitioners describe them as *unique outcomes*.[231] And strengths practitioners simply refer to them as *successes*.[232] However, the goal for each is the same. They seek events that depict competence and capacity in the face of the problem,[233] as well as in other areas of the client's life unrelated to the problem.[234] As these empowering supplementary events are added to the clients' alternative narrative of their life events, the postmodern practitioner prompts clients to reflect upon what these events reveal about the client's identity.[235] This will involve asking clients to articulate their personal agency involved in making these events come to pass.[236] As the empowering identity arising from this configuration of events takes shape, the postmodern practitioner directs the client to consider possible near-term future actions that would also be reflective of this empowering identity serving as the theme of the emerging configured narrative.[237] These imagined future possibilities then become objectives to accomplish between sessions, which serve to promote a plot of progress for the emerging configured narrative.[238] The image of a journey of self-discovery is often evoked by these postmodern practitioners to describe the nature, and consciousness-raising aspects, of this configuration process.[239]

The configuration process taking place in postmodern interventions is succinctly summarized by these words of Michael White and David Epston: "when persons seek therapy, an acceptable outcome would be the identification or generation of alternative stories that enable them to perform new meanings, bringing with them desired possibilities—new meanings that persons will experience as more helpful, satisfying, and open-ended."[240] The generation of these alternative stories, and the alternative social constructions that they spawn, is experienced by clients as a liberating act of freedom, one in which they assume greater control over defining their life stories.[241] The goal of the social worker is to inspire clients in this newfound freedom to create rich and thick descriptions of their lives and relationships, that is, descriptions that generate many possibilities for action in ways that were previously never considered.[242]

Let's now turn back to the case study of Nick as a means to illustrate various elements of the configuration process.[243] White started the first session by asking Nick and his parents to relate how the problem was impacting their lives and relationships; White describes this as an endeavor at *mapping the influence of the problem*. This process revealed the family's prefigurative understanding of their situation. They had embraced the dominant social constructions arising from their knowledge of the normative functioning of six-year-olds: "Normal/good boys are able to control their bowel movements," and, "competent parents are able to potty train their children by age six." The intense shame felt at failing to meet these normative standards had the effect of getting the family members to police their own behavior: Nick withdrew from socializing with other children; the parents stopped inviting family and friends over for visits; and the topic of Nick's incidents began to dominate the conversations between Sue and Ron, leaving little time to nurture their own relationship.

White then proceeded to employ the technique of externalizing the problem. He invited Nick and his parents to begin considering the encopresis as their nemesis. Nick even granted his nemesis the name "Sneaky Poo." This move mirrors that of the theme "women are messed over, not messed up" stated by Carol Hanisch when describing the workings of the women's consciousness-raising groups. Externalizing the problem in such terms takes the implicit prefigurative understanding of "I'm messed up" and makes it explicit by setting it in contrast to a new theme of "I'm messed over" by the problem. Next, after getting the family to consider their actions within this new theme of a struggle against one's nemesis, White began to help the family explore their personal agency at work in resisting the demands of Sneaky Poo.

White describes this line of questioning as *mapping the influence of persons* on the problem, which he begins by asking the family members about their acts of resistance in the face of the problem, what he terms *unique outcomes*. Nick proceeds to "recall a number of occasions during which he had not allowed Sneaky Poo to 'outsmart' him. These were occasions during which Nick could have cooperated by 'smearing,' 'streaking,' or 'plastering,' but declined to do so."[244] Sue describes times in which she chose not to let an incident drive her into misery. The fact that Nick has experienced various "incidents" remains as the constituent event making up the plot of this story as a life struggle. However, these various acts of resistance become supplementary events in the new alternative narrative being constructed, replacing the prefigurative supplementary events of failure and incompetence. White describes this process as follows:

> After identifying Nick's, Sue's, and Ron's influence in the life of Sneaky Poo, I introduced questions that encouraged them to perform meaning in relation to these examples, so that they might "re-author" their lives and relationships.
>
> How had they managed to be effective against the problem in this way? How did this reflect on them as people and on their relationships? What personal and relational attributes were they relying upon in these achievements? Did this success give them any ideas about further steps that they might take to reclaim their lives from the problem? What difference would knowing what they now knew about themselves make to their future relationship with the problem?[245]

Consequently, from these supplementary events of resistance, a new theme arises along the lines of "good/smart boys fight against Sneaky Poo." The effects of embracing this new social construction are profound. Under the prefigurative social construction of "normal six-year-olds are able to control their bowel movements," Nick would have to completely resolve his problem before regaining the status of "normal." Until this occurs, he suffers under the negative identity conclusion of being abnormal, or a failure. Yet under the new social construction of "good/smart boys fight against Sneaky Poo," Nick immediately becomes liberated from such negative identity conclusions and dons the mantle of "good/smart boy." As such, this alternative social construction begins to undercut the power of the previously dominant prefigurative social construction. This process echoes Paulo Freire's assertion that once conscientization becomes firmly rooted in the mind of the individual, simply acting to resist the oppressive structures immediately sets one on the transformative path to becoming more fully human and empowered.[246] The same can be said as taking place with the parents dethroning the prefigurative social construction of "competent parents are able to potty train their children by six years old" and embracing the new social construction of "competent parents fight against Sneaky Poo."

By being placed in the role of protagonist/hero(ine) of one's story, each family member is able to move away from self-blame and its accompanying negative identity conclusion, and instead, embrace the empowering image of oneself as heroically defying an overwhelming force in one's life. In turn, these supplementary events of resistance engender hope that such acts of resistance may continue into the future and even be improved upon. Thus, each family member is invited to consider possible future acts of resistance they might take against the problem, providing a source of future supplementary events to be added to the story. Nick stated that he is ready to resist further Sneaky Poo's invitations to become its playmate. Sue expressed additional ideas on how she would resist Sneaky Poo from driving her to misery. And Ron felt ready to take the risk of sharing with his co-workers his family's struggle with Nick's encopresis as a means to resist the isolating influence of Sneaky Poo.

White set the second meeting for two weeks later. Upon arriving for the second meeting, Nick reported that he only had a single incident in the intervening time span. Ron and Sue expressed similar successes in their efforts. This case study serves as an excellent example of the power of conscientization. After only a single session, family members were able to achieve tremendous progress versus a previously intractable problem.

Refiguration: Reflection in Action

I encouraged Nick, Sue, and Ron to reflect on and speculate about what this success said about the qualities that they possessed as people and about the attributes of their relationships. I also encouraged them to review what these facts suggested about their current relationship with Sneaky Poo. In this discussion, family members identified further measures that they could take to decline Sneaky Poo's invitations to support it.[247]

Whereas configuration evokes the image of client as author of alternative narratives of their life experiences, refiguration evokes the image of persons as audience members. And within the configuration–refiguration process, the role of audience member is crucial.[248] If a narrative of a person's life experiences is generated but there is no audience to receive it and react to it, then it is bereft of all power to transform the individual.[249] For it is a theory of epistemology which speaks to how we know our knowledge of reality is accurate. And within the postmodern discourse, the theory of epistemology is social constructionism. Audience members provide the social component of the construction process, thus turning the generated narrative into a social construction. When sharing a narrative with an audience and the audience's reaction is that the narrative both makes sense and is believable, epistemologically they begin to affirm the verisimilitude of the newly configured narrative. This is turn lends power to the newly configured social construction, which then serves to empower the individual to perform future actions consistent with its theme: for example, valiantly defying the influence of one's problem. This resonates with Paulo Freire's articulation of hope within the conscientization process. In addition, it resonates with Aristotle's emphasis on the importance of hope, in which, when hope is lacking, individuals will view their "who I want to be" as being unobtainable and thus will not act toward attaining it.

Similar to the writing process, the configuration–refiguration process involves producing an initial draft, followed by frequent rewrites.[250] Thus, configuration and refiguration act in sync, producing a feedback loop within which the newly emerging socially constructed narrative is fine-tuned and honed. Within the social work helping situation, the first audience member who is appealed to is the social work practitioner.[251] In their role as editor, the social work practitioner first seeks to communicate to the clients that their problem-saturated description of their life struggles makes for a poor story; in effect, it does not accurately reflect who they are as a person and in fact may be covering up their "true" selves.[252] This occurs through asking questions that seek exceptions to the problem, unique outcomes, and strengths. These questions serve as invitations to begin the configuration process.

Next, as audience member, the social work practitioner will paraphrase the elements of the configured narrative as they emerge as a means to check for understanding, which in turn serves to acknowledge the viability of the alternative narrative. This will be followed by questions seeking greater detail, particularly concerning the client's personal agency at work, as a means to solidify the configured narrative through providing a fuller, richer description of its events.[253] This then leads to the social work practitioner asking questions that invite clients to reflect upon the newly emerging configured narrative, in effect recruiting them to be audience members to their own story.[254] In future sessions, as clients begin adding more unique outcomes to their emergent narrative, the social work practitioner as audience member may offer compliments[255] or seek to celebrate with the client their accomplishments,[256] each of which serves to further solidify and affirm the verisimilitude of the client's newly configured narrative.

Stemming from the work of the literary theorists Algirdas Julien Greimas and Joseph Courtes, White describes this invitation to clients to become audience members to their own story as comprising *landscape of action* questions and *landscape of consciousness* questions posed to the client.[257] Landscape of action questions invite the client to examine gaps in their story development, prompting them as author to then begin providing richer detail to their narrative.[258] Landscape of consciousness questions invite clients to reflect upon the various supplementary events of the configured narrative (i.e., exceptions, unique outcomes, and strengths) in terms of what they reveal about the protagonist (i.e., the client) regarding the qualities that they possess, the values that they hold, and the underlying motivation for future acts.[259] This prompts clients to articulate preferred identity claims, which, now being explicit, can be further validated by additional audience members in the form of significant others and the social worker.[260] Coming at it from a different angle, Steve De Shazer draws upon the work of Ludwig Wittgenstein and his theory of language games to conceptualize this process of validating preferred identity claims and preferred outcomes by others.[261]

As the configuration–refiguration process becomes established between the client and social worker, the next step is to broaden the scope of audience members invited to participate in this process.[262] With only the client and social worker as audience members, the emerging narrative is still weak and vulnerable to being swept aside by the dominant narrative.[263] Once again drawing upon social constructionism as the theory of epistemology, it tells us that the greater the social network contributing to the social construction, the greater the validation of said social construction as being accurate and representative of reality. Thus, an effort is made to build this social network by inviting as audience members family members, friends, co-workers, and other significant persons in the client's life.

This can be accomplished in a number of different ways. One is to include significant others symbolically or virtually.[264] This entails asking the client to step into the shoes of someone that they know in order to describe what they believe this person's reaction would be to the social construction. For example, asking the client to identify someone who would be least surprised to learn the following: the client's recent accomplishments in defying the problem, the particular value held by the client that is motivating the client to reach for said accomplishments, or particular qualities possessed by the client that are contributing toward achieving these accomplishments.[265]

Another technique is to ask the client to write letters (or emails) to these significant persons sharing these accomplishments, values, and qualities.[266] In one particularly creative example, Michael White was working with a child who had suffered trauma and had identified the value of fairness as being particularly important to her in guiding her actions. In exploring the history played by this value in the child's life, the client identified her favorite book (*Pipi Longstocking*) as being particularly inspirational in this regard. White then helped the child write a letter to this book's author, acknowledging this author's contribution toward her development of her value of fairness.[267]

Of course, the traditional route of inviting significant persons into the therapy sessions is another means to recruit audience members. In addition, as a between-session task clients may be asked to share their emergent narrative with significant persons in their life.[268] As is the case with the social worker as audience member, these significant persons may also join in the celebrations of accomplishments, as well as provide compliments as audience member reactions, which then further strengthen the emerging narrative. This approach does not have to be limited to family members. Group work, for example, provides a ready audience for clients to share their newly configured narrative.[269] In addition, individuals sharing a common problem do not have to be limited to those currently experiencing the problem. In what Michael White refers to as "outsider witnesses," narrative practitioners will invite former clients who successfully overcame their problem, and thus now play the role of experts in this regard.[270] Not only does this provide a sympathetic audience for the current client's configured narrative but also it further reinforces the former clients' image of themselves as a success. White describes this entire process as engaging in a definitional ceremony, a ceremony of storytelling in which the newly defined image of the client's "who I am" is acknowledged and validated.[271]

Moral Blind Spots of the Postmodern discourse

In each of the previous chapters describing social work practices in the Colonial Era, the Premodern Era, and the Modern Era, I ended the chapter with an examination of the moral blind spots to practice arising from that particular discourse. I will not attempt to do the same for the Postmodern discourse. This is not due to the belief that the Postmodern discourse does not have any moral blind spots, as all discourses do. Rather, it is due to the fact that the Postmodern discourse has yet to achieve a dominant status; as such, the moral blind spots arising from such dominance have yet to be revealed. I will leave that task to a future historian, should it come to pass that the Postmodern discourse ascends to dominance.

Reflections Phases of the Helping Process

The practice of social work is about facilitating positive change in the client. As such, one's theory of how change occurs (i.e., theory of causality) will structure how the helping process will proceed. This structure is typically conceived in terms of phases to the helping process. Postmodern practice approaches embrace mimesis as their theory of change, whereas modernist approaches embrace cause–effect. Hence, it will be no surprise that the postmodern practice approaches call for a new conceptualization of the phases of practice. Within the Modern Discourse, these broad phases are study, diagnose, treatment; these phases directly mirror the broad phases of the scientific method. While no declarative statements addressing the issue of unique phases have been made in the academic literature concerning postmodern practice, I would argue that the phases of treatment within the Postmodern discourse can be conceived of as follows: *confront, generate, solidify.* These postmodern phases of treatment seek to mirror the broad phases of phenomenological inquiry. Before exploring these phases further, it will be useful to review the phases of treatment in the Modern Discourse to set a point of contrast with what follows.

The Modern Discourse: Study, Diagnose, Treatment

In Chapter 7, it was discussed how during the 1950s the Council on Social Work Education (CSWE) was formed and that one of their first tasks was to articulate a common base for all of social work. Turning to the medical field for inspiration, the CSWE embraced the medical model as a defining feature of social work and saw the practice phases of study, diagnose, and treatment stemming from the medical model as representing a commonality among all social work interventions. With the medical model being heavily grounded upon the scientific method, it is no surprise that the practice phases of study, diagnose, and treatment mirrored the main steps of the scientific method: observe, form a hypothesis, and then test the hypothesis. Over the subsequent years, the term *medical model* began taking on negative connotations, so the more neutral term *problem-solving process* replaced *medical model* to describe the overall conceptual framework guiding the phases of social work practice.

In addition, while various practice phases would be added over the years (such as evaluation), the practice phases of study, diagnose, treatment remain central to social work practice within the Modern Discourse and continue to serve as a commonality representing all social work interventions. However, seeking to shed their overly medicalized connotations stemming from their association with the medical model, these core phases of social work practice—while remaining unchanged in substance—were also rebranded. Thus, the process of gathering information from the client that took place in the study phase now occurs in the rebranded phase of *engagement*, wherein not only the gathering of information is emphasized but also the building of trust in the helping relationship. The analysis of this collected information in order to form cause–effect linkages of the presenting problem, which before took place in the diagnose phase, now takes place in the *assessment* phase. And the development and implementation of a plan for intervention, which before took place in the treatment phase, now occurs in the *intervention* phase. The continued centrality of these phases to social work practice within the Modern Discourse is demonstrated by the CSWE's most recent accreditation standards: the *2015 Educational Policy and Accreditation Standards* (EPAS). Within the 2015 EPAS, nine overall competencies are identified as being essential for social workers to possess, four of which (numbers 6, 7, 8, and 9) relate to direct practice: *Engagement* comprises competency 6, *assessment* comprises competency 7, and *intervention* comprises competency 8 (with competency 9 being *evaluation*).

Lastly, worthy of mention is the development of ecological systems theory in the 1970s, its articulation into person-in-environment, and then its subsequent widespread adoption as the de facto conceptual model defining social work practice. Based upon ecological systems found in nature, person-in-environment conceives of individuals existing in a social environment, wherein the biological and psychological aspects of the person interact with the social aspects of the environment. The main theme arising from this model is that of adaptation. When clients come to receive social work services, their presenting problem is viewed as the result of a maladaptation to their social environment. Thus, putting it all together, within the Modern Discourse the problem-solving approach—built upon the scientific method—provides the overall conceptual framework guiding the social work practice phases of engagement (study), assessment (diagnose), and intervention (treatment), whereas the concept of adaptation from ecological systems theory provides the overall theme directing these phases.

The Postmodern discourse: Confront, Generate, Solidify

The above summary will now serve as a useful contrast to the shape of social work practice within the Postmodern discourse wherein the three core phases of practice can be described as *confront*, *generate*, and *solidify*. Similar to the Modern Discourse, these three phases stem from the Postmodern discourse's understanding of causality: that being mimesis. And just as the scientific method arose as the means to investigate concerns over cause–effect (the theory of causality for the Modern Discourse), Paul Ricœur's description of the mimetic process—comprised of the stages of prefiguration, configuration, and refiguration—serves as the means to investigate concerns over mimesis (the theory of causality for the Postmodern discourse). The process of conscientization—built upon the mimetic process—provides the overall conceptual framework guiding the postmodern social work practice phases of confront, generate, and solidify. As postmodern practice seeks to target change in the client's phenomenological essence, the idea of becoming (achieving a higher or better state of being) acts as the theme directing these phases within the mimetic process.

Prefiguration represents the stage in which clients enter the helping relationship. Under the current societal understanding of social work within the Modern Discourse, the criterion for triggering social work services is that the client is experiencing some form of maladaptation, or dysfunction. For those persons experiencing the same life struggles (e.g., depression), this is what distinguishes those who do not need social work services from those deemed to need them: Those who are effectively addressing their life struggle are seen as capable and possessing appropriate coping strategies and/or a responsive environment allowing them to adapt on their own; those in need of social services are seen as experiencing significant dysfunction arising from not adequately being able to adapt to their environment according to scientifically based and societal norms of functioning. Typically, this prefigurative understanding of why one needs social work services carries with it a disempowering social construction yielding negative identity conclusions depicting the client as abnormal, weak, and/or dysfunctional. This was illustrated in the case study of Nick by the social construction, "good/normal six-year-old boys do not soil their underwear."

Thus, this normative social construction exerts an oppressive influence on clients' phenomenological essence. Their image of "who I am" is depicted in a disempowering light. This in turn undercuts their hope of achieving their image of "who I would like to be." As their image of "who I would like to be" motivates present actions, such an oppressive social construction serves to restrict individuals from effectively addressing and moving beyond their current life struggle. Thus, the task of the postmodern practitioner becomes that of helping the client to *confront* this oppressive social construction. This occurs through the process of deconstruction wherein—by using such techniques as the miracle question, externalizing the problem, or a strengths assessment—the postmodern practitioner seeks to open clients' minds to the possibility of creating alternative social constructions by organizing their lived experiences in a different manner.

This then leads to the next mimetic stage of configuration. Herein, the goal of the postmodern practitioner is to inspire the client to *generate* alternative social constructions that depict the client's phenomenological essence in an empowering light. This serves to empower the client's image of "who I am," thus fostering hope that the client's image of "who I would like to be" is attainable and motivating the client's actions to begin moving toward this change. In turn, these empowered actions then become new supplementary events to be added to the alternative social construction being generated by the client, and thus serve to provide richer detail to the social construction.

This then leads to the mimetic stage of refiguration. Refiguration involves the postmodern practitioner helping the client to recruit an audience for the client's emerging social construction being generated via configuration. As important people in the client's life begin to listen to and affirm this new organization of the client's lived experiences into a configured narrative, the empowering social construction arising from this narrative strengthens, and its verisimilitude begins to *solidify*. Termination of services occurs when the verisimilitude of the empowering social construction has solidified to the extent that it takes over as clients' default understanding, thus becoming the new prefigurative understanding which clients use to help them navigate their world.

Value-Based Practice

Another point of contrast to consider is that of knowledge generation. Postmodern approaches have offered themselves as a "value-based alternative" to evidence-based practice.[272] On the surface, this point of contrast may simply yield confusion. Evidence-based social work practice has never disavowed social work values. Quite the opposite, throughout the Modern Era the social work profession has strongly embraced its value base as being a central part of practice. Similarly, these value-based postmodern approaches have never disavowed scientific evidence and the knowledge derived from such evidence. In fact, many postmodern scholars have used scientific investigation to produce evidence of the effectiveness of their approaches.[273] So where does the point of contrast lie then?

I believe that what is being contrasted is the type of knowledge generated (objective vs. subjective) that is used to plan and implement interventions. Evidence-based practice relies upon objective knowledge targeting the client's properties of existence: biological, psychological, and social functioning. The understanding of cause–effect linkages concerning the client's biological, psychological, and social functioning in relation to the presenting problem is what drives the development and shape of the intervention plan. Social work values are then used to circumscribe the boundaries within which the knowledge gathering and intervention take place. So, for example, in their role as sovereign consumer, clients may elect not to proceed with the first intervention plan created through objective knowledge of their situation. Applying the social work value of self-determination, the social worker must then respect the client's decision in their role as sovereign consumer and seek to offer an alternative intervention plan more amenable to the client.

Conversely, the value-based practice of postmodern approaches relies upon subjective knowledge targeting the client's phenomenological essence. Hence, the understanding of the mimetic process as it relates to the client's conscientization of the presenting problem is what drives the development and shape of the intervention plan. This involves the application of social work values to produce subjective knowledge. So, for example, the social work value of self-determination paired with the mimetic understanding that one's image of "who I would like to be" is what motivates one's present actions leads the postmodern practitioner to view the client as the expert concerning "who they would like to be." This is captured in the stance that the client's ultimate goal is held inviolable.[274] Movement toward obtaining the client's aspiration of "who they would like to be" is then what guides the development and shape of the intervention plan. Scientific, objective knowledge is then utilized to circumscribe the boundaries within which this intervention takes place. So, for example, returning to the case study of Mrs. J,[275] she stated her ultimate goal of "who I would like to be" as that of being like the queen of England. This goal was held inviolable by the case manager. However, objective knowledge clearly revealed the impossibility of Mrs. J gaining the actual status of being a queen. This then led the case manager to inquire into Mrs. J's understanding of what it meant to be queen as the means to capture the essence it held for Mrs. J. This in turn led to the development of the intervention plan seeking to capture this essence: moving in with a close friend who would provide companionship, organize volunteer activities for Mrs. J, and help with her day-to-day organizational needs.

Summing up the contrast between evidence-based practice and value-based practice, we have the following. Evidence-based practice adopts the Modern Discourse's premise that knowledge of the True (in the form of objective knowledge of reality) is necessary to achieve knowledge of the Good (a desired state of being for the client). Meanwhile, social constructionism's premise of multiple realities undercuts the notion of a purely objective knowledge of reality; thus, in postmodern practice concern is directed away from establishing an objective truth and toward establishing the verisimilitude of a particular subjective truth. Hence, value-based practice adopts the Postmodern discourse's premise that knowledge of the Good (in the form of subjective knowledge of a client's desired state of being) is inspired by knowledge of the Beautiful—the client utilizing aesthetic judgment to create an empowering narrative and identity. In fact, by adopting the moniker that "the client is the expert," value-based practice places faith in clients' ability to utilize their aesthetic judgment to articulate their unique personal good. Knowledge of this unique personal good is then necessary to direct efforts at establishing the verisimilitude of the client's chosen, particular reality.

Final thoughts

Friendship is unnecessary, like philosophy, like art . . . It has no survival value; rather it is one of those things which give value to survival.

—C. S. Lewis[276]

This poetic truth offered by C. S. Lewis speaks well to the contrast between social work practice under the Modern Discourse and social work practice under a Postmodern discourse.

Within the Modern Discourse, social work practice has as its focus the adaptation of the organism to its environment. Person-in-environment provides the hoped-for norm—that of homeostasis, or proper functioning—which speaks to survival of the organism. When employing evidence-based practice, exploring what gives value to this survival is not essential to achieving its end. So, for example, a person who is suffering from depression seeks services. The goal of the intervention is to restore the person to proper functioning by alleviating the debilitating aspects of depression. It is not necessary to explore what the client would be doing differently if they were no longer depressed, the goals and aspirations they would like to achieve. The focus on adaptation as the means of survival drives the treatment process.

The value-based practice of postmodern social work squarely puts its emphasis on what gives value to one's survival. It is about helping the client in exploring their process of becoming. Survival in and of itself is not the goal. Rather, the aspirations and dreams of the client are examined as the means to learn and foster what gives value and aesthetic beauty to the client's existence.

Notes

1. De Shazer, *Patterns of Brief Family*; De Shazer, *Keys to Solution*.
2. White, *Selected Papers*.
3. Rapp and Chamberlain, "Case Management Services"; Weick et al., "A Strengths Perspective."
4. De Jong and Kim Berg, *Interviewing for Solutions*.
5. White and Epston, *Narrative Means*.
6. Rapp, *The Strengths Model*; Saleebey, *The Strengths Perspective*.
7. De Shazer and Dolan, *More than Miracles*, 1.

8. White, *Selected Papers*, 3–4.

9. Saleebey and Weick, personal communication, May 12, 2004.

10. De Jong and Kim Berg, *Interviewing for Solutions*, 9, 263; White, *Commentary*, 121–22.

11. Rapp, *The Strengths Model*, 30–31; White, *Maps of Narrative Practice*, 103–07.

12. Kim Berg and De Jong, "Solution Building Conversations," 376; Saleebey, "Strengths Approach to Practice," 88–89.

13. De Jong and Kim Berg, *Interviewing for Solutions*, 16–17; White, *Maps of Narrative Practice*, 220, 232.

14. Saleebey, *The Strengths Perspective* (editions 1–4), final chapter; White, "Narrative Practice and Community," 22; White, "Narrative Practice and Unpacking," 36.

15. White, *Maps of Narrative Practice*, 194–95.

16. White, 194–95.

17. White and Epston, *Narrative Means*, 139–42.

18. De Jong and Kim Berg, "Co-Constructing Cooperation"; White, "Children, Trauma, and Subordinate."

19. De Jong and Kim Berg, *Interviewing for Solutions*, 85; Lipchik and De Shazer, "The Purposeful Interview," 88–89; Wade, "Small Acts of Living," 35.

20. Parry and Doan, *Story Re-Visions*, 52–55; White and Epston, *Narrative Means*, 19–24; Winslade and Cheshire, "School Counseling," 217.

21. Rapp, *The Strengths Model*, 78; Saleebey, "Introduction: Power" (1st ed.), 3; Weick, "The Philosophical Context," 554–55.

22. Parry and Doan, *Story Re-Visions*, 142.

23. White and Epston, *Narrative Means*, 19–20, 71.

24. White and Epston, 24.

25. White and Epston, 20–22.

26. Weick. "The Philosophical Context," 554–55; Weick et al., "A Strengths Perspective," 352.

27. Epston, White, and Ben, "Consulting Your Consultants," 278; White, *Maps of Narrative Practice*, 61.

28. De Jong and Kim Berg, *Interviewing for Solutions*, 85; Lipchik and De Shazer, "The Purposeful Interview," 89–90.

29. Drewery and Winslade, "The Theoretical Story," 34–35; White and Epston, *Narrative Means*, 28–31.

30. Rapp, *The Strengths Model*, 26; Saleebey, "The Estrangement of Knowing," 556; Weick and Pope, "Knowing What's Best," 16.

31. Drewery and Winslade, "The Theoretical Story," 34–35.

32. De Jong and Kim Berg, *Interviewing for Solutions*, 4; Drewery and Winslade, 34–35.

33. White, "Children, Trauma, and Subordinate," 11; White, "Folk Psychology," 20; White, *Maps of Narrative Practice*, 26–27.

34. Poertner and Ronnau, "A Strengths Approach," 115; Saleebey, "Introduction: Power" (1st ed.), 1; Weick et al., "A Strengths Perspective," 351.

35. Winslade and Smith, "Countering Alcoholic Narratives," 190.

36. White, *Maps of Narrative Practice*, 61.

37. Lipchik and De Shazer, "The Purposeful Interview," 189–90; White, "Narrative Practice and Community," 20; White, *Maps of Narrative Practice*, 266.

38. Parry and Doan, *Story Re-Visions*, 27–28, 118–20; White and Epston, *Narrative Means*, 75; White, "Deconstruction and Therapy," 47.

39. Parry and Doan, 54–58.

40. White and Epston, *Narrative Means*, 30.

41. White and Epston, 29; White, *Maps of Narrative Practice*, 27; Winslade and Smith, "Countering Alcoholic Narratives," 190.

42. Cowger, "Assessing Client Strengths" (2nd ed.), 60–61; Holmes, "The Strengths Perspective," 152.

43. White, *Maps of Narrative Practice*, 266.

44. Parry and Doan, *Story Re-Visions*, 61; Walter and Peller, *Becoming Solution-Focused*, 100; Winslade and Cheshire, "School Counseling," 219–20.

45. Freire, *Pedagogy of the Oppressed*, 47–48.

46. Kisthardt, "The Strengths Perspective," 168.

47. Walter and Peller, *Becoming Solution-Focused*, 67–68.

48. De Jong and Kim Berg, *Interviewing for Solutions*, 82; De Shazer and Dolan, *More than Miracles*, 39; Walter and Peller, 28.

49. Epston, White, and Ben, "Consulting Your Consultants," 277; Parry and Doan, *Story Re-Visions*, 46.

50. Fast and Chapin, "The Strengths Model," 118; Rapp, *The Strengths Model*, 58; Saleebey, "Introduction: Power" (1st ed.), 5.

51. Kim Berg and De Jong, "Co-Constructing Cooperation," 366; De Shazer and Dolan, *More than Miracles*, 39; Walter and Peller, *Becoming Solution-Focused*, 68.

52. Epston, White, and Ben, "Consulting Your Consultants," 277; Parry and Doan, *Story Re-Visions*, 123.

53. Fast and Chapin, *Strengths-Based Care Management*, 24; Kisthardt, "The Strengths Perspective," 181; Rapp, *The Strengths Model*, 50.

54. Kim Berg and De Jong, "Co-Constructing Cooperation," 363; De Jong and Kim Berg, *Interviewing for Solutions*, 79; De Shazer and Dolan, *More than Miracles*, 39.

55. Epston, White, and Murray, "A Proposal," 111; White, "Deconstruction and Therapy," 56.

56. Fast and Chapin, *Strengths-Based Care Management*, 13; Rapp, *The Strengths Model*, 93; Weick et al., "A Strengths Perspective," 354.

57. De Shazer and Dolan, *More than Miracles*, 65.

58. De Shazer and Dolan, 29.

59. Cowger, "Assessing Client Strengths" (1st ed.), 142; Parry and Doan, *Story Re-Visions*, 123; Rapp, *The Strengths Model*, 61.

60. Bricker-Jenkins, "Building a Strengths Model," 131; Fast and Chapin, *Strengths-Based Care Management*, 151; Saleebey, "Introduction: Power" (2nd ed.), 11.

61. Epston, White, and Ben, "Consulting Your Consultants," 277; Parry and Doan, *Story Re-Visions*, 46, 120, 171.

62. Kim Berg and De Jong, "Co-Constructing Cooperation," 364; Kim Berg and De Jong, "Solution-Building Conversations," 388; Walter and Peller, *Becoming Solution-Focused*, 28.

63. Rapp, *The Strengths Model*, 104.
64. Kim Berg and De Jong, "Co-Constructing Cooperation," 363; Monk, "How Narrative Therapy Works," 15–16; Walter and Peller, *Becoming Solution-Focused*, 28.
65. De Jong and Kim Berg, *Interviewing for Solutions*, 19; Parry and Doan, *Story Re-Visions*, 120; Rapp, *The Strengths Model*, 30.
66. De Jong and Kim Berg, 19; White and Epston, *Narrative Means*, 41–45; White, *Maps of Narrative Practice*, 219–20.
67. Kisthardt, "The Strengths Perspective," 166; Saleebey, "Introduction: Power" (1st ed.), 5; Walter and Peller, *Becoming Solution-Focused*, 28;
68. De Jong and Kim Berg, *Interviewing for Solutions*, 20–21; Kim Berg and De Jong, "Co-Constructing Cooperation," 364; Hoyt and Kim Berg, "Solution-Focused Couple Therapy," 205.
69. Harker, "Therapy and Male Sexual," 250; Monk, "How Narrative Therapy Works," 25; Parry and Doan, *Story Re-Visions*, 122, 146.
70. Saleebey, "Introduction: Power" (1st ed.), 12–13; Weick, "Building a Strengths Perspective," 23.
71. Anderson and Goolishian, "The Client," 29.
72. Klempner, "Socrates and the Oracle," 1.
73. McAvoy, *The Profession of Ignorance*, 19.
74. De Jong and Kim Berg, *Interviewing for Solutions*, 21; De Shazer and Dolan, *More than Miracles*, 64.
75. Harker, "Therapy and Male Sexual," 244; Monk, "How Narrative Therapy Works," 26; Parry and Doan, *Story Re-Visions*, 122, 146.
76. Cowger, "Assessing Client Strengths" (2nd ed.), 63; Holmes, "The Strengths Perspective," 152.
77. De Jong and Kim Berg, *Interviewing for Solutions*, 53; Kim Berg and De Jong, "Solution-Building Conversations," 388.
78. De Jong and Kim Berg, 20.
79. De Jong and Kim Berg, 90.
80. Parry and Doan, *Story Re-Visions*, 120–22; White and Epston, *Narrative Means*, 83.
81. White, "Deconstruction and Therapy," 56.
82. Monk, "How Narrative Therapy Works," 26; Parry and Doan, *Story Re-Visions*, 120–22.
83. Fast and Chapin, "The Strengths Model," 120; Kisthardt, "The Strengths Perspective," 164–65; Saleebey, "Introduction: Power" (1st ed.), 7, 11–12.
84. Rapp, *The Strengths Model*, 105.
85. Cowger, "Assessing Client Strengths" (2nd ed.), 63; Saleebey, "Introduction: Power" (1st ed.), 6; Weick, "Building a Strengths Perspective," 24.
86. Silvester, "Appreciating Indigenous Knowledge," 234; White, "Narrative Practice and Community," 25.
87. De Jong and Kim Berg, *Interviewing for Solutions*, 223; Wade, "Small Acts of Living," 24; Walter and Peller, *Becoming Solution-Focused*, 159.
88. Saleebey, "Introduction: Beginnings," 41.
89. Fast and Chapin, *Strengths-Based Care Management*, 1; Saleebey, "Introduction: Power" (1st ed.), 9; Weick, "Building a Strengths Perspective," 23.

90. White and Epston, *Narrative Means*, 65; White, "Deconstruction and Therapy," 59; White, *Maps of Narrative Practice*, 269.

91. De Jong and Kim Berg, *Interviewing for Solutions*, 225; De Shazer and Dolan, *More than Miracles*, 4; Walter and Peller, *Becoming Solution-Focused*, 160.

92. De Jong and Kim Berg, 365–66; Walter and Peller, 24; White, "Children, Trauma, and Subordinate," 14–15.

93. Cowger, "Assessing Client Strengths" (2nd ed.), 63; Fast and Chapin, "The Strengths Model," 123.

94. White and Epston, *Narrative Means*, 65; White, "Children, Trauma, and Subordinate," 13–14; White, "Folk Psychology," 8, 13.

95. De Shazer and Dolan, *More than Miracles*, 4; Shilts, Rambo, and Hernandez, "Clients Helping Therapists," 125–30; Walter and Peller, *Becoming Solution-Focused*, 107, 159.

96. De Jong and Kim Berg, *Interviewing for Solutions*, 16, 112; Shilts, Rambo, and Hernandez, 120; Walter and Peller, 12, 162;

97. McKenzie and Monk, "Learning and Teaching Narrative," 109; Parry and Doan, *Story Re-Visions*, 27–28; White, *Maps of Narrative Practice*, 219–20.

98. White, "Narrative Practice and Community," 25.

99. White and Epston, *Narrative Means*, 65; White, *Maps of Narrative Practice*, 232, 269.

100. Chapin, "Supporting the Strengths," 184; Rapp, "The Strengths Perspective," 51; Weick, "Building a Strengths Perspective," 24–25.

101. Epston, White, and Ben, "Consulting Your Consultants," 278; White and Epston, *Narrative Means*, 45; White, *Maps of Narrative Practice*, 219–20.

102. Kim Berg and De Jong, "Co-Constructing Cooperation," 365; Wade, "Small Acts of Living," 24; Walter and Peller, *Becoming Solution-Focused*, 68.

103. White, *Maps of Narrative Practice*, 232.

104. De Jong and Kim Berg, *Interviewing for Solutions*, 123–24; De Shazer and Dolan, *More than Miracles*, 8; Walter and Peller, *Becoming Solution-Focused*, 119.

105. Walter and Peller, 218–25.

106. Walter and Peller, 218.

107. Walter and Peller, 220.

108. Walter and Peller, 221.

109. Walter and Peller, 224.

110. Walter and Peller, 224–25.

111. De Jong and Kim Berg, *Interviewing for Solutions*, 216, 234; Miller, "Systems and Solutions," 19–20; Walter and Peller, 29.

112. White, "Children, Trauma, and Subordinate," 13; White, "Folk Psychology," 19; White, *Maps of Narrative Practice*, 10–17.

113. Fast and Chapin, *Strengths-Based Care Management*, 7; Saleebey, "Introduction: Power" (4th ed.), 8; Sullivan and Rapp, "Environmental Context," 253.

114. Freire, *Pedagogy of Hope*, 1.

115. Sullivan and Rapp, "Environmental Context," 253.

116. Cowger, "Assessing Client Strengths" (1st ed.), 141; De Jong and Kim Berg, *Interviewing for Solutions*, 84; Saleebey, "Introduction: Power" (1st ed.), 5.

117. De Shazer and Dolan, *More than Miracles*, 39; Walter and Peller, *Becoming Solution-Focused*, 24.

118. De Jong and Kim Berg, *Interviewing for Solutions*, 19, 124; Shilts, Rambo, and Hernandez, "Clients Helping Therapists," 120; Walter and Peller, 68–82.

119. De Jong and Kim Berg, 87; De Shazer and Dolan, *More than Miracles*, 8; Walter and Peller, 18–19.

120. De Jong and Kim Berg, 124; De Shazer and Dolan, 8; Walter and Peller, 116, 119.

121. De Jong and Kim Berg, 117; De Shazer and Dolan, 145–47; Walter and Peller, 210–11.

122. Shilts, Rambo, and Hernandez, "Clients Helping Therapists," 131.

123. Parry and Doan, *Story Re-Visions*, 53; White and Epston, *Narrative Means*, 16; White, *Maps of Narrative Practice*, 26–27.

124. McKenzie and Monk, "Learning and Teaching Narrative," 109; White and Epston, 16; White, 219–20.

125. White and Epston, 46.

126. White, "Folk Psychology," 22; White, *Maps of Narrative Practice*, 165–66; White, "Children, Trauma, and Subordinate," 17.

127. Parry and Doan, *Story Re-Visions*, 167–68; White, *Maps of Narrative Practice*, 181–201; White and Epston, *Narrative Means*, 188–92.

128. Epston, White, and Murray, "A Proposal," 100; White and Epston, 12–16, 41; White, 165.

129. Rapp, *The Strengths Model*, 107–11.

130. Kisthardt, "A Strengths Model," 69–75; Rapp, 102.

131. Kisthardt, 60–62; Rapp, 125; Sullivan, "Reconsidering the Environment," 154.

132. Rapp, *The Strengths Model*, 104.

133. Cowger, "Assessing Client Strengths" (1st ed.), 144–46; Kisthardt, "A Strengths Model," 60–62; Rapp, 94–97.

134. Cowger, 146; Kisthardt, 62; Rapp, 118.

135. Fast and Chapin, *Strengths-Based Care Management*, 21; Rapp, 69.

136. De Jong and Kim Berg, *Interviewing for Solutions*, 92–95.

137. De Jong and Kim Berg, 150–52.

138. De Jong and Kim Berg, 153–54.

139. De Jong and Kim Berg, 157.

140. De Jong and Kim Berg, 157–58.

141. Hoyt and Kim Berg, "Solution-Focused Couple Therapy," 205; Saleebey, "Strengths Approach to Practice," 78; White, *Maps of Narrative Practice*, 4.

142. Rapp and Goscha, *The Strengths Model*, 97; Sullivan and Rapp, "Honoring Philosophical Traditions," 271; Walter and Peller, *Becoming Solution-Focused*, 141.

143. Rapp and Goscha, 97–102; Walter and Peller, 141; White, *Maps of Narrative Practice*, 4.

144. Walter and Peller, 162; White, "Children, Trauma, and Subordinate," 13–14; Winslade, Crocket, and Monk, "The Therapeutic Relationship," 70.

145. Walter and Peller, 159.

146. White, "Deconstruction and Therapy," 59.

147. White, *Maps of Narrative Practice*, 269.
148. Walter and Peller, *Becoming Solution-Focused*, 169.
149. White and Epston, *Narrative Means*, 4.
150. Epston, White, and Murray, "A Proposal," 97.
151. Saleebey, "Strengths Approach to Practice," 84; Walter and Peller, *Becoming Solution-Focused*, 67.
152. White, *Maps of Narrative Practice*, 232.
153. Walter and Peller, *Becoming Solution-Focused*, 78.
154. Kim Berg and De Jong, "Solution-Building Conversations," 377–78; Rapp and Goscha, *The Strengths Model*, 97–102; White, *Maps of Narrative Practice*, 4..
155. Walter and Peller, *Becoming Solution-Focused*, 83.
156. Walter and Peller, 119.
157. Rapp, *The Strengths Model*, 107–08.
158. Rapp, 107–08.
159. White, "Deconstruction and Therapy," 36–37.
160. White, "Deconstruction and Therapy," 37.
161. Drewery and Winslade, "The Theoretical Story," 42; McKenzie and Monk, "Learning and Teaching Narrative," 95.
162. Epston, White, and Murray, "A Proposal," 108–09; Parry and Doan, *Story Re-Visions*, 128.
163. De Shazer and Dolan, *More than Miracles*, 177; McKenzie and Monk, "Learning and Teaching Narrative," 95; White, *Maps of Narrative Practice*, 219.
164. De Jong and Kim Berg, *Interviewing for Solutions*, 109–10; Saleebey, "Introduction: Power" (1st ed.), 3–4.
165. Drewery and Winslade, "The Theoretical Story," 34–35; Weick et al., "A Strengths Perspective," 351; White, *Maps of Narrative Practice*, 26–27.
166. Epston, White, and Murray, "A Proposal," 100–01; Parry and Doan, *Story Re-Visions*, 120–21.
167. Drewery and Winslade, "The Theoretical Story," 41; Epston, White, and Murray, 108–09.
168. De Shazer and Dolan, *More than Miracles*, 101; Drewery and Winslade, 39.
169. De Shazer and Dolan, 101–02; Drewery and Winslade, 39–41.
170. McKenzie and Monk, "Learning and Teaching Narrative," 95; White, "Deconstruction and Therapy," 53, 59.
171. Epston, White, and Ben, "Consulting Your Consultants," 280; Parry and Doan, *Story Re-Visions*, 120.
172. Monk, "How Narrative Therapy Works," 15–16; White, "Deconstruction and Therapy," 24; White, *Maps of Narrative Practice*, 31.
173. De Shazer and Dolan, *More than Miracles*, 177; Parry and Doan, *Story Re-Visions*, 55; Winslade and Cheshire, "School Counseling," 217–20.
174. Parry and Doan, *Story Re-Visions*, 45.
175. White and Epston, *Narrative Means*, 43.
176. White and Epston, 44.
177. Drewery and Winslade, "The Theoretical Story," 43; Saleebey, "Strengths Approach to Practice" (4th ed.), 90.

178. Hanisch, "The Personal Is Political," 1, 4; Napikoski, "Feminist Consciousness-Raising Groups."

179. Hanisch, "The Personal Is Political."

180. Blakemore, "Consciousness-Raising Groups," 2nd paragraph; Hanisch, "The Personal Is Political," 2–3; Napikoski, "Feminist Consciousness-Raising Groups," subheading, "What Happened in a CR Group?"

181. Hanisch, 3.

182. Drewery and Winslade, "The Theoretical Story," 34–35; Napikoski, "Feminist Consciousness-Raising Groups," subheading, "Effects of Consciousness-Raising."

183. Hanisch, "The Personal Is Political," 1; White and Epston, *Narrative Means*, 24.

184. Drewery and Winslade, "The Theoretical Story," 43; Napikoski, "Feminist Consciousness-Raising Groups."

185. Hanisch, "The Personal Is Political," 2; Parry and Doan, *Story Re-Visions*, 58.

186. Hanisch, 4; White, *Maps of Narrative Practice*, 26–27.

187. Napikoski, "Feminist Consciousness-Raising Groups," subheading, "Effects of Consciousness-Raising"; White, *Maps of Narrative Practice*, 266–68.

188. Blakemore, "Consciousness-Raising Groups," 2nd paragraph; White, "Narrative Practice and Unpacking," 33–34.

189. Napikoski, "Feminist Consciousness-Raising Groups," subheading, "The Genesis of Consciousness-Raising in New York"; Parry and Doan, *Story Re-Visions*, 53.

190. Hanisch, "The Personal Is Political," 4; White, "Deconstruction and Therapy," 59.

191. Napikoski, "Feminist Consciousness-Raising Groups," subheading, "Effects of Consciousness-Raising"; Winslade and Smith, "Countering Alcoholic Narratives," 190.

192. Hanisch, "The Personal Is Political," 4

193. Hanisch, 3; White, *Maps of Narrative Practice*, 181.

194. Hanisch, 4; White and Epston, *Narrative Means*, 30.

195. Napikoski, "Feminist Consciousness-Raising Groups," subheading, "Effects of Consciousness-Raising"; White, *Maps of Narrative Practice*, 219.

196. Saleebey, *The Strengths Perspective* (editions 1–4), final chapter; White, "Narrative Practice and Community," 22; White, "Narrative Practice and Unpacking," 36.

197. Hanisch, "The Personal Is Political," 3.

198. White and Epston, *Narrative Means*, 29; Winslade and Smith, "Countering Alcoholic Narratives," 190.

199. De Shazer and Dolan, *More than Miracles*, 38.

200. De Jong and Kim Berg, *Interviewing for Solutions*, 91.

201. De Jong and Kim Berg, 91.

202. White and Epston, *Narrative Means*, 30.

203. White and Epston, 38.

204. Parry and Doan, *Story Re-Visions*, 53; White, "Deconstruction and Therapy," 34.

205. White, "Deconstruction and Therapy," 53; White, *Maps of Narrative Practice*, 27, 179, 268.

206. White and Epston, *Narrative Means*, 16; White, *Maps of Narrative Practice*, 9.

207. White, "Deconstruction and Therapy," 31, 34; White, *Maps of Narrative Practice*, 26–27.

208. White and Epston, *Narrative Means*, 40–41; White, *Maps of Narrative Practice*, 59.
209. White and Epston, 16, 65; White, 103.
210. Harker, "Therapy and Male Sexual," 207; White, *Maps of Narrative Practice*, 9; White, "Narrative Practice and Unpacking," 34.
211. Rapp and Goscha, *The Strengths Model*, 94.
212. Rapp and Goscha, 98–102.
213. Rapp and Goscha, 98.
214. Rapp and Goscha, 91, 96, 102.
215. Rapp and Goscha, 95.
216. Rapp and Goscha, 107.
217. Rapp and Goscha, 107.
218. Parry and Doan, *Story Re-Visions*, 45; White and Epston, *Narrative Means*, 40–41; White, *Maps of Narrative Practice*, 27.
219. De Jong and Kim Berg, *Interviewing for Solutions*, 57; Rapp and Goscha, *The Strengths Model*, 109; White, 269–71.
220. Parry and Doan, *Story Re-Visions*, 48, 119; White and Epston, *Narrative Means*, 9–10.
221. Epston, White, and Murray, "A Proposal," 100; Parry and Doan, 120; Winslade and Smith, "Countering Alcoholic Narratives," 185.
222. De Jong and Kim Berg, *Interviewing for Solutions*, 57; Walter and Peller, *Becoming Solution-Focused*, 67, 204; White and Epston, *Narrative Means*, 41.
223. Ricœur, *Time and Narrative* (vol. 1), 52–54.
224. Abbot, *Cambridge Introduction to Narrative*, 20–21.
225. Saleebey, "The Strengths Perspective," 279, 283; Weick, Kreider, and Chamberlain, "Solving Problems," 122.
226. Abbot, *Cambridge Introduction to Narrative*, 20–21.
227. Abbot, 88–89.
228. Abbot, 128–31; Drewery and Winslade, "The Theoretical Story," 34–39; White, *Maps of Narrative Practice*, 80–82.
229. Saleebey, "Introduction: Power" (2nd ed.), 3–4; White, "Children, Trauma, and Subordinate," 14; 20; White, "Narrative Practice and Unpacking," 31–34.
230. De Jong and Kim Berg, *Interviewing for Solutions*, 112; Shilts, Rambo, and Hernandez, "Clients Helping Therapists," 120; Walter and Peller, *Becoming Solution-Focused*, 82–83.
231. McKenzie and Monk, "Learning and Teaching Narrative," 109; Parry and Doan, *Story Re-Visions*, 27–28; White, *Maps of Narrative Practice*, 219–20.
232. Rapp and Goscha, *The Strengths Model*, 94–97; Saleebey, "Strengths Approach to Practice," 82–84; Weick, Kreider, and Chamberlain, "Solving Problems," 117–19.
233. De Shazer and Dolan, *More than Miracles*, 41; Parry and Doan, *Story Re-Visions*, 66; Saleebey, "Introduction: Power" (2nd ed.), 9.
234. Kim Berg and De Jong, "Solution-Building Conversations," 380; Rapp and Goscha, *The Strengths Model*, 97–98; White, *Maps of Narrative Practice*, 61.
235. De Jong and Kim Berg, *Interviewing for Solutions*, 84; Saleebey, "Introduction: Power" (2nd ed.), 8; White, 80.
236. Walter and Peller, *Becoming Solution-Focused*, 159–60; Saleebey, "Strengths Approach to Practice," 88–89; White, 103.

237. De Jong and Kim Berg, *Interviewing for Solutions*, 48; Monk, "How Narrative Therapy Works," 21; Rapp and Goscha, *The Strengths Model*, 141–43.

238. De Shazer and Dolan, *More than Miracles*, 41; Rapp and Goscha, 159–60; White and Epston, *Narrative Means*, 8.

239. De Jong and Kim Berg, *Interviewing for Solutions*, 83; Rapp and Goscha, 31–33; White, *Maps of Narrative Practice*, 7.

240. White and Epston, *Narrative Means*, 15.

241. Epston, White, and Ben, "Consulting Your Consultants," 280; Epston, White, and Murray, "A Proposal," 111; White, "Deconstruction and Therapy," 47.

242. White, *Maps of Narrative Practice*, 166; White, "Narrative Practice and Unpacking," 33.

243. White and Epston, *Narrative Means*, 43–48.

244. White and Epston, 46.

245. White and Epston, 47.

246. Freire, *Pedagogy of the Oppressed*, 47–48.

247. White and Epston, *Narrative Means*, 48.

248. Parry and Doan, *Story Re-Visions*, 160; Winslade, Crocket, and Monk, "The Therapeutic Relationship," 68–70; Winslade and Smith, "Countering Alcoholic Narratives," 189.

249. De Shazer and Dolan, *More than Miracles*, 47; Monk, "How Narrative Therapy Works," 20–21; Parry and Doan, 157.

250. Epston, White, and Murray, "A Proposal," 100; Parry and Doan, 127.

251. Winslade and Smith, "Countering Alcoholic Narratives," 189.

252. White, "Narrative Practice and Unpacking," 31–34.

253. De Jong and Kim Berg, *Interviewing for Solutions*, 9, 26–27; Parry and Doan, *Story Re-Visions*, 173; Wade, "Small Acts of Living," 24.

254. Winslade, Crocket, and Monk, "The Therapeutic Relationship," 66; White and Epston, *Narrative Means*, 45.

255. De Jong and Kim Berg, *Interviewing for Solutions*, 37–39; De Shazer and Dolan, *More than Miracles*, 8; Walter and Peller, *Becoming Solution-Focused*, 116.

256. Epston, White, and Ben, "Consulting Your Consultants," 277; Fast and Chapin, "The Strengths Model," 21; Rapp, *The Strengths Model*, 69;

257. White, *Maps of Narrative Practice*, 77–78.

258. McKenzie and Monk, "Learning and Teaching Narrative," 109; White, "Deconstruction and Therapy," 36–37.

259. White, 37; White, *Maps of Narrative Practice*, 78–79.

260. White, "Folk Psychology," 19–22; White, *Maps of Narrative Practice*, 59; Winslade, Crocket, and Monk, "The Therapeutic Relationship," 55.

261. De Shazer and Dolan, *More than Miracles*, 101, 108, 134.

262. McKenzie and Monk, "Learning and Teaching Narrative," 110; Monk, "How Narrative Therapy Works," 20–21; White and Epston, *Narrative Means*, 17, 41.

263. Parry and Doan, *Story Re-Visions*, 157–58; Winslade and Smith, "Countering Alcoholic Narratives," 185–87.

264. Kim Berg and De Jong, "Co-Constructing Cooperation," 368; De Jong and Kim Berg, *Interviewing for Solutions*, 192; McKenzie and Monk, "Learning and Teaching Narrative," 111.
265. De Jong and Kim Berg, *Interviewing for Solutions*, 111; McKenzie and Monk, 111; White, "Folk Psychology," 17.
266. Parry and Doan, *Story Re-Visions*, 151; White and Epston, *Narrative Means*, 138–41.
267. White, "Children, Trauma, and Subordinate," 17.
268. Walter and Peller, *Becoming Solution-Focused*, 170; White, "Folk Psychology," 30.
269. Silvester, "Appreciating Indigenous Knowledge," 245.
270. Parry and Doan, *Story Re-Visions*, 172; White, *Maps of Narrative Practice*, 179.
271. White, 165, 185.
272. Weick, "Building a Strengths Perspective," 25.
273. De Jong and Kim Berg, *Interviewing for Solutions*, 245–51; Rapp and Goscha, *The Strengths Model*, 71.
274. Rapp, *The Strengths Model*, 104.
275. Rapp, 105.
276. Lewis, *Four Loves*, 71.

References

Abbott, H. Porter. *The Cambridge Introduction to Narrative*. Cambridge: Cambridge University Press, 2002.

Anderson, Harlene, and Harold Goolishian. "The Client Is the Expert: A Not-Knowing Approach to Therapy." In *Therapy as Social Construction*, edited by Sheila McNamee and Kenneth J. Gergen, 25–39. Thousand Oaks, CA: Sage, 1992.

Berg, Insoo Kim, and Peter De Jong. "Solution-Building Conversations: Co-Constructing a Sense of Competence with Clients." *Families in Society* 77 (1997): 376–91.

Berg, Insoo Kim, and Peter De Jong. "Co-Constructing Cooperation with Mandated Clients." *Social Work* 46 (2001): 361–74.

Blakemore, Erin. "Consciousness-Raising Groups and the Women's Movement." JSTOR Daily, March 11, 2021, https://daily.jstor.org/consciousness-raising-groups-and-the-womens-movement/.

Bricker-Jenkins, Mary. "Building a Strengths Model of Practice in the Public Social Services." In *The Strengths Perspective in Social Work Practice*, edited by Dennis Saleebey, 122–36. 1st ed. White Plains, NY: Longman, 1992.

Campbell, Joseph. *The Hero with a Thousand Faces*. Bollingen Series, 17. Princeton, NJ: Princeton University Press, 1968. First published 1949.

Caputo, Richard, William Epstein, David Stoesz, and Bruce Thyer. "Postmodernism: A Dead End in Social Work Epistemology." *Journal of Social Work Education* 51 (2015): 638–47.

Chapin, Rosemary. "Supporting the Strengths of Older Women." In *Building on Women's Strengths: A Social Work Agenda for the Twenty-First Century*, edited by Jean K. Peterson and Alice A. Lieberman, 169–96. 2nd ed. New York: Haworth Social Work Practice Press, 2001.

Cowger, Charles D. "Assessing Client Strengths." In *The Strengths Perspective in Social Work Practice*, edited by Dennis Saleebey, 139–47. 1st ed. White Plains, NY: Longman, 1992.

Cowger, Charles D. "Assessing Client Strengths." In *The Strengths Perspective in Social Work Practice*, edited by Dennis Saleebey, 59–73. 2nd ed. White Plains, NY: Longman, 1997.

De Jong, Peter, and Insoo Kim Berg. *Interviewing for Solutions*. 4th ed. Belmont, CA: Brooks/Cole, 2013.

De Shazer, Steve. *Patterns of Brief Family Therapy: An Ecosystemic Approach*. New York: Guilford Press, 1982.

De Shazer, Steve. *Keys to Solution in Brief Therapy*. New York: W. W. Norton and Company, 1985.

De Shazer, Steve. "Some Thoughts on Language Use in Therapy." *Contemporary Family Therapy* 19 (1997): 133–41.

De Shazer, Steve, and Insoo Kim Berg. "Doing Therapy: A Post-Structuralist Re-vision." *Journal of Marital and Family Therapy* 18 (1992): 71–81.

De Shazer, Steve, and Yvonne Dolan. *More than Miracles: The State of the Art of Solution-Focused Brief Therapy*. New York: Routledge, 2007.

Drewery, Wendy, and John Winslade. "The Theoretical Story of Narrative Therapy." In *Narrative Therapy in Practice: The Archeology of Hope*, edited by Gerald Monk, John Winslade, Kathie Crocket, and David Epston, 32–52. San Francisco: Jossey-Bass, 1997.

Epston, David, and Michael White. "Consulting Your Consultants: The Documentation of Alternative Knowledges." *Dulwich Centre Newsletter* 4 (1990): 25–35.

Epston, David, Michael White, and Kevin Murray. "A Proposal for a Re-authoring Therapy: Rose's Revisioning of Her Life and Commentary." In *Therapy as Social Construction*, edited by Sheila McNamee and Kenneth J. Gergen, 96–115. Thousand Oaks, CA: Sage, 1992.

Fast, Becky, and Rosemary Chapin. "The Strengths Model with Older Adults: Critical Practice Components." In *The Strengths Perspective in Social Work Practice*, edited by Dennis Saleebey, 115–32. 2nd ed. White Plains, NY: Longman, 1997.

Fast, Becky, and Rosemary Chapin. *Strengths-Based Care Management for Older Adults*. Baltimore: Health Professions Press, 2000.

Freire, Paulo. *Pedagogy of the Oppressed*. Translated by Myra Bergman Ramos. New York: Continuum International Publishing, 2000. First published 1968.

Freire, Paulo. *Pedagogy of Hope: Reliving Pedagogy of the Oppressed*. Translated by Robert Barr. London: Bloomsbury Academic, 2014. First published 1992.

Gergen, Kenneth J. "Toward Generative Theory." *Journal of Personality and Social Psychology* 36 (1978): 1344–60.

Hanisch, Carol. "The Personal Is Political: The Women's Liberation Movement Classic with a New Explanatory Introduction." January 2006, http://www.carolhanisch.org/CHwritings/PersonalIsPol.pdf. First published February 1969.

Harker, Tim. "Therapy and Male Sexual Abuse Survivors: Contesting Oppressive Life Stories." In *Narrative Therapy in Practice: The Archeology of Hope*, edited by Gerald Monk, John Winslade, Kathie Crocket, and David Epston, 193–214. San Francisco: Jossey-Bass, 1997.

Hoyt, Michael F., and Insoo Kim Berg. "Solution-Focused Couple Therapy: Helping Clients Construct Self-Fulfilling Realities." In *Case Studies in Couple and Family Therapy*, edited by Frank M. Dattilio and Marvin R. Godfried, 203–32. New York: Guilford Press, 1998.

Kisthardt, Walter E. "A Strengths Model of Case Management: The Principles and Functions of a Helping Partnership with Persons with Persistent Mental Illness." In *The Strengths Perspective in Social Work Practice*, edited by Dennis Saleebey, 59–83. 1st ed. White Plains, NY: Longman, 1992.

Kisthardt, Walter E. "The Strengths Perspective in Interpersonal Helping: Purpose, Principles, and Functions." In *The Strengths Perspective in Social Work Practice*, edited by Dennis Saleebey, 163–85. 3rd ed. Boston: Allyn and Bacon, 2002.

Klempner, Geoffrey. "Socrates and the Oracle of Delphi." Ask a Philosopher, September 9, 2011. https://askaphilosopher.org/2011/09/09/socrates-and-the-oracle-of-delphi/ #:~:text=1%29%20The%20Oracle%20of%20Delphi%20pronounced%20Socrates%20 the,begins%20to%20question%20the%20accepted%20wisdom%20of%20tradition.

Lewis, C. S. *The Four Loves*. New York: Harcourt Brace, 1960.

Lipchik, Eve, and Steve De Shazer. "The Purposeful Interview." *Journal of Strategic and Systemic Therapies* 5 (1986): 88–99.

McAvoy, Martin. *The Profession of Ignorance: With Constant Reference to Socrates*. Lanham, MD: University Press of America, 1999.

McKenzie, Wally, and Gerald Monk. "Learning and Teaching Narrative Ideas." In *Narrative Therapy in Practice: The Archeology of Hope*, edited by Gerald Monk, John Winslade, Kathie Crocket, and David Epston, 82–120. San Francisco: Jossey-Bass, 1997.

Miller, Gale. "Systems and Solutions: The Discourses of Brief Therapy." *Contemporary Family Therapy* 19 (1997): 5–22.

Monk, Gerald. "How Narrative Therapy Works." In *Narrative Therapy in Practice: The Archeology of Hope*, edited by Gerald Monk, John Winslade, Kathie Crocket, and David Epston, 3–31. San Francisco: Jossey-Bass, 1997.

Napikoski, Linda. "Feminist Consciousness-Raising Groups: Collective Action Through Discussion." ThoughtCo. Last modified October 14, 2019, https://www.thoughtco. com/feminist-consciousness-raising-groups-3528954.

Parry, Alan, and Robert E. Doan. *Story Re-Visions: Narrative Therapy in a Postmodern World*. New York: Guilford Press, 1994.

Poertner, John, and John Ronnau. "A Strengths Approach to Children with Emotional Disabilities." In *The Strengths Perspective in Social Work Practice*, edited by Dennis Saleebey, 111–21. 1st ed. White Plains, NY: Longman, 1992.

Rapp, Charles. "The Strengths Perspective of Case Management with Persons Suffering from Severe Mental Illness." In *The Strengths Perspective in Social Work Practice*, edited by Dennis Saleebey, 45–58. 1st ed. White Plains, NY: Longman, 1992.

Rapp, Charles. *The Strengths Model: Case Management with People Suffering from Severe and Persistent Mental Illness*. New York: Oxford University Press, 1998.

Rapp, Charles, and Rhonda Chamberlain. "Case Management Services to the Chronically Mentally Ill." *Social Work* 30 (1985): 417–22.

Rapp, Charles, and Richard Goscha. *The Strengths Model: Case Management with People Suffering from Severe and Persistent Mental Illness*. 2nd ed. New York: Oxford University Press, 2006.

Ricœur, Paul. *Time and Narrative*. Vol. 1. Chicago: University of Chicago Press, 1984.

Saleebey, Dennis. "The Estrangement of Knowing and Doing: Professions in Crisis." *Social Casework: The Journal of Contemporary Social Work* 70 (1989): 556–63.

Saleebey, Dennis. "Introduction: Power in the People." In *The Strengths Perspective in Social Work Practice*, edited by Dennis Saleebey, 3–17. 1st ed. White Plains, NY: Longman, 1992.

Saleebey, Dennis. "Introduction: Beginnings of a Strengths Approach to Practice." In *The Strengths Perspective in Social Work Practice*, edited by Dennis Saleebey, 41–44. 1st ed. White Plains, NY: Longman, 1992.

Saleebey, Dennis. "Theory and the Generation and Subversion of Knowledge." *Journal of Sociology and Social Welfare* 20 (1993): 5–25.

Saleebey, Dennis. "Introduction: Power in the People." In *The Strengths Perspective in Social Work Practice*, edited by Dennis Saleebey, 3–20. 2nd ed. White Plains, NY: Longman, 1997.

Saleebey, Dennis. "Power in the People: Strengths and Hope." *Advances in Social Work* 1 (2000): 127–36.

Saleebey, Dennis. "The Strengths Approach to Practice." In *The Strengths Perspective in Social Work Practice*, edited by Dennis Saleebey, 77–92. 4th ed. Boston: Allyn and Bacon, 2006.

Saleebey, Dennis. "The Strengths Perspective: Possibilities and Problems." In *The Strengths Perspective in Social Work Practice*, edited by Dennis Saleebey, 279–303. 4th ed. Boston: Pearson/Allyn and Bacon, 2006.

Shilts, Lee, Anne Rambo, and Laurie Hernandez. "Clients Helping Therapists Find Solutions to Their Therapy." *Contemporary Family Therapy* 19 (1997): 117–32.

Silvester, Glen "Appreciating Indigenous Knowledge in Groups." In *Narrative Therapy in Practice: The Archeology of Hope*, edited by Gerald Monk, John Winslade, Kathie Crocket, and David Epston, 233–51. San Francisco: Jossey-Bass, 1997.

Sullivan, William P. "Reconsidering the Environment as a Helping Resource." In *The Strengths Perspective in Social Work Practice*, edited by Dennis Saleebey, 148–57. 1st ed. White Plains, NY: Longman, 1992.

Sullivan, William P., and Charles Rapp. "Environmental Context, Opportunity, and the Process of Recovery: The Role of Strengths-Based Practice and Policy." In *The Strengths Perspective in Social Work Practice*, edited by Dennis Saleebey, 247–63. 3rd ed. Boston: Allyn and Bacon, 2002.

Sullivan, William P., and Charles Rapp. "Honoring Philosophical Traditions: The Strengths Model and the Social Environment." In *The Strengths Perspective in Social Work Practice*, edited by Dennis Saleebey, 261–78. 4th ed. Boston: Allyn and Bacon, 2002.

Taylor, Edward. "The Weaknesses of the Strengths Model: Mental Illness as a Case in Point." *Best Practices in Mental Health* 2 (2006): 1–30.

Taylor, Robert. "The Social Control Function in Casework." *Social Casework* 1 (1958): 17–21.

Trattner, Walter I. *From Poor Law to Welfare State: A History of Social Welfare in America.* 4th ed. New York: Free Press, 1989.

Van Gennep, Arnold. *Rites of Passage.* Translated by Monika B. Vizedom and Gabrielle L. Caffee. Chicago: Chicago University Press, 1960. First published 1909.

Wade, Allen. "Small Acts of Living: Everyday Resistance to Violence and Other Forms of Oppression." *Contemporary Family Therapy* 19 (1997): 23–39.

Walter, John L., and Jane E. Peller. *Becoming Solution-Focused in Brief Therapy.* New York: Brunner/Mazel. 1992.

Weick, Ann. "The Philosophical Context of a Health Model of Social Work." *Social Casework: The Journal of Contemporary Social Work* 67 (1986): 551–59.

Weick, Ann. "Building a Strengths Perspective for Social Work." In *The Strengths Perspective in Social Work Practice*, edited by Dennis Saleebey, 18–26. 1st ed. White Plains, NY: Longman, 1992.

Weick, Ann, James Kreider, and Ronna Chamberlain. "Solving Problems from a Strengths Perspective." In *The Strengths Perspective in Social Work Practice*, edited by Dennis Saleebey, 16–127. 4th ed. Boston: Pearson/Allyn and Bacon, 2006.

Weick, Ann, and Loren Pope. "Knowing What's Best: A New Look at Self-Determination." *Social Casework* 69 (1988): 10–16.

Weick, Ann, Charles Rapp, Patrick Sullivan, and Walter Kisthardt. "A Strengths Perspective for Social Work Practice." *Social Work* 34 (1989): 350–54.

White, Michael. *Selected Papers*. Adelaide, Australia: Dulwich Center Publications, 1989.

White, Michael. "Deconstruction and Therapy." In *Therapeutic Conversations*, edited by Stephen Gilligan and Reese Price, 22–61. New York: W. W. Norton, 1993.

White, Michael. "Commentary: The Histories of the Present." In *Therapeutic Conversations*, edited by Stephen Gilligan and Reese Price, 121–35. New York: W. W. Norton, 1993.

White, Michael. "The Mouse Stories." In *The Personal Is the Professional: Therapists Reflect upon their Families, Lives, and Work*, edited by Cheryl White and Jane Hales, 105–13. Adelaide, Australia: Dulwich Centre Publications, 1997.

White, Michael. "Folk Psychology and Narrative Practice." *Dulwich Centre Journal* 2 (2001): 3–37.

White, Michael. "Narrative Practice and the Unpacking of Identity Conclusions." *Gecko* 1 (2001): 28–55.

White, Michael. "Narrative Practice and Community Assignments." *International Journal of Narrative and Community Work* 2 (2003): 17–56.

White, Michael. "Children, Trauma, and Subordinate Storyline Development." *International Journal of Narrative and Community Work* 3/4 (2005): 10–21.

White, Michael. *Maps of Narrative Practice*. New York: W. W. Norton, 2007.

White, Michael, and David Epston. *Narrative Means to Therapeutic Ends*. New York: W. W. Norton, 1990.

Winslade, John, and Aileen Cheshire. "School Counseling in a Narrative Mode." In *Narrative Therapy in Practice: The Archeology of Hope*, edited by Gerald Monk, John Winslade, Kathie Crocket, and David Epston, 215–32. San Francisco: Jossey-Bass, 1997.

Winslade, John, Kathie Crocket, and Gerald Monk. "The Therapeutic Relationship." In *Narrative Therapy in Practice: The Archeology of Hope*, edited by Gerald Monk, John Winslade, Kathie Crocket, and David Epston, 53–81. San Francisco: Jossey-Bass, 1997.

Winslade, John, and Lorraine Smith. "Countering Alcoholic Narratives." In *Narrative Therapy in Practice: The Archeology of Hope*, edited by Gerald Monk, John Winslade, Kathie Crocket, and David Epston, 158–92. San Francisco: Jossey-Bass, 1997.

10
Social Welfare at a Crossroads

Although social work has only recently (in historical terms) achieved the status of a profession, social welfare has been administered by individuals since the first pilgrims arrived to colonize our shores. In Chapter 1 of this book the question was posed, "Is the practice of social welfare morally progressing?" The historical evidence presented herein speaks to a nuanced, both "yes" and "no" response to this question. What has clearly been demonstrated is that the history of the Discourse on social welfare is cyclical in nature: As society evolves and grows, new pressing needs arise. In attempting to meet these new pressing needs, and the overall existential urgent need, a new conceptualization of social welfare takes shape—and, consequently, a new conceptualization as to what comprises an effective intervention takes shape.

This new conceptualization of social welfare grants social welfare agents a new vantage through which to critically examine past practices. This new vantage lays bare the previous moral blind spots that plagued past practices, providing a moral progression of knowledge that can be built upon. So, for example, after transitioning from the Premodern Discourse to the Modern Discourse, it became quite apparent from the vantage of the Modern Discourse that moral education efforts could easily devolve into proselytizing. Our awareness of this historical fact makes it inconceivable that social welfare agents will once again fall prey to this particular moral hazard in any future Discourses that may arise. So, in this respect, we can state that the practice of social welfare is morally progressing.

This does not mean that social work scholars are incapable of offering critiques of current practices of their era. However, due to the dominance of the Discourse, these critiques become muted; their call to action is never fully realized. Again, taking an example from the Premodern Era, it did not take long after the embrace of institutionalization for social welfare agents to realize that this model for intervention was highly flawed and contained many moral hazards. However, the dominance of the existing Discourse made it extremely difficult to conceive of a better alternative. Hence, critiques by social welfare scholars and activists (such as Dorothea Dix's efforts at reforming insane asylums) did not entail questioning the underlying premise for institutionalization as an effective intervention but, rather, centered upon its implementation by poorly trained agents.[1] For example, it was viewed that the warden of an institution needed to be trained

A Genealogy of the Good and Critique of Hubris. Phillip Dybicz, Oxford University Press. © Oxford University Press 2023. DOI: 10.1093/oso/9780197670071.003.0010

in moral philosophy to fully appreciate and exploit the positive attributes of institutionalization as an effective social welfare intervention and that a failure on that score was a main contributor to the various flaws and moral hazards that arose.[2] Additionally, with the exception of the child saving movement adopting a foster care approach as an alternative to orphanages,[3] social welfare agents of that era were unable to conceive of any better alternatives to institutionalization. They accepted the many inherent flaws and dubious results simply because they were unable to think of any better alternatives. It took the transition to the Modern Discourse, and the new vantage that it provided, to spur the development of better alternatives to institutionalization. Consequently, it was during the Modern Era that the various institutions began to disappear, being replaced by alternatives that circumvented the flaws of institutionalization and its moral hazards—with the penitentiary being the sole remaining holdout.

Similarly, as was described in Chapter 7, throughout the decades of the Modern Era social work scholars have repeatedly critiqued the inherent social control function in current social work practice. Yet the underlying premise of the medical/problem-solving model as an effective intervention approach is never seriously questioned; rather, its implementation is critiqued. As such, refinements to the model merely amount to window dressing: such as calling the individual seeking services the "client" or "consumer" rather than the "patient" or renaming the model the "problem-solving approach" rather than the "medical model." Hence, scholars positioning themselves within the Modern Discourse were unable to think of better alternatives to the medical model. It took the recent emergence of the Postmodern discourse and the new vantage that it provides to offer an alternative model in the form of the "not-knowing" approach that seeks to overcome the moral hazards of the problem-solving approach.

So, getting back to the response to the question "Is social welfare practice morally progressing?" the cyclical nature of discourses achieving dominance creates a new vantage in which to examine past practices. And this new vantage is able to easily lay bare the various moral hazards inherent in these past practices. However, the rise of a new dominant Discourse brings with it moral blind spots of its own. Hence, in that vein, moral progress does not occur, thus representing the "no" side to the above question.

One thing we can state with historical certainty is that societies will always continue to evolve and change. And, as was demonstrated in the previous chapters, this accumulation of changes will eventually reach a point where the current dominant Discourse in social welfare will no longer be adequately able to address the needs that arise from them, and a new discourse will arise to achieve dominance. Thus, building upon this premise, it is readily apparent that the current Modern Discourse on social welfare does not represent the pinnacle of humankind's achievement in the area of social welfare, and thus its final end.

Rather, just like the Discourses before it, it too shall pass. It is a question not of whether the Modern Discourse will fall from dominance but rather of when.

Additionally, it now appears that the social work profession stands at a crossroads between continuing to practice within the Modern Discourse and taking a new path in the form of the Postmodern Discourse[a] rising to dominance. One conclusion the historical record has illustrated quite clearly is that one cannot traverse both paths simultaneously. It is not uncommon to find calls in the social work literature to shun notions of dichotomy between these two discourses and to equally embrace insights from each. Yet, heeding calls to have simultaneously one foot in the Modern Discourse and one foot in the Postmodern discourse would entail operating within two paradigms simultaneously. The social worker would need to operate with two competing versions of reality, epistemology, and causality at the same time; this would appear to me to be an impossible task.

And, as has been historically demonstrated in previous chapters, when competing discourses arise, one of two positions emerges. If the social worker continues to operate within the current Dominant discourse, insights arising from the competing discourse get reinterpreted and repurposed to fit within the paradigm of the current Dominant discourse. Inevitably, this leads to the watering down and loss of the true power behind such insights. We saw this in the Premodern Era when the charity organization society workers attempted to practice "scientific" charity. In our present times, we explored how this currently occurs when attempting to employ notions such as strengths while continuing to operate within the social engineering approach of the Modern Discourse.

If the social worker decides to position themselves within the arising discourse, similarly, the insights and knowledge from the preceding discourse get transformed. We saw this happening with the rise of the Modern Discourse. The insights stemming from the moral knowledge of the Premodern Discourse were dethroned from their position of prominence and rather put to use in a supporting role. Thus, within the Modern Discourse moral knowledge is no longer used to plan the steps of the intervention itself—scientific knowledge, in the form of social engineering, is used for that purpose (i.e., evidence-based practice). Rather, this moral knowledge was transformed into a vibrant code of ethics which now serves the purpose of helping social workers respect the process and circumscribe the boundaries within which the intervention takes place. Similarly, those social workers now practicing from within a Postmodern discourse seek to dethrone scientific (i.e., objective) knowledge from its position of prominence in directing the helping process and repurpose it to help social workers respect the process and circumscribe the boundaries within which the intervention takes place. Instead, they seek to advance the prominence of

---

[a] I am using a capital "D" here to denote its status of dominance.

subjective knowledge in outlining the steps of the intervention plan itself (i.e., value-based practice).

Examining Scenarios on the Fate of the Postmodern Discourse

In recent decades, a new discourse has begun to emerge and develop: the Postmodern discourse on social welfare. It offers the first legitimate challenge to the Modern Discourse on social welfare and its position of dominance. Thus, further examination of this challenge may shed some light on the question of when the Modern Discourse will fall from dominance. I see three possibilities for us to consider. First is that the Postmodern discourse will never achieve dominance; while having its day in the sun currently as challenger, it will ultimately fall into obscurity, and it will be a different discourse down the road that will usurp the Modern Discourse's dominance. In this scenario, it is conceivable that the Modern Discourse would maintain its dominance for some time to come, perhaps equaling or exceeding the two hundred-year duration of the Colonial Discourse. Thus, it would be at least another century or more (2120 or beyond) before it falls from dominance.

The second possibility is that the Modern Discourse will be replaced by the Postmodern discourse; however, this might not occur for another seventy to eighty years. From the investigations laid out in this book, we have one historical example of such a scenario occurring. During the 1730s–1740s the First Great Awakening occurred. The First Great Awakening offered a new conceptual understanding of democratic equality—however, its application was restricted to the spiritual sphere of society only. Without similar changes taking place in the other aspects of society, this movement became short-lived; its key insight of democratic equality was seen as a threat to the existing social order of that time.[4]

However, while successfully suppressed, this insight was never snuffed out. It would emerge anew by the end of the eighteenth century as the Second Great Awakening, and its key insight of democratic equality would find much more fertile intellectual ground upon which to gain wide acceptance.[5] The Revolutionary War brought dramatic change to the political sphere, and the advent of the Industrial Revolution prompted massive change in the economic sphere. The concept of democratic equality was now finding expression among multiple spheres of society, contributing heavily to the Premodern Discourse's rise to dominance: Societal conditions and needs had changed to the extent that the Premodern Discourse was better positioned to offer solutions to these new societal problems. So if the Postmodern discourse followed a similar scenario, it would be a matter of decades (2170–2190) before societal conditions and needs changed to the extent that the Modern Discourse fell from dominance and was replaced by the Postmodern Discourse.

The third possibility is that this current challenge by the Postmodern discourse is marking a transition phase between the Modern Discourse and the Postmodern Discourse; the conditions and needs of society have changed significantly to the point where the Modern Discourse is quickly becoming unable to adequately meet them. In this scenario, the Postmodern discourse is on the verge of replacing the Modern Discourse, requiring only a decade or two (2030–2040) before it rises to dominance. Let us now examine each of these three possibilities.

Scenario One: The Postmodern discourse Fades to Obscurity

The first possibility—wherein the Postmodern discourse begins to emerge but then fades into obscurity before ever having achieved dominance, never to return—seems the most remote. When examining the historical investigations that comprise this book, the historical record does not reveal a single instance where a similar scenario occurred. Furthermore, one of the broad themes of the Postmodern discourse—the devolution of power to the user/client/consumer—resonates with changes in society already taking place in the social sphere (with the rise of social media) and the economic sphere (with the rise of things such as cryptocurrency and ecommerce). It would require the radical reversal of such trends to undermine the strength of the Postmodern discourse to the extent that its aspects lose their relevance, and hence cause it to fade into obscurity. Outside of doomsday scenarios that would radically alter the societal landscape, it is difficult to conceive how and why such a radical reversal would take place. Additionally, there is no parallel event occurring during the Colonial Era where a competing discourse arose to challenge the Colonial Discourse, failed, and then faded into obscurity, never to return. In summary, the lack of supporting evidence makes this scenario flimsy at best, thus making it highly unlikely.

Scenario Two: Elements of the Postmodern Discourse Are Early on the Scene

The second possibility—that the Postmodern discourse is early on the scene and that its time has not yet come—does have a supporting example in the historical record. As mentioned above, the First Great Awakening of the 1730s–1740s shares the characteristics of this scenario. Thus, there are a number of parallels. The first parallel is that the religious scholars of the Colonial Era—in the form of priests and pastors—viewed the tenets of the Great Awakening as dangerous to society, and thus were vehemently opposed to their acceptance in any form.[6] Similarly, some social work scholars (i.e., hard-hat scientists firmly rooted in the Modern Discourse) have issued dire warnings in the academic literature concerning the dangers of adopting a postmodern approach to social work practice for both the client and the profession.[7]

Additionally, the First Great Awakening solely concerned itself with spiritual matters. Thus, it could be described as representing merely a fragment of the Premodern Discourse to come. Arguments can be made that a similar situation applies to the current rise of postmodern social work practices, in that the vast majority of the proponents of postmodern practice approaches—as reflected in the academic literature—ground their inspiration solely upon social constructionism. Very little has been written on how phenomenology informs these approaches, and to date, writings on how mimesis informs these approaches appear to be limited solely to this author. Unless this condition changes, it is quite conceivable that the legitimacy of postmodern practice approaches will continue to be suppressed for decades to come before finally arising anew once more and gaining dominance as a complete Discourse.

Yet there are areas of dissonance with this comparison as well. When the First Great Awakening arose to challenge the existing colonial social order, there were no broad societal movements taking place which resonated with its broad theme of democratic equality. It would take the events of the Revolutionary War and the birth of the United States several decades later to thrust the theme of democratic equality into the forefront of social consciousness once more. By contrast, the Postmodern discourse's broad theme of the devolution of power resonates strongly with the digital revolution taking place in our time; and, as stated above, social media and ecommerce represent broad movements in society already taking place which embrace this theme of the devolution of power. A second point of contrast is that the First Great Awakening mostly represented a movement of the common people rising up to challenge existing elites in the form of these common people laying claim to the right to become a preacher if they were touched by the Holy Spirit, whereas the battle between proponents of the Modern Discourse and proponents of the Postmodern discourse represents a clash between social work scholars for the hearts and minds of professionals.

Another piece of historical evidence which might support this scenario is that the Modern Discourse shares an affinity with the Colonial Discourse in that both view society as relatively stable and thus both possess an urgent need centered upon maintenance of the existing social structure. The fact that the Colonial Discourse lasted for approximately two hundred years speaks to the proposition that Discourses possessing an urgent need centered upon maintenance may be relatively more stable than their alternative counterparts (such as the Premodern Discourse), and hence, tend to retain dominance for a considerably longer period. Therefore, it is conceivable that the Modern Discourse could extend to a similar length as well. However, it is just as easy to ascribe the extended time period of the Colonial Discourse as being due to the fact that society evolved and changed at a much slower pace in that era. Even so, this scenario appears much more probable than the first as there is a modicum of historical evidence supporting its thesis.

Scenario Three: Transition Period

The final scenario to consider is that the current rise of the Postmodern discourse marks a transition period between the dominant Discourse and its soon-to-be successor. The historical record shows that these transition periods inevitably happen. So the question becomes, "In what ways do our current events share a similarity with prior transition phases?" Let us examine the various conditions of society along with the dissemination of intellectual thought as the means to answer this question.

As was discussed in Chapter 8, a number of recent changes in society have occurred which seem to favor and support the Postmodern discourse. First, we may examine the various challenges that have arisen due to changes that have occurred regarding how geography limits and influences transportation, communication, and demographics. Regarding transportation, there has yet to be a transformative change, and thus there is no new challenge arising from such change. This would seem to indicate a continued dominance of the Modern Discourse.

Regarding communication, however, such a transformation has taken place due to the rapid rise and development of the internet. The challenge arising from the internet is that it can be a conduit for building/maintaining a sense of community, but also it can serve to isolate the individual. As was discussed in Chapter 8, the Modern Discourse's embrace of liberal individualism seems to feed the latter: facilitating an isolation of the individual. This is because liberal individualism's propensity to view persons as generic individuals—while ensuring individual rights—also possesses a darker side, which leads to persons becoming radically situated. Being radically situated handicaps one's ability to form the communal bonds that give life meaning. And being treated as a generic individual while interacting with others on the internet serves to exacerbate one's condition of being radically situated. Contrast this with the Postmodern discourse's embrace of responsive communitarianism. The dark side of communitarianism is that of totalitarianism, where individual rights are unduly sacrificed for an authoritarian's vision of the common good. In this instance, the internet serves to undermine this darker side rather than exacerbate it, due to the internet serving as a powerful tool in the free and open dissemination of information. Thus, the societal challenges arising from the internet seem to favor the Postmodern discourse achieving dominance.

Regarding demographics, societal challenges have begun to arise due to the United States transitioning from a country comprising a solid White majority with various racial minorities to a country containing no clear racial majority. Such a transition brings with it many new voices seeking to offer their contribution as to what comprises American values and what it means to be an American (rather than a proscribed hyphenated American). Embedded in the Modern Discourse, liberal individualism and scientific management—which aim at subsuming the individual to a greater whole—are not well positioned to address such an ongoing multivoiced societal conversation on these issues, whereas embedded in the Postmodern discourse, normative cultural relativism—which aims at the creation of a shared value system comprised from the input of multiple cultures—is well situated to facilitate such an ongoing multivoiced societal conversation on American values and identity. Thus, this societal condition seems to favor the Postmodern discourse's rise.

Regarding political conditions in society, there have yet to appear any definitive challenges arising from transformative changes taking place, although an aspiring consideration for such a challenge may be that of the extreme political bipolarization that has arisen in recent years and the accompanying legislative gridlock it spawns. In terms of a discourse rising to meet such a challenge of political bipolarization, it would appear that the Modern Discourse has a slight edge. The past few decades has seen the rise of neoliberalism. Neoliberalism is a political stance in which a more hands-off approach is adopted concerning the scientific management of society in the form of public policy. Thus, political gridlock serves as an ally in achieving these ends; consequently, the Modern Discourse would seem to exert its power to maintain this political bipolarization.

Yet if political gridlock is viewed as problematic to society, then neoliberalism is not contributing anything toward its resolution. Conversely, identity politics—with its emphasis on issues of identity—is a product of the Postmodern discourse. In recent years within the current demographic makeup of society, it has acted as a lightning rod spurring increased political bipolarization, thus exacerbating the problem rather than ameliorating it. Yet, identity politics hold the promise—as of yet unrealized—of promoting bipartisanship by bringing people together over shared experiences of oppression.

The changing economic conditions related to globalization and ecommerce clearly throw their support behind the Postmodern discourse's movement of seeking to extend the devolution of power to the individual. As explained in Chapter 8, the Modern Discourse's embrace of neoliberalism as its form of scientific management has resulted in market fundamentalism. It is this response of market fundamentalism to globalization that has spurred an ever-increasing disparity of wealth to emerge in US society. Thus, the Modern Discourse's response to this societal change is resulting in the growth of a social problem. By contrast, the growth of ecommerce and cryptocurrency contributes to the devolution of economic power back to the consumer. For example, the definance movement in cryptocurrency seeks to cut out banks as the middlemen scientifically managing the economic exchange. And the rise of social entrepreneurship can be seen as working in opposition to a greater move toward disparity in wealth. As the Postmodern discourse seems to promote the nobler side of capitalism, the above societal economic changes taking place strongly support its rise.

Next to consider are the various social changes occurring. The birth of a new form of media—social media—and its explosive growth and development clearly mark the largest social change occurring in present society. As was the case with globalization, the growth of social media appears to strongly support the Postmodern discourse's rise. Once again, it appears that the Modern Discourse's embrace of scientific management feeds the darker side of this societal change; it typically takes the form of trying to scientifically manage and promote a particular viewpoint (regardless of the facts supporting it) in what amounts to propaganda. This can be seen as one of the primary factors contributing to political bipolarization, whereas by lending voice to common individuals and facilitating their ability to organize, social media has been instrumental in the advancement of numerous social causes. Additionally, in the area of ecommerce, it serves to devolve power back to the consumer regarding product messaging. The foundational premise of social media rests upon this devolution of power to the individual—a hallmark trait of the Postmodern discourse.

Lastly, while there is limited data upon which to make this assertion, the various dominant Discourses, like the swing of a pendulum, seem to alternate between stability and instability. The urgent need of the Colonial Discourse was that of maintaining the stability of society in the form of preserving the social hierarchy. Conversely, the urgent need of the Premodern Discourse was focused upon addressing instability in society brought on by the Industrial Revolution in the form of attending to the moral integration of society. For the Modern Discourse, the urgent need has swung back to maintaining the stability of society in the form of maintaining and enhancing the functioning of society through social engineering. Starting with the dawn of the twenty-first century, we appear to be entering a period of instability once more, this time being brought on by the digital revolution. If these developments do presage a sustained period of societal instability ahead, then the Postmodern discourse's urgent need of attending to the cohesiveness of society would seem to be better positioned to address this instability.

In summary, regarding this third scenario of the current time period representing a transition phase between discourses, there appears to be much historical evidence in support of this view, marking it, I believe, as the strongest possibility. If this scenario is indeed the case, this would predict the rise of the Postmodern discourse to dominance sometime in the next decade or two (2030s–2040s).

The Evolution of Democratic Equality

One of the interesting discoveries from this historical investigation, unlooked for as it is but tangentially related to social welfare, is that of the flowering of democratic equality in the United States that has occurred across the various eras studied. It has been revealed that the moral progression of social welfare has been cyclical in nature, with each new cycle resolving the moral lapses of the previous, yet at the same time creating new moral lapses of its own. By contrast, the moral progression of democratic equality in the United States seems to have followed an evolutionary path. Admittedly, the topic of democratic equality was not the focus of this study; and hence, a deeper investigation into the topic might reveal cyclical tendencies not present in this study. Nonetheless, this evolutionary path is worthy of note as it illustrates an alternative path that moral progression might take, depending upon the element of society being studied.

When the Pilgrims arrived on America's shores, they brought with them a monarchy. The vast distance separating these subjects from the monarch and seat of government fostered a hefty dose of political freedom in local rule. Yet any notions of democratic equality only found expression through the social hierarchy, limiting the expression of democratic equality to those occupying the top tier. Thus, for example, White male landowners were allowed to freely speak at a town hall meeting.[8] Additionally, this notion of democratic equality only extended itself to the political sphere. While toward the end of the Colonial Era, the Revolutionary War ushered in a democratic republic to replace the monarchy, political participation remained limited to those elites occupying the top tier of the hierarchy. As was noted in Chapter 3, only 6% *of the population* was eligible to vote in the first election in 1789.[9] In addition, as was noted in Chapter 2 as well as above, the First Great Awakening of the 1730s–1740s unsuccessfully attempted to extend this notion of democratic equality to the spiritual/religious sphere of society.[10] So for the Colonial Era, the expression of democratic equality was limited due to it finding expression within the social hierarchy.

The Premodern Era ushered in an era highlighted by suffrage movements. These suffrage movements were ultimately successful in extending the expression of democratic equality within the political sphere to all adult citizens. Passed in 1920, the Nineteenth Amendment to the Constitution granting women the right to vote marked both the end of this era as well as the final missing piece to the full expression of democratic equality in the political sphere.[b] Additionally, as noted in Chapter 4, the notion of democratic equality found expression in the spiritual/religious sphere through the movement of the Second Great Awakening. Thus, we can see the beginnings of an evolution beyond the political sphere in the expression of democratic equality taking place.

Building upon the previous eras, the Modern Era is distinguished by the advancement of civil rights. Now we can see the expression of democratic equality within the social and the economic spheres of society taking place. Within the social sphere, the eradication of miscegenation laws which prohibited interracial marriage is but one such example. Within the economic sphere, we have examples such as the passage of the Equal Opportunity Act. Hence, the expression of democratic equality in the United States in current times now extends to all the major spheres of society.

With the dawn of the twenty-first century, a number of revolutionary technological developments in communication—known as the *digital revolution*—have served to advance and support the goal of a truly open society, as articulated by Karl Popper and George Soros.[11] This current evolutionary pulse in the expression of democratic equality involves the devolution of power from governments back into the hands of the people. Thus, instead of relying solely on the government to ensure the expression of democratic equality through the enshrinement of rights, people are now able to pursue the expression of democratic equality through appealing directly to other members of society.

So, for example, in the economic sphere you have the development of software platforms such as Kickstarter and Patreon, which allow budding entrepreneurs and artists to directly appeal to interested members of society to provide funding for their project, as opposed to having to seek funding through financial services, where their right to seek funding is ensured by the government but not the granting of funds. The various social media platforms go beyond the government's guarantee of the right of free speech; they provide individuals with the power and means to reach out directly to their target audience. These aspects of the open society further enhance opportunities for individuals to participate in society, and thus mark a further flowering of the expression of democratic equality.

[b] This full expression entailed the enshrinement of the right to vote. As was discussed in Chapter 5, abridgment of this right for racial minorities occurred into the Modern Era, primarily throughout the Southern states.

Social Welfare and Its Current Challenges

As was concluded in the beginning of this chapter, when a new discourse rises and supplants the existing dominant Discourse on social welfare, this new discourse carries within itself moral blind spots of its own. This presents a sobering realization for professional social workers: It does not matter how we position ourselves within a Discourse, there will always be moral hazards to which we are blind. Thus, despite possessing good intentions, a measure of expertise, and strong professional ethics in the form of social work values, we may still unintentionally visit harm upon those we serve. By their very nature, blind spots are concealed areas that lay outside our scope of awareness. This historical realization should plant a seed of doubt, cautioning ourselves in all that we do.

Yet serve we must; social workers are not ones to stand idly by while the most tortured, oppressed, and vulnerable in society experience suffering and call out for help. And by far, the historical record attests to the multitude of positive contributions social welfare agents over the years have made to alleviate such suffering and to empower individuals to take greater control over their lives. Belonging to a service profession (or a *calling* in earlier times), social welfare agents have always been the first to jump into the breach and attempt to address social problems as they arise. We are constantly challenged to learn as we go; and hence, we are constantly challenged to act while possessing incomplete knowledge. Therefore, it is not surprising that the historical record contains numerous examples of social workers falling prey to moral hazards. When we lose sight of the fact that we are acting with incomplete knowledge and begin to hubristically think we "know" the reality of the client's situation, too often history has shown that bad consequences for the client have followed. Acting while possessing a level of uncertainty carries with it a level of uncomfortableness. As social workers, we must learn to become comfortable with this level of uncomfortableness. This then leads social workers to focus more upon respecting the process of the helping situation, rather than solely focusing upon the desired result.

Notes

1. Deutsch, *The Mentally Ill*, 158–85; Lightner, *Asylum, Prison, and Poorhouse*, 109–10.
2. Kirkbride, *On the Construction*, 293–94; Rothman, *Discovery of the Asylum*, 204–05, 265–68, 285–87.
3. Merill, "State Public Schools," 204; Minton, "Family Life," 37–53.
4. Kidd, *The Great Awakening*.
5. Hankins, *The Second Great Awakening*, 50–55; Schneewind, *Sidgwick's Ethics and Victorian*, 4, 13–15.

6. Kidd, *The Great Awakening*.
7. Caputo et al., "Postmodernism."
8. Goodman, *Essays in American Colonial*, 144–45; Morgan, *The Puritan Family*, 71–72.
9. Northern California Citizen Project, "U.S. Voting Rights Timeline," 1.
10. Kidd, *The Great Awakening*.
11. Popper, *The Open Society*; Soros, *Open Society*.

References

Caputo, Richard, William Epstein, David Stoesz, and Bruce Thyer. "Postmodernism: A Dead End in Social Work Epistemology." *Journal of Social Work Education* 51 (2015): 638–47.

Deutsch, Albert. *The Mentally Ill in America: A History of Their Care and Treatment*. New York: Doubleday, Doran & Company, 1937.

Goodman, Paul. *Essays in American Colonial History*. New York: Holt Rinehart and Winston, 1967.

Hankins, Barry. *The Second Great Awakening and the Transcendentalists*. Greenwood Guides to Historic Events 1500–1900. Santa Barbara: Greenwood, 2004.

Kidd, Thomas S. *The Great Awakening: A Brief History with Documents*. New York: Bedford/ St. Martin's, 2007.

Kirkbride, Thomas. *On the Construction, Organization, and General Arrangements of Hospitals for the Insane*. New York: Arno Press, 1880.

Lightner, David. *Asylum, Prison, and Poorhouse: The Writings and Reform Work of Dorothea Dix in Illinois*. Carbondale: Southern Illinois University Press, 1971.

Merill, Gildea. "State Public Schools for Dependent and Neglected Children." In *History of Child Saving in the United States: At the Twentieth National Conference of Charities and Correction in Chicago, June, 1893*. Report of the Committee on the History of Child-Saving Work, 204–26. Boston: Geo H. Ellis, 1893. https://books.google.com/books?id= 6KIzAQAAMAAJ&printsec=frontcover&dq#v=onepage&q&f=false

Minton, Sophie. "Family Life Versus Institution Life." In *History of Child Saving in the United States: At the Twentieth National Conference of Charities and Correction in Chicago, June, 1893*. Report of the Committee on the History of Child-Saving Work, 37–53. Boston: Geo H. Ellis, 1893. https://books.google.com/books?id=6KIzAQAAM AAJ&printsec=frontcover&dq#v=onepage&q&f=false

Morgan, Edmund S. *The Puritan Family: Essays on Religion and Domestic Relations in Seventeenth-Century New England*. Eastford, CT: Martino Fine Books, 1944.

Northern California Citizen Project. "U.S. Voting Rights Timeline." 2004. Accessed June 8, 2017, https://a.s.kqed.net/pdf/education/digitalmedia/us-voting-rights-timel ine.pdf.

Popper, Karl. *The Open Society and Its Enemies*. Princeton, NJ: Princeton University Press, 1950.

Rothman, David. *The Discovery of the Asylum: Social Order and Disorder in the New Republic*. 3rd ed. New York: Walter de Gruyter, 1971.

Schneewind, Jerome B. *Sidgwick's Ethics and Victorian Moral Philosophy*. Oxford: Oxford University Press, 1977.

Soros, George. *Open Society: Reforming Global Capitalism*. London: Little Brown, 2000.

Index